Effortless Attention

Effortless Attention

A New Perspective in the Cognitive Science of Attention and Action

edited by Brian Bruya

A Bradford Book
The MIT Press
Cambridge, Massachusetts
London, England

© 2010 Massachusetts Institute of Technology

All rights reserved. No part of this book may be reproduced in any form by any electronic or mechanical means (including photocopying, recording, or information storage and retrieval) without permission in writing from the publisher.

MIT Press books may be purchased at special quantity discounts for business or sales promotional use. For information, please email special_sales@mitpress.mit.edu or write to Special Sales Department, The MIT Press, 55 Hayward Street, Cambridge, MA 02142.

This book was set in Stone Sans and Stone Serif by Toppan Best-set Premedia Limited. Printed and bound in the United States of America.

Library of Congress Cataloging-in-Publication Data
Effortless attention : a new perspective in the cognitive science of attention and action / edited by Brian Bruya.
   p. cm.
"A Bradford book."
Includes bibliographical references and index.
ISBN 978-0-262-01384-0 (hardcover : alk. paper)—ISBN 978-0-262-51395-1 (pbk. : alk. paper)
   1. Attention. 2. Cognitive neuroscience. I. Bruya, Brian, 1966–
QP405.E33 2010
612.8'233—dc22

                                        2009030469

10 9 8 7 6 5 4 3 2

For Yuling and Giorgio

Contents

Introduction: Toward a Theory of Attention That Includes Effortless Attention and Action   1
Brian Bruya

1   Effortful Attention Control   29
    Brandon J. Schmeichel and Roy F. Baumeister

2   The Benefits and Perils of Attentional Control   51
    Marci S. DeCaro and Sian L. Beilock

3   Effortless Motor Learning?: An External Focus of Attention Enhances Movement Effectiveness and Efficiency   75
    Gabriele Wulf and Rebecca Lewthwaite

4   The Impact of Anticipated Cognitive Demand on Attention and Behavioral Choice   103
    Joseph T. McGuire and Matthew M. Botvinick

5   Grounding Attention in Action Control: The Intentional Control of Selection   121
    Bernhard Hommel

6   Implicit versus Deliberate Control and Its Implications for Awareness   141
    Chris Blais

7   Effortless Attention, Hypofrontality, and Perfectionism   159
    Arne Dietrich and Oliver Stoll

8   Effortless Attention in Everyday Life: A Systematic Phenomenology   179
    Mihaly Csikszentmihalyi and Jeanne Nakamura

9   Developing an Experimental Induction of Flow: Effortless Action in the Lab   191
    Arlen C. Moller, Brian P. Meier, and Robert D. Wall

10 The Physiology of Effortless Attention: Correlates of State Flow and Flow Proneness   205
Fredrik Ullén, Örjan de Manzano, Töres Theorell, and László Harmat

11 Apertures, Draw, and Syntax: Remodeling Attention   219
Brian Bruya

12 Toward an Empirically Responsible Ethics: Cognitive Science, Virtue Ethics, and Effortless Attention in Early Chinese Thought   247
Edward Slingerland

13 Flow Experience Explained on the Grounds of an Activity Approach to Attention   287
Yuri Dormashev

14 Two to Tango: Automatic Social Coordination and the Role of Felt Effort   335
Joshua M. Ackerman and John A. Bargh

15 The Thalamic Gateway: How the Meditative Training of Attention Evolves toward Selfless Transformations of Consciousness   373
James H. Austin

16 Training Effortless Attention   409
Michael I. Posner, Mary K. Rothbart, M. R. Rueda, and Yiyuan Tang

Contributors   425
Index   429

Introduction: Toward a Theory of Attention That Includes Effortless Attention and Action

Brian Bruya

Attention and action require effort, and, under normal circumstances, the higher the demands of a course of action, the greater the effort required to sustain a level of efficacy (Grier et al. 2003; Kahneman 1973). Although a clear distinction is rarely made, effort is generally presumed to be both objective (as calories consumed) and subjective (as experienced effortfulness). There are times, however, when attention and action seem to flow effortlessly,[1] allowing a person to meet an increase in demand with a sustained level of efficacy but without an increase in felt effort—even, at the best of times, with a decrease (Csikszentmihalyi 1975; Csikszentmihalyi and Csikszentmihalyi 1988; Dobrynin 1966).

Under normal circumstances, the expectation is that expenditure of effort increases with the level of demands until effort reaches a maximum point at which no more increase is possible (Kahneman 1973; see figure I.1).

Sometimes, however, when the level of demand reaches a point at which one is fully engaged, one is given over to the activity so thoroughly that action and attention seem effortless (see figure I.2).

That subjective effort can follow this path of unexpected decrease without a decrement in performance is clearly supported by the literature (Csikszentmihalyi, this volume; 1975; Dormashev, this volume; Ullén, this volume; Csikszentmihalyi and Csikszentmihalyi 1988; Dobrynin 1966; Jackson and Csikszentmihalyi 1999). Whether objective effort follows the same path is less clear, but there is evidence to suggest that it is possible (Wulf and Lewthwaite, this volume). Either way, because the objective–subjective distinction is rarely made in regard to discussions about effort, evidence shows that the accepted theoretical framework of increased effort to meet increased demand falters. This failure of our accepted framework to accommodate effortlessness has likely been the reason for its long neglect as a subject of serious investigation and for artists and philosophers to attribute its causes to the mystical, the divine, or the Freudian unconscious.

Mihaly Csikszentmihalyi (1975) identified the phenomenon of effortlessness as autotelic experience—when a person's full engagement in an activity provides ongoing

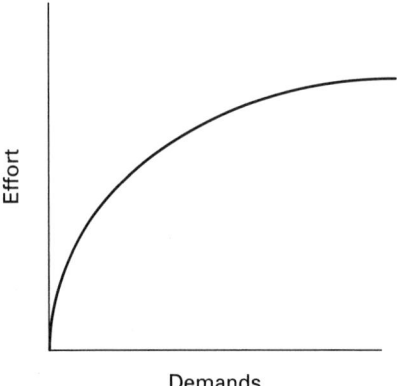

Figure I.1
Effort versus demands in effective action—normal experience.

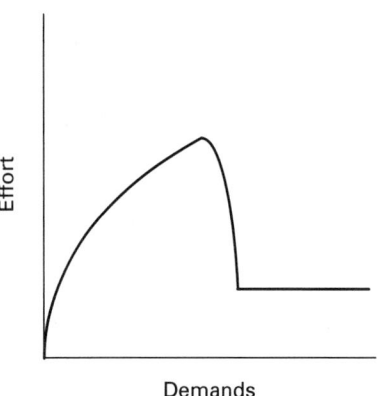

Figure I.2
Effort versus demands in effective action—effortless experience.

impetus for attention and action—and found it across a wide variety of activity domains, from rock climbing to chess, from factory line working to intimate conversation.[2] Using a novel data collection procedure (Hektner, Schmidt, and Csikszentmihalyi 2007) that allowed for better monitoring of naturalistic activities, Csikszentmihalyi achieved a great deal on the descriptive level, isolating the phenomenon and detailing the manner of its occurrence, its duration, its depth, its phenomenal characteristics, its variability, its breadth across populations, its parameters of occurrence, and its psychological value. Through his work, autotelic experience (commonly known as "flow") has entered both the scientific and the vernacular vocabularies (see box I.1 for

Box I.1

> **Example**
>
> A professor who has given the same classroom lecture 10 times over the past five years gives it again on two occasions over two semesters.
>
> **Effortful Experience**
> Outside of class, the professor is struggling with a particularly trying bit of research, a student he failed for cheating has taken the matter to the administration, a recent faculty meeting exploded in accusations and acrimony, and a close family member is ill. Inside of class, he is in an unfamiliar room, his new shoes are hurting his feet, the temperature is unusually warm, and students are lethargic. Under these conditions,* the professor experiences a frustrating lecture. Examples fall flat, insightful points come haltingly, if at all, and conclusions feel awkward and indecisive. Unexpected questions from students are met with hems and haws. There is a feeling of self-consciousness—that the lecture is not going well. There is a feeling of interminability during the lecture and of relief and fatigue after the lecture.
>
> **Effortless Experience**
> Outside of class, the professor just sent off a revised manuscript for publication, he recently won an award for teaching excellence, and his new research assistant is buoyant and eager. Inside of class, conditions are familiar, and students are responsive. The lecture goes smoothly, punctuated at appropriate moments by examples and insightful asides that meet bright eyes and nods of understanding. Unexpected questions are deftly assimilated to the material with humor and aplomb. Conclusions neatly wrap up sections and lead naturally to subsequent sections. There is no feeling of self-consciousness during the lecture but a retrospective feeling of diminished sense of time and that the lecture came off automatically and with ease. There is a feeling after the lecture of zest and that it could have been continued indefinitely without fatigue.
>
> * There are many possible obstacles to effortlessness; others could be extreme demands, low demands, lack of interest, unexpected interruptions, lethargy, negative affect, and so on. (The effect of unfavorable conditions is not a necessary one. Conceivably, in the first experience the professor could have overcome the obstacles and experienced an effortless lecture.)

an illustration of how the same activity can be carried out with and without a feeling of flow).

Because of its occurrence largely in naturalistic settings, however, and perhaps due to its vestigial mysteriousness, autotelic experience has been resistant to explanatory analysis. Therefore, fundamental questions regarding the cognitive science of effortlessness have, until now, been neither asked nor answered.

In a separate program in the Soviet Union, descriptive research was conducted by N. F. Dobrynin, D. I. Gatkevich, and N. V. Lavrova (Dobrynin 1966; Dormashev, this volume) under the rubric of postvoluntary attention—attention that was neither voluntary (effortful) nor involuntary (automatic). Postvoluntary attention is characterized in the literature as attention that has been captured by an absorbing, interesting, and meaningful activity and that can be sustained willingly and productively for a long period of time. Unfortunately, the bulk of this literature remains untranslated.

Despite the difficult questions remaining, research into effortless attention and action should be viewed not as an esoteric discipline but instead as a welcome challenge to test, refine, and even alter current models of attention and action. In order for any model of behavior to be considered comprehensive, it must be able to account for all types of human action. As Daniel Kahneman and Anne Treisman have said, "While we continue to work within the old framework [of attention], we should remain alert to the possibility that it could soon become obsolete" (Kahneman and Treisman 1984, p. 57). Bernhard Hommel recommends that in order to make future advances in developing a full model of human action, our most basic concepts must be clarified (Hommel 2007). The present volume submits the concept of effortless attention for such consideration.

In this introduction, I isolate seven topics concerning which scholars have produced theories and results pertinent to a nascent theory of effortlessness. I offer a summary of these ("Overview"), show how the topic of effortlessness may reveal gaps in the current literature and challenge current theoretical models ("Challenges–Gaps"), delineate potential aspects of a future theory of effortless attention and action ("Theory"), and discuss how the chapters in this volume mark advances in that direction ("Advances"). The categories do not necessarily reflect the intentions of the contributors or fully encompass current paradigms in cognitive science, and they are best considered one possible attempt at a heuristic for approaching this unwieldy topic. Further, the "Advances" discussions are necessarily brief and discuss how each chapter contributes to our understanding of only one issue in particular. Readers will find that the chapters are usually broader than that, often speaking importantly on several of these issues.

Topic 1: Effort

Overview

Two general kinds of effort have been distinguished in the literature—mental effort and physical effort (Smit, Eling, Hopman, and Coenen 2005), which are conceptually dissociable. For instance, in the development of overlearned action, the same level of physical effort is subject to decreasing amounts of mental effort. Nevertheless, mental effort must also have a physiological basis and has been approached by researchers and theorists under two general headings: attention and self-regulation (see box I.2 for terminology relevant to this field of inquiry).

William James defined attention as the effortful holding of something before one's mind (James 1983). Daniel Kahneman (1973) identified attention as mental effort, postulating that maintenance of attention can be under voluntary control but intensity of attention cannot. William Sarter has delineated a neuronal model of "attentional effort" that describes the mechanisms for initiation of top–down control of attention (Sarter, Gehring, and Kozak 2006). According to Sarter, when attention is threatened, performance monitoring (prefrontal–anterior cingulate) and motivational (mesolimbic) systems are recruited and integrated, manifesting as attentional effort.

Philosophers have long used "will" as a term that indicates subjective effort (Schulkin 2007). Research psychologists have preferred "self-regulation" or "self-control" (Baumeister and Vohs 2005; Rothbart 2005; Vohs and Baumeister 2004)—the

---

Box I.2

Working Definitions

Objective effort (exertion)   an increase in the metabolic or physiological processes of movement (physical effort) or thought (mental effort).

Subjective effort   the feeling of exertion.

Effortful   description of attention or action in which there is subjective effort under normal conditions.

Autotelic   description of an experience in which one feels that the activity provides the impetus for action, involving a challenging activity that requires skill, the merging of action and awareness, clear goals and immediate feedback, concentration on the task at hand, a feeling of being in control, a loss of self-consciousness, and an altered sense of time.

Effortless   description of attention or action that (1) is not experienced as effortful or (2) involves exertion and, due to the autotelicity of experience, subjective effort is lower than in normal conditions, with effectiveness maintained at a normal or elevated level.

Postvoluntary   effortless (2).

ability to accomplish one's goals and to refrain from actions that contravene one's goals. Studies have shown that self-regulation is a limited resource, that this resource can be depleted through prior effort (e.g., choices), and that its maintenance can be affected by cognitive states such as bias or a feeling of autonomy (Baumeister, Bratslavsky, Muraven, and Tice 1998; Inzlicht 2006; Moller, Deci, and Ryan 2006; Muraven, Tice, and Baumeister 1998; Schmeichel and Baumeister, this volume).

Challenges–Gaps
Current theories of attention identify attention with effort and rarely distinguish between objective and subjective effort. Such theories are unable to account for attention that is high in intensity but low in subjective effort. Is a synchronic decrease in *objective* effort also possible without a performance decrement? If so, is it akin to, or dependent on, the efficiency of overlearned action achieved diachronically? How can the two be distinguished on functional and physiological levels?

Further, the phenomenon of effortlessness complicates the notion of executive control. In autotelic experience, subjects report that they are able to exert exceptional control over the subtlest responses in an activity but without a *feeling* of executive control. They report that they can be completely focused on a task but feel as if only a slight effort is expended (Csikszentmihalyi 1975; Csikszentmihalyi and Csikszentmihalyi 1988). Lionel Naccache and colleagues report that executive control and the feeling of effort are dissociable (Naccache et al. 2005; see also Lafargue, Paillard, Lamarre, and Sirigu 2003).

These two challenges to current models raise many fundamental questions about the relationship between attention and effort and even about the nature of mental effort, itself.

Theory
Nearly five decades ago Gunnar Borg (1962) demonstrated a reliable correlation between objective and subjective physical effort that is still the basis of psychophysiological instruments today. A similar correlation between objective and subjective mental effort has been presumed but not verified. Several scales of subjective workload are used in human factors research, but none of the major scales distinguish clearly between mental and physical subjective effort (Rubio, Díaz, Martín, and Puente 2004). Any presumption of an outright correlation between objective and subjective mental effort appears to have been contradicted by Csikszentmihalyi's and Dobrynin's findings.[3] A theory of effortlessness will have to clearly define objective and subjective mental effort by delineating their functional and physiological features.

Advances
1. *Shared resources of self-regulation and attention* In their chapter for this volume, Brandon Schmeichel and Roy Baumeister demonstrate that under normal circum-

stances attention and self-regulation draw from a shared limited resource. Research with colleague Gailliot (Gailliot et al. 2007) suggests that this resource is glucose. Thus, under normal circumstances, objective mental effort (in the form of attention and self-regulation), like objective physical effort, appears to have a measurable and manipulable physiology.

2. *Decrease in objective effort during attention*   Gabriele Wulf and Rebecca Lewthwaite show in this volume that the normal reduction in physical and mental objective effort (coupled with an increase in efficacy) that is achieved through typical diachronic practice can be enhanced synchronically. Through a slight shift in the focus of attention—from internal to external—subjects have consistently decreased their objective effort while increasing their efficacy. In other words, there is a direct correspondence between attention and effort such that both physical and mental effort can be reduced while one's prior level of attention is maintained.

Topic 2: Decision Making

Overview

The study of decision making is now a mainstay of economics research (Tomlin et al. 2006) and moral psychology (Greene, Nystrom, Engell, Darley, and Cohen 2004). Less attention has been focused on the fact that every action a person makes involves a choice of some kind, whether fully conscious or not. Jeffrey Schall has shown that choice (selection from among alternatives) is conceptually dissociable from both decision making (deliberation about selection) and action (overt indication of selection; Schall 2001).

Working within a more traditional framework, Mariano Sigman and Stanislaus Dehaene have reported that of the three stages of an action (perceptual, central, and motor), the first and third can work in parallel on different stages of different tasks, and only the central must work serially, hence accounting for time delay in deliberative action (Sigman and Dehaene 2005).

A link between the autonomic nervous system and automatic action was rarely considered until Antonio Damasio and colleagues demonstrated that the autonomic nervous system plays a crucial role in some forms of decision making that lead to action (Damasio 1996, 1994). In essence, the autonomic nervous system sets the body and mind in proper form for reacting to uncertain but familiar circumstances.

A key component of automaticity is an individual's level of response inhibition. Antoine Bechara, working with Damasio, has conducted seminal research into the role of response inhibition in decision making (Bechara, Damasio, Tranel, and Damasio 1997; Bechara, Damasio, and Damasio 2000, 2003; Bechara 2004). In impulsive behavior, according to Bechara, response inhibition fails, the decision-making process never engages, and a response based on previous success is initiated automatically. Different areas of the brain, he says, may be active, depending on which of three types of decision (under certainty, under risk, and under ambiguity) is being made. If decisions under ambiguity are more likely, they will involve the orbitofrontal region and thereby engage the autonomic nervous system, which would slow processing down considerably.

Arne Dietrich has postulated that autotelic experience involves a decrease of neural activity in executive regions of the brain, specifically the anterior cingulate cortex (Dietrich 2004), which has been confirmed to be directly associated with the feeling of effort (Mulert, Menzinger, Leicht, Pogarell, and Hegerl 2005).

Challenges–Gaps
The above findings suggest that a complete theory of choice and decision making in human behavior would do well to include the actual neurophysiology of such processes. Effortless attention complicates any such model because the distinction between executive control and decision making vanishes. Decision making in flow is fast and precise, implicating automatic action, but also creative and flexible, implicating processes that are normally associated with executive control—though executive control processes are generally considered slow. Monitoring activation of brain areas in effortless attention may shed some light.

Theory
Recognizing Schall's distinction between choice, decision making, and action and then identifying the neural mechanisms underlying each may be important in accounting for the precision of effortless action and the rapid choices that precede it. Under Sigman and Dehaene's model, does effortless action (where rapid and accurate responses are characteristic) leave out the middle—deliberative—step, is it somehow integrated in a parallel fashion, or is there another way to account for it? Damasio and Bechara's work may point to an important role for something like confidence in effortlessness—familiarity with an activity and confidence in one's ability may (artificially?) push the subjective level of engagement from ambiguity toward certainty.

Advances
1. *Response conflict, effort, and decision making* In their contribution to this volume, Joseph McGuire and Matthew Botvinick show that an integral part of the decision-making process involves evaluating the demand for cognition in a prospective task. Drawing on numerous studies, they postulate that the anterior cingulate cortex and nearby medial frontal cortex monitor the current output of cognitive resources and compare that to expected demand, resulting in a projected increase or decrease in needed cognition. This projected amount of control is then balanced against projected reward (nucleus accumbens), resulting in either an adjustment in cognitive resources

to meet expected demand or in avoidance. McGuire and Botvinick demonstrate, therefore, that mental effort is dissociable from cognitive control. Cognitive control is an ongoing process, and subjective mental effort is associated with the change in that process rather than with the process, itself. This shows us how it is possible that there can be a high level of cognitive control but a low level of subjective effort.

2. *Effort in deliberative problem solving* It is natural to think that the greater the effort applied to a task, especially one that is exclusively cognitive, the better the outcome will be. Marci DeCaro and Sian Beilock demonstrate that although effortful (i.e., linear, rule-based) problem-solving strategies often result in better performance, under real-world conditions they can lose out to less effortful (i.e., associative, heuristic) strategies. Such results provide another avenue for demonstrating that effortful attention and performance are dissociable.

3. *Executive control is not necessarily conscious* The status of executive control as a defining feature of the explicit processing system is called into question by Chris Blais. Blais shows through his research and studies by others that an instance of executive control that is generally taken as a paradigm case of executive control by researchers actually occurs outside of conscious awareness. Blais, therefore, calls into question the need for a distinction between explicit and implicit systems of control. The very phenomenon of effortless attention, as explained above, seems to lead in the same direction, and Blais's work may help in resolving this conundrum.

Topic 3: Action Syntax

Overview

Joaquín Fuster has examined the temporal role of executive function in attention and action, in which the automated behavior that is integrated into lower neural stages (premotor cortex, basal ganglia, hypothalamus, or other subcortical structures) is activated and modulated by the anterior cingulate cortex (high motivation, resolution of conflict), areas of lateral prefrontal convexity (set, integration of information across time), and orbital areas (inhibitory control). Temporal integration of behavior, Fuster says, is closely related to negotiating a syntax. Although syntax is most commonly associated with language, Fuster says that "linguistic syntax and motoric syntax seem to have a common phyletic origin" (Fuster 2003, p. 180). If the perception–action cycle involves the same, or functionally similar, neural mechanisms as those that allow us to negotiate grammar, it would go a long way in explaining certain elements of effortless action.

Matthew Botvinick (Botvinick and Plaut 2004; Botvinick 2007) has developed a recurrent connectionist network model that accounts for decision-making behavior in everyday routine tasks through transient, flexible hierarchies that rely on concurrent representation rather than enduring schemas. The resulting hierarchies are context dependent and, as such, are appropriately vulnerable to distraction errors common in everyday behavior. Such a computational model may help elucidate the role of attention in complex sequential actions.

Among other things (Ivry and Helmuth 2003), sequential actions involve neural timing mechanisms, particularly in the cerebellum (Ivry 1997; Ivry and Richardson 2002; Ivry, Spencer, Zelaznik, and Diedrichsen 2002; Ivry and Spencer 2004a; Ivry and Spencer 2004b; Spencer, Ivry, and Zelaznik 2005), neural systems for force control and special trajectory planning (Diedrichsen, Verstynen, Hon, Zhang, and Ivry 2007; Spencer et al. 2005), and response selection (Bischoff-Grethe, Ivry, and Grafton 2002; Diedrichsen, Verstynen, Hon, Lehman, and Ivry 2003).

Challenges–Gaps

Syntax consists in a set of goals arranged in a hierarchy (within a circumscribed domain) that is constituted by defeasible rules temporally executed. Since effortless action is most often achieved in a well-demarcated activity, with constitutive rules, effortlessness (of attention and action) may be closely related to the process of negotiating syntax. The notion of action syntax is still a novel one and must be integrated into any comprehensive model of action (Costanzo 2002). One important issue that it brings to the fore is the distinction between explicit rule following and optimal action within constraints (Langlois 1998). When adding cream and sugar to a cup of coffee (Botvinick and Plaut 2004), how does one decide which to add first? When playing a sequence of notes on the piano, how does one decide on the particular dynamics? Assimilating explicit rules (Bunge 2004) is only one step in executing action. Another step is applying the rules appropriately according to context, which can never be completely identical from one instance to the next.

Theory

A theory of effortlessness should embrace action syntax and explain at functional and physiological levels what it means to negotiate a syntax. It should distinguish between explicit rule syntax and constraint–parameter syntax and thereby account for the role of appropriateness in effective action (how quickly to stir, how much arc to put on the basketball, how to express a chord, whether to bluff or not, etc.). Such a theory should also elucidate the role of attention in complex, sequential actions. Where, when, and how is attention directed to relevant cues, and how is that relevance determined? Further, determining these aspects of attention will have important implications for training and education.

Advances

1. *Action representation drives attention* Where is one's attention in downhill skiing? The pace of the activity is too fast for deliberation in conscious processing, and yet we

do attend fleetingly to this curve and that bump. Bernhard Hommel offers a theory for conceiving of attention not as necessarily consciousness driven and not as a system for managing scarce cognitive resources but as a "by-product of action control in a distributed processing system" (chapter 5, this volume). Hommel demonstrates that at its most fundamental level, attention is the process of perceptual systems filling parameters in preestablished action programs as those action programs successively come online. A skier (on a good day) attends effortlessly to curves and bumps as needed to maintain success. Attention, according to Hommel, is normally experienced as effortless, and it is only when something comes between endogenous motivation and relevant external cues (as in artificial laboratory tasks) that it is experienced as effortful. The apparent integration of perception and action in a single representational system appears to allow for immediate action-driven processing of syntactic cues.

2. *Effortlessness as domain specific* Through their unique methods of measuring dimensions of activities under normal circumstances, Mihaly Csikszentmihalyi and Jeanne Nakamura in their contribution to this volume demonstrate that effortless attention is most likely to be achieved under domain-specific conditions: clear, sequential, short-term goals; immediate feedback; and a balance between opportunities for action and the individual's ability to act. When these conditions are met under conducive circumstances, effortless attention is most likely to ensue. Further, they show that in circumstances of high attention experienced as effortless (as opposed to high attention experienced as effortful), subjects feel more involved, in control, unselfconscious, relaxed, and as if they are putting their skills to more use.

3. *Effortless attention in the lab* Can these conditions be replicated in the laboratory? While Hommel suggests that the limitations of the laboratory setting are problematic in understanding effortless attention, and while Csikszentmihalyi and Nakamura have overcome those limitations by taking their research outside the lab, there is still something to be said for the prospect of introducing a naturalistic activity into the lab such that effortless attention can be induced in a setting that would allow for more systematic study and more intense monitoring. In their contribution to this volume, Arlen Moller, Brian Meier, and Robert Wall examine the attempts of several laboratories, including their own, to induce flow by manipulating the balance between challenge and skills for subjects playing video games. While these teams have been successful in inducing many of the features of flow, the laboratory setting, itself, still presents a number of challenges. Moller, Meier, and Wall go on to examine such challenges and formulate suggestions for future research.

4. *Syntax and the draw of attention* In his contribution, Brian Bruya offers a new model of attention. Rather than a spotlight, or a filter, and so on, this model posits that attention may be profitably conceived of as a mechanism of sensitization that draws information relevant to dynamic contextual structures of reference through dynamic processing pathways. Contextual structures of reference compete spontaneously for

predominance in processing pathways, with predominance shifting rapidly and constantly over time, accounting for transient selective attention. A semblance of sustained, focused attention may be precariously achieved by inhibiting the intrusions of competing structures of reference, usually experienced as effortful to some degree. Occasionally, activity domains stabilize as temporary, predominant structures, inhibiting competing structures of reference by virtue of the activity's autotelicity, thereby allowing for sustained, focused attention that feels effortless.

Topic 4: Agency

Overview

David LaBerge's triangular circuit theory of attention (LaBerge 1995, 1998, 2000) postulates an important role for the thalamus in attentional processing. According to the triangular circuit theory, attention just is conscious attention, or what LaBerge more precisely calls awareness. This theory postulates an internal representation of the self directly associated with the thalamus that provides the motivation or interest that amplifies preattentively selected stimuli for sustained attention.

Walter Freeman views the brain as a fundamentally intentional system (in the tradition of John Dewey) that essentially creates itself through goal-directed activity. Freeman views brain waves as the multiple manifestations of self-organizing nonlinear dynamic systems rooted in the electrochemical activity of neuron populations. Freeman's data (Freeman 2004a, 2004b, 2005, 2006), he says, support a view that neuron populations are self-organizing systems in which transient activity arises spontaneously, spreads across populations following basins of attraction, and then subsides, to be replaced by the next wave of activity. These basins of attraction represent confluences of meaning. One of the characteristics of effortless attention and action is heightened sensitivity to domain-specific stimuli. Freeman's theory of nonlinear dynamic systems in neuron populations provides a model for this kind of readiness, or preafference, as he calls it (Freeman 1999, 2000).

Transient selfhood has been a central concern of the philosopher Thomas Metzinger, who has developed a theory of the self that coheres with the latest results of neuroscientific research, especially research related to the broad functionality of the motor system (Metzinger and Gallese 2003; Metzinger 2003). According to his work, we can consider the self a unitary entity only in a phenomenal sense. In a functional sense, it is constructed and continuously remade (determined at the physiological level by particular neural processes).

Susan Hurley created a model of intentional action that links action, imitation, and simulation, and she speculated widely on the implications for this research with regard to social philosophy and ethics (e.g., Hurley and Chater 2005; Hurley 2005).

A decision to act is not isolated but arises as a response to past events and in expectation of future events. Marc Jeannerod, working closely with philosophical theory on the one hand and neuroscientific studies on the other, has contributed significantly to the transformation of our understanding of the motor functions of the brain from noncognitive action deployment to full-blown centers of planning, perception, prediction, and complex social behavior (Jacob and Jeannerod 2003; Jeannerod 1988, 1997, 2006). How the sense of agency is constructed and maintained is one of Jeannerod's primary concerns because it appears to be at the heart of motor cognition. Without agency, there is no goal setting or subject of simulation or prediction.

Challenges–Gaps
A core challenge that effortlessness research poses to current models of attention and action is to answer the following question: When a decision to act is made, who is doing the deciding? Effortlessness brings to the foreground two issues fundamental to action: (1) When an act is attributed to a self, what exactly is a self, and (2) as mentioned above, is there really a clear demarcation between executive control and automaticity? There are obviously distinct neuronal systems handling overlearned actions on the one hand and executive control on the other; effortless action highlights the need to study their integration because in this highly achieved form of action, a person seems to draw from them both with exquisite mastery. Freeman's dynamic systems framework may help close these gaps by supplying to current models a kind of spontaneous sensitivity (see Alicia Juarrero 1999 for an insightful examination of dynamic systems theory, agency, and action).

LaBerge points out that awareness involving a self-representation is distinct from self-awareness. Nonetheless, the same question asked above may be asked here (applicable also to Jeannerod): How can such a theory account for the commonly reported phenomenon of a dropping away of a distinct sense of self in effortless attention and action? Also, is a self-representation solely a function of the thalamus, or are there important contributions from other specific areas of the brain, such as the medial cingulate where attributions to self and other are formed (Tomlin et al. 2006)?

When attention is invested in an activity, it can be perceived as purely voluntary or carry a sense of compulsion. According to Csikszentmihalyi (1978) and Dobrynin (1966), effortless action is more likely achieved when attention is not only highly focused but also entirely voluntary—in pursuits that a person finds intrinsically worthwhile. Because effortlessness is often reported as a desirable state for both the enjoyment and the efficacy of action that it affords (Csikszentmihalyi 1975), it exposes a gap in current literature with regard to the optimal structuring of an individual's life. How can the achievement of effortless attention, on personal, pedagogical, and managerial levels (Dobrynin 1966) be cultivated and encouraged for the sake of the acting agent?

Moving from the individual agent to the social agent, social behavior involves executing appropriate actions according to complex circumstances—evaluating subtle cues and responding without time for deliberation. Insofar as mirror neurons have been implicated in social action, as Hurley (among others) has done, many questions can be asked with regard to how much of social behavior is automatic and how much is voluntary and with how much robustness this distinction can even be maintained. Are the same mechanisms of effortless action also at work in social action (see also under "Automaticity" below)? If so, given that effortless attention and action are often cultivated in a practice regime, what are the implications for the possibility of achieving expertise in social action? Could such knowledge be applied at a personal or even a pedagogical level? What are the ethical implications?

Theory
Effortless attention and action may simply be the free running of Freeman's intentional system, but what does that mean for a persistent sense of self, especially if such a sense of self falls away during effortless activity? Because reports of effortlessness often involve the loss of coherence of a phenomenal sense of self (Csikszentmihalyi 1975; Csikszentmihalyi and Csikszentmihalyi 1988; the feeling that the piano is playing itself or one is on "autopilot"), some aspects of functional selfhood seem to dissociate also. A comprehensive theory of perception and action would account not only for the role of the self in motivation but for the dissolution of the self in effortless attention and action. Further, it would explore the implications of "nonagentive" action in ethics, education, law, and public policy.

Advances
1. *Self and the thalamus*   An important repository of anecdotal and speculative literature regarding effortless attention and action lies in the Asian philosophical traditions. In Zen Buddhism, for example, there are countless stories of acolytes who have practiced meditation for long periods and then, on encountering an unexpected, nondescript stimulus, suddenly experience a number of the hallmarks of effortless attention. In his contribution to this volume, neurologist James Austin considers how the sudden experience of a dropping away of a sense of self may have direct neurophysiological correlates. Drawing on research that distinguishes two attentional systems, he shows that distinct pathways between thalamic nuclei and the two attentional systems are likely implicated in the experience of a loss of a sense of self. He suggests that the blinking out of self-consciousness in a Zen enlightenment experience, and in effortless attention and action more broadly, may be due to deafferented cortical areas of the dorsal (egocentric) attentional system, traceable to deactivated thalamic nuclei. The

entire process is achieved, he suggests, through long practice regimens and their resulting neurophysiological effects.

2. *Ethics and agency* The findings in cognitive science that call into question the traditional conception of a unitary rational agent have profound implications for contemporary ethical theory. In his contribution to this volume, Edward Slingerland integrates results from the cognitive science of action with an ethical theory that takes effortless action to be the epitome of virtuous action. Through a detailed examination of philosophical and cognitive scientific accounts of human action, Slingerland concludes that ethical human action is best characterized on a descriptive level in terms of a virtue ethics broadly construed. In other words, he says, humans generally act not from active cognitive control but from self-activating effortless dispositions that can be cultivated through introspection and education.

3. *The person level in activity* Researchers in twentieth-century Russian psychology recognized the primary importance of syntax in attention and action, adopting the rubric *activity theory* to describe their overall psychological framework. Yuri Dormashev, in addition to giving an extraordinary introduction to activity theory in general and postvoluntary attention in particular, explains in his contribution to this volume that attention is best understood in terms of activity, functioning as a *gestalt* and focused on a limited range of objects. In postvoluntary attention, activity is organized at the person level, or *personality* (understood as the focal point of the driving hierarchy of motives in the cultural sphere). On this basis, Dormashev suggests that an important element missing from accounts of autotelic experience is that of *personal taste*—the interest, or broad aesthetic sense, that acts as a motivating force outside of organic and social motivations. The sense of transactional, embedded attention and action inherent in this view serves to unify the autonomous individual with the social and organic milieus in which—and through which—the individual develops.

Topic 5: Automaticity

Overview

Kahneman and Treisman point out that there has been a running debate among researchers of attention as to the role of automaticity in attention, with some researchers emphasizing early onset attention (selective processing–filtering) and some late onset (mental set/efficiency of action), and suggest that research into automaticity may help us bring the two closer together and away from mutual exclusivity (Kahneman and Treisman 1984; see also Pashler 1998).

In his analysis of available data, Marc Jeannerod (2006) suggests that the automated steps of an action come in for conscious access when there is discord between intention and actuality—when the perceptual representation does not match the action representation.

John Bargh, researching the automaticity of social behavior, has concluded that much more of behavior than previously thought is outside of voluntary consciousness (Bargh 2000; Bargh and Chartrand 1999). He has recently proposed that a cascade model of language be applied to behavior (Bargh 2006; Ackerman and Bargh, this volume), explaining how actions proceed spontaneously from parallel processed goal activation, just as conversation occurs spontaneously while also being goal directed and falling within strict syntactic and semantic parameters.

Related to the cascade model is the theory of event coding put forward by Hommel, Müsseler, Aschersleben, and Prinz (2001; Hommel, this volume). Working in the tradition of Dewey (1896) and Gibson (1979), they suggest, as discussed briefly above, that perception and action are encoded in the brain in unitary fashion, accounting for the functional linking of the two as one. One result of this model is the postulate that actions are encoded in terms of their effects rather than in terms of explicitly understood movements. The practical result of this is that attention in learning an action must be focused not on the intentional, voluntary aspect of a movement but on the effects of the movement (Wulf 2001, this volume).

Challenges–Gaps

These theories and findings, coupled with those under "Agency" and "Action Syntax" above, highlight a shift in research models from stimulus–response to what one might call sensitivity–responsiveness. Whereas the behaviorist model cut out intentional agency completely, the new models replace it with a multimodal agent, which, while not exactly being metaphysically free, is a bundle of preafference and readiness potentials created in a complex array of self-organized neuronal populations, with their representational (or other) associations constantly arranged and rearranged through phylogenetic and historical factors. In many circumstances, the responsiveness of the agent appears to be a function of these associations.

Theory

If Jeannerod is correct that actions come into consciousness when perception does not match intention, it would help explain why effortless action, which reportedly occurs when expectations are consistently met, often seems outside of conscious awareness. On the other hand, it would also seem to leave high-level effortless action as purely automated, thereby seeming to preclude credit to a subject for creativity, insight, emotional expression, and so forth. A cascade model of behavior may work well for effortless action; in fact, effortless action, being generally domain dependent, may prove to be the best testing ground for establishing the basis for such a theory. The theory of event coding may help explain why the precision of effortless action can appear "nonintentional" while attention is intensely focused on rapidly arising cues.

Advances

1. *Social automaticity* In their contribution to this volume, Joshua Ackerman and John Bargh review the extensive literature on the automaticity of social coordination, suggesting three general mechanisms that may account for it: simple dynamical systems at the level of mechanics (e.g. synchronized rocking in rocking chairs), shared perception–action representations (e.g., priming), and active motivations. They conclude that the automaticity of social coordination has several qualities that may be relevant to corollary qualities in flow: reduced experience of effort, transcendence of the negative aspects of the self, positive affect, and interpersonal fluency. Ackerman and Bargh go on to make a case for flow's being a special case of automaticity, explaining that the conscious awareness does not, itself, drive the experience of flow and is, instead, a passive spectator.

Topic 6: Expertise

Overview

Attention and its relation to performance have been an intense topic of research, exemplified by the conference and volume *Attention and Performance*'s appearing biennially since 1966. There appears to be a very close link between expert performance and effortlessness. Although the learning of a highly refined skill involves intense effort over extended periods (Ericsson and Lehmann 1996), its execution at the highest level is often characterized from a first-person perspective as feeling effortless and from a third-person perspective as appearing effortless. How to build this level of expertise and how it is executed have been the object of a number of interesting lines of research.

For instance, Sian Beilock and colleagues (Beilock, Bertenthal, McCoy, and Carr 2004; Beilock, Carr, MacMahon, and Starkes 2002) have found, when comparing sport performance of novices and experts, that experts perform better at full attentional capacity, even if their attention is occupied by irrelevant details, such as distractors or an artificial speed requirement.

Focused attention is attention that is voluntarily concentrated on a single domain of stimuli. The limited attention of lower animals can be understood as involuntarily focused attention. Ethologist Reuven Dukas (2002) has suggested that limited attention in lower animals may have an adaptive advantage, and Csikszentmihalyi (1978) has noted the advantages of focused attention in autotelic experience. Drawing from a series of studies involving computer simulations, Dehaene and Changeux (2005) have postulated that when human attention is captured in high-level cortical activity, the processing of domain-specific stimuli is facilitated while that of other stimuli is inhibited, perhaps accounting for the phenomenon of inattentional blindness.

Challenges–Gaps

Effortlessness is often characterized by an experience of completely focused attention. It is a mystery, however, as to why attempting to give full attention to an activity at which one is completely competent and which *does not require* full attention should result in a performance decrement. It may be that sustaining full attention in a task that does not demand it is simply not possible for any length of time (but why?) and that free cognitive resources will be involuntarily drawn to competing targets of attention, drawing with them some of the cognitive resources required for the original task.

Theory

The Dehaene and Changeux model (2005) seems to most easily match autotelic experience—as opposed to normal experience—because full attention that inhibits non-domain stimuli is difficult to maintain outside of autotelic experience. A theory of effortlessness should include the mechanisms for the capture and release of full attention in autotelicity and seek to answer the question of whether the capturing can be facilitated or the releasing can be inhibited through training.

Advances

1. *The explicit system and perfectionism*   Related to the chapters by Austin, DeCaro and Beilock, and Wulf and Lewthwaite mentioned above, the contribution to this volume from Arne Dietrich and Oliver Stoll considers evidence, first, for the downregulation of specific brain areas during effortless attention and, second, for the important relationship between attention and performance. Dietrich and Stoll begin by explaining the explicit–implicit distinction in cognitive processing and suggest that some activities can facilitate a neurophysiological process that shuts down modules of the explicit system. They then weigh in on the long-standing issue of the value of perfectionism by distinguishing two kinds, one of which draws processing through the explicit system and the other through the implicit system—the former being deleterious in attempts to achieve flow.

2. *The physiology of flow*   Related to the work of Moller, Meier, and Wall described above, Fredrik Ullén, Örjan de Manzano, Töres Theorell, and László Harmat have successfully induced flow in the lab and examined its physiological correlates. Through these studies, they have found that the physiological correlates (measured in skin conductance, electromyography of facial muscles, and respiratory and cardiovascular dimensions) of effortless attention are, indeed, unique, sharing some features with the state of joyous arousal and importantly distinct from the state of effortful attention. Through further measurements of personality traits, including flow proneness, they found that flow proneness is not correlated with the capacity for sustained effortful attention, nor with general intelligence in leisure activities, and is negatively correlated with general intelligence in maintenance and professional activities.

Introduction

Topic 7: Mental Training

Overview

In the West, expertise has traditionally been viewed as a combination of inborn ability and effortful practice. While some valuable attempts have been made on a descriptive level (Jackson and Csikszentmihalyi 1999; Kremer and Scully 1994; Moran 1996) and while there have been calls for a program of research in this area (Moran 1996)—and while popular psychology has been flooded with speculation and anecdotal evidence of the efficacy of mental training (Grout and Perrin 2004; Kauss 2001; Kuehl, Kuehl, and Tefertiller 2005; Millman 1999)—just as with the topic of effortlessness, comparatively little progress has been made in explaining scientifically the processes and effectiveness of mental training. In the East, we find a situation in which effortlessness and mental training have been topics of philosophical speculation for millennia. Edward Slingerland (2003) has documented a direct concern with effortless action across numerous schools of thought in ancient China, Brian Bruya (2010) has taxonomized effortlessness as spontaneity in early China and identified allied notions in the history of Western philosophy, and volumes too numerous to mention have been written on the methods of meditation and mindfulness in Hindu and Buddhist philosophy.

Over the past few decades, these methods and concerns have gradually been trickling into the cognitive science literature—for example, in Maturana and Varela's concept of autopoiesis (Maturana and Varela 1980), Ellen Langer's work on mindfulness (Langer 1989), and James Austin's neurological analysis of meditation (Austin 1998, 2006, this volume).

Autotelic effortlessness involves two important characteristics: (1) focused attention and (2) a dropping away of a salient sense of self. Meditation practices involve the cultivation of these two mental states, and recent research has shown that neural plasticity in adult humans is more extensive than previously believed. Bengtsson and Ullén have shown that piano practice can influence white matter structure well into adulthood (Bengtsson et al. 2005). In separate studies, Lutz and colleagues (Lutz, Greischar, Rawlings, Ricard, and Davidson 2004) and Davidson and colleagues (Davidson et al. 2003) have shown that long-term meditators can alter neuronal structures that are implicated in high-attention states. Their results show that their subjects are able to voluntarily induce not only high-amplitude gamma oscillations but also long-distance gamma synchrony. Equally important is that these subjects' baseline EEG spectral profiles differed significantly from those of the control subjects, demonstrating the possibility of long-term neural changes through meditative practice.

B. Rael Cahn and John Polich undertook a comprehensive review of neurological studies of meditation (Cahn and Polich 2006) that confirms the positive effects of meditation on attention. B. Alan Wallace, a former Tibetan Buddhist monk and now an active scholar, has produced a series of books that explain the elements of attentional training in the Buddhist idiom (Wallace and Houshmand 1992; Wallace and Houshmand 1999) and has more recently attempted to interpret these in relation to advances in cognitive science (Wallace 2003; Wallace and Tsoçn-kha-pa Blo-bzaçn-grags-pa 2005; Wallace 2007). According to Wallace, Buddhists view meditation as a metaskill, a skill that is applicable to multiple domains. This skill, he says, can be cultivated by anyone and begins with a concerted effort to diminish self-centeredness. The result of the training, he says, is extensive cognitive–affective control, positive affect, and a robust prosocial attitude.

John Kabat-Zinn reports that an 8- to 10-week group program in mindfulness meditation training can produce short- and long-term positive results in reducing anxiety and pain (Kabat-Zinn et al. 1992; Miller, Fletcher, and Kabat-Zinn 1995). Wallace claims that it takes six months to a year of full-time meditation practice, under conducive conditions and with appropriate preparation and instruction, for a person to achieve a state of sustainable effortless attention (Wallace and Houshmand 1999).

Challenges–Gaps

While researchers have had significant success in examining the neural correlates of attention on the one hand and the parameters for improving performance within a domain of activity on the other, the neural confluence of these two topics has been relatively neglected. According to Marc Jeannerod (2006), evidence supports the hypothesis that representing an action and executing it are distinct but functionally equivalent. If representing an action is essentially practicing an action, then visualization, observation, and any steps that support or promote these will have an impact on cultivating skills that contribute to high-level effortless action.

In the East, many claims have been made regarding taxonomies of higher levels of focused attention/concentration/absorption, but there is little agreement on particular terminology or functional demarcations. It is unclear with how much precision we can conceptualize any natural neurological and developmental boundaries of different kinds of attention and of levels of focused attention for objective study.

Theory

A question that a theory of effortlessness must attempt to answer is to what extant mental training conducted in one domain is transferable to other domains. Further, is there such a thing as metamental training—mental training that is conducted outside of a specific domain but which is applicable across domains? Anecdotal evidence from Buddhist publications suggests that meditation and mindfulness training could offer such a metamethod. If such a claim turns out to be supported by empirical evidence, it could have broad implications for clinical application, formal education, and other kinds of training.

A complete theory of effortless attention and action would include not only precise definitions of basic terms of attention but also a taxonomy of stages of attentional training.

Advances

1. *Evidence for improved attention through general training*   In their contribution, Michael Posner, Mary Rothbart, M. R. Rueda, and Yiyuan Tang trace measurements of temperamental effortful control in parents and children to specific brain networks and the brain networks to specific gene alleles, demonstrating natural individual differences in attentional capacity. They go on to demonstrate that these differences can be significantly influenced through environmental factors. Testing the potential of attentional training, Posner and colleagues found that five days of computerized task training in young children can result in increased activity in the anterior cingulate cortex, a general and persistent increase in IQ, and an increase in affective regulation. In adults, in a double-blind study in which subjects were trained for only 20 minutes per day over five days in a systematic method of mind–body attention, subjects showed improvement in executive attention, lower negative affect, lower fatigue, and lower stress compared to both controls and subjects who underwent generic relaxation training.

Conclusion

The phenomena of effortless attention and action provide an unexplored opportunity to test and probe current models of attention and action and extend them in directions that not only are valuable academically but could potentially have a significant impact on human flourishing. Each of the chapters in this volume has implications that bear on a variety of different aspects of attention and action discussed above.

Notes

1. Reduction in effort is often associated with a concomitant reduction in attention (Dehaene, Kerszberg, and Changeux 2001). Here, however, "effortless" means a reduction of felt effort only, with attention preserved or even enhanced.

2. Action in autotelic experience should be distinguished from overlearned action. Overlearned action is a reduction in effort in the face of a sustained high level of challenge within a domain *diachronically*, whereas action in autotelic experience is a reduction in effort in the face of a sustained high level of challenge *synchronically*. The execution of action in autotelic experience typically depends on overlearned action, whereas overlearned action does not necessarily entail the achievement of autotelic experience. Also, overlearned action seems to reduce effort by bring-

ing action out of attention, freeing up cognitive resources for other things, whereas autotelicity is marked by the paradox of minutely sensitized attention coupled with a diminution of subjective will.

3. If objective effort in autotelic experience is found to decrease along with subjective effort, while efficacy is maintained, the standard models would be challenged even more radically.

References

Austin, J. H. 1998. *Zen and the brain: Toward an understanding of meditation and consciousness*. Cambridge: MIT Press.

Austin, J. H. 2006. *Zen-Brain Reflections*. Cambridge: MIT Press.

Bargh, J. A. 2000. Beyond behaviorism: On the automaticity of higher mental processes. *Psychol. Bull.* 126:925–945.

Bargh, J. A. 2006. Agenda 2006: What have we been priming all these years? On the development, mechanisms, and ecology of nonconscious social behavior. *Eur. J. Soc. Psychol.* 36:147–168.

Bargh, J. A., and T. L. Chartrand. 1999. The unbearable automaticity of being. *Am. Psychol.* 54:462–479.

Baumeister, R. F., E. Bratslavsky, M. Muraven, and D. M. Tice. 1998. Ego depletion: Is the active self a limited resource? *J. Pers. Soc. Psychol.* 74:1252–1265.

Baumeister, R. F., and K. D. Vohs. 2005. *Handbook of self-regulation: Research, theory, and applications*. New York: Guilford Press, 2004.

Bechara, A. 2004. The role of emotion in decision-making: Evidence from neurological patients with orbitofrontal damage. *Brain Cogn.* 55:30–40.

Bechara, A., H. Damasio, and A. R. Damasio. 2000. Emotion, decision making and the orbitofrontal cortex. *Cereb. Cortex* 10:295–307.

Bechara, A., H. Damasio, and A. R. Damasio. 2003. Role of the amygdala in decision-making. *Ann. N. Y. Acad. Sci.* 985:356–369.

Bechara, A., H. Damasio, D. Tranel, and A. R. Damasio. 1997. Deciding advantageously before knowing the advantageous strategy. *Science* 275:1293–1295.

Beilock, S. L., B. I. Bertenthal, A. M. McCoy, and T. H. Carr. 2004. Haste does not always make waste: Expertise, direction of attention, and speed versus accuracy in performing sensorimotor skills. *Psychon. Bull. Rev.* 11:373–379.

Beilock, S. L., T. H. Carr, C. MacMahon, and J. L. Starkes. 2002. When paying attention becomes counterproductive: Impact of divided versus skill-focused attention on novice and experienced performance of sensorimotor skills. *J. Exp. Psychol. Appl.* 8:6–16.

Bengtsson, S. L., Z. Nagy, S. Skare, L. Forsman, H. Forssberg, and F. Ullén. 2005. Extensive piano practicing has regionally specific effects on white matter development. *Nat. Neurosci.* 8:1148–1150.

Bischoff-Grethe, A., R. B. Ivry, and S. T. Grafton. 2002. Cerebellar involvement in response reassignment rather than attention. *J. Neurosci. the Official Journal of the Society for Neuroscience* 22:546–553.

Borg, G. 1962. *Physical performance and perceived exertion.* Lund: C. W. K. Gleerup.

Botvinick, M., and D. C. Plaut. 2004. Doing without schema hierarchies: A recurrent connectionist approach to normal and impaired routine sequential action. *Psychol. Rev.* 111:395–429.

Botvinick, M. M. 2007. Multilevel structure in behaviour and in the brain: A model of Fuster's hierarchy. *Philos. Trans. R. Soc. Lond. B Biol. Sci.* 362:1615–1626.

Bruya, B. 2010. The rehabilitation of spontaneity: A new approach in the philosophy of action. *Philos. East West* 60 (2).

Bunge, S. A. 2004. How we use rules to select actions: A review of evidence from cognitive neuroscience. *Cogn. Affect. Behav. Neurosci.* 4:564–579.

Cahn, B. R., and J. Polich. 2006. Meditation states and traits: EEG, ERP, and neuroimaging studies. *Psychol. Bull.* 132:180–211.

Costanzo, P. 2002. Social exchange and the developing syntax of moral orientation. In *Social exchange in development*, ed. B. Laursen and W. G. Graziano. San Francisco: Jossey-Bass, 41–52.

Csikszentmihalyi, M. 1975. *Beyond boredom and anxiety.* 1st ed. San Francisco: Jossey-Bass.

Csikszentmihalyi, M. 1978. Attention and the holistic approach to behavior. In *The stream of consciousness*, ed. K. S. Pope and J. L. Singer. New York: Plenum, 335–358.

Csikszentmihalyi, M., and I. S. Csikszentmihalyi. 1988. *Optimal experience: Psychological studies of flow in consciousness.* Cambridge: Cambridge University Press.

Damasio, A. R. 1996. The somatic marker hypothesis and the possible functions of the prefrontal cortex. *Philos. Trans. R. Soc. Lond. B Biol. Sci.* 351:1413–1420.

Damasio, A. R. 1994. *Descartes' error: Emotion, reason, and the human brain.* New York: Putnam.

Davidson, R. J., J. Kabat-Zinn, J. Schumacher, M. Rosenkranz, D. Muller, S. Santorelli, F. Urbanowski, A. Harrington , K. Bonus , and J. F. Sheridan. 2003. Alterations in brain and immune function produced by mindfulness meditation. *Psychosom. Med.* 65:564–570.

Dehaene, S., M. Kersberg, and J. Changeux. 2001. A neuronal model of a global workspace in effortful cognitive tasks. In *Cajal and consciousness: Scientific approaches to consciousness on the centennial of Ramón y Cajal's Textura*, ed. P. C. Marijuán. New York: New York Academy of Sciences, 152–165.

Dehaene, S., and J. P. Changeux. 2005. Ongoing spontaneous activity controls access to consciousness: A neuronal model for inattentional blindness. *PLoS Biol.* 3:e141.

Dewey, J. 1896. The reflex arc concept in psychology. *Psychol. Rev.* 3:357–370.

Diedrichsen, J., T. Verstynen, A. Hon, S. L. Lehman, and R. B. Ivry. 2003. Anticipatory adjustments in the unloading task: Is an efference copy necessary for learning? *Experimental Brain Research. Experimentelle Hirnforschung. Experimentation Cerebrale* 148:272–276.

Diedrichsen, J., T. D. Verstynen, A. Hon, Y. Zhang, and R. B. Ivry. 2007. Illusions of force perception: The role of sensori-motor predictions, visual information, and motor errors. *J. Neurophysiol.* 97:3305–3313.

Dietrich, A. 2004. Neurocognitive mechanisms underlying the experience of flow. *Consciousness and Cognition: An International Journal* 13:746–761.

Dobrynin, N. 1966. *Basic problems of the psychology of attention: Psychological science in the USSR.* Washington, DC: U.S. Dept. of Commerce, Clearinghouse for Federal Scientific and Technical Information, 274–291.

Dukas, R. 2002. Behavioural and ecological consequences of limited attention. *Philos. Trans. R. Soc. Lond. B Biol. Sci.* 357:1539–1547.

Ericsson, K. A., and A. C. Lehmann. 1996. Expert and exceptional performance: Evidence of maximal adaptation to task constraints. *Annu. Rev. Psychol.* 47:273–305.

Freeman, W. J. 1999. Consciousness, intentionality and causality. *J. Conscious. Stud.* 6 (11–12): 143–172.

Freeman, W. J. 2000. *How brains make up their minds.* New York: Columbia University Press.

Freeman, W. J. 2004a. Origin, structure, and role of background EEG activity: I. Analytic amplitude. *Clin. Neurophysiol.: Official Journal of the International Federation of Clinical Neurophysiology* 115:2077–2088.

Freeman, W. J. 2004b. Origin, structure, and role of background EEG activity: II. Analytic phase. *Clin. Neurophysiol.: Official Journal of the International Federation of Clinical Neurophysiology* 115:2089–2107.

Freeman, W. J. 2005. Origin, structure, and role of background EEG activity: III. Neural frame classification. *Clin. Neurophysiol.: Official Journal of the International Federation of Clinical Neurophysiology* 116:1118–1129.

Freeman, W. J. 2006. Origin, structure, and role of background EEG activity: IV. Neural frame simulation. *Clin. Neurophysiol.: Official Journal of the International Federation of Clinical Neurophysiology* 117:572–589.

Fuster, J. M. 2003. *Cortex and mind: Unifying cognition.* New York: Oxford University Press.

Gailliot, M. T., R. F. Baumeister, C. N. DeWall, J. K. Maner, E. A. Plant, D. M. Tice, L. E. Brewer, and B. J. Schmeichel. 2007. Self-control relies on glucose as a limited energy source: Willpower is more than a metaphor. *J. Pers. Soc. Psychol.* 92:325–336.

Gibson, J. J. 1979. *The ecological approach to visual perception.* Boston: Houghton Mifflin.

Greene, J. D., Nystrom, L. E., Engell, A. D., Darley, J. M., and Cohen, J. 2004. The neural basis of cognitive conflict and control in moral judgment. *Neuron* 44:389–400.

Grier, R. A., J. S. Warm, W. N. Dember, G. Matthews, T. L. Galinsky, J. L. Szalma, et al. 2003. The vigilance decrement reflects limitations in effortful attention, not mindlessness. *Hum. Factors* 45:349–359.

Grout, J., and S. Perrin. 2004. *Mind games: Inspirational lessons from the world's biggest sports stars.* Chichester, UK: Capstone.

Hektner, J. M., J. A. Schmidt, and M. Csikszentmihalyi. 2007. *Experience sampling method: Measuring the quality of everyday life.* Thousand Oaks, CA: Sage.

Hommel, B., J. Müsseler, G. Aschersleben, and W. Prinz. 2001. The theory of event coding (TEC): A framework for perception and action planning. *Behav. Brain Sci.* 24:849–878.

Hommel, B. 2007. Consciousness and control: Not identical twins. *Consciousness Studies* 14 (1–2):155–176.

Hurley, S. L. 2005. Bypassing conscious control: Media violence, unconscious imitation, and freedom of speech. In *Does consciousness cause behavior? An investigation of the nature of volition,* ed. S. Pockett, W. Banks, and S. Gallagher. Cambridge: MIT Press, 301–338.

Hurley, S. L., and N. Chater. 2005. *Perspectives on imitation: From neuroscience to social science.* Cambridge: MIT Press.

Inzlicht, M. 2006. Stigma as ego depletion: How being the target of prejudice affects self-control. *Psychol. Sci.* 17:262–269.

Ivry, R. 1997. Cerebellar timing systems. *Int. Rev. Neurobiol.* 41:555–573.

Ivry, R. B., and L. Helmuth. 2003. Representations of neural mechanisms of sequential movements. In *Taking action: Cognitive neuroscience perspectives on intentional acts,* ed. S. H. Johnson-Frey. Cambridge: MIT Press, 221–257.

Ivry, R. B., and T. C. Richardson. 2002. Temporal control and coordination: The multiple timer model. *Brain Cogn.* 48:117–132.

Ivry, R. B., and R. M. Spencer. 2004a. Evaluating the role of the cerebellum in temporal processing: Beware of the null hypothesis. *Brain: A Journal of Neurology* 127(Pt 8), E13.

Ivry, R. B., and R. M. Spencer. 2004b. The neural representation of time. *Curr. Opin. Neurobiol.* 14:225–232.

Ivry, R. B., R. M. Spencer, H. N. Zelaznik, and J. Diedrichsen. 2002. The cerebellum and event timing. *Ann. N. Y. Acad. Sci.* 978:302–317.

Jackson, S. A., and M. Csikszentmihalyi. 1999. *Flow in sports.* Champaign, IL: Human Kinetics.

Jacob, P., and M. Jeannerod. 2003. *Ways of seeing: The scope and limits of visual cognition.* New York: Oxford University Press.

James, W. 1983. *The principles of psychology*. Cambridge: Harvard University Press.

Jeannerod, M. 1988. *The neural and behavioural organization of goal-directed movements*. Oxford: Clarendon Press.

Jeannerod, M. 1997. *The cognitive neuroscience of action*. Oxford: Blackwell.

Jeannerod, M. 2006. *Motor cognition: What actions tell to the self*. New York: Oxford University Press.

Juarrero, A. 1999. *Dynamics in action: Intentional behavior as a complex system*. Cambridge: MIT Press.

Kabat-Zinn, J., A. O. Massion, J. Kristeller, L. G. Peterson, K. E. Fletcher, L. Pbert, et al. 1992. Effectiveness of a meditation-based stress reduction program in the treatment of anxiety disorders. *Am. J. Psychiatry* 149:936–943.

Kahneman, D. 1973. *Attention and effort*. Englewood Cliffs, NJ: Prentice-Hall.

Kahneman, D., and A. Treisman. 1984. Changing views of attention and automaticity. In *Varieties of attention*, ed. R. Parasuraman and D. R. Davies. Orlando: Academic Press, 29–61.

Kauss, D. R. 2001. *Mastering your inner game*. Champaign, IL: Human Kinetics.

Kremer, J. M. D., and D. M. Scully. 1994. *Psychology in sport*. London: Taylor & Francis.

Kuehl, K., J. Kuehl, and C. Tefertiller. 2005. *Mental toughness: A champion's state of mind*. Chicago: I.R. Dee.

LaBerge, D. 1998. Defining awareness by the triangular circuit of attention. *Psyche (Stuttg.)* 4 (7), Retrieved May 20, 2007, from http://psyche.cs.monash.edu.au/v4/psyche-4-07-laberge.html.

LaBerge, D. 2000. Clarifying the triangular circuit theory of attention and its relations to awareness: Replies to seven commentaries. *Psyche (Stuttg.)* 6 (6), Retrieved May 20, 2007, from http://psyche.cs.monash.edu.au/v6/psyche-6-06-laberge.html.

LaBerge, D. 1995. *Attentional processing: The brain's art of mindfulness*. Cambridge: Harvard University Press.

Lafargue, G., J. Paillard, Y. Lamarre, and A. Sirigu. 2003. Production and perception of grip force without proprioception: Is there a sense of effort in deafferented subjects? *Eur. J. Neurosci.* 17:2741–2749.

Langer, E. J. 1989. *Mindfulness*. Reading: Addison-Wesley/Addison Wesley Longman.

Langlois, R. N. 1998. Rule-following, expertise, and rationality: A new behavioral economics? In *Rationality in economics: Alternative perspectives*, ed. K. Dennis. Dordrecht: Kluwer Academic, 57–80.

Lutz, A., L. L. Greischar, N. B. Rawlings, M. Ricard, and R. J. Davidson. 2004. Long-term meditators self-induce high-amplitude gamma synchrony during mental practice. *Proc. Natl. Acad. Sci. USA* 101:16369–16373.

Maturana, H. R., and F. J. Varela. 1980. *Autopoiesis and cognition: The realization of the living.* Dordrecht: D. Reidel.

Metzinger, T., and V. Gallese. 2003. The emergence of a shared action ontology: Building blocks for a theory. *Consciousness and Cognition: An International Journal. Special Issue: Self and Action.* 12:549–571.

Metzinger, T. 2003. *Being no one: The self-model theory of subjectivity.* Cambridge: MIT Press.

Miller, J. J., K. Fletcher, and J. Kabat-Zinn. 1995. Three-year follow-up and clinical implications of a mindfulness meditation-based stress reduction intervention in the treatment of anxiety disorders. *Gen. Hosp. Psychiatry* 17:192–200.

Millman, D. 1999. *Body mind mastery: Creating success in sport and life.* Rev. ed. Novato, CA: New World Library.

Moller, A. C., E. L. Deci, and R. M. Ryan. 2006. Choice and ego-depletion: The moderating role of autonomy. *Pers. Soc. Psychol. Bull.* 32:1024–1036.

Moran, A. P. 1996. *The psychology of concentration in sport performers: A cognitive analysis.* Hove, UK: Psychology Press.

Mulert, C., E. Menzinger, G. Leicht, O. Pogarell, and U. Hegerl. 2005. Evidence for a close relationship between conscious effort and anterior cingulate cortex activity. *Int. J. Psychophysiol.* 56:65–80.

Muraven, M., D. M. Tice, and R. F. Baumeister. 1998. Self-control as limited resource. *J. Pers. Soc. Psychol.* 74(3):774–789.

Naccache, L., S. Dehaene, L. Cohen, M. O. Habert, E. Guichart-Gomez, D. Galanaud, et al. 2005. Effortless control: Executive attention and conscious feeling of mental effort are dissociable. *Neuropsychologia* 43:1318–1328.

Pashler, H. E. 1998. *The psychology of attention.* Cambridge: MIT Press.

Rothbart, M. K. 2005. The development of effortful control. In *Developing individuality in the human brain: A tribute to Michael I. Posner,* ed. U. Mayr, E. Awh, and S. W. Keele. Washington, DC: American Psychological Association, 167–188.

Rubio, S., E. Díaz, J. Martín, and J. M. Puente. 2004. Evaluation of subjective mental workload: A comparison of SWAT, NASA-TLX, and workload profile methods. *Applied Psychology: An International Review* 53(1):61–86.

Sarter, M., W. J. Gehring, and R. Kozak. 2006. More attention must be paid: The neurobiology of attentional effort. *Brain Res. Rev.* 51(2):145–160.

Schall, J. D. 2001. Neural basis of deciding, choosing and acting. *Nat. Rev. Neurosci.* 2:33–42.

Schulkin, Jay. 2007. *Effort: A behavioral neuroscience perspective on the will.* Mahwah, NJ: Erlbaum.

Sigman, M., and S. Dehaene. 2005. Parsing a cognitive task: A characterization of the mind's bottleneck. *PLoS Biol.* 3:e37.

Slingerland, E. G. 2003. *Effortless action: Wu-wei as conceptual metaphor and spiritual ideal in early China.* Oxford: Oxford University Press.

Smit, A. S., P. Eling, M. T. Hopman, and A. Coenen. 2005. Mental and physical effort affect vigilance differently. *Int. J. Psychophysiol.* 57:211–217.

Spencer, R. M., R. B. Ivry, and H. N. Zelaznik. 2005. Role of the cerebellum in movements: Control of timing or movement transitions? *Experimental Brain Research. Experimentelle Hirnforschung. Experimentation Cerebrale* 161:383–396.

Tomlin, D., M. A. Kayali, B. King-Casas, C. Anen, C. F. Camerer, S. R. Quartz, et al. 2006. Agent-specific responses in the cingulate cortex during economic exchanges. *Science* 312:1047–1050.

Vohs, K. D., and R. F. Baumeister. 2004. Ego depletion, self-control, and choice. In *Handbook of experimental existential psychology*, ed. J. Greenberg, S. L. Koole, and T. Pyszczynski. New York: Guilford, 398–410.

Wallace, B. A. 2003. *Buddhism and science: Breaking new ground.* New York: Columbia University Press.

Wallace, B. A. 2007. *Contemplative science: Where Buddhism and neuroscience converge.* New York: Columbia University Press.

Wallace, B. A., and Z. Houshmand. 1992. *A passage from solitude: Training the mind in a life embracing the world: A modern commentary on Tibetan Buddhist mind training.* Ithaca, NY: Snow Lion.

Wallace, B. A., and Z. Houshmand. 1999. *Boundless heart: The four immeasurables.* Ithaca, NY: Snow Lion.

Wallace, B. A., and Tsoçn-kha-pa Blo-bzaçn-grags-pa. 2005. *Balancing the mind: A Tibetan Buddhist approach to refining attention* [formerly titled *Bridge of quiescence*]. Ithaca, NY: Snow Lion.

Wulf, G. 2001. Directing attention to movement effects enhances learning: A review. *Psychon. Bull. Rev.* 8:648–660.

1 Effortful Attention Control

Brandon J. Schmeichel and Roy F. Baumeister

"Pay attention!"

This familiar directive reveals an important clue about attention: Sometimes it exacts a cost. But under what conditions is attention costly? And what currency is spent when a person "pays attention"? In this chapter, we review evidence that the effortful control of attention exacts a psychological cost that is paid by a temporary reduction in the capacity for self-control.

External and Internal Determinants of the Focus of Attention

Attention has two masters. Its first and most formidable master is the external world, or the environment that stimulates the senses to form the bricks and mortar of conscious awareness. (Note that "external" does not refer only to stimuli outside the person. Physical sensations and emotional states, for example, have an experiential quality that resides inside the person but nonetheless may become an object of attention much like other, external stimuli.) Loud noises, pungent odors, and beautiful strangers all have the power to attract attention quickly and effortlessly. The list of stimuli that capture attention can be expanded to include a whole host of biologically relevant objects and events that have populated the environment throughout human evolutionary history. Snakes, fire, and lightning are on the list, and so are infants' cries, moans of pleasure, and novel aromas. In fact, novel stimuli of all kinds capture attention (e.g., Shiffrin and Schneider 1977). People pay attention to these stimuli literally without trying, without expending effort. When detected by the senses, such stimuli grab attention and quickly earn a preferential place in conscious awareness. This is true even when attention is intently focused on something else. For example, consider a motorist navigating an automobile down a busy highway. Although attending to the road ahead and anticipating one's next driving maneuver is challenging enough to fully occupy attentional resources, a salient external stimulus such as a collision off to the side of the road is likely to warrant at least a glance in the direction of the collision.

The directive to "pay attention" does not refer to these fast, automatic forms of attending, except perhaps in a metaphorical sense, as if the collision were to say "You had better pay attention to me!" A person does not need to be told to pay attention to a stimulus that captures attention quickly and effortlessly. Rather, admonitions to pay attention are necessary in precisely the opposite circumstance, in which attention is diverted away from a task or event by a stimulus that captures attention. If a driver is attending to the remains of a collision off to the side of a busy and unfamiliar road, for example, the passengers in the car are likely to demand that the driver pay attention to the road! It is in these circumstances—the ones in which the person must train attention away from attention-grabbing stimuli and toward other tasks or events—that "paying attention" is necessary. We suggest that moving attention away from attention-grabbing events exacts a psychological cost because this entails the self-control of attention.

The second master of attention, then, is the person who does the attending. Whereas the external environment may capture attention and thereby determine where attention is placed, the person may intentionally shift attention or maintain focus elsewhere. We are not the first to make this distinction, of course (cf. Norman and Shallice 1986). Several theorists distinguish between bottom–up versus top–down influences on attention, meaning, respectively, those that filter up from the senses to influence conscious awareness versus those that filter down from the person's intentions and goals (e.g., Desimone and Duncan 1995). That distinction corresponds to our external versus internal distinction. Other theorists contrast exogenous control versus endogenous control of attention (e.g., Jonides 1981), which also relates to the external–internal distinction we have made.

It is important to note that not all internal (top–down, endogenous) determinants of the focus of attention are expected to exact a psychological cost. For example, a person's motivations and goals help to determine what stimuli will capture attention (e.g., Lang 1995), and these are properly considered internal determinants of the focus of attention. However, attending to what one is motivated to attend to while ignoring other stimuli typically does not require self-control.

We propose that attention control exacts a cost when it entails counteracting or resisting what one is compelled to do by internal (e.g., motivational) forces or by powerful external stimuli that automatically capture attention. In other words, attention must be controlled when the stimulus the person is attending to is a stimulus the person is not otherwise inclined to attend to. In such instances, paying attention may exact a cost because it requires self-control.

Self-Control, Attention Control, and Limited Resources

We define self-control as the capacity to override or alter one's predominant response tendencies. Self-control is commonly understood as resisting immediate gratifications for the sake of long-term gains or goals (e.g., Fujita, Trope, Liberman, and Levin-Sagi 2006; Metcalfe and Mischel 1999), but in our usage self-control refers more broadly to any instance in which a subdominant response is deliberately substituted for a dominant one.

Attention control is one form of self-control. Other forms include emotion regulation, behavioral inhibition, and impulse control. Some theorists have suggested that attention control is the single most important or influential form of self-control because it contributes to all the other forms (e.g., Baumeister, Heatherton, and Tice 1994). Attention control refers to efforts to override or alter one's predominant attentional focus or tendency. Researchers have identified at least three forms of attention control. *Selective attention* refers to the act of focusing attention on one subset of the environment while avoiding or ignoring other attention-grabbing aspects of the environment. As we described earlier, some stimuli capture attention effortlessly and automatically. To ignore such stimuli or to divert attention away from them requires selective attention. *Divided attention* is a second form of attention control. This refers to attending and responding to multiple streams of information simultaneously. Insofar as the dominant mode of attention is to follow one stream of information at a time, attention control is required to split attention between two or more information streams. A third form of attention control is *sustained attention*, which refers to focusing attention on a stimulus or activity for an extended period of time. Generally speaking, novel stimuli capture attention. To sustain attention on the same well-worn stimulus or activity, then, requires an element of effortful persistence and attention control.

The benefits of successful self-control are difficult to overstate. Research has indicated that success at self-control contributes to subjective well-being, satisfying interpersonal relationships, and high levels of academic achievement (Duckworth and Seligman 2005; Kelly and Conley 1987; Tangney, Baumeister, and Boone 2004). Success at self-control is also commonly associated with resisting temptation, breaking bad habits, and performing well under pressure. Conversely, failures of self-control are associated with intellectual underachievement, interpersonal conflict, irrepressible appetites or addictions, and many other adverse outcomes (see Baumeister and Vohs 2004).

The main thesis of this chapter is that attention control exacts a psychological cost, paid in the form of a temporary reduction in the capacity for self-control. This view was inspired by the strength model of self-control (Muraven and Baumeister 2000). According to the strength model, the capacity to override or alter one's predominant response tendencies (including attentional tendencies) operates like a limited inner resource or strength. The sufficiency of this strength for overriding responses is determined in part by the person's previous behavior. If the person has recently exercised self-control, then strength may be temporarily depleted and hence the capacity for further self-control may be diminished.

Support for the strength model has come from experiments assessing performance on consecutive self-control tasks. In one memorable experiment, for example, self-control was manipulated by instructing hungry participants to eat only radishes while faced with the tempting sight and smell of chocolate. Soon afterward, self-control was measured on an unrelated task that involved solving challenging and frustrating puzzles. Participants who had resisted the temptation to consume chocolate more quickly gave up trying to solve the puzzles, compared to other hungry participants who had been free to eat chocolate without restriction (Baumeister, Bratslavsky, Muraven, and Tice 1998). This experiment and several others have supported the strength model by finding that initial efforts at self-control temporarily impair subsequent volitional efforts, as though the initial efforts reduced the strength of the impulse-control mechanism (for a review, see Baumeister, Schmeichel, and Vohs 2007).

In our view, attention control is a form of self-control. Consequently, we expect that acts of attention control consume and deplete the limited resource or strength that underlies self-control. By the same token, acts of attention control should vary in effectiveness according to the state of this limited resource, such that success at attention control should be less likely following other, unrelated acts of self-control.

Attention Control Depletes Resources

We begin by reviewing evidence that effortful attention control causes a temporary reduction in self-control. The basic experimental strategy used to test this hypothesis is as follows. Participants are asked to perform one of two tasks at the start of the experiment. One task requires attention control and the other one does not; otherwise the tasks are alike. Later in the experiment, all participants perform a test of self-control. Insofar as attention control exacts a cost that is paid with a reduction in self-control, participants who initially exercised attention control should perform worse on the self-control task later in the experiment, compared to participants who did not initially exercise attention control.

Because there is no single, gold-standard method to assess self-control, several different methods have been used to test the hypothesis that attention control causes a reduction in self-control. These range from tests of logical reasoning to assessments of the voluntary regulation of emotional expressions. By the same token, attention control is multifaceted, and so researchers have sought to manipulate the presence versus absence of attention control using different tasks. Before diving into the literature review, we will describe in detail the two main tasks that have been used to manipulate the presence versus absence of effortful attention control.

The first task, which we will call the *attention-control video task,* is adapted from an experiment by Gilbert, Krull, and Pelham (1988). For this task, participants watch a video clip depicting a woman being interviewed by an off-camera interviewer. The clip is played without audio, purportedly because the experimenter is interested in how participants form impressions based on others' nonverbal behavior. In addition to the woman being interviewed, a series of one-syllable words appear at the bottom of the screen. The words are meant to mimic the running tickers that have become ubiquitous on cable news, finance, and sports channels.

In the typical experiment using the attention-control video task, participants are randomly assigned to watch the interview clip in one of two ways. In one condition, participants are instructed simply to watch the interview and are given no instruction regarding the words at the bottom of the screen. We will refer to this as the effortless attention condition because participants in this condition are free to attend to any and all parts of the viewing screen. In the other condition, participants are instructed to focus on the woman being interviewed and to ignore any words that appear on the screen. Because attention automatically orients toward novel stimuli (Shiffrin and Schneider 1977), participants in this condition must exercise attention control to focus on the woman and to ignore the words that appear on the screen. We will refer to this as the effortful attention condition.

The experiments we review below used this attention-control video task to compare the aftereffects of effortful versus effortless attention. All participants in these experiments viewed the same video stimulus; the key difference between conditions was in how participants attended to it. In support of the view that the two viewing conditions entail differing degrees of attention control, the effortful attention condition is consistently rated as being more difficult and requiring more effort than the effortless attention condition. Insofar as paying attention exacts a psychological cost, this experimental manipulation provides a reasonable strategy to detect that cost.

The second major task that has been used to manipulate the presence versus absence of effortful attention control is the Stroop color-naming task (Stroop 1935). This task requires participants to name the ink color of a series of words as quickly and as accurately as possible. In the effortful attention condition, the words and ink colors are mismatched (e.g., GREEN is printed in blue ink). The predominant response tendency upon viewing a printed word is to read the word (i.e., "green"). Because this response tendency produces an incorrect response (in the example, the correct response is "blue"), participants must focus their attention on the ink color and away from the predominant reading response.

In the effortless attention conditions, participants also name ink colors but the specifics beyond color-naming vary across experiments. In some experiments, the words and ink colors match, so that the predominant tendency (to read the text) produces the same correct responses as naming the ink color (e.g., GREEN is printed in green ink). Here, there is no need to override the predominant response tendency. In other experiments, the effortless attention condition entails naming the ink color of a string of Xs. In this instance, there is no response interference to contend with (i.e., no word to be read), and so participants can simply name the ink color. Indeed, participants are perfectly capable of naming the ink color of a string of Xs quickly and automatically.

In support of the idea that the Stroop color-naming task requires attention control, research has indicated that individual differences in the capacity to control attention predict performance on mismatched or incongruent trials of the task (e.g., Kane and Engle 2003). Hence, experiments that compare the aftereffects of the two versions of the color-naming task provide a valuable context in which to detect any costs associated with effortful attention control.

Evidence That Attention Control Undermines Subsequent Acts of Self-Control

Cognitive Aftereffects of Attention Control

A series of experiments to test the hypothesis that attention control exacts a psychological cost that may be detected on subsequent tasks was reported by Schmeichel, Vohs, and Baumeister (2003). They predicted that prior efforts at attention control would impair some (but not all) forms of intelligent thought. Specifically, they predicted that relatively simple forms of thinking would be largely unimpaired, whereas more complex thought processes would show substantial impairments following effortful attention control.

Schmeichel and colleagues (2003) used the attention-control video task to manipulate initial efforts at attention control. Following the attention-control manipulation, participants completed portions of the Graduate Record Exam (GRE), a standard test given to aspirants to graduate study in the United States. One portion of the GRE—the Analytical subtest—required participants to construct mental models, make inferences, and derive logical conclusions on the basis of a set of postulates. Another portion of the GRE—the Reading Comprehension subtest—required participants to read and comprehend a dense passage and then to elaborate on their understanding of the text to answer relatively difficult questions about it. Participants who had previously exercised attention control were less successful at these challenges. In contrast, prior efforts at attention control had little effect on performance of a short-term memory test, which required participants to encode novel information into memory and recall it a short while later. For example, in one study, participants encoded a list of nonsense syllables and attempted to recall them a short while thereafter. Prior efforts at attention control did not influence performance on this test of short-term memory. Thus, apparently, some forms of thought are unaffected by prior efforts at attention control, whereas other (more complex) processes suffer when a person "pays attention."

These results were broadly consistent with the view that attention control temporarily reduces the capacity for self-control. To perform well on tests of complex

Effortful Attention Control

cognitive processing requires a degree of self-control to persist at problem solving when the correct answer is not immediately apparent. By contrast, success at the simpler cognitive tasks required less self-control and could be accomplished on the basis of automatic processes and well-practiced habits, such as those involved in encoding information into short-term memory. Thus, prior efforts at attention control undermined performance of complex cognitive tasks.

One complex cognitive process that is closely associated with self-control is thought suppression. A study by Gailliot, Schmeichel, and Baumeister (2006, study 3) tested the hypothesis that effortful attention control reduces the capacity to suppress thoughts and therefore increases the salience of thoughts related to death.

Research based on terror management theory suggests that people are motivated to keep thoughts of death out of conscious awareness (Arndt, Greenberg, Solomon, Pyszczynski, and Simon 1997; Greenberg, Pyszczynski, and Solomon 1986). One proximal or immediate response to being reminded about death is, therefore, to suppress or ignore death-related thought. Thought suppression requires self-control, however, so prior efforts to control attention may undermine the capacity to keep death-related thoughts out of awareness. Among individuals who have recently attempted to control attention, then, a reminder of death may cause an increase in death-related thought, even though this is precisely what they are motivated to avoid.

Gailliot and colleagues (2006) used the attention-control video task described previously. When the video had ended, all participants were shown a drawing and asked to list the first 10 thoughts that came to mind while looking at the drawing. The image in the drawing was ambiguous, such that it could be perceived either as two men sitting at a table enjoying a bottle of wine, or as a skull, with the head of the two men serving as the eye sockets and the table's legs serving as the teeth of the skull.

The prediction was that, compared to the absence of such efforts, prior efforts at attention control would cause participants to perseverate on the death-related content of the image (i.e., the skull). They did. Participants who had previously exercised attention control listed more death-related thoughts than did participants who had not previously exercised attention control. These results supported the idea that attention control has as a cost, a relative inability to keep unwanted thoughts from mind. In the case of this experiment, the specific cost of "paying attention" was an increase in thoughts associated with death.

Effortful attention control has also been linked to subsequent increases in racially biased responding. A study by Govorun and Payne (2006) manipulated initial efforts at attention control by having participants perform the Stroop task either for a brief period of time (approximately 1 minute) or for a longer period of time (approximately 15 minutes). After the Stroop task, participants completed an ostensibly unrelated study dealing with how people make quick decisions. More specifically, participants attempted to classify objects appearing on a screen as either guns or tools. Immediately prior to the appearance of each object, a face flashed on the screen for 200 milliseconds. Participants were instructed to treat the face as a warning signal that an object was about to appear on the screen. When the object appeared, participants were to respond as quickly as possible by pressing a key labeled either "gun" or "tool."

Some of the faces that flashed on the screen depicted white males and some depicted black males. Previous research had shown that people are more likely to identify harmless tools as guns when they are preceded by the face of a black man versus a white man. Hence, the faces served to prime racially biased responses. Govorun and Payne predicted that effortful attention control would reduce the capacity to control the influence of the primes on categorization behavior, and indeed it did. Automatic biases linking black males with weapons were more likely to guide behavior on the "quick decisions" task following a lengthy exertion of attention control. Following a much less taxing exertion of attention control, however, the automatic biases were controlled and hence served as less influential guides of behavior.

Prior efforts at attention control, therefore, appear to reduce the capacity to inhibit thoughts about death (Gailliot et al. 2006) and racially biased responses (Govorun and Payne 2006). Subsequent research sought to extend these findings by testing the more general hypothesis that initial efforts at attention control undermine subsequent efforts at attention control.

In one study by Schmeichel (2007), attention control was manipulated using the attention-control video task described previously. After watching the interview clip, participants completed a cognitive task that is commonly used to assess the capacity to control attention. This task, known as the Operation Span (OSPAN) task (Turner and Engle 1989), required participants to shift their attention between solving mathematical equations and encoding and recalling target words. For example, participants saw *Is (9 × 3) − 1 = 2?* and had to indicate ("Yes" or "No") whether the given answer was correct. Then participants read a target word (e.g., *house*) for later recall. One target word was presented after each equation. Thus, participants read an equation, evaluated whether it was correct, read a target word, and then advanced to the next equation, the next target word, and so on. Participants saw two, three, four, or five equation–word pairings before being prompted to recall the target words in the set. Participants worked through 15 sets totaling 48 equation–word pairings in all.

If attention control operates like a limited resource, then performance on the OSPAN task should vary according to how participants watched the woman being interviewed during the first phase of the experiment. Participants who had controlled their attention to ignore words during the interview should perform worse than participants who did not have to ignore words while watching the interview. This is precisely what happened. Participants who had kept their attention focused on the interviewee while ignoring the words on the screen subsequently performed more poorly on a test of divided attention. More specifically, they were less successful at simultaneously encoding target words and solving mathematical equations. Hence, it appeared that one cost of paying attention (by focusing on the interviewee) is a reduction in the capacity to pay attention to two tasks simultaneously (storing words in memory while solving math problems). In other words, initial efforts at a selective attention task undermined subsequent efforts to divide attention. This pattern is consistent with the idea that effortful attention causes a temporary reduction in self-control, including the self-control of attention.

A follow-up experiment by Schmeichel (2007, experiment 3) indicated that attention control could undermine subsequent efforts to control emotional responses. Initial efforts at attention control were manipulated by having participants perform either a task that required them to encode and recall words (i.e., a simple short-term memory task) or a more challenging task that required them to encode and recall words while also solving mathematical equations (i.e., the OSPAN task described above). Although success at both tasks requires effort and attention, the working memory test required a great deal more attention control. After their respective tests, participants viewed an emotionally charged film clip under instructions to inhibit all outward expressions of emotional response. Participants' faces were videotaped and subsequently coded for visible expressions of emotion. The prediction was that, relative to participants who had performed a short-term maintenance task, those who had performed a working memory task would be less successful at inhibiting their emotional responses (i.e., they would express more emotion), as though the attention-control task temporarily depleted the capacity for emotion regulation.

Within this basic framework, this experiment also sought to address an alternate account of the predicted results, namely, that performing any effortful or difficult task reduces the capacity for self-control. According to this account, expending effort undermines subsequent self-control regardless of whether the initial effort was devoted to attention control. Schmeichel (2007) investigated this possibility by comparing the aftereffects of three different tasks that varied in difficulty. In one condition, participants performed a divided attention task that required them to coordinate performance on two tasks at once (i.e., the OSPAN task). In the other two conditions, participants performed tasks that required them to maintain information in short-term memory. The two short-term memory tasks differed in terms of difficulty, but neither of them required a great deal of attention control. If effort expenditure or the difficulty of a task is responsible for subsequent decrements in self-control, then performance on the emotion inhibition task should reveal a linear pattern such that inhibition is poorest after the divided attention task and best after the easy short-term memory task, with inhibition after the moderately difficult short-term memory task falling somewhere in between. If, however, only efforts at attention control reduce the capacity for self-control, then inhibition ability should be poorest after the divided attention task but equally good after the two short-term memory tasks.

To make the comparison between the aftereffects of effort expenditure versus attention control even more rigorous, the short-term memory tasks were made to last approximately six minutes longer than the divided attention task. If performing the divided attention task impairs response inhibition relative to performing the more time-consuming short-term memory tasks, then the conclusion that exerting attention control, rather than effort, is responsible for depleted self-control would be considerably strengthened.

The results convincingly supported the attention-control view. That is, participants who had completed the divided attention task were less successful at inhibiting emotional expressions during the subsequent video clip, compared to participants who had completed the short-term memory tests. Crucially, emotional expressivity did not differ between the two short-term memory groups: Those who had completed the difficult short-term memory task expressed just as little emotion as participants who had completed the easy short-term memory task. The two short-term memory tasks differed in difficulty (both according to participants' self-reports and according to participants' performance), so task difficulty was not responsible for the subsequent decrement in the self-control of emotional responses. The key distinction between the short-term memory tasks and the divided attention (i.e., OSPAN) task was the degree of attention control required. The task that required the most attention control had the most detrimental effect on the subsequent inhibition of emotional responding.

Interpersonal Consequences of Attention Control

Vohs and colleagues extended research on the aftereffects of attention control by considering the effects of attention control on interpersonal processes. They examined the extent to which the exercise of attention control made people prefer to engage in unlikable or maladaptive interpersonal styles. For example, one study by Vohs, Baumeister, and Ciarocco (2005, study 7) examined the effects of attention control on the preferred intimacy level of self-disclosure. Upon first meeting somebody or in the early stages of a relationship, a moderate level of intimacy in self-disclosure is often seen as likable because it indicates that one wants to increase the level of closeness in the relationship without overwhelming the other person with overly intimate details and without underwhelming the other person with impersonal trivia or an aloof attitude. Adaptive, likable interactions with a new acquaintance, then, often entail a moderate degree of self-disclosure.

People differ in how willing or comfortable they are in disclosing information about themselves, however. People with an avoidant attachment style are prone to avoid closeness. As a result, they tend to disclose relatively impersonal or nonintimate information about themselves to others, particularly under stressful conditions. People with an anxious–ambivalent attachment style, by contrast, are eager for closeness and therefore tend to disclosure intimate or personal information about themselves to others under stressful conditions.

Vohs and colleagues (2005) tested the hypothesis that initial efforts at attention control would undermine adaptive self-presentation and cause participants to migrate toward their predisposed desires for intimacy. They reasoned that efforts at attention control would cause avoidant individuals to become particularly impersonal or non-intimate in their preferred level of self-disclosure, whereas anxious–ambivalent individuals would prefer overly intimate or particularly personal self-presentations after an exercise in attention control. Put differently, the researchers anticipated that the cost of "paying attention" would be to bias self-presentations in a direction consistent with participants' characteristic attachment styles—and away from the most adaptive and likable degree of self-presentation (i.e., moderately intimate).

Participants first performed the Stroop task or a similar task that did not require attention control (name the color of Xs). Next, participants were provided with a list of topics from the Relationship Closeness Induction Task (RCIT; Sedikides, Campbell, Reeder, and Elliot 1998). The RCIT is typically used to create an increasingly intimate interaction between unacquainted individuals. The RCIT entails first asking and answering a series of nonintimate, low-disclosure questions, then progressing to moderate-disclosure questions, and, finally, higher disclosure questions. Vohs and colleagues (2005) presented participants with a list of questions from the RCIT in random order, such that low-, moderate-, and high-disclosure questions were intermixed throughout the list. Participants were asked to indicate how much they would like to discuss each topic. Because the topics on the RCIT list vary in intimacy (Sedikides et al. 1998), the researchers could quantify how willing (or unwilling) participants were to discuss intimate topics with a stranger.

As expected, exercising attention control at the start of the study caused participants to prefer levels of self-disclosure that veered away from adaptive, moderate levels of self-disclosure. Anxious–ambivalent individuals, who are prone to overly intimate self-disclosures, reported preferring more intimate self-disclosures after they had completed the attention-control task compared to the simpler, non-attention-control task. And participants with an avoidant attachment style preferred less intimate disclosures after the Stroop task versus the simpler, non-attention-control task.

These results indicated that the self-disclosure preferences of insecurely attached individuals were influenced by the prior exercise of attention control. In the absence of effortful attention control, however, all participants tended to favor moderately intimate self-disclosures—the kind that are typically the most pleasant and appropriate when interacting with a new acquaintance and that make the best impression.

Another study by Vohs and colleagues (2005, study 8) indicated that effortful attention control causes an increase in narcissistic self-descriptions (which, like inappropriate disclosures, tend to make bad impressions on interaction partners). Attention control was manipulated using the attention-control video task described previously. Shortly after watching the videotape, participants completed a self-report measure of narcissism known as the Narcissistic Personality Inventory (NPI; Raskin and Terry 1988). The NPI asked participants to respond True or False to statements such as "If I ruled the world it would be a much better place" and "I am going to be a great person." The prior exercise of attention control caused participants to endorse more narcissistic statements on the NPI. Given that narcissism is often viewed by others as an undesirable, unlikable personality characteristic, it seems fair to say that one cost of "paying attention" may be an inflated view of self that may be detrimental to interpersonal relationships.

Research by Vohs and Faber (2007) tested the impact of attention control on consumer behavior. They manipulated initial efforts at attention control using the attention-control video task. After viewing the videotaped interview, participants studied pictures of several expensive products and were asked to indicate the price they would be willing to pay for each product. The list of products included boats, cars, stoves, and watches, among other items. The total amount of money participants were willing to pay for all the products was the dependent variable. The results indicated that participants who had previously exercised attention control assigned higher prices to the products compared to participants who had not previously exercised attention control. Hence, this study suggests that "paying attention" may have a financial cost, insofar as it leads to an increased willingness to pay more for potential purchases.

Effects of Attention Control on Task Persistence
The evidence presented so far suggests that attention control (and effortful self-control more generally) depletes some inner energy that is required for subsequent self-control tasks. One study by Wallace and Baumeister (2002) tested an alternative explanation for the psychological cost associated with attention control. Wallace and Baumeister reasoned that perhaps the results could be explained by the fact that the exercise of attention control leads people to experience failure or to view themselves as poor at attention control. Attention control is often experienced as effortful and difficult, and so after exercising attention control participants may feel as though they did not perform as well as they should have performed. In this view, poorer self-control following an attention-control task may reflect the person's response to failing at the initial attention-control task rather than the depletion of resource for self-control. To test this hypothesis, Wallace and Baumeister gave participants explicit feedback about their performance on an initial attention-control task and then measured their self-control on a subsequent task. If attention control impairs subsequent performance because people believe they failed at the initial attention-control task, then those who receive success feedback should not show any impairment on a subsequent task. On the other hand, if the costs of attention control arise because of the depletion of an

inner resource for self-control, then the impairment should occur regardless of the feedback participants receive.

In the first phase of the experiment, some participants completed a version of the Stroop color-naming task that required them to exercise attention control, whereas other participants completed a similar color-naming task that did not require attention control. Participants who had completed the attention-control version of the color-naming task received either positive feedback, negative feedback, or no feedback about their performance on the task. Participants in the positive feedback condition were told that they had made fewer errors and had performed much more quickly than most other participants (thus, they had performed better all around). Participants in the negative feedback condition were told that they had made more errors and had performed much more slowly than most other participants (thus, they had performed worse than others). Participants in the no-feedback condition proceeded directly to the next task, which constituted the dependent measure in this experiment. For this task, participants attempted to trace a figure without retracing any lines and without lifting their pen from the paper (from Glass and Singer 1972). Participants were instructed to work on the puzzle until they had solved it or until they grew weary of the task. Unbeknownst to participants, the figure was impossible to trace as instructed. The experimenter timed how long participants attempted to solve the unsolvable figure-tracing puzzle to serve as the dependent measure of self-control. Persistence in the face of failure has long been a standard measure of self-control, because one is discouraged and frustrated and would like to quit, so the impulse to quit must be overridden in order for the person to keep working.

Participants who performed the attention-control version of the color-naming task persisted for less time at the subsequent figure-tracing puzzle than participants who had performed the simpler (no attention control) version of the color-naming task. Hence, one cost of "paying attention" appears to be reduced persistence at subsequent challenges. Furthermore, the cost of attention control was unaltered by performance feedback. Receiving positive feedback about performance on an attention-control task did not increase subsequent persistence, and receiving negative feedback did not reduce subsequent persistence, relative to receiving no feedback about attention-control performance. Thus, the results argued against the idea that the self-perception of failure at attention control leads to impairments on subsequent, ostensibly unrelated tasks. Rather, they lent additional support to the view that effortful attention control depletes an inner resource or strength that is required for subsequent acts of self-control, which in this case entailed forcing oneself to persist at a difficult task.

A clever experiment by Webb and Sheeran (2003) revealed a way to minimize or reduce the psychological cost of attention control. Participants were asked to perform the Stroop color-naming task in one of three ways. All participants viewed a series of words that were presented in different colors of ink. In the no-attention-control condition, participants simply read the words. In the attention-control condition, participants named the ink color in which the words were printed, and as is common in the Stroop color–word interference task, the words and the ink color mismatched. Participants in a third condition were also asked to name the ink color of a series of words, but these participants were further asked to form an implementation intention pertaining to the task. These participants were instructed to tell themselves: "As soon as I see the word I will ignore its meaning (for example, by concentrating on the second letter only) and I will name the color ink it is printed in."

Webb and Sheeran (2003) reasoned that the implementation intention could make otherwise effortful attention less effortful. Previous research had indicated that implementation intentions pass control of behavior from the self to anticipated environmental cues (Gollwitzer 1999). Thus, once the implementation intention is formed, the relevant behavior (e.g., naming the ink color) is elicited quickly and automatically by the relevant environmental cue (e.g., the word). If that is correct, then participants should be able to exercise effective attention control without experiencing a decline in subsequent performance.

After performing their respective color-naming tasks, all participants attempted to solve figure-tracing puzzles. As in the experiment by Wallace and Baumeister (2002), the puzzles were unsolvable and the main dependent variable was the duration for which participants persisted at trying to solve the puzzles. The results replicated the Wallace and Baumeister finding: Participants who performed the attention-control version of the color-naming task persisted less on the subsequent task than participants who performed the version of the task that did not require attention control. More important, the results indicated that the implementation intention eliminated the psychological cost of attention control: Participants who had formed implementation intentions to exercise attention control persisted just as long at the unsolvable puzzles as participants who had not previously exercised attention control. These findings suggest that making attention control more automatic, such as by forming specific intentions (how and when) to exercise attention control, helps to reduce the psychological cost of attention control.

Physiological Consequences of Attention Control

An ambitious series of studies by Gailliot and colleagues specified a physiological cost of attention control—reduced glucose in the bloodstream. Glucose is a vital fuel for the brain's functions. Gailliot and colleagues hypothesized that attention control (and self-control more generally) may be a particularly taxing brain function that draws on and consumes larger amounts of glucose than other, simpler mental operations.

In a first study linking attention control to glucose (Gailliot, Baumeister, et al. 2007, study 1), participants reported to a laboratory, and an experimenter assessed their baseline blood glucose levels with a blood sampling lancet. Blood glucose levels were measured (mg/dL) using an Accu-Chek compact meter. Next, the exercise of attention control was manipulated using the attention-control video task. After participants watched the video, the experimenter assessed blood glucose levels a second time.

Blood glucose levels were lower after participants had exercised attention control while watching a video—lower than their own levels before the video and lower than those of participants who had just watched the same video without controlling attention. These results provided the first evidence that attention control may be costly in a physiological sense, such that the exercise of attention control consumes large amounts of glucose.

A follow-up study (Gailliot, Baumeister, et al. 2007, study 3) tested the hypothesis that the drop in blood glucose following effortful attention control helps to explain some of the psychological costs of controlling attention. Once again, a baseline measure of blood glucose levels was collected, and then all participants watched a videotaped interview under instructions to ignore any words that might appear on the screen. (Note that all participants in this experiment were instructed to exercise attention control.) Following a second glucose measurement, participants completed the Stroop color-naming task, which is a popular measure of attention control. As described previously, the Stroop task requires the participant to override an incipient response (i.e., to read aloud the name of the word) in order to say instead the color in which the word is printed, and in that sense it requires participants to control their attention. The hypothesis was that lower blood glucose should impair Stroop performance in the sense of causing the person to take longer to get the right answer and in terms of making more errors along the way.

As predicted, lower glucose after having watched the video was associated with poorer Stroop performance. Specifically, the lower the person's glucose levels after exercising attention control, the more time it took to complete the Stroop task. Number of errors on the Stroop task showed a similar though nonsignificant pattern, such that lower glucose was associated with making more errors.

An additional study (Gailliot, Baumeister, et al. 2007, study 7) indicated that restoring glucose to the bloodstream eliminated the psychological cost of attention control. In this study, participants first completed 20 Stroop trials as a baseline measure of Stroop ability. They then were administered the attention–control video task, with half simply watching the videotaped interview and the other half being instructed to keep their attention focused on the woman and not on the words while watching it. After watching the tape, participants rated how often they had looked at the woman and the words, respectively. Next, participants were given 14 ounces of lemonade sweetened with either sugar (glucose condition) or a sugar substitute (placebo condition). Participants and the experimenter were blind to condition. Participants then completed filler questionnaires to allow time for the glucose from the drink (if they had any) to be metabolized. Last, participants completed 80 Stroop trials separated into four blocks. Speed and errors on the Stroop task constituted the dependent measures of self-control performance.

In the placebo condition, attention-control participants made more errors than watch normally participants. Once again, prior efforts at attention control undermined subsequent performance on the Stroop task (this time in terms of number of errors). This was not the case in the glucose condition, however. The glucose drink eliminated the tendency for initial efforts at attention control to impair Stroop performance. These results supported the hypothesis that glucose replenishes what has been depleted by effortful attention control and thereby attenuates the psychological costs of "paying attention."

Summary

The research reviewed in this section indicates that effortful attention control temporarily reduces the capacity for self-control. This psychological cost of paying attention was evident in impaired performance on tests of logical reasoning and reading comprehension, an increase in thoughts related to death, an increase in racially prejudiced responding, a reduced capacity to suppress emotional expressions, an increase in preferences to engage maladaptive self-presentational styles, increased narcissism, an increase in the price consumers were willing to pay for expensive products, reduced levels of glucose in the bloodstream, and reduced persistence at difficult challenges. These findings are consistent with the limited resource model of self-control insofar as acts of attention control appear to consume and deplete an inner resource required for further volitional efforts.

If attention control relies on the same limited resource as other forms of self-control, then acts of attention control should vary in effectiveness according to the state of this limited resource. More precisely, success at attention control should be less likely following other, unrelated acts of self-control. In the next section, we review the evidence pertaining to this hypothesis.

Evidence That Self-Control Undermines Subsequent Acts of Attention Control

Here we review evidence that acts of self-control cause a temporary reduction in the operation of attention control. The basic experimental strategy used to test this hypothesis is as follows. Participants are asked to perform one of two tasks at the start of the experiment. One task requires self-control and the other one does not; otherwise the tasks are alike. Later in the experiment, all participants perform a test of attention control. Insofar as self-control and attention control rely on the same underlying resource, then participants who initially exercised self-control should perform worse on the attention-control task later in the experiment, compared to participants who did not initially exercise self-control.

Important evidence that acts of self-control may undermine subsequent efforts to control attention was reported by Richeson and Shelton (2003). They found that racial interactions may undermine efforts at attention control. In one study white participants engaged in an interaction with either a black person (interracial interaction) or a white person (same-race interaction). After the interaction, all participants completed the Stroop color-naming task. The results indicated that performance on the Stroop task was undermined by a prior interracial interaction, particularly among participants who harbored relatively higher levels of racial bias. The authors argued that, compared to relatively nonbiased participants, white participants who harbored higher levels of racial bias would have to exercise self-control during an interracial interaction. Indeed, the evidence suggested that efforts to inhibit racial bias during the interaction were responsible for subsequent impairments in attention control on the Stroop task.

The findings reported by Richeson and Shelton (2003) represent the converse of the results reported later by Govorun and Payne (2006). Whereas Govorun and Payne found that performing the Stroop task undermined efforts to inhibit racially biased responding subsequently, Richeson and Shelton observed that efforts to inhibit racial bias led to poorer performance on the Stroop task subsequently. In tandem, these results strongly suggest a connection between attention control (as required by the Stroop color-naming task) and the self-control of racially biased behaviors, and they lend support to the view that attention control and other forms of self-control draw upon the same underlying resource or energy.

An experiment by Gailliot et al. (2006, study 7) found that inhibiting unwanted thoughts undermines subsequent efforts at attention control. Upon being reminded of the inevitability of their own personal death, people often attempt to suppress thoughts of death from conscious awareness (Arndt et al. 1997). Thought suppression depletes the limited resource for self-control, so a reminder of death should undermine the capacity to control attention. Gailliot and colleagues tested this hypothesis by prompting participants to ponder their own inevitable death or to ponder an aversive topic that was unrelated to death. A short time later, all participants attempted the Stroop color-naming task. On some trials, the meaning of words was mismatched with the ink color in which the words were printed, and so naming the ink color required participants to exercise attention control. On other trials, the words' meaning and ink color were matched, so that naming the ink color did not require attention control.

As predicted, participants who had pondered their own death performed worse than participants who had pondered a topic that was unrelated to death, but only on trials that required attention control (i.e., mismatched or incongruent color-naming trials). Performance on the congruent trials was unaffected by the manipulation of mortality salience. These findings supported the view that efforts to suppress troubling thoughts of death temporarily undermine the capacity to control attention.

The experiments reviewed thus far share some common elements. They all used a form of response inhibition as the initial self-control task, and they measured subsequent attention-control performance using the Stroop color-naming task. To provide converging evidence for the view that acts of self-control temporarily undermine subsequent efforts at attention control, Schmeichel (2007, experiment 4) used an initial self-control task that required response exaggeration (not inhibition) and a different dependent measure of attention-control capacity.

The experiment by Schmeichel (2007) revealed that emotion regulation undermines subsequent performance on a divided attention task. Participants in this experiment viewed two distressing film clips—one that depicted an eye surgery and one that depicted children discussing tragedies that had befallen their families. Participants were instructed to view the film clips in one of two randomly assigned ways. One group was instructed to exaggerate their emotional response to the film clips, whereas the other group was instructed simply to view the film clips. Subsequently, all participants attempted the OSPAN task, a widely used and well-validated measure of the capacity to control attention. The prediction was that exaggerating emotional responses would deplete the capacity for attention control and so disrupt performance on the OSPAN task. It did. Exaggerators scored significantly worse than other participants, consistent with the notion that prior efforts at emotion regulation have a negative impact on attention control. These results also suggested that efforts at emotion regulation had a greater impact on attention control than did negative mood. Participants in the two groups reported experiencing equally negative mood states in response to the film clips, so it appeared that attention control was impaired by prior efforts to regulate emotional responses above and beyond any effect of negative mood that stemmed from watching the distressing film clips.

Summary

The research reviewed in this section indicates that acts of self-control undermine subsequent efforts to control attention. Performance on tests of attention-control capacity was undermined by prior acts of inhibiting racial bias, inhibiting thoughts of death, and exaggerating emotional expressions. Furthermore, attention-control capacity was measured in two different ways, including the Stroop color-naming task and the OSPAN task. These findings are consistent with the limited resource model of self-control insofar as diverse acts of self-control appear to consume and deplete an inner resource required for subsequent attention control.

Implications and Conclusions

The findings we have reviewed indicate that control of attention draws on the same resources as needed for other acts of self-control. We saw that controlling attention led to subsequently poorer self-control on other, unrelated tasks. Conversely, we saw that a variety of basic self-control tasks led to subsequent impairments in the control of attention. These two complementary patterns indicate that the first act of self-control depletes some resource, leaving less left over for the second task. Either or both tasks may involve control of attention.

We also reported some evidence about what this resource is. The glucose studies by Gailliot, Baumeister, et al. (2007) indicate that blood glucose levels are highly relevant to success at self-control and attention control. Primarily converted from ingested nutrients, glucose is transmitted throughout the body via blood. Glucose provides fuel for the activities of both the body and the brain. Brain processes that are involved in controlling attention (and self-control generally) use more of this fuel than routine or automatic brain processes.

Recent evidence suggests that, with practice, self-control may become less effortful and less depleting to perform. For example, Gailliot, Plant, Butz, and Baumeister (2007) observed that regular exercises in self-control help to make effortless what was once an effortful act of control. With enough practice, overriding a response tendency may itself become the predominant tendency. In this way, deliberate self-control may pave the way for relatively effortless, automatic forms of self-regulation to emerge. Limited resources for self-control can then be devoted to other, more difficult, challenges.

We started this chapter by considering the familiar command "Pay attention!" We can perhaps now see why payment was chosen as an appropriate metaphor for directing awareness and mental processes toward some particular event or stimulus. Controlling attention not only requires effort, but this effort depletes a limited resource of body and mind. As with real money, people have a limited amount and can get into difficulties if they have expended too much. Willpower, and, perhaps, blood glucose, constitutes the coin in which attention is paid.

References

Arndt, J., J. Greenberg, S. Solomon, T. Pyszczynski, and L. Simon. 1997. Suppression, accessibility of death-related thoughts, and cultural worldview defense: Exploring the psychodynamics of terror management. *J. Pers. Soc. Psychol.* 73:5–18.

Baumeister, R. F., E. Bratslavsky, M. Muraven, and D. M. Tice. 1998. Ego depletion: Is the active self a limited resource? *J. Pers. Soc. Psychol.* 74:1252–1265.

Baumeister, R. F., T. F. Heatherton, and D. M. Tice. 1994. *Losing control: How and why people fail at self-regulation.* San Diego, CA: Academic Press.

Baumeister, R. F., B. J. Schmeichel, and K. D. Vohs. 2007. Self-regulation and the executive function: The self as controlling agent. In *Social psychology: Handbook of basic principles.* 2nd ed., ed. A. W. Kruglanski and E. T. Higgins. New York: Guilford, 516–539.

Baumeister, R. F., and K. D. Vohs. 2004. *Handbook of self-regulation: Research, theory, and applications*. New York: Guilford.

Desimone, R., and J. Duncan. 1995. Neural mechanisms of selective visual attention. *Annu. Rev. Neurosci.* 18:193–222.

Duckworth, A. L., and M. E. Seligman. 2005. Self-discipline outdoes IQ in predicting academic performance of adolescents. *Psychol. Sci.* 16:939–944.

Fujita, K., Y. Trope, N. Liberman, and M. Levin-Sagi. 2006. Construal levels and self-control. *J. Pers. Soc. Psychol.* 90:351–367.

Gailliot, M. T., R. F. Baumeister, C. N. DeWall, J. K. Maner, E. A. Plant, D. M. Tice, L. E. Brewer, and B. J. Schmeichel. 2007. Self-control relies on glucose as a limited energy source: Willpower is more than a metaphor. *J. Pers. Soc. Psychol.* 92:325–336.

Gailliot, M. T., E. A. Plant, D. A. Butz, and R. F. Baumeister. 2007. Increasing self-regulatory strength can reduce the depleting effect of suppressing stereotypes. *Pers. Soc. Psychol. Bull.* 33:281–294.

Gailliot, M. T., B. J. Schmeichel, and R. F. Baumeister. 2006. Self-regulatory processes defend against the threat of death: Effects of self-control depletion and trait self-control on thoughts and fears of dying. *J. Pers. Soc. Psychol.* 91:49–62.

Gilbert, D. T., D. S. Krull, and B. W. Pelham. 1988. Of thoughts unspoken: Social inference and the self-regulation of behavior. *J. Pers. Soc. Psychol.* 55:685–694.

Glass, D. C., and J. E. Singer. 1972. *Urban stress: Experiments on noise and social stressors*. New York: Academic Press.

Gollwitzer, P. M. 1999. Implementation intentions: Strong effects of simple plans. *Am. Psychol.* 54:493–503.

Govorun, O., and B. K. Payne. 2006. Ego-depletion and prejudice: Separating automatic and controlled components. *Soc. Cogn.* 24:111–136.

Greenberg, J., T. Pyszczynski, and S. Solomon. 1986. The causes and consequences of a need for self-esteem: A terror management theory. In *Public self and private self*, ed. R. F. Baumeister. New York: Springer-Verlag, 189–212.

Jonides, J. 1981. Voluntary versus automatic control over the mind's eye's movement. In *Attention and performance IX*, ed. J. B. Long and A. D. Baddely. Hillsdale, NJ: Erlbaum, 187–203.

Kane, M. J., and R. W. Engle. 2003. Working-memory capacity and the control of attention: The contributions of goal neglect, response competition, and task set to Stroop interference. *J. Exp. Psychol. Gen.* 132:47–70.

Kelly, E. L., and J. J. Conley. 1987. Personality and compatibility: A prospective analysis of marital stability and marital satisfaction. *J. Pers. Soc. Psychol.* 52:27–40.

Lang, P. J. 1995. The emotion probe: Studies of motivation and attention. *Am. Psychol.* 50:372–385.

Metcalfe, J., and W. Mischel. 1999. A hot/cool-system analysis of delay of gratification: Dynamics of willpower. *Psychol. Rev.* 106:3–19.

Muraven, M., and R. F. Baumeister. 2000. Self-regulation and depletion of limited resources: Does self-control resemble a muscle? *Psychol. Bull.* 126:247–259.

Norman, D. A., and T. Shallice. 1986. Attention to action: Willed and automatic control of behavior. In *Consciousness and self regulation*, ed. R. J. Davidson, G. E. Schwartz, and D. Shapiro. New York: Plenum, 1–17.

Raskin, R., and H. Terry. 1988. A principal-components analysis of the Narcissistic Personality Inventory and further evidence of its construct validity. *J. Pers. Soc. Psychol.* 54:890–902.

Richeson, J. A., and J. N. Shelton. 2003. When prejudice does not pay: Effects of interracial contact on executive function. *Psychol. Sci.* 14:287–290.

Schmeichel, B. J. 2007. Attention control, memory updating, and emotion regulation temporarily reduce the capacity for executive control. *J. Exp. Psychol. Gen.* 136:241–255.

Schmeichel, B. J., K. D. Vohs, and R. F. Baumeister. 2003. Ego depletion and intelligent performance: Role of the self in logical reasoning and other information processing. *J. Pers. Soc. Psychol.* 85:33–46.

Sedikides, C., W. K. Campbell, G. Reeder, and A. J. Elliot. 1998. The self-serving bias in relational context. *J. Pers. Soc. Psychol.* 74:378–386.

Schneider, W., and R. M. Shiffrin. 1977. Controlled and automatic human information processing: I. Detection, search, and attention. *Psychol. Rev.* 84:1–66.

Stroop, J. R. 1935. Studies of interference in serial verbal reactions. *J. Exp. Psychol.* 18:643–662.

Tangney, J. P., R. F. Baumeister, and A. L. Boone. 2004. High self-control predicts good adjustment, less pathology, better grades, and interpersonal success. *J. Pers.* 72:271–324.

Turner, M. L., and R. W. Engle. 1989. Is working memory capacity task dependent? *J. Mem. Lang.* 28:127–154.

Vohs, K. D., R. F. Baumeister, and N. J. Ciarocco. 2005. Self-regulation and self-presentation: Regulatory resource depletion impairs impression management and effortful self-presentation depletes regulatory resources. *J. Pers. Soc. Psychol.* 88:632–657.

Vohs, K. D., and R. J. Faber. 2007. Spent resources: Self-regulatory resource availability affects impulse buying. *J. Consum. Res.* 33:537–547.

Wallace, H. M., and R. F. Baumeister. 2002. The effects of success versus failure feedback on further self-control. *Self. Ident.* 1:35–41.

Webb, T. L., and P. Sheeran. 2003. Can implementation intentions help to overcome ego-depletion? *J. Exp. Soc. Psychol.* 39:279–286.

2 The Benefits and Perils of Attentional Control

Marci S. DeCaro and Sian L. Beilock

Executive attention is involved in the learning and performance of an array of complex cognitive and motor skills, ranging from reading comprehension (Turner and Engle 1989) to mathematical problem solving (Beilock, Kulp, Holt, and Carr 2004) to learning a new sports skill (Beilock, Carr, MacMahon, and Starkes 2002). Although investigations of the link between executive attention and behavior have spanned diverse areas of psychological science, most of this work has yielded surprisingly similar conclusions regarding the role of this cognitive construct in high-level performance—the more attentional resources one is able to devote to performance at a given time, the higher one's success rate will be on the types of learning, problem solving, and comprehension tasks encountered in both the confines of the laboratory and the complexity of the real world (Engle 2002).

Executive attention allows memory representations to be maintained in a highly active state in the face of distraction (Conway et al. 2005) and is a key component of the working-memory system. By pairing domain-general executive attention resources with domain-specific (e.g., verbal and visual) short-term storage and processing resources, *working memory* functions to control, regulate, and actively maintain a limited amount of information with immediate relevance to the task at hand (Miyake and Shah 1999).

Working memory is thought to be "so central to human cognition that it is hard to find activities where it is not involved" (Ericsson and Delaney 1999, 259). In support of this idea, numerous studies have shown a positive relation between an individual's working-memory capacity and performance on an array of complex cognitive activities (Conway et al. 2005). And one's executive attention ability—the ability to attend to the most important information, while inhibiting irrelevant information—has been shown to drive this relation between individual differences in working memory and performance (Conway et al. 2005; Engle 2002; Kane, Bleckley, Conway, and Engle 2001; Kane and Engle 2000, 2003). For this reason, working-memory capacity is often conceptualized as executive attention (Engle 2002), and we do so in this chapter as well.

As mentioned above, working-memory capacity is positively related to higher level cognitive functions such as general intellectual ability, reasoning, and analytic skill and is touted as one of the most powerful predictive constructs in psychology (Conway et al. 2005). Despite its well-established utility, however, recent work suggests that increased attentional control can sometimes have a downside. In this chapter, we discuss research across a variety of tasks—problem solving, category learning, language learning, and correlation perception—to contrast the renowned benefits of attentional control with its potential pitfalls. In doing so, we demonstrate that *less* executive attention devoted to the planning and unfolding of performance is sometimes better than more.

Problem Solving

"A problem exists when a living organism has a goal but does not know how this goal is to be reached" (Duncker 1945, 2). Problem solving involves creating new knowledge in order to achieve a specific goal, not just extracting existing knowledge. As such, successful problem solving builds on other aspects of cognition, including perception, language, and working memory. When solving problems under normal conditions, individuals with higher working-memory capacity have an increased ability to maintain complex problem information in a transient store, while inhibiting ancillary information that might compete for attention. In contrast, individuals with less working-memory capacity are more apt to spread their attention superficially across multiple aspects of the performance environment rather than focusing intently on a subset of task information.

Support for the idea that individual differences in working memory capture variation in attentional control ability comes from an investigation of dichotic listening by Conway, Cowan, and Bunting (2001). These researchers asked individuals lower and higher in working memory to listen to a message in one ear and ignore a message in the other ear. In the irrelevant, to-be-ignored message, the participant's name was sometimes mentioned. Of interest was whether an individual noticed his or her name, despite being instructed to ignore the message in which his or her name was played. Conway et al. found that individuals lower in working-memory capacity were more likely to detect their name in the irrelevant message than were those higher in working memory.

This ability of higher working-memory individuals to selectively control attention, so that ancillary information is blocked out, is typically viewed as an aid to problem solving—facilitating a planned, deliberate memory search for problem solutions and supporting the online execution of a series of problem steps. In contrast, simultaneously attending to information both focal and disparate to the task at hand typically leads to suboptimal performance. However, this is not always the case. We begin by describing situations in which higher working memory is useful for problem solving and how performance suffers when this cognitive control capability is compromised. We then go on to demonstrate that performance on some types of problems actually benefits when one has less opportunity or less ability to exert attentional control.

In many problem-solving situations, the more working-memory capacity individuals bring to the table, the better they perform. As an example, Beilock and Carr (2005; see also Beilock and DeCaro 2007) asked individuals to complete a demanding mental arithmetic task called modular arithmetic and looked at their performance as a function of individual differences in working memory. Modular arithmetic involves judging the truth-value of equations such as "34 = 18 (mod 4)." Although there are several ways to solve modular arithmetic equations, Beilock and Carr taught their participants a problem-solving method that involves two key problem steps. First, the problem's middle number is subtracted from the first number (i.e., 34 − 18), and then this difference is divided by the last number (i.e., 16 ÷ 4). If the result is a whole number (here, 4), the statement is true. If not, the statement is false. As one can see, successful performance on this task requires the ability to allocate attentional resources to multiple problem steps and the ability to work with and manipulate this information in memory (e.g., holding 16 in mind while dividing it by 4).

Individual differences in working memory were measured using two common assessment tools: Operation Span (OSPAN; Turner and Engle 1989) and a modified Reading Span (RSPAN; Daneman and Carpenter 1980). In the OSPAN, individuals are asked to solve a series of arithmetic equations while remembering a list of unrelated words. Equation–word combinations are presented one at a time on the computer screen (e.g., "(3 × 4) − 2 = 8? CAT"), and individuals are asked to read the equation aloud and verify whether it is correct. Individuals then read the word aloud. At the end of a series of two to five of these strings, participants are asked to write down the series of words, in the correct order. The RSPAN follows the same general procedure, except instead of verifying equation accuracy and reading a word, individuals verify whether a sentence makes sense and then read a letter aloud for later recall (e.g., "On warm sunny afternoons, I like to walk in the park.? G"). Working-memory scores on these tasks consist of the total number of words/letters recalled from all series in which recall was 100% accurate. The ability to maintain this type of information (e.g., the words/letters) in the face of distraction (e.g., equation or sentence verification) is said to reflect executive attention, or working-memory capacity (Engle 2002).

What Beilock and Carr (2005) found was quite consistent with the idea that more working memory is better than less. The higher individuals' working memory, the more accurately they solved the modular arithmetic problems. Attention benefits performance on this type of multistep mental arithmetic task. Beilock and DeCaro (2007, experiment 1) have recently replicated this effect (see figure 2.1, top line) and also shed light on why these working-memory differences might occur. To do this, we

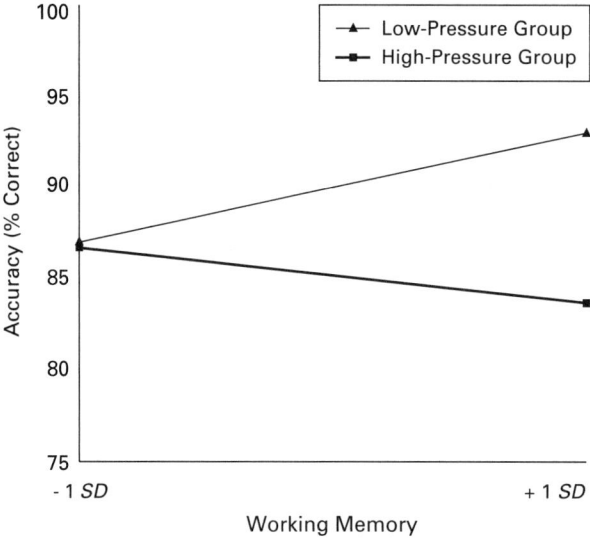

Figure 2.1
Mean modular arithmetic problem accuracy (percentage correct) as a function of individual differences in working memory and pressure condition. Nonstandardized coefficients are plotted at ±1 *SD*.
Adapted from Beilock and DeCaro 2007, experiment 1.

prompted individuals to describe the steps and processes they used to solve a selection of the modular arithmetic problems. Despite the fact that modular arithmetic is based on common subtraction and division procedures, there are shortcut strategies that can be employed to derive the correct answer, some of the time, without requiring a multistep problem-solving algorithm. For example, if one automatically responded to problems with all even numbers as "true," this strategy would result in a correct answer some of the time (as in the problem above), but not always (e.g., 52 = 16 (mod 8)). Successfully computing a multistep algorithm (i.e., subtract, then divide) would result in a correct answer every time.

We hypothesized that individuals with lower working-memory capacity, and therefore with less capacity to maintain and execute the complex procedures the algorithm required, would rely on shortcut strategies to circumvent this demand on attentional control (cf. Siegler 1988). On the other hand, individuals who can execute the algorithm with ease, those higher in working-memory capacity, would be more likely to do so in order to attain the highest accuracy possible. Consistent with this idea, we found that individuals lower in working-memory capacity were less likely to report using complex multistep strategies to solve the math problems than were their higher

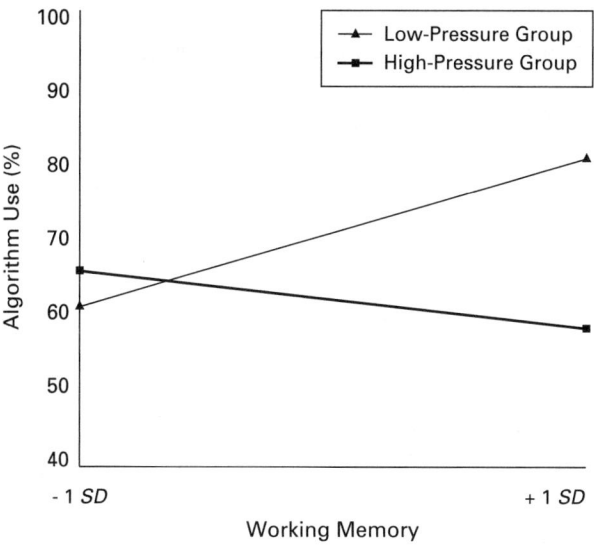

Figure 2.2
Proportion of rule-based algorithm use as a function of individual differences in working memory and pressure condition. Nonstandardized coefficients are plotted at ±1 *SD*.
Adapted from Beilock and DeCaro 2007, experiment 1.

capacity counterparts (see figure 2.2, top line). When these individuals were not using the complex strategies, they were using shortcuts. Use of shortcuts resulted in less accurate performance overall.

Given these findings, one might think that individuals higher in working memory should always outperform their low-capacity counterparts when solving difficult problems. What happens, however, if a particular performance situation compromises one's attentional resources? As an example, testing situations that elicit pressure to perform at a high level oftentimes lead to worries about performing poorly. These worries have been shown to consume attention and working-memory resources needed to successfully solve difficult math problems (Ashcraft and Kirk 2001; Beilock 2008; Beilock, Kulp, et al. 2004). One possibility is that all individuals, regardless of working-memory capacity, are equally impacted by pressure. Everyone's performance might drop by the same amount when the pressure is on. If so, then higher working-memory individuals will still outperform those with less capacity. A second possibility, however, is that because individuals higher in working-memory capacity rely heavily on this important resource for their typical success at demanding tasks like math, they might have more to lose in a pressured testing situation. That is, under pressure, individuals higher in working memory may perform as if they were lower in working memory in the first place, precisely because pressure-induced worries co-opt the very working-memory resources that higher capacity individuals normally use to showcase superior performance.

We have tested these ideas using the same modular arithmetic problems described above (Beilock and DeCaro 2007). After performing a set of practice problems during which individuals were merely instructed to perform as quickly and accurately as possible, participants were given a scenario intended to elicit commonly experienced pressures such as social evaluation, peer pressure, and a potential outcome-dependent reward. Specifically, individuals were told that if they could improve their problem-solving speed and accuracy by 20% relative to the first set of problems, they could earn a monetary reward. This reward, however, was said to be part of a "team effort," and both the participant and a "partner" needed to improve in order for both parties to receive the reward. The partner, however, was said to have already participated in the study and improved by the required amount, leaving the rewards for both participants dependent on the present individuals' performance. Individuals were also videotaped by an experimenter and informed that the footage would be examined by math teachers and students in order to examine how individuals learn this type of math skill. After hearing these stakes, participants completed the second set of math problems.

In line with the idea that our type of pressure situation compromises the attentional resources of those who typically rely on this capacity the most, individuals higher in working memory performed the modular arithmetic problems significantly worse under high-pressure compared to low-pressure tests. As shown in figure 2.1 (bottom line), under pressure the performance of higher working-memory individuals (right side of the graph) was at the same level as individuals lower in this capacity. The performance of those lower in working-memory capacity (left side of the graph) was not affected by pressure—their performance was equivalent in both high- and low-pressure testing environments.

Why might the performance of low working-memory individuals be so resilient to pressure's negative effects? And why might the performance of high-working-memory individuals fall under pressure? As mentioned previously, in normal situations individuals lower in working memory are less likely to solve the math problems with a complex algorithm. And when individuals were not using complex strategies, they used shortcuts that circumvent the heavy demand on attentional control. Under pressure, lower working-memory individuals were still able to use these shortcut strategies (see figure 2.2, bottom line), given that they are not attention-demanding in the first place. This simpler problem-solving approach allows individuals to maintain adequate, above-chance (but less-than-perfect) problem-solving accuracy (see figure 2.1). As shown in figure 2.2, higher working-memory individuals under high pressure also adopted the problem-solving shortcuts used by their lower capacity counterparts. Pressure limited high-working-memory individuals' ability to use the intensive problem-solving approach. When working memory was compromised by environmental demands, those who typically perform at the top (i.e., higher working-memory individuals) showed the largest performance decline (see also Kane et al. 2001; Kane and Engle 2002; Rosen and Engle 1997). Here again, we see the necessity of executive attention resources for problem solving—when these resources are taken away by environmental distractions, performance falters relative to where one was under normal, low-stakes conditions.

As we saw in Conway et al.'s (2001) dichotic listening study, where lower working-memory individuals were more likely to notice their name in the message they were supposed to be ignoring than their higher working-memory counterparts, instead of focusing intently on a subset of task information, individuals with lower working-memory capacity are more apt to spread their attention superficially across multiple aspects of the performance environment (Conway et al. 2001). For these individuals, learning and skill execution may be more associative in nature, less dependent on controlled effort, and rely more on shortcuts or heuristics. Of course, attending to information both focal and disparate to the task at hand typically leads to suboptimal performance, such as when performing modular arithmetic problems requiring attention to multiple task steps. However, a diffuse attentional focus may not always prove harmful. Having less ability to maintain complex information in the focus of attention may, in some situations, lead to more inventive problem-solving approaches than would be discovered if attention were more stringently controlled.

Beilock and DeCaro (2007, experiment 2) examined this idea by asking individuals to complete a series of water jug problems (Luchins 1942). In this task, three jugs are shown on a computer screen, each able to hold a different maximum capacity and labeled as jugs A, B, and C (see figure 2.3). Individuals must use the capacity of these three jugs to derive a goal quantity of water. A mathematical formula is used to denote a solution, and importantly, individuals are instructed to use the simplest strategy possible, without the aid of pencil and paper. Six problems were used in total. The first three can only be solved with a complex algorithm (i.e., $B - A - 2C$). These complex problems require multiple problem steps (e.g., computing different subtraction operations while also maintaining the results of prior calculations in transient memory) and therefore rely heavily on attentional resources. Each of the last three problems, however, can be solved in two different ways: with the same complex algorithm as the first three problems or with a much simpler formula (i.e., $A - C$ or $A + C$). The latter solution is more optimal in this case, because it is the simplest solution in terms of the number of steps involved. Notably, the formula given as a problem solution is directly reflective of one's problem-solving strategy. Of interest is whether these problem-solving strategies vary as a function of working-memory capacity—specifically whether individuals continue to use the more complex problem solution or whether they switch to the simpler, shortcut strategy when it is available.

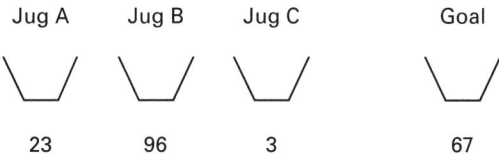

Figure 2.3
Water jug display. Participants derived a formula to obtain a "goal" quantity of water using jugs of various capacities. The first three problems were only solvable by the formula B – A – 2C (i.e., Fill jug B, pour out enough to fill jug A, then pour the remaining into jug C twice, leaving the goal quantity in jug B). The last three problems were solvable by this same difficult formula in addition to a much simpler formula (e.g., A – C). Individuals were informed that the water supply was unlimited and not all jugs had to be used.

We found that lower working-memory individuals were *more* likely to switch to the simpler solution when it became available. In contrast, individuals higher in working memory were more likely to persist in using the complex problem solution. Such persistence is known as *mental set* and, here, represents a negative artifact of previous experience in which individuals who are used to performing a task in a particular way tend to repeat this behavior in lieu of a more efficient strategy (Wiley 1998). Having a greater ability to execute multiple problem steps in memory seems to lead higher working-memory individuals to set in on a narrower problem-solving approach in line with their high capabilities. This is true even though, at the outset of the water jug task, we asked all subjects to solve the problems using the *simplest* strategy possible.

Such mental set effects can be especially pronounced when one is not only high in working memory but also has a lot of experience in a given domain. Ricks, Turley-Ames, and Wiley (2007) nicely demonstrated this phenomenon in the domain of baseball. They asked baseball experts and novices (as determined by a baseball knowledge test) to perform a creative problem-solving task called the Remote Associates Task (RAT; Mednick 1962). In this task, individuals view three words (e.g., "cadet, crawl, ship") and are asked to discover a fourth word (i.e., "space") that can be combined into a meaningful phrase with each of the three other words (i.e., "space cadet," "crawlspace," "spaceship"). The test words were either baseball neutral, having no obvious association with any aspect of baseball (as in the previous example), or baseball misleading. Baseball-misleading stimuli have one word that can be associated with baseball, but not in a way that would likely lead to a correct solution. For example, given the words "plate, broken, shot," a baseball expert might quickly retrieve the word "home" as associated with "plate," when the correct answer (i.e., glass) actually has no association with baseball at all.

To the extent that greater attentional control enables efficient retrieval and testing of multiple problem solutions, while inhibiting previously tested or ineffective solutions (Rosen and Engle 1997), one would expect higher working memory to be related to more successful performance on this problem-solving task. Indeed, for the neutral stimuli, the higher individuals' working memory, the better their solution accuracy (regardless of baseball expertise). A different pattern of results was seen for the baseball-misleading problems, however. First, expertise played a detrimental role. Baseball experts were outperformed by novices on the baseball-misleading problems. Experts have been shown to fixate on problem solutions that are activated by their extensive prior knowledge, leading to a negative mental set on this type of task (Wiley 1998). Moreover, the higher baseball experts' working memory, the worse they performed on the baseball-misleading problems. Working memory appears to have exacerbated the strategy rigidity commonly associated with expertise, by allowing hyperfocus on the incorrectly selected problem solution.

However it is triggered, whether from prior facility with a solution path or extensive knowledge of a particular domain, working memory supports a persistent approach in ways that are sometimes too selective. Such reliance on cognitive control not only may limit the discovery of new problem-solving approaches but may also lead to an attention-dependent learning strategy that overrides a more optimal associative strategy. We now turn to an example of the latter case in the category learning domain.

Category Learning

Similar to most problem-solving tasks, there are various ways one can go about learning the many categories that exist in our world. For example, individuals encountering new information, objects, or even people can explicitly test various hypotheses about the categories to which these belong. In order to learn to categorize objects in this way, individuals must form and test hypotheses about the potentially relevant features of the stimulus, move on to new hypotheses if current ones prove incorrect, and refrain from reexamining the hypotheses that have already been tested. This kind of complex process relies heavily on executive attention (Dougherty and Hunter 2003). However, there are other category learning strategies that are less attention-demanding, and in such cases, trying to devote executive attention resources to performance can actually result in a less-than-optimal learning situation.

When definitive rules can be applied to determine category membership, the best strategy is typically to hypothesize about the features that determine category membership. Tasks used to resemble this process in the lab are called *rule-based category learning* tasks (Ashby and Maddox 2005). Individuals usually see a series of categorization stimuli one at a time and are instructed to categorize each into category "A" or "B." Following each categorization choice, individuals usually receive feedback. The idea is that, over a series of categorization trials, individuals will learn to correctly categorize the stimuli to some criterion (e.g., eight correct categorization responses in a row; Waldron and Ashby 2001). A variety of categorization stimuli have been used for these tasks. For example, Waldron and Ashby (2001) created 16 stimuli, each a square with an embedded symbol in it. Each stimulus had four dimensions, with one of two levels of each dimension: square–background color (yellow or blue), embedded symbol shape (circle or square), symbol color (red or green), and number of embedded symbols (1 or 2). For a rule-based task, stimuli are correctly categorized based on an easily verbalizable rule regarding one of these features (e.g., "If the embedded symbol is a circle, choose category A; if the symbol is a square, choose category B"). The specific rule is established beforehand by the experimenter, and the individual discovers it over a series of learning trials.

Because generating and selecting different rules about category membership, while inhibiting previously selected features, relies extensively on working-memory resources (Ashby and O'Brien 2005), it is not surprising that individuals with more of this capacity outperform lower working-memory individuals on this type of rule-based learning task (see figure 2.4, left side; DeCaro, Thomas, and Beilock 2008). Moreover, when

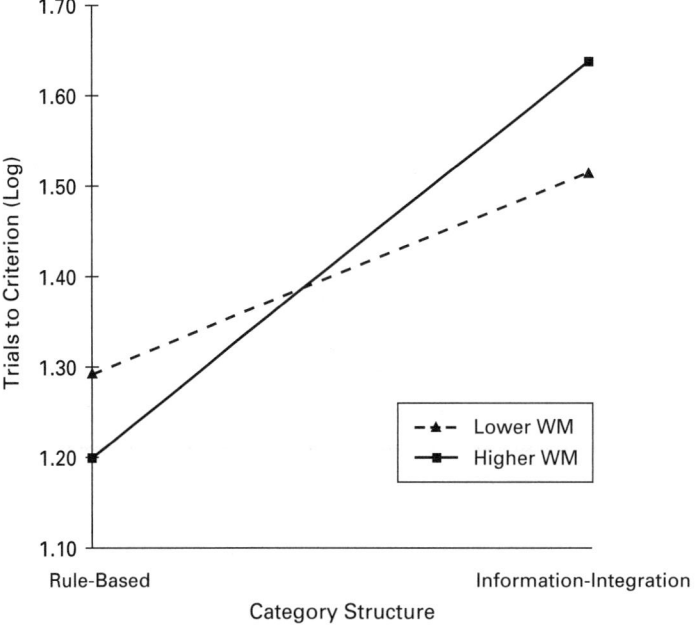

Figure 2.4
Mean number of trials taken to learn categories to a criterion of eight correct categorization responses in a row (log transformed), as a function of category structure and individual differences in working memory (WM). WM was measured as a continuous variable—nonstandardized regression coefficients are plotted at ±1 SD.
Adapted from DeCaro, Thomas, and Beilock 2008.

working-memory capacity is limited by a requirement to perform another demanding task simultaneously (Waldron and Ashby 2001; Zeithamova and Maddox 2006), or by a distracting high-pressure situation (Markman, Maddox, and Worthy 2006), the ability to learn rule-based categories is diminished.

Other categories are better learned without such reliance on attentional control. Indeed, when learning categories based on stimulus–response combinations too complex to occur within the bounds of explicit awareness, attentional control can simply get in the way. *Information-integration category learning* tasks are used to investigate this type of learning (Maddox and Ashby 2004). For example, the same 16 stimuli used in the rule-based task mentioned above can be grouped into similarity-based information-integration categories. To do so, one of the four stimulus dimensions is selected to be irrelevant, and each level of the remaining dimensions is randomly assigned a +1 or –1 value (e.g., a blue background could be assigned a +1 and a yellow background a –1). Then the dimension values for each stimulus are added together. If the sum of the three numbers is greater than one, that stimulus belongs to Category A; otherwise it belongs to Category B (Waldron and Ashby 2001). As can be seen, information-integration categories are not easily verbalized but instead rely on similarities between items and their respective categories that are associated over a series of learning events. This type of learning is believed to rely extensively on the procedural learning system (Maddox and Ashby 2004).

When new categories of any type are learned, it is thought that individuals employ both of the learning processes mentioned above—explicitly testing hypotheses about category membership while also accruing procedural-based associations between items and their respective categories. Whichever strategy accomplishes learning the fastest wins out (Zeithamova and Maddox 2006). As long as explicit hypothesis testing is occurring, however, this strategy will dominate responding. Therefore, in a rule-based task, individuals will typically successfully test different hypotheses about category membership until an explicit rule is discovered. However, in an information-integration task, individuals are actually slower to learn the categories the longer they persist in testing different rules—they are better off abandoning rule-based testing and responding only as guided by the procedural learning system (Markman et al. 2006; Zeithamova and Maddox 2006).

To the extent that individuals higher in working-memory capacity are better able to carry out complex hypothesis testing (Dougherty and Hunter 2003), they may be more likely to persist in using these multistep rules even when such a strategy is not ideal. In support of this idea, DeCaro, Thomas, and Beilock (2008) demonstrated that individuals higher in working-memory capacity took significantly longer to learn information-integration category structures than individuals lower in working memory (see figure 2.4). Similarly, Markman, Maddox, and Worthy (2006) found that in a high-pressure situation in which working-memory capacity is consumed, information-integration learning performance actually improved relative to a low-pressure testing condition. Distracting attentional resources away from category learning appears to have reduced the ability to hypothesis test, leading individuals to abandon this strategy sooner and allowing the procedural learning system to dominate categorization responses. Recently, Maddox and colleagues (2008) found that more detailed feedback after each categorization trial (i.e., the correct category assignment is displayed in addition to the minimal feedback labels "correct" or "incorrect") hurt information-integration category learning but helped rule-based learning. The additional information seems to have led individuals to rely on rule-based processing, to the detriment of a learning task that operates more optimally outside explicit attentional control.

Much like problem-solving tasks for which the optimal approach involves dissipating attention and allowing simpler strategies to become apparent, learning how to categorize new information or objects can sometimes be best accomplished by *not* thinking too much. Individual cognitive capabilities or situational factors that lead one to attend more explicitly to the factors determining category membership can serve to impair this type of learning.

Language Learning

Information-integration category learning is similar in nature to other tasks requiring the gradual accrual of environmental regularities, such as language learning or the perception of correlation. It is widely known that adults have more difficulty adeptly learning a new language than do children (Cochran, McDonald, and Parault 1999). One hypothesis of language learning (Newport 1990) posits that the limited cognitive resources of children may facilitate the learning of new language. In order to learn language, one must be able to correctly select from a stream of conversation not only words and their combinations but also the simple morphemes that change the meanings of words (e.g., adding an "s" to a word to denote plurality). Analyzing the errors made by adults versus children learning a second language, Newport discovered that adults are more likely to rely on unanalyzed wholes—words or phrases that often appear together in a particular context but may not always be appropriate in a new context. Children are more adept at the componential analysis that eventually results in better grasp of the language—they pick up the pieces of the complex linguistic input to which they have been exposed and flexibly learn to use them correctly.

Several studies have supported the idea that "less is more" when learning language (Newport 1990). Kersten and Earles (2001) found that adults learn a miniature artificial language better when initially presented with small segments of language rather than the full complexity of language, purportedly allowing them to process language as if their cognitive resources were more limited in the first place. Other work has found that language learning improves if an adult concurrently performs another task designed to consume working-memory resources (Cochran et al. 1999).

It should be noted that the exact role of executive attention in language learning has not yet been fully unpacked. Some use the term "working memory" (e.g., Kersten and Earles 2001), and others use terms like "maturational state" (Newport 1990). Moreover, Newport and others primarily describe the potential benefits of working-memory limitations in language learning in terms of the limited storage capacity to perceive and remember small segments of language, highlighting the short-term storage aspects of working memory more than the attentional control capabilities central to this construct. Yet, although the specific role of the executive attention component of working memory has not been central to this theory of language learning, this initial research does point to the potential negative impact of greater attentional control abilities and is consistent with research in similar domains such as information-integration category learning and, as will be seen below, correlation perception.

Correlation Perception

Research on the perception of correlation, or statistical regularities between two events, has also found an advantage of limited processing capacity. In one demonstration of this effect, Kareev, Lieberman, and Lev (1997) presented participants with a large bag containing 128 red and green envelopes and asked them to select one envelope at a time. Inside each envelope was a coin, marked with either an "X" or an "O." When selecting each envelope, individuals were asked to predict which marking would appear on the coin, based on the color of the envelope. If the prediction was correct, participants earned the coin in the envelope. Counterintuitively, individuals performing worse on a digit span task, a measure of short-term memory, rated the correlations between envelope color and coin marking more accurately than those performing well at the memory task. Kareev and colleagues explained that individuals with less cognitive capacity are more likely to perceive narrow "windows" of events out of an expansive experience with co-occurring events—that is, lower capacity individuals will perceive and remember only a small chunk of these trials. Smaller subsets of trials are more likely to be highly skewed, and therefore lower capacity individuals will perceive correlations as more extreme, facilitating performance on this type of task (for a debate of these findings, see Anderson et al. 2005; Cahan and Mor 2007; Juslin and Olsson 2005; Kareev 2005).

Gaissmaier, Schooler, and Rieskamp (2006) replicated Kareev and colleagues' key findings but offered an interpretation based on strategy differences between individuals lower and higher in cognitive resources. Specifically, high-span individuals are said to employ complex hypothesis testing such as *probability matching*, in which the next event to be predicted in a series is judged from the overall probability that the event has been shown to occur in the past. For example, if event "A" has occurred about

70% of the time up to the current trial, an individual using a probability matching strategy will choose this event about 70% of the time on the following trials. To follow this strategy, one must constantly mentally update the probabilities of past event occurrences and nonoccurrences and hypothesize about the likelihood of subsequent event occurrences based on this information. Although an impressive capability of higher capacity individuals, this strategy, on average, leads to lower accuracy (e.g., 58% in the previous example) than much less intensive strategies (Gaissmaier et al. 2006).

One less intensive strategy, *maximizing*, involves simply remembering which event has occurred most frequently in the past and always predicting that this dominant event will happen next. This simple strategy will generally produce greater accuracy than the more complicated probability matching approach. For example, if an event that has occurred 70% of the time is always predicted to occur next, one would be correct about 70% of the time. Of course, an individual using this strategy would not calculate this 70% probability, as he or she only gauges that one event seems to be happening more than the other. As noted by Gaissmaier and colleagues (2006), prior research has demonstrated that this simpler strategy is more often adopted by less intelligent individuals (Singer 1967), children (Derks and Paclisanu 1967), and even monkeys (Wilson and Rollin 1959) and pigeons (Herrnstein and Loveland 1975; Hinson and Staddon 1983). Consistent with the idea that maximizing is a simpler alternative to probability matching, Gaissmeier and colleagues found that individuals lower in short-term memory capacity were more likely to adopt this strategy.

Implementing a dual-task methodology often used to disrupt attentional control, Wolford and colleagues (2004) found a similar relation between decreased attentional control and the adoption of a simpler, but more effective, strategy. Specifically, in a probability-guessing paradigm similar to the correlation detection tasks mentioned above (Gaissmaier et al. 2006), individuals given a concurrent verbal-based task increased their use of maximizing relative to those in a single-task condition. Use of this less-demanding strategy improved probability-guessing performance. The previously mentioned studies (i.e., Kareev et al. 1997; Gaissmaier et al. 2006) linked strategy selection tendencies to individual difference measures rather than experimentally reduced attentional control. Thus, the finding from Wolford et al. of improved performance across all individuals when a secondary task is imposed provides a nice piece of converging evidence that decreased attentional capabilities elicit shortcut strategies that are sometimes better suited to the task at hand (Beilock and DeCaro 2007).

Toward a Comprehensive Understanding of the Benefits and Perils of Attentional Control

We have seen that individuals with greater attentional capacity available to them are inclined to use it, even when a task might benefit from less attentional control. For example, individuals with greater attentional control ability are sometimes more likely to focus selectively on less efficient problem solutions (Beilock and DeCaro 2007; Ricks et al. 2007), override the veritable responses of associative-based category learning (DeCaro et al. 2008; Markman et al. 2006), encode phrases of a new language holistically rather than analyzing important components (Newport 1990), and unnecessarily search for complicated patterns in a series of events (Wolford et al. 2004). Because the positive aspects of attentional control are so commonly seen, attention's accompanying pitfalls often receive little acknowledgment.

One question such work brings to the surface, however, is how to understand when "less is less" and "less is more." Fortunately, there is a literature one can look at to develop a more comprehensive understanding of attentional control and performance. The dual-process literature describes two types of cognitive processes used for performance across domains, differing specifically in their reliance on attentional control. By conceptualizing the tasks presented in this chapter in light of these overarching dual processes, we may begin to abstract a more comprehensive understanding of when explicit attention devoted to performance will hurt and when it will help.

Dual-process theories have become common across many domains, such as social cognition (Smith and DeCoster 2000), judgment and reasoning (De Neys 2006; Evans 2003; Sloman 1996; Stanovich and West 2000), attention (Barrett et al. 2004; Schneider and Shiffrin 1977; Shiffrin and Schneider 1977), and categorization (Ashby et al. 1998; Maddox and Ashby 2004), to name a few. The details and terminology vary from one particular theory to another, but recently there has been a drive to abstract generalities across the domain-specific dual-process theories (Kahneman 2003; Sloman 1996; Smith and DeCoster 2000). Most dual-process theories posit that optimal skill execution can differentially rely on one of two types of cognitive processes, generally believed to be functionally divided by separate neural pathways (Maddox and Ashby 2004; Smith and DeCoster 2000; see also Poldrack and Packard 2003). What we will refer to as *associative processing* (also referred to as implicit, automatic, intuitive, heuristic, procedural, or System 1) is said to operate automatically, without heavy use of working-memory resources (if any), largely outside of conscious awareness, and based on domain-specific stimulus–response pattern recognition and retrieval. In contrast, *rule-based processing* (also called explicit, controlled, analytic, algorithmic, declarative, or System 2) is thought to operate effortfully and sequentially, require attention and working-memory resources, and be available to conscious awareness, and it can (but does not necessarily always) utilize more domain-general symbolic processing (Sloman 1996; Smith and DeCoster 2000).

Associative and rule-based processes are said to operate separately, with both systems generating their own computational products such as problem solutions, category selections, or task approaches. Many times these systems act in concert, deriving the same output (De Neys 2006). For example, when viewing a robin for the first time, associative processing, using experiences with other animals with similar physical characteristics, would likely lead the robin to be classified as a bird. And the rule-based system, using sequential deliberation or hypothesis testing of the various features that constitute relevant categories, would likely arrive at the same conclusion. As another example, recall the math problem-solving work described earlier in this chapter (Beilock and DeCaro 2007). Individuals were asked to derive a solution to a math problem involving multiple steps, say $(42 - 6) \div 6$, and determine whether there is a remainder. A rule-based processing approach might entail performing the subtraction step first, using a borrow operation, and then dividing the result by 6, concluding that there is no remainder. An associative heuristic might instead easily derive an answer without heavy use of working-memory resources. Based on experiences where problems with all even numbers do not have remainders, an associatively derived answer of "no remainder" in this case would be consistent with that derived by rule-based processes.

Associative and rule-based processes may at other times conflict, deriving different responses to the same stimuli. For example, when asked to classify a dolphin, the associative system may readily derive the "fish" category, given the similarity of this animal to commonly encountered fish. The rule-based response, following a sequence of rules leading instead to a "mammal" classification, would therefore conflict with the associative-based response. Similarly, when asked whether $(42 - 6) \div 8$ has a remainder, the rule-based response would be "yes." However, the aforementioned associatively driven heuristic concerning all even numbers would incorrectly determine that "no," there is no remainder.

Situations in which rule-based and associative processes lead to conflicting solutions are of special interest, because they allow one to discern how these separate systems interact (Beilock and DeCaro 2007). Given that only one response can win out, in these conflicting situations we can ascertain whether the outcome is consistent with a rule-based or an associative processing strategy. If a solution is consistent with rule-based processing, then one might say that an approach involving explicit attentional control has been favored over more associatively driven and less attention-demanding processes. And the opposite can be said when results consistent with associative processes are seen.

Across the domains discussed in this chapter, we have seen countless examples of situations in which rule-based and associatively derived responses differentially lead to "correct" performance on a task. Attention-demanding rule-based processes prove successful for multistep computations in math problem solving (Beilock and DeCaro 2007) and the complex hypothesis testing required for rule-based categorization (DeCaro, et al. 2008; Markman et al. 2006). On the other hand, associatively driven processes lead to more efficient math problem solving on the water jug task (Beilock and DeCaro 2007; Gasper 2003) and quicker information-integration category learning (Ashby and Maddox 2005).

When conceptualizing rule-based processes as attention-demanding and associative processes as nondemanding, one might speculate as to when attention will hurt or harm performance on a particular task. Less-than-optimal skill performance may occur in those situations in which a mismatch between optimal and actual processing approaches occurs. For example, an individual solving multistep math problems with associative-based heuristics will generally perform more poorly than if he or she followed through with the complex rules required for the highest level of performance (Siegler 1988). Or an individual learning information-integration categories too complex to integrate within the bounds of working memory will learn even more slowly if trying to push a rule-based process on this more associative-based task (Zeithamova and Maddox 2006). The latter situation is an example of when less attention is more optimal for a task than an attention-demanding approach. Construing the findings reviewed in this chapter in this way, then, we may begin to establish a general rule about when attention will be beneficial versus harmful—attentional control will benefit tasks relying on attention-demanding rule-based processes but will hamper performance that more optimally relies on associative processing.

Of course the question remains—how do we know whether a task relies on rule-based or associative processes? There is little consensus regarding the defining characteristics of tasks that demand one or the other type of processing. Certain stimuli may evoke more associative processes by their physical similarity to objects stored in memory, whereas tasks requiring convoluted computations may demand rule-based processing (Kahneman 2003). If a task is believed to rely on rule-based processes, then concurrently performing an attention-demanding secondary task should disrupt performance (Kahneman 2003; Sloman 1996).

A further question centers on how we can determine whether a task is *best* performed by relying on rule-based or associative processes (e.g., Gaissmaier et al. 2006). "Optimal" performance is necessarily defined somewhat subjectively, with characteristics such as accuracy and speed factored into the equation. Cognitive economy can also play a role, in that a process used is described as the most optimal if the least amount of cognitive effort (e.g., attentional control) is exerted for the most adequate (e.g., quickest and most accurate) outcome. Although standards of optimality are widely debated (e.g., Gigerenzer and Todd 1999; Stanovich and West 2000), denoting the characteristics of rule-based versus associative processes can allow us to at least generally determine whether performance has been driven more so by one or the other processing strategy.

Considering tasks in terms of the processes required for successful performance also carries implications for skill types beyond those reviewed in this chapter. For example, high-level sensorimotor skill performance such as golf putting or soccer dribbling can be hurt or helped by attentional control depending on the level of practice an individual has with the skill. Novice performers rely on attention to execute the steps of a skill—knowledge about that skill is held in working memory and attended in a step-by-step fashion (Anderson 1982; Fitts and Posner 1967; Proctor and Dutta 1995). Thus, if attention cannot be sufficiently devoted to a novice skill, performance suffers. However, as a skill develops, its execution becomes more automatic, or procedural, in nature. The unintegrated control structures of the novice performer become integrated, running largely outside of conscious control (Anderson 1982; Fitts and Posner 1967). Thus, if an expert explicitly attends to the step-by-step performance of the skill itself, performance suffers (Beilock and Carr 2001; Beilock, Bertenthal, McCoy, and Carr 2004; Gray 2004; Jackson, Ashford, and Norsworthy 2006; Lewis and Linder 1997). Attending to the components of a procedural skill essentially reverts execution back to the unintegrated control processes of novices (Masters 1992).

Thus, a dual-process perspective offers one way skill success and failure across disparate domains such as problem solving and sensorimotor skills may be understood by the common thread of attentional control. Notably, when considering skill execution in terms of rule-based versus associative processes, the traditional distinction between cognitive and motor tasks becomes blurred. Sports tasks such as expert soccer dribbling become classified with language learning and information-integration category learning, as all rely on associative processing and respond to attentional control in much the same way. With studies such as those reviewed here, we may also better inform existing dual-process theories by exposing the individual difference and situational factors that may impact the type of processing required and utilized for a given task. Whether associative processing is optimal, and whether rule-based processing wins out instead, will be determined by factors such as individual differences in attentional control, expertise, aspects of the performance environment, and the particular task itself. Such work allows us to begin to cut across research domains, not only speaking to a possible overarching theory of attentional control and skill performance but also providing a framework by which to inform future research endeavors.

Conclusion

It is commonly believed that the more extensively information is processed and attended to, the more optimal performance will be (Hertwig and Todd 2003). Such assertions are supported by the plethora of research demonstrating that working memory and attention are vital to performance across skill domains (Conway et al. 2005). Cognitive control abilities are held in such high esteem that the performance of those with more of these capabilities (i.e., individuals higher in intellectual or working-memory capacity) has been deemed the standard by which performance should be measured: "…whatever the 'smart' people do can be assumed to be right" (De Neys 2006, 432; Stanovich and West 2000). Even individuals who do not have the capacity to successfully perform working-memory-demanding processes are thought to adhere to the same norm as those higher in working memory, but they simply fall short in the capability to do so (De Neys 2006). As shown in this chapter, however, greater attentional control capabilities can impede performance, and individuals with less cognitive control can excel beyond their higher capacity counterparts by effectively utilizing simpler strategies. Such findings call into question the validity of characterizing attention-demanding processing strategies as the standard for rational or optimal behavior. They instead speak to the importance of considering not only cognitive capacity but also task demands and aspects of the performance environment when delineating the most "optimal" use of attention in any given performance scenario.

Acknowledgment

This research was supported by Institute of Education Sciences grant R305H050004 and National Science Foundation grant DRL-0746970 to Sian Beilock.

References

Anderson, J. R. 1982. Acquisition of cognitive skill. *Psychol. Rev.* 89:369–406.

Anderson, R. B., M. E. Doherty, N. D. Berg, and J. C. Friedrich. 2005. Sample size and the detection of correlation—A signal detection account: Comment on Kareev (2000) and Juslin and Olsson (2005). *Psychol. Rev.* 112:268–279.

Ashby, F. G., and W. T. Maddox. 2005. Human category learning. *Annu. Rev. Psychol.* 56:149–178.

Ashby, F. G., and J. B. O'Brien. 2005. Category learning and multiple memory systems. *Trends Cogn. Sci.* 9:83–89.

Ashby, F. G., L. A. Alfonso-Reese, A. U. Turken, and E. M. Waldron. 1998. A neuropsychological theory of multiple systems in category learning. *Psychol. Rev.* 105:442–481.

Ashcraft, M. H., and E. P. Kirk. 2001. The relationships among working memory, math anxiety, and performance. *J. Exp. Psychol. Gen.* 130:224–237.

Barrett, L. F., M. M. Tugade, and R. W. Engle. 2004. Individual differences in working memory capacity and dual-process theories of the mind. *Psychol. Bull.* 130:553–573.

Beilock, S. L. 2008. Math performance in stressful situations. *Curr. Dir. Psychol. Sci.* 17:339–343.

Beilock, S. L., and T. H. Carr. 2001. On the fragility of skilled performance: What governs choking under pressure? *J. Exp. Psychol. Gen.* 130:701–725.

Beilock, S. L., and T. H. Carr. 2005. When high-powered people fail: Working memory and "choking under pressure" in math. *Psychol. Sci.* 16:101–105.

Beilock, S. L., and M. S. DeCaro. 2007. From poor performance to success under stress: Working memory, strategy selection, and mathematical problem solving under pressure. *J. Exp. Psychol. Learn. Mem. Cogn.* 33:983–998.

Beilock, S. L., T. H. Carr, C. MacMahon, and J. L. Starkes. 2002. When paying attention becomes counterproductive: Impact of divided versus skill-focused attention on novice and experienced performance of sensorimotor skills. *J. Exp. Psychol. Appl.* 8:6–16.

Beilock, S. L., B. I. Bertenthal, A. M. McCoy, and T. H. Carr. 2004. Haste does not always make waste: Expertise, direction of attention, and speed versus accuracy in performing sensorimotor skills. *Psychon. Bull. Rev.* 11:373–379.

Beilock, S. L., C. A. Kulp, L. E. Holt, and T. H. Carr. 2004. More on the fragility of performance: Choking under pressure in mathematical problem solving. *J. Exp. Psychol. Gen.* 133:584–600.

Cahan, S., and Y. Mor. 2007. The effect of working memory capacity limitations on the intuitive assessment of correlation: Amplification, attenuation, or both? *J. Exp. Psychol. Learn. Mem. Cogn.* 33:438–442.

Cochran, B. P., J. L. McDonald, and S. J. Parault. 1999. Too smart for their own good: The disadvantage of a superior processing capacity for adult language learners. *J. Mem. Lang.* 41:30–58.

Conway, A. R. A., N. Cowan, and M. F. Bunting. 2001. The cocktail party phenomenon revisited: The importance of working memory capacity. *Psychon. Bull. Rev.* 8:331–335.

Conway, A. R. A., M. J. Kane, M. F. Bunting, D. Z. Hambrick, O. Wilhelm, and R. W. Engle. 2005. Working memory span tasks: A methodological review and user's guide. *Psychon. Bull. Rev.* 12:769–786.

Daneman, M., and P. A. Carpenter. 1980. Individual differences in working memory and reading. *J. Verbal Learn. Verbal Behav.* 19:450–466.

De Neys, W. 2006. Dual processing in reasoning: Two systems but one reasoner. *Psychol. Sci.* 17:428–433.

DeCaro, M. S., R. D. Thomas, and S. L. Beilock. 2008. Individual differences in category learning: Sometimes less working memory capacity is better than more. *Cognition* 107:284–294.

Derks, P. L., and M. I. Paclisanu. 1967. Simple strategies in binary prediction by children and adults. *J. Exp. Psychol.* 73:278–285.

Dougherty, M. R. P., and J. E. Hunter. 2003. Hypothesis generation, probability judgment, and individual differences in working memory capacity. *Acta Psychol. (Amst.)* 113:263–282.

Duncker, K. 1945. On problem-solving. *Psychol. Monogr.* 58:1–113.

Engle, R. W. 2002. Working memory capacity as executive attention. *Curr. Dir. Psychol. Sci.* 11:19–23.

Ericsson, K. A., and P. R. Delaney. 1999. Long-term working memory as an alternative to capacity models of working memory in everyday skilled performance. In *Models of working memory: Mecha-*

nisms of active maintenance and executive control, ed. A. Miyake and P. Shah. New York: Cambridge University Press, 257–297.

Evans, J. St. B. T. 2003. In two minds: Dual-process accounts of reasoning. *Trends Cogn. Sci.* 7:454–459.

Fitts, P. M., and M. I. Posner. 1967. *Human performance*. Belmont, CA: Brooks/Cole.

Gaissmaier, W., L. J. Schooler, and J. Rieskamp. 2006. Simple predictions fueled by capacity limitations: When are they successful? *J. Exp. Psychol. Learn. Mem. Cogn.* 32:966–982.

Gasper, K. 2003. When necessity is the mother of invention: Mood and problem solving. *J. Exp. Soc. Psychol.* 39:248–262.

Gigerenzer, G., and P. M. Todd. 1999. Fast and frugal heuristics: The adaptive toolbox. In *Simple heuristics that make us smart*, ed. G. Gigerenzer and P. M. Todd and the The ABC Research Group. New York: Oxford University Press, 3–34.

Gray, R. 2004. Attending to the execution of a complex sensorimotor skill: Expertise differences, choking, and slumps. *J. Exp. Psychol. Appl.* 10:42–54.

Herrnstein, R. J., and D. H. Loveland. 1975. Maximizing and matching on concurrent ratio schedules. *J. Exp. Anal. Behav.* 24:107–116.

Hertwig, R., and P. M. Todd. 2003. More is not always better: The benefits of cognitive limits. In *Thinking: Psychological perspectives on reasoning, judgment and decision making*, ed. D. Hardman and L. Macchi. Chichester, UK: Wiley, 213–231.

Hinson, J. M., and J. E. R. Staddon. 1983. Matching, maximizing and hillclimbing. *J. Exp. Anal. Behav.* 40:321–331.

Jackson, R. C., K. J. Ashford, and G. Norsworthy. 2006. Attentional focus, dispositional reinvestment, and skilled motor performance under pressure. *J. Sport Exerc. Psychol.* 28:49–68.

Juslin, P., and H. Olsson. 2005. Capacity limitations and the detection of correlations: Comment on Kareev (2000). *Psychol. Rev.* 112:256–267.

Kahneman, D. 2003. A perspective on judgment and choice: Mapping bounded rationality. *Am. Psychol.* 58:697–720.

Kane, M. J., and R. W. Engle. 2000. Working-memory capacity, proactive interference, and divided attention: Limits on long-term memory retrieval. *J. Exp. Psychol. Learn. Mem. Cogn.* 26:336–358.

Kane, M. J., and R. W. Engle. 2002. The role of prefrontal cortex in working-memory capacity, executive attention, and general fluid intelligence: An individual-differences perspective. *Psychon. Bull. Rev.* 9:637–671.

Kane, M. J., and R. W. Engle. 2003. Working-memory capacity and the control of attention: The contributions of goal neglect, response competition, and task set to Stroop interference. *J. Exp. Psychol. Gen.* 132:47–70.

Kane, M. J., K. M. Bleckley, A. R. A. Conway, and R. W. Engle. 2001. A controlled-attention view of working-memory capacity. *J. Exp. Psychol. Gen.* 130:169–183.

Kareev, Y. 2005. And yet the small-sample effect does hold: Reply to Juslin and Olsson (2005) and Anderson, Doherty, Berg, and Friedrich (2005). *Psychol. Rev.* 112:280–285.

Kareev, Y., I. Lieberman, and M. Lev. 1997. Through a narrow window: Sample size and the perception of correlation. *J. Exp. Psychol. Gen.* 126:278–287.

Kersten, A. W., and J. L. Earles. 2001. Less really is more for adults learning a miniature artificial language. *J. Mem. Lang.* 44:250–273.

Lewis, B., and D. E. Linder. 1997. Thinking about choking? Attentional processes and paradoxical performance. *Pers. Soc. Psychol. Bull.* 23:937–944.

Luchins, A. S. 1942. Mechanization in problem solving: The effect of Einstellung. *Psychol. Monogr.* 54:1–95.

Maddox, W. T., and F. G. Ashby. 2004. Dissociating explicit and procedural-learning based systems of perceptual category learning. *Behav. Processes* 66:309–332.

Maddox, W. T., B. C. Love, B. D. Glass, and J. V. Filoteo. 2008. When more is less: Feedback effects in perceptual category learning. *Cognition* 108:578–589.

Markman, A. B., W. T. Maddox, and D. A. Worthy. 2006. Choking and excelling under pressure. *Psychol. Sci.* 17:944–948.

Masters, R. S. 1992. Knowledge, knerves, and know-how: The role of explicit versus implicit knowledge in the breakdown of complex motor skill under pressure. *Br. J. Psychol.* 83:343–358.

Mednick, S. 1962. The associative basis of the creative process. *Psychol. Rev.* 69:220–232.

Miyake, A., and P. Shah. 1999. *Models of working memory: Mechanisms of active maintenance and executive control*. Cambridge: Cambridge University Press.

Newport, E. L. 1990. Maturational constraints on language learning. *Cogn. Sci.* 14:11–28.

Poldrack, R. A., and M. G. Packard. 2003. Competition among memory systems: Converging evidence from animal and human brain studies. *Neuropsychologia* 41:245–251.

Proctor, R. W., and A. Dutta. 1995. *Skill acquisition and human performance*. Thousand Oaks, CA: Sage.

Ricks, T. R., K. J. Turley-Ames, and J. Wiley. 2007. Effects of working memory capacity on mental set due to domain knowledge. *Mem. Cognit.* 35:1456–1462.

Rosen, V. M., and R. W. Engle. 1997. The role of working memory capacity in retrieval. *J. Exp. Psychol. Gen.* 126:211–227.

Schneider, W., and R. M. Shiffrin. 1977. Controlled and automatic human information processing: I. Detection, search, and attention. *Psychol. Rev.* 84:1–66.

Shiffrin, R. M., and W. Schneider. 1977. Controlled and automatic human information processing: II. Perceptual learning, automatic attending, and a general theory. *Psychol. Rev.* 84:127–190.

Siegler, R. S. 1988. Individual differences in strategy choices: Good students, not-so-good students, and perfectionists. *Child Dev.* 59:833–851.

Singer, E. 1967. Ability and the use of optimal strategy in decisions. *Am. J. Psychol.* 80:243–249.

Sloman, S. A. 1996. The empirical case for two systems of reasoning. *Psychol. Bull.* 119:3–22.

Smith, E. R., and J. DeCoster. 2000. Dual-process models in social and cognitive psychology: Conceptual integration and links to underlying memory systems. *Pers. Soc. Psychol. Rev.* 4:108–131.

Stanovich, K. E., and R. F. West. 2000. Individual differences in reasoning: Implications for the rationality debate? *Behav. Brain Sci.* 23:645–665.

Turner, M. L., and R. W. Engle. 1989. Is working memory capacity task dependent? *J. Mem. Lang.* 28:127–154.

Waldron, E. M., and F. G. Ashby. 2001. The effects of concurrent task interference on category learning: Evidence for multiple category learning systems. *Psychon. Bull. Rev.* 8:168–176.

Wiley, J. 1998. Expertise as mental set: The effects of domain knowledge in creative problem solving. *Mem. Cognit.* 26:716–730.

Wilson, W. A., Jr., and A. R. Rollin. 1959. Two-choice behavior of rhesus monkeys in a noncontingent situation. *J. Exp. Psychol.* 58:174–180.

Wolford, G., S. E. Newman, M. B. Miller, and G. S. Wig. 2004. Searching for patterns in random sequences. *Can. J. Exp. Psychol.* 58:221–228.

Zeithamova, D., and W. T. Maddox. 2006. Dual-task interference in perceptual category learning. *Mem. Cognit.* 34:387–398.

3 Effortless Motor Learning?: An External Focus of Attention Enhances Movement Effectiveness and Efficiency

Gabriele Wulf and Rebecca Lewthwaite

Skilled movement entails learned motor patterns that are produced with a high degree of accuracy, consistency, and efficiency. The classic definition of skill by Guthrie (1952) captures these important characteristics. According to Guthrie, skill "consists in the ability to bring about some end result with maximum certainty and minimum outlay of energy, or of time and energy" (p. 136.). This definition implies that with skill movement goals are achieved with high reliability. In addition, movements are performed fluently and efficiently, or with relatively little (physical or mental) effort. This can also result in faster movement executions, or time savings. These aspects of skill are seen in experienced performers. For example, skilled golfers typically hit the ball closer to the hole than novice players, and they do so consistently. In addition, an expert golfer is able to hit the ball farther than a novice by generating greater club head speed achieved through fluid, seemingly effortless, motion; indeed, attempts to produce maximal force typically reduce swing fluidity and speed at ball contact. Likewise, the coordination patterns displayed by skilled cross-country skiers are more effective and economical than those demonstrated by most recreational skiers. Skilled individuals have learned to produce the appropriate forces at the right time and in the right directions; they have learned to avoid counterproductive cocontractions and to exploit passive forces, such as gravity. Thus, as a result of practice, movements are produced with less muscular energy—or physical effort (e.g., Lay, Sparrow, Hughes, and O'Dwyer 2002; Sparrow, Hughes, Russell, and Le Rossignol 1999; for a review, see Sparrow and Newell 1998). Moreover, the mental effort associated with movement production lessens with practice (e.g., Abernethy 1988; Leavitt 1979; Smith and Chamberlin 1992), and the movement is thought to become automated—that is, able to be generated without the conscious control of the mover. As the control of movements becomes more automatic, at least some of the available attentional resources can be directed elsewhere (e.g., the traffic in driving, the strategy in ball games, or the artistic expression in ice skating). Thus, relative effortlessness is a defining characteristic of motor skill—even though, somewhat paradoxically, learning is often marked by more, rather than less, effort (Lee, Swinnen, and Serrien 1994; Salmoni, Schmidt, and Walter 1984; Schmidt 1991; Schmidt and Lee 2005).

Attentional processes and focus have been studied from a wide variety of perspectives and paradigms. The concept of limited attentional capacity or finite attentional resources (e.g., Pashler 1994), often considered to result in the need for selective attention (Sarter, Gehring, and Kozak 2006), has been the subject of much research. Included in this set are studies that overload performers' or learners' attentional capacities to the point of primary task performance disruption, often by dual-task or distracting conditions (e.g., Abernethy 1988; Wilson, Chattington, Marple-Horvat, and Smith 2007). Other researchers have referred to the direction, content, or focus of attention. In this chapter, we discuss a particular line of evidence within the attentional focus literature related to movement that draws a subtle but important distinction between the instructionally induced internal (body-related) and external (movement-effect-related) content of performers' and learners' thoughts.

Research into the effects of attentional focus has shown that an external focus of attention results in more effective performance and learning than an internal focus (see Wulf 2007a, 2007b); moreover, the enhanced outcome seems to be achieved with less effort. Wulf, Höß, and Prinz (1998) first defined an *internal focus* as one that is directed at the performer's own body movements and an *external focus* as one that is directed at the effects that his or her movement have on the environment. Learners, instructors, and theorists do not commonly distinguish between an internal and external focus, haphazardly adopting one or the other without any hard data about effectiveness. In many training situations (e.g., in sports, physical therapy, music), individuals are given instructions about the correct movement pattern—with references being made to the coordination of their body movements. The view that, at the beginning of the learning process, performers need to direct their attention to coordination of their movements can also be seen in the current literature (e.g., Beilock and Carr 2001; Beilock, Carr, MacMahon, and Starkes 2002; Gray 2004). Yet, numerous studies conducted over the past decade or so have provided considerable evidence that an external focus of attention is beneficial not only for more advanced performers but for the inexperienced or novice as well. An external focus is not only more effective for performance and learning, compared to an internal focus, but also results in greater movement economy. That is, an external focus appears to speed the learning process so that a higher skill level is achieved sooner (Wulf 2007b).

To explain the effects of internal versus external foci of attention, Wulf and colleagues put forward the "constrained action hypothesis" (McNevin, Shea, and Wulf 2003; Wulf, McNevin, and Shea 2001; Wulf, Shea, and Park 2001). According to this view, individuals who try to consciously control their movements (i.e., adopt an internal attentional focus) tend to *constrain* their motor system and interfere with automatic control processes. That is, the automatic control mechanisms that have the capacity to control movements effectively and efficiently are disrupted. In contrast, focusing on the movement's effect allows for a more automatic mode of control. It promotes the utilization of unconscious, fast, and reflexive control processes, with the result that the desired outcome is achieved almost as a by-product.

In this chapter, we examine findings related to the effects of different attentional foci. Specifically, we review findings related to how movement effectiveness ("ability to bring about some end result with maximum certainty"; Guthrie 1952, 136) and movement efficiency ("minimum outlay of energy, or of time and energy"; Guthrie, 136) are affected by the learner's attentional focus. While most studies have been concerned with the former aspect—that is, performance outcomes such as movement accuracy or consistency—as a function of a person's focus of attention (see reviews by Wulf 2007a, 2007b), in this chapter we will particularly focus on the latter aspect. As outlined above, the efficiency of the movement—as indicated by its fluidity or smoothness—is another important criterion of skill. This is often accompanied by subjective feelings of relative effortlessness (e.g., Lay et al. 2002; Sparrow et al. 1999). We will review evidence that a focus on the movement's effects enhances movement efficiency, compared to a focus on the movement per se—which is central to the claim that the adoption of an external focus can speed the learning process (Wulf 2007b).

Attentional Focus and Movement Effectiveness

Most studies have used outcome measures—such as the accuracy in hitting a target or the minimization of deviations from a balanced position—thus examining participants' "ability to bring about some end result" (Guthrie 1952, 136). This was also the case in the first study that demonstrated the superiority of an external relative to an internal focus (Wulf et al. 1998). In that study, the learning of two dynamic balance tasks was enhanced when participants' attention was directed to the movements of the platform on which they were standing as compared to the movements of their feet. Despite minor difference in the instructions given to different groups, those who focused on the effects their movements had on the support surface (external focus) demonstrated more effective learning than those who focused on their body movements (i.e., feet; internal focus). Specifically, on a ski-simulator task (Wulf et al. 1998, experiment 1), where the goal was to produce slalom-type movements with the largest possible amplitudes, participants who were instructed to focus on exerting pressure on the wheels of the platform under their feet produced larger amplitudes than those who were instructed to exert pressure with their feet. On the stabilometer task (Wulf et al. 1998, experiment 2), learners who directed their attention to markers attached to the platform in front of their feet (without looking at them) were more proficient at keeping the platform in a horizontal position than those who directed attention to their feet. Those group differences were seen on delayed retention tests without focus reminders, suggesting that they reflected differential effects on learning. Since the publication of the paper by Wulf et al., numerous other studies using balance tasks and populations as diverse as children (Thorn 2006) and persons who had experienced a stroke (Fasoli, Trombly, Tickle-Degnen, and Verfaellie 2002) or who had Parkinson's disease (e.g., Landers, Wulf, Wallmann, and Guadagnoli 2005; Wulf, Landers, Lewthwaite, and Töllner 2009) have replicated the advantages of instructing learners to adopt an external focus of attention.

Other studies have demonstrated learning benefits of external versus internal foci for a variety of sport skills. The accuracy of golf shots has been shown to be enhanced when the performers' attention is directed to the swinging motion of the club rather than to the swing of their arms (Wulf, Lauterbach, and Toole 1999). Interestingly, this is the case not only for novices but even for expert golfers (Wulf and Su 2007). Furthermore, movement accuracy has also been shown to increase with an external focus in basketball free-throw shooting (Al-Abood, Bennett, Hernandez, Ashford, and Davids 2002; Zachry, Wulf, Mercer, and Bezodis 2005), dart throwing (Marchant, Clough, and Crawshaw 2007), football kicks (Zachry 2005), and volleyball serves and soccer kicks (Wulf, McConnel, Gärtner, and Schwarz 2002). Table 3.1 provides an overview of the tasks used, focus instructions given to participants, and the results of some studies examining attentional focus effects. Overall, learning benefits of an external compared to an internal focus—in terms of greater movement accuracy or improved balance performance, for example—have been shown for a variety of skills, levels of expertise, and age groups, as well as for healthy individuals and those with motor impairments, suggesting that this a general and reliable phenomenon (for a review, see Wulf 2007a, 2007b).

Attentional Focus and Movement Efficiency

An important criterion in Guthrie's (1952) definition of skill is minimal energy expenditure. This can be interpreted as energy savings related to either *physical* (metabolic) or *mental* energy. If the same movement outcome is achieved with less energy, the movement pattern is considered more efficient or economical (distinctions between these terms can be made [e.g., Sparrow and Newell 1998], but for our purposes they are used interchangeably). While movement efficiency typically refers to the metabolic energy required for goal achievement, this concept can also be applied to the mental energy invested in the achievement of the movement goal. If a motor skill is produced with fewer attentional resources (i.e., controlled with a greater degree of automaticity), for example—as is characteristic of skilled performance—one can argue that this is mentally more economical. It can further be suggested that the extent of self-regulatory activity invested in thought and affect management—including that produced by self-focused attention (e.g., Carver and Scheier 1978)—surrounding movement

Table 3.1

Task, instructions provided in internal focus (IF), external focus (EF), and control (C) conditions, and results of selected previous studies

Study	Task	Instructions			Results
		Internal focus	External focus	No focus (control)	
Wulf et al. 1998, experiment 1	*Ski simulator*: Produce slalom-type movements with largest possible amplitude and frequency	Exert pressure with outer foot	Exert pressure on outer wheels (under feet)	None	Largest amplitude and frequency for EF group (IF = C)
Wulf and McNevin 2003	*Stabilometer*: Keep platform in a horizontal position	Keep your feet horizontal	Keep markers (in front of feet) horizontal	None	Smallest deviations from horizontal for EF group (IF = C)
Wulf et al. 2002, experiment 1	*Volleyball serves*: Hit target area	For example, shift your weight from the back leg to the front leg	For example, shift your weight toward the target		Greater accuracy for EF group
Wulf et al. 2002, experiment 2	*Soccer kicks*: Hit target area	Position your foot below the ball's midline to lift the ball	Strike the ball below its midline to lift it, that is, kick underneath it		Greater accuracy for EF group
Wulf and Su 2007	*Golf*: Pitch shot	Focus on swing of arms	Focus on swing of club	None	Greatest accuracy for EF group (IF = C)

Table 3.1
(continued)

Study	Task	Instructions			Results
		Internal focus	External focus	No focus (control)	
Zachry et al. 2005	*Basketball free-throws*	Focus on wrist motion	Focus on rim		Greater accuracy for EF group
Wulf et al. 2007, experiment 1	*Jump-and-reach*: Jump as high as possible	Focus on finger (touching the rungs)	Focus on rungs (to be touched with finger)	None	Greatest jump height for EF groups (IF = C)
Freedman et al. 2007	*Force production/oral-motor control*: Exert a given amount of pressure on bulb in mouth	Focus on your tongue	Focus on the bulb		Greater accuracy for EF group
Fasoli et al. 2002	*Individuals after stoke*: Remove a can from a shelf and place it on a table	Pay attention to your arm: Think about how much you straighten your elbow and how your wrist and fingers move	Pay attention to the can: Think about where it is on the shelf and how big or heavy it is		Shorter movement times, greater peak velocities for EF group
Totsika and Wulf 2003	*Pedalo*: Ride as fast as possible	Focus on pushing your feet forward	Focus on pushing the platforms (under each foot) forward		Greater speed for EF group

performance and learning contributes to the mental effort, and sense of mental effort, for the motor task (we discuss this proposition further in a later section). Skilled performance is presumably associated with reduced need to engage in active suppression or change of maladaptive thoughts and affective reactions.

From the performer's point of view, increases in movement efficiency are accompanied by feelings of greater effortlessness (e.g., Lay et al. 2002; Sparrow et al. 1999). Given that organisms seem to have a natural propensity to try to conserve energy, it has been argued that they follow the principle of "least effort" (e.g., Hull 1943; Tolman 1932). Interoceptive sensory information about energy expenditure is seen as a means that governs the organism's choice of motor response and that results in the fine-tuning of responses with practice: "…organisms select the least effortful coordination and control function, and, with practice, the selected control parameters are refined to attain the task goal with less metabolic energy expenditure" (Sparrow and Newell 1998, 190).

In the following sections, we describe how an individual's focus of attention influences energy expenditure in the production of motor skills. Specifically, we focus on the physical and mental effort associated with different foci.

Energy Expenditure

Physical Effort
The physical energy required to produce movements can be measured by various metabolic indices, such as heart rate or oxygen consumption. Studies that have examined energy expenditure as a function of practice have shown that movement efficiency indeed increases. For example, in a series of studies using a rowing ergometer, the metabolic energy required to produce a given power output decreased across practice days (e.g., Durand, Geoffroi, Varray, and Prefault 1994; Lay et al. 2002; Sparrow et al. 1999). Specifically, decreases were found in heart rate and oxygen consumption. As a consequence of the reduction in oxygen consumption, movement economy (as measured by oxygen consumption at a given workload) increased (Lay et al. 2002). Furthermore, muscle activation—that is, integrated electromyographic (iEMG) activity—decreased across practice days. Finally, perceived exertion—or subjective estimate of effort—was found to decrease with practice (Lay et al. 2002; Sparrow et al. 1999). These changes in energy expenditure are presumably a function of increased movement efficiency brought about by greater movement stability (e.g., Lay et al. 2002), minimized cocontractions, and generally more economical muscle activation patterns.

Although not many studies have directly examined movement efficiency as a function of attentional focus, several studies have compared EMG activity when participants adopted an internal or external focus while performing a motor task. One can argue that if the same outcome is achieved with less muscular activity, the movements that are producing the outcome are more efficient. In the first study that measured EMG activity under different focus conditions, Vance, Wulf, Töllner, McNevin, and Mercer (2004) had participants perform biceps curls with a bar that was weighted with a mass equivalent to an estimated 50% of each participant's maximal force. All participants performed two sets of 10 repetitions under both internal and external focus conditions, with the order of conditions being counterbalanced. In internal focus conditions, participants were instructed to concentrate on their *arms*, whereas under external focus conditions, they were instructed to focus on the *curl bar*. Figure 3.1 shows iEMG activity of the biceps and triceps brachii muscles across repetitions and sets under the two focus conditions. (Only repetitions 2-9 are shown, as the first repetition started from a static position and the last repetition ended in a static position, making them mechanically different from the other repetitions.) As expected, with increasing repetitions of an energy-demanding task, iEMG activity generally increased across repetitions, and, at least for the triceps, iEMG significantly increased from set 1 to set 2. These findings reflect an increase in muscular effort to produce the same result. Importantly, iEMG activity of both biceps and triceps muscles was consistently lower under the external compared to the internal focus condition. This result supports the view that the adoption of an external focus (i.e., on the weight to be lifted) allows the motor system to operate more efficiently—perhaps by recruiting only the absolutely necessary number of motor units required for the task.

Marchant, Greig, Scott, and Clough (2006) replicated and extended these findings (see also Marchant, Greig, and Scott forthcoming). Their study included a control condition, allowing them to examine whether external focus instructions would increase movement efficiency not only compared to internal focus instructions but also compared to a "natural" condition. Given that weightlifting is a relatively uncomplicated task in terms of motor coordination, one might not necessarily expect to find greater movement efficiency just by changing performers' focus of attention relative to what they normally do, yet Marchant et al. (2006) found that instructions to focus on the bar (external focus), indeed, resulted in less iEMG as well as peak EMG activity in the biceps muscle, compared with instructions to focus on their arms (internal focus) or no focus instructions (control). The latter finding is particularly interesting in that it shows that adopting an external focus reduced muscular activity—or increased movement efficiency—even compared to normal conditions.

In another study examining EMG activity as a function of attentional focus, Zachry, Wulf, Mercer, and Bezodis (2005) used a task that had a clear goal as well as a measurable outcome in terms of movement accuracy. In that study, the participants' task was to shoot basketball free throws under either external focus (rim of the basket) or internal focus (wrist flexion) conditions. The results showed that shooting accuracy was greater with an external focus (see figure 3.2, top), replicating the findings of

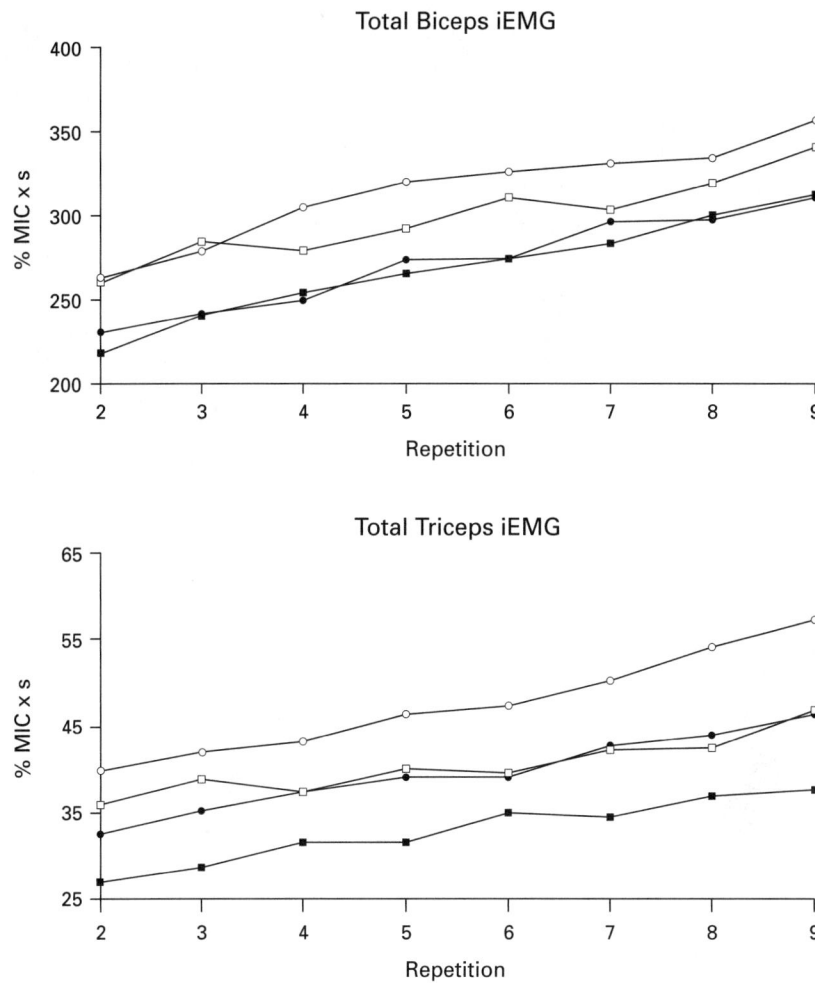

Figure 3.1
Total biceps (top) and triceps (bottom) muscle iEMG activity across sets and repetitions of biceps curls for the internal and external focus conditions in the study by Vance et al. (2004, Experiment 1). MIC, maximal-effort isometric contraction; s, second.

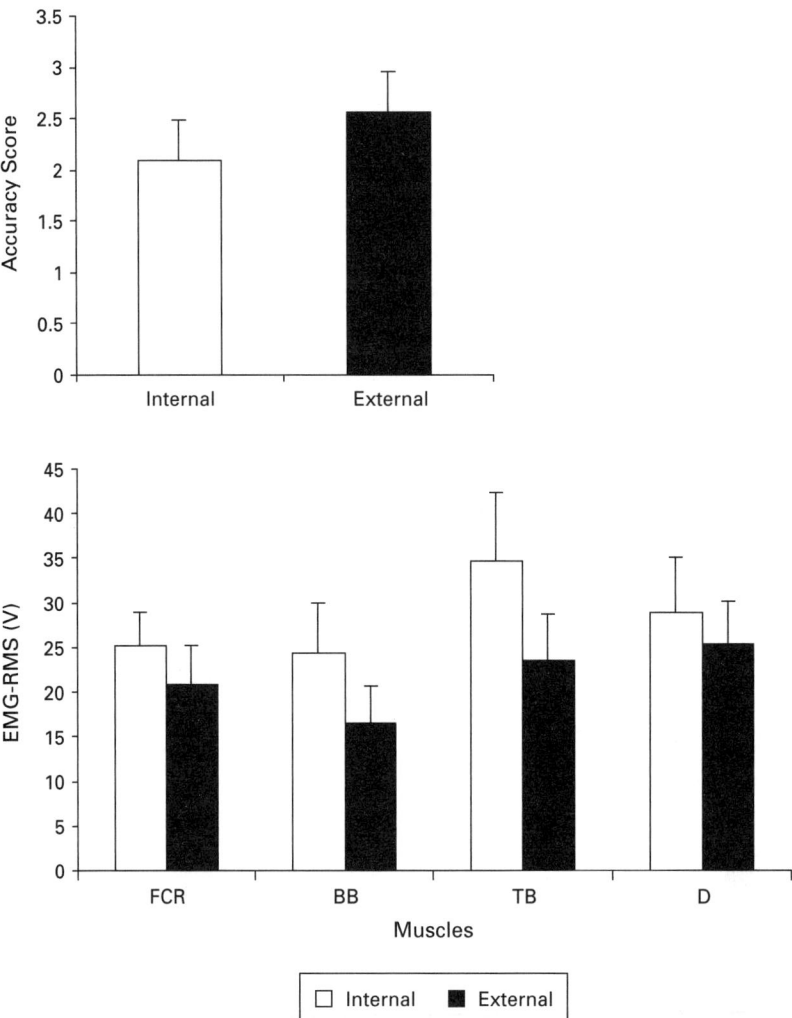

Figure 3.2
Average free-throw accuracy scores (higher scores indicate greater accuracy) (top) and EMG root mean square errors (RMSE) of the internal and external focus groups for the four muscle groups (bottom) in the study by Zachry et al. (2005). FCR, flexor carpi radialis; BB, biceps brachii; TB, triceps brachii; D, deltoid.

previous studies (for reviews, see Wulf 2007a, 2007b). In addition, EMG activity in the biceps and triceps muscles was reduced compared to that in the internal focus condition (see figure 3.2, bottom). This study was the first to show that reduced EMG activity with an external focus condition was accompanied by greater movement accuracy. Zachry et al. (2005) argued that increased "noise" in the motor system (i.e., increased EMG activity) resulting from a focus on body movements may hamper fine movement control with the consequence that the movement outcome (e.g., movement accuracy) is less reliable. In other words, an external focus appears to result in more effective and efficient movement patterns, and, as a consequence, movement accuracy is enhanced.

Another interesting finding in the Zachry et al. (2005) study was the fact that attentional focus differences in EMG occurred in muscle groups that participants were not specifically instructed to focus on (i.e., biceps, triceps). This suggests that the effects of attentional focus on the motor system are rather general in nature— "spreading" to muscle groups that are not in the performer's focus of attention. Even though participants were instructed to focus on the wrist flexor (flexor carpi radialis) in the internal focus condition, significant differences in EMG activity occurred in the biceps and triceps brachii muscles. That is, the focus on a certain part of the body (e.g., hand) had an influence on the control of other parts of the motor system as well (see also McNevin and Wulf 2002; Wulf, Mercer, McNevin, and Guadagnoli 2004; Wulf, Weigelt, Poulter, and McNevin 2003). Thus, the constraining effect on the motor system induced by an internal focus appeared to be relatively general in nature.

Aside from producing a given amount of force with greater efficiency, a minimization of cocontractions between agonist and antagonist muscle groups or an optimized recruitment of motor units can also result in increased maximum force. The production of maximal forces requires an optimal activation pattern of agonist and antagonist muscle groups, as well as optimal muscle fiber recruitment within a muscle (Hollmann and Hettinger 2000). Inaccuracies in the timing of these forces, unnecessary cocontractions, or "noise" in the motor system would result in a less-than-maximal force output. In addition, the timing and direction of the generated forces must be optimal in tasks that require maximum force production. This includes tasks in which an object (e.g., shot, discus, football) or one's own body has to be propelled (e.g., high jump, long jump, volleyball block) or even static force production tasks (e.g., dynamometer). Thus, if an individual produces different amounts of maximum force under external versus internal focus conditions, this can only be attributed to different coordination patterns within or between muscles.

Studies demonstrating increased force production when individuals are instructed to focus on the movement's effect (i.e., externally; Marchant, Greig, and Scott 2009; Wulf and Dufek 2009; Wulf, Zachry, Granados, and Dufek 2007) therefore provide further evidence for increased movement efficiency with the adoption of an external focus. In a series of experiments, Wulf et al. (2007; Wulf and Dufek 2009; Wulf, Dufek, Lozano, and Pettigrew forthcoming) used a maximum vertical jump-and-reach task to examine effects of attentional focus. Because they used a within-participant design, in which all participants performed the task under counterbalanced internal and external conditions (and under a control condition in Wulf et al. 2007, experiment 1), any differences in jump height would have to be due the coordination of the forces between and/or within muscles. The measurement device used to record maximal vertical jump-and-reach height consisted of plastic rungs at different heights that the participant reached for during the jumps. While no attentional focus instructions were given in the control condition, participants were instructed to concentrate on the tips of their fingers in the internal focus condition and on the rungs in the external focus condition. The results of Wulf et al. showed that participants jumped significantly higher in the external focus condition than in both the internal focus or control conditions, while the latter two resulted in similar jump height. In addition, the vertical displacement of the center of mass (COM) was greatest when participants were instructed to adopt an external focus, providing preliminary evidence that the increase in jump height was due to increased force production.

In a follow-up study, Wulf and Dufek (2009) showed that in addition to jump height and COM displacement, the impulses produced as well as joint moments about the ankle, knee, and hip joints were significantly greater in the external focus condition. Thus, the results provided conclusive evidence that the increased jump height with an external focus was achieved through greater force production. Interestingly, the greater joint moments observed in the external versus internal focus condition (Wulf and Dufek 2009) correspond to the increased joint moments found by Vanezis and Lees (2005) for good versus poor jumpers performing a vertical jump. Vanezis and Lees argued that neuromuscular activity was presumably coordinated more effectively (i.e., the coactivation of antagonists was reduced) in the group of good jumpers (although they could not exclude other explanations due to the between-participants design they used). These findings are in line with the view that giving learners instructions that induce an external, rather than internal, focus of attention creates better performance earlier in skill acquisition, effectively accelerating the learning process so that an advanced level of performance is achieved sooner (Wulf 2007b).

A recent study by Marchant et al. (2009) also showed beneficial effects of an external focus on maximum force production. Using an isokinetic dynamometer, these researchers had participants produce maximum voluntary contractions of the elbow flexors under internal focus (i.e., focus on arm muscles) or external focus (i.e., focus on the crank hand bar) conditions. They found that participants produced significantly greater peak joint torque when they focused externally as compared to internally. Interestingly, this was achieved with significantly *less* muscular (EMG) activity (see also Marchant et al. forthcoming).

A study by Schücker, Hagemann, Strauß, and Völker (2009) showed differential effects of a performer's attentional focus on movement efficiency for a different task. In that study, experienced long-distance runners ran on a treadmill at an individual target speed (corresponding to 75% of their maximum oxygen consumption) under each of three different attentional focus conditions: (1) their running movements (internal focus: motor system), (2) their breathing (internal focus: breathing), or (3) a video clip showing an urban running course from the perspective of a runner (external focus: surroundings). The external focus condition resulted in significantly less oxygen consumption than both internal focus conditions. Also, participants rated that condition as the "easiest" one.

These studies provide converging evidence that movement efficiency—or the physical effort exerted to produce a given outcome—varies greatly with an individual's focus of attention. When an individual adopts an external focus, movements not only are more effective (e.g., Zachry et al. 2005) but also are produced more economically—with the consequence that the resultant maximum forces are greater (Marchant et al. 2009; Wulf et al. 2007; Wulf and Dufek 2009), the same forces are produced with less muscular energy (Marchant et al. 2006, forthcoming; Vance et al. 2004; see also Zachry et al. 2005), and oxygen consumption for a given output is reduced (Schücker et al. 2009). Thus, an external focus seems to exploit the energy-conserving nature of the body. Findings showing reduced postural sway with an external compared to an internal focus, for instance, are in line with this view as well (e.g., Wulf et al. 2009; McNevin and Wulf 2002; Wulf et al. 2004). Bringing the center of gravity back to a central position requires more energy if the deviations from this central position are greater. For a motor system to exploit these energy-conserving characteristics, the system has to be sensitive to the movement effects it produces. If attention is directed to the outcome of an action (external focus), there may be a greater coherence between the outcome and the sensory consequences of that action—which allows the motor system to adjust more adaptively to task demands (McNevin and Wulf 2002; McNevin et al. 2003).

Mental Effort

In addition to reducing physical effort, an external focus has been shown to result in greater automaticity in movement control—thus reducing attentional demands, or mental effort. Wulf, McNevin, and Shea (2001) measured participants' probe reaction times (RTs) while they were performing a dynamic balance task (stabilometer) after being given external or internal focus instructions. Dual-task methods are often used to assess the amount of attention required to perform a certain (primary) task (e.g., Li and Wright 2000; McLeod 1978, 1980; Monno, Chardenon, Temprado, Zanone, and Laurant 2000; Posner and Keele 1969; Salmoni, Sullivan, and Starkes 1976; Temprado, Zanone, Monno, and Laurent 1999; Wright and Kemp 1992; Wrisberg and Shea 1978). Performance on the secondary probe RT task is assumed to be related to the attentional demands of the primary task, with poorer secondary task performance, or longer probe RTs, being interpreted as an indication that the primary task required more attention (e.g., Abernethy 1988). Participants in the Wulf, McNevin, and Shea (2001) study were asked to balance on the stabilometer and to press a response key as quickly as possible when a tone occurred. As can be seen in figure 3.3 (top), participants who were instructed to focus on keeping markers on the platform horizontal (external focus) demonstrated more effective balance learning than participants instructed to focus on keeping their feet horizontal (internal focus). Furthermore, probe RTs generally decreased across practice, indicating that attentional demands of the balance task were reduced as learners became more skilled. More importantly, probe RTs were generally shorter for the external focus group, compared to the internal focus group (see figure 3.3, bottom). This difference in attentional demand was seen not only throughout the two-day practice phase but also on a delayed retention test without instructions. These findings show that the external focus reduced the mental effort associated with the balance task from the beginning of practice, compared to an internal focus. They support the idea that with an external focus of attention, a greater degree of automaticity is achieved sooner than would be the case with an internal focus. Furthermore, the retention results indicated that this advantage was relatively permanent and thus represented a learning effect.

Another piece of evidence for the facilitation of automaticity through an external focus comes from analyses of the frequency of movement adjustments produced by performers who were given external or internal focus instructions. In some of the studies using balance tasks, power spectral analyses were used to determine the dominant frequency components of the movement patterns (e.g., McNevin, Shea, and Wulf 2003; Wulf, McNevin, and Shea 2001; Wulf, Shea, and Park 2001). Faster movement adjustments indicate the utilization of reflexive feedback loops that operate at an automatic or unconscious level. In contrast, relatively slow adjustments reflect the use of more conscious feedback loops. Analyses of the balance records indeed revealed that learners instructed to adopt an external focus (i.e., markers on the stabilometer platform) made more frequent and, as a result, smaller corrections in maintaining their balance than did learners instructed to focus internally (i.e., on their feet; Wulf, McNevin, and Shea 2001; Wulf, Shea, and Park 2001). Figure 3.4 shows the position–time curves of the stabilometer platform across 90-second trials for representative participants in the internal focus (top) and in the external focus (bottom) groups in the Wulf, McNevin, and Shea study. As can be seen, the external focus participant

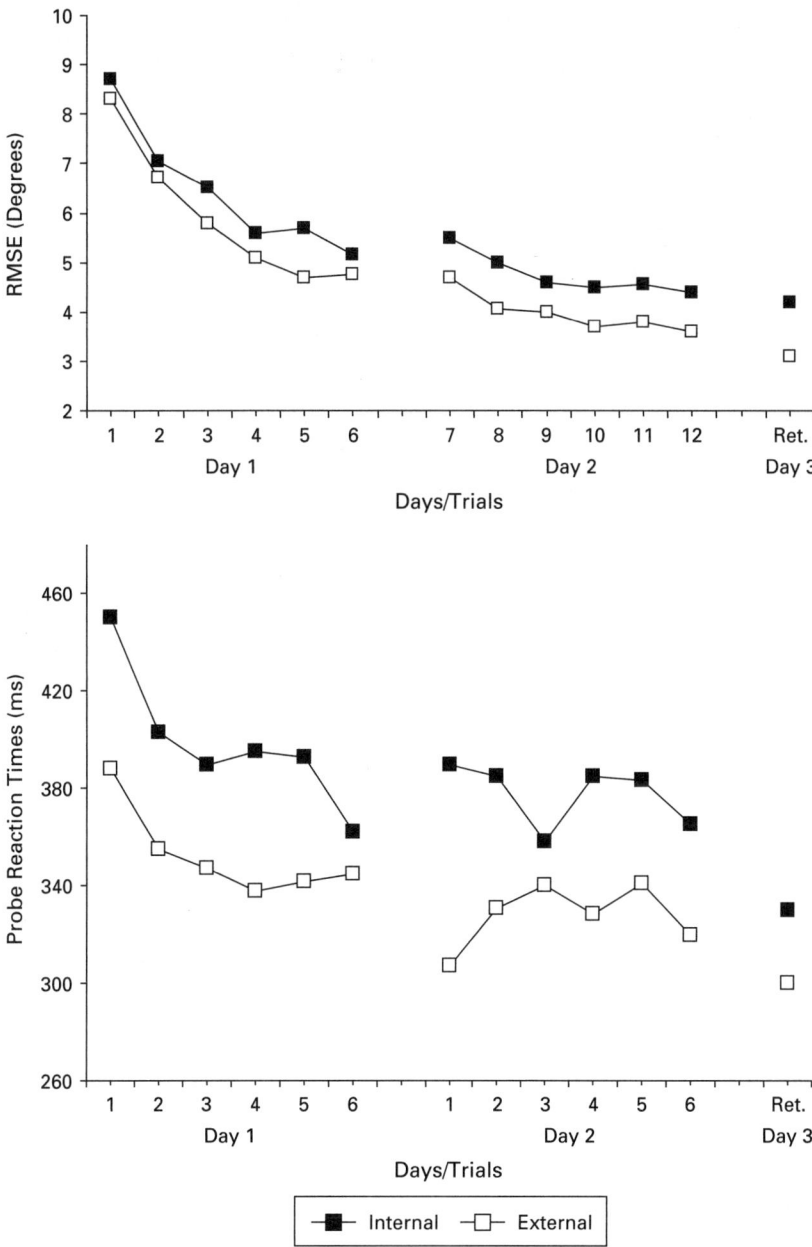

Figure 3.3
Balance performance (i.e., platform deviations from the horizontal; root-mean-square errors, RMSE) (top) and probe reaction times (RTs) (bottom) for the internal and external focus groups with auditory stimuli during practice (days 1 and 2) and in retention (day 3) in the study by Wulf, McNevin, and Shea (2001). Ret., retention.

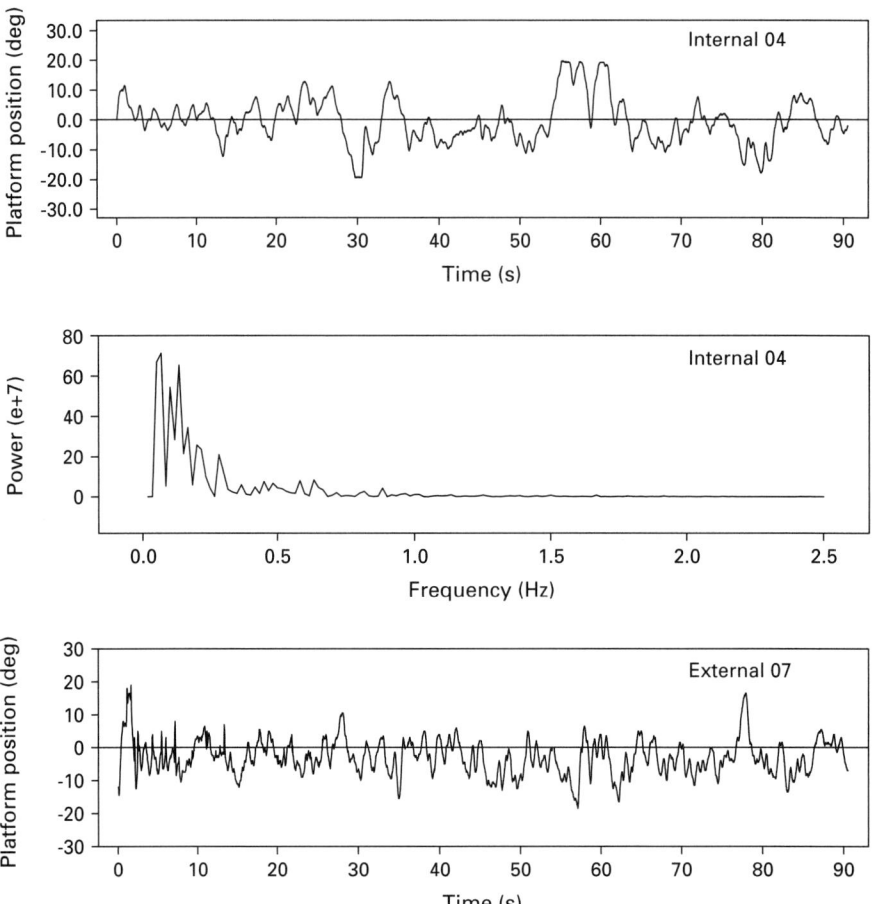

Figure 3.4
Examples of platform displacements on a retention trial for one participant in the internal (top) and external (bottom) condition in the study by Wulf, McNevin, and Shea (2001).

displayed higher frequency adjustments than did the internal focus participant. The results of a frequency analysis of the platform movements confirmed this effect, indicating significantly greater frequencies (i.e., mean power frequencies) when learners adopted an external focus.

Interestingly, this effect was even more pronounced in groups of participants that focused on markers that were further away from participants' feet, as compared to participants who focused on markers close to their feet (McNevin et al. 2003). That is, focusing on the more remote movement effects—which are presumably more easily distinguishable from the body movements—resulted in even higher frequencies of responding, and thus greater automaticity, than focusing on effects closer to the body or adopting an internal focus. Thus, there is converging evidence that a focus on the desired movement effect, or outcome, facilitates automatic control processes—thereby reducing mental effort.

Time and Energy Expenditure

Skilled performance is characterized by the fluidity and smoothness of the movements that are performed. This, in turn, may result in faster movement execution. For example, the well-timed coordination of the arm and leg actions in breaststroke swimming will result in a relatively constant velocity, thereby allowing the performer to swim faster with a given amount of metabolic energy expenditure. In his definition of skill, Guthrie also included as a criterion the capability of achieving the movement goal with a "minimum outlay .... of time and energy" (Guthrie 1952, 136).

Only a few studies that examined the effects of attentional focus used movement speed as a dependent variable (Freudenheim et al. 2009; Totsika and Wulf 2003; Vance et al. 2004), and these studies showed increases in movement speed with external compared to internal focus instructions. In the Vance et al. (2004) study discussed earlier, participants spontaneously executed the biceps curls faster (i.e., with greater angular velocity) when they adopted an external relative to an internal focus (experiment 1). (In experiment 2, the timing was kept constant through the use of a metronome.) The finding that movements were performed more rapidly when participants focused on the curl bar, rather than their arms, is in line with the automaticity notion (e.g., Wulf, McNevin, and Shea 2001). A more automatic mode of control typically results in more fluid movement patterns and, consequently, can increase the speed of movement production.

This effect was seen more directly in a study by Totsika and Wulf (2003). In that study, two groups of participants practiced riding a pedalo. The pedalo consists of two platforms (one for each foot) between sets of wheels. It moves by alternately pushing the upper platform forward and downwards, similar to the pedals on a bicycle. Totsika and Wulf asked participants to ride a distance of 15 m at their "own pace," with instructions to focus either on pushing their feet forward (internal focus) or on pushing the platforms forward (external focus). While both groups of participants increased their speed with practice, those who were instructed to adopt an external focus were significantly faster than those who adopted an internal focus. This was the case during the practice phase as well as on various transfer tests, which included (1) riding as fast as possible, (2) riding as fast as possible while counting backward by threes from a two-digit number, and (3) riding backward as fast as possible. These findings show that external focus can result in greater movement speed, facilitated by smoother and more fluid movements. In addition, they indicate that the benefits of practicing with an external focus are generalizable to novel situations (i.e., time pressure, riding backward) and persist when participants' attention was directed elsewhere (i.e., to counting backward).

Freudenheim et al. (2009) recently showed that swimming speed (16 m crawl) can be increased by instructing swimmers to focus on pushing the water back (external) instead of pulling their hands back (internal), or pushing the water down (external) instead of pushing the instep down (internal). With all participants performing under both external and internal focus conditions, swimming times were generally reduced when the swimmers focused on the water. Again, a minor difference in the wording of instructions presumably resulted in greater movement efficiency and, as a consequence, shorter movement times.

Thus, from the available evidence, it appears that an external focus indeed has the capacity to result in time savings. The automaticity in movement control induced by an external focus of attention seems to have concomitant effects on the fluidity and, consequently, speed of motion. Overall, it is clear that, compared to focusing on a movement, focusing on a movement's effect enhances movement effectiveness and economy—speeding the learning process so that a higher skill level is achieved sooner (Wulf 2007b). In the following section, we discuss potential mechanisms underlying this effect.

Mechanisms Underlying the Constrained Action Hypothesis

Why Do Minor Wording Differences in Instructions Induce Performance and Learning Effects?

A number of commentators have posed explanations for attentional focus effects (Hossner and Wenderoth 2007). These explanations range from presumed visual advantages (Hodges and Ford 2007; Maurer and Zentgraf 2007; Russell 2007) to a greater functional relevance (e.g., Hommel 2007; Künzell 2007; Wrisberg 2007; Ziessler 2007) to reduced information-processing demands of an external relative to an internal focus (Poolton, Maxwell, Masters, and van der Kamp 2007). However, several studies reviewed above within the attentional focus line of inquiry provide evidence that the external focus advantage cannot be attributed to any of those factors (see

Wulf 2007c). For example, visual information is usually kept constant between focus conditions by having participants look straight ahead on balance tasks (e.g., McNevin et al. 2003; Wulf et al. 1998; Wulf, McNevin, and Shea 2001) or by having them close their eyes (McNevin and Wulf 2002). The concept that an external focus of attention facilitates use of more functionally relevant, goal-directed actions is perhaps the most commonly expressed notion regarding the external focus advantage. It might be argued, for example, that external foci may make use of action-oriented capabilities of the neuromuscular system, enabling biomechanical advantages of anticipatory postural adjustments or goal-directed synergies (such as a raised head oriented toward the environmental target). A greater goal relatedness of an external versus internal focus of attention, however, cannot explain some key findings, for instance, differential balance performance when the focus is on the feet as opposed to boards (Totsika and Wulf 2003), rectangles (Landers et al. 2005), disk (Wulf et al 2009) or wheels (Wulf et al. 1998) under one's feet, or differences in muscle activity via EMG recordings as a function of attentional focus (e.g., Marchant et al. 2006; Vance et al. 2004). Finally, it is difficult to argue that the movement-related information-processing demands of internal compared with external focus conditions cause the ongoing differential effects on performance and learning, as proprioceptive and outcome information must be processed under both conditions (for further arguments against this view, see Wulf 2007c).

If the explanations discussed above cannot account for key findings, what might? The explanation might be so straightforward as to note that under internal focus conditions participants simply follow instructions that cause them to deconstruct available automated control sequences into chunks marked by bodily sensations, which presumably cannot well utilize transitions between parts in ways that long strings of linked and automated sequences can. External focus instructions may prevent this decomposition or facilitate performance and learning in other, currently unexplicated, ways.

Here, we speculate about a new perspective on the highly reliable attentional focus effects. This perspective involves what can be called the "self-invoking trigger" and is consistent with our already proffered constrained action hypothesis (see above) but addresses a potential proximal cause of more automatic or conscious control of movements. It is important at this point to recall that external and internal attentional focus effects can occur as the result of as little as one- or two-word differences in instruction (see table 3.1; e.g., Wulf and Su 2007; "Focus on the swing of your arms" [internal] vs. "Focus on the swing of the club" [external]). Wording differences in instructions have been shown in other circumstances (e.g., Cimpian, Acre, Markman, and Dweck 2007; Jourden, Bandura, and Banfield 1991) to result in a range of self-evaluative and behavioral effects. In the case of the movement-related attentional focus literature described in this chapter, external focus instructions often involve a movement's effect on a "natural" sport-related (e.g., Wulf et al. 1999) or home-related (Fasoli et al. 2002) implement, an artificial target for external focus such as rectangles under one's feet (see table 3.1), or a metaphor (e.g., Wulf et al. 2002). Conversely, internal focus instructions typically contain references to body parts (feet, arms). Thus, the primary distinction between these sets of attentional focus instructions is whether or not they involve the human body.

We speculatively suggest that the mere mention within the internal focus instructions of the participant's body ("your fingers," "your arm," "your feet") or bodily sensation (Marchant et al. 2007; "the feel of the dart") provokes implicit, probably unconscious, access to the self. The self construct has increasingly been recognized in a variety of circumstances to "lurk" within social environments, including all movement contexts and laboratory experimental settings, influencing thoughts, actions, and behavior (see Bargh and Morsella 2008; Stapel and Blanton 2004; Leary 2004).

Self-consciousness or self-focus may lead readily to self-evaluation and activate self-regulatory processes in attempts to manage thoughts and affective responses (Carver and Scheier 1978). It is assumed that this sequence of self-related processing may at times be unconscious (Bargh and Morsella 2008; Chartrand and Bargh 2002), although it may often rise into consciousness. This activity may produce what amounts to a series of ongoing "microchoking" episodes with attempts to right thoughts and bring emotions under control. A number of researchers have posed hypotheses about the nature of the relationship between attentional control for automated skills and for self-regulatory activities (e.g., Beilock et al. 2002; Kanfer and Stevenson 1985). When movement skills are automated, some degree of self-regulatory activity may be accommodated through available "excess" attentional capacity (e.g., Beilock et al. 2002). However, cognitive and affective activity ensuing from ubiquitous social influences (e.g., Stapel and Blanton 2004) and self-evaluation may eventually redirect attention to active attempts at negative thought and emotion suppression or substitution. The switching of attention to this self-regulatory activity may necessitate or activate a switching of control for the concurrent motor task from a more automatic mode to one requiring conscious control in efforts to reestablish control over movement. Alternatively, efforts to manage self-related thoughts and emotions may be so demanding that available attentional capacity is exceeded and performance suffers, prompting the individual to attempt task- and self-related regulatory activity, which may promote a more conscious control of both movement and self-regulatory activities (see Sarter et al. 2006).

A number of social-cognitive variables with ties to the self—including anxiety, fear, performance pressure, and self-efficacy—have been found to influence or correlate with the neuromuscular coordination or control of movement tasks and skills (e.g., Adkin, Frank, Carpenter, and Peysar 2002; Gray 2004; Pijpers, Oudejans, and Bakker

2005; Slobounov, Yukelson, and O'Brien, 1997; Williams, Vickers, and Rodrigues 2002). These findings are consistent with the proposition that a more negative self-focus (reflected in higher anxiety and fear levels and lower levels of self-efficacy) is associated with more widespread, inefficient activation of the muscular system, disruption of automaticity, and the use of more conscious control over ongoing movement. Exploration of the possible role of positive self-evaluations and affective responses for facilitation of automatic control is currently limited. It may be that active self-regulatory activities do not ensue, or at least demand less effort and attention, when positive self-regard and optimal task performance are experienced. As noted earlier, the self-invoking trigger potentially associated with internal focus instructions is speculative and has not been directly examined, nor have the potential sequelae of self-regulatory activity and subsequent impacts on conscious control of movement. Investigation of the mechanisms involved in the external focus advantage will likely involve not only the experimental and behavioral methods utilized thus far but the methods of social-cognitive psychology and social-cognitive affective neuroscience (Lieberman 2007; Ochsner and Gross 2008; Sarter et al. 2006) as well as the continued application of neurophysiological and biomechanical approaches.

Summary and Conclusion

From the findings reviewed in this chapter, it is clear that the effectiveness and efficiency of motor skill performance is affected by the individual's focus of attention. In particular, focusing on the movement's effect (i.e., adopting an external focus) has been shown to result not only in greater accuracy but also in enhanced efficiency of movement—both physically and mentally. The production of the same outcome (e.g., weight lifted, distance run) with reduced muscular activity or reduced oxygen consumption, or even greater maximum force production, when the performer adopts an external relative to an internal focus is an indication of decreased physical effort. In addition, an external focus appears to reduce mental effort—as indicated, for example, by improved secondary-task performance. Finally, there is evidence that movements are executed faster with an external focus, presumably as a result of greater fluidity and smoothness in movement production.

To account for the differential effects of external versus internal foci of attention, we originally proposed the constrained action hypothesis, according to which an external focus promotes automaticity in movement control (Wulf, McNevin, and Shea 2001). Here we expanded this view by suggesting a possible self-invoking trigger that may accompany an internal focus of attention or be prevented by an external focus. Regardless of cause, an external focus of attention appears to produce more effective performance achieved with minimizations of physical and mental effort. Ironically, however, it seems that a focus on achieving effortlessness (arguably an internal sensation) might result in a Sisyphean frustration in which a state of effortlessness is never reached.

References

Abernethy, B. 1988. Dual-task methodology and motor skills research: Some applications and methodological constraints. *Journal of Human Movement Studies* 14:101–132.

Adkin, A. L., J. S. Frank, M. G. Carpenter, and G. W. Peysar. 2002. Fear of falling modifies anticipatory postural control. *Exp. Brain Res.* 143:160–170.

Al-Abood, S. A., S. J. Bennett, F. M. Hernandez, D. Ashford, and K. Davids. 2002. Effects of verbal instructions and image size on visual search strategies in basketball free throw shooting. *J. Sports Sci.* 20:271–278.

Bargh, J. A., and E. Morsella. 2008. The unconscious mind. *Perspect. Psychol. Sci.* 3:73–79.

Beilock, S. L., and T. H. Carr. 2001. On the fragility of skilled performance: What governs choking under pressure? *J. Exp. Psychol. Gen.* 130:701–725.

Beilock, S. L., T. H. Carr, C. MacMahon, and J. L. Starkes. 2002. When paying attention becomes counterproductive: Impact of divided versus skill-focused attention on novice and experienced performance of sensorimotor skills. *J. Exp. Psychol. Appl.* 8:6–16.

Carver, C. S., and M. F. Scheier. 1978. Self-focusing effects of dispositional self-consciousness, mirror presence, and audience presence. *J. Pers. Soc. Psychol.* 36:324–332.

Chartrand, T. L., and J. A. Bargh. 2002. Nonconscious motivations: Their activation, operation, and consequences. In *Self and motivation: Emerging psychological perspectives*, ed. A. Tesser, D. A. Stapel, and J. V. Wood. Washington, DC: American Psychological Association, 13–41.

Cimpian, A., H.-M. C. Acre, E. M. Markman, and C. S. Dweck. 2007. Subtle linguistic cues affect children's motivation. *Psychol. Sci.* 18:314–316.

Durand, M., V. Geoffroi, A. Varray, and C. Prefault. 1994. Study of the energy correlates in the learning of a complex self-paced cyclical skill. *Hum. Mov. Sci.* 13:785–799.

Fasoli, S. E., C. A. Trombly, L. Tickle-Degnen, and M. H. Verfaellie. 2002. Effect of instructions on functional reach in persons with and without cerebrovascular accident. *Am. J. Occup. Ther.* 56:380–390.

Freedman, S.E., E. Maas, M. P. Caligiuri, G. Wulf, and D. A. Robin. 2007. Internal vs. external: Oral-motor performance as a function of attentional focus. *Journal of Speech, Language, and Hearing Science.* 56:131–136.

Freudenheim, A. M., G. Wulf, F. Madureira, U. C. Corrêa, and B. U. Corrêa. 2009. An external focus of attention results in greater swimming speed. Manuscript submitted for publication.

Gray, R. 2004. Attending to the execution of a complex sensorimotor skill: Expertise differences, choking, and slumps. *J. Exp. Psychol. Appl.* 10:42–54.

Guthrie, E. R. 1952. *The psychology of learning.* New York: Harper & Row.

Hodges, N. J., and P. Ford. 2007. Skillful attending, looking and thinking. In Wulf on attentional focus and motor learning [Special issue], ed. E.-J. Hossner and N. Wenderoth. *Bewegung und Training,* 1:23–24. Retrieved August 13, 2008, from http://www.ejournal-but.de/doks/wulf_2007.pdf

Hollmann, W., and T. Hettinger. 2000. *Sportmedizin—Grundlagen für Arbeit, Training und Präventivmedizin (Sports medicine—Fundamentals for work, exercise, and preventative medicine).* 4th ed. Stuttgart: Schattauer-Verlag.

Hommel, B. 2007. Goals, attention, and the dynamics of skill acquisition: Commentary on Wulf. In Wulf on attentional focus and motor learning [Special issue], ed. E.-J. Hossner and N. Wenderoth. *Bewegung und Training,* 1:25–26. Retrieved August 13, 2008, from http://www.ejournal-but.de/doks/wulf_2007.pdf

Hossner, E.-J., and N. Wenderoth, eds. 2007. Gabriele Wulf on attentional focus and learning [Special issue]. *Bewegung und Training,* 1. Retrieved August 13, 2008, from http://www.ejournal-but.de/Journal/reader.asp?Doc=wulf_2007.pdf

Hull, C. L. 1943. *Principles of behavior.* New York: Appleton-Century.

Jourden, F. J., A. Bandura, and J. T. Banfield. 1991. The impact of conceptions of ability on self-regulatory factors and motor skill acquisition. *J. Sport Exerc. Psychol.* 8:213–226.

Kanfer, F. H., and Stevenson, M. K. 1985. The effects of self-regulation on concurrent cognitive processing. *Cogn. Ther. Res.* 9:667–684.

Künzell, S. 2007. Optimal attentional focus in practical sport settings: Always external or task specific? In Wulf on attentional focus and motor learning [Special issue], ed. E.-J. Hossner and N. Wenderoth. *Bewegung und Training,* 1:27–28. Retrieved August 13, 2008, from http://www.ejournal-but.de/doks/wulf_2007.pdf

Landers, M., G. Wulf, H. Wallmann, and M. A. Guadagnoli. 2005. An external focus of attention attenuates balance impairment in Parkinson's disease. *Physiotherapy* 91:152–185.

Lay, B. S., A. W. Sparrow, K. M. Hughes, and N. J. O'Dwyer. 2002. Practice effects on coordination and control, metabolic energy expenditure, and muscle activation. *Hum. Mov. Sci.* 21:807–830.

Leary, M. R. 2004. *The curse of the self: Self-awareness, egotism, and the quality of human life.* New York: Oxford University Press.

Leavitt, J. L. 1979. Cognitive demands of skating and stickhandling in ice hockey. *Can. J. Appl. Sport Sci.* 4:46–55.

Lee, T. D., S. P. Swinnen, and D. J. Serrien. 1994. Cognitive effort and motor learning. *Quest* 46:328–344.

Li, Y., and D. L. Wright. 2000. An assessment of the attention demands during random- and blocked-practice schedules. *Q. J. Exp. Psychol.* 53A:591–606.

Lieberman, M. D. 2007. Social cognitive neuroscience: A review of core processes. *Annu. Rev. Psychol.* 58:259–289.

Marchant, D., P. Clough, and M. Crawshaw. 2007. The effects of attentional focusing strategies on novice dart throwing performance and their task experiences. *International Journal of Sport and Exercise Psychology* 5:291–303.

Marchant, D. C., M. Greig, C. Scott, and P. J. Clough. 2006. Attentional focusing strategies influence muscle activity during isokinetic bicep curls. Poster presented at the annual conference of the British Psychological Society, Cardiff, UK.

Marchant, D.C., M. Greig, and C. Scott. 2009. Attentional focusing strategies influence bicep EMG during isokinetic biceps curls. *Athletic Insight.* Retrieved July 11, 2009, from http://www.athleticinsight.com/Vol10Iss2/MuscularActivity.htm.

Marchant, D. C., M. Greig, and C. Scott. Forthcoming. Attentional focusing instructions influence force production and muscular activity during isokinetic elbow flexions. *Journal of Strength and Cenditioning Research.*

Maurer, H., and K. Zentgraf. 2007. On the how and why of the external focus learning advantage. In Wulf on attentional focus and motor learning [Special issue], ed. E.-J. Hossner and N. Wenderoth. *Bewegung und Training,* 1:31–32. Retrieved August 13, 2008, from http://www.ejournal-but.de/doks/wulf_2007.pdf

McLeod, P. D. 1978. Does probe RT measure central processing demand? *Q. J. Exp. Psychol.* 80:83–89.

McLeod, P. D. 1980. What can probe RT tell us about the attentional demands of movements? In *Tutorials in motor behavior,* ed. G. E. Stelmach and J. Requin. Amsterdam: North-Holland, 579–589.

McNevin, N. H., C. H. Shea, and G. Wulf. 2003. Increasing the distance of an external focus of attention enhances learning. *Psychol. Res.* 67:22–29.

McNevin, N. H., and G. Wulf. 2002. Attentional focus on supra-postural tasks affects postural control. *Hum. Mov. Sci.* 21:187–202.

Monno, A., A. Chardenon, J. J. Temprado, P. G. Zanone, and M. Laurant. 2000. Effects of attention on phase transitions between bimanual coordination patterns: A behavioral and cost analysis. *Neurosci. Lett.* 283:93–96.

Ochsner, K. D., and J. J. Gross. 2008. Cognitive emotion regulation: Insights from social cognitive and affective neuroscience. *Curr. Dir. Psychol. Sci.* 17:153–158.

Pashler, H. 1994. Dual-task interference in simple tasks: Data and theory. *Psychol. Bull.* 116:220–244.

Pijpers, J. J., R. R. Oudejans, and F. C. Bakker. 2005. Anxiety-induced changes in movement behavior during the execution of a complex whole-body task. *Q. J. Exp. Psychol.* 58A:421–445.

Poolton, J. M., J. P. Maxwell, R. S. W. Masters, and J. van der Kamp. 2007. Moving with an external focus: Automatic or simply less demanding? In Wulf on attentional focus and motor learning [Special issue], ed. E.-J. Hossner and N. Wenderoth. *Bewegung und Training*, 1:43–44. Retrieved August 13, 2008, from http://www.ejournal-but.de/doks/wulf_2007.pdf

Posner, M. I., and S. W. Keele. 1969. Attentional demands of movement. In *Proceedings of the 16th Congress of Applied Psychology*. Amsterdam: Swets and Zeitlinger.

Russell, D. M. 2007. Attentional focus on the invariant control variables. In Wulf on attentional focus and motor learning [Special issue], ed. E.-J. Hossner and N. Wenderoth. *Bewegung und Training*, 1:47–48. Retrieved August 13, 2008, from http://www.ejournal-but.de/doks/wulf_2007.pdf

Salmoni, A. W., R. A. Schmidt, and C. B. Walter. 1984. Knowledge of results and motor learning: A review and critical reappraisal. *Psychol. Bull.* 95:355–386.

Salmoni, A. W., S. J. Sullivan, and J. L. Starkes. 1976. The attention demands of movements: A critique of the probe technique. *J. Mot. Behav.* 8:161–169.

Sarter, M., W. J. Gehring, and R. Kozak. 2006. More attention must be paid: The neurobiology of attentional effort. *Brain Res. Brain Res. Rev.* 51:145–160.

Schücker, L., N. Hagemann, B. Strauß, and K. Völker. 2009. The effect of attentional focus on running economy. *Journal of Sports Sciences*. 27:1241–1248.

Schmidt, R. A. 1991. Frequent augmented feedback can degrade learning: Evidence and interpretations. In *Tutorials in motor neuroscience*, ed. J. Requin and G. E. Stelmach. Dordrecht: Kluwer Academic, 59–75.

Schmidt, R. A., and T. D. Lee. 2005. *Motor control and learning: A behavioral emphasis*. 4th ed. Champaign, IL: Human Kinetics.

Slobounov, S., D. Yukelson, and R. O'Brien. 1997. Self-efficacy and movement variability of Olympic-level springboard divers. *J. Appl. Sport Psychol.* 9:171–190.

Smith, M. D., and C. J. Chamberlin. 1992. Effect of adding cognitively demanding tasks on soccer skill performance. *Percept. Mot. Skills* 75:955–961.

Sparrow, A. W., K. M. Hughes, A. P. Russell, and P. F. Le Rossignol. 1999. Effects of practice and preferred rate on perceived exertion, metabolic variables and movement control. *Hum. Mov. Sci.* 18:137–153.

Sparrow, A. W., and K. M. Newell. 1998. Metabolic energy expenditure and the regulation of movement economy. *Psychon. Bull. Rev.* 5:173–196.

Stapel, D. A., and H. Blanton. 2004. From seeing to being: Subliminal social comparisons affect implicit and explicit self-evaluations. *J. Pers. Soc. Psychol.* 87:468–481.

Temprado, J. J., P. G. Zanone, A. Monno, and M. Laurent. 1999. Attentional load associated with performing and stabilizing preferred bimanual patterns. *J. Exp. Psychol. Hum. Percept. Perform.* 25:1579–1594.

Thorn, J. 2006. *Using attentional strategies for balance performance and learning in nine through 12 year olds.* Unpublished doctoral dissertation, Florida State University, Tallahassee.

Tolman, E. C. 1932. *Purposive behavior in animals and men.* New York: Century.

Totsika, V., and G. Wulf. 2003. The influence of external and internal foci of attention on transfer to novel situations and skills. *Res. Q. Exerc. Sport* 74:220–225.

Vance, J., G. Wulf, T. Töllner, N. H. McNevin, and J. Mercer. 2004. EMG activity as a function of the performer's focus of attention. *J. Mot. Behav.* 36:450–459.

Vanezis, A., and A. Lees. 2005. A biomechanical analysis of good and poor performers of the vertical jump. *Ergonomics* 48:1594–1603.

Williams, A. M., J. Vickers, and S. Rodrigues. 2002. The effects of anxiety on visual search, movement kinematics and performance in table tennis: A test of Eysenck and Calvo's processing efficiency theory. *J. Sport Exerc. Psychol.* 24:438–455.

Wright, D. L., and T. Kemp. 1992. The dual-task methodology and assessing the attentional demands of ambulation with walking devices. *Phys. Ther.* 72:306–312.

Wilson, M., M. Chattington, D. E. Marple-Horvat, and N. C. Smith. 2007. A comparison of self-focus versus attentional explanations of choking. *J. Sport Exerc. Psychol.* 29:439–456.

Wrisberg, C. A. 2007. An applied sport psychological perspective on the relative merits of an external and internal focus of attention. In Wulf on attentional focus and motor learning [Special issue], ed. E.-J. Hossner and N. Wenderoth. *Bewegung und Training,* 1:53–54. Retrieved August 13, 2008, from http://www.ejournal-but.de/doks/wulf_2007.pdf

Wrisberg, C. A., and C. H. Shea. 1978. Shifts in attention demands and motor program utilization during motor learning. *J. Mot. Behav.* 2:149–158.

Wulf, G. 2007a. Attentional focus and motor learning: A review of 10 years of research (Target article). In Wulf on attentional focus and motor learning [Special issue], ed. E.-J. Hossner and N. Wenderoth. *Bewegung und Training,* 1:4–14. Retrieved August 13, 2008, from http://www.ejournal-but.de/doks/wulf_2007.pdf

Wulf, G. 2007b. *Attention and motor skill learning.* Champaign, IL: Human Kinetics.

Wulf, G. 2007c. Methods, findings, explanations, and future directions: Response to commentaries on "Attentional focus and motor learning." In Wulf on attentional focus and motor learning [Special issue], ed. E.-J. Hossner and N. Wenderoth. *Bewegung und Training,* 1:57–64. Retrieved August 13, 2008, from http://www.ejournal-but.de/doks/wulf_2007.pdf

Wulf, G., and J. S. Dufek. 2009. Increased jump height with an external attentional focus is due to augmented force production. *J. Motor Behav.* 41:401–409.

Wulf, G., J. S. Dufek, L. Lozano, and C. Pettigrew. Forthcoming. Increased jump height and reduced EMG activity with an external focus of attention. *Hum. Mov. Sci.*

Wulf, G., M. Höß, and W. Prinz. 1998. Instructions for motor learning: Differential effects of internal versus external focus of attention. *J. Mot. Behav.* 30:169–179.

Wulf, G., M. Landers, R. Lewthwaite, and T. Töllner. 2009. External focus instructions reduce postural instability in individuals with Parkinson disease. *Phys. Ther.* 89:162-168.

Wulf, G., B. Lauterbach, and T. Toole. 1999. Learning advantages of an external focus of attention in golf. *Res. Q. Exerc. Sport* 70:120–126.

Wulf, G., N. McConnel, M. Gärtner, and A. Schwarz. 2002. Enhancing the learning of sport skills through external-focus feedback. *J. Mot. Behav.* 34:171–182.

Wulf, G., and N. H. McNevin. 2003. Simply distracting learners is not enough: More evidence for the learning benefits of an external focus of attention. *Eur. J. Sport Sci.* 3:1–13.

Wulf, G., N. H. McNevin, and C. H. Shea. 2001. The automaticity of complex motor skill learning as a function of attentional focus. *Q. J. Exp. Psychol.* 54A:1143–1154.

Wulf, G., J. Mercer, N. H. McNevin, and M. A. Guadagnoli. 2004. Reciprocal influences of attentional focus on postural and supra-postural task performance. *J. Mot. Behav.* 36:189–199.

Wulf, G., C. H. Shea, and J.-H. Park. 2001. Attention in motor learning: Preferences for and advantages of an external focus. *Res. Q. Exerc. Sport* 72:335–344.

Wulf, G., and J. Su. 2007. An external focus of attention enhances golf shot accuracy in beginners and experts. *Res. Q. Exerc. Sport* 78:384–389.

Wulf, G., M. Weigelt, D. R. Poulter, and N. H. McNevin. 2003. Attentional focus on supra-postural tasks affects balance learning. *Q. J. Exp. Psychol.* 56:1191–1211.

Wulf, G., T. Zachry, C. Granados, and J. S. Dufek. 2007. Increases in jump-and-reach height through an external focus of attention. *International Journal of Sports Science & Coaching* 2:275–284.

Zachry, T. 2005. *Effects of attentional focus on kinematics and muscle activation patterns as a function of expertise.* Unpublished master's thesis, University of Nevada, Las Vegas.

Zachry, T., G. Wulf, J. Mercer, and N. Bezodis. 2005. Increased movement accuracy and reduced EMG activity as the result of adopting an external focus of attention. *Brain Res. Bull.* 67:304–309.

Ziessler, M. 2007. Effect codes are important for learning and control of movement patterns. In Wulf on attentional focus and motor learning [Special issue], ed. E.-J. Hossner and N. Wenderoth. *Bewegung und Training,* 1:55–56. Retrieved August 13, 2008, from http://www.ejournal-but.de/doks/wulf_2007.pdf

4 The Impact of Anticipated Cognitive Demand on Attention and Behavioral Choice

Joseph T. McGuire and Matthew M. Botvinick

Information-processing tasks vary in their associated levels of cognitive demand. Highly demanding tasks require strong input from cognitive or executive control, input typically associated with a subjective sense of mental effort. In addition to being partly dictated by the situation, effort can also, of course, be regulated volitionally. Within the context of a single task, people can decide to increase or decrease their level of controlled information processing. Greater control, with its associated experience of effort, can be empirically observed in behavioral adjustments or in such manifestations of physiological arousal as skin conductance, cardiovascular activity, and pupil diameter (Kahneman 1973). In regulating their level of mental effort, people take account of both demand and incentives; in one study, a large preparatory cardiovascular response occurred only if the upcoming task was moderately difficult *and* was highly likely to earn a payoff (Wright and Gregorich 1989). Even subtle changes to the task environment can affect people's choices about how much mental effort to tolerate. For example, effort goes down (indexed by performance) when the introduction of a tiny monetary incentive nullifies a task's intrinsic reward (Heyman and Ariely 2004). Effort also goes down (indexed by task-related physiological arousal) when fatigue makes success less probable (Wright, Martin, and Bland 2003). Emphasizing that effort depends jointly on motivation and task demand, Sarter, Gehring, and Kozak (2006) suggested conceptualizing attentional effort as a "cognitive incentive."

The choice of how much effortful control to impose on a moment-to-moment basis constitutes one type of *demand-based decision making*, as it depends partly on the amount of control demanded by the task. There is also a second form of demand-based decision making. Since different situations impose different amounts of demand, people can regulate their experience of mental effort proactively in choosing which situations they will enter. A person might face two behavioral options, one of which will be more cognitively demanding than the other. The anticipated level of demand is likely to be one factor that influences which option the person chooses.

As an example, consider a major purchase such as a car. One person in need of a car might embark on an extensive research project that involves seeking and integrating information, judging the accuracy of sources, making trade-offs, resolving contradictions, and holding goals in mind. Another person faced with the same task could take a less mentally taxing approach, simply visiting dealerships until something satisfactory is found.

In considering how people choose between strategies, it is worth noting that a more intensive approach is often more likely to optimize the final outcome—the more thorough individual is more likely to end up with a better car or a better bargain.[1] This raises the question of why a person would not *always* accept the maximum level of demand. The fact that an easier task would ever be selected (or, in our example, that a person would ever buy an automobile without thorough research) suggests that additional factors are in play. Specifically, it implies that cognitive demand gives rise to subjective *costs*. Even within a single task, people appear to accept only as much effort as is required in order to meet reasonable performance criteria. Cardiovascular activity prior to task performance is only high if the task is expected to be difficult (Contrada, Wright, and Glass 1984), and cognitive control appears to be upregulated only when a task becomes more demanding (Gratton, Coles, and Donchin 1992).

It is a long-standing behavioral principle that people and animals avoid physical exertion when all else is equal (Hull 1943). We will discuss experimental evidence that an equivalent principle applies to prospective choices regarding cognitive, rather than physical, work (Kool, McGuire, Rosen, and Botvinick 2009; Botvinick 2007). An aversion to mental effort could serve the useful purpose of biasing behavior toward the most efficient available tasks or strategies.

If cognitive demand imposes costs, then long-term demand-based decisions involve trade-offs between the tangible gains that high-demand situations afford and the intrinsic costs that such situations impose. Trade-offs of this kind have been considered in detail before. Wilcox (1993) proposed that people approach economic decisions by first choosing a decision algorithm and then applying that algorithm to the information at hand. More intensive algorithms are more accurate for certain kinds of complex decisions but are also more costly; these algorithms become advantageous when stakes are high. Relatedly, Camerer and Hogarth (1999) have proposed a "capital–labor–production framework," in which effort is analogous to economic labor resources and interacts with people's abilities (which are analogous to capital resources) to improve their performance. Effort-associated resources will be invested so long as they yield net gains in either tangible or intrinsic rewards, but such gains may be minor if a person's relevant abilities are either very high (so that further effort is superfluous) or very low (rendering further effort useless).

Overview

In the present chapter we review recent behavioral and neuroscientific evidence concerning both immediate and long-term demand-based decision making. We first consider evidence that people make continuous decisions about how much cognitive control to exert, adjusting their level of control online in reaction to demand. We then discuss the idea that people choose strategies and tasks so as to minimize demand proactively. One point that we shall emphasize is that both these forms of demand-based decision making require a mechanism for *evaluating* the levels of cognitive demand associated with specific task contexts. Brain imaging studies identify a neural system serving such a demand-monitoring function, and this system appears to participate both in online adjustments and in proactive demand avoidance. We conclude by considering the possible contribution of this demand-monitoring system to situations where high effort is sought, or where demanding tasks appear to take on an effortless subjective character.

Monitoring Demand in Order to Modulate Control

We have stated that people continuously choose how much control to exert. One class of relevant evidence shows that people respond to fluctuating cognitive demand by making short-term adjustments. People notice when their level of cognitive control is falling short of the level demanded by the situation, and they react by effortfully applying such control in order to preserve performance. Such adjustments constitute an immediate, reactive form of demand-based decision making.

A demonstration was provided by Gratton et al. (1992). Participants in this study performed a *flanker task*: they were to respond based on the identity of the central letter in a display, while ignoring flanking letters that could be either incongruent (HHSHH) or congruent (SSSSS) with the correct response. Incongruent flankers are more demanding and elicit slower and less accurate responses. Of primary relevance, however, is the observation of sequential effects. If two incongruent trials are presented in a row, performance is better on the second trial (compared to performance on an incongruent trial that was preceded by a congruent trial). This simple observation suggests that people react to cognitive demand by exerting greater control and that this ability can facilitate performance if demand remains high (see Botvinick, Cohen, and Carter 2004 for a review of related findings).

Related evidence comes from studies using the *Stroop task* to manipulate cognitive demand. Participants performing this task must name the color in which a word is printed, which can be incongruent with the word itself (saying "green" to the word RED printed in green) or can be congruent (saying "green" to GREEN printed in green). As in the flanker task, people tend to respond more slowly when the word and color provide conflicting information. Here again, however, people can adapt to high situation-imposed demand. Performance on high-demand trials is worst when such trials are infrequent. If incongruent stimuli occur frequently, the associated response slowing grows smaller (Lowe and Mitterer 1982). Interestingly, individual differences in abilities (i.e., in working memory capacity) only impact Stroop performance when high-demand trials are rare and cannot be adapted to (Kane and Engle 2003).

There is even evidence that sequential adjustments in control can extend across tasks. For example, an incongruent flanker trial appears to facilitate performance of a subsequent incongruent Stroop trial (Freitas, Bahar, Yang, and Banai 2007, but for opposing data see Mayr, Awh, and Laurey 2003). This would support a view that sequential effects reflect acclimation to an overall level of cognitive demand rather than the priming of a specific task or stimulus.

Sequential adjustment effects may be related to the phenomenon of *posterror slowing*. In one study (Rabbitt 1966), errors in a sequential choice task tended to be faster than correct responses, but responses to trials that followed errors were unusually slow. One interpretation is that when participants detected their own errors, they responded by applying a greater amount of cognitive control on the next trial.

Such effects indicate that people continuously evaluate the demand imposed on them. How might continuous demand evaluation be implemented computationally? In previous work, Botvinick, Braver, Barch, Carter, and Cohen (2001) have proposed that the unmet demand present in a situation can be quantitatively indexed by the amount of *response* (or *decision*) *conflict* the situation creates (see also Botvinick et al. 2004). Response conflict encodes the extent to which two incompatible response tendencies are active. The quantitative formulation of response conflict arises from simulation models that assign a scalar activation value to each potential response. The activation of a given response represents the amount of evidence that has accumulated in favor of enacting that response (see, e.g., Bogacz 2007; Cohen, Dunbar, and McClelland 1990). Conflict arises during incompatible flanker or Stroop trials because there is perceptual evidence supporting both a correct and incorrect action (e.g., flankers indicate one response while the target indicates another; a word's color indicates "green," but word reading indicates "red"). Conflict can be diminished by applying cognitive control, which privileges relevant information at the expense of distracting information. The occurrence of conflict thus indicates a demand for control that is not yet adequately met.

A monitoring mechanism sensitive to response conflict (and, by extension, to unmet cognitive demand) could trigger the application of top–down control. Elevated control, in turn, would reduce conflict and facilitate coherent action. Computational modeling work has shown that sequential effects observed in the flanker and Stroop tasks, as well as posterror slowing, can be accounted for using exactly this type of conflict-triggered adjustment. Elevated control increases the influence of the central target relative to the flankers, or of word-color information relative to word-reading information, reducing conflict and improving subsequent performance (Botvinick et al. 2001). Modeling work further makes clear that the detection of conflict and the direct, proximate application of control are potentially separable components of the total process.

Evidence suggests that conflict-monitoring computations are indeed performed in the human brain. Neuroimaging data have associated conflict monitoring with specific anatomical structures, most notably the anterior cingulate cortex (ACC), which is located on the medial surface of the frontal lobes. Activity in the ACC and adjacent medial frontal regions is greater when task-imposed demand rises, including during incongruent flanker trials (Botvinick, Nystrom, Fissell, Carter, and Cohen 1999) and incongruent Stroop trials (MacLeod and MacDonald 2000; Pardo, Pardo, Janer, and Raichle 1990). ACC-associated activity can be elicited by many other manipulations of difficulty, including the simple addition of instructions that impose time pressure in a choice task (Mulert, Menzinger, Leicht, Pogarell, and Hegerl 2005).

If the ACC plays a role in evaluating conflict, then it is well-positioned to trigger sequential adjustments in control. Data in favor of such a role come from a functional magnetic resonance imaging (fMRI) study by Kerns et al. (2004). Congruent and incongruent Stroop trials were intermixed, and the central analyses concerned occasions when two incongruent trials occurred in a row. The second of two incongruent trials tended to be facilitated (i.e., to be responded to more quickly than the first incongruent trial), suggesting conflict-triggered adjustments in control consistent with previous findings. Furthermore, ACC activity was associated with trial-to-trial variability in the size of this facilitation effect. A portion of the ACC was significantly more active during those incongruent trials that produced the largest subsequent adjustment effects. In addition, a region of the dorsolateral prefrontal cortex was more active during the trials in which large adjustment effects actually occurred, and this dorsolateral activity was positively correlated with previous-trial ACC activity. This pattern is consistent with a model in which the ACC detects elevated demand and triggers dorsolateral regions to apply increased task control (as proposed by Botvinick et al. 2001). Kerns (2006) reported a similar pattern of results using a different cognitive task. Here again, greater ACC activity predicted larger subsequent behavioral adjustments.

Demand Avoidance

In the previous section we considered one form of demand-based decision making: deciding how much control to recruit based on a conflict signal that signifies unmet demand. These short-term decisions appear to rely on continuous demand monitoring by the ACC. As established at the outset of this chapter, another important form of demand-based decision making involves using long-term knowledge about task demand to choose which tasks to undertake and which to avoid.

The Costliness of High Demand

Several lines of evidence suggest that people generally prefer to avoid highly cognitively demanding situations—that is, that human behavior is well-characterized by a *law of least mental effort* (cf. Hull 1943). A bias against demanding situations is strongly implied by the cost–benefit framework outlined earlier in this chapter. If the rewards associated with two situations are equal and one situation imposes less cognitive demand than the other, then it should yield a more favorable trade-off and should be more likely to be chosen.

One relevant observation is that ease of perceptual processing is linked to positive affect. Incipient smiles, detectable using electromyography, are elicited by pictures presented in a visually fluent manner (Winkielman and Cacioppo 2001).

There is also direct evidence that people take cognitive demand into account when choosing strategies. MacLeod, Hunt, and Mathews (1978) gave participants a sentence–picture verification task that could be accomplished by manipulating either visual or verbal information. Individual participants tended to adopt whichever strategy best suited their own abilities. The visual strategy was frequently chosen by people with high spatial abilities but was almost never chosen by those with low spatial abilities. This pattern reflects an intuitive form of demand minimization. Stated according to the economic metaphor of Camerer and Hogarth (1999), people chose to work in a domain, visual or verbal, where they possessed stronger capital (i.e., abilities) and therefore could do with less labor (i.e., effort).

In a different approach to demonstrating demand-related costs, our lab has recently obtained brain imaging evidence that cognitive demand counts negatively within a neural cost–benefit analysis (Botvinick, Huffstetler, and McGuire 2009). Specifically, we found that a neural signature of reward was weaker if rewards were associated with high demand. We reasoned that the outcome of an internal cost–benefit analysis should be reflected by activity in the nucleus accumbens, a value-sensitive region in the ventral striatum. The nucleus accumbens responds to both primary and secondary rewards. Its activity is greater when rewards are unpredicted (Berns, McClure, Pagnoni, and Montague 2001). It also exhibits temporal discounting, responding less strongly to a signal of delayed than immediate future reward (McClure, Laibson, Loewenstein, and Cohen 2004). The nucleus accumbens thus registers relatively complex value computations and is a reasonable candidate to incorporate the impact of effort on a situation's net value.

Botvinick, Huffstetler, and McGuire (2009) presented participants with a number-judgment task in an MRI scanner. Depending on the color in which a number was shown, participants were to make a judgment about either its magnitude (high vs. low) or its parity (odd vs. even). Switching between two types of judgments is slower

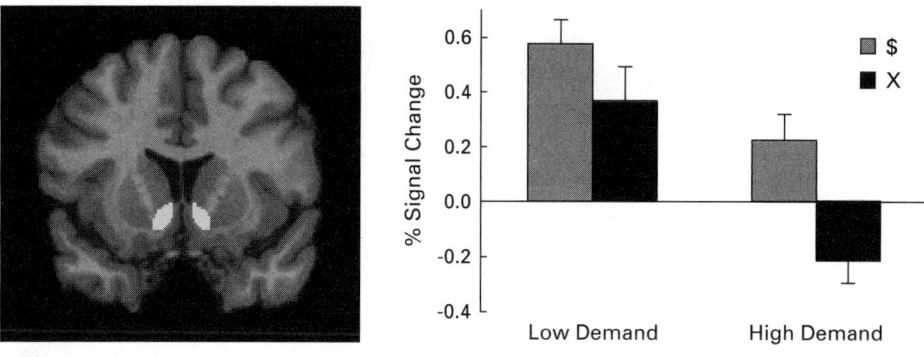

Figure 4.1
The left-hand panel shows the value-sensitive region of interest in the nucleus accumbens (NAcc in white). The right-hand panel shows the response in this region to reward cues that followed task blocks. There was a main effect of reward, such that reward elicited a greater response than nonreward. There was also a main effect of the preceding block's demand level. Reward cues elicited a smaller response when they represented payment for a high-demand task, a pattern referred to as *effort discounting*. Error bars reflect standard error of the mean. Data from Botvinick, Huffstetler, and McGuire (2009).

and less efficient than repeating judgments of the same type (see, e.g., Rogers and Monsell 1995). Each task block could impose either high demand (alternating between magnitude and parity judgments, requiring frequent task switches) or low demand (repeating judgments of a single type). Participants then received a signal that they were paid either $1 or $0 for the just-completed block. The response of the nucleus accumbens to this reward cue was the primary dependent variable. Consistent with past findings, activity was greater when participants were paid than when they received nothing. In addition, however, there was a main effect of the preceding cognitive task: The accumbens responded more strongly to reward cues for low-demand blocks than for high-demand blocks (see figure 4.1). This finding confirmed our expectation that the nucleus accumbens would encode an integrated value spanning the task block episode and, moreover, that cognitive demand would contribute negatively to that net value. Accumbens activity was found to reflect *effort discounting*.

Furthermore, there was also evidence that the ACC is a potential source of demand-related information. Trial-to-trial correlations were observed between signal levels in the ACC and nucleus accumbens. Even among trials of the same explicit demand level, trials that evoked greater ACC activity (presumably reflecting a greater experience of conflict or unmet demand) were associated with a lower *subsequent* reward-related response in the nucleus accumbens. Such correlations were specific to the ACC and were not observed for a control region, an area of dorsolateral prefrontal cortex that showed activity during the demanding task but is not generally implicated in conflict detection.

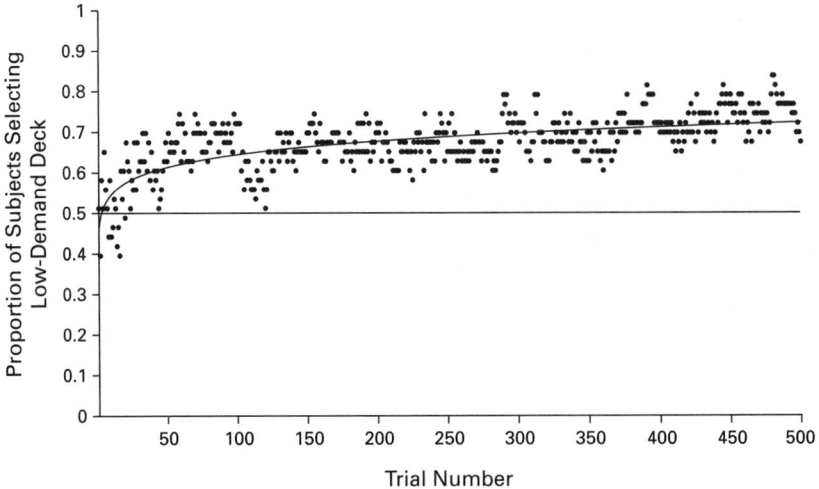

Figure 4.2
Over the course of a 500-trial session, participants gradually developed a bias toward a deck of cards that imposed a smaller amount of cognitive demand. Data from Kool, McGuire, Rosen, and Botvinick (2009).

Behavioral Avoidance of Demand

The evidence discussed so far indicates that unmet cognitive demand brings about an aversive experience. Findings associating demand with negative affect (Winkielman and Cacioppo 2001), strategy modification (MacLeod et al. 1978), and diminished neurally coded value (Botvinick, Huffstetler, and McGuire 2009) all imply that people will make behavioral decisions so as to minimize the amount of unmet cognitive demand they encounter.

We have recently used a *demand selection* paradigm to provide direct evidence for behavioral avoidance of demanding task-switching (Kool, McGuire, Rosen, and Botvinick 2009). In this paradigm, participants are given choices between two options that impose different levels of demand. Participants choose between two decks of cards on each trial. The chosen deck then displays a single digit which, depending on its color, requires either a magnitude or a parity judgment. The high-demand deck requires frequent switches between magnitude and parity judgments, while the low-demand deck generates strings of trials requiring the same type of judgment. The law of least mental effort predicts that given a free choice, subjects will develop a bias toward the deck imposing less switching-related demand. As shown in figure 4.2, this is what is observed.

Successful avoidance of demand implies that participants in the demand selection experiment can accurately *anticipate* the level of cognitive demand that their choices

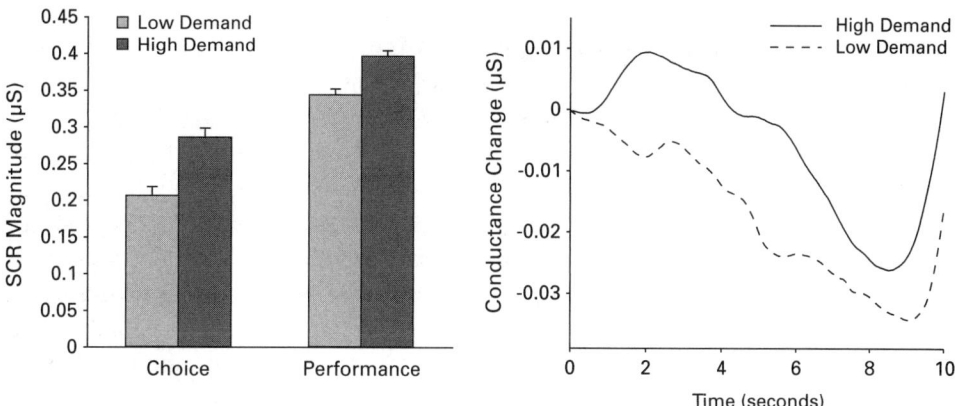

Figure 4.3
The left-hand panel shows skin-conductance response (SCR) amplitudes (base to peak) during the decision period (before the participant chose a deck) and during the performance period (while the participant performed the task). SCRs were greater during both the performance and the anticipation of high-demand trials. The right-hand panel shows the skin-conductance time course during the anticipatory decision phase. Data from Botvinick and Rosen (2008).

will entail. Mechanisms for demand anticipation may be integral to the ability to avoid demand. Botvinick and Rosen (2008) recently obtained direct evidence for a physiological response in anticipation of high task demand. In a modified demand selection paradigm, skin-conductance responses were recorded while participants made their choices between decks. Skin-conductance responses provide an index of phasic bodily arousal. A larger anticipatory skin-conductance response occurred during choices from the high-demand than the low-demand deck, and this anticipatory response was distinct from the physiological response during actual task performance (see figure 4.3).

It has been proposed that anticipatory physiological arousal is important for facilitating the avoidance of negative outcomes. According to the *somatic marker hypothesis* (Bechara, Tranel, Damasio, and Damasio 1996), bodily arousal supplies or enhances an internal signal that an upcoming action should be reconsidered. This proposal has been advanced in the context of an experimental task in which participants chose between decks of cards carrying monetary outcomes. Some decks were safer, providing a reliable stream of small payoffs, while others were dangerous, providing sizable gains that were wiped out by occasional large losses. Participants normally developed a skin-conductance response before choices from risky decks, and gradually learned to avoid making these disadvantageous choices. By contrast, neuropsychological patients who lacked anticipatory skin-conductance responses failed to avoid the dangerous decks, even though they could express knowledge that the decks produced bad outcomes (Bechara, Damasio, Tranel, and Damasio 1997).

Interestingly, the ACC is part of the circuit for generating both avoidance-related and demand-related physiological responses. Naccache et al. (2005) have described a patient with a large left medial frontal lesion encompassing the ACC. This patient lacked anticipatory skin-conductance responses during the Bechara gambling task. Like previously reported patients, she could explicitly describe which decks produced bad outcomes but failed to avoid selecting them. In addition, this patient completely lacked normal skin-conductance responses to cognitively demanding tasks such as incongruent Stroop trials. This deficit appeared despite normal behavioral performance costs on such trials, and despite normal skin-conductance responsiveness to overtly emotional stimuli.

Neuroimaging studies strengthen the link between ACC and demand-related bodily arousal. Critchley, Tang, Glaser, Butterworth, and Dolan (2005) identified a dorsal ACC area that responded both to performance errors and to the resulting arousal, as well as a more ventral ACC area that was associated with arousal irrespective of errors. It has been proposed that this latter area, the forward part of the ACC, is selectively involved in affective processing (Bush, Luu, and Posner 2000). The possibility of distinct affective and cognitive ACC components has stimulated proposals that the region as a whole provides an *interface* between cognitive performance and motivational, physiological, or interoceptive processes (Critchley et al. 2005; Paus 2001).

It appears, therefore, that the ACC's demand-detection function is closely associated with physiological responses to demand (such as those observed by Botvinick and Rosen 2008). It further appears that physiological arousal may directly contribute to avoidance behavior. This raises the possibility that the ACC is involved in guiding *choices* that proactively minimize cognitive demand (such as the effort-averse choices reported by Kool, McGuire, Rosen, and Botvinick).

In fact, a largely separate body of data implicates the ACC in value-based behavioral choices more generally. Animal work has suggested that medial frontal cortex is involved in estimating what rewards will follow from a prospective action or set of actions (see Rushworth, Walton, Kennerley, and Bannerman 2004 for a review). Under one account, the rat ACC is critical for reaching a decision that a future reward is valuable enough to merit immediate physical effort (Walton, Kennerley, Bannerman, Phillips, and Rushworth 2006). Medial frontal cortex is activated by a variety of generically negative events; among these are subjective pain (Rainville, Duncan, Price, Carrier, and Bushnell 1997), the sight of aversively conditioned stimuli (Büchel, Morris, Dolan, and Friston 1998), and monetary losses (Gehring and Willoughby 2002). This suggests that the ACC could be computationally well-positioned to promote value-guided actions, especially the behavioral avoidance of negative outcomes. In direct support of this possibility, one study found that rats acquired a tendency to avoid locations in which direct ACC stimulation was applied (Johansen and Fields 2004).

The colocalization of aversion learning to the same brain structure as response conflict detection suggests an intriguing possibility: The detection of unmet cognitive demand, like pain, might drive long-term avoidance. As Botvinick (2007) has recently discussed, such an account holds potential to unify two existing concepts of ACC function, conflict monitoring (Botvinick et al. 2001) and outcome integration (Rushworth et al. 2004). It suggests a more elaborate way in which the ACC might computationally contribute to performance optimization. Beyond mediating the *reactive* application of cognitive control discussed in the first part of this chapter, the ACC might additionally promote a more *proactive* form of conflict minimization, causing the organism to avoid situations where response conflict is expected. Just as pain detection can produce a behavioral bias against dangerous or anxiogenic situations, conflict detection would generate a bias against effortful and inefficient tasks and strategies. This proposal assigns the ACC an active role encoding the aversiveness of mental effort.

This proposal suggests two further hypotheses in need of confirmation. One is that anticipatory physiological responses to cognitive demand are indeed mediated by ACC activity. The other is that the magnitude of ACC activation relates directly to the strength of a person's behavioral aversion toward a given demanding situation. These possibilities await empirical testing. Future research will also need to delineate more clearly the circumstances in which the ACC does and does not show anticipatory activity. Extant findings suggest it can anticipate pain (Büchel et al. 1998), errors (Brown and Braver 2005, 2007), and simple task onset (Murtha, Chertkow, Beauregard, Dixon, and Evans 1996), but findings of anticipatory activity are not unanimous (Nieuwenhuis, Schweizer, Mars, Botvinick, and Hajcak 2007).

Summary

To recap, evidence suggests that the human brain contains a system for detecting ongoing levels of unmet cognitive demand and that the ACC is a key anatomical component of this system. We propose that the impact of this detection mechanism is twofold. First, demand detection facilitates reactive adjustments. People apply cognitive control in order to preserve performance when demand rises. There is evidence that such adjustments are mediated by interactions between the ACC and dorsolateral prefrontal cortex. Second, the detection mechanism registers the negative valence of situations in which unmet demand occurs. It provides a basis for long-term knowledge, causing people to avoid returning to inefficient situations if all else is equal. In line with this second role, the ACC may be able to anticipate levels of demand and may factor demand-related costs into a larger cost–benefit analysis via interactions with the ventral striatum.

Pursuing High Demand

What does this account reveal about the *pursuit* of mental effort? As noted by Wong and Csikszentmihalyi (1991), there are two broad ways of explaining why a person might seek out a demanding situation. It may be that expected future rewards simply outweigh the costs of effortful performance and that approaching effort amounts to accepting a worse outcome now for a better outcome later. The alternative possibility would be that some type of reward inheres directly in the experience of exertion.

The position presented in this chapter, that demand-based decisions involve a trade-off between expected benefits and intrinsic costs, naturally accommodates the first type of explanation. Under this view, the choice to enter a mentally demanding situation would be analogous to a rat's rational decision to climb a high barrier only when the food on the other side is worth the work (as in experiments by Walton et al. 2006).

Trading effort for reward can have an interesting side effect. Effort, in some cases, seems to increase the subjective value of subsequently occurring outcomes. In a phenomenon reminiscent of *effort justification* (Aronson and Mills 1959), animals sometimes appear to place a higher value on rewards that they encounter while in a depleted state (Clement, Feltus, Kaiser, and Zentall 2000; Kacelnik and Marsh 2002; Pompilio, Kacelnik, and Behmer 2006; but see Vasconcelos, Urcuioli, and Lionello-DeNolf 2007 for a failure to replicate). If effortful exertion can put people in a state that makes subsequent outcomes seem more pleasant by comparison, then effort-associated rewards could become inflated in value and be more likely to win future cost–benefit trade-offs. However, magnification of rewards would not change the fact that, under this category of explanation, effort carries negative value in need of some counterbalancing incentive.

A related possibility is that the sensation of effort itself, in some contexts, develops a conditioned association with positive reinforcers. A relevant idea has arisen in connection with the personality characteristic of *need for cognition* (NFC; Cacioppo and Petty 1982). NFC includes a tendency to engage spontaneously in mental work, such as imposing structure on incoming information. Having observed a positive correlation between NFC and intelligence, Cacioppo and Petty (1982) speculated that intelligent individuals might more frequently experience rewarding outcomes produced by their own mental work and might become more inclined toward spontaneous mental exertion for that reason. Conditioned associations between reward and sensations of effort also form the basis for a theory of *learned industriousness* (Eisenberger 1992). Again, however, such theories suggest that high-demand situations will be pursued when other factors counterbalance their intrinsic aversiveness. Rewards can attach to mental effort just as they can attach to physically effortful activities such as weightlifting. This perspective is entirely consistent with a cost–benefit framework for demand-based decision making.

Demand, Subjective Effort, and Performance

What relationship might exist between the literature we have discussed and the idea of effortless attention, the topic of this volume? Wong and Csikszentmihalyi (1991, 568) describe effortless attention as "a state in which people's skills are in accord with the challenge presented by the activity." Although the conflict-monitoring hypothesis was not formulated to address this particular situation, it does expressly account for cases in which both task demand and cognitive control are high, and therefore *unmet* demand, indexed by cognitive conflict, is low. Researchers interested in effortless attention might find the mechanics of such situations to be relevant.

Conflict monitoring explicitly dissociates the proximate implementation of task control from the demand-detection mechanisms that lead control to be triggered. The two mechanisms are segregated both computationally and neuroanatomically. In the original formulation of the hypothesis (Botvinick et al. 2001), the ACC was assigned the function of monitoring conflict and triggering the direct regulation of control by other brain regions, such as areas of dorsolateral prefrontal cortex. Task control can be triggered by other means as well. For example, MacDonald, Cohen, Stenger, and Carter (2000) found that a signal of high upcoming demand elicited activity in the dorsolateral region but not in the ACC. This was interpreted to reflect the preparatory upregulation of control, absent any occurrence of conflict. Relatedly, Botvinick et al. (1999) identified a region of the cingulate that showed greater activity to incongruent than congruent trials, and still greater activity to incongruent trials if congruent trials preceded them. That is, activity in this region was highest when high demand was encountered at a low level of preparedness.

Such findings support the idea that the ACC response conflict signal encodes *unmet* demand for cognitive control (Botvinick et al. 2001). If a conflict-inducing event is well anticipated (due either to an informative cue or other recent demanding events), unmet demand will be low because an adequate level of control already exists. We have proposed in this chapter (see also Botvinick 2007) that the ACC response to unmet demand participates in encoding the costliness of mental effort. Under this framework, therefore, a demanding but well-anticipated situation can entail strong control in the absence of effort-related aversion.

A converging observation comes from the neuropsychological patient described by Naccache et al. (2005). As discussed earlier, this patient lacked physiological responses relating to cognitive demand and also failed to avoid disadvantageous decisions during a gambling task. Naccache and colleagues further noted that their patient's subjective experience differed starkly from the experience of control subjects, in that she denied experiencing any subjective sense of difficulty attached to demanding tasks. The patient could readily identify that incongruent Stroop trials took longer to respond to, but, unlike control subjects, consistently declined to describe such trials as feeling uniquely difficult. This report links the ACC-mediated demand monitoring mechanism, together with the associated physiological reactivity, to the subjective sensation of effortful exertion.

In conclusion, activity in the ACC and nearby medial frontal cortex marks situations in which the engagement of cognitive control is not equal to task-imposed demand. Two potentially adaptive responses to such situations are to increase efforts in the near term and to learn to avoid such situations in the long term. We have proposed that the ACC participates in each of these responses. The conflict-monitoring hypothesis establishes a role for the ACC in continuously monitoring unmet demand and triggering reactive adjustments (Botvinick et al. 2001). We further propose that the costliness of effort, which facilitates proactive demand avoidance, arises from the same ACC-mediated signal of unmet demand. This account explains how, if demand is high but is met by an adequate level of control, intensive performance could occur without involving ACC-based conflict detection and its associated motivational costs.

Note

1. Even a viewpoint that calls the value of focused, effortful deliberation into question (Dijksterhuis and Nordgren 2006) still acknowledges that complex decisions benefit from the thorough and systematic gathering of relevant information.

References

Aronson, E., and J. Mills. 1959. The effect of severity of initiation on liking for a group. *J. Abnorm. Soc. Psychol.* 59:177–181.

Bechara, A., H. Damasio, D. Tranel, and A. R. Damasio. 1997. Deciding advantageously before knowing the advantageous strategy. *Science* 275:1293–1295.

Bechara, A., D. Tranel, H. Damasio, and A. Damasio. 1996. Failure to respond autonomically to anticipated future outcomes following damage to prefrontal cortex. *Cereb. Cortex* 6:215–225.

Berns, G. S., S. M. McClure, G. Pagnoni, and P. R. Montague. 2001. Predictability modulates human brain response to reward. *J. Neurosci.* 21:2793–2798.

Bogacz, R. 2007. Optimal decision-making theories: Linking neurobiology with behaviour. *Trends Cogn. Sci.* 11:118–125.

Botvinick, M. M. 2007. Conflict monitoring and decision making: Reconciling two perspectives on anterior cingulate function. *Cogn. Affect. Behav. Neurosci.* 7:356–366.

Botvinick, M. M., T. S. Braver, D. M. Barch, C. S. Carter, and J. D. Cohen. 2001. Conflict monitoring and cognitive control. *Psychol. Rev.* 108:624–652.

Botvinick, M. M., J. D. Cohen, and C. S. Carter. 2004. Conflict monitoring and anterior cingulate cortex: An update. *Trends Cogn. Sci.* 8:539–546.

Botvinick, M. M., S. Huffstetler, and J. T. McGuire. 2009. Effort discounting in human nucleus accumbens. *Cognitive, Affective & Behavioral Neuroscience* 9:16–27.

Botvinick, M. M., L. E. Nystrom, K. Fissell, C. S. Carter, and J. D. Cohen. 1999. Conflict monitoring versus selection-for-action in anterior cingulate cortex. *Nature* 402:179–181.

Botvinick, M. M., and Z. B. Rosen. 2008. Anticipation of cognitive demand during decision-making. *Psych. Res.*

Brown, J. W., and T. S. Braver. 2005. Learned predictions of error likelihood in the anterior cingulate cortex. *Science* 307:1118–1121.

Brown, J. W., and T. S. Braver. 2007. Risk prediction and aversion by anterior cingulate cortex. *Cogn. Affect. Behav. Neurosci.* 7:266–277.

Büchel, C., J. Morris, R. J. Dolan, and K. J. Friston. 1998. Brain systems mediating aversive conditioning: An event-related fMRI study. *Neuron* 20:947–957.

Bush, G., P. Luu, and M. Posner. 2000. Cognitive and emotional influences in anterior cingulate cortex. *Trends Cogn. Sci.* 4:215–222.

Cacioppo, J. T., and R. E. Petty. 1982. The need for cognition. *J. Pers. Soc. Psychol.* 42:116–131.

Camerer, C., and R. Hogarth. 1999. The effects of financial incentives in experiments: A review and capital–labor–production framework. *J. Risk Uncertain.* 19:7–42.

Clement, T. S., J. R. Feltus, D. H. Kaiser, and T. R. Zentall. 2000. "Work ethic" in pigeons: Reward value is directly related to the effort or time required to obtain the reward. *Psychon. Bull. Rev.* 7:100–106.

Cohen, J. D., K. Dunbar, and J. L. McClelland. 1990. On the control of automatic processes: A parallel distributed processing account of the Stroop effect. *Psychol. Rev.* 97:332–361.

Contrada, R. J., R. A. Wright, and D. C. Glass. 1984. Task difficulty, type A behavior pattern, and cardiovascular response. *Psychophysiology* 21:638–646.

Critchley, H. D., J. Tang, D. Glaser, B. Butterworth, and R. Dolan. 2005. Anterior cingulate activity during error and autonomic response. *Neuroimage* 27:885–895.

Dijksterhuis, A., and L. F. Nordgren. 2006. A theory of unconscious thought. *Perspect. Psychol. Sci.* 1:95–109.

Eisenberger, R. 1992. Learned industriousness. *Psychol. Rev.* 99:248–267.

Freitas, A. L., M. Bahar, S. Yang, and R. Banai. 2007. Contextual adjustments in cognitive control across tasks. *Psychol. Sci.* 18:1040–1043.

Gehring, W. J., and A. R. Willoughby. 2002. The medial frontal cortex and the rapid processing of monetary gains and losses. *Science* 295:2279–2282.

Gratton, G., M. G. H. Coles, and E. Donchin. 1992. Optimizing the use of information: Strategic control of activation of responses. *J. Exp. Psychol. Gen.* 121:480–506.

Heyman, J., and D. Ariely. 2004. Effort for payment: A tale of two markets. *Psychol. Sci.* 15:787–793.

Hull, C. L. 1943. *Principles of behavior.* New York: Appleton-Century-Crofts.

Johansen, J. P., and H. L. Fields. 2004. Glutamatergic activation of anterior cingulate cortex produces an aversive teaching signal. *Nat. Neurosci.* 7:398–403.

Kacelnik, A., and B. Marsh. 2002. Cost can increase preference in starlings. *Anim. Behav.* 63:245–250.

Kahneman, D. 1973. *Attention and effort.* Englewood Cliffs, NJ: Prentice-Hall.

Kane, M. J., and R. W. Engle. 2003. Working-memory capacity and the control of attention: The contributions of goal neglect, response competition, and task set to Stroop interference. *J. Exp. Psychol. Gen.* 132:47–70.

Kerns, J. G. 2006. Anterior cingulate and prefrontal cortex activity in an fMRI study of trial-to-trial adjustments on the Simon task. *Neuroimage* 33:399–405.

Kerns, J. G., J. D. Cohen, A. W. MacDonald, III, R. Y. Cho, V. A. Stenger, and C. S. Carter. 2004. Anterior cingulate conflict monitoring and adjustments in control. *Science* 303:1023–1026.

Kool, W., J. T. McGuire, Z. Rosen, and M. M. Botvinick. 2009. *Action selection based on anticipated cognitive demand: A test of "the law of least mental effort."* Under review.

Lowe, D. G., and J. O. Mitterer. 1982. Selective and divided attention in a Stroop task. *Can. J. Psychol.* 36:684–700.

MacDonald, A. W., III, J. D. Cohen, V. A. Stenger, and C. S. Carter. 2000. Dissociating the role of the dorsolateral prefrontal and anterior cingulate cortex in cognitive control. *Science* 288:1835–1838.

MacLeod, C. M., E. B. Hunt, and N. N. Mathews. 1978. Individual differences in the verification of sentence–picture relationships. *J. Verbal Learn. Verbal Behav.* 17:493–507.

MacLeod, C. M., and P. A. MacDonald. 2000. Interdimensional interference in the Stroop effect: Uncovering the cognitive and neural anatomy of attention. *Trends Cogn. Sci.* 4:383–391.

Mayr, U., E. Awh, and P. Laurey. 2003. Conflict adaptation effects in the absence of executive control. *Nat. Neurosci.* 6:450–452.

McClure, S. M., D. I. Laibson, G. Loewenstein, and J. D. Cohen. 2004. Separate neural systems value immediate and delayed monetary rewards. *Science* 306:503–507.

Mulert, C., E. Menzinger, G. Leicht, O. Pogarell, and U. Hegerl. 2005. Evidence for a close relationship between conscious effort and anterior cingulate cortex activity. *Int. J. Psychophysiol.* 56:65–80.

Murtha, S., H. Chertkow, M. Beauregard, R. Dixon, and A. Evans. 1996. Anticipation causes increased blood flow to the anterior cingulate cortex. *Hum. Brain Mapp.* 4:103–112.

Naccache, L., S. Dehaene, L. Cohen, M. O. Habert, E. Guichart-Gomez, D. Galanaud, et al. 2005. Effortless control: Executive attention and conscious feeling of mental effort are dissociable. *Neuropsychologia* 43:1318–1328.

Nieuwenhuis, S., T. S. Schweizer, R. B. Mars, M. M. Botvinick, and G. Hajcak. 2007. Error-likelihood prediction in the medial frontal cortex: A critical evaluation. *Cereb. Cortex* 17:1570–1581.

Pardo, J. V., P. J. Pardo, K. W. Janer, and M. E. Raichle. 1990. The anterior cingulate cortex mediates processing selection in the Stroop attentional conflict paradigm. *Proc. Natl. Acad. Sci. USA* 87:256–259.

Paus, T. 2001. Primate anterior cingulate cortex: Where motor control, drive and cognition interface. *Nat. Rev. Neurosci.* 2:417–424.

Pompilio, L., A. Kacelnik, and S. Behmer. 2006. State-dependent learned valuation drives choice in an invertebrate. *Science* 311:1613–1615.

Rabbitt, P. M. 1966. Errors and error correction in choice-response tasks. *J. Exp. Psychol.* 71:264–272.

Rainville, P., G. H. Duncan, D. D. Price, B. Carrier, and M. C. Bushnell. 1997. Pain affect encoded in human anterior cingulate but not somatosensory cortex. *Science* 277:968.

Rogers, R. D., and S. Monsell. 1995. Costs of a predictable switch between simple cognitive tasks. *J. Exp. Psychol. Gen.* 124:207–231.

Rushworth, M. F. S., M. E. Walton, S. W. Kennerley, and D. M. Bannerman. 2004. Action sets and decisions in the medial frontal cortex. *Trends Cogn. Sci.* 8:410–417.

Sarter, M., W. J. Gehring, and R. Kozak. 2006. More attention must be paid: The neurobiology of attentional effort. *Brain Res. Brain Res. Rev.* 51:145–160.

Vasconcelos, M., P. J. Urcuioli, and K. M. Lionello-DeNolf. 2007. Failure to replicate the "work ethic" effect in pigeons. *J. Exp. Anal. Behav.* 87:383–399.

Walton, M. E., S. W. Kennerley, D. M. Bannerman, P. E. M. Phillips, and M. F. S. Rushworth. 2006. Weighing up the benefits of work: Behavioral and neural analyses of effort-related decision making. *Neural Netw.* 19:1302–1314.

Wilcox, N. T. 1993. Lottery choice: Incentives, complexity and decision time. *Econ. J.* 103:1397–1417.

Winkielman, P., and J. T. Cacioppo. 2001. Mind at ease puts a smile on the face: Psychophysiological evidence that processing facilitation elicits positive affect. *J. Pers. Soc. Psychol.* 81:989–1000.

Wong, M. M., and M. Csikszentmihalyi. 1991. Motivation and academic achievement: The effects of personality traits and the duality of experience. *J. Pers.* 59:539–574.

Wright, R. A., and S. Gregorich. 1989. Difficulty and instrumentality of imminent behavior as determinants of cardiovascular response and self-reported energy. *Psychophysiology* 26:586–592.

Wright, R. A., R. E. Martin, and J. L. Bland. 2003. Energy resource depletion, task difficulty, and cardiovascular response to a mental arithmetic challenge. *Psychophysiology* 40:98–105.

5 Grounding Attention in Action Control: The Intentional Control of Selection

Bernhard Hommel

My first poster presentation at a scientific meeting was no success. I offered a new theoretical framework on stimulus and response representation (the later theory of event coding; Hommel, Müsseler, Aschersleben, and Prinz 2001a) together with supportive data and hoped to attract the interest of all the big shots working on stimulus–response compatibility. But no one came. One year later I presented a much less inspired study but made one crucial move: I put the A-word in the title, with the effect that my poster was one of the most crowded, and long after the session was over I was still heavily engaged in discussions. This is just one of many examples demonstrating that cognitive scientists love attention as a topic. In contrast to sensory and motor processes, say, which rather smell like hardware and mechanics, the concept of attention seems to directly connect to what makes us human, as it somehow expresses our individual needs and wishes, preferences, and interests. The drawback of this attractiveness is that the concept is more often than not used as a wastebasket, a container that serves as a pseudo-explanation for the phenomena we still fail to understand—so that "attention" is explained by the workings of an "attentional system."

One of the more successful strategies to tackle this problem is to focus on the function of attentional processes, that is, to ask what attention does rather than what it is. Indeed, the modern cognitive sciences have benefited greatly from this strategy, even though over the years we have seen rather dramatic changes in the way the functions of attention have been characterized. In the following, I will briefly discuss some of the more influential perspectives, which all have their benefits and their drawbacks. This discussion (for broader treatments, see Allport 1993; Neumann 1987; and Schneider 1995) will reveal that early approaches emphasized attentional function subserving higher order cognition and consciousness, whereas more recent approaches increasingly appreciate the importance of attentional processes for action (selection for action). In this chapter, I would like to push this trend one step further by arguing that attention not only subserves action-control processes but may actually have emerged to solve action-control problems in a cognitive system that relies on distributed representations and multiple, loosely connected processing streams.

The Functions of Attention

Most of the grand, influential attentional theories have considered attention as a mechanism that administers and organizes scarcity. In the 19th century authors were mainly impressed by the limits of consciousness, which was assumed to be restricted to the representation of only one thought or event at a time (e.g., James 1890). Given the emphasis on introspective methods, this limitation was rarely systematically investigated but rather taken for granted, and attention was thought to make the best of it. The main idea was that if consciousness can only contain one event, then attention better ensures that this event is of optimal use, which can be guaranteed by directing attention to relevant events (the endogenous aspect of attention) and having attention attracted by interesting events (the exogenous aspect of attention).

Even though modern cognitive approaches more or less did away with introspective methods, the assumed function of attention did not change much. In view of the increasing importance and availability of computers, researchers like Broadbent (1958) replaced consciousness with working memory as the central processing unit, which, however, was considered to be equally limited in processing capacity. Accordingly, attentional mechanisms were thought of as filters that discriminate between relevant and irrelevant information and effectively gate out the latter in order to prevent working memory from being overloaded. Again, the filters were thought to be endogenously controlled in principle, but this control could be overruled by overlearned or highly important stimuli. Emphasis on the coordinative and administrative aspects of attention was replaced by capacity theories (e.g., Kahneman 1973), which considered the flexible use of attentional resource policies and selection strategies in multiple task performance and everyday life. However, the main function of attention was again to prevent a central processing unit from being overloaded by gating out irrelevant information.

Recent attentional theories are more broadly informed by neuroscientific knowledge about the structure and processing characteristics of the primate brain and thus are necessarily more complex. Some theories are particularly interested in the spatial limitations of attention or, more precisely, in the apparent limitation of the brain to integrate information from only one point in space at one time (e.g., Treisman 1988; Wolfe 1994). Other approaches are less pessimistic with regard to strict spatial limitations, but they do assume that attended locations are processed at a higher spatial resolution (e.g., Bundesen, Habekost, and Kyllingsbaek 2005). Even though such theories are much more elaborated than their predecessors, they still share the basic logic that limited capacity must be administered and that attention has the job of doing that.

All of the approaches that I have discussed so far not only share the limited-capacity notion but also consider consciousness, or some philosophically less laden equivalent (like working memory or the central processor), as the system that suffers from these limitations and has thus to be saved from overload. A few approaches have questioned this latter implication, however. Authors like Allport (1987) and Neumann (1987) have considered that it may not, or not so much, be conscious representation that constitutes the functionally important bottleneck but rather our action potentialities. As an example, visual attention may selectively focus on one of many apples on an apple tree not because one's conscious awareness would otherwise be overloaded but, rather, because one can actively pick only one apple at a time anyway. On the one hand, these approaches differ from the main tradition by considering action as more important than consciousness, culminating in the claim that selection is for action. On the other hand, however, the limited-capacity notion is not given up, as it is still scarcity (of action possibilities) that represents the main problem and attention that solves it.

In this chapter, I want to challenge not only the assumption that attention functions to prevent consciousness from overload (an aim that I share with selection-for-action approaches) but also that the management of scarcity has anything to do with the original biological function of attention. In particular, I will argue that attention is a direct derivative of mechanisms subserving the control of basic motor actions. I'm aware that this is an extreme statement that is likely to require modification in the light of new findings, but at the same time I believe that it can be inspiring and helpful by generating new insights and research questions. To motivate my suggestion, I will first set the theoretical stage by discussing the implications of the primate brain's preference to represent stimulus events and action plans in a distributed, feature-based fashion and to process information concurrently along multiple pathways. Then, I will discuss a number of empirical findings that support the general idea that action planning and action control can affect perception and attention, and I will develop a preliminary theoretical framework that grounds attention in action control.

Distributed Representations and Common Coding

Artificial intelligence, philosophical approaches, and many psychological models assume that the basic units of human cognition can be considered as symbols, so that cognitive processes can be reconstructed as symbol manipulation. Increasing evidence and deeper insights into the structure of the primate cortex suggest a different picture, however. Visual objects, for instance, are known to be coded in terms of their features, which are concurrently analyzed on various feature maps specialized in the processing of orientation, shape, color, motion, and more (DeYoe and Van Essen 1988). Even at higher representational levels, objects do not seem to be represented by single units but rather by composites of codes representing the parts and elements of objects (Tanaka 2003). This does not rule out the possibility that symbolic representations exist in addition to that, but it does point to the fact that the human brain has a strong tendency to represent perceptual events in a distributed, feature-based fashion. This tendency is not restricted to perceptual coding. Separate neural networks code, among other things, the direction of an arm movement (Georgopoulos 1990), its force (Kalaska and Hyde 1985), and distance (Riehle and Requin 1989), suggesting that action plans are composites of codes of separately specified action features.

The distributed, feature-based representation of perceptual events and action plans is also reflected in numerous behavioral observations. For instance, searching for a single visual feature (a particular shape, say) in perceptually crowded scenes or arrays is much easier than searching for a feature conjunction (a particular shape in a particular color; Treisman and Gelade 1980), and if people are to report feature conjunctions under attentionally demanding conditions, they tend to fabricate illusionary conjunctions (Treisman and Schmidt 1982). With regard to action planning, different parameters of manual movements can be precued separately and through different stimuli, with the eventual reaction time decreasing as a function of the number of precues (e.g., Rosenbaum 1980; Lépine, Glencross, and Requin 1989). Even interactions between stimuli and actions provide evidence for feature-based representations: For instance, stimulus events prime responses, and action plans affect perceptual processes, if and to the degree that stimuli and responses share features, such as location (Hommel et al. 2001a; Kornblum, Hasbroucq, and Osman 1990).

Especially these latter observations—that stimulus representations and response representations can interact, and that these interactions depend on feature overlap—have important implications with regard to the question of how stimuli and responses are cognitively represented and how these representations are related. According to Hommel et al. (2001a), both perceived events (i.e., stimuli) and to-be-produced events (i.e., action plans) are represented by cognitive codes of their distal features and, thus, in a common format. These codes are composites of sensorimotor units, which relate perceived action effects to the motoric means employed to produce them (Elsner and Hommel 2001). According to this logic, seeing a red pen on one's desk, say, is the result of having directed one's eyes, and perhaps even one's head and body, toward the location of the pen, so that the visual information the pen provides is the action effect of these motor movements and will thus be integrated with them. Perceiving and acting is thus the same process, consisting of moving one's body in order to generate particular perceptions. If so, there is no qualitative difference between the representation of a stimulus event (which includes the action that has given rise to it) and the representation of an action plan (which includes the perceptual event the action aims at—the action goal, that is).

If perceptual events and action plans are represented in a common format, and if this format refers to bundles or bindings of perceptual features and motor parameters (Hommel 2004), one would expect that control processes operating on these cognitive representations have characteristics that reflect this distributed, feature-based format. Indeed, there is increasing evidence that input and output control (i.e., attentional and intentional selection) operates on feature dimensions. For instance, when people search complex visual scenes for visually deviant targets (i.e., stimuli that pop out because of their unique color, shape, etc.), their performance will be better if they can anticipate the feature dimension on which an upcoming target will deviate (e.g., Müller, Heller, and Ziegler 1995). This suggests that people can strategically increase the weights or "gain" of a particular feature dimension in order to facilitate the coding of features falling on it (Found and Müller 1996). The same conclusion is suggested by observations from studies on task switching. In such studies, subjects often carry out responses to stimuli that are defined by one of multiple feature dimensions, such as to the color versus the meaning of colored color words (Allport, Styles, and Hsieh 1994) or to the horizontal versus vertical location of stimuli (e.g., Meiran 1996). Performance is much better if the task-relevant feature dimension is repeated than if it is alternated, suggesting that switching between different task sets takes time and effort. Importantly for our purposes, implementing a new task set is assumed to include directing attention to the target-defining stimulus dimension (Logan and Gordon 2001) and the response-defining action dimension (Meiran 2000). That is, executive control operates on feature dimensions, presumably by altering the weights that determine the degree to which features coded on these dimensions are considered by, or affect, cognitive processes.

Multiple Processing Pathways

There is increasing evidence that the human brain not only codes perceived and produced events in a distributed fashion but also concurrently processes different aspects of events along different neural pathways. One of the best known distinctions between parallel processing codes is that between the dorsal and the ventral pathway (Ungerleider and Mishkin 1982). Early approaches have characterized these two pathways in terms of "where" versus "what" processing. Whereas the dorsal pathway was considered to process spatial attributes of perceived events, the ventral pathway was thought to process identity-related attributes, such as shape and color. Later approaches, Milner and Goodale (1995) in particular, have suggested an alternative interpretation in terms of action-related (or pragmatic) processing versus perception-related processing. That is, the dorsal pathway was considered to directly feed into action control, without being accessible for conscious perception, whereas the ventral pathway was thought to mainly subserve conscious and unconscious perceptual processes. In view of increasing evidence that is not quite consistent with this particular subdivision, recent reformulations have suggested an interpretation in terms of online control of action—attributed to the dorsal pathway—versus action planning—

a presumably ventral activity (Glover 2004; Hommel, Müsseler, Aschersleben, and Prinz 2001b).

Interestingly, these neuroscientifically motivated considerations fit well with theoretical developments in the domain of action planning and control. Modern cognitive approaches were driven by the insight that human action is commonly goal driven and must, thus, be controlled by some kind of internal representation (Lashley 1951). Authors like Keele (1968) have pushed this possibility to an extreme and assumed that all muscle parameters and commands of a movement are stored and used to construct motor programs that prestructure all aspects of a movement in advance. Others, however, have pointed out that this possibility would put too high a demand on storage and render action planning very inflexible, as each slight change of a movement would require a separate program (Schmidt 1975). Theoretically more reasonable are hybrid approaches that assume that only some structural or invariant features of an action are stored and used for later programming, whereas more variable features are specified by online information (e.g., Schmidt 1975). Consistent with this consideration, studies have shown that transferring from one task to another is easier if the two tasks share invariant features, whereas changes in variant features do not affect performance much (see Heuer 1991).

Behavioral and neuroscientific approaches thus converge on the idea that action control is comprised of two processes: *action planning*, which consists of specifying the basic structure of an action, including its most relevant, invariant features, and which can be performed online as well as offline (i.e., some time before the action is executed), and online *action adjustment*, which consists of fine-tuning the action by specifying the remaining features and open parameters. A particularly elegant illustration of the interplay between action planning and action adjustment is provided by studies using the so-called double-step paradigm. For instance, in a study by Prablanc and Pélisson (1990), subjects were asked to move their right index finger from a home position to a light spot, and the spatial and temporal parameters of the movement were measured. In some trials, the target spot was moved a little further away from the subject while he or she was already moving. Importantly, the target was moved during an eye movement, so that subjects were unable to see the change. The most relevant outcome was that, first, the finger correctly reached the target even in change trials and that, second, this was achieved without any measurable hesitation of the moving hand. In a manner of speaking, the hand was smarter, better informed, and more adaptive than the mind. Thus, even though we can assume that goal-directed reaching movements are prepared and programmed in advance, a slight change in the location of the target does not require time-consuming modifications of the program or complete reprogramming. This means that the original program did not include specific information about the target location but left the specification of the details to online routines that adjusted the action on the fly.

Distributing the labor over different processing channels has obvious advantages: Storage and preplanning are minimized, and yet the resulting action is as precise as necessary. However, just as distributed representations create binding problems (Treisman 1996), distributed processing creates coordination problems. In one way or another, action-planning processes need to inform action-adjustment processes about which parameters to fill or specify and how to do so. For instance, Milner and Goodale (1995) claim that their dorsal action pathway does not have any memory capacity and does not interact with, nor is it informed by, ventrally mediated, conscious or unconscious decision making. This would imply that the channel that is dedicated to action control has no way to plan any action, has no way to retrieve or access any action plan, and cannot have any idea about currently relevant action goals. It is difficult to see how such a channel can do the job it is supposed to do: to select relevant sensory features and feed them into the action programs. Obviously, coherent, goal-directed action requires some kind of coordination between planning and adjustment processes, so that the latter can provide what the former leave open.

This chapter is devoted to this kind of coordination problem, and I will present a principled approach to how it might be solved. An important insight pointing to a possible solution is that concurrent processing streams need to be conditionalized by the current action goal. Action goals, so I will assume, govern the selection and planning of appropriate actions, and this planning process biases concurrent processing streams, such as the one in charge of action adjustments, toward information that is suitable to specify the action parameters that planning processes left open. A particularly interesting implication of this line of thought is that it requires action-related processes to affect perception and attention to perceptual input. Indeed, as the next section shows, there are numerous findings suggesting that action planning does affect perception and attention.

Action Control and Attention

An early suggestion that visual attention may be affected by action planning emerged from studies on the so-called meridian effect (Rizzolatti, Riggio, Dascola, and Umiltà 1987). This effect can be observed in studies that use attentional cues. Consider, for instance, a subject focusing on a central spot in a visual display, which further consists of four possible target locations marked by small frames, two at the left and two at the right of fixation. Now assume that, in each trial, one of the four locations is precued with high validity—that is, the subject knows in which of the four frames the target is likely to appear. If the target then actually appears in the precued frame, reaction times can be expected to be fast, suggesting that subjects "moved their attention" to the frame (Posner 1980). However, what if the target appears in an uncued frame? As Rizzolatti et al. (1987) observed, reaction times are not only slower in this case but depend on the spatial relation between the cued frame and the eventual target location. If, for instance, one of the two inner frames was cued, performance was better if the target frame was located on the same side of the cue rather than on the opposite side. In other words, moving attention further into the same direction was less costly than changing the direction. According to the authors, this may suggest that attention is moved by programming (but not necessarily executing) an eye movement, which may require the sequential specification of a direction parameter and a distance parameter—in this order. If the direction stays the same (as when, say, the inner left frame is cued but the target appears in the outer left frame), only the distance parameter needs to be modified, which can be done faster than modifying the direction parameter or both parameters.

Further evidence for the general idea that the programming of eye movements is involved in directing visual attention to locations in space (see also Klein 1980) stems from Deubel and Schneider (1996; Schneider and Deubel 2002). Their subjects were to carry out saccades to visual targets on the left or right of a fixation point. Before moving their eyes, they were briefly flashed with a visual string of stimuli containing a to-be-discriminated target symbol. As it turned out, performance was good only if the location of the visual target coincided with the goal of the saccade, suggesting that programming the saccade involves moving attention to the goal location in advance of the saccade—which then facilitates the processing of stimuli appearing there. These observations are consistent with the premotor theory of attention but go beyond previous findings in directly demonstrating that saccade programming actually matters for spatial selection.

Interactions between the programming of eye movements and attentional selection support the idea that action planning affects attentional control, but they are too restricted to provide a basis for a comprehensive action-based theory of attention. First, even though linking overt and covert visual attention (i.e., attending by moving the physical versus the "mind's" eye) has a long tradition in psychology (e.g., James 1890; Posner 1980), this may be due to the particularly strong and straightforward subcortical connections between retinal input processing and movements of the eyeballs. This raises the question of whether other than oculomotor action planning can affect attention. Second, the observed interactions between action and attention were restricted to spatial selection. Even though the spatial selection of relevant information plays an important role in perception and action, human attention subserves more functions than that—just think of object-based selection, action selection, and integration (Schneider 1995). Fortunately, however, there is increasing evidence of interactions between manual and verbal action planning and attentional functions other than spatial selection.

First evidence for the impact of manual action planning on visual processing was provided by Müsseler and colleagues. Müsseler and Hommel (1997), for instance, had participants prepare a left- or right-hand key press and carry it out whenever they felt ready. To signal their readiness, they pressed a spatially neutral readiness key before performing the prepared action. Pressing the readiness key triggered the presentation of a masked visual arrowhead that pointed to the left or right. At the end of the trial, participants reported at leisure in which direction the arrowhead pointed, which, given the masking procedure, was difficult and attention demanding. The important observation was that the accuracy of the perceptual report was dependent on the relation between the prepared response and the direction of the arrowhead. If participants prepared and carried out a left-hand response, they had substantially more difficulty detecting a left-pointing than a right-pointing arrowhead, and the opposite was true for right-hand responses. In other words, planning a spatially defined manual action "blinded" the participants to perceptual events that shared features with the action.

Even though this finding seems counterintuitive, it fits with the idea that action planning consists in the binding of distributed feature codes that specify the action's relevant characteristics (Stoet and Hommel 1999). Planning a left-hand action would thus require the binding of a <left> code with other relevant codes specifying, say, the speed, force, and extent of the key press. If we further assume that perceptual and action-related features are coded in the same format (Hommel et al. 2001a; Prinz 1990), "occupying" (Stoet and Hommel 1999) a given feature by binding it into an action plan should indeed impair the creation of another binding to represent a feature-overlapping perceptual event—such as a spatially compatible arrowhead. Other observations confirmed that this line of reasoning is not restricted to manual action plans or spatial relationships. For instance, planning a manual left or right action "blinds" participants to compatible left- or right-pointing arrowheads but not to the words "left" or "right," whereas planning a vocal action (i.e., saying aloud "left" or "right") impairs the perception of compatible words but not arrowheads (Hommel and Müsseler 2006).

Another demonstration of interactions between manual action planning and visual attention was provided by Craighero, Fadiga, Rizzolatti, and Umiltà (1999). They had participants manually grasp invisible objects that were tilted to the left or right. The type of grasp was planned ahead of time, but the execution had to await the presentation of a go signal. The orientation of this go signal did or did not match the orientation of the to-be-grasped object. It turned out that participants responded faster if the invisible target object and the go signal matched in orientation (and even if the go signal was responded to by foot), suggesting that planning a grasping action prepared the visual system for the processing of target-related features. Similarly, Bekkering and Neggers (2002) had participants detect and grasp (vs. point to) visual targets defined by a conjunction of orientation and color features. The findings revealed that fewer orientation errors were committed when participants prepared for grasping as compared to pointing, whereas color errors were rare in all conditions. The authors argue that planning a particular movement enhances the processing of features that specify the target of this movement. At first sight, these observations do not seem to fit with the inverse effect on feature overlap reported by Müsseler and Hommel (1997). However, while Müsseler and Hommel required participants to consciously perceive and report the perceptual events, participants in the Craighero et al. and Bekkering and Neggers studies were only using these events for triggering a more or less prepared response—a situation that is unlikely to require feature binding.

Let us summarize so far. The apparent distribution of labor between offline action-planning processes and online action adjustment introduces a control problem and raises the question of how action planning can make sure that adjustment processes select the appropriate sensory information and feed it into the relevant motor-control structures. We have seen a number of empirical phenomena suggesting that planning an action has a direct impact on attentional and perceptual processes, and we have also seen that this holds for oculomotor, manual, and vocal actions, and corresponding perceptual dimensions. In principle, it thus seems possible that action planning processes not only specify the task-relevant characteristics of a given action but also bias action-adjustment routines toward the relevant perceptual dimensions. And yet, there is one fly in the ointment: Whereas research on visual attention suggests that task goals lead to the priming and stronger weighting of appropriate perceptual *dimensions*, at least most of the available evidence for action-attention interactions points to stimulus-specific biases (e.g., the priming of one particular orientation in Craighero et al. 1999). The theoretical challenge thus consists in explaining why and how action planning can bias perceptual processing toward perceptual dimensions that provide information for specifying the open parameters of the action in question.

Intentional Control of Attention: A New Framework

The theoretical framework I want to propose here was motivated by an observation of Schubotz and von Cramon (2001, 2002). They had participants carry out an oddball task while lying in an fMRI scanner. Sequences of stimuli that followed a particular rule were presented (e.g., a repeated sequence of particular colors, locations, or shapes), and the participant was to report at leisure at the end of the trial whether one of the stimuli violated the rule. The important observation was that this perceptual monitoring task consistently activated the lateral premotor cortex, even in the absence of any motoric response. A meta-analysis of these and similar observations revealed systematic relationships between the task-relevant perceptual dimension and the particular area in the premotor cortex where the activation was located (Schubotz and von Cramon 2003). Three of these relations were particularly systematic: Location-relevant perceptual monitoring engaged premotor areas that are involved in the control of saccades and reaching movements, the monitoring of object-related features (such as color or shape) activated premotor areas involved in the control of grasping movements, and the monitoring of rhythmic events engaged premotor areas responsible for controlling vocal actions and manual tapping. As the authors point out, these relationships suggest that action-related brain areas are directly involved in the control of attention and, in particular, in directing attention toward action-related perceptual dimensions.

These considerations were further developed by Fagioli, Hommel, and Schubotz (2007a). Preparing for a reaching movement, these authors reasoned, should sensitize the perceptual system for features of dimensions that are relevant for specifying the open parameters of reaching movements. Most likely, this criterion is met by location information. Preparing for a grasping movement, in turn, should sensitize the system for processing information about the final phase of the grasp, such as the size of the object signaling the hand's aperture. To test these hypotheses, the authors had participants reach toward or grasp an object in front of them. Before the action was executed, however, participants were presented with a sequence of stimuli following a particular rule, as in the setup of Schubotz and von Cramon (2001), and they were to detect possible oddballs. If an oddball occurred, the prepared reaching or grasping movement was carried out. As expected, the reaction times for these movements varied with the perceptual dimension on which the oddball was defined. Whereas reaching movements were initiated faster with location oddballs than with size oddballs, the opposite applied to grasping movements. To rule out that this effect was due to the oddball-induced priming of the movement, another experiment was carried out in which the detection of the oddball was signaled by a foot response. Again, preparing for a reaching movement facilitated the detection of location oddballs, and preparing for a grasping movement facilitated the detection of size oddballs.

These observations are consistent with the idea that action control encompasses the priming of perceptual dimensions, but one may argue that this connection is less direct than suggested here. For instance, it may be that a general executive control system not only selects appropriate responses but also implements a particular attentional set. Indeed, Logan and Gordon (2001) have suggested that executive control functions both bias attention toward task-relevant perceptual dimensions and specify the necessary stimulus–response rules without directly relating these two processes to each other or even deriving the attentional bias from action-control demands. In an attempt to provide more specific evidence for action-induced attentional biases, Fagioli, Ferlazzo, and Hommel (2007b) investigated whether the biases observed by Fagioli, Hommel, and Schubotz require active action planning. If activating an action plan is sufficient to induce the stronger weighting of related perceptual dimensions, they reasoned, such weighting should also be observed if the action plan is activated involuntarily. Participants again monitored sequences of stimuli and were to press a foot pedal as soon as they detected an oddball. They did not carry out any other action;

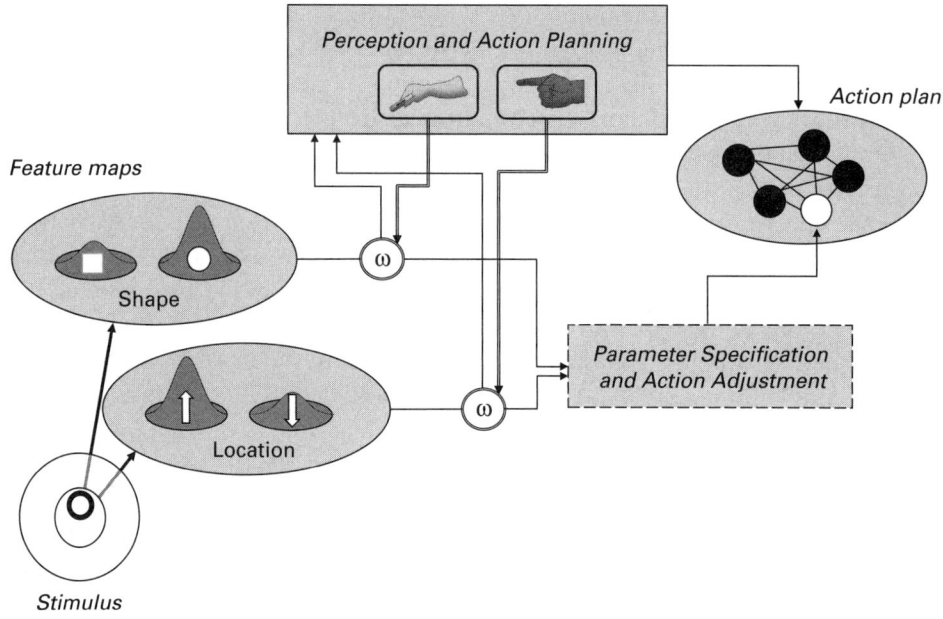

Figure 5.1
A process model of action-induced attention.

in particular, it should be noted that they made no reaching or grasping movement. However, prior to the stimulus sequences, short video clips that showed a person carrying out a reaching or grasping movement were presented. These videos were not relevant to the task and did not predict or inform about the stimulus sequences or the correct responses. Nevertheless, participants were faster at detecting location oddballs after seeing a reaching movement and size oddballs after seeing a grasping movement. Apparently, the videos activated reaching- and grasping-related action plans and this activation was sufficient to increase the weights of reaching- and grasping-related perceptual dimensions.

Taken together, these findings support the idea that the mere activation of an action plan—whether through top–down processes in the service of the current action goal or bottom–up, stimulus-induced processes—leads to an increase on the weights of those perceptual dimensions that allow for the specification of action parameters commonly left open by action planning. Figure 5.1 summarizes the theoretical implications of this consideration. As pointed out above, stimuli are assumed to be coded on feature maps, with each feature activating a code on the respective feature dimension (or multiple codes competing for coding the stimulus: Reynolds, Chelazzi, and Desimone 1999). In the example given, a circular object at some top location is coded on a shape and a location map—a drastic simplification that is not meant to deny the existence of numerous other feature maps (such as color, motion, etc.), of multiple spatial maps (coding for, e.g., allocentric, egocentric, and retinal location), and of other sensory modalities.

This information is propagated to two different processing pathways, one subserving perception and action planning (similar but not identical to the ventral pathway of Milner and Goodale 1995, and comparable to the action-planning pathway of Glover 2004) and one subserving online action adjustments (comparable to Milner and Goodale's dorsal pathway and Glover's action-control pathway). Activating an action plan, such as for grasping or reaching (symbolized by the grasping and pointing hands in the figure), increases the weight (ω) of the output of particular feature maps, which increases the impact of information coded there on further information processes (i.e., perception and action planning on the one hand and action adjustment on the other). Following the theory of event coding (Hommel et al. 2001a), perception and action planning are not further differentiated, which acknowledges that these two functions highly interact and can be considered two sides of the same coin.

Perception and action planning create action plans reflecting the current goal. Action plans consist of specified parameters (structural features of the planned action that are relevant for reaching the goal) and not-yet-specified parameters that are to be filled by online adjustment processes; in the figure, these parameters are symbolized by black and white circles, respectively. The open parameters are specified by continuously transmitting sensory information from feature maps to ongoing actions. This transmission is weighted by the output weight ω of the respective dimensions. Accordingly, given that planning a grasping action increases the weights for shape information, action-adjustment processes will mainly consider information provided by the shape map and use it to specify the remaining grasping parameters (such as hand aperture).

Note that the output weights have two functions in this model. On the one hand, they help to overcome the control problem posed by the existence of multiple concurrent processing streams by biasing online adjustment processes toward goal-relevant perceptual dimensions. On the other hand, they also bias perception and action planning toward these dimensions, a characteristic that is important in accounting for the findings of Fagioli et al. (2007a, 2007b). These findings suggest that planning an action leads to the faster conscious detection of stimuli varying on action-relevant perceptual dimensions, which implies that planning must have affected perceptual processes. Recent findings support the idea that action planning modulates conscious perception in systematic ways. Wykowska, Schubö, and Hommel (2009) presented participants with visual-search displays that contained to-be-detected pop-out targets—that is, stimuli that differed from all other stimuli of the display on one dimension. As in the studies of Fagioli and colleagues, participants prepared either a reaching or a grasping action, and the target-defining dimensions were luminance (which was considered more important for reaching than for grasping) and size (which was considered more important for grasping than for reaching). If participants knew in advance on which perceptual dimensions a target would pop out, the prepared action biased attention systematically: Preparing a reach facilitated the detection of luminance-defined targets, and preparing a grasp facilitated the detection of size-defined targets. However, this effect was not observed when participants did not know the target-defining dimension in advance. Under this kind of uncertainty, participants are known to not prepare for a particular perceptual dimension but to rely on saliency signals—that is, they respond to any departure from homogeneity in the visual field without identifying the dimension on which it occurs (Bacon and Egeth 1994). Given the absence of action-induced biases in this type of processing, it makes sense to assume that these biases target the output of feature-map coding, but not the input or processes preceding or circumventing feature coding.

Theoretical Implications

The proposed framework has a number of interesting theoretical implications that break with the main line of reasoning underlying traditional attentional research. Most importantly, it denies that attentional functions emerged to distribute sparse cognitive resources to prevent the cognitive system from being overloaded. In contrast, it proposes that attentional functions originally evolved to deal with control problems arising from distributed representation and processing and from the share of labor between offline, anticipatory action planning and online action adjustment in particular. Once these functions were available, they could also be used for other purposes—that is, the weights of perceptual dimensions could be manipulated for other reasons than action adjustment and without actually preparing overt actions. It is this generalization that makes people good performers in visual-search experiments and related tasks. However, outside of the psychological laboratory, there are not too many occasions in which selective attention is needed for other purposes than action control—we commonly do not detect feature conjunctions in complex visual environments for the sake of detecting them but do so in the service of particular action goals. Considering this, selection-for-action approaches (Allport 1987; Neumann 1987) go in the right direction in emphasizing the theoretical importance of actions. However, the available evidence allows for an even more radical interpretation, according to which attentional functions not only consider action opportunities but may be a mere by-product of action control in a distributed processing system.

Given the systematic interactions between particular types of actions and particular perceptual dimensions, it is interesting to ask where this systematicity comes from. One possibility is phylogenetic development—that is, the discovery that some perceptual dimensions are more important for some actions than others may be an evolutionary achievement that became genetically coded over time. Alternatively, the selective use of perceptual dimensions may be an ontogenetic discovery. Consider, for instance, a learning process that is sensitive to the success of actions. In the beginning, actions may be carried out on the basis of any available information, with a noisy and random weighting of information provided by the available feature maps and very mixed results. The open parameters of an action—a grasp, say—would thus be randomly filled with all sorts of feature information. However, extensive experience will reveal that using size information renders grasping actions more successful than, say, using color information, and correlation learning would be sufficient to detect the relationship between different perceived sizes of the grasped object and the hand aperture in the final phase of a grasp. In other words, exploration in infancy and early childhood may allow for the discovery of optimal relationships between the consideration of particular perceptual dimensions on the one hand and particular action categories on the other.

Let us conclude by considering the implications of this suggested theoretical framework for the topic of this book, the issue of whether and when attentional processes are effortful or effortless. According to the suggested framework, attentional operations themselves are not effortful but are more or less automatically triggered by action-control processes, which again are coordinated by the current action goal (see Fagioli et al. 2007b). Hence, the selection, representation, and maintenance of an action goal would be a necessary precondition for attentional processes to operate, and these processes are commonly considered effortful. The most common task used to investigate goal implementation requires participants to switch between different, mutually incompatible action goals (e.g., Monsell 2003). Using this task has revealed two major findings that are important for our purposes. First, performance is strongly impaired in trials that require a goal switch, which has been taken to reflect time demands associated with establishing the new goal before going on with the task details (e.g., Rogers and Monsell 1995; Meiran 1996). Second, even task repetitions have been found to show performance decreases over time, suggesting that goal maintenance requires some effort (e.g., Altmann 2002). Even though such observations seem to make a strong case for effortful goal operations, there are reasons not to jump to conclusions. Waszak, Hommel, and Allport (2003) provided evidence that task goals can become associated with particular stimuli, so that these stimuli can act as exogenous retrieval cues for these goals. Along the same lines, Logan and Bundesen (2003) observed that most of the difficulty in switching between different goals is due to a shift in the task cues that signal the different goals—again suggesting that goal selection can become stimulus driven under appropriate circumstances. Indeed, Bargh and Gollwitzer (1994; Bargh, Gollwitzer, Chai, Barndollar, and Troetschel 2001) have claimed that everyday behavior is often driven by external cues, which would allow for effortless goal selection. Similarly, even if goal maintenance turned out to require effort in artificial laboratory tasks, the goals we maintain in everyday life are commonly consistent with, and thus supported by, long-term motives and overarching goals as well as by environmental cues. Indeed, in situations in which the available stimuli are specifically associated with different tasks, switching between tasks and goals was not found to be effortful or performance costly (Jersild 1927). Taken altogether, it may thus be possible that the frequent use of artificial tasks that are not deeply anchored in the participant's motivational structure and not supported by environmental cues has led to a rather drastic overestimation of the cognitive effort needed to deal with everyday life.

Acknowledgment

Support for this research by the European Commission (PACO+, ISTFP6-IP-027657) is gratefully acknowledged.

References

Allport, A. 1987. Selection for action: Some behavioral and neurophysiological considerations of attention and action. In *Perspectives on perception and action*, ed. H. Heuer and A. F. Sanders. Hillsdale, NJ: Erlbaum, 395–419.

Allport, D. A. 1993. Attention and control: Have we been asking the wrong questions? A critical review of twenty-five years. In *Attention and performance XIV: Synergies in experimental psychology, artificial intelligence, and cognitive neuroscience*, ed. D. E. Meyer and S. Kornblum. Cambridge: MIT Press, 183–218.

Allport, A., E. A. Styles, and S. Hsieh. 1994. Shifting intentional set: Exploring the dynamic control of tasks. In *Attention and performance XV: Conscious and nonconscious information processing*, ed. C. Umilta and M. Moscovitch. Cambridge: MIT Press, 421–452.

Altmann, E. M. 2002. Functional decay of memory for tasks. *Psychol. Res.* 66:287–297.

Bacon, W. F., and H. E. Egeth. 1994. Overriding stimulus-driven attentional capture. *Percept. Psychophys.* 55:485–496.

Bargh, J. A., and P. M. Gollwitzer. 1994. Environmental control over goal-directed action. *Nebr. Symp. Motiv.* 41:71–124.

Bargh, J. A., P. M. Gollwitzer, A. L. Chai, K. Barndollar, and R. Troetschel. 2001. Automated will: Nonconscious activation and pursuit of behavioral goals. *J. Pers. Soc. Psychol.* 81:1014–1027.

Bekkering, H., and S. F. W. Neggers. 2002. Visual search is modulated by action intentions. *Psychol. Sci.* 13:370–374.

Broadbent, D. E. 1958. *Perception and communication*. London: Pergamon.

Bundesen, C., T. Habekost, and S. Kyllingsbaek. 2005. A neural theory of visual attention: Bridging cognition and neurophysiology. *Psychol. Rev.* 112:291–328.

Craighero, L., L. Fadiga, G. Rizzolatti, and C. A. Umiltà. 1999. Action for perception: A motor-visual attentional effect. *J. Exp. Psychol. Hum. Percept. Perform.* 25:1673–1692.

Deubel, H., and W. X. Schneider. 1996. Saccade target selection and object recognition: Evidence for a common attentional mechanism. *Vision Res.* 36:1827–1837.

DeYoe, E. A., and D. C. Van Essen. 1988. Concurrent processing streams in monkey visual cortex. *Trends Neurosci.* 11:219–226.

Elsner, B., and B. Hommel. 2001. Effect anticipation and action control. *J. Exp. Psychol. Hum. Percept. Perform.* 27:229–240.

Fagioli, S., F. Ferlazzo, and B. Hommel. 2007b. Controlling attention through action: Observing actions primes action-related stimulus dimensions. *Neuropsychologia* 45:3351–3355.

Fagioli, S., B. Hommel, and R. I. Schubotz. 2007a. Intentional control of attention: Action planning primes action related stimulus dimensions. *Psychol. Res.* 71:22–29.

Found, A., and H. J. Müller. 1996. Searching for unknown feature targets on more than one dimension: Investigating a "dimension weighting" account. *Percept. Psychophys.* 58:88–101.

Georgopoulos, A. P. 1990. Neurophysiology of reaching. In *Attention and performance XIII: Motor representation and control*, ed. M. Jeannerod. Hillsdale, NJ: Erlbaum, 227–263.

Glover, S. 2004. Separate visual representations in the planning and control of action. *Behav. Brain Sci.* 27:3–24.

Heuer, H. 1991. Invariant relative timing in motor-program theory. In *The development of timing control and temporal organization in coordinated action*, ed. J. Fagard and P. H. Wolff. Amsterdam: North-Holland, 37–68.

Hommel, B. 2004. Event files: Feature binding in and across perception and action. *Trends Cogn. Sci.* 8:494–500.

Hommel, B., and J. Müsseler. 2006. Action-feature integration blinds to feature-overlapping perceptual events: Evidence from manual and vocal actions. *Q. J. Exp. Psychol.* 59:509–523.

Hommel, B., J. Müsseler, G. Aschersleben, and W. Prinz. 2001a. The theory of event coding (TEC): A framework for perception and action planning. *Behav. Brain Sci.* 24:849–878.

Hommel, B., J. Müsseler, G. Aschersleben, and W. Prinz. 2001b. Codes and their vicissitudes. *Behav. Brain Sci.* 24:910–927.

James, W. 1890. *The principles of psychology*. New York: Dover Publications.

Jersild, A. T. 1927. Mental set and shift. *Archive of Psychology,* whole no. 89.

Kahneman, D. 1973. *Attention and effort*. Englewood Cliffs, NJ: Prentice-Hall.

Kalaska, J. F., and M. L. Hyde. 1985. Area 4 and area 5: Differences between the load direction-dependent discharge variability of cells during active postural fixation. *Exp. Brain Res.* 59:197–202.

Keele, S. W. 1968. Movement control in skilled motor performance. *Psychol. Bull.* 70:387–403.

Klein, R. 1980. Does oculomotor readiness mediate cognitive control of visual attention? In *Attention and performance VIII*, ed. R. S. Nickerson. Hillsdale, NJ: Erlbaum, 259–276.

Kornblum, S., T. Hasbroucq, and A. Osman. 1990. Dimensional overlap: Cognitive basis of stimulus–response compatibility—A model and taxonomy. *Psychol. Rev.* 97:253–270.

Lashley, K. S. 1951. The problem of serial order in behavior. In *Cerebral mechanisms in behavior*, ed. L. A. Jeffress. New York: Wiley, 112–146.

Lépine, D., D. Glencross, and J. Requin. 1989. Some experimental evidence for and against a parametric conception of movement programming. *J. Exp. Psychol. Hum. Percept. Perform.* 15:347–362.

Logan, G. D., and C. Bundesen. 2003. Clever homunculus: Is there an endogenous act of control in the explicit task-cuing procedure? *J. Exp. Psychol. Hum. Percept. Perform.* 29:575–599.

Logan, G. D., and R. D. Gordon. 2001. Executive control of visual attention in dual-task situations. *Psychol. Rev.* 108:393–434.

Meiran, N. 1996. Reconfiguration of processing mode prior to task performance. *J. Exp. Psychol. Learn. Mem. Cogn.* 22:1423–1442.

Meiran, N. 2000. Modeling cognitive control in task-switching. *Psychol. Res.* 63:234–249.

Milner, A. D., and M. A. Goodale. 1995. *The visual brain in action*. Oxford: Oxford University Press.

Monsell, S. 2003. Task switching. *Trends Cogn. Sci.* 7:134–140.

Müller, H. J., D. Heller, and J. Ziegler. 1995. Visual search for singleton feature targets within and across feature dimensions. *Percept. Psychophys.* 57:1–17.

Müsseler, J., and B. Hommel. 1997. Blindness to response-compatible stimuli. *J. Exp. Psychol. Hum. Percept. Perform.* 23:861–872.

Neumann, O. 1987. Beyond capacity: A functional view of attention. In *Perspectives on perception and action*, ed. H. Heuer and A. F. Sanders. Hillsdale, NJ: Erlbaum, 361–394.

Posner, M. I. 1980. Orienting of attention. *Q. J. Exp. Psychol.* 32:3–25.

Prablanc, C., and D. Pélisson. 1990. Gaze saccade orienting and hand pointing are locked to their goal by quick internal loops. In *Attention and performance XIII: Motor representation and control*, ed. M. Jeannerod. Hillsdale, NJ: Erlbaum, 653–676.

Prinz, W. 1990. A common coding approach to perception and action. In *Relationships between perception and action: Current approaches*, ed. O. Neumann and W. Prinz. Berlin: Springer, 167–201.

Reynolds, J. H., L. Chelazzi, and R. Desimone. 1999. Competitive mechanisms subserve attention in macaque areas V2 and V4. *J. Neurosci.* 19:1736–1753.

Riehle, A., and J. Requin. 1989. Monkey primary motor and premotor cortex: Single-cell activity related to prior information about direction and extent of an intended movement. *J. Neurophysiol.* 61:534–549.

Rizzolatti, G., L. Riggio, I. Dascola, and C. Umiltà. 1987. Reorienting attention across the horizontal and vertical meridians: Evidence in favor of a premotor theory of attention. *Neuropsychologia* 25:31–40.

Rogers, R. D., and S. Monsell. 1995. Costs of a predictable switch between simple cognitive tasks. *J. Exp. Psychol. Gen.* 124:207–231.

Rosenbaum, D. A. 1980. Human movement initiation: Specification of arm, direction and extent. *J. Exp. Psychol. Gen.* 109:444–474.

Schmidt, R. A. 1975. A schema theory of discrete motor skill learning. *Psychol. Rev.* 82:225–260.

Schneider, W. X. 1995. VAM: A neuro-cognitive model for visual attention control of segmentation, object recognition, and space-based motor action. *Vis. Cogn.* 2:331–376.

Schneider, W. X., and H. Deubel. 2002. Selection-for-perception and selection-for-spatial-motor-action are coupled by visual attention: A review of recent findings and new evidence from stimulus-driven saccade control. In *Attention and performance XIX: Common mechanisms in perception and action*, ed. W. Prinz and B. Hommel. Oxford: Oxford University Press, 609–627.

Schubotz, R. I., and D. Y. von Cramon. 2001. Functional organization of the lateral premotor cortex: fMRI reveals different regions activated by anticipation of object properties, location and speed. *Brain Res. Cogn. Brain Res.* 11:97–112.

Schubotz, R. I., and D. Y. von Cramon. 2002. Predicting perceptual events activates corresponding motor schemes in lateral premotor cortex: An fMRI study. *Neuroimage* 15:787–796.

Schubotz, R. I., and D. Y. von Cramon. 2003. Functional–anatomical concepts of human premotor cortex: Evidence from fMRI and PET studies. *Neuroimage* 20:S120–S131.

Stoet, G., and B. Hommel. 1999. Action planning and the temporal binding of response codes. *J. Exp. Psychol. Hum. Percept. Perform.* 25:1625–1640.

Tanaka, K. 2003. Columns for complex visual object features in the inferotemporal cortex: Clustering of cells with similar but slightly different stimulus selectivities. *Cereb. Cortex* 13:90–99.

Treisman, A. 1988. Features and objects: The Fourteenth Bartlett Memorial Lecture. *Q. J. Exp. Psychol.* 40A:201–237.

Treisman, A. 1996. The binding problem. *Curr. Opin. Neurobiol.* 6:171–178.

Treisman, A., and G. Gelade. 1980. A feature-integration theory of attention. *Cognit. Psychol.* 12:97–136.

Treisman, A., and H. Schmidt. 1982. Illusory conjunctions in the perception of objects. *Cognit. Psychol.* 14:107–141.

Ungerleider, L. G., and M. Mishkin. 1982. Two cortical visual systems. In *Analysis of visual behaviour*, ed. D. J. Ingle, M. A. Goodale, and R. J. W. Mansfield. Cambridge, MA: MIT Press, 549–586.

Waszak, F., B. Hommel, and A. Allport. 2003. Task-switching and long-term priming: Role of episodic stimulus-task bindings in task-shift costs. *Cognit. Psychol.* 46:361–413.

Wolfe, J. M. 1994. Guided Search 2.0: A revised model of visual search. *Psychon. Bull. Rev.* 1:202–238.

Wykowska, A., A. Schubö, and B. Hommel. 2009. How you move is what you see: Action planning biases selection in visual search. *J. Exp. Psychol. Hum. Percept. Perform.* 35:1755–1769.

6 Implicit versus Deliberate Control and Its Implications for Awareness

Chris Blais

Overview

Research on cognitive control tends to focus on deliberate forms of control. This is strangely peculiar considering that most of our day-to-day behavior is driven by forms of control that are far from deliberate. This chapter begins with a brief discussion of the mechanisms involved in recruiting deliberate control, which serves as a framework for how nondeliberate, or adaptive, forms of control may be recruited. I then discuss whether the mechanisms involved in deliberate control might be more correctly descriptive of adaptive control. This discussion centers on the proportion congruency effect in Stroop and related selective attention paradigms and shows that the long-held strategic explanation of this effect is incorrect. The chapter ends with a discussion which considers the functional consequences of awareness.

Introduction

Cognitive control refers to the large set of processes that underlie our ability to regulate our thoughts and actions with respect to our internal goals and the prevailing external circumstances. Many of these processes involved in regulating behavior are inflexible, "automatic" processes operating below our level of awareness. How do these automatic processes support the flexible thoughts, actions, and behavior that constitute human behavior?

Several lines of research have shown that the prefrontal cortex plays a critical role in the implementation and application of cognitive control (Cohen, Braver, and O'Reilly 1996; Fuster 1980; Herd, Banich, and O'Reilly 2006; Knight, Grabowecky, and Scabini 1995; Stuss and Benson 1984). This chapter focuses on important extensions to an influential theory (Botvinick, Braver, Barch, Carter, and Cohen 2001) which outlines how the prefrontal cortex "knows" to intercede or, more generally, how and why certain mechanisms are emphasized over others on a trial-by-trial, second-by-

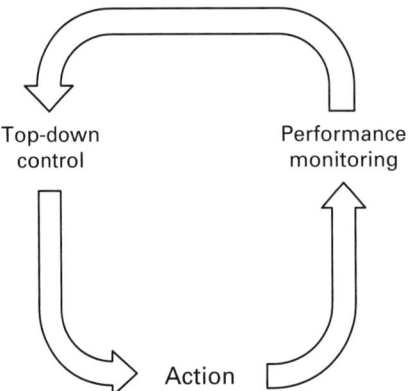

Figure 6.1
A simplified version of the cognitive control cycle.

second basis. To begin, I will outline the general cognitive control cycle (see figure 6.1).

Top–down control is a general heuristic for thinking about the mechanisms underlying cognitive control. The idea became popular with Desimone and Duncan's (1995) idea of top–down biasing of attention. The term is used here to refer to those mechanisms which allow us to flexibly shape and constrain our thoughts and actions with respect to our internal goals and prevailing external circumstances. A number of mechanisms which play a role in performing these duties are argued to be housed in the prefrontal cortex, including working memory (D'Esposito et al. 1995), selective attention (Knight, Hillyard, Woods, and Neville 1981), behavioral inhibition (Kumar, Schapiro, Haxby, Grady, and Friedland 1990), and response selection (Granon, Vidal, Thinus-Blanc, Changeux, and Poucet 1994). Although researchers have always been keen to explore these processes, data has been increasing at a seemingly exponential rate as many of the scientists turn to functional magnetic resonance imaging (fMRI).

In this diagram, *action* refers to nearly any thought or behavior. Although research in cognitive psychology typically involves decomposing the action into its (often automatic) subcomponents, at this stage it is much easier to consider the action as a whole. In this context, an action includes complex behavior such as operating a helicopter, as well as relatively simpler actions such as reaching across the table to pick up a drinking glass. This latter example is much more tractable for our purpose.

Among a host of other processes, picking up a drinking glass involves visually identifying the position of the glass, implementing a motor program to coordinate the muscles in the arm and hand to reach out and grasp the drinking glass, and applying this motor program. While this action is occurring, a *performance-monitoring* mechanism scrutinizes the action and assesses the fit between the actual behavior and the desired behavior. In this example, the performance monitor may detect that someone has just placed a different glass along the path of your arm's trajectory. In such a situation, the performance monitor would detect the discrepancy between the desired goal of getting the drinking glass and the current action's ability to complete that goal, and it informs the top–down control system. The top–down control system evaluates the situation and modifies the action accordingly. It is argued that this cycle operates continually.

The process is much more complicated than I have outlined, and there are better specified accounts of this cycle, including the important perception mechanisms (e.g., the self-monitoring model; Frith, Rees, and Friston 1998). However, the model in figure 6.1 is easy to follow and contains the gist of most models of cognitive control. That said, there is a serious philosophical problem associated with many of these accounts: Without specifying *how* the performance monitor recruits the top–down control system, it is difficult to avoid the homunculus problem. That is, the model provides no explanation of how cognitive control is recruited; it is just a repetition of the original problem.

Matthew Botvinick and his colleagues outlined an influential solution to this problem (Botvinick et al. 2001; Botvinick, Braver, et al. 2004; Botvinick, Cohen, and Carter 2004; Botvinick, Nystrom, Fissell, Carter, and Cohen 1999). They suggest that the performance-monitoring mechanism is situated in the anterior cingulate cortex (ACC) and that it recruits top–down control as a function of the amount of conflict it detects. Others have contended that rather than conflict, the process is accomplished by detecting the probability of committing an error (Brown and Braver 2005). Regardless of the specifics, each hypothesis is important in that it avoids the homunculus problem.

With respect to cognitive control, most of the empirical work that has gone into developing this model has been, explicitly or implicitly, tied to a form of *deliberate* control. That is, subjects are described as applying a strategy, or optimizing their behavior to a set of contingencies in the environment which they have detected. Most often this comes in the form of the retrieval and application of specific rules (Bunge 2004). The remainder of this chapter discusses implicit control, shows that one effect long ascribed to strategic control is more accurately described by implicit control, and suggests that deliberate control should only be offered as an explanation after implicit control no longer provides an accurate description of the data.

Implicit Control

The first time I heard the term *implicit control* and its cousin, *automatic control*, I was baffled. It was the first time I could recall coming across an oxymoron in the psychology literature. To be sure, in its most common use in cognitive psychology, implicit is used to describe forms of learning or memory to which the learner has no access (e.g., learning to ride a bicycle). This implicit form of learning is contrasted with more explicit forms in which cognitive control gives one the feeling of being in charge of one's own actions. Explicit control typically implies choice, and in cognitive psychology it is often associated with the application of a rule or strategy.

By virtue of the fact that one can override one's habits when they lead to inefficient behavior, despite the fact that one is not deliberately, or even aware of, doing so, it seems likely that implicit control is intimately involved with behavioral adaptation and learning in general. The idea of implicit control is not limited to explaining cognitive processes. John Bargh, for example, has long advocated that our social behaviors are guided by automatic processes (Bargh and Ferguson 2000), and more recently Iris Mauss (Mauss, Cook, and Gross 2007) has shown that people can automatically regulate their emotions.

To be clear, I am not denying the presence of deliberate control. In most situations behavior appears to be driven by both deliberate and implicit forms of control.[1] The difference is that awareness of one's actions is an essential component of deliberate control but not of implicit control. Further consideration of this phenomenon yields an important insight: Because we are not always aware of the control, implicit control must always be operating. If it were not, we would never be able to adapt to a situation since all situations are new in the sense that we can never be in exactly the same situation twice.[2] Consider a familiar task such as driving home from work. At some point a deliberate goal will have come to mind. Upon looking at the clock, for instance, I realize that I will be late unless I leave now. I was conscious of the decision to leave and implemented a series of actions to accomplish this goal. Once I begin driving, though, my deliberate thoughts—my conscious attention—may be completely task irrelevant: daydreaming, people watching, hunger, and so on. I rarely catch myself explicitly attending to the task of operating the vehicle, navigating the congested streets, avoiding the adjacent vehicles. I have never been in this exact situation before (i.e., the cars are always in different places traveling at different speeds, etc). Clearly, this demanding task involves control. However, I am not aware of each subtle nuance of the continuously changing environment because my thoughts are otherwise occupied. Thus, I am not deliberately controlling my actions, so I must be controlling them implicitly. Again, the simple difference is that for deliberate control I am aware of choosing to explicitly modulate my actions; implicit control is not privy to that information.

The majority of the cognitive control literature follows a simple formula: Utilize a selective attention task, and ask participants to respond to a nondominant dimension. The most common examples employ various forms of the Stroop task, in which subjects respond to the print color of a color word (e.g., saying "yellow" to the word *green* printed in yellow); the Simon task, in which subjects respond to a stimulus using lateralized response keys (e.g., using a standard keyboard, responding to A or L, which appear on the left or right side of the screen); or the flanker task, in which subjects respond to a central stimulus that is flanked on both sides by a task-relevant distractor (e.g., respond to the central arrow of >><>>). All of these situations produce robust behavior in which the task-irrelevant information has an impact on the subjects' ability to perform the task. That is, virtually all subjects show a pattern of behavior such that the word impacts color naming (the Stroop effect; Stroop 1935), the location of the target impacts responding to its identity (the Simon effect; Simon and Small 1969), and the surrounding characters impact responding to a central target (the flanker effect; Eriksen and Eriksen 1974).

Although the cause of these effects is disputed, an accurate portrayal involves an appeal to the fact that the task is simple enough to not require our full attentional capacity. This leftover capacity is obligatorily allocated to the distractors, causing them to be processed and compete for response (see Lavie 1995). This type of research on cognitive control seeks to identify factors which can adjust the focus of selective attention to be more biased toward early selection (i.e., less interference from the ignored information) or toward late selection (i.e., more interference from the ignored information). Two factors which have been heavily used to exploit this property of cognitive control are proportion effects and sequential effects.

Proportion effects have been shown across Stroop (Logan and Zbrodoff 1979), Simon (Toth et al. 1995), flanker (Chen, Zhang, and Zhou 2006), and a range of other selective attention tasks. The near-universal finding is that as the proportion of congruent trials increases, the size of the interference effect also increases (Jacoby, Lindsay, and Hessels 2003; Lindsay and Jacoby 1994; Logan and Zbrodoff 1979; Logan, Zbrodoff, and Williamson 1984; Toth et al. 1995). Stated differently, a high proportion of trials in which the task-irrelevant information leads to the same response as the task-relevant information biases the system to engage in late selection. Conversely, as the proportion of congruent trials decreases, the size of the interference effect also decreases; a low proportion of trials in which the task-irrelevant information leads to the same response as the task-relevant information biases the system to engage in early selection.

The Gratton effect (Gratton, Coles, and Donchin 1992) refers to the observation that following an incongruent trial, the size of the interference effect decreases; conversely, following a congruent trial, the size of the interference effect increases. Stated differently, the presentation of an incongruent trial biases the system to engage in early selection, and the presentation of a congruent trial biases the system to engage in late selection. This also demonstrates that control operates quite rapidly on a trial-by-trial basis.

Both of these effects have been argued to engage a common underlying mechanism, namely, the performance monitor that operates via conflict detection (e.g., response conflict, stimulus conflict, the conflict caused by underdetermined responses, etc.; Botvinick et al. 2001). When presented with an incongruent trial, a conflict signal produced by the mismatch between the two dimensions begins to accumulate in the response system. This signal rapidly modifies how much top–down control is utilized by the task (Botvinick et al. 1999). In Stroop, this involves adjusting the emphasis placed on the *attend to the color* rule represented in dorsolateral prefrontal cortex (DLPFC; MacDonald, Cohen, Stenger, and Carter 2000). Both proportion effects and Gratton effects are readily explained by this hypothesis.

Consider the response time to an incongruent trial presented within a sequence of Stroop trials. According to the conflict-monitoring hypothesis, on a congruent trial there is very little response conflict between the task-relevant color and the task-irrelevant word. Thus, a congruent trial functionally turns down the selectivity between the color and the word, causing more resources to be allocated toward processing the word. Conversely, on an incongruent trial, there is considerable response conflict between the color and the word. Thus, an incongruent trial essentially turns up the selectivity between the color and the word, causing fewer resources to be allocated to the word, which allows for better filtering of the distracting information. Keep in mind that the system is unable to completely repress what occurred on the previous trial. Thus, within a sequence of trials, it follows from the conflict-monitoring hypothesis that, if the preceding trial was incongruent, then the response time to the current incongruent trial will be faster because the preceding incongruent trial configured the system to attend more selectively to the color (and ignore the irrelevant word less effectively). Conversely, if the preceding trial was congruent, then the response time to the current incongruent trial will be slower because the preceding congruent trial configured the system to attend less selectively to the color (and better ignore the irrelevant word). The same logic applies when the current trial is congruent. The net result is that when the response times in each of these four conditions are compiled, we see a smaller Stroop effect following incongruent trials than following congruent trials, exactly as described by Gratton et al. (1992).

It should be evident that this same mechanism can explain the proportion effect. The standard proportion analysis involves measuring the size of the Stroop effect when there are many congruent trials compared to when there are relatively few congruent trials. When there are many congruent trials, we have a situation in which the system is bombarded with information indicating that the word is beneficial and there is no need to apply a strong filter. In this situation, the rare incongruent trial will take a relatively long time to resolve, leading to a very large Stroop effect. Conversely, when there are few congruent trials, we have a situation in which the system is bombarded with information indicating that the word is harmful, so we apply as strong a filter as possible. In this situation, the rare congruent trial will again take a relatively long time to resolve because it gets less help from the word because of the strong filter, which leads to a smaller Stroop effect.

With respect to the issue of deliberate control, the standard account of the proportion effect is either explicitly strategic or implied to be strategic (e.g., Logan, Zbrodoff, and Williamson 1984). Proponents of this account argue that subjects detect and/or become aware of the contingency between the color and the word. When this contingency is high, subjects (choose to) attend to the word because it helps their overall performance. When the contingency is low, subjects do their best to (choose to) ignore the word because it hurts their overall performance. This strategic account is hard to refute based on the fact that proportion manipulation usually occurs at the level of a block or list of trials. That is, subjects will get one block of trials that are made up of items that are each 25% congruent and another block of trials in which each block is made up of items that are 75% congruent. The strategic account applies well in this setting because it is conceivable that subjects can detect the contingency between the color and the word. Interestingly, if this contingency is withheld from subjects—for example, by masking the word in a temporally segregated version of the task—then subjects fail to show a proportion congruency effect despite showing a Stroop effect (Cheesman and Merikle 1986). This implies a dissociation between awareness of the proportion of congruent trials and showing a proportion congruency effect in that awareness is a necessary prerequisite for producing a proportion effect (but see below). However, it tells us little about the level at which the effect manifests. A surprising result by Larry Jacoby and his colleagues, discussed below, is much more informative in this regard.

Item-Specific Control

The Gratton effect demonstrates a clear example of online trial-to-trial control (but see Mayr, Awh, and Laurey 2003; Nieuwenhuis et al. 2006; with a defense in Ullsperger, Bylsma, and Botvinick 2005). In addition to this online control, Jacoby et al. (2003) provide evidence that control is also directed to specific *items*. Their experiments vary the proportion of congruent trials at the level of specific items (i.e., a specific pairing of a color word and color) while keeping the list-level congruency proportion at 50%. They report that "mostly congruent" items showed a larger Stroop effect than "mostly incongruent" items. When proportion is manipulated like this, subjects have no way of knowing which item is coming next, so it is difficult to see how a *general* strategy of "attending more to 'the' color" could explain this result. This result demands a much more focused, or local, form of control. Before describing this model, I will note that this item-specific control has been shown across a range of selective attention tasks (Crump, Gong, and Milliken 2006; Crump, Vaquero, and Milliken 2008) and analyses have been performed which indicate that it is unlikely that the effect is the result of simple priming (Crump et al. 2006).

To be clear, my goal is to show that the "deliberate" model of control I outlined earlier is more likely an ideal candidate for a general, implicit model of control. Recall that the model has three main components: the action or behavior itself, performance monitor, and top–down control, which interact to flexibly adapt our behavior to the environment. A concrete diagram of this model as it applies to the Stroop task is shown in figure 6.2.

Let me restate this strategic account more explicitly in the context of a computational model of the conflict-monitoring hypothesis. The vast majority of Stroop experiments instruct subjects to respond to the print color of the color word (it is also typical to instruct them to ignore the meaning of word). The model simulates this by activating the "attend to the color" rule prior to each trial or continuously throughout the simulation. On a congruent trial, such as green in green, both the color and the word activate the same concept in the response layer, which creates a weak conflict signal in ACC. This weak signal is sent to DLPFC, which turns down the gain on the "respond to the color" rule, allowing the "respond to the word" rule to also be quite active. Conversely, on an incongruent trial, such as blue in green, the color and the word activate different concepts in the response layer, creating a strong conflict signal in the ACC. This strong signal is sent to DLPFC, which turns up the gain on the "respond to the color" rule, causing the "respond to the word" rule to be strongly suppressed, thus minimizing the influence of the word on performance.

Blais, Robidoux, Risko, and Besner (2007) demonstrate that this account cannot explain Jacoby's item-specific proportion congruent (ISPC) effect and propose a model in which control occurs at the item level rather than globally across the entire pathway (see figure 6.2). Specifically, rather than DLPFC exerting equivalent amounts of control to all colors and words in their respective pathways, it sends signals that are proportional to the amount of conflict associated with each item. At a conceptual level, it approximates more specific rules such as "attend to the color red." A similar account is offered by Verguts and Notebaert (2008) via a conflict-modulated Hebbian learning mechanism. Both of these implementations mesh well with the ACC's established role in reward-based learning (Rushworth, Buckley, Behrens, Walton, and Bannerman 2007), particularly given that much of this literature uses animal models for which high performance in specific contexts with specific stimuli leads to the largest rewards and the fastest learning. Following detection of this conflict, the ACC recruits regions in the DLPFC that implement the specific rule via the top–down control signal.

Perhaps the most interesting result to emerge from this model is that Blais et al. (2007) reveal that deliberate control is unnecessary to explain the proportion effect (see Blais et al. 2007, simulation 2). A single mechanism implementing control at the item level explains "global" list-level effects just as well as the traditional mechanism that implements control at a "strategic" level. Given that the former is required to explain the ISPC, eliminating the general strategic rule is certainly more parsimonious. It is also consistent with recent data (Schmidt and Besner 2008; Schmidt, Crump, Cheesman, and Besner 2007) showing that awareness of the proportion of congruent

Implicit versus Deliberate Control

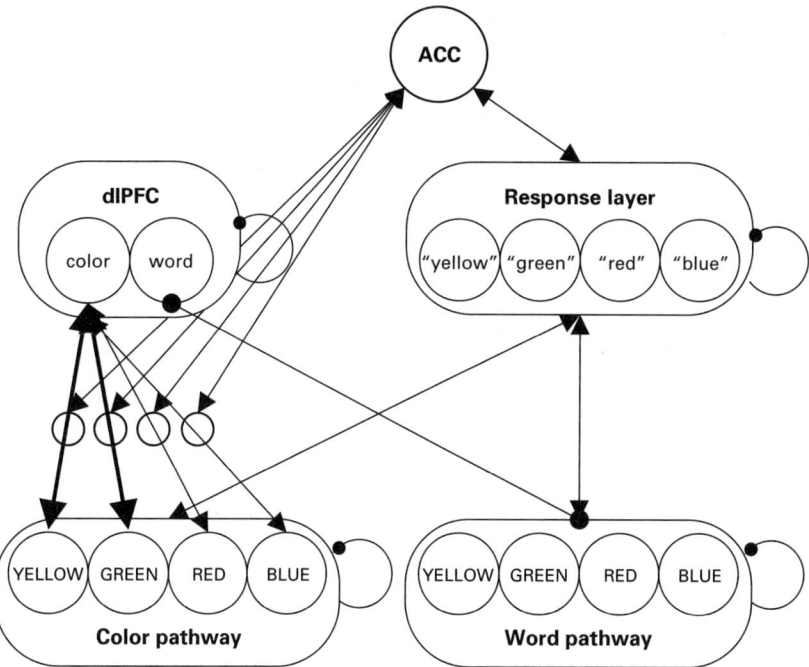

Figure 6.2
A model of Stroop performance based on Blais et al. (2007) in which control is allocated to specific items. The color pathway, word pathway, and response layer comprise the action cycle, while the anterior cingulate cortex (ACC) and dorsolateral prefrontal cortex (dlPFC) form the performance monitor and top–down control, respectively. The heavier lines from the color rule to the colors yellow and green indicate that the model will attend more to these colors, causing them to show a reduced Stroop effect. Some connections have been omitted to remove clutter. There are connections between nodes representing the same concept between the color pathway and the response layer and between the word pathway and the response layer. In addition, the ACC affects the connections between the dlPFC and the word pathway in the same way as shown along the color pathway.

trials in a Stroop-like task has no impact on the size of the cueing effect (but note Cheesman and Merikle 1986).

The culmination of this work prompts the question of whether there is a global proportion effect or, more specifically, whether awareness of the proportion of congruent trials has an additional effect. This question was addressed recently by Blais, Risko, and Bunge (2008). Their within-subjects experiment contained both item-level and list-level proportion manipulations. Each subject received three blocks of trials whose order was counterbalanced. The proportion of congruent trials at the list level was 30%, 50%, or 70%. This is like the typical experiment investigating the effects of proportion congruency, but within each of these blocks one set of items was presented congruently on 50% of trials. The other set of items was congruent on either 10%, 50%, or 90% of the trials to yield the aforementioned list-level proportion. Given the highly robust ISPC effect, we of course find differences within the 30% and 70% blocks which are consistent with the operation of an item-specific, adaptive, form of control. The interesting comparison is of the 50% conditions across blocks. If there is a global effect that operates above and beyond the item-level effect, we would expect that the 50% items in the 30% and 70% blocks would show a Stroop effect similar to the other items within that block (the 10% and 90% items, respectively). Specifically, in the 30% block, the 50% items should show a smaller Stroop effect because they are paired with items that are congruent on 10% of trials. Similarly, in the 70% block, the 50% items should show a larger Stroop effect because they are paired with items that are congruent on 90% of trials.

As shown in figure 6.3, we find no evidence for a global effect that operates independently from the item effects. The size of the Stroop effect for items presented congruently on 50% of the trials is the same regardless of whether they were presented in the same block as 10%-, 50%-, or 90%-congruent items. The finding is surprising in that it has demonstrated that the intuitive strategic account for proportion effects is false. This finding has been replicated and extended in an fMRI experiment (Blais and Bunge, in press). Together, these findings demonstrate that areas in the ACC-DLPFC network that are attributed to the conflict-monitoring loop also respond exclusively to conflict at the level of the specific item.

Is Awareness Functionally Relevant?

What role does awareness play in cognition? The terminology in this area is murky at best, so I will provide the gist of the argument in common language where possible. With respect to the *function* of consciousness, a relatively common view, particularly in neuropsychology, is that it is an epiphenomenon. That is, mental states are the by-products of physical changes in the brain. Epiphenomenalism grew out of a problem facing dualism, namely, how does the mental realm affect the physical? The strongest

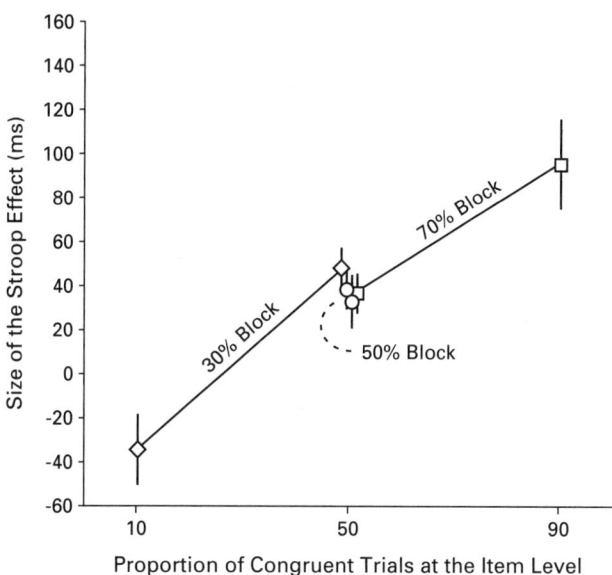

Figure 6.3
The size of the Stroop effect in milliseconds as a function of the proportion of congruent trials at the item level. Of particular relevance here is the fact that the size of the Stroop effect is the same across the 50%-congruent condition regardless of whether it was mixed with 10%-, 50%-, or 90%-congruent trials.

version of this view states that all mental states are causally irrelevant in that they have no ability to affect the electrical or chemical properties of the brain and thus cannot impact behavior. Proponents of this account often cite the *readiness potential* as evidence. This effect refers to the observation that the electrical activity related to voluntary actions can be recorded up to two seconds before the subject is aware of taking a decision to perform the action (Libet 1985). Since these data support the idea that subliminal processing becomes conscious experience, these results have been interpreted to suggest that people are capable of action before conscious experience of the decision to act occurs (Wegner 2002). That is, the feeling of choosing to act could not cause the action to occur because the action happens before the decision.

However, the readiness potential is also taken as evidence against the view that consciousness is an epiphenomenon. First, consider what is required of the subject performing a readiness potential experiment. The subject is asked to report the point in time at which the conscious experience to initiate an action occurs. This action relies on two abilities. First, the subject must be able to consciously perform an action. Second, the conscious experience must be effective enough to prompt a response. Both of these abilities contradict the claim that consciousness has no effects and therefore cannot be measured. Thus, any experiment which detects whether or when a conscious effect occurs argues strongly against, not for, epiphenomenalism (Flanagan 1994).

More recently, Green (2003) has noted that epiphenomenalism does not even provide a satisfactory solution to the problem of the mind–brain interaction posed by dualists. According to Green, epiphenomenalism implies a one-way form of interactionism that is just as hard to conceive of as the two-way form embodied in substance dualism. Specifically, if the dualism problem is how mental events can causally influence physical events, why is it any less of a problem for how physical events can influence mental ones? Scientists might be quick to argue that physical events (e.g., brain activity) have some sort of primacy over mental ones (e.g., the experience of pain), likely because the former are more tangible and readily measured with reliable scientific instrumentation.

The outcome of this debate is particularly important with respect to the issue of free will and determinism. For scientists studying the mechanisms of human behavior, it seems to be given that we must deny the existence of free will. Specifically, we search for the causal mechanisms of behavior. We believe that every effect has a cause and if we can reproduce the context (i.e., all the causes) exactly, a person's behavior will be identical each time. There appears to be little room for free will in the science of psychology (Wegner 2002) but rather deterministic causes that have yet to be discovered.

I certainly do not think this brief discussion will end a centuries-old debate. However, I wish to use it to advocate two avenues of research which might provide the evidence needed to tease apart the elements of this debate. The first involves a more systematic analysis of the function of awareness. To do this, one might carefully investigate the role proportion plays in modulating the size of the Stroop effect. I chose proportion because we already know quite a bit about this effect. Basically, as the proportion of congruent trials increases, the size of the Stroop effect increases (apparently linearly). An underlying assumption for all of the research on this effect is that subjects can detect the contingency between the word and the color. To test this, we could give subjects a very large number of small blocks of Stroop trials in which each block would have a different proportion of trials. We could then obtain both objective measures of performance, such as the size of the Stroop effect, in each small block of trials, and subjective measures, such as estimating the proportion of congruent trials in each block, but more importantly subjects' confidence about their proportion estimate. If we were to do this, it would allow us to assess whether awareness "adds" anything. That is, do subjects "use" information in a qualitatively different way depending on whether they are unconsciously versus consciously aware of that information? Unfortunately, I do not have the answers to these questions, as I am only beginning to test these ideas.

A second avenue of research, for which I do have findings, concerns the fate of conflict in the absence of awareness of its cause: If a source of conflict is presented below the level of subjective awareness, what, if anything, is modulated by control? I have begun to assess this in the context of a temporally segregated Stroop task (Blais, Tudela, and Bunge 2007). In this task, subjects are asked to respond to a color patch that is preceded by a masked color word. The duration of the color word is calibrated individually for each subject, and we use two different masks. Critically, one mask is associated with more conflict than another mask by having one mask appear with mostly incongruent trials in which only 33% of the color patches match the masked word. The other mask is associated with mostly congruent trials in which 66% of the color patches match the masked word. In addition to this, there is a condition in which only the mask is presented, without the word. Consistent with one's intuitions, when the word is present, we find that the 33%-congruent condition is slower than the 66%-congruent condition. This is not surprising given that we are averaging many slow incongruent trials with few fast congruent trials in the 33%-congruent condition and averaging many fast congruent trials with few slow incongruent trials in the 66%-congruent condition. However, in the absence of any actual conflict, because no word is presented, we find evidence that the system is attributing the source of conflict to the mask. Specifically, subjects are faster to respond to the color patch when preceded by the 33%-congruent mask associated with more conflict than when preceded by the 66% mask associated with relatively less conflict. Essentially, the system detects the conflict and uses it to signal control in the most adaptive, to an informed observer, way possible (at least in this task).

Conclusion

The majority of research into cognitive control, either implicitly or explicitly, focuses on deliberate forms of control—those forms which assume awareness. However, as scientists, we must be parsimonious. We must first show that implicit control cannot offer a satisfactory explanation of the effect before offering an account based on deliberate control. This is especially true given the large body of evidence showing that our behavior can be driven by thoughts and actions to which we have no conscious access. We must be diligent in ruling out these implicit forms of control before we can offer an account based on deliberate control.

Acknowledgments

This research was supported by a postdoctoral fellowship grant from the Natural Sciences and Engineering Research Council of Canada (NSERC). I thank Silvia Bunge for valuable criticism on a draft of this chapter.

Notes

1. I suspect that some (Wegner 2002) may argue that deliberate control is nothing more than an illusion.

2. This is not to say that deliberate control cannot allow for adaptability to novel situations but rather to acknowledge that even in the absence of deliberate control, we are quite exemplary at adapting to our environment.

References

Bargh, J. A., and M. J. Ferguson. 2000. Beyond behaviorism: on the automaticity of higher mental processes. *Psychol. Bull.* 126:925–945. Medline:11107883 doi:10.1037/0033-2909.126.6.925

Blais, C., and S. Bunge. In press. Behavioral and neural evidence of item-specific performance monitoring. *J. Cogn. Neurosci.*

Blais, C., E. F. Risko, and S. Bunge. 2008. *Cognitive control: Item specific and rapid.* Paper presented at the 15th Annual Cognitive Neuroscience Society Meeting, San Francisco, CA.

Blais, C., S. Robidoux, E. F. Risko, and D. Besner. 2007. Item specific adaptation and the conflict monitoring hypothesis: A computational model. *Psychol. Rev.* 114:1076–1086. Medline:17907873 doi:10.1037/0033-295X.114.4.1076

Blais, C., P. Tudela, and S. Bunge. 2007. *Proportion congruency and the neural correlates of consciousness.* Paper presented at the Annual meeting of the Society for Neuroscience, San Diego, CA.

Botvinick, M., T. S. Braver, D. M. Barch, C. S. Carter, and J. D. Cohen. 2001. Conflict monitoring and cognitive control. *Psychol. Rev.* 108:624–652. Medline:11488380 doi:10.1037/0033-295X.108.3.624

Botvinick, M., T. S. Braver, N. Yeung, M. Ullsperger, C. S. Carter, and J. D. Cohen. 2004. Conflict monitoring: Computational and empirical studies. In *Cognitive neuroscience of attention*, ed. M. I. Posner. New York: Guilford, 91–102.

Botvinick, M., J. D. Cohen, and C. S. Carter. 2004. Conflict monitoring and anterior cingulate cortex: An update. *Trends Cogn. Sci.* 8:539–546. Medline:15556023 doi:10.1016/j.tics.2004.10.003

Botvinick, M., L. E. Nystrom, K. Fissell, C. S. Carter, and J. D. Cohen. 1999. Conflict monitoring versus selection-for-action in anterior cingulate cortex. *Nature* 402:179–181. Medline:10647008 doi:10.1038/46035

Brown, J. W., and T. S. Braver. 2005. Learned predictions of error likelihood in the anterior cingulate cortex. *Science* 307:1118–1121. Medline:15718473 doi:10.1126/science.1105783

Bunge, S. A. 2004. How we use rules to select actions: a review of evidence from cognitive neuroscience. *Cogn. Affect. Behav. Neurosci.* 4:564–579. Medline:15849898 doi:10.3758/CABN.4.4.564

Cheesman, J., and P. M. Merikle. 1986. Distinguishing conscious from unconscious perceptual processes. *Can. J. Psychol.* 40:343–367. Medline:3502878 doi:10.1037/h0080103

Chen, Q., M. Zhang, and X. Zhou. 2006. Effects of spatial distribution of attention during inhibition of return (IOR) on flanker interference in hearing and congenitally deaf people. *Brain Res.* 1109:117–127. Medline:16859649 doi:10.1016/j.brainres.2006.06.043

Cohen, J. D., T. S. Braver, and R. C. O'Reilly. 1996. A computational approach to prefrontal cortex, cognitive control and schizophrenia: Recent developments and current challenges. *Philos. Trans. R. Soc. Lond. B Biol. Sci.* 351:1515–1527. Medline:8941963 doi:10.1098/rstb.1996.0138

Crump, M. J., Z. Gong, and B. Milliken. 2006. The context-specific proportion congruent Stroop effect: Location as a contextual cue. *Psychon. Bull. Rev.* 13:316–321. Medline:16893001

Crump, M. J., J. M. Vaquero, and B. Milliken. 2008. Context-specific learning and control: The roles of awareness, task relevance, and relative salience. *Conscious Cogn.* 17:22–36.

D'Esposito, M., J. A. Detre, D. C. Alsop, R. K. Shin, S. Atlas, and M. Grossman. 1995. The neural basis of the central executive system of working memory. *Nature* 378:279–281. Medline:7477346 doi:10.1038/378279a0

Desimone, R., and J. Duncan. 1995. Neural mechanisms of selective visual attention. *Annu. Rev. Neurosci.* 18:193–222. Medline:7605061 doi:10.1146/annurev.ne.18.030195.001205

Eriksen, B. A., and C. W. Eriksen. 1974. Effects of noise letters upon the identification of a target letter in a nonsearch task. *Percept. Psychophys.* 16:143–149.

Flanagan, O. 1994. *Consciousness reconsidered.* Cambridge: MIT Press.

Frith, C., G. Rees, and K. Friston. 1998. Psychosis and the experience of self: Brain systems underlying self-monitoring. *Ann. N. Y. Acad. Sci.* 843:170–178. Medline:9668657 doi:10.1111/j.1749-6632.1998.tb08213.x

Fuster, J. M. 1980. *The prefrontal cortex: Anatomy, physiology, and neuropsychology of the frontal lobe.* New York: Raven Press.

Granon, S., C. Vidal, C. Thinus-Blanc, J. P. Changeux, and B. Poucet. 1994. Working memory, response selection, and effortful processing in rats with medial prefrontal lesions. *Behav. Neurosci.* 108:883–891. Medline:7826511 doi:10.1037/0735-7044.108.5.883

Gratton, G., M. G. Coles, and E. Donchin. 1992. Optimizing the use of information: Strategic control of activation of responses. *J. Exp. Psychol. Gen.* 121:480–506. Medline:1431740 doi:10.1037/0096-3445.121.4.480

Green, C. 2003. *The lost cause: Causation and the mind–body problem.* Oxford: Oxford Forum.

Herd, S. A., M. T. Banich, and R. C. O'Reilly. 2006. Neural mechanisms of cognitive control: An integrative model of Stroop task performance and FMRI data. *J. Cogn. Neurosci.* 18 (1):22–32. Medline:16417680 doi:10.1162/089892906775250012

Jacoby, L. L., D. S. Lindsay, and S. Hessels. 2003. Item-specific control of automatic processes: Stroop process dissociations. *Psychon. Bull. Rev.* 10:638–644. Medline:14620358

Knight, R. T., M. F. Grabowecky, and D. Scabini. 1995. Role of human prefrontal cortex in attention control. In *Epilepsy and the functional anatomy of the frontal lobe*, ed. H. Jasper, S. Riggio, P. S. Goldman-Rakic. New York, NY; 21–36.

Knight, R. T., S. A. Hillyard, D. L. Woods, and H. J. Neville. 1981. The effects of frontal cortex lesions on event-related potentials during auditory selective attention. *Electroencephalogr. Clin. Neurophysiol.* 52:571–582. Medline:6172256 doi:10.1016/0013-4694(81)91431-0

Kumar, A., M. B. Schapiro, J. V. Haxby, C. L. Grady, and R. P. Friedland. 1990. Cerebral metabolic and cognitive studies in dementia with frontal lobe behavioral features. *J. Psychiatr. Res.* 24 (2):97–109. Medline:2213642 doi:10.1016/0022-3956(90)90050-Z

Lavie, N. 1995. Perceptual load as a necessary condition for selective attention. *J. Exp. Psychol. Hum. Percept. Perform.* 21:451–468. Medline:7790827 doi:10.1037/0096-1523.21.3.451

Libet, B. 1985. Unconscious cerebral initiative and the role of conscious will in voluntary action. *Behav. Brain Sci.* 8:529–566.

Lindsay, D. S., and L. L. Jacoby. 1994. Stroop process dissociations: The relationship between facilitation and interference. *J. Exp. Psychol. Hum. Percept. Perform.* 20:219–234. Medline:8189189 doi:10.1037/0096-1523.20.2.219

Logan, G. D., and N. J. Zbrodoff. 1979. When it helps to be misled: Facilitative effects of increasing the frequency of conflicting stimuli in a Stroop-like task. *Mem. Cognit.* 7:166–174.

Logan, G. D., N. J. Zbrodoff, and J. Williamson. 1984. Strategies in the color-word Stroop task. *Bull. Psychon. Soc.* 22 (2):135–138.

MacDonald, A. W., III, J. D. Cohen, V. A. Stenger, and C. S. Carter. 2000. Dissociating the role of the dorsolateral prefrontal and anterior cingulate cortex in cognitive control. *Science* 288:1835–1838. Medline:10846167 doi:10.1126/science.288.5472.1835

Mauss, I. B., C. L. Cook, and J. J. Gross. 2007. Automatic emotion regulation during anger provocation. *J. Exp. Soc. Psychol.* 43:698–711. doi:10.1016/j.jesp.2006.07.003

Mayr, U., E. Awh, and P. Laurey. 2003. Conflict adaptation effects in the absence of executive control. *Nat. Neurosci.* 6:450–452. Medline:12704394

Miller, E. K., and J. D. Cohen. 2001. An integrative theory of prefrontal cortex function. *Annu. Rev. Neurosci.* 24:167–202. Medline:11283309 doi:10.1146/annurev.neuro.24.1.167

Nieuwenhuis, S., J. F. Stins, D. Posthuma, T. J. Polderman, D. I. Boomsma, and E. J. de Geus. 2006. Accounting for sequential trial effects in the flanker task: Conflict adaptation or associative priming? *Mem. Cognit.* 34:1260–1272. Medline:17225507

Rushworth, M. F., M. J. Buckley, T. E. Behrens, M. E. Walton, and D. M. Bannerman. 2007. Functional organization of the medial frontal cortex. *Curr. Opin. Neurobiol.* 17:220–227. Medline:17350820 doi:10.1016/j.conb.2007.03.001

Schmidt, J. R., and D. Besner. 2008. The Stroop effect: Why proportion congruent has nothing to do with congruency and everything to do with contingency. *J. Exp. Psychol. Learn. Mem. Cogn.* 34:514–523. Medline:18444752 doi:10.1037/0278-7393.34.3.514

Schmidt, J. R., M. J. Crump, J. Cheesman, and D. Besner. 2007. Contingency learning without awareness: Evidence for implicit control. *Conscious. Cogn.* 16:421–435. Medline:16899377 doi:10.1016/j.concog.2006.06.010

Simon, J. R., and A. M. Small, Jr. 1969. Processing auditory information: Interference from an irrelevant cue. *J. Appl. Psychol.* 53:433–435. Medline:5366316 doi:10.1037/h0028034

Stroop, J. R. 1935. Studies of interference in serial verbal reactions. *J. Exp. Psychol.* 18:643–662.

Stuss, D. T., and D. F. Benson. 1984. Neuropsychological studies of the frontal lobes. *Psychol. Bull.* 95:3–28. Medline:6544432 doi:10.1037/0033-2909.95.1.3

Toth, J. P., B. Levine, D. T. Stuss, A. Oh, G. Winocur, and N. Meiran. 1995. Dissociation of processes underlying spatial S–R compatibility: Evidence for the independent influence of what and where. *Conscious. Cogn.* 4:483–501. Medline:8750420 doi:10.1006/ccog.1995.1052

Ullsperger, M., L. M. Bylsma, and M. M. Botvinick. 2005. The conflict adaptation effect: It's not just priming. *Cogn. Affect. Behav. Neurosci.* 5:467–472. Medline:16541815 doi:10.3758/CABN.5.4.467

Verguts, T., and W. Notebaert. 2008. Hebbian learning of cognitive control: Dealing with specific and nonspecific adaptation. *Psychol. Rev.* 115 (2):518–525. Medline:18426302 doi:10.1037/0033-295X.115.2.518

Wegner, D. M. (2002). *The illusion of conscious will*. Cambridge: MIT Press.

7 Effortless Attention, Hypofrontality, and Perfectionism

Arne Dietrich and Oliver Stoll

Autotelic experiences, popularly known as flow, are associated with enhanced or even optimal performance. They occur when one becomes so deeply engrossed in a task and pursues it with such passion that all else disappears, including any sense of the passage of time or the worry of failure. Attention and action in such an autotelic state seem to flow effortlessly, and the task, whichever it may be, is performed without strain or effort to the best of the person's ability.

In sports competition, for instance, such a performance-enhancing state of mind is, for rather obvious reasons, highly desirable. Although no lives are at stake in the literal sense, as there are, for instance, in the skilled movements of a surgeon in the operating theater, winning or losing in sports is, in contemporary society at least, not a minor matter. There can be an extraordinary monetary benefit to be had for professional athletes and their entourages, along with a whole host of other perks, such as prestige and social status, to say nothing of things like national pride. It is not surprising, then, that no effort is being spared in optimizing athletic performance on the part of the people who have a stake in it. This includes, obviously, the desire to use this somewhat peculiar alteration to mental status known as flow as a way to tap into superior performance, preferably at will.

There is, as there has to be, only one minor hitch. We don't know, you see, what makes flow come and go, so to speak. Without some decent grasp of how to induce it, preferably on command, and maintain it, preferably in those all-important critical moments, athletes cannot reliably take advantage of it on their way to glory, gold, or other rewards, to say nothing of that place in history.

There are several reasons why we don't understand the underlying mechanisms, cognitive or neural, of autotelic experiences. Even compared to other altered states of consciousness that are equally difficult to nail down in terms of neurocognitive mechanisms—meditation, hypnosis, daydreaming, or the runner's high—flow states have escaped, in more ways than one, the attention of cognitive neuroscientists. The main reason for this oversight is perhaps the fact that the phenomenon is somewhat of a paradox and remains difficult to explain according to traditional theories of attention and mental effort for the simple reason that they assume that better performance, on any task, is associated with increased conscious effort allocated to that task. Theories of attention and action, such as those by Kahneman (1973) or Sanders (1997), assume that higher task demands require more effort, both objectively, in terms of caloric consumption by the brain, and subjectively, in terms of perceived mental effort. In flow, however, the opposite appears to be the case. Here the perceived mental effort decreases, sometimes to the point of utter effortlessness, yet such seemingly automatic action is associated with superior performance. In other words, increased task demands are met not by an increase in mental effort but by a decrease. In flow states, in fact, action seems to be entirely outside of conscious awareness—the experience is often described as if it happens by itself, without any effort at all. What, then, might explain how a decrease in mental effort, especially in terms of attentional resources (according to Kahneman and Sanders), improves task performance?

This chapter starts by summarizing previous work in the cognitive neurosciences that might account for this phenomenon. To understand the neurocognitive mechanisms underlying the flow state requires that we fully appreciate the fact that the brain runs two functionally and anatomically distinct information-processing systems, the explicit and implicit systems, and that we rigorously apply the flexibility–efficiency trade-off that exists between these two systems to the computational problem of skilled motor performance. In addition, the transient hypofrontality theory is briefly outlined, which can account for the phenomenological features of autotelic experiences, such as, for instance, the merging of awareness and action, the exclusion from consciousness of distractions, the loss of the sense of time passing, and the lack of worry of possible failure. These are all higher order metacognitive processes that require, in order to be subtracted from consciousness, the downregulation of brain regions, primarily in the prefrontal cortex, that play a key role in the computation of these higher order thoughts and feelings in the first place.

Finally, this chapter ends with a specific example from the sports sciences of how our understanding and appreciation of these mechanisms can inform training strategies to improve performance. To that end, we review the evidence linking perfectionism to success in competition. This is relevant because athletes who show negative perfectionist tendencies—that is, are overly self-critical, preoccupied with mistakes, and feel that a discrepancy exists between expectation and result—often fail to perform at their best. Their frequent inability to enter a state of effortless action, especially when the stakes are high, informs our understanding, in mechanistic terms, of how personality characteristics and individual differences influence the brain processes that control the execution of a skilled movement.

I Don't Know How to Do It, but My Body Does

A key to understanding the neurocognitive underpinnings of the flow state, its phenomenology included, arises from the well-known but apparently underappreciated distinction made between the explicit and implicit information-processing systems. Briefly, the brain operates two distinct information-processing systems to acquire, represent, and implement knowledge. The explicit system is rule-based, its content can be expressed by verbal communication, and it is tied to conscious awareness. In contrast, the implicit system is skill or experience based, its content is not verbalizable and can only be conveyed through task performance, and it is inaccessible to conscious awareness (Ashby and Casale 2002; Dienes and Perner 1999; Schacter and Bruckner 1998). Research on animals, patients with brain damage, and neuroimaging studies of healthy subjects have shown that these systems can be dissociated from each other functionally and anatomically (Schacter and Bruckner 1998; Squire 1992).

The explicit system is a sophisticated system that represents knowledge in a higher order format; that is, it represents additional information about the information, such as the fact that it contains the information it contains. This permits the information to be broadcast to a global work space, making it usable for other parts of the system. The complexity involved in organizing information in propositional and abstract terms is beyond any single brain structure's computational ability. Thus, the explicit system depends on several brain structures, each specialized in performing a particular step of information processing. Grossly oversimplified, the prefrontal cortex handles working memory, the hippocampus helps in the consolidation of that information, and permanent storage occurs in a plethora of cortical networks.

The implicit system is a more primitive and evolutionarily ancient system that does not form higher order representations. As a consequence, the explicit system, or any other functional system in the brain, does not know about knowledge imprinted in the implicit system, making it unavailable for representation in working memory and, thus, consciousness. For implicit knowledge to reach consciousness, it must first be explicated, which cannot proceed, due to its concrete-operational organization, through a bottom–up process. We must perform or execute implicit knowledge, which allows the explicit system to observe it and extract its essential components. Because the implicit system precludes metarepresentations, it is not burdened by the computational complexity that comes with higher order thought, and a single brain structure, such as the basal ganglia or cerebellum, can handle all information-processing steps (Dietrich 2004a). This makes knowledge execution in the system highly efficient and fast, albeit only to its specific application. Smooth sensorimotor integration leading to purposeful motion must occur in real time, and this is the domain of the implicit system, responding to environmental stimuli in a rapid and accurate manner (Dietrich 2004a).

This efficiency of implicit knowledge is paramount to motor skills because purposeful movement must occur in real time. As an example, consider the lightening-fast escape maneuvers of a squirrel. Lacking an overall strategy or plan, the squirrel gets to safety entirely by relying on moment-to-moment adjustments. Such smooth feedback-driven sensorimotor integration can produce extremely complex movement patterns that can serve an overall and/or higher goal (safety) yet require no more than the reaction to immediately preceding input. This is not unlike an outfielder trying to catch a fly ball. Starting with only a vague idea as to the ball's ultimate location, the player progressively approximates that location by continuously adjusting his or her movements based on updates of the ball's trajectory and speed as it approaches (McLeod et al. 2001). Because these are fluid situations occurring in real time, they require, first and foremost, efficiency. A system is most efficient if it represents knowledge in a fully implicit manner—that is, it codes the application of the knowledge within the procedure and refrains from buffering any other property of the information in a higher order representation. On the flip side, this setup is the reason why motor behavior must progress stepwise from immediately preceding input. The lack of metarepresentation precludes the system from calculating hypothetical future scenarios that would enable it to anticipate several steps in advance.

Framed in computational terms, it becomes clear why such metarepresentation is unattainable for movement. Even for squirrels, the number of possible next moves is so astronomically high that future projections would quickly multiply to infinity. Such a nonlinear calculation is unpredictable, rendering the calculation of hypothetical future scenarios useless. Accordingly, the combinatorial complexity of skilled movement, coupled with the real-time speed requirement of its production, make it impossible to micromanage such a system explicitly. However, the explicit system can exert influence by steering events toward a strange attractor. For instance, a tennis match is a dynamic system with two moving targets. Although moment-to-moment events are completely unpredictable, the explicit system might settle to one or more strange attractors, such as the opponent's weak backhand. The explicit system can guide motor output toward such a strange attractor as long as the attractor is of a complexity that does not challenge the capacity limit of working memory.

This flexibility–efficiency trade-off between the explicit and implicit systems is critical in understanding the control of skilled movement. The explicit system has evolved to increase cognitive flexibility but is limited, exactly because of its ability to deal with computational complexity, to tasks that must be solved outside real time and that can be broken up into chunks of complexity that do not exceed the capacity limit of working memory. Since this is not the case for skilled movement, the implicit system must handle real-time movements, which it does on a moment-by-moment basis (Dietrich 2004a). This is especially so for complex patterns that have been automated through hours of repetition. The more a motor skill is practiced and becomes habitual, a learning effect often known by the unfortunate misnomer muscle memory, the more the details of its execution come under the control of the implicit system in the basal ganglia, supplementary motor cortex, and lower brain centers in the brain stem (Jenkins et al. 1994).

Because a highly practiced skill is still performed by a conscious person, it is possible for the explicit system to partake in the skill's moment-to-moment execution. To stay with the example of tennis, this occurs when a player buffers any part of the game—consciously reflecting on the strokes, for instance—in a higher order representation and allows such analysis to guide movements. However, due to the explicit system's inefficiency and capacity limit, it should be obvious that any amount of transfer of the actual motor execution from implicit to explicit control gravely affects its quality. Indeed, it has been proposed that the degree of implicitness of motor competence is positively related to the quality of the performance (Dietrich 2004a).

Let's take a concrete example to illustrate the deleterious effect of such a transfer. A movement can be executed by the explicit system and/or the implicit system, but an explicit-predominant movement proceeds from a mental representation that is, for all we know, different in kind from one that is implicit predominant. Transferring the control of the motion from implicit to explicit has rather profound consequences for its speed and efficiency. Take Roger Federer's tennis serve, for instance, which, during competition, is entirely driven by his implicit system. None of the task's requirements are, presumably, explicit in consciousness as he performs the serve. To find out how much the explicit system actually knows about how to do a tennis serve, we can introduce a slight change. All we have to do is to ask Federer to perform the serve with his other arm. Now the explicit system must take over. The problem is that a tennis serve is too fast and too complicated to be executed by a mental representation that is general in nature and needs to apply its abstract knowledge, in real time no less, to a specific example. The resulting tennis serve would bear little resemblance to a world-class one, and neither would the brain activation.

In sum, the implicit system owes its efficiency and speed to the fact that it does not form costly higher order representations of its knowledge. This very feature, however, also limits its use to the specific application in which it is embedded. The explicit system owes its flexibility to exactly this abstract representational format, which is the very feature that limits its use for applications, such as skilled movements, where time is of the essence. Each system can have a representation of the task requirements, and there is, of course, a lot of anatomical cross-wiring, for various reasons, at several levels between these two systems, but their respective motor representations are still fundamentally different (Dietrich 2008), one being general, context independent (explicit), and the other specific and context dependent (implicit; Dietrich 2004a).

This allows us to look at the paradox of effortless performance from a different angle. Traditional models of attention have assumed that superior performance, in any task, is associated with increased attentional effort allocated to that task (Kahneman 1973; Sanders 1997). Experiments on experts—skilled athletes, in most cases—have shown that once a motor skill is perfected, directing attention to a motor task is detrimental to its execution (e.g., Beilock and Carr 2005; Ravizza 1977). Wulf and Lewthwaite (chapter 3, this volume) have also found that directing attention to the effect of an action increases performance, irrespective of skill level, but this is different from directing attention to the actual execution of the movement. This literature has broadly supported an inverse, instead of a linear, relationship between conscious attention to movement and performance (Fitts and Posner 1973). Indeed, recent computational models have shown that such an inverse relationship between focusing the mind on motor execution and actual motor execution is inherent in any dynamic system that operates with time-delayed feedback and is subjected to random perturbations (Milton et al., forthcoming; Insperger 2006). According to these models, optimal performance requires that an optimal amount of attention be allocated to a task, and the optimal amount of attention for an expert is, apparently, as little as possible, while the optimal amount of attention for a novice is, apparently, as much as possible.

Thus, optimal performance, by an expert, of a well-learned, real-time, sensorimotor integration task is associated with maximal implicitness of the task's execution. Put another way, effortless attention is an inherent feature of superior performance in such situations.

The computational perspective on the explicit–implicit distinction also accounts for some of the phenomenal features of the flow state. People have described these autotelic experiences, saying that action and awareness are merged, the surrounding events are excluded from consciousness, there is no worry of failure, the movements feel as if executed automatically, self-consciousness disappears, or the sense of time becomes distorted. These are all examples of metacognitive processes that require explicit, higher order processing. In other words, they are *about* the motor task. If any of these processes were activated and allowed to feed into the computation of the actual motor plan, the performance level would suffer due to the inherent loss of efficiency of applying general knowledge to a specific movement.

The flow experience, then, precipitates that those metacognitive processes are downregulated. This, as we will see in a later section, is easier for some people than for others. Given that the explicit system which computes such higher order thought is subserved by prefrontal regions, flow experiences must occur during a state of transient hypofrontality that can bring about the inhibition of the explicit system

(Dietrich 2003, 2004b, 2006). To see how this might take place, a brief, general overview of the transient hypofrontality theory (THT) might be helpful.

Transient Hypofrontality

The THT proposes a common neural mechanism for altered states of consciousness. The theory is explicitly based on functional neuroanatomy and views consciousness as composed of various attributes, such as self-reflection, attention, memory, perception, and arousal, which are ordered in a functional hierarchy with the frontal lobe necessary for the top attributes. Although this implies a holistic view in which the entire brain contributes to consciousness, it is evident that not all neural structures contribute equally to conscious experience. This layering concept localizes the most sophisticated levels of consciousness in the zenithal higher order structure: the prefrontal cortex. From such considerations, the THT of altered states of consciousness can be formulated, which attempts to unify all altered states into a single theoretical framework (Dietrich 2003, 2007).

Because the prefrontal cortex is the neural substrate of the topmost layers, any change to conscious experience should affect, first and foremost, this structure, followed by a progressive shutdown of brain areas that contribute more basic cognitive functions. Put another way, the highest layers of consciousness are most susceptible to change when brain activity changes. It follows from this "onion-peeling" principle, as we might call it, that higher cognitive processes such as working memory, sustained and directed attention, and temporal integration are compromised first when an alteration to mental status occurs. All altered states share phenomenological characteristics whose proper functions are regulated by the prefrontal cortex, such as time distortions, disinhibition from social norms, or a change in focused attention. This suggests that the neural mechanism common to all altered states is the transient downregulation of functional networks in the prefrontal cortex.

The reduction of specific contents of conscious experience is known as phenomenological subtraction. The deeper an altered state becomes, induced by the progressive downregulation of prefrontal regions, the more of those subtractions occur and people experience an ever greater departure from their normal phenomenology. In altered states that are characterized by severe prefrontal hypoactivity—various drug states such as those induced by LSD or PCP, for instance—this change results in an extraordinarily bizarre phenomenology—hallucinations and delusions, most prominently. In altered states that are characterized by less prefrontal hypoactivity, such as long-distance running, meditation, or hypnosis, the modification to consciousness is much more subtle. In any event, the idea is that an individual simply functions on the highest layer of phenomenological consciousness that remains fully operational.

A consequence of the THT is that full-fledged consciousness is the result of a fully operational brain. Thus, and despite popular belief to the contrary, default consciousness is the highest possible manifestation of consciousness, and all altered states represent, by virtue of being an alteration to a fully functional brain, a reduction in consciousness. Altered states of consciousness that are often presumed to be "higher" forms of consciousness, such as, for instance, transcendental meditation or the experiences reported after taking "mind-expanding" drugs, are therefore really "lower" states of consciousness, as they, functionally speaking, all reduce cognitive processes—attention, working memory, temporal integration, and so forth—that are associated with the highest forms of consciousness. This view is also in contrast to the theories of, for instance, William James (1890) and Charles Tart (1972), who maintained that normal consciousness is not qualitatively different from any other state of consciousness. It is difficult to imagine how "higher consciousness," whatever that might be, would look in terms of brain activity or feel in terms of phenomenology, but shouldn't it entail an enhancement of mental abilities ascribed to the prefrontal cortex rather than, as is the case in the above examples, their subtraction?

If all altered states share this common neural mechanism, why, then, does each feel unique? To anyone who frequents them, the experience of, say, hypnosis is unmistakably distinct from that of dreaming or meditation. How can we reconcile this with the proposal that prefrontal downregulation is the underlying cause for all altered states? A clue may be found in the induction procedure. There are several ways by which a change in mental status is achieved. We can use a variety of behavioral methods; for instance, we can take advantage of our ability to control executive attention, a method we use to enter the states of daydreaming, hypnosis, or meditation. This is also the route by which flow occurs—by a change in attentional focus. Alternatively, we can use our ability to engage in prolonged, rhythmic motion, such as running or dancing, to get into a trance state. One altered state, dreaming, we enter entirely involuntarily through a circadian rhythm controlled by the brain stem. And then there is the direct manipulation of neurotransmitter systems by taking psychoactive substances. It is almost certainly the case that these different techniques alter brain function in different ways, but the overall effect should, given the similarities in phenomenological subtractions, be the same. That is, according to the THT, mental functions computed at the level of the prefrontal cortex that comprise the top layers of consciousness are altered first, followed by a progressive downregulation of mental functions lower in the hierarchy. What accounts for the distinct experience of each state is that each induction method targets different sets of prefrontal networks which remove quite specific mental faculties from the conscious experience (Dietrich 2007).

Given the focus of this chapter on the experience of effortless action, especially in skilled motor performance during sports competition, we need to explore further the induction method that alters consciousness by using bodily motion, as it appears that this method changes overall brain function in a unique way. Complex locomotion, especially that involving large muscle groups, is an extremely demanding task in *computational* terms—that is, to be clear, for the brain, not the body. Movement has never been understood, certainly not in cognitive psychology, as a biocomputation of the highest order. And, if one continues to think, as is customary in many fields, that motor control is a minor part of the brain's daily chores, it will be difficult to understand the consequences of movement for all regions of the brain, including—or especially—those not directly involved in moving the body.

Thus, to help you along and make you more familiar with the seemingly counter-intuitive realities of a computational perspective, we provide you with a few intriguing facts designed, primarily, to help you with conceivability. These will then be followed by some of the empirical evidence showing that the simple act of, say, running activates vast areas of the brain and thus requires the redistribution of much of the brain's metabolic resources. For starters, consider artificial intelligence, a field in which motion is readily recognized as a huge computational problem. Human artificers have managed to make machines that beat you in chess in eight-and-a-half moves with half of their transistors unplugged; yet they can't make a robot that walks nicely on two feet, let alone one that does a slam dunk. It certainly isn't because they can't make the movable equipment—arms, legs, joints, and so on (the main problem seems to be balance—Kuo et al. 2005). The reason is that sensorimotor integration, in real time, requires an astronomical amount of number crunching. Even for the simple act of walking, the brain must control umpteen millions of muscle fibers to precise specification, with every twitch affecting the strength of the contraction of the next. This is computationally, and thus metabolically, very costly, even when the movement is controlled mostly by lower brain centers. Programming an analogous movement into a robot is a real headache and has yet to be done successfully (Kuo et al. 2005).

Next, consider the brain's motor system. By simply listing the number of structures devoted to movement, you can get an appreciation of the complexity of moving the body around: primary motor cortex, secondary motor cortices (i.e. premotor and the supplementary motor area or SMA), basal ganglia, the motor thalamus, cerebellum, red nucleus, substantia nigra, the massive pathway systems, and the motor neurons all along the spinal cord, among rather many others. This represents not just an enormous amount of brain volume but also a very high number, in percentage terms, of neurons. Why, for instance, does the cerebellum have more neurons than any other structure in the brain, including *the entire cerebral cortex*?! What do you think all these neurons do? They do the brunt of the work of fine motor coordination, the very thing for which brute computational power is so critically needed. And then, let's not forget, movement occurs through space, so any motor activity must integrate sensory processes, and soon we are at yet another, nearly equally long list of brain structures that must be activated in order to process the relevant perceptual information during exercise. However, we haven't yet finished because there are also those nuclei mediating autonomic regulation such as, for instance, in the hypothalamus, the reticular formation, and many nuclei in the medulla. At this point, all the person is doing with all this massive brain activation, I remind you, is simply moving!

Let's try a third, slightly more sensitive intriguing fact. The male human brain is about 150 grams heavier than the female one. It is universally understood that this is due to the male's higher body mass. However, let's stop for a moment and think about what this really means. The male brain has, on average, 8% to 10% more brain mass only so that he can throw around what amounts to no more than a few more kilos of body mass. It is hard to believe that moving around a few more kilos of muscle and bone requires so much additional brain mass, especially in percentage terms, given that we are animals who are already copiously equipped with neuronal goo. But it does.

Finally, also keep in mind that the human motor system is more highly evolved than that of other animals. Animals with much smaller brains can produce very complex movements, movements we find extraordinary, but what they cannot do is learn motor acts for which they are counterprepared, let alone to such a state of perfection the way humans can. Just think of our ability to swim butterfly, pole vault, or play the violin, all actions we are not evolved to perform. Try teaching these to a chimp.

Such crutches for the imagination are not, of course, sound evidence as far as neuroscience goes; we simply offer them here to help you start thinking of motion in terms of its neural costs. We must understand movement as a computational issue that requires vast amounts of resources *for the brain*, even if the movement is well automated and thus driven mostly by the implicit system and/or lower brain centers.

All this is underscored by the evidence. Several techniques such as ^{133}Xe washout, radioactive microsphere, and autoradiography, as well as EEG, single photon emission computed tomography (SPECT), near infrared spectroscopy (NIRS), and positron-emission tomography (PET), have been used to measure brain activity during exercise. Converging evidence from these studies indicates that exercise is associated with profound regional changes in motor, sensory, and autonomic regions of the brain (Holschneider et al. 2003; Sokoloff 1991; Vissing et al. 1996). Physical exercise, then, requires massive neural activation in a large number of neural structures across the entire brain. It follows that prolonged movement, especially involving the entire body, requires the *sustained* activation of a large amount of neural tissue (Dietrich 2006).

Yet during exercise, global blood flow to the brain, along with global cerebral metabolism and uptake of oxygen, remains constant (Ide and Secher 2000; Sokoloff 1992) or increases slightly (Secher et al. 2008). Thus, contrary to expectation, there is no evidence to suggest that the brain is the recipient of significant additional resources to offset the seemingly enormous metabolic demands that physical activity appears to require. So what, then, are the consequences for the brain of such a computationally demanding task without getting any, or only little, additional fuel?

The central idea behind the THT is that the brain, in order to drive the bodily motion, is forced to make profound changes to the way it allocates its metabolic resources. This follows from the facts that the brain has a finite energy supply and that movement is an extremely demanding task in *computational* terms. In other words, as the brain sustains, during exercise, the massive and widespread neural activation that runs motor units, assimilates sensory inputs, and coordinates autonomic regulation, it must take metabolic resources, given their limited availability, away from neural structures whose functions are not critically needed at the time, which are, according to the THT, areas of the prefrontal cortex and, perhaps, limbic system (Dietrich 2003, 2004a, 2006). This is supported by several lines of evidence in animals and humans using a multitude of techniques, such as EEG, event-related potentials, SPECT, PET, NIRS, radioactive microsphere, single-cell recording, autoradiography as well as several cognitive studies (Dietrich 2006, Dietrich and Sparling 2004, Tashiro et al. 2001).

The THT, then, simply proposes the following. When the brain is under strain, it starts to reserve its limited metabolic resources for operations that are critically needed at the time, which results, necessarily, in the downregulation of neural structures whose computations are not critical for the task at hand. As the strain continues, the brain is forced to go ever deeper into safe mode, and the THT simply suggests that this decline progresses from brain areas supporting the highest cognitive functions, down the functional hierarchy, one phenomenological subtraction at a time, to brain areas supporting the most basic ones. Thus, the prefrontal cortex, being the most zenithal higher order structure, is the first region whose computations are no longer supported sufficiently to reach muscles or consciousness. Prolonged physical exercise is simply one example of a general neural mechanism that accounts for the phenomenology of all altered states of consciousness, as, indeed, the experience of timelessness, living in the here and now, reduced awareness of one's surroundings, and diminished analytical or attentional capacities—all subtle modifications of mental functions that are typically ascribed to the prefrontal cortex—is consistent with a state of frontal hypofunction (Dietrich 2003). In most conditions or techniques producing alterations to mental function, prefrontal hypoactivity is all that is necessary, hence the name of the theory. However, if the strain continues, and, to stay with exercise, the person keeps on moving, say, running the 135-mile Badwater Ultramarathon, he or she is, sooner or later, reduced—in an onion-peeling principle of sorts—to his or her most basic mental capabilities.

This means, to come back to the topic of effortless attention and action, that sustained physical motion of the kind we see in many sports is particularly good at engendering flow states. The metabolic stress the brain is under during prolonged bodily motion causes a cascading ripple effect throughout the brain that facilitates—necessitates, actually—the inhibition of mental processes in the explicit system, which are, to repeat, supported primarily by computations in the prefrontal cortex. This eliminates metacognitive processes about the task more readily than when the exclusion of the same processes from phenomenal consciousness must be achieved purely by the muscle of focused attention, as is the case, for instance, in golf, meditation, or playing a musical instrument (see Dietrich 2003). In other words, a powerful physiological mechanism helps the person keep distractions out, which makes the task readily controlled by the implicit system, as it should be anyway for optimal execution. It is perhaps this additional mechanism that explains why autotelic experiences seem to be reported nowhere as frequently as in the arena of sports and exercise.

Perfectionism

A well-learned task is performed best if it is controlled maximally by the implicit system. As explained above, any interference by the explicit system in the actual execution of the task is detrimental to quality. Such interference can take many forms. While some people must guard against letting their explicit knowledge of the actual movement infringe on the action, others seem to be having more problems with avoiding buffering in working memory factors completely extraneous to the movement, such as worry about failure, and letting these considerations enter the motor plan execution. It is the latter kind of problem that interests us next.

Perfectionism is the disposition to regard anything short of perfection as unacceptable. Individuals possessing high levels of this trait strive for flawlessness and set excessively high standards for performance. This is accompanied by a pronounced tendency to be overly critical in evaluating their own behavior (Flett and Hewitt 2002; Frost et al. 1990). How perfectionism affects performance is highly debated in the sports sciences (Hall 2006). While some researchers have identified perfectionism as a positive trait that makes Olympic champions (Gould et al. 2002), others see perfectionism as a maladaptive trait that undermines, rather than helps, athletic performance (Flett and Hewitt 2005; Hall 2006).

The weight of the evidence suggests, however, that two major dimensions of perfectionism must be differentiated (Enns and Cox 2002; Stoeber and Otto 2006). The first dimension has been described as positive-striving perfectionism (Frost et al. 1993) and captures those facets of perfectionism that relate to perfectionist strivings, such as having high personal standards, setting exact benchmarks for one's performance, and having the drive to achieve excellence. This dimension is positively correlated with indicators of good adjustment, such as positive affect, endurance, and high academic performance (Bieling et al. 2003; Frost et al. 1993; Stumpf and Parker 2000).

The other, second, dimension has been described as self-critical perfectionism (Dunkley et al. 2003) and captures those facets of perfectionism that relate to critical self-evaluations of one's performance, such as constant concern over mistakes and negative feelings when expectations do not match results. This dimension is positively correlated with indicators of maladjustment, such as depression, stress, and anxiety (Stoeber and Otto 2006).

In sport and exercise psychology, the differentiation between positive-striving perfectionism and self-critical perfectionism is crucial because the evidence supporting perfectionism as detrimental to performance (Flett and Hewitt 2005; Hall 2006) is true only for those aspects of perfectionism associated with the self-critical dimension of perfectionism. This is not necessarily the case for those aspects that are associated with the positive-striving dimension, which is linked with positive characteristics and outcomes.

One example of this is the athlete burnout syndrome. Comparing a group of junior elite tennis players with high levels of burnout with a control group on dimensions of perfectionism, Gould and colleagues (2002) found that burned-out players reported higher levels of concern over mistakes and lower personal standards than players in the control group. As concern over mistakes is a core aspect of the self-critical dimension of perfectionism and personal standards a core aspect of the positive-striving dimension, the results suggest that only self-critical perfectionism is related to athlete burnout, while positive-striving perfectionism is not.

A similar conclusion can be drawn out from the link between perfectionism and goal orientation in athletes. Two cognitive dispositions can be distinguished here: task orientation and ego orientation (Duda and Nicholls 1992). Task orientation refers to an athlete's emphasis on mastering a task and on improving ability. This makes task orientation a good predictor of athletic development. In contrast, ego orientation represents an emphasis on outperforming others and demonstrating one's ability in comparison to others. While this emphasis may, on the one hand, motivate athletes to perform at a higher level, it may also increase the fear of failure or other such negative, external factors (Elliot 1997). A strong and exclusive ego orientation must be regarded as a potential risk to competitive performance (Ommundsen 2004).

Yet another example of this interaction is the link between perfectionism and competitive anxiety (Frost and Henderson 1991; Hall et al. 1998; Koivula et al. 2002; Stoeber et al. 2007). In general, perfectionism in athletes has been associated with higher levels of competitive anxiety (Flett and Hewitt 2005; Hall 2006). Upon closer inspection, however, only two tendencies, the concern over mistakes and negative reactions to imperfection, show a consistent relationship with high competitive anxiety as well as low self-confidence in competitions. Other aspects of perfectionism do not show this pattern (Stoeber et al. 2007). For instance, personal goals and striving for perfection show an inverse relationship with competitive anxiety as well as a positive relationship with self-confidence. These findings suggest that athletes who strive for perfection without preoccupying themselves with failure or mistakes experience lower levels of anxiety and higher levels of confidence in competitions (Craft et al. 2003).

Before these data are brought into contact, in the last section, with the neurocognitive mechanism described earlier, one final example underscores the necessity to differentiate between these two dimensions of perfectionism. The research described above relied on expert athletes. However, during the acquisition of a new task, everyone is a novice, and a new task is not yet controlled by the implicit system because it has not had the exposure to the task demands to build a mental representation of the task's requirements, which can only be done by doing the task. As a consequence, extraneous factors cannot as readily mess up performance because the acquisition of a new motor task is heavily controlled by the explicit system anyway. In this situation, some positive perfectionist tendencies can be outright beneficial. For instance, Stoll and colleagues (2008) investigated how perfectionism relates to performance by measuring performance increments over a series of trials in a new basketball training task. Two aspects of the perfectionism dimension were distinguished: (1) striving for perfection, representing the positive dimension, and (2) negative reactions to imperfection, representinging the self-critical dimension. The findings showed that perfectionism is not necessarily a maladaptive characteristic that undermines sport performance. Rather, during the learning of a new task, perfectionism may enhance performance and lead to greater progress over time. This meshes well with results from other fields in which striving for perfection is associated with higher grades in students (Bieling et al. 2003; Stoeber and Rambow 2007) and better predicts results on aptitude tests (Stoeber and Kersting 2007). Again, the critical factor here seems to be that such tests, like novel tasks, are handled mostly by the explicit system, and interference by external factors, especially when they relate to positive striving and motivation, can enhance task performance, which is less likely for tasks that have been automated and thus executed implicitly.

Conclusion

How, then, can we approach these findings in the context of the neural and cognitive explanations of effortless action? How do such personality characteristics facilitate or inhibit a state of effortless attention during sports competition? During the performance of a well-learned task, optimal performance is associated with maximal implicitness (Dietrich 2004a). It should follow from this that any interference by explicit mental processes in implicitly controlled action decreases the smoothness of the performance. This straightforward conclusion must be mitigated, however, for the simple reason that there are a whole host of other factors that also figure in the equation here, most prominently individual differences in working memory capacity (Beilock and Carr 2005) and how well the task difficulty matches the skill level. For the purpose of this chapter, however, we will pursue a different variable.

To that end, let's consider once more the characteristics that constitute autotelic experiences. The defining feature of this multifaceted phenomenon is the intrinsically rewarding experiential involvement in moment-to-moment activity that is accompanied by a positive experience quality. This main feature is responsible for further features, such as the merging of action and awareness, the altered sense of time, and the sense of control. In this state of effortless attention, the individual is completely absorbed in the activity itself and is no longer aware of being separate from the action. Although the person feels fully in control, things seem to flow as if fully automatic.

Some flow characteristics directly influence performance because they are inherently performance enhancing. For example, high concentration and a sense of control have often been cited as facilitators of performance (Eklund 1994, 1996; Williams and Krane 1997). Flow, then, is a functional state that facilitates performance directly. Indirect influences on performance have also been suggested. These involve the rewarding effects of the positive experience that accompanies flow. According to Csikszentmihalyi and colleagues (2005, 602), this positive experience is a powerful motivating force: "When individuals are fully involved in an activity, they tend to find the activity enjoyable and intrinsically rewarding." Because activities that have been rewarded are more likely to be performed again, the experience of effortlessly performing a task is likely to have a strong positive effect on motivation. As the activity is performed again, individuals find greater challenges in the task, which results in further skill development, more competence, and greater performance (Csikszentmihalyi and Larson 1987; Wong and Csikszentmihalyi 1991). In other words, the positive experience quality of flow has an indirect effect on performance by first influencing the motivation to perform the activity again, which then, in a second step, directly enhances the performance itself.

We can now attempt to disentangle a bit the effects of perfectionist tendencies on effortless action. Individuals with a negative disposition of perfectionism are extrinsically motivated, and their action is driven by a focus on outcomes and consequences (worrying about failure, ruminating, outperforming others, comparing themselves with others, experiencing competitive anxiety, having negative reactions to imperfection, being overly self-critical, etc.). Because these are factors external to the actual action, they, when activated, interfere with the quality of the execution. In other words, they are metacognitive processes that are computed in the explicit system and, as such, undermine the smoothness of a well-learned, implicitly controlled sensorimotor task.

Individuals with a positive disposition of perfectionism, on the other hand, are intrinsically motivated, and their action is driven by a focus not on ultimate objectives but rather on the quality of the activity itself. Because these cognitive processes concern themselves with the action per se, they cannot be regarded as metacognitive processes *about* the task. In other words, these cognitive processes are not superfluous to the motor plan; indeed, they represent the very features that characterize the flow state. As such, they do not decrease the efficiency of a skilled movement and might even have the potential, in a novel task that is not yet implicitly executed, to enhance its acquisition.

For individuals with negative perfectionist thinking patterns, the problem is compounded by the following set of circumstances. As explained above, to enter a state of flow, explicit metacognitive processes have to be inhibited. This necessitates that the prefrontal cortex, which plays a key role in their computation, be downregulated. This, however, is more difficult for individuals with perfectionist personality traits because they have, as it is, an elevated baseline activity in prefrontal regions compared to others (Damasio et al. 2000; Baxter 1990), which is, of course, the very source of their perfectionist thinking habits. In people suffering from full-blown obsessive–compulsive disorder, this hyperactivity in prefrontal regions is particularly pronounced (Baxter 1990). This excessive prefrontal activity acts like a double whammy for them. First, they have a longer way to go, so to speak, before the prefrontal cortex is sufficiently inhibited to keep thoughts extraneous to the activity from entering consciousness. Second, in those all important moments during competition, when everything is on the line, the predisposition to worry, to be anxious, and to think about the possible consequences of one's action is more readily reactivated because these are just the situations that tend to generate such thoughts in the first place.

References

Ashby, G. F., and M. B. Casale. 2002. The cognitive neuroscience of implicit category learning. In *Attention and implicit learning*, ed. L. Jiménez. Amsterdam: John Benjamins, 109–141.

Baxter, L. R. 1990. Brain imaging as a tool in establishing a theory of brain pathology in obsessive–compulsive disorder. *J. Clin. Psychiatry* 51 (Suppl.):22–25.

Beilock, S. L., and T. H. Carr. 2005. When high-powered people fail: Working memory and "choking under pressure." *Math Psychological Science* 16:101–105.

Bieling, P. J., A. Israeli, J. Smith, and M. M. Antony. 2003. Making the grade: The behavioral consequences of perfectionism in the classroom. *Pers. Individ. Dif.* 35:163–178.

Csikszentmihalyi, M., and R. Larson. 1987. Validity and reliability of the Experience Sampling Method. *J. Nerv. Ment. Dis.* 175:526–536.

Csikszentmihalyi, M., S. Abuhamdeh, and J. Nakamura. 2005. Flow. In *Handbook of competence and motivation*, ed. A. J. Elliot and C. S. Dweck. New York: Guilford, 598–608.

Craft, L. L., T. M. Magyar, B. J. Becker, and D. L. Feltz. 2003. The relationship between the Competitive State Anxiety Inventory–2 and sport performance: A meta-analysis. *J. Sport Exerc. Psychol.* 25:44–65.

Damasio, A. R., T. J. Grabowski, A. Bechera, H. Damasio, L. L. B. Ponto, J. Parvizi, and R. D. Hichwa. 2000. Subcortical and cortical brain activity during the feeling of self-generated emotions. *Nat. Neurosci.* 3:1049–1056.

Dietrich, A. 2003. Functional neuroanatomy of altered states of consciousness: The transient hypofrontality hypothesis. *Conscious. Cogn.* 12:231–256.

Dietrich, A. 2004a. Neurocognitive mechanisms underlying the experience of flow. *Conscious. Cogn.* 13:746–761.

Dietrich, A. 2004b. The cognitive neuroscience of creativity. *Psychon. Bull. Rev.* 11:1011–1026.

Dietrich, A. 2006. Transient hypofrontality as a mechanism for the psychological effects of exercise. *Psychiatry Res.* 145:79–83.

Dietrich, A. 2007. *Introduction to consciousness*. London: Palgrave Macmillan.

Dietrich, A. 2008. Imaging the imagination: The trouble with motor imagery. *Methods* 45:319–324.

Dietrich, A., and P. B. Sparling. 2004. Endurance exercise selectively impairs prefrontal-dependent cognition. *Brain Cogn.* 55:516–524.

Dienes, Z., and J. Perner. 1999. A theory of implicit and explicit knowledge. *Behav. Brain Sci.* 5:735–808.

Duda, J. L., and J. G. Nicholls. 1992. Dimensions of achievement motivation in schoolwork and sport. *J. Educ. Psychol.* 84:290–299.

Dunkley, D. M., D. C. Zuroff, and K. R. Blankstein. 2003. Self-critical perfectionism and daily affect: Dispositional and situational influences on stress and coping. *J. Pers. Soc. Psychol.* 84:234–252.

Eklund, R. C. 1994. A season long investigation of competitive cognition in collegiate wrestlers. *Res. Q. Exerc. Sport* 65:169–183.

Eklund, R. C. 1996. Preparing to compete: A season-long investigation with collegiate wrestlers. *Sport Psychol.* 10:111–131.

Elliot, A. J. 1997. Integrating the "classic" and "contemporary" approaches to achievement motivation: A hierarchical model of approach and avoidance achievement motivation. In *Advances in motivation and achievement*. vol. 10. ed. P. Pintrich and M. Maehr. Greenwich, CT: JAI Press, 143–179.

Enns, M. W., and B. J. Cox. 2002. The nature and assessment of perfectionism: A critical analysis. In *Perfectionism: Theory, research, and treatment*, ed. G. L. Flett and P. L. Hewitt. Washington, DC: American Psychological Association, 33–62.

Fitts, P. M., and M. I. Posner. 1973. *Human performance*. London: Prentice-Hall.

Flett, G. L., and P. L. Hewitt. (2002). Perfectionism and maladjustment: An overview of theoretical, definitional, and treatment issues. In *Perfectionism: Theory, research, and treatment*, ed. G. L. Flett and P. L. Hewitt. Washington, DC: American Psychological Association, 5–13.

Flett, G. L., and P. L. Hewitt. 2005. The perils of perfectionism in sports and exercise. *Curr. Dir. Psychol. Sci.* 14:14–18.

Frost, R. O., R. G. Heimberg, C. S. Holt, J. I. Mattia, and A. L. Neubauer. 1993. A comparison of two measures of perfectionism. *Pers. Individ. Dif.* 14:119–126.

Frost, R. O., and K. J. Henderson. 1991. Perfectionism and reactions to athletic competition. *J. Sport Exerc. Psychol.* 13:323–335.

Frost, R. O., P. Marten, C. Lahart, and R. Rosenblate. 1990. The dimensions of perfectionism. *Cognit. Ther. Res.* 14:449–468.

Gould, D., K. Dieffenbach, and A. Moffett. 2002. Psychological characteristics and their development in Olympic champions. *J. Appl. Sport Psychol.* 14:172–204.

Hall, H. K. 2006. Perfectionism: A hallmark quality of world class performers, or a psychological impediment to athletic development? In *Essential processes for attaining peak performance*. vol. 1. ed. D. Hackfort and G. Tenenbaum. Oxford, UK: Meyer & Meyer, 178–211.

Hall, H. K., A. W. Kerr, and J. Matthews. 1998. Precompetitive anxiety in sport: The contribution of achievement goals and perfectionism. *J. Sport Exerc. Psychol.* 20:194–217.

Holschneider, D. P., J.-M. I. Maarek, J. Yang, J. Harimoto, and O. U. Scremin. 2003. Functional brain mapping in freely moving rats during treadmill walking. *J. Cereb. Blood Flow Metab.* 23:925–932.

Ide, K., and N. H. Secher. 2000. Cerebral blood flow and metabolism during exercise. *Prog. Neurobiol.* 61:397–414.

Insperger, T. 2006. Act-and-wait concept for time-continuous control systems with feedback delay. *IEEE Trans. Contr. Syst. Technol.* 14:974–977.

James, W. 1890. *Principles of psychology*. New York: Holt.

Jenkins, I. H., D. J. Brooks, P. D. Nixon, R. S. J. Frackowiak, and R. E. Passingham. 1994. Motor sequence learning: A study with positron emission tomography. *J. Neurosci.* 14:3775–3790.

Kahneman, D. 1973. *Attention and effort*. Englewood Cliffs, NJ: Prentice-Hall.

Koivula, N., P. Hassmén, and J. Fallby. 2002. Self-esteem and perfectionism in elite athletes: Effects on competitive anxiety and self-confidence. *Pers. Individ. Dif.* 32:865–875.

Kuo, A. D., J. M. Donelan, and A. Ruina. 2005. Energetic consequences of walking like an inverted pendulum: Step-to-step transitions. *Exerc. Sport Sci. Rev.* 33:88–97.

McLeod, P., N. Reed, and Z. Dienes. 2001. Towards a unified fielder theory: What we do not yet know about how people run to catch a ball. *J. Exp. Psychol. Hum. Percept. Perform.* 27:1347–1355.

Milton, J. G., J. L. Cabrera, and T. Ohira. Unstable dynamical systems: Delays, noise, and control. *Europhys. Lett.* Forthcoming.

Ommundsen, Y. 2004. Self-handicapping related to task and performance-approach and avoidance goals in physical education. *J. Appl. Sport Psychol.* 16:183–197.

Ravizza, K. 1977. Peak performances in sports. *J. Humanist. Psychol.* 4:35–40.

Sanders, A. F. 1997. A summary of resource theories from a behavioral perspective. *Biol. Psychol.* 45:5–18.

Schacter, D. L., and R. L. Bruckner. 1998. On the relationship among priming, conscious recollection, and intentional retrieval: Evidence from neuroimaging research. *Neurobiol. Learn. Mem.* 70:284–303.

Secher, N. H., T. Seifert, and J. J. Van Lieshout. 2008. Cerebral blood flow and metabolism during exercise: Implications for fatigue. *J. Appl. Physiol.* 104:306–314.

Squire, L. R. 1992. Memory and the hippocampus: A synthesis from findings with rats, monkeys and humans. *Psychol. Rev.* 99:195–231.

Sokoloff, L. 1991. Measurements of local cerebral glucose utilization and its relation to functional activity in the brain. *Adv. Exp. Med. Biol.* 291:21–42.

Sokoloff, L. 1992. The brain as a chemical machine. *Prog. Brain Res.* 94:19–33.

Stoeber, J., and M. Kersting. 2007. Perfectionism and aptitude test performance: Testees who strive for perfection achieve better test results. *Pers. Individ. Dif.* 42:1093–1103.

Stoeber, J., and K. Otto. 2006. Positive conceptions of perfectionism: Approaches, evidence, challenges. *Pers. Soc. Psychol. Rev.* 10:295–319.

Stoeber, J., K. Otto, E. Pescheck, C. Becker, and O. Stoll. 2007. Perfectionism and competitive anxiety in athletes: Differentiating striving for perfection and negative reactions to imperfection. *Pers. Individ. Dif.* 42:959–969.

Stoeber, J., and A. Rambow. 2007. Perfectionism in adolescent school students: Relations with motivation, achievement, and well-being. *Pers. Individ. Dif.* 42:1379–1389.

Stoll, O., A. Lau, and J. Stoeber. 2008. Perfectionism and performance in a new basketball training task: Does striving for perfection enhance or undermine performance? *Psychol. Sport Exerc.* 9:620–629.

Stumpf, H., and W. D. Parker. 2000. A hierarchical structural analysis of perfectionism and its relation to other personality characteristics. *Pers. Individ. Dif.* 28:837–852.

Tart, C. T. 1972. States of consciousness and state-specific sciences. *Science* 176:1203–1210.

Tashiro, M., M. Itoh, T. Fujimoto, T. Fujiwara, H. Ota, K. Kubota, M. Higuchi, et al. 2001. 18F-FDG PET mapping of regional brain activity in runners. *J. Sports Med. Phys. Fitness* 41:11–17.

Vissing, J., M. Anderson, and N. H. Diemer. 1996. Exercise-induced changes in local cerebral glucose utilization in the rat. *J. Cereb. Blood Flow Metab.* 16:729–736.

Williams, J. M., and V. Krane. 1997. Psychological characteristics of peak performance. In *Applied sport psychology: Personal growth to peak performance*. vol. 3. ed. J. M. Williams. Mountain View, CA: Mayfield, 158–170.

Wong, M. M., and M. Csikszentmihalyi. 1991. Motivation and academic achievement: The effects of flow on performance effects of personality traits and the quality of experience. *J. Pers.* 59:539–574.

8 Effortless Attention in Everyday Life: A Systematic Phenomenology

Mihaly Csikszentmihalyi and Jeanne Nakamura

All living organisms, in order to continue living, must have access to information relevant to their survival. A mouse that cannot sense the vicinity of a cat, or find its way to food or to a mate, is less likely to survive and to pass on its genes compared to the mouse that can. In a sense, evolution is a process that selects organisms increasingly more proficient at securing and using information (Campbell 1960; Miller 1983; Tooby and Cosmides 1990, 408).

In most species, organisms respond to information according to biologically predetermined stimulus–response pathways. Our dog, much as we love him, does not seem very interested in the world—except for those aspects of it that natural selection has programmed him to attend to, such as other dogs, certain smells, food, his human companions; to the rest he is rather indifferent. Primates, and humans especially, move in a much broader world of information—less intense, perhaps, but more diverse.

At the human level, because of the rapid changes that cultural development has made possible, biological evolution has not had a chance to select stimulus–response pathways that ensure a more likely survival. For instance, hunter–gatherers may have prospered more if their attention was constantly flitting to provide information about potential prey or predators. However, with the advent of agriculture, this way of attending would have been less advantageous; farmers with more focused attention were more likely to prosper. Finally, in our "knowledge economy," the way of getting information that benefited hunter–gatherers might be diagnosed as attention deficit disorder.

Lacking a stable measure of what a human must do to achieve adaptive success, biological selection has to rely on a different strategy for determining how and what is worth attending to. Instead of built-in instructions as to what is interesting, organisms that live in rapidly changing environments must develop an independent information-processing organ. The human brain has provided one such evolutionary solution. To work well in a diversified *Umwelt*, the brain needs to be fairly flexible and, to a certain extent, must have its own self-directing capacity. Too much built-in software would be a detriment under the rapidly changing conditions typical of lifestyles based on culture—that is, on knowledge and technologies that change at rates many orders of magnitude faster than our physical environment and biology change.

Attention as Psychological Resource

The mechanism by which our brain registers information is what we call attention. The topic of attention is one of the oldest in psychology, starting with the writings of William James (1890) or Henri Ribot (1890).

All through the long history of research on attention, on one topic most writers agree, namely, that attention is in scarce supply. The implications of this fact are vividly expressed by the evolutionary psychologists Tooby and Cosmides: "Animals subsist on information. The single most limiting resource to reproduction is not food or safety or access to mates, but what makes them each possible: The information required for making adaptive behavioral choices" (Tooby and Cosmides 1990, 408). Of course, it is not just the presence or absence of information that matters but the organism's ability to recognize the relevant information before making an "adaptive behavioral choice." And this ability, in turn, depends on how the organism uses attention.

In the present context we focus on *experience* itself, defined as *what appears in consciousness when a person turns attention to the quality and texture of his or her momentary situation in the world*. In order to experience joy, love, sadness, awe, or understanding, we must allocate some attention to these internal states.

Because attention is needed to have experiences in the first place, and to accomplish any task that requires conscious effort, we may think of it as *psychic capacity*, a definition that highlights the narrow bandwidth of information we can process at any given time, or as *psychic energy*, a definition that foregrounds the fact that any complex mental "work" requires the input of attention. These definitions are only heuristic; they remind us that attention is a limited resource that must be allocated to becoming aware of what we experience at the moment and to determine what experiences we shall have in the future, thus shaping the quality of our lives.

Therefore, we might say that attention holds the key to experience and, hence, to life as we subjectively know it. William James (1890) recognized that the quality of our lives depends on the habits of attention we cultivate moment by moment. In a similar vein, approximately 100 years later Daniel Kahneman could write: "An assessment of a person's objective happiness over a period of time can be derived from a dense record of the quality of experience at each point" (Kahneman 1999, 3).

The Uses of Attention and the Quality of Life

The way we use attention is not only a means for having various experiences but can also become an experience in itself. For instance, various forms of meditation and religious practice rely on focusing attention in ways that produce ecstasy, or at least a sense of serene contentment. In contrast, diffuse attention—what the Buddhists call the *monkey mind*, jumping from one stimulus to the other—is generally experienced as a less desirable state.

In our studies of "optimal experience," one fundamental finding has been that when people enjoy most what they are doing—from playing music to playing chess, from reading good books to having a good conversation, from working their best to trying to beat their own record in sport—they report a state of effortless concentration so deep that they lose their sense of time, of themselves, of their problems. We have called this the "flow experience," because so many of the persons describing it used the analogy of being effortlessly carried by a current—of being in a flow (Csikszentmihalyi 1975, 1990; Nakamura and Csikszentmihalyi 2002).

Later studies have confirmed that the flow experience is reported in similar terms by persons from different cultures, ages, and educational levels, even though the activities that produce the experience may be very diverse, from meditating on religious texts to racing motorcycles (Csikszentmihalyi and Csikszentmihalyi 1988). Apparently, our brain experiences a complete involvement that requires intense concentration of attention as rewarding. The evolutionary benefits of such an adaptation seem obvious and will not be elaborated here. Rather, we shall present some results concerning the prevalence of effortless attention in everyday life, as well as the conditions in which such experiences occur and their psychological consequences.

The Use of Attention in Daily Life

Before presenting some of the findings, it will be necessary to provide a brief description of how the data were collected. For several decades now, our laboratory (first at the University of Chicago, then at Claremont Graduate University) has pioneered a method for studying the quality of subjective experience by means of what we have come to call the Experience Sampling Method (ESM). This method consists of triggering subjective self-reports about eight times a day at random moments, usually for a week, using a pager or other signaling device. Participants in the study report their experience at the time of the signals, using various scales and open-ended items, assessing such aspects as the level of concentration, the ease of concentrating, and the moods felt at the moment. Each participant completes about 40 to 50 reports during the week, which provide a dense account of their subjective states as they were involved in the business of living—working, eating, watching TV, being with partners and children, and so on. Our lab has collected several hundred thousand such reports, and investigators around the world have added at least the same number.

Although the data generated by this method consist of subjective self-reports and hence, are open to all sorts of potential distortions, it turns out that what people say they do and feel during the day appears to be an accurate reflection of their actual experiences. Without going here into the psychometric properties of this method, which have been described elsewhere (Csikszentmihalyi and Larson 1987; Hektner, Schmidt, and Csikszentmihalyi 2006), it suffices to say that it both confirms the obvious (e.g., that people concentrate more at work or whenever the perceived challenges are greater) and reveals the unexpected (e.g., how easily attention turns to painful feelings when it is not engaged by outside stimuli).

Attention not only is a scarce resource but is one that ordinarily takes effort to use. In everyday life, people report concentrating their attention mostly when they are working or when they are under stress. Samuel Johnson's quip: "…when a man knows he is to be hanged in a fortnight, it concentrates his mind wonderfully" (Boswell 1873, 338) is not far off the mark: Most of the time the content of consciousness moves hither and yon, thus requiring effort to keep it stable and focused.

The findings reported here are based on an ESM study of several hundred middle and high school students from around the United States—the Sloan Study of Youth and Social Development (Csikszentmihalyi and Schneider 2000), which provides a unique window on attentional states in daily life. Adolescents are a particularly informative and important population for study because they are still in the process of forming attentional habits and their days are spent in settings that vary widely in their attentional demands.

We are used to thinking of focused attention—full concentration—as a signature or essential quality of the optimal flow state. However, when a distinction is made between times when we feel that we must work at concentrating and times when we feel that our attention is held by an activity easily, without strain and felt expenditure of effort, we realize that the definition of this signature quality of the flow state can be made more precise. There is a phenomenological difference between subjective experience when full attention is effortful and when it is effortless, and we hypothesize that it is specifically the experience of complete but also *effortless* attention that is associated with being in the enjoyable state of flow.

The Sloan Study data let us compare the phenomenology of effortful and effortless attention in situ. This is because along with reporting other subjective states, the participants in the study responded to the following two items: (1) "How well were you concentrating?" (rated on a scale from 1, *not at all*, to 10, *very much*) and (2) "Was it hard to concentrate?" (rated on the same 1 to 10 scale, reverse scored as "ease of concentration" so that 10 indicates maximal ease).

In the analysis presented here, 858 teenagers reported both how intensely they felt they were concentrating and how easily they felt they were doing so, for a total of 25,948 different moments during an average week. Looking across all these occasions, the mean levels of subjective concentration and ease of concentration were both above their scale midpoints (mean concentration = 6.3, SD = 3.1; mean ease of concentration = 7.7, SD = 2.8). However, the relationship between the two conditions at this momentary level—the degree to which the two covaried within the sample of almost 26,000 occasions—was low and negative ($r = -.04$), reflecting a slight tendency for concentration to be harder at times when it is higher.

In the kind of ESM analyses to be reported, an individual's responses to an item are standardized prior to analysis; that is, the raw scores for the week are converted so that the mean of the person's responses to an item is 0 and the standard deviation is 1. One benefit of this transformation is greater ease of interpretation, in that a positive score indicates that the individual at that moment was above average for the week, and a negative score indicates that the individual was below average for the week. In order to identify moments of effortless and effortful attention, individuals' scores were standardized for the items, "How well were you concentrating?" and "Was it hard to concentrate?" The top third of the resulting z scores on the two items then were designated *high concentration* and *high ease of concentration*, respectively, while the bottom third were designated *low concentration* and *low ease of concentration*. When high concentration coincided with high ease of concentration for a response, it was classified as an instance of *effortless attention*; when concentration was rated high but ease of concentration low, it was treated as an instance of *effortful attention*.

Each time they were signaled, the teenagers rated the following dimensions of experience, which according to theory are simultaneously high in the optimal flow state: feeling involved (vs. detached), in control of the situation, clear (vs. confused), and self-conscious or embarrassed (reverse scored); they also provided responses on three indices of the "autotelic" (intrinsically rewarding) character of the experience: finding the activity interesting, wishing to be doing something else (reverse scored), and enjoying what they were doing.

According to theory, when challenges and skills are both above average and in balance, flow is more likely. In contrast, being overchallenged is associated with experiencing anxiety and being underchallenged is associated with feeling bored. Thus, four additional dimensions are of interest: participants' reports on the perceived challenges, their skills in the activity, and how relaxed (vs. tense) and excited (vs. bored) they felt at the time.

The quality of subjective experience is markedly different when attention is effortful compared to when it is effortless, and it is so in line with theoretical expectations. To examine the essential comparison, effortless and effortful attention were defined so that concentration is high in both conditions. The mean is a full standard deviation above average in both cases. However, the relative *ease* of this concentration—the effort that it is perceived to require—is on average two standard deviations apart in these two conditions, and this makes a dramatic difference in the teenagers' quality of experience. Each of the experiential dimensions associated in theory with the flow state is significantly higher under the condition of effortless attention than it is under the condition of effortful attention.

Furthermore, teenagers are significantly more relaxed rather than tense, yet also more excited rather than bored, when attention is effortless than when it is effortful. Finally, the students report the most favorable combination of challenges and skills when their concentration feels high but effortless. Much higher perceived challenges, in conjunction with average levels of skill, are associated with effortful attention. It is not surprising, therefore, that adolescents report that they are succeeding at times of effortless attention compared to when attention is high but effortful.

These stark differences in the quality of experience derive in part from differences in the kinds of activities associated with effortless and effortful attention. Examining first the teenagers' reports of what they are doing in moments of effortless as contrasted with effortful attention, a much greater proportion of the former moments arise in activities that feel freely chosen ("wanted to," 46.9% vs. 30.9%) and a much smaller proportion in activities that feel obligatory ("had to," 29.6% vs. 49.0%). These differences appear to reflect differences in the objective activities that the teenagers report under the two attentional conditions. When attention is effortless, the teenagers are less likely to be engaged in "productive" activities, primarily comprising *schoolwork* (34.2% vs. 51.3%); they are more likely to be engaged in *leisure* (45.1% vs. 33.5%). Thus, it is possible that the differences in the quality of experience derive from these differences in the proportions of time spent in productive versus leisure activities.

To address this possibility, we examined the experiences of effortless and effortful attention but looking only at the times when the teenagers were engaged in schoolwork (see table 8.1). It is evident that academic activities depress teenagers' moods. For example, when doing schoolwork, the average levels of intrinsic motivation (wish to be doing the activity) and enjoyment do not get better than average in either attentional condition. Nevertheless, when doing schoolwork and using their attention effortlessly, students feel more involved, in control, unselfconscious, and even more interested than they do on average across all activities for the week.

The ESM results confirm the fact that, on the whole, when people say they are concentrating their attention and also report that doing so is hard, their quality of experience is generally unpleasant. This is in part due to the fact that high levels of concentration typically occur when a person is doing something that he or she would not voluntarily do absent constraints. For young people, this occurs in school, often in math or science classes, when taking tests or doing difficult homework. Adults also

Table 8.1
Average quality of schoolwork experience when attention is effortful versus effortless

	Effortful		Effortless			
	M	SD	M	SD	t^1	df
Concentration	0.93	0.41	0.84	0.40		
Ease of concentration	−1.24	0.79	0.61	0.32		
Involved	0.08	0.70	0.14	0.69	1.46	494
Interested	−0.09	0.75	0.13	0.73	4.98***	520
In control	−0.11	0.77	0.13	0.72	5.36***	522
Not self-conscious	−0.15	0.85	0.15	0.63	5.86***	467
Clear (vs. confused)	−0.24	0.84	0.06	0.76	5.78***	496
Excited (vs. bored)	−0.25	0.75	−0.09	0.69	3.69***	495
Relaxed (vs. tense)	−0.23	0.85	−0.06	0.75	3.44**	490
Wish to do [i.e., intrinsic motivation]	−0.53	0.70	−0.26	0.69	6.30***	520
Enjoyment	−0.49	0.77	−0.21	0.75	6.61***	527

[1]Paired t tests; ***$p < .001$, **$p < .01$. Scores were standardized on individual means for the week across all activities. For the analyses restricted to schoolwork experiences, effortful attention is defined by above average concentration and below average ease of concentration, and effortless attention is defined by above average concentration and ease of concentration.

focus their attention most often under compulsory situations—high-stakes situations at work. Not surprisingly, such moments are not particularly happy ones. The focus of attention is maintained with effort, and it would be relaxed immediately if the external conditions were to change. Just visualize what happens to a classroom full of schoolchildren after the bell sounds: The silent concentration on their books explodes into a riot of liberation.

Yet the direct relationship between concentration and effort does not always hold. In fact, some of the highest levels of concentration are reported to be effortless. These tend to be moments when a person is engaged in a freely chosen activity—a hobby, a sport, playing music or chess, and so on. However, often people also report such effortless concentration in their work, or when studying, or when engaged in other activities that are normally experienced as obligatory and, therefore, effortful.

These moments are relatively rare but tend to be intense and memorable. They are the moments when we feel most fully alive, engaged with the world, and in harmony with ourselves. As the data reported in this chapter suggest, when concentration is effortless, even difficult and obligatory activities—such as studying—can become significantly more enjoyable. Clearly, our quality of life could be greatly enhanced by learning to devote effortless attention to what we need to do in everyday life.

Effortless Attention and Automaticity

It is sometimes assumed that effortless attention is achieved through developing habitual patterns of response to certain stimuli. Automatic behavior saves effort by producing a learned response to a given range of stimuli without having to process a great deal of information. A chess player who has memorized dozens of openings can afford to move his or her pieces with a minimum of thinking at the start of a game, because the player is familiar with all the options and their consequences.

While flow experiences often rely on automating sequences of action, this happens so as to allow *more* attention to be invested in the essential aspects of the activity. For instance, surgeons—who generally consider their work as being their deepest source of enjoyment—automate as many of the routine aspects of an operation as possible, so as to be able to notice any unusual response in the patient's body that might require an emergency intervention.

Thus, effortless attention is rarely fully automatic. In fact, it is likely that in flow a person is more open, more alert and flexible, *within the attentional structure of the activity*. In other words, surgeons doing a difficult operation may indeed be unaware for hours of how tired and hungry they are, or what time of day it is, because this information is irrelevant to the operation, and they need all the attention they have to cope with the task at hand. While all the extraneous information disappears from awareness, their attention is processing a stream of complex and often ambiguous information that must be interpreted online, so to speak, and that must be responded to appropriately.

Some Conditions for Effortless Attention

Thus, effortless attention does not mean that the person is paying less attention—to the contrary, the amount of information being processed is usually higher than at other moments. What makes the experience effortless is not that there is *less* attention expended but that investing *more* attention is experienced as requiring less effort.

How is this possible? Here again, the phenomenology of the flow experience can help explain this paradox. The conditions that make flow possible are also the ones that facilitate effortless attention. Studies of flow during the past three decades have found that three conditions are generally present in activities that result in deep and effortless concentration. These are: clear goals, immediate feedback, and a balance between opportunities for action and the individual's ability to act.

The first of these conditions, *clear goals*, is one that is often misunderstood. What counts is not that the overall goal of the activity be clear but rather that the activity present a clear goal for the next step in the action sequence, and then the next, on and on, until the final goal is reached. What focuses a mountain climber's mind is not the intention of reaching the top of the climb but the problem of which outcrop of rock to use for the next handhold and where to place next the toe of the boot. It is not winning the game that keeps the chess player's attention—that is too distant a goal—but the next move, and a few after that. What focuses the pianist's mind is not the goal of finishing the piece, but the chord, the next cluster of notes to be played just right.

However, clear goals do not sustain attention unless the activity also provides *immediate feedback*. If, for instance, I cannot hear myself playing the piano, my attention is likely to wander. Why pay attention if I can't tell what difference my actions make? Of course, one can train oneself to act without feedback, but acting in this way requires ongoing effort—whereas if we get information about how well we are doing, attention will focus spontaneously on the ongoing action. The feedback to the climber is seeing that every move brings him or her higher up the rock face; the feedback to the chess player is seeing the strategic position on the board change as a result of the last move. Surgeons say that one reason operations are so enjoyable is that they provide immediate information—if there is blood in the cavity, the scalpel must have slipped.

Finally, attention is most focused when environmental challenges are in balance with the person's skills. In this condition every additional investment of attention can have the most immediate effect. If the challenges are much greater than the skills (e.g., 60/40), the person either has to produce an extraordinary effort to overcome the odds or will give up trying and, thus, diffuses attention. In the opposite case, where skills outweigh challenges, the person does not need to pay much attention and gets distracted for that reason. Phenomenologically, these three alternatives translate into flow, anxiety, and boredom, respectively. Experiences that one believes are in the neighborhood of a 50/50 balance are experienced as enjoyable; the other two are stressful.

This analysis might be seen to suggest that effortless attention, which momentarily is the most rewarding condition we can experience, is the result of conditions outside the person: the clarity of goals, the availability of feedback, the ratio of challenges to skills. However, environmental conditions rarely affect us directly. It is the *Umwelt* cocreated through our experiences that screens external stimuli and transforms them into information. For a person who has never climbed, Yosemite's wonderful slabs of rock are just featureless granite, at most to be admired on an aesthetic level. For an expert climber, they present innumerable challenges, and goals that result in years of preparation, and then an ascent that might provide the high point of a lifetime.

Similarly, a man lying with his ribcage open to reveal his inner organs will just freak out most people, whereas the same view will mobilize a surgeon's skills to start a challenging operation. Thus, it would be absurdly reductionistic to claim that effortless attention is caused by external events—unless we take into account the more important contribution of the person's prepared mind as well.

Can Effortless Attention Be Enhanced?

If effortless attention improves the quality of everyday experience as much as our studies suggest, it would seem that increasing its frequency should become one of the main paths to a better life. There are two kinds of approaches to enhancing effortless attention. Neither one is easy, but both have promise for those who are determined to follow them.

The first approach is what we might call the *direct path* to effortless attention. It consists in any of a variety of mental disciplines, ranging from Zen Buddhist practices to mindfulness meditation, that were developed in the Far East over the centuries and are now pursued all around the world. These approaches have the advantage of providing viable methods for focusing attention, and disciplines for controlling it. Although at first requiring great effort, with continued practice these direct methods become relatively effortless (Brown and Ryan 2003).

The downside of the direct path is that it risks taking over the person's entire supply of attentional energy. Instead of being a means to an end, control of attention may become the very goal of existence. A person who learns to live in a more or less continuous state of effortless attention is likely to have a very high quality of experience. However, one might question whether such a life would be meaningful in the long run if all the person achieved was a detached serenity of experience.

The second, or *indirect path*, focuses on doing something as well as possible and producing the serenity of effortless attention as an indirect consequence. People who love what they are doing, who are interested and involved in their work or their hobby, get the domain-specific benefits that meditation provides without directly trying.

Of course, the indirect path can also lead nowhere: If a person dedicates his or her life to mastering a trivial task, the resulting life will be trivial, too. Effortless attention will improve the quality of experience but not necessarily its value. Whether one invests attention directly or indirectly, it is the object of attention that determines whether one's life is meaningful or not.

References

Boswell, J. 1873. *The life of Samuel Johnson, LL.D.* Ed. W. Wallace. Edinburgh: William P. Nimmo.

Brown, K. W., and R. M. Ryan. 2003. The benefits of being present: Mindfulness and its role in psychological well-being. *J. Pers. Soc. Psychol.* 84:822–848.

Campbell, D. 1960. Blind variation and selective retention in creative thought as in other knowledge processes. In *The Philosophy of Karl Popper*, ed. P. A. Schlipp. La Salle, IL: Open Court.

Csikszentmihalyi, M. 1975. *Beyond boredom and anxiety: The play experience in work and games*. San Francisco: Jossey-Bass.

Csikszentmihalyi, M. 1990. *Flow: The psychology of optimal experience*. New York: HarperCollins.

Csikszentmihalyi, M., and I. S. Csikszentmihalyi, eds. 1988. *Optimal experience: Psychological studies of flow in consciousness*. New York: Cambridge University Press.

Csikszentmihalyi, M., and R. Larson. 1987. Validity and reliability of the Experience Sampling Method. *J. Nerv. Ment. Dis.* 175:526–536.

Csikszentmihalyi, M., and B. Schneider. 2000. *Becoming adult: How teenagers prepare for the world of work*. New York: Basic Books.

Hektner, J., J. Schmidt, and M. Csikszentmihalyi. 2006. *Experience Sampling Method: Measuring the quality of everyday life*. Thousand Oaks, CA: Sage.

James, W. 1890. *Principles of psychology*. New York: Holt.

Kahneman, D. 1999. Objective happiness. In *Well-being: The foundations of hedonic psychology*, ed. D. Kahneman, E. Diener, and N. Schwartz. New York: Russell Sage, 3–25.

Miller, G. A. 1983. *Informavore*. Ed. F. Machlup and U. Mansfield. New York: Wiley.

Nakamura, J., and M. Csikszentmihalyi. 2002. The concept of flow. In *Handbook of positive psychology*, ed. C. R. Snyder and S. J. Lopez. New York: Oxford University Press, 89–105.

Ribot, T. A. 1890. *The psychology of attention*. Chicago: Open Court.

Tooby, J., and L. Cosmides. 1990. The past explains the present: Emotional adaptations and the structure of ancestral environments. *Ethol. Sociobiol.* 11:375–424.

9 Developing an Experimental Induction of Flow: Effortless Action in the Lab

Arlen C. Moller, Brian P. Meier, and Robert D. Wall

Intuitively, one might presume that the more challenging an activity, the more effort will be exerted. That is, an easy task is often assumed to require less effort relative to an otherwise comparable yet more difficult task. However, despite its intuitive appeal, anecdotal reports and evidence from correlational research on subjective experience do not uniformly affirm this basic and intuitive principle. Sometimes, it seems, greater challenge results in less subjective effort and resulting self-regulatory fatigue. For instance, Kubey and Csikszentmihalyi (1990; also see Csikszentmihalyi and Kubey 1981) have reported that although participants found watching television less challenging than reading, reading resulted in significantly higher feelings of potency (i.e., greater alertness, more strength, and less passivity).

Anecdotally, people report that when they are optimally challenged, as when immersed in creating a work of art or dancing fluidly across a stage, the experience can feel as though it requires no effort at all. Professional basketball player Pat Garrity describes an experience wherein "the ball feels so light, and your shots are *effortless* [italics added]" ("How It Feels to Be on Fire," 2005). Csikszentmihalyi and colleagues (Csikszentmihalyi 1975, 1990; Nakamura and Csikszentmihalyi 2002) have identified this subjective experience as *flow* and defined it as an optimal state in which one's skills are matched to the challenges demanded by a given activity. According to Nakamura and Csikszentmihalyi (2002), there are at least six aspects that characterize the flow state: (1) intense and focused concentration on the task at hand; (2) a merging of action and awareness; (3) loss of reflective self-consciousness, (4) elevated sense of control or self-efficacy, (5) distorted perception of time (typically, a reflective sense that time passed more quickly than normal), and (6) autotelic or intrinsic motivation; the activity or process itself is perceived as rewarding for its own sake.

One of the interesting features of the research literature on flow is that, despite over 30 years of empirical attention, nearly all of the research done to this point has been correlational in nature (Csikszentmihalyi 1975; Keller and Bless 2008). Historically, the concept of flow originated from observational and interview-based research on the creative process (Getzel and Csikszentmihalyi 1976). Csikszentmihalyi observed that when artists were painting most effectively, they seemed to enter a state of mind that allowed them to focus deeply on their work while ignoring hunger, fatigue, and discomfort. These intense periods of creative production were described as highly enjoyable and subjectively effortless, in the sense that the artists' energy seemed to flow forth without requiring force of will or exertion.

In the years since, the flow concept has been elaborated extensively using primarily a variety of correlational methods. In particular, in the 1980s and 1990s the Experience Sampling Method became a widely employed tool for studying the flow state in naturalistic contexts (Csikszentmihalyi and Csikszentmihalyi 1988; Inghilleri 1999; Massimini and Carli 1988; Massimini and Delle Fave 2000). This approach involves providing participants with pagers or handheld devices that randomly beep several times a day over the course of several weeks. When paged, participants are asked to report on their experiences at that moment. This methodology provides a detailed examination of people's everyday thoughts, feelings, and behavior, as well as the factors that precede and follow such experiences. Research employing this method in a variety of contexts (e.g., aesthetic, athletic, and academic), with both children and adults, has helped to refine a model of flow, identifying its antecedents and consequences. Indeed, the flow concept has proven to be a robust and generative one. However, the heavy reliance on correlational methods has long been a shortcoming of the flow research literature. Related weaknesses include unresolved questions about causality and the direction of relations observed between flow and other contextual and person-level variables (Spencer, Zanna, and Fong 2005). For example, it would be incorrect to assume from correlation data that an optimal degree of challenge is causally related to the experience of flow (although this is a common assumption), as it could reasonably be the case that some third variable is causally influencing both perception of optimal challenge and flow in similar directions. Furthermore, as psychology increasingly turns its attention as a field toward understanding the neural underpinnings of intrapsychic phenomena, the demand for reliable experimental induction methods for studying flow has increased. While it is infeasible, at the moment, to attach a high-resolution brain scanner—for example, functional magnetic resonance imaging (fMRI) technology—to an athlete or artist's head and have him or her wander around until an episode of flow sets in, a widely applicable flow manipulation would facilitate significant advancement in terms of exploring the neuroscience of flow.

Thus, the advantages of exploring the flow concept using experimental methods are clear and numerous, yet the lack of experimental methodology in this literature is not accidental. Unfortunately, for a variety of reasons, inducing flow under controlled lab conditions has proven difficult. To paraphrase the pioneering flow researcher Mihalyi Csikszentmihalyi, trying to induce flow in the lab is a bit like trying to make someone relax in a dentist's chair (M. Csikszentmihalyi, personal communication,

August 17, 2007). While it is certainly possible, the task is far from easy, as the cold laboratory context often seems less than conducive, and the flow experience can be elusive, even under seemingly optimal conditions. Nevertheless, recently a small group of researchers from a number of independent laboratories have accepted this challenge and begun the process of developing the first experimental procedures for inducing flow (Cabo, Kleiman, McCauley, and Parks 2004; Engeser and Rheinberg 2008; Keller and Bless 2008; Moller, Csikszentmihalyi, Nakamura, and Deci 2007; Parks and Victor 2006; Rheinberg and Vollmeyer 2003). The primary focus of this chapter will be to explore the complexities inherent to this task and to examine the cutting-edge findings that are emerging, as well as to offer insight into future directions for this research and speculate on how existing approaches might be improved upon.

Experimentally Inducing Flow

Csikszentmihalyi and colleagues (Csikszentmihalyi, Abuhamdeh, and Nakamura 2005; Nakamura and Csikszentmihalyi 2002) have identified two basic conditions that are correlated with a flow state. The first condition, as noted above, concerns *a perception* that the challenges of a task are well matched to one's capacities; when the demands of a task require one to stretch or extend existing skills, entering into flow becomes more likely. A second condition concerns the structure of a task. People tend to enter into flow more easily when a task has clear proximal goals and offers immediate informational feedback on one's progress (Csikszentmihalyi and Rathunde 1993). These two categories of contextual factors identified by Csikzentmihalyi and colleagues' flow model have been the basis from which several attempts at experimentally inducing flow have been designed. We explore these factors, as well as several additional contextual factors, including task importance, autonomy, and varieties of distraction.

Balancing Challenge and Skill

The most popular approach that has been used for inducing flow in the lab has involved manipulating the difficulty level of simple videogames (Cabo et al. 2004; Engeser and Rheinberg 2008; Keller and Bless 2008; Moller et al. 2007; Parks and Victor 2006; Rheinberg and Vollmeyer 2003). To the best of our knowledge, the earliest studies to employ this strategy were conducted by Rheinberg and Vollmeyer (2003). Two different videogames were used: in the first study, a game called Roboguard; in the second study, a game called Pac-Man. In the Roboguard game, players moved a spaceship on the computer screen, trying to avoid a collision with either enemy rockets or meteors. In the Pac-Man game, players moved a yellow mouth on the computer screen, trying to "eat" as many dots as possible while avoiding ghosts. In each case, the difficulty level of the game was varied through the amount of obstacles (enemy rockets and meteors in Roboguard; ghosts in Pac-Man) and how quickly these obstacles were moving (game speed). In both studies, within-participant designs were employed, such that each participant played a game at three different levels of difficulty: very easy, optimal, and very difficult. Each session included five trials, each trial lasting for five minutes, in the following sequence: optimal, difficult, optimal, easy, and optimal. After each trial, participants complicated a Flow Short Scale questionnaire, which included subscales assessing task fluency and absorption (Rheinberg, Vollmeyer, and Engeser, 2002, 2003). The results were consistent across the two studies: Participants reported significantly greater flow (task fluency and absorption) in the optimal trials relative to the very easy and very difficult trials.

Since these early studies by Rheinberg and Vollmeyer (2003), there have been a number of follow-up attempts made at perfecting an experimental induction of flow using simple videogames—in particular, versions of the internationally popular videogame Tetris (Cabo et al. 2004; Keller and Bless 2008; Moller et al. 2007; Parks and Victor 2006). This game involves manipulating geometric objects falling vertically from the top of a computer screen. Participants rotate these objects with the goal being to make them fit together so as to create complete lines, which then disappear and earn the participant points. This computer-based activity has proven particularly suitable to the demands of experimental designs insofar as the level of difficulty can be adjusted based on a single and easily quantifiable dimension of the game—that is, the speed at which the objects are falling from the top of the screen.

Cabo et al. (2004) examined the relationship between mood and flow by experimentally inducing positive and negative moods in participants and then measuring levels of flow experienced while playing Tetris. In this case, the level of difficulty was a function of participants' ongoing performance (i.e., game speed increased if participants performed well). The authors found that negative mood inhibited the experience of flow while playing Tetris, but positive mood did not significantly promote it. This pattern was later replicated by Parks and Victor (2006), again using Tetris to induce flow in the lab.

Keller and Bless (2008) have published the most extensive validation of an experimental flow induction to date, again using a version of the Tetris computer game. In this case, Keller and Bless used a between-participants design, contrasting three experimental conditions, which they labeled boredom, adaptive playing mode, and overload. The three conditions differed in several ways in addition to game speed (or difficulty). In the boredom condition, the geometric objects fell at a very slow rate, regardless of the player's performance, and the player had no option (see below) available to accelerate the falling speed of the objects at will. In the adaptive (flow) condition, the speed at which the geometric objects fell adapted to the player's performance. All the participants assigned to the adaptive condition began the game with geometric objects falling at a medium rate. If and when the player successfully created five lines

Developing an Experimental Induction of Flow 195

or more (using a minimal number of 30 consecutive objects), the speed was automatically increased by one step. If and when the player accomplished only three lines or fewer (using a maximal number of 30 consecutive objects), the speed was decreased by one step. In addition, participants in the adaptive condition were given the option to press the down arrow key to increase the speed of a dropping object. In the overload condition, objects initially started falling at a relatively rapid rate, and the speed was increased to an even faster rate if the player managed to fill five lines. Thus, the three conditions differed in terms of (1) the speed the game was initially set at, (2) access to a tool for speeding up game play, and (3) whether game speed adapted to performance.

After playing Tetris for a period of eight minutes, participants completed several measures designed to assess different dimensions of flow, including perception of time, perceived control, involvement–enjoyment, and perceived fit of skills and task demands. Across two studies, Keller and Bless (2008) found that participants in the adaptive playing mode (flow) condition performed better (i.e., number of lines completed), perceived that they were playing for less time, perceived greater control, reported greater involvement–enjoyment, and reported greater fit between their skills and the demands of the task relative to the boredom and overload conditions. There were no significant differences found between participants in the boredom and overload conditions with respect to any of these five outcomes.

The work by Keller and Bless (2008) represented an important and significant advance toward developing a reliable induction procedure for inducing flow experimentally; however, this is not to say that the procedure could not be improved. One drawback to their study is that the induction procedure included several confounded factors that varied across conditions, namely, the speed the game was initially set at, access to a tool for speeding up game play, and whether game speed adapted to performance.

Yet another experimental induction procedure using a variation of Tetris was developed by Moller et al. (2007). This induction procedure differed from the Keller and Bless (2008) approach in two important ways. First, across three conditions—underwhelming, optimal (flow), and overwhelming—just one dimension was varied, namely, game speed (i.e., task difficulty). Second, while all previous attempts at using videogames to induce flow set different levels of difficulty across conditions relative to an average player's ability (at least with regard to the speed set at the game's onset), Moller et al. set the different levels of difficulty across conditions relative to each individual player's baseline ability. In other words, in this case, the challenge–skill balance was individually calibrated in all three experimental conditions.

In the first phase (i.e., the calibration phase) of their study, Moller et al. (2007) had all participants play Tetris for six minutes under conditions that closely resembled the adaptive playing mode condition used by Keller and Bless (2008; i.e., game speed could increase or decrease based on participants' performance). Relative to players' performance during the calibration phase, each player was then assigned a game speed that would represent an optimal level of difficulty or challenge. Next, participants were randomly assigned to one of three experimental conditions: underwhelming, optimal (flow), or overwhelming. In the second phase of the study participants played Tetris for six minutes with the game speed fixed (no longer changing based on performance). The fixed game speed during the second phase of the study was either (1) one-third the rate of that participant's individually calibrated optimal level (underwhelming), (2) at his or her optimal level (optimal challenge), or (3) three times the rate of the participant's individually calibrated optimal level (overwhelming). None of the participants were given an option to accelerate the falling speed of the objects. Balance between challenge and skill was the sole factor varied by condition.

After playing the second game of Tetris, participants completed several self-report measures related to flow experience while playing, including: the Flow State Scale—2 (FSS–2; Jackson and Eklund 2002) and a measure of interest–enjoyment (McAuley, Duncan, and Tammen 1989). The FSS–2 is a 36-item measure that has nine subscales (4 items per subscale), mapping onto various aspects of the flow experience: (1) challenge–skill balance, (2) action–awareness merging, (3) clear goals, (4) unambiguous feedback, (5) concentration on task, (6) sense of control, (7) loss of self-consciousness, (8) time transformation, and (9) autotelic experience. As predicted, participants assigned to the optimal challenge condition reported experiencing significantly greater overall or composite flow and interest–enjoyment for the activity relative to the underwhelming and overwhelming conditions. They also reported significantly greater balance between challenge and skill and greater autotelic experience relative to those in the two comparison conditions. Further, those in the optimal challenge condition reported significantly higher levels of concentration relative to the underwhelming condition but no difference relative to the overwhelming condition, and significantly greater sense of control relative to those in the overwhelming condition but no difference relative to those in the underwhelming condition. However, not all subscales from the FSS–2 were significantly related to the experimental condition. The relations between experimental condition and action–awareness merging, clarity of goals, ambiguity of feedback, self-consciousness, and time transformation were all nonsignificant.

Although manipulating the balance between challenge and skill has now been shown to be a reasonably successful approach toward inducing flow, it is important to note that many authors have acknowledged that this factor *alone* cannot be expected to reliably induce flow (Keller and Bless 2008; Moller et al. 2007). We next consider additional factors that may contribute to inducing the flow experience.

Task Instrumentality

Recently, research by Engeser and Rheinberg (2008) has begun to explore the potential for task instrumentality (or extrinsic utility) to moderate the well-established relation between difficulty–skill balance and the experience of flow. Specifically, across three studies, the authors found support for their assertion that a match between difficulty and skill was most relevant when the instrumentality of the task was low (e.g., during a game of Pac-Man in study 2). During an activity with higher instrumentality (e.g., an obligatory statistics course, in study 1), high levels of flow were experienced even when skills were greater than perceived difficulty. Based on these findings, the authors recommend exercising additional caution with regard to equating difficulty–skill balance with flow. A further recommendation that can be extrapolated from this research is that experimental induction procedures which focus on manipulating the balance between task difficulty and skill (e.g., Keller and Bless 2008; Moller et al. 2007) might be improved by explicitly downplaying the extrinsic instrumentality of the activity. For example, making extrinsic rewards (like money or course credit) contingent on participants' performance may increase instrumentality yet undermine flow when difficulty and skill are evenly matched. Thus, features like performance-contingent rewards should be downplayed or eliminated from experimental flow inductions.

Task Structure: Clarity of Goals and Feedback

In comparison to experimentally manipulating the balance between challenge and skill, the issue of experimentally manipulating aspects of task structure, including goal clarity and informational feedback, has been relatively neglected. The single published study to have directly explored this factor experimentally was conducted by Mannell and Bradley (1986). In this experiment, participants were asked to manipulate blocks in order to replicate a geometric pattern from memory. In the low-structure condition, after a brief demonstration, participants were simply told to take several cards with patterns printed on them (number unspecified) and to work until time was called. In the high-structure condition, participants were given a set number of cards (four), and a set of scoring guidelines that they might consider in creating their patterns. However, participants in both conditions were told that it did not matter how well they performed and that no score would be recorded. The results confirmed that participants in the high-structure condition reported significantly greater psychological involvement and flow.

Thus, the empirical literature suggests that task structure, specifically clarity of goals, may be an important contextual feature to consider when designing an experimental flow induction procedure. Certainly, the activities that have been used for inducing flow in past research (e.g., Tetris, Pac-Man, Roboguard) have included a medium to relatively high degree of task structure, in the sense that the standards for good performance are made clear in the instructions. However, given the paucity of research on task structure and flow, more work has to be done, especially in terms of exploring the upper limits of this contextual factor—that is, in tasks that are so highly structured that the range of appropriate action is severely restricted. This issue seems especially relevant, given the significant literature and historical roots linking the experience of flow to creative expression (Csikszentmihalyi 1975; Csikszentmihalyi et al. 2005; Nakamura and Csikszentmihalyi 2002). At some point, the level of structure, in terms of goal clarity, may begin to limit the range of potential action, thereby restricting creativity and the accompanying experience of flow. Thus, just as the relation between challenge and flow is understood to be curvilinear (i.e., challenge increases flow, but only until skill is approximately equal to challenge; as challenge becomes greater than skill, flow decreases; Csikszentmihalyi et al. 2005), so too may be the relation between structure and flow. This, however, remains a speculative hypothesis to be tested by future research.

Autonomy Support at the Context Level
In addition to optimal challenge and task structure, the degree to which an induction procedure supports versus thwarts autonomy may be an important factor. One characteristic aspect of the flow experience involves autotelic or intrinsic motivation; that is, flow experiences are motivated by the reward inherent in performing the task itself as opposed to some extrinsic reward or punishment. The research literature on intrinsic motivation—in particular, self-determination theory—has long recognized the importance of supporting people's psychological need for autonomy (Deci, Koestner, and Ryan 1999; Deci and Moller 2005; Deci and Ryan 1985). Autonomy, as defined by self-determination theory, involves the experience of freely endorsing one's action without feeling coerced by any internal or external pressures. Providing an autonomy-supportive context in the lab would involve using such strategies as (1) providing a rationale which conveys why it is personally meaningful to do the activity effectively, (2) acknowledging people's feelings about the activity, and (3) using language that conveys choice rather than control. For example, participants might be told a fictitious cover story suggesting that Tetris is a form of cognitive exercise shown to improve problem-solving ability after playing (i.e., rationale). The experimenter might be instructed to ask for participants' feelings about Tetris and to use language that emphasizes choice (e.g., "can," "may," or "if you like") as opposed to control (e.g., "must" or "have to"). Experimenters may also emphasize the fact that participation in the study is voluntary.

Each of these strategies designed to support autonomy should not be considered antithetical in any way to efforts toward providing a high degree of task structure, as autonomy and structure are conceptually independent. Mannell and Bradley (1986) experimentally manipulated both objective freedom of choice and task structure independently. High-choice participants were told that the senior author was allowing the experimenter to ask them to try one of several games, and it was stressed that the participants did not have to play and that they had a choice of games or could sit and read. By contrast, participants in the low-choice condition were told that they were required to play and that the experimenter was sorry he could not allow them to sit and read or to have a choice of games. The results confirmed that participants in the high-choice condition experienced greater task absorption and flow relative to those in the low-choice condition.

Minimizing Distractions
One general category of contextual factors relevant for facilitating flow in the lab involves eliminating task-irrelevant stimuli that may be distracting. One form of distraction involves stimuli that enhance reflective self-awareness. As noted above, loss of reflective self-consciousness has been identified as a defining feature of the flow experience (Jackson and Eklund 2002; Nakamura and Csikszentmihalyi 2002). Thus, it follows straightforwardly that researchers interested in inducing flow should take every step to eliminate stimuli known to increase reflective self-awareness. This includes removing mirrors and cameras from the lab (Wicklund and Duval 1971; Plant and Ryan 1985) as well as removing any audience from the flow induction context, including the experimenter (Carver and Scheier 1978; Lepper and Green 1975). If the flow-inducing activity does not require interpersonal interaction, then other people are extrinsic distractions, likely to inhibit the experience of flow.

One particular aspect of interpersonal context that deserves greater empirical attention involves the role of competition in either facilitating or inhibiting the experience of flow. Although many prototypic examples of flow, especially in sport, often involve direct competition, there is reason to exercise caution and consider the possibility that sometimes competition may, in fact, be a form of distraction and thus inhibit the experience of flow. A number of studies have now demonstrated that direct competition has the potential to undermine intrinsic motivation (Deci, Betley, Kahle, Abrams, and Porac 1981; Reeve and Deci 1996; Vansteenkiste and Deci 2003). The issue is a complex one, insofar as direct face-to-face competition can offer excellent online informational feedback about one's performance; and informational feedback is an aspect of task structure, which has been shown to facilitate flow (Csikszentmihalyi and Rathunde 1993; Mannell and Bradley 1986). However, while the informational aspects of direct face-to-face competition may facilitate flow, the extrinsic aspects of competition—in particular, competition for an extrinsic reward—are very likely to be distracting from the task itself, and thus not conducive to the kind of task absorption characteristic of flow. Based on our understanding of these two competing forces that accompany competition, we can offer two recommendations. First, competition with an unseen opponent should almost certainly be eliminated from any procedure designed to experimentally induce flow, because making the opponent remote eliminates the beneficial opportunities for online, informational feedback. Second, if and when competition is a necessary component of an activity, the competition itself should be de-emphasized, and the use of tangible, competitively contingent rewards should be avoided, as these features of the activity have the potential to be distracting as well as controlling (Vansteenkiste and Deci 2003).

Person-Level Moderators of Flow Induction

Given that we understand the flow experience to be an elusive one, when researchers bring participants into the lab with the intention of inducing flow, it may prove useful to consider the person-level characteristics of their sample. Specifically, the empirical literature has identified a number of personality traits that may interact with contextual factors in producing flow.

One trait that has received recent attention in the flow literature is action orientation and, more specifically, the volatility–persistence component of action orientation (Keller and Bless 2008). This personality variable reflects the ability to stay in an action-oriented mode while engaged in a task, to maintain focused attention on an activity, and to persevere until a task is finished (Diefendorff, Hall, Lord, and Strean 2000; Kuhl 1994). Keller and Bless (2008) found a significant interaction between action orientation and their experimental manipulation of the skills–demand balance, such that those participants who were lower in action orientation (higher volatility, lower in persistence) were less sensitive to the compatibility of skills and task demands. Specifically, within the experimental condition designed to represent an optimal challenge, action-state orientation was positively related to involvement and enjoyment during the Tetris game. Keller and Bless surmised that the volatility–persistence component of action orientation was positively related to flow given that this trait contributes to one's readiness to experience deep involvement during task engagement. The action-orientation trait has also been shown to moderate the depleting impact of tasks that require high cognitive demands (Jostmann and Koole 2007). Thus, it may be that those high in action orientation are able to experience a demanding task as less *effortful* by virtue of more readily experiencing flow while engaged in such an activity.

Another person-level factor with significant implications for designing sample-appropriate experimental inductions of flow involves individual differences in achievement motivation. Engeser and Rheinberg (2008, study 1) assessed both implicit and explicit achievement motivation, including hope for success and fear of failure, and found that achievement motivation moderated the relation between difficulty–skill balance and flow during an obligatory course in statistics. Specifically, those higher in implicit hope of success reported experiencing greater flow when there was balance between difficulty and skill. However, the reverse pattern was found for explicit fear of failure, such that those participants higher in explicit fear of failure reported experiencing less flow when there was balance between difficulty and skill. The data suggest that for those high in explicit fear of failure, having skills that exceed difficulty may be more conducive to experiencing flow, while balance is potentially threatening and thus less conducive to flow. This line of research has important implications for designing experimental inductions of flow which extend beyond tailoring induction procedures to individuals or characteristics of a sample. Although hope for success and fear of failure are operationalized as person-level variables, the hierarchical model of achievement motivation posits that these person-level motive constructs exert their influence through the adoption of context-specific achievement goals (Elliot 1997; Elliot and Church 1997). Given that achievement goals have been shown to be effectively manipulated in experimental settings, it follows that future efforts to induce flow in the lab may incorporate goal settings that are approach related (as opposed to avoidance related) in orientation by emphasizing the potential for success. Lending further support for this recommendation are numerous studies that have already documented a positive relation between approach goals and intrinsic motivation—one aspect of the flow experience (Rawsthorne and Elliot 1999).

As a larger theme, we recommend that researchers interested in experimentally inducing flow also examine trait-level moderators, both for the sake of tailoring induction procedures to their specific sample and with an eye toward translating trait-level constructs into context-level manipulations whenever possible. We believe that this can be a generative approach toward further refining and advancing the experimental exploration of flow.

Conclusions

Although experimental procedures for inducing flow in the lab are still in the early stages of development, the existing empirical literature offers researchers significant promise. The research we review has typically manipulated the balance between demands and skills in an attempt to alter state levels of flow. While this methodology has been effective in manipulating some components of flow, we suggest that researchers continue to experimentally examine other aspects of the flow experience, such as task structure, importance, autonomy, and trait-level moderators. We hope that this chapter can help guide and inspire future investigations that will contribute to the next generation of flow research—in the lab, in the fMRI magnet, and beyond.

Acknowledgments

We gratefully acknowledge the support of the John Templeton Foundation and the Positive Psychology Institute at the University of Pennsylvania. We also wish to express our gratitude to Jessica Chen, Michelle Heroux, Darcy Johnson, Tony

Vargas, and J. Scott Willey for their important contributions collecting data reported herein.

References

Cabo, R., M. Kleiman, A. McCauley, and A. C. Parks. 2004, May. *Mood and flow*. Poster presented at the 16th Annual Convention of the American Psychological Society.

Carver, C. S., and M. F. Scheier. 1978. Self-focusing effects of dispositional self-consciousness, mirror presence, and audience presence. *J. Pers. Soc. Psychol.* 36:324–332. doi:10.1037/0022-3514.36.3.324

Csikszentmihalyi, M. 1975. *Beyond boredom and anxiety: The experience of play in work and games*. San Francisco: Jossey-Bass.

Csikszentmihalyi, M. 1990. *Flow: The psychology of optimal experience*. New York: HaperCollins.

Csikszentmihalyi, M., S. Abuhamdeh, and J. Nakamura. 2005. Flow. In *Handbook of competence motivation*, ed. A. Elliot and C. Dweck. New York: Plenum Press, 598–609.

Csikszentmihalyi, M., and Csikszentmihalyi, I. S., eds. 1988. *Optimal experience: Psychological studies of flow in consciousness*. New York: University of Cambridge Press.

Csikszentmihalyi, M., and R. Kubey. 1981. Television and the rest of life: A systematic comparison of subjective experience. *Public Opin. Q.* 45:317–328. doi:10.1086/268667

Csikszentmihalyi, M., and K. Rathunde. 1993. The measurement of flow in everyday life: Toward a theory of emergent motivation. In *Nebraska symposium on motivation*. vol. 40. *Developmental perspectives on motivation*, ed. J. J. Jacobs. Lincoln: University of Nebraska Press, 57–97.

Deci, E. L., G. Betley, J. Kahle, L. Abrams, and J. Porac. 1981. When trying to win: Competition and intrinsic motivation. *Pers. Soc. Psychol. Bull.* 7:79–83. doi:10.1177/014616728171012

Deci, E. L., R. Koestner, and R. M. Ryan. 1999. A meta-analytic review of experiments examining the effects of extrinsic rewards on intrinsic motivation. *Psychol. Bull.* 125:627–668. Medline:10589297 doi:10.1037/0033-2909.125.6.627

Deci, E. L., and A. C. Moller. 2005. The concept of competence: A starting place for understanding intrinsic motivation and self-determined extrinsic motivation. In *Handbook of competence motivation*, ed. A. Elliot and C. Dweck. New York: Plenum Press, 579–597.

Deci, E. L., and R. M. Ryan. 1985. *Intrinsic motivation and self-determination in human behavior*. New York: Plenum Press.

Diefendorff, J. M., R. J. Hall, R. G. Lord, and M. L. Strean. 2000. Action-state orientation: Construct validity of a revised measure and its relation to work-related variables. *J. Pers. Soc. Psychol.* 85:250–263.

Elliot, A. J. 1997. Integrating "classic" and "contemporary" approaches to achievement motivation: A hierarchical model of approach and avoidance achievement motivation. In *Advances in motivation and achievement*. vol. 10. ed. P. Pintrich and M. Maehr. Greenwich, CT: JAI Press, 143–179.

Elliot, A. J., and M. A. Church. 1997. A hierarchical model of approach and avoidance achievement motivation. *J. Pers. Soc. Psychol.* 72:218–232. doi:10.1037/0022-3514.72.1.218

Engeser, S., and F. Rheinberg. 2008. *Flow, performance and moderators of challenge–skill balance.* Manuscript submitted for publication.

Getzel, J. W., and Csikszentmihalyi, M. (1976). *The creative vision: A longitudinal study of problem finding in art.* New York: Wiley.

How it feels to be on fire. 2005, February 21. *Sports Illustrated*, Retrieved June 11, 2008, from http://vault.sportsillustrated.cnn.com/vault/article/magazine/MAG1106119/index.htm

Inghilleri, P. 1999. *From subjective experience to cultural change.* New York: Cambridge University Press.

Jackson, S. A., and R. C. Eklund. 2002. Assessing flow in physical activity: The Flow State Scale—2 and Dispositional Flow Scale—2. *J. Sport Exerc. Psychol.* 24:133–150.

Jostmann, N. B., and S. L. Koole. 2007. On the regulation of cognitive control: Action orientation moderates the impact of high demands in Stroop interference tasks. *J. Exp. Psychol. Gen.* 136:593–609. Medline:17999573 doi:10.1037/0096-3445.136.4.593

Keller, J., and H. Bless. 2008. Flow and regulatory compatibility: An experimental approach to the flow model of intrinsic motivation. *Pers. Soc. Psychol. Bull.* 34:196–209. Medline:18212330 doi:10.1177/0146167207310026

Kubey, R., and M. Csikszentmihalyi. 1990. *Television and the quality of life: How viewing shapes everyday experience.* Hillsdale, NJ: Erlbaum.

Kuhl, J. 1994. Action versus state orientation: Psychometric properties of the action control scale (ACS–90). In *Volition and personality: Action versus state orientation*, ed. J. Kuhl and J. Beckmann. Seattle, WA: Hogrefe & Huber, 47–59.

Lepper, M. R., and D. Green. 1975. Turning play into work: Effects of adult surveillance and extrinsic rewards on children's intrinsic motivation. *J. Pers. Soc. Psychol.* 31:479–486. doi:10.1037/h0076484

Massimini, F., and M. Carli. 1988. The systematic assessment of flow in daily experience. In *Optimal experience: Psychological studies of flow in consciousness*, ed. M. Csikzentmihalyi and I. S. Csikzentmihalyi. New York: Cambridge University Press, 266–287.

Mannell, R. C., and W. Bradley. 1986. Does greater freedom always lead to greater leisure? Testing a Person × Environment model of freedom and leisure. *J. Leisure. Res.* 18:215–230.

Massimini, F., and Delle Fave, A. 2000. Individual development in a bio-cultural perspective. *Am. Psychol.*, 55:24–33.

McAuley, E., T. Duncan, and V. V. Tammen. 1989. Psychometric properties of the Intrinsic Motivation Inventory in a competitive sport setting: A confirmatory factor analysis. *Res. Q. Exerc. Sport* 60:48–58. Medline:2489825

Moller, A. C., M. Csikszentmihalyi, J. Nakamura, and E. L. Deci. 2007, February. *Developing an experimental induction of flow.* Poster presented at the Society for Personality and Social Psychology Conference, Memphis, TN.

Nakamura, J., and M. Csikszentmihalyi. 2002. The concept of flow. In *Handbook of positive psychology*, ed. C. R. Snyder and S. J. Lopez. New York: Oxford University Press, 89–105.

Parks, A. C., and H. A. Victor. 2006, May. *Are positive and negative moods causes or correlates of flow?* Poster presented at the 18th Annual Convention of the American Psychological Society.

Plant, R. W., and R. M. Ryan. 1985. Intrinsic motivation and the effects of self-consciousness, self-awareness, and ego-involvement: An investigation of internally controlling styles. *J. Pers.* 53:435–449. doi:10.1111/j.1467-6494.1985.tb00375.x

Rawsthorne, L. J., and A. J. Elliot. 1999. Achievement goals and intrinsic motivation: A meta-analytic review. *Pers. Soc. Psychol. Rev.* 3:326–344. Medline:15661680 doi:10.1207/s15327957pspr0304_3

Reeve, J., and E. L. Deci. 1996. Elements within the competitive situation that affect intrinsic motivation. *Pers. Soc. Psychol. Bull.* 22:24–33. doi:10.1177/0146167296221003

Rheinberg, F., and R. Vollmeyer. 2003. Flow-Erleben in einem computerspiel unter experimentell variierten bedingungen [Flow experience in a computer game under experimentally varied conditions]. *Zeitschrift für Psychologie* 221:161–170.

Rheinberg, F., Vollmeyer, R., and Engeser, S. (2002). Measuring components of flow: the flow-short-scale. In *Poster presented at the first international positive psychology summit*. Washington, DC.

Rheinberg, F., R. Vollmeyer, and S. Engeser. 2003. Die Erfassung des Flow-Erlebens [The assessment of flow]. In *Diagnostik von Motivation und Selbstkonzept*, ed. J. Stiensmeier-Pelster and F. Rheinberg. Göttingen: Hogrefe, 261–279.

Spencer, S. J., M. P. Zanna, and G. T. Fong. 2005. Establishing a casual chain: Why experiments are often more effective than mediational analyses in examining psychological processes. *J. Pers. Soc. Psychol.* 89:845–851. Medline:16393019 doi:10.1037/0022-3514.89.6.845

Vansteenkiste, M., and E. L. Deci. 2003. Competitively contingent rewards and intrinsic motivation: Can losers remain motivated? *Motiv. Emot.* 27:273–299. doi:10.1023/A:1026259005264

Wicklund, R. A., and S. Duval. 1971. Opinion change and performance facilitation as a result of objective self-awareness. *J. Exp. Soc. Psychol.* 7:319–342. doi:10.1016/0022-1031(71)90032-1

10 The Physiology of Effortless Attention: Correlates of State Flow and Flow Proneness

Fredrik Ullén, Örjan de Manzano, Töres Theorell, and László Harmat

When in flow, a person is highly concentrated and absorbed in an ongoing activity—yet, there is no subjective feeling of mental effort (Csikszentmihalyi 1990). The term *effortless attention* has been proposed for this type of attentive state to distinguish it from more well-studied states of high attention during mental effort (see, e.g., Bruya, Introduction, this volume). The main purpose of this chapter is to investigate whether high attention during flow is not only phenomenologically but also physiologically different from effortful attention. As a background, we first relate the concepts *flow* and *flow proneness* to current theories of emotion, attention, and expertise. Thereafter we survey the at present relatively small literature on psychological and physiological correlates of flow, and proneness for flow experiences, and examine whether it is in line with the view that attention during flow is distinct from attention during mental effort. We conclude with a brief discussion of how the psychophysiology of flow may explain links between flow and health.

The Flow State and Flow Proneness

Flow is a subjective experience of enjoyment and concentration that typically occurs during performance of tasks that are challenging but matched in difficulty to the person's skill level. Research in social psychology has identified nine elements in verbalizations of this state (Csikszentmihalyi 1990): (1) *challenge–skill balance* (the task is challenging but matched in difficulty to the skill of the person); (2) *action–awareness merging* (actions feel automatic, and few or no attentional resources are required for executing action sequences); (3) *clear goals*; (4) *unambiguous feedback*; (5) *high concentration*; (6) *sense of control*; (7) *loss of self-consciousness* (self-reflective thoughts and fear of social evaluation are absent); (8) *transformation of time* (time may seem to move either faster or slower than usual); and (9) *autotelic experience* (performance is accompanied by positive affect, which may be part of an intrinsic reward response—that is, performing the task becomes a goal in itself).

Flow proneness as a trait refers to the tendency of a person to experience flow states. It can be measured by questionnaires where participants indicate how frequently they have experiences with the various characteristics of the flow state summarized above (see, e.g., the Activity Experience Scale of Jackson and Eklund; Jackson and Eklund 2004). Two other traits that presumably are closely related to flow proneness will also be discussed here: *intrinsic enjoyment* and *boredom coping* (Hamilton, Haier, and Buchsbaum 1984). Intrinsic enjoyment refers to a tendency to perform activities because they are rewarding in themselves rather than because they are linked to external rewards. Boredom coping is a disposition to relate to and perform potentially boring tasks in such a way as to make them more intrinsically rewarding. A fourth proposed higher order trait, *autotelic personality*, appears related to all three of these constructs (Csikszentmihalyi 1990; Nakamura and Csikszentmihalyi 2009).

Flow, Flow Proneness, and Emotion

Before we can discuss the physiological underpinnings of flow and flow proneness, these concepts need to be related to relevant established knowledge on emotion, attention, and expertise.

Enjoyment is a central aspect of the flow experience. Furthermore, several other elements of flow are dependent on emotional state: Challenge appraisals and task engagement vary as a function of affect (Maier, Waldstein, and Synowski 2003); emotional stimuli can modulate attentional processes along the dimensions of valence and arousal (Brosch, Sander, Pourtois, and Scherer 2008; Jefferies, Smilek, Eich, and Enns 2008; see below); perceived personal control is related to greater self-reported coping ability prior to a task and lower self-reported stressfulness afterwards (Weinstein and Quigley 2006); positive emotions have been found to reduce self-conscious awareness of, for example, pain (Roy, Peretz, and Rainville 2008); and sense of time is altered such that highly arousing stimuli with positive valence are perceived as having shorter duration than negative, low-arousing stimuli (Droit-Volet and Meck 2007; Noulhiane, Mella, Samson, Ragot, and Pouthas 2007). Using the well-known two-dimensional affective space of valence and arousal (Lang 1995), a flow state would thus be associated with the upper right quadrant—that is, the flow experience includes an emotional state characterized by moderate to high levels of both dimensions.

Interestingly, the dimensions of valence and arousal are commonly found to also organize somatophysiological responses. Hence, by locating flow in the affective space, it is possible to yield a hypothesis about how psychophysiological measures of emotion correlate with state flow. Many studies have used electromyographical recordings of activity in facial muscles to differentiate between emotional states (see, e.g., Ravaja, Saari, Salminen, Laarni, and Kallinen 2006; Witvliet and Vrana 1995). Two commonly probed muscles in this context are the *corrugator supercilii* (CS), which is used during frowning, and the *zygomaticus major* (ZM), which is activated during smiling. CS activity increases during negative affect and decreases during positive affect. ZM mainly responds to decreases in negative affect (Larsen, Norris, and Cacioppo 2003). Activity in these muscles also depends on arousal: CS activity is highest during negatively valent low-arousal states, while ZM activity is maximal during positive, high-arousal (joyous) states (Witvliet and Vrana 1995). Arousal is also reflected in respiratory measures. Excited and aroused states are associated with rapid deep breathing accompanied by a high inspiratory flow rate (Gomez and Danuser 2004; Wientjes 1992). Cardiovascular measures, too, demonstrate emotion-specific autonomic activation: High-arousal emotions (such as joy) are reliably associated with decreased heart period (interval between beats) and increased systolic blood pressure (Ekman, Levenson, and Friesen 1983; Schwartz, Weinberger, and Singer 1981; Sinha, Lovallo, and Parsons 1992; Witvliet and Vrana 1995).

In addition, we can formulate hypotheses about the relation between flow proneness and other psychological traits that influence emotional processing. Specifically, one would predict a negative correlation between flow proneness and neuroticism. This higher order personality trait, which is highly consistent across various models of personality, including the currently dominating five-factor model of McCrae and Costa (1990), is characterized by a number of features that would tend to interfere with the affective component of flow states— in particular, a high reactivity to negative stimuli and a proneness to worry and negative affect (Gray and McNaughton 2000; McCrae and Costa 1990).

Flow, Flow Proneness, and Attention

Attention is a central component of human cognition and a prerequisite for being able to maintain goals and execute goal-oriented action (for a review, see Raz and Buhle 2006). As mentioned, an interesting aspect of the flow state is effortless attention: a subjective experience of heightened, unforced concentration and absorption in the ongoing performance. We suggest that this may occur as a result of an interaction between positive valence and attention. Positive valence can distract away from negative and even painful stimuli (Roy, Peretz, and Rainville 2008), that is, a task of great attentional load may be experienced as less effortful in a state of positive affect. This transient neglect could be explained by a propensity of brain systems to respond differently to a stimulus depending on whether attention is focused on sensory- or affect-related properties—for example, intensity or pleasantness (Grabenhorst and Rolls 2008).

In terms of psychophysiology, attention in the sense of mental effort is accompanied by higher activity in the CS (the "frown muscle"; Cohen, Davidson, Senulis, Saron, and Weisman 1992; Waterink and van Boxtel 1994), fast and shallow respiration (Backs and Seljos 1994; Veltman and Gaillard 1998; Wientjes 1992), and decreased heart period and increased systolic blood pressure, together with a decreased variability in these measures (Berntson, Cacioppo, and Quigley 1993; Middleton, Sharma, Agouzoul, Sahakian, and Robbins 1999; Porges and Byrne 1992; Richter, Friedrich, and Gendolla 2008; Veltman and Gaillard 1996, 1998), all of which points to an increased activation of the sympathetic nervous system. However, it should be noted that studies on individual differences in physiological response to, for example, working memory- and attention-demanding tasks show better performance to be associated with relatively greater—that is, less suppressed—heart rate variability related to vagal influence—that is, the parasympathetic component of the heart rate variability spectrum (Hansen, Johnsen, and Thayer 2003). The coupling between mental effort and shallow respiration is particularly interesting, since joyous states typically show deep respiration (see above). One could thus hypothesize that this measure distinguishes between states of effortful and effortless attention. In general, deep breathing is associated with decelerated heart rate and lowered blood pressure—something underscoring the importance of deep breathing to parasympathetic activation (see, for instance, von Schéele, von Schéele, Hansson, Winman, and Theorell 2005).

At a trait level, performance on tests of effortful, sustained attention show a substantial positive correlation with psychometric general intelligence (Schweizer and Moosbrugger 2004; Schweizer, Moosbrugger, and Goldhammer 2005). It is therefore of interest to examine whether flow proneness also shows a relation with intelligence and performance in sustained attention tasks. If this is the case, it would indicate that individual differences in the capacity for effortful and effortless attention share neural substrates. If not, it would provide further support for the hypothesis that effortless attention differs from effortful attention, perhaps because the absorption in a task during flow is more dependent on expertise—that is, a high level of skill in particular tasks that induce the flow experience—than on general cognitive ability (see below).

Expertise and Flow

Flow occurs during performance of tasks when the challenge of the task is on par with the skill level of the subject. An additional requirement appears to be that the task is at least moderately complex and challenging in absolute terms; too simple tasks are not flow promoting (Csikszentmihalyi 1990). What is most flow promoting for a given person will thus depend on the particular domains of expertise of that person. More generally, expertise, implemented as stored long-term representations in the brain, will guide planning and expectations (Ericsson and Lehmann 1996) and even influence sensory processing to attend to task-relevant cues (Summerfield, Lepsien, Gitelman, Mesulam, and Nobre 2006). Since top–down processes can modulate attentional focus and filtering processes, expertise can presumably also facilitate sustained attention and reduce distractibility in a domain-specific manner.

Another important aspect of expertise is automaticity (Ericsson, Charness, Feltovich, and Hoffman 2006). Nonautomatic behavioral routines can be gradually automated by extended training, practice, repetition, and overlearning. With greater automaticity, there is less need for higher order cognitive functions to micromanage sequential sensory and motor processes, which enables the automated processes to be carried out faster and more accurately while also being less vulnerable to attentional shifts. Focus can instead be allocated to speed and/or other more qualitative aspects of motor output, also making challenge per se qualitatively different at different levels of ability. Expertise also involves domain-specific changes in attentional function. An extraneous dual task can thus degrade performance in novices but not necessarily in experts. Furthermore, effortful attention to skill execution in experts can actually interfere with performance (Beilock, Bertenthal, McCoy, and Carr 2004; Beilock, Carr, MacMahon, and Starkes 2002; Gray 2004). These observations appear to support the idea that effortless attention during skilled performance in flow is different in nature from effortful attention to task.

Correlates of Flow

The existing literature thus allows one to make a number of predictions with regard to the underlying biology of flow and flow proneness. To summarize, physiological correlates of state flow should include decreased heart period, increased cardiac output, increased respiratory rate, increased respiratory depth, and differential activation of facial muscles involved in expression of emotion—that is, increased activity in the ZM and decreased activity in the CS. Flow proneness and related traits may show relations to numerous other traits influencing attentional and emotional processing, but we have focused here on two main traits: general intelligence, where we expect a positive correlation to the extent that effortless attention overlaps with mechanisms for effortful sustained attention, and neuroticism, where we predict a negative relation.

Very few studies have so far directly tested these predictions. To our knowledge, a recent study from our own group is the only one investigating physiological correlates of state flow while controlling for other variables that may influence physiology (de Manzano, Theorell, Harmat, and Ullén in press). In this study, the subjects ($n = 21$) were all professional concert pianists. Physiological measures included electromyograms of the CS and ZM muscles, heart rate, blood pressure, and thoracic respiration. During the experiment, the pianist played the same self-chosen musical piece (three to seven minutes' duration) repeatedly for five trials, thus keeping all sensorimotor processing and physical effort that could influence physiology essentially constant. Flow was measured after each trial using self-reports and then compared to physiological measures obtained during each trial. In line with the previously stated hypotheses, we found performance with higher flow to be associated with a decreased heart period, higher activity in ZM, and larger respiratory depth. No effect was found for CS activity or respiratory rate.

Correlates of Flow Proneness

A few studies have investigated psychological correlates of flow proneness and related traits. Hamilton and coworkers measured intrinsic enjoyment and boredom coping in 160 subjects, who were divided into subgroups that were subject to different sets of additional measurements and tests (Hamilton, Haier, and Buchsbaum 1984). In one subsample of 18 students, the frequency of experiences relating to state flow was measured using the Experience Sampling Method (Csikszentmihalyi and Larson 1987). Intrinsic enjoyment was significantly related to several of these measures—that is, this trait seems substantially related to flow proneness. Trends for boredom coping did not reach significance in this relatively small subsample. Furthermore, intrinsic enjoyment was significantly related to higher *internal locus of control* (Rotter 1966), a trait which in turn is negatively correlated with neuroticism (Clarke 2004; Horner 1996). In a second subsample of 48 college students, a test of sustained attention (the continuous performance task) showed no relation to intrinsic enjoyment, and a modest positive relation to boredom coping ($r = .4$) was found.

We recently measured general intelligence (Raven's Standard Progressive Matrices Plus), personality (NEO Personality Inventory—Revised), and flow proneness in three domains of activity (professional, leisure time, and maintenance activities) in a sample of 76 university students (Madison, de Manzano, Forsman, and Ullén, in preparation). Interestingly, no relations between flow proneness and intelligence were found in this sample. In contrast, flow proneness during leisure showed a significant negative relation to neuroticism ($r = -.4$). A negative relation between neuroticism and flow proneness was also found in a sample ($n = 126$) of music students (Avsec and Smolej Fritz 2008). Clearly, further studies on relations between flow proneness and other traits in larger and demographically different (e.g., older) samples would be of interest.

The Physiology of Flow and Effortless Attention—Preliminary Observations

Conclusions regarding the biological basis of flow still have to be made with great caution, given that so few studies have been performed. However, the existing data support several of our hypotheses regarding differences in the underlying physiology of effortful and effortless attention. Our own study on pianists suggests that an increased activation of the sympathetic branch of the autonomic nervous system in combination with deep breathing is characteristic of the flow state. In other words, flow is a state of arousal, but it is accompanied not by the shallow respiration characteristic of mental effort but rather by the deep respiration typical of joyous states. This is compatible with our proposal that the flow state is the result of an interaction between positive affect and attention. Intuitively, too little or too much arousal in relation to task difficulty should decrease flow. One might speculate that this is reflected in the challenge–skill balance dimension and that arousal, thus, is related to optimal performance and flow as predicted by an inverted U-shaped relationship as in the much debated Yerkes–Dodson law (Hanoch and Vitouch 2004).

These findings also suggest that regulation of sympathetic and parasympathetic activity levels may be of importance for state flow. In general, the parasympathetic system can be regarded as a system that counterregulates a general stress–arousal reaction. Indirect evidence for concomitant activation of the sympathetic and parasympathetic systems in music performing professionals comes from a study of a singing lesson in which professional singers were compared to amateurs (Grape, Sandgren, Hansson, Ericson, and Theorell 2003). During singing, the increase in heart rate was very similar in the two groups. However, in the professionals heart rate variability increased markedly, whereas no such increase was observed in the amateurs. This was particularly pronounced for low-frequency power, which has been assumed to reflect a mixture of parasympathetic and sympathetic activity (Porges and Byrne 1992), but it was noticeable also in high-frequency power, which reflects parasympathetic activity. Preliminary data on piano performance from our group are also in line with this. In three of the pianists participating in the above-mentioned study (de Manzano et al. in press), additional physiological measurements—continuous recordings of electrocardiogram and pCO_2 in exhaled air—were made during performance of both the self-selected, well-learned piece and a difficult, unknown piece (the fourth movement of György Kurtág's *Splinters*) that had to be played *a prima vista*. During playing of the unknown piece, as compared to the self-selected piece, all three pianists showed an increase of high-frequency power in heart rate variability, and also a longer heart period, a higher respiratory rate, and a lower $pCO_2.$ These findings suggest that the professional pianists were able to immediately activate the parasympathetic system in the difficult *prima vista* situation. It appears possible, therefore, that the ability of experts to regulate the level of activity in both sympathetic and parasympathetic branches of the autonomous nervous system during performance is of importance for state flow, but further research is obviously needed to test this idea.

Differences in physiology suggest differences in neurophysiology. Further work is needed to elucidate the neural correlates of the flow experience, but an interesting speculation is that flow may have commonalities with states experienced during deep meditation and that the anterior cingulate cortex may play important roles for the coordination of autonomic responses and cognitive control in such states (Posner, Rothbart, Rueda, and Tang, chapter 16, this volume; Siegel 2007).

That the affective component of flow is essential for effortless attention is also supported by the fact that flow proneness is related to emotional stability (i.e., low neuroticism) and internal locus of control (Avsec and Smolej Fritz 2008; Hamilton, Haier, and Buchsbaum 1984; Madison, de Manzano, Forsman, and Ullén, in preparation). The lack of a positive correlation between flow proneness and intelligence in our sample of young adults (Madison et al.) as well as between flow proneness and sustained attention (Hamilton et al.) is a further indication that there are essential differences in the mechanisms underlying effortful and effortless attention. One explanation for this may be that the absorption in an activity during flow is less dependent on general cognitive ability than on high skills in particular domains—that is, expertise—which allows the person to perform specific flow-promoting tasks at a high level. This would be in line with sociological studies showing that flow experiences are common among people at different educational levels but that the flow-promoting activities differ depending on the expertise of the subjects (Csikszentmihalyi 1990). The importance of intelligence for expertise remains a question of debate, but it appears uncontroversial that for most domains practice is a better predictor of expert performance than cognitive ability (Ericsson, Charness, Feltovich, and Hoffman 2006). To get a more conclusive picture of the relation between flow proneness, intelligence, and expertise, however, studies on larger cohorts with a wide range of cognitive ability as well as expertise in different domains would be important.

The Psychophysiology of Flow and Health

There are several published studies which show that there is a positive relationship between health and a high prevalence of positive emotions in daily life. If we assume that flow would increase the prevalence of positive emotions, this would be of relevance. For instance, in one study (Theorell, Ahlberg-Hulten, Jodko, Sigala, and de la Torre 1993) female health care staff were asked to record emotions every hour during an ordinary working day. Blood pressure was recorded on all these occasions. The findings indicated a strong relationship between a high prevalence of joyful feelings and a low blood pressure level during working hours as well as at rest and during leisure hours. In a large prospective cohort study, Kubzansky, Sparrow, Vokonas, and Kawachi (2001) showed that optimism in general was associated with a markedly reduced incidence of coronary heart disease (after adjustment for other risk factors). Of more direct relevance is the observation by Bygren, Konlaan, and Johansson (1996) based upon a cohort study of randomly selected Swedish participants. They were asked whether they participated at least once a week in cultural activities (which should increase the number of flow experiences) or not. Those who did so had a better survival during follow-up than other participants in the study. This association remained significant after adjustment for education, income, health at start, and life habits (such as smoking) that are of relevance to survival and which may also be related to participation in cultural activities. In a small randomized study by our own group (Grape, Sandgren, Hansson, Ericson, and Theorell 2003), adult beginners in choir singing showed increased saliva testosterone concentration and reported increased vitalization during the initial months. The control group showed no such increase. Moderate increase in saliva testosterone is an indicator of improved cell regeneration and therefore of relevance to this question. Furthermore, as we speculated above, parasympathetic mechanisms may be of importance for flow. During recent years, it has been pointed out that activation of the parasympathetic system is helpful in the recovery phase after an arousal reaction and that this stops inflammatory reactions that stimulate, for instance, the atherosclerotic process (Gidron et al. 2007). The ability to activate the parasympathetic system could thus be of importance for flow as well as long-term health and longevity. In summary, there is indirect but no direct evidence that a high prevalence of flow experiences could benefit health.

Acknowledgments

The authors would like to thank Mihaly Csikszentmihalyi and Jeanne Nakamura for valuable discussions. Fredrik Ullén and Örjan de Manzano were supported by grants from the Söderberg Foundation, Stockholm Brain Institute, and the Freemasons in Sweden Foundation for Children's Welfare during the preparation of this chapter.

References

Avsec, A., and B. Smolej Fritz. 2008. Traits as predictors of flow experience in music students, *4th European Conference on Positive Psychology* (pp. 277). Opatija, Croatia: Faculty of Arts and Sciences, University of Rijeka, Rijeka, Croatia.

Backs, R. W., and K. A. Seljos. 1994. Metabolic and cardiorespiratory measures of mental effort: The effects of level of difficulty in a working memory task. *Int. J. Psychophysiol.* 16:57–68.

Beilock, S. L., B. I. Bertenthal, A. M. McCoy, and T. H. Carr. 2004. Haste does not always make waste: Expertise, direction of attention, and speed versus accuracy in performing sensorimotor skills. *Psychon. Bull. Rev.* 11:373–379.

Beilock, S. L., T. H. Carr, C. MacMahon, and J. L. Starkes. 2002. When paying attention becomes counterproductive: Impact of divided versus skill-focused attention on novice and experienced performance of sensorimotor skills. *J. Exp. Psychol. Appl.* 8:6–16.

Berntson, G. G., J. T. Cacioppo, and K. S. Quigley. 1993. Respiratory sinus arrhythmia: Autonomic origins, physiological mechanisms, and psychophysiological implications. *Psychophysiology* 30 (2):183–196.

Brosch, T., D. Sander, G. Pourtois, and K. R. Scherer. 2008. Beyond fear: Rapid spatial orienting toward positive emotional stimuli. *Psychol. Sci.* 19:362–370.

Bygren, L. O., B. B. Konlaan, and S. E. Johansson. 1996. Attendance at cultural events, reading books or periodicals, and making music or singing in a choir as determinant of survival: Swedish fourteen-year cohort follow-up. *BMJ* 313:1577–1580.

Clarke, D. 2004. Neuroticism: Moderator or mediator in the relation between locus of control and depression? *Pers. Individ. Dif.* 37:245–258.

Cohen, B. H., R. J. Davidson, J. A. Senulis, C. D. Saron, and D. R. Weisman. 1992. Muscle tension patterns during auditory attention. *Biol. Psychol.* 33:133–156.

Csikszentmihalyi, M. 1990. *Flow: The psychology of optimal experience.* New York: Harper & Row.

Csikszentmihalyi, M., and R. Larson. 1987. Validity and reliability of the Experience Sampling Method. *J. Nerv. Ment. Dis.* 175:526–536.

de Manzano, Ö., T. Theorell, L. Harmat, and F. Ullén. In press. The psychophysiology of the flow during piano playing. *Emotion.*

Droit-Volet, S., and W. H. Meck. 2007. How emotions colour our perception of time. *Trends Cogn. Sci.* 11:504–513.

Ekman, P., R. W. Levenson, and W. V. Friesen. 1983. Autonomic nervous system activity distinguishes among emotions. *Science* 221:1208–1210.

Ericsson, K. A., N. Charness, P. J. Feltovich, and R. R. Hoffman, eds. 2006. *The Cambridge handbook of expertise and expert performance.* New York: Cambridge University Press.

Ericsson, K. A., and A. C. Lehmann. 1996. Expert and exceptional performance: Evidence of maximal adaptation to task constraints. *Annu. Rev. Psychol.* 47:273–305.

Gidron, Y., N. Kupper, M. Kwaijtaal, J. Winter, and J. Denollet. 2007. Vagus–brain communication in atherosclerosis-related inflammation: A neuroimmunomodulation perspective of CAD. *Atherosclerosis* 195 (2):e1–e9. Epub 2006 Nov 13.

Gomez, P., and B. Danuser. 2004. Affective and physiological responses to environmental noises and music. *Int. J. Psychophysiol.* 53:91–103.

Grabenhorst, F., and E. T. Rolls. 2008. Selective attention to affective value alters how the brain processes taste stimuli. *Eur. J. Neurosci.* 27:723–729.

Grape, C., M. Sandgren, L. O. Hansson, M. Ericson, and T. Theorell. 2003. Does singing promote well-being? An empirical study of professional and amateur singers during a singing lesson. *Integr. Physiol. Behav. Sci.* 38 (1):65–74.

Gray, J. A., and N. McNaughton. 2000. *The neuropsychology of anxiety: An inquiry into the functions of the septo–hippocampal system.* Oxford: Oxford University Press.

Gray, R. 2004. Attending to the execution of a complex sensorimotor skill: Expertise differences, choking, and slumps. *J. Exp. Psychol. Appl.* 10:42–54.

Hamilton, J. A., R. J. Haier, and M. S. Buchsbaum. 1984. Intrinsic enjoyment and boredom coping scales: Validation with personality, evoked potential and attention measures. *Pers. Individ. Dif.* 5:183–193.

Hanoch, Y., and O. Vitouch. 2004. When less is more—Information, emotional arousal and the ecological reframing of the Yerkes–Dodson law. *Theory Psychol.* 14:427–452.

Hansen, A. L., B. H. Johnsen, and J. F. Thayer. 2003. Vagal influence on working memory and attention. *Int. J. Psychophysiol.* 48:263–274.

Horner, K. L. 1996. Locus of control, neuroticism, and stressors: Combined influences on physical illness. *Pers. Individ. Dif.* 21:195–204.

Jackson, S. A., and R. C. Eklund. 2004. *The Flow Scales manual*. Morgantown: Publishers Graphics.

Jefferies, L. N., D. Smilek, E. Eich, and J. T. Enns. 2008. Emotional valence and arousal interact in attentional control. *Psychol. Sci.* 19:290–295.

Kubzansky, L. D., D. Sparrow, P. Vokonas, and I. Kawachi. 2001. Is the glass half empty or half full? A prospective study of optimism and coronary heart disease in the normative aging study. *Psychosom. Med.* 63:910–916.

Lang, P. J. 1995. The emotion probe: Studies of motivation and attention. *Am. Psychol.* 50:372–385.

Larsen, J. T., C. J. Norris, and J. T. Cacioppo. 2003. Effects of positive and negative affect on electromyographic activity over zygomaticus major and corrugator supercilii. *Psychophysiology* 40:776–785.

Madison, G., Ö. de Manzano, L. Forsman, and F. Ullén. Flow proneness, intelligence and personality. Manuscript in preparation.

Maier, K. J., S. R. Waldstein, and S. J. Synowski. 2003. Relation of cognitive appraisal to cardiovascular reactivity, affect, and task engagement. *Ann. Behav. Med.* 26:32–41.

McCrae, R. R., and P. T. J. Costa. 1990. *Personality in adulthood*. New York: Guilford.

Middleton, H. C., A. Sharma, D. Agouzoul, B. J. Sahakian, and T. W. Robbins. 1999. Contrasts between the cardiovascular concomitants of tests of planning and attention. *Psychophysiology* 36:610–618.

Nakamura, J., and M. Csikszentmihalyi. 2009. Flow theory and research. In *Oxford handbook of positive psychology*, ed. C. R. Snyder and S. J. Lopez Rev. ed. of *Handbook of positive psychology* (pp. 195–206). Oxford: Oxford University Press.

Noulhiane, M., N. Mella, S. Samson, R. Ragot, and V. Pouthas. 2007. How emotional auditory stimuli modulate time perception. *Emotion* 7:697–704.

Porges, S. W., and E. A. Byrne. 1992. Research methods for measurement of heart rate and respiration. *Biol. Psychol.* 34:93–130.

Ravaja, N., T. Saari, M. Salminen, J. Laarni, and K. Kallinen. 2006. Phasic emotional reactions to video game events: A psychophysiological investigation. *Media Psychol.* 8:343–367.

Raz, A., and J. Buhle. 2006. Typologies of attentional networks. *Nat. Rev. Neurosci.* 7:367–379.

Richter, M., A. Friedrich, and G. H. Gendolla. 2008. Task difficulty effects on cardiac activity. *Psychophysiology* 45:869–875.

Rotter, J. B. 1966. Generalized expectancies for internal vs. external control of reinforcement. *Psychol Monogr: Gen Appl* 80 (1):1–28.

Roy, M., I. Peretz, and P. Rainville. 2008. Emotional valence contributes to music-induced analgesia. *Pain* 134 (1–2):140–147.

Schwartz, G. E., D. A. Weinberger, and J. A. Singer. 1981. Cardiovascular differentiation of happiness, sadness, anger, and fear following imagery and exercise. *Psychosom. Med.* 43:343–364.

Schweizer, K., and H. Moosbrugger. 2004. Attention and working memory as predictors of intelligence. *Intelligence* 32:329–347.

Schweizer, K., H. Moosbrugger, and F. Goldhammer. 2005. The structure of the relationship between attention and intelligence. *Intelligence* 33:589–611.

Siegel, D. J. 2007. Mindfulness training and neural integration: Differentiation of distinct streams of awareness and the cultivation of well-being. *Soc. Cogn. Affect. Neurosci.* 2 (4):259–263.

Sinha, R., W. R. Lovallo, and O. A. Parsons. 1992. Cardiovascular differentiation of emotions. *Psychosom. Med.* 54:422–435.

Summerfield, J. J., J. Lepsien, D. R. Gitelman, M. M. Mesulam, and A. C. Nobre. 2006. Orienting attention based on long-term memory experience. *Neuron* 49:905–916.

Theorell, T., G. Ahlberg-Hulten, M. Jodko, F. Sigala, and B. de la Torre. 1993. Influence of job strain and emotion on blood pressure in female hospital personnel during workhours. *Scand. J. Work Environ. Health* 19 (5):313–318.

Veltman, J. A., and A. W. Gaillard. 1996. Physiological indices of workload in a simulated flight task. *Biological Psychology* 42:323–342.

Veltman, J. A., and A. W. Gaillard. 1998. Physiological workload reactions to increasing levels of task difficulty. *Ergonomics* 41:656–669.

von Schéele, I., B. von Schéele, G. Hansson, A. Winman, and T. Theorell. 2005. Psychosocial factors and respiratory and cardiovascular parameters during psychophysiological stress profiling in working men and women. *Applied Psychophysiology and Biofeedback* 30:125–136.

Waterink, W., and A. van Boxtel. 1994. Facial and jaw-elevator EMG activity in relation to changes in performance level during a sustained information processing task. *Biol. Psychol.* 37:183–198.

Weinstein, S. E., and K. S. Quigley. 2006. Locus of control predicts appraisals and cardiovascular reactivity to a novel active coping task. *J. Pers.* 74:911–931.

Wientjes, C. J. 1992. Respiration in psychophysiology: Methods and applications. *Biol. Psychol.* 34:179–203.

Witvliet, C. V., and S. R. Vrana. 1995. Psychophysiological responses as indices of affective dimensions. *Psychophysiology* 32:436–443.

11 Apertures, Draw, and Syntax: Remodeling Attention

Brian Bruya

Because psychological studies of attention and cognition are most commonly performed within the strict confines of the laboratory or take cognitively impaired patients as subjects (Parasuraman 1998b; Pashler 1998; Posner 2004; Underwood 1993), it is difficult to be sure that resultant models of attention adequately account for the phenomenon of effortless attention. The problem is not only that effortless attention is resistant to laboratory study (but see Moller, Meier, and Wall, chapter 9, this volume). A further issue is that because the laboratory is the most common way to approach attention, models resulting from such studies are naturally the most widely propagated, these models naturally tend to be biased toward features of attention most amenable to laboratory study, and these models by their implications set the agenda for future study that leads back to the laboratory. In this self-reinforcing system, features of attention not amenable to laboratory study are naturally neglected by researchers. Being that they are neglected, one can surmise that they are not adequately accounted for in current models, and such models, therefore, fail to indicate potentially important areas for future study. In this chapter, I will suggest an alternative model of attention as a heuristic for opening paths to further profitable research. The features of attention emphasized in this model are not new, but the synthesis is novel and sheds some light on issues relevant to the topic of effortless attention.

I begin with the five following observations:

1. One naturally pays attention to a task of current interest.
2. There are (at least) two distinct modes of attention—selective and diffuse.
3. Attention is a constantly shifting avenue for the assimilation of information.
4. Information is not forced in from outside but is captured through internal sensitization.
5. Human information processing is fundamentally syntactic.

Combining these five observations yields an explanatory model of attention that is not only consistent with the data from the many studies on attention in recent decades but also allows us to investigate the neglected phenomenon of effortless

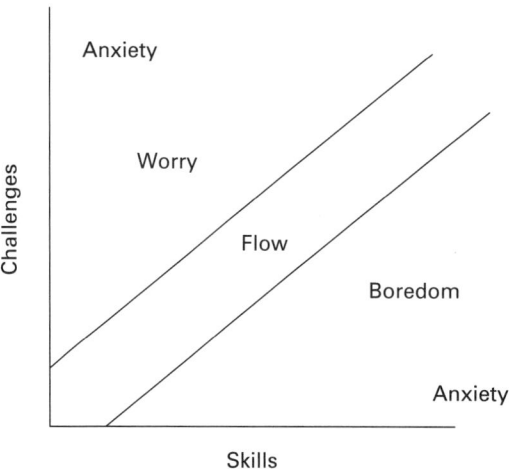

Figure 11.1
Psychological states related to challenge and skill balance (Csikszentmihalyi and Csikszentmihalyi).

attention. The model relies on the notions of apertures, draw, and syntax (ADS, for short) and will be explicated by addressing each of the above observations in turn. In the final part of the chapter, I shall explore how the model expands our understanding of effortless attention.

Interest and Effortless Attention

Csikszentmihalyi and Csikszentmihalyi (1988, 49) postulated a *flow channel* that accounts for effortless attention and action in terms of a balance between challenges and skills (see figure 11.1):

Massimini and Carli (Csikszentmihalyi 1997, 31) revised this model, specifying further states related to the imbalance of challenges and skills (see figure 11.2).

Under these interpretations, the states of arousal, flow, control, and relaxation are all positive affective states. This positive affect partially explains natural human motivation for pursuing and achieving activities that engender flow. However, positive affect alone does not tell the whole story.

Under normal circumstances, attention is most easily maintained if one is actively interested, so an obvious place to turn is the notion of interest. Paul Silvia (2006) summarizes his own work and the work of other recent research programs in the behavioral psychology of interest, concluding that interest is distinct from curiosity, attention, importance, and intrinsic motivation. He further concludes that no clear

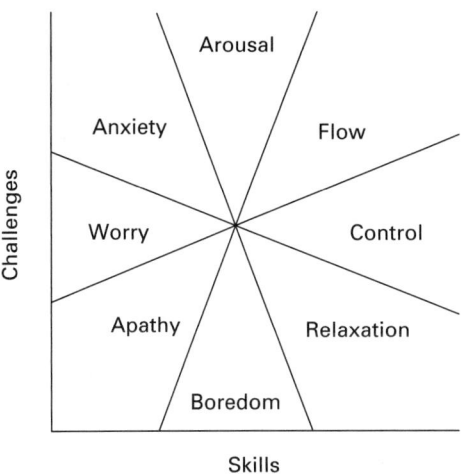

Figure 11.2
Psychological states related to challenge and skill balance (Massimini and Carli).

distinction is warranted between cognitive and emotional interest. What is most relevant to building a complete model of attention is the number of studies he cites demonstrating that "interest motivates the development of knowledge and skills" (209). This should come as no surprise, but it highlights the need to take interest into account as an important variable in the processes that subtend effortless attention, which are so closely associated with skill acquisition. Because current models of attention arise from laboratory studies in which tasks are exogenously motivated, interest rarely plays a part in such studies.

Are there any general elements of activities toward which interest turns attention when engaged in an activity? If activities can be broken down into elements and it is found that certain general elements attract attention, then it may be possible to account for interest and investigate its role in flow activities. But what does it mean for an external stimulus to attract attention? Without an accurate model of attention, this question will be impossible to answer. Therefore, we will turn first to attention and return to specific elements of activities and their relation to interest in the "Implications of the Aperture, Draw, Syntax Model" section below.

Modes of Attention

One way researchers taxonomize attention is into selective attention and vigilance (Parasuraman 1998b). *Selective attention* refers to choosing one task of attention from among many, and *vigilance* to sustaining attention on a chosen task. Selective attention is widely studied by cognitive scientists attempting to map its functional

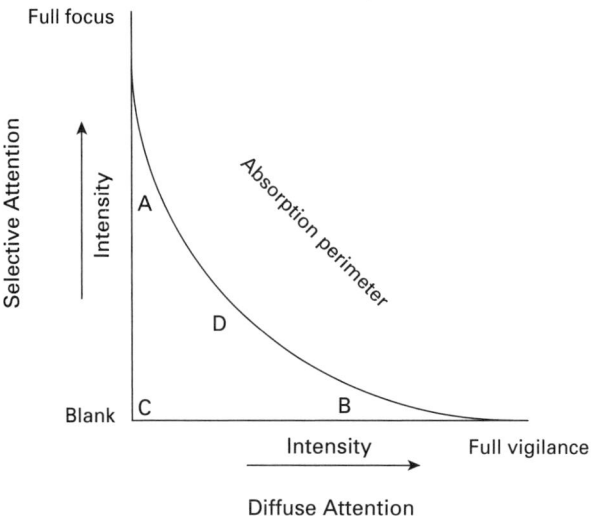

Figure 11.3
Selective versus diffuse attention under normal conditions.

and neurophysiological features, and vigilance is often studied in relation to pathologies, such as attention-deficit/hyperactivity disorder. Here we'll try to understand the relationship between selective attention and vigilance.

When one concentrates on a task, one's concentration may be slight or intense (Kahneman 1973). Let us call intense selective attention *focused*. The term *vigilance* presumes a level of success, so let us call the kind of attention that expectantly observes a field of stimuli *diffuse attention* (Faglioni 1990) and say that high intensity of diffuse attention is *vigilance*. In a conscious person, these two modes of attention are always simultaneously in operation (Faglioni 1990). Thus, we can run them as axes in a phase-space diagram (see figure 11.3) to analyze their relationship. Diffuse attention begins at blank attention (C), and increased intensity of attention leads to full vigilance (B). Selective attention begins at blank attention (C), and increased intensity leads to full focus (A).

Any position near either axis and toward the blank side seems within the range of normalcy. As one approaches the absorption perimeter, the outer limit of attentional capacity, evidence suggests that attention tends to one axis rather than the other (Parasuraman 1998a), as illustrated—increase in intensity of focus results in a decrease in intensity of vigilance, and vice versa.

A dimension not depicted in this figure is effort. What is the relation of effort to intensity? Intuitively, there would be a direct correlation—the more effort, the more intense one's attention. We could plot the two different kinds of attention against effort as follows (see figure 11.4).

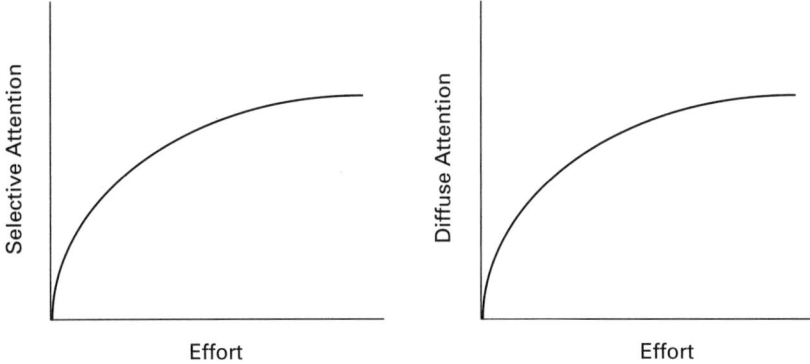

Figure 11.4
Attention versus effort under normal conditions.

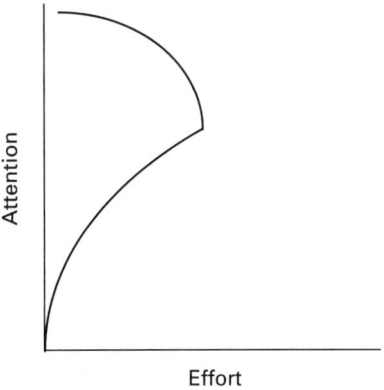

Figure 11.5
Attention versus effort under flow conditions.

In these diagrams, intensity increases with effort until attention asymptotes regardless of increases in effort. An important finding in flow research, however, is that subjects report an increase in absorption and a decrease in effort (Csikszentmihalyi and Nakamura, chapter 8, this volume; Csikszentmihalyi 1975; see figure 11.5).

An increase in intensity over normal circumstances suggests that flow may facilitate the extension outward of the absorption perimeter, and perhaps even the orientation of its parabola (see figure 11.6).

An important dimension not depicted here is the scope of one's attention. While selective attention implies a narrow scope and diffuse attention a broad scope, there is no indication in this depiction of how broad either scope is. For instance, if I am

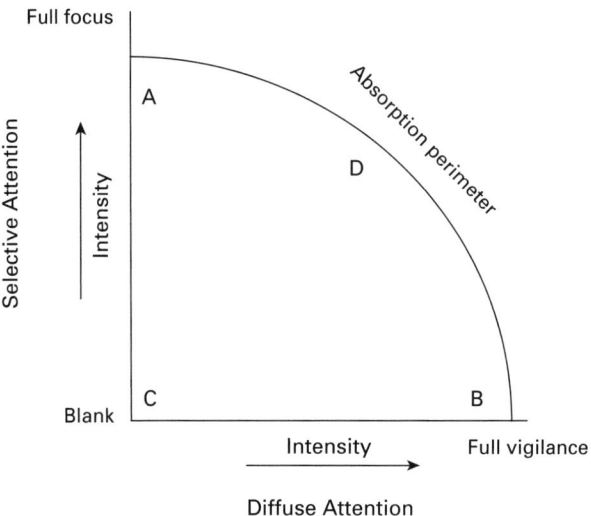

Figure 11.6
Selective versus diffuse attention under flow conditions.

attending to detail x of activity M and am vigilant to other potential details of activity M (suppose my attention is close to point D), there is no indication of how vigilant I am to details of activity N. With respect to activity N, it could be that I am closer to point C—I am not paying attention to any details of activity N nor am I vigilant to future potential details. For instance, suppose five men are playing cards in one room while their wives are convening a book club in another room, both groups of spouses within earshot of the other. All could be near point D with respect to their own activity but near point C with respect to the other.

This observation is consistent with research demonstrating that attention is not an all-or-nothing proposition with regard to domains of activity—that the field of one's attention and the field of one's perception are importantly distinct. Attention is conceived here as domain specific, and all subjects will fall somewhere on the selective–diffuse attention scale with respect to all current and potential domains of activity within their perceptual field. It's not the case that just because a stimulus is within one's field of perception it is also within one's field of attention (Treisman and Gelade 1980).

Apertures and Structures

What do these modes of attention suggest about the functional mechanisms of attention? Most models of attention focus on the selective aspect of attention, which is

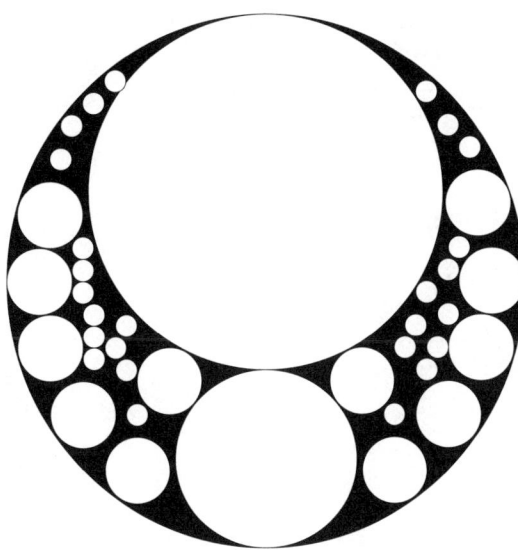

Figure 11.7
Apertures of attention, two-dimensional view.

often depicted as a beacon of light illuminating the object or field of attention. Such a metaphor implies a single control mechanism directing the beam of light and controlling its intensity. Under a typical behaviorist model, the beam would be controlled by external stimuli. Under a voluntarist model, the beam would be controlled by subjective choice. Most such models make room for both "top–down" and "bottom–up" mechanisms.

There are other metaphors for selective attention, as well. The common filter theory goes back to Broadbent's Y-shaped tube model (Broadbent 1957). Zenon Pylyshyn (1989) has proposed an INSTantiation FINger (FINST) model of visual attention. These models, and others, generally do not attempt to account for diffuse attention, focusing instead on various features of and controversies around selective attention. I propose that we view diffuse attention as an *aperture* (see figure 11.7)—not just as a single aperture, however, but as multiple subapertures within one larger aperture—in other words, as multiple avenues of information processing within a single larger avenue. Selective attention will operate within the main aperture only,[1] although nonattentive processing could be operating in any number of apertures simultaneously.

Attention is understood here as an avenue for the mind to consciously process and assimilate information.[2] Under the beam-of-light metaphor, the beacon shines on that part of the information that the brain processes in consciousness. Such a metaphor fails to account not only for the separation of information that occurs but also for the

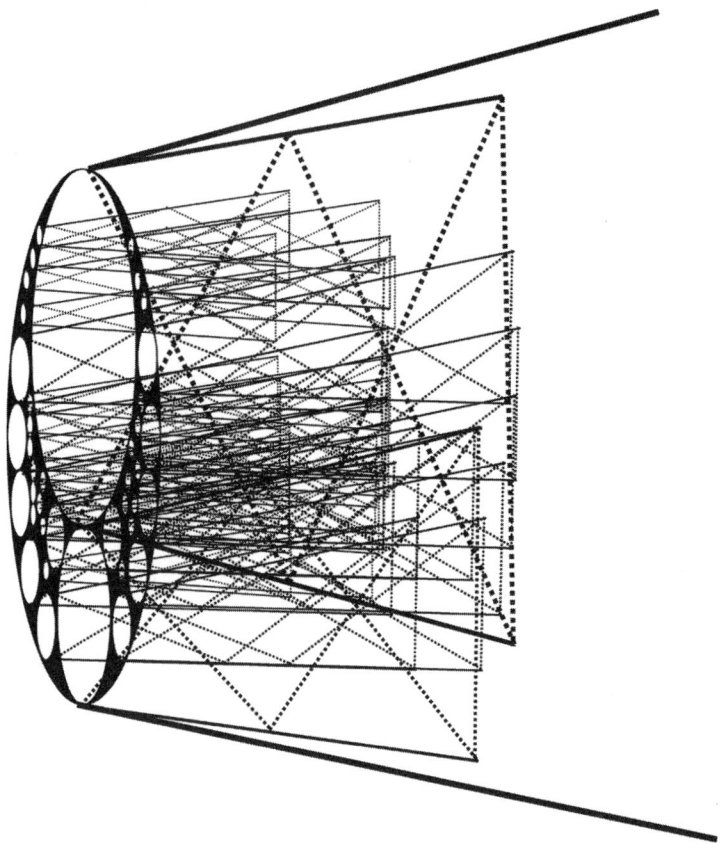

Figure 11.8
Apertures of attention, three-dimensional view.

competing demands of attention, for the negotiation of competing demands, and for special attentive states such as flow and meditative absorption.

Under the aperture model, the outer perimeter depicts full attentional capacity (which may or may not be elastic). Inside this perimeter lie the subapertures of attention. These apertures are not mere windows.

An old, and enduring, idea of the way information is processed is via associative maps, studied in cognitive psychology under such monikers as hierarchical schemata (Houghton and Hartley 1995) and central motive states (Bindra 1974), and recently updated as dynamic connectionist contexts (Botvinick and Plaut 2004). Different terminology has been used over the years. I will call them structures of reference. If we rotate figure 11.7 to peer behind the apertures (see figure 11.8), we will not find a black box with a spotlight shining on a stage but rather a network of structures of reference constructed such that each is uniquely sensitized to potential stimuli within overlapping, dynamic domains of activity. The structures are both apertures and avenues of processing.

The glue that binds the elements of each of these structures of reference is their association with each other within a specific domain of activity—one may call it a *context*. Within a contextual structure of reference (CSR), attending to an activity involves processing information, setting expectations, evaluating relevant cues, responding through established pathways within the structure, and constructing new pathways according to new developments. The claim is that all conscious attending in human cognition occurs within the context of an activity (see Yuri Dormashev's chapter 13 in this volume for a closely related perspective).

The context is a pathway of processing with links having been established in the past that allow for rapid processing of responses. A context sets expectations regarding what should be attended to (diffuse attention); when a matching cue arises, there is selective attention; relevance of this cue to immediate and long-term goals is calculated according to accumulated information embedded in the structure (long-term memory, habit); a response is formulated and executed accordingly; new expectations arise. This is a rough accounting of what occurs within one CSR aperture pathway. Other CSR aperture pathways will be open simultaneously, and how wide will depend on their relevance to the immediate and long-term goals of the subject. One of the CSR aperture pathways may be termed *fight or flight*, one may be termed *curiosity*, and yet another, *romance*. These are some of the hardwired CSRs, which, no matter how much attention is driven through other CSRs, are likely always open to a degree and ready to expand with a salient cue.

It should be emphasized that the apertures are understood as dilating and contracting in a constant flux as attention shifts from one activity to another over milliseconds. What drives one CSR to gain ascendance over the others, and how is such competition adjudicated? CSRs may be linked to a larger hierarchical goal structure where input through the CSRs goes for further relevance evaluation. Alternatively, they may compete in a Darwinian way for ascendancy,[3] with the larger goal hierarchy playing some role in which wins out. How factors within the CSRs that drive ascendancy match up with particular internal or external stimuli (Botvinick and Plaut 2004) must also be an integral part of the process. My use of the term *structure* may lend an unintended sense of stasis to the model, but these structures are envisioned as dynamic—in constant flux with constantly shifting boundaries. Thus, an element within one structure may also belong to other structures.

Let us look at an example. A young man in a technologically primitive society (say, in the highlands of Borneo) is on a lookout platform in the forest.[4] His job is to lash some spearheads to spears while keeping watch for any sign of marauding warriors from another tribe. He is new to both tasks and not expecting much excitement. When taking up his position, he surveys the surroundings. At this point, a CSR aperture pathway that we might call *defense* opens widest. Expectations are raised for signs of danger that he has been taught or has encountered before, all of which have been integrated into this pathway—such things as birds taking flight, sounds of snapping twigs, signature hoots of neighboring tribes, and so forth. This CSR has primed him to respond with urgency to such cues.

After surveying the surroundings, he squats down to begin lashing a spearhead to a shaft, a task he has only seen others do and is now trying for the first time. His defense CSR contracts, and his "spear-making" CSR dilates, but this CSR is still rather empty, and this lack of skill makes it difficult for him to recognize and adjust to appropriate cues in the task. On top of this, the previous evening he had had a riveting encounter with a young woman at a ceremonial dance. His romance CSR keeps crowding out his spear-making and defense CSRs.

While making his first spear and daydreaming about his love interest, the defense CSR, though comparatively small, is still open, and before the first spear is complete, the sound of a snapping twig catches his attention. The romance CSR immediately contracts, crowded out by the dilating defense CSR. Without moving, the boy scans the surroundings with ears and eyes. A flock of birds takes to the air. He identifies this through his defense CSR as another danger signal. He hears a hoot that he can't place—another bad sign identified through the defense CSR. These accumulated dangers prompt his defense CSR to temporarily integrate with his fight-or-flight CSR, and his heart begins beating faster, his adrenaline flows, and he realizes his unfinished spear could be very useful if finished. The integrated defense/fight-or-flight CSR is near full dilation until he turns attention to the nascent spear, at which time his spear-making CSR dilates, forcing contraction of the integrated defense/fight-or-flight CSR.[5] Both CSRs contract and dilate as he shifts attention back and forth. The more he concentrates on his spear, the less he is able to attend completely to signals from the forest, and vice versa.

We see in this example that selective attention is activated within an activity domain which drives diffuse attention. The temporary persistence of diffuse attention allows for the integration and assimilation of relevant information via selective attention.

A more contemporary example would be a male college student at a football game. Actively competing CSRs would likely be *socializing, analyzing the game, cheering*, and *sustenance*.[6] Other CSRs that would simultaneously be open but minimized might be *unfinished homework* and, of course, *romance*. Imagine if, to the student's surprise, a professor or a friend of his (stern) father sat down next to him. Now, in addition to his *socialize with elders* CSR's dilating, it will elide with his *socialize with friends* CSR, channeling his responses away from remarks and behavior suspected to be deemed distasteful by his neighbor.

To be more specific, imagine two alternative versions of this scenario. In one, before the elder arrives, a referee makes a controversial call unfavorable to the home team. The male fan in question, gesticulating threateningly toward the field, shouts a string of obscenities. In the alternative version, the same call is made but after the elder arrives, in which case the student's response would be more mild: "I can't believe that," throwing his hands up. Same cue, different response, guided by a qualitatively different CSR.

Now suppose something salient occurs, such as a siren blaring. Salience is often considered the mark of an entirely externally driven stimulus. The current model, however, would require that every attended cue be processed through a CSR and be dependent on two things: the availability of the CSR with respect to other CSRs and the sensitivity of the stimulus within the CSR. Depending on the listener, a siren could conceivably enter through a curiosity CSR (as with a young child), through a public safety CSR (for a distant motorist), or through a danger CSR (for a criminal). At a football game, it may enter through a cheering CSR. The CSR through which it enters depends on one's prior experience. For someone new to football games, it would likely enter through a public safety CSR and then be integrated into a cheering CSR relevant to the football game. The actual intention of the siren operator would bear no necessary relation to the CSR aperture pathways of listeners, but the most seasoned fans would be the quickest to channel the sound through the football CSR and respond appropriately. A particularly nerdy, though seasoned, fan sitting in the upper bleachers concentrating on calculus problems might have the siren enter through a cheering CSR and not attend to it at all—not even remember hearing it if questioned about it later.

Again, salience, under this model, is not an independent variable in attention and is, instead, predicated upon CSRs. It may be true that we are hardwired with certain CSRs, such as fight or flight, through which loud noises are attributed salience. But it is also true that such noises will be selected for attention depending only on their relevance within a CSR and the status of other competing CSRs. A straightforward way of challenging the notion of the inevitability of salient stimuli is to consider external context: A neon Coca-Cola sign will be much more salient in the middle of farmland than in downtown Tokyo. Another way to challenge it, however, is by considering internal contextual structure: The bouncing cheerleaders on the sidelines of the football game will be more salient to our heterosexual male fan than to his homosexual friend, who through his romance CSR finds more salience in the physiques of the players running and jumping on the field.

Draw

The postulate above is that the internal conditions of CSRs, in conjunction with *relevant* external stimuli, drive attention. As such, the main drivers of attention are internal rather than external. A salient phenomenon in the environment is best characterized not as a stimulus (thereby implying a behaviorist response) but as a cue, implying that there is a preexisting structure of responsiveness sensitized to the recognition and processing of the phenomenon.

One could try to argue counterfactually that without the stimulus there would be no attention to it and therefore attention begins in the stimulus, but if it is true that the CSR is always open to some extent and that it is appropriately sensitized to external phenomena, then stimulus or not, there is always diffuse attention. Ruth Garrett Millikan, discussing language and cognition under a theory she calls biosemantics, suggests that we do best to understand biological organisms not as representation producers but as representation consumers—a representation has meaning only as understood by the system—so consumption is primary (Millikan 1989). Likewise, I would argue, a stimulus has the potential to be attended to only insofar as it can be assimilated into and processed by an open CSR.

If the salience of external phenomena is dependent on internal constructions, how are we to conceive of the flow of information? Traditionally, sense data are conceived to impinge on our senses like so many projectiles flying through space; our sensory organs let them in, and then our processing pathways filter some out and let others through. The problem with the projectile view of information flow is that the information is, again, originating externally. What many studies in inattentional blindness (Mack, Pappas, Silverman, and Gay 2002; Mack and Rock 1998) have shown, however, is that often we simply do not see phenomena that are obviously open to view. Mack and Rock (1998, 228) conclude that the most important factor in an object's capturing attention "is the meaningfulness or signal value of the stimulus." In other words, it is not that irrelevant stimuli are filtered out but that only relevant stimuli are drawn in.

The projectile view of information flow presupposes that the information will be processed unless rejected. The view presented here is that there is no information until there is a CSR ready to assimilate and process it (i.e., if NPR is being broadcast in the forest and there is no one around to hear it, there is no news there in the forest). Does this open me up to a chicken-and-egg objection? No, because an evolutionary-developmental view of the human being posits a certain amount of hardwiring that begins with rudimentary CSRs and allows for them to gradually mature and differentiate (Gopnik and Schulz 2004; Millikan 1989).

I introduce the notion of draw as a way of emphasizing the fundamental role of sensitivity in attention. There are two basic claims: (1) We attend only to those phenomena to which we are cognitively capable of attending, and (2) once we are capable of attending, there is an active internal mechanism that struggles for predominance against other active internal mechanisms to receive and process relevant information.

How can we make sense of a cognitive draw? How can there be a pulling force from inside the head that acts on things outside the head? Action at a distance was a common problem in early theories of physics—how could it be, for instance, that electricity suddenly flows through a channel when there is nothing obviously pushing it along? The answer lies in there being a particular difference between one place and another. If the voltage on one end of an electrical channel is identical to the voltage on the other end, there will be no flow of electricity. Only when the voltage increases on one end do electrons flow toward that end. One way of understanding it is that the voltage differential establishes a draw that enables the flow of electricity. Just as voltage is known more accurately as electric potential, attentional sensitivity in cognition could be conceived as *information potential*.

Electricity isn't the only occurrence of a draw due to a differential in a potential channel of a flowing medium. A similar set of phenomena power the flow of air in the form of wind. Aside from global processes, such as the Coriolis force, wind is generally understood as the flow of air through a channel of pressure differentials, from a high-pressure area to a low-pressure area. One way to understand it is that the low-pressure area sets up a draw from the high-pressure area. For instance, when a window breaks in movie depictions of airplane disasters, the reason that the air is depicted as being sucked outwards from within the plane is that the air pressure at an altitude of 33,000 feet is much lower than the artificially pressurized cabin.

A third way to think of draw is through economic demand. The analogy of cognitive information flow to economics is felicitous in that the appearance of a product on the market originates from the supply end, just as stimuli originate externally to the agent. However, just as a product will not move through market channels until there is the draw of consumer demand, so information will not flow through cognitive channels until there is the draw of attentional sensitivity.

We see still more examples of the action-at-a-distance effect of draw in the cases of heat and dissolved substances. In human attention, it may be best to think of raw sense data (sound waves, photons, etc.) as the channel of the information stream, the infrastructure, that is always there and of information as the medium that flows through the channel. Attention is not a sensitivity to photons but to the information that photons carry.

The metaphors, whether explicit or implicit, of attention as a spotlight and of sense data as projectiles that would strike and register if not filtered are pervasive in the cognitive science literature. What differentiates the model expounded here is the realization that attention follows not sense data but rather information. Broadbent (1958) distinguished between stimuli and information some five decades ago, but the idea still persists today that we will be overwhelmed (even by information) without a filtering mechanism. Briefly going back to the beginnings can help put this idea to rest.

A simple stone is bombarded by sound, heat, and the entire range of stimuli from the electromagnetic spectrum. Does it feel overwhelmed? Of course not. When life formed and successfully opened the first window of sensitivity to its environment, was it overwhelmed with so much incoming sensory stimuli? No, because the window was open only to a single kind of information that was ultimately adaptive. To everything else, it was like a stone. As creatures became more complex, new sensitivities opened up to enable creatures to process new information, but only to the extent that it was ultimately adaptive. At no step was there a gush of data that required filtering, and that goes for humans, too. William James gave us the term "blooming, buzzing confusion," and we have the common intuition that when babies are born they are overwhelmed by sensory stimuli that they cannot interpret. It's more likely, however, that infants are born with a limited number of active domains of activity within which they are naturally responsive to what we would consider primitive information. Sensitivity and responsiveness would then expand in tandem.

As our sensitivity expands within domains of activity, the specific circumstances combined with specific internal conditions of the CSR together select information as needed. There is no perceived bombardment and no filter. Pylyshyn's (1989) FINSTs that point outward, index, and track features of visual stimuli are similar in that they are endogenously prepared to respond to specific kinds of features of the external world rather than accepting everything and then dumping what is not needed.

Syntax

The claim is made above that all human attention arises within a domain of activity, so it is important to inquire into what is meant by the term *activity*. An activity is understood here as a set of constraints that are related in such a way that they facilitate the accomplishment of a goal.[7] This set of related constraints is understood as a syntax because it provides a dynamic structure for an unfolding concatenation of actions (including thoughts).[8] The syntax of daily etiquette is implicit, whereas the syntax of chess is more explicit, with its large body of rules, but the suggestion here is that the syntax of any activity goes beyond any explicit set of rules to encompass all constraints on thought and action relevant to the activity as a situational, temporal, autopoietic enterprise. Thus, the syntax of competitive downhill skiing includes not only the international rule book but also the resistance of its moguls and gates and the implicit rules of socializing among competitors.

Constraints are parameters within which one may respond to a cue.[9] Cues are recognized according to the total set of constraints, the syntax. How good one is at negotiating a syntax will often depend on one's amount of experience within that syntax. Cues gain and lose salience accordingly, and responses become more or less automatic accordingly. Cues are phenomena the appropriate response to which advances one toward a goal. They can be external or internal, perceived or cognized, and sensitive or insensitive to response. A cue can be a rock on a cliff face, a move in a mental chess game, a batting eyelash, and so on. Each of these cues is recognized within a syntax, and a response follows according to the constraints of that syntax.

The final element in this formulation of an activity is the response. Once the goals and syntax are organized in a functional way and one is able to recognize relevant cues, two things occur in cognition: predictions are made, according to which responses are primed to possible future cues, and immediate responses are executed (the effects of which may become future cues). This should not suggest, however, that potential responses are temporally secondary to the recognition and assimilation of cues. The capacity to respond—the syntax of response—may play an active, and even necessary, role in establishing the initial sensitivity to the cue, itself (see Borghi 2005; Hommel, chapter 5, this volume). A response would then be functionally inseparable from a cue, even though in real time a response may be temporally separate or may not even arise at all. In this sense, a cue would entail at least a potential and approximate response in order to be a genuine cue. This conceptual necessity linking response to cue, does not, however, mean that the response is *actually* necessary, or that a non-habituated action may not be identified post hoc as an appropriate response.

For everyone but a newborn (perhaps even a newborn), every activity involves some amount of prior cognitive habituation. Habituation is the Hebbian facilitation of response through repetition to a general cue within the general constraints of a syntax and according to generalized situational demands. An initial step in the habituation process is recognizing a cue as general—as something the likes of which may occur again under similar circumstances and require a similar response. A related step, formulation of a response, is established in the same context. If the context is novel, response formulation will happen haphazardly at first, arrived at by navigation through related but not identical CSRs, which elide in and out until appropriate responses are arrived at and incorporated into a nascent new CSR. Habituation is viewed here as the construction and reinforcement of the pathways of a CSR.

In addition to syntax, goals, and response, the final element of an activity relevant to this model is how the response is executed. William Calvin posited the notion of the ballistic thought (Calvin 1993), suggesting that cognition involved in time-constrained, complex serial actions is a borrowing of the same cerebral mechanisms that allow us to accurately hurl a projectile at a target. Launching mental calculations is like launching a series of actions that once started cannot be adjusted via feedback and response, because the response time is too long. I suggest that the real-time negotiation of the syntax of a CSR is just this kind of ballistic thought, except that in an activity, it is more open to revision than in an action, itself. It's difficult to think of a human response that is not in some sense ballistic, that does not involve the initiation of a concatenation of cerebral activity that proceeds in some way on its own.

Habituation involves the automation of the links in the concatenation. Thus, each of the three steps of response involves the possibility of habituation: the recognition of cues (*what* to be sensitive to), choosing a response (*why* this response and not another), and the cognitive and motor activity that are the response (*how* to execute it and *when*—i.e., timing). The provisional answers to the what, why, how, and when of an action are the syntax of a CSR and allow for the smooth unfolding of the perception–action cycle.

Implications of the Aperture, Draw, Syntax Model

As I suggested at the start of this chapter, adopting any particular model of attention will entail specific available inferences from the model. What is the payoff for using the ADS model? I think there are many.

Given the elements of an activity—the goals, the syntax, and the response—we can begin to envision a theory of optimization of action. The obvious avenues of intervention are at any of the four opportunities in the process of habituation of a response just noted: the *what*, the *why*, the *how*, and the *when*. These may be more or less important depending on the weightings of certain aspects within a syntax. In chess, the *why* is most important; in figure skating, it is the *how*; in urban warfare, it is the *what*; and the *when* is crucial in all of these examples (though less obviously so in chess).

As discussed, the use of the term *syntax* should not give the sense of an intransigence to modification. Not only is a CSR constantly open to modification but its place in the competitive hierarchy for attentional predominance is also constantly open to modification. As a CSR becomes richer through experience, assuming at least a moderate level of associated positive affect, it will compete more successfully for attention, and an interest may develop.

In this model, *interest* is best understood as motivation through enjoyment. An underappreciated corollary to Csikszentmihalyi's theory of flow is his distinction between enjoyment and pleasure. The full passage is worth rehearsing:

Playing a close game of tennis that stretches one's ability is enjoyable, as is reading a book that reveals things in a new light, as is having a conversation that leads us to express ideas we didn't know we had. Closing a contested business deal, or any piece of work well done, is enjoyable. None of these experiences may be particularly pleasurable at the time they are taking place, but afterward we think back on them and say, "That really was fun" and wish they would happen again. After an enjoyable event, we know that we have changed, that our self has grown: in some respect, we have become more complex as a result of it.

Experiences that give pleasure can also give enjoyment, but the two sensations are quite different. For instance, everybody takes pleasure in eating. To enjoy food, however, is more difficult. A gourmet enjoys eating, as does anyone who pays enough attention to a meal so as to discriminate the various sensations provided by it. As this example suggests, we can experience pleasure without any investment of psychic energy, whereas enjoyment happens only as a result of unusual investments of attention. (Csikszentmihalyi and Csikszentmihalyi 1988, 46)

A person is interested in activities that lead to enjoyment but not necessarily to pleasure. One is interested in gardening but not shooting heroin. Drinking wine in an enjoyable way may further develop an interest that enriches the enjoyment. Drinking wine in a pleasurable way leads to inebriation. Enjoyment and pleasure are not mutually exclusive, but interest is associated with enjoyment, not pleasure. Further, people are not interested in activities that do not yield any enjoyment whatsoever. Researchers who study interest confirm that interest is closely associated with the understanding of enjoyment offered here, but because they do not make the enjoyment–pleasure distinction, conclusions in the literature state that "interest and enjoyment are distinct positive emotions" (Silvia 2006, 29). The confluence of enjoyment and interest, in my view, is that they both enrich CSRs in a constructive way.

There is obviously a tight correlation, probably a mutually reinforcing relationship, between interest, enjoyment, and flow. Achievement of one, therefore, likely yields achievement of the others, suggesting that if one wishes to cultivate or increase interest in an activity, engendering flow would be of some assistance. Achieving flow intentionally, however, can be elusive. For this reason, it would help to understand potential obstacles to flow.

Because flow depends on a balance of challenge and skill (and assuming timely feedback), any imbalance would diminish chances of achievement. Thus, two primary obstacles to flow are high challenge/low skill and, conversely, low challenge/high skill. A third obstacle is distractions (internal or external), and finally, even if there is a balance of challenge and skill and an absence of distractions, flow may still be difficult to achieve if there is a lack of interest.

In most activities, when the first two obstacles are encountered, adjustments in challenge level are the easiest to make, and practice results in an increase in skill. The most difficult adjustment to make is when the level of skill is too high in relation to the level of challenge, as in monotonous assembly-line or office work. Csikszentmihalyi relates the story of an assembly-line worker who increased the challenge level of his work activity by fabricating personal challenges with relation to the demands of his job (Csikszentmihalyi 1990, 39). Something similar can be observed in children at play, and this may actually be one of the functions of play—to build CSRs through incrementally more difficult challenges.

Why does Johnny climb on the low walls, avoid cracks, and kick rocks while walking home from school, instead of walking like a typical adult? One explanation is that he increases the level of challenge. He has already mastered walking, and just walking is boring—there is no sense of enjoyment. By fabricating challenges and meeting those challenges, he increases his level of enjoyment, in addition to his skills of balance, locomotion, and so on. This natural desire to meet challenges and the natural satisfaction gained from achieving goals may go a long way in explaining why children learn so readily. It also goes a long way in explaining how to overcome the obstacle of low challenge.

At the level of the CSR, the introduction of new challenges adds complexity to the activity's syntax. A sports coach, for instance, keeps the attention of players while emphasizing fundamentals by creating a number of high-challenge training exercises and keeping the players moving from one exercise to the next. However, this process is extrinsic to the players. To make the activity autotelic, the athlete must, himself or herself, incorporate such challenges into his or her own CSR. The self-motivated athlete must work on the cognitive level as well as the somatic—building challenges into an otherwise boring workout routine.

Distractions are an interesting case and a good illustration of the usefulness of the aperture model of attention. Under the aperture model, when one is fully engaged in an activity, that activity's CSR aperture pathway widens until nearly all attentive processing capacity is monopolized by that CSR, blocking out competing CSRs—the would-be distractions. Competing CSRs can distract only when the desired activity's CSR has not grown to ascendancy or when that ascendancy cannot easily be maintained.

William James said that there is no such thing as sustained attention, only attention renewed. This is consistent with the aperture model of attention in which different CSRs are competing for ascendancy under normal conditions and, from a subjective point of view, it therefore takes effort to sustain (repeatedly renew) any one CSR for an extended period of time. I suggest that when a CSR is opened to ascendancy, its predominance is usually precarious because it is vulnerable to other CSRs' attempting to simultaneously dilate. Mental effort can be understood as the deployment of cognitive resources to renew conscious attention to an activity. The more vulnerable an ascendant CSR is relative to the strength of competing CSRs, the greater the effort required to maintain attention. One can analogize the process to pedaling a bicycle. To maintain momentum on a flat surface (normal conditions), one must exert energy by pedaling. To maintain momentum on an upward incline (distracted conditions), one must pedal harder. To maintain momentum going downhill, however, no expenditure is required. Flow activities, by monopolizing attentive capacities, achieve a stable momentum such that they endure without external propulsion and so can persist despite incursions from other CSRs. Effortless attention, then, is constituted by the autotelic maintenance of a CSR. The syntax is so tightly constructed, the facility of responses so automatic, and the information flow so large, that the momentum created dominates the entire perception–action cycle, thereby inhibiting the rise of other CSRs.

As discussed above, the fourth obstacle to flow—lack of interest—is related to enrichment of a CSR and positive affect from enjoyment. Interest in activities is often neglected as a subject of study, I believe, because it is understood as subjective, like taste: To say that one is interested in baseball is like saying one has a taste for spicy food or impressionist painting. As such, it is written off, like taste, to unanalyzable personal preference (see Dormashev, chapter 13, this volume for a different and more subtle view of personal taste, which is closer to my notion of interest). Interest, I am suggesting, however, increases in an activity with the complexity of one's CSR (assuming concomitant positive affect). But what are the ways in which one's CSR may be complex and increase in complexity? There may be many; below I describe two: formality of actions and syntax of actions.

Formality in an action refers to the narrowness of the parameters of movement—the lower the amount of flexibility (the fewer correct[10] ways to make the movement), the higher the formality. Consider dance. For teenagers at a high school dance, the degree of formality in any one movement is low. For a traditional ballerina, however, the degree of formality in each movement is extremely high—there are precise ways in which to execute each movement, and going outside those parameters would be perceived as incorrect.

Syntax in a set of actions refers to the parameters constraining how one action is concatenated with the next and is directly related to syntax in a CSR; since CSRs are functionally intermodal and internal cognition eventuates in external action, it makes sense that syntax in an action is part of the syntax of a CSR. Again, consider dance. For teenagers at a high school dance, how one strings one action of the dance to the next generally makes little difference, and so the degree of syntax is low. For the ballerina in a tightly choreographed classical dance, however, there is a very high degree of syntax, and if one move is out of order, even if the formality of the movement is executed with virtuosic brilliance, it will be perceived as incorrect.

Let us distinguish an activity from an action. Swinging a bat is an action, while playing baseball is an activity. We may categorize all *activities* based on the degree of formality of the *actions* that constitute them. Imagine a continuum with completely formal activities (i.e. those composed of highly formal actions), such as choreographed dance, martial arts forms, or acrobatics, on one end. On the other end will be completely informal, or open-ended, activities (those with informal actions), such as a high school dance or eating a grape.[11] Most activities will have both formal and informal components, and, therefore, fall somewhere between the two extremes. Entertaining guests, for instance, would appear toward the informal end, while driving and making pottery might appear somewhere in the middle.

We may also categorize activities according to another continuum, namely, the amount of syntax involved in connecting the actions together within the activity. Activities with a higher degree of syntax may be called *more syntactic*, and those with a lower degree of syntax *less syntactic*. We can also place activities on this continuum with respect to others. For instance, a classical ballet dance would be highly syntactic,

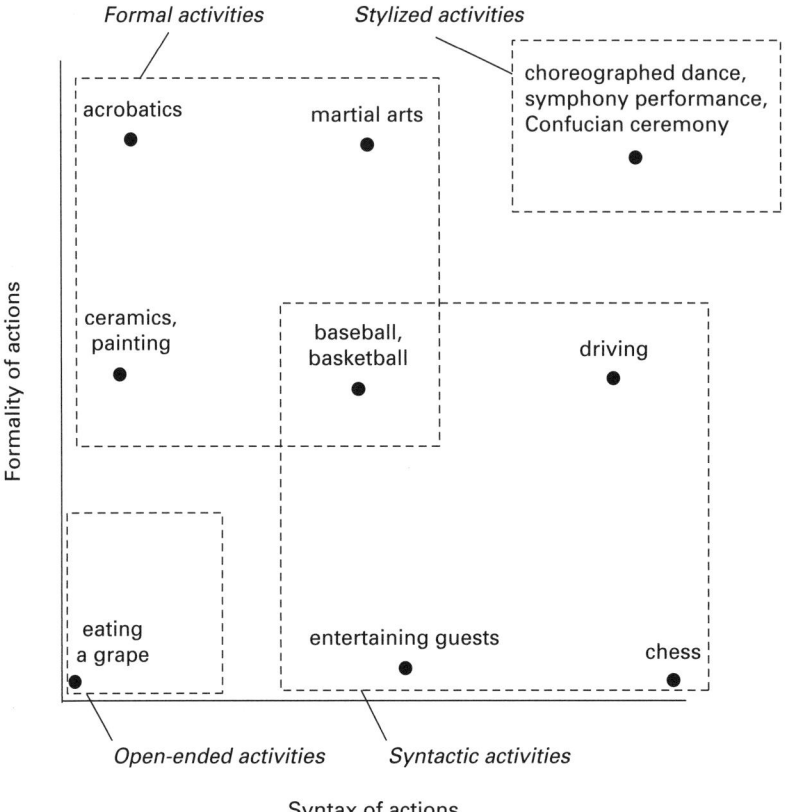

Figure 11.9
Action diagram: formal versus syntactic activities.

as would chess and, perhaps, driving. Entertaining guests and executing martial arts moves would be moderately syntactic, and eating a grape, making pottery, and executing unchoreographed acrobatic moves less syntactic.

Let us now combine these two continua into two axes in a phase-space diagram (see figure 11.9)—formality being the vertical axis and syntax being the horizontal axis. Fully formal and highly syntactic activities, such as a symphony performance or a highly ritualized ceremony, will fall at the top right, while informal nonsyntactic activities, such as eating a grape, will fall at the bottom left. Elsewhere on the grid, we will find driving (middle right—lots of syntax, less formality), martial arts practice (top middle—lots of formality, less syntax), chess and other games (bottom right—lots of syntax, very little formality), painting, sculpture, and other arts (middle left—some formal techniques but little syntax), and baseball and other sports (center—a moderate amount of both formal actions and syntax). We can now identify activities as belonging to one of four groups: *formal* (top left), *syntactic* (bottom right), *stylized*—both syntactic and formal (top right)—and *open-ended*—neither syntactic nor formal (bottom left).

Studying this diagram, one may surmise that among the general populace flow is most commonly found in syntactic and formal activities. Activities with the highest probability of engendering flow likely fall at the intersection of these two squares, where we find such activities as playing popular music, ballroom dancing, and all kinds of sports. Outside of these two squares, in the stylized activities and the open-ended activities, is where we find flow the most difficult to achieve, on the one hand because challenges are too high, and on the other because challenges are too low.

With the help of this way of conceptualizing the relationship between activities and flow, we can get a bit more purchase on the question of overcoming obstacles to flow. Consider, first, what it takes to achieve flow in open-ended activities, such as leisurely walking to a destination, washing the dishes, taking a shower. In activities such as these, in which the degree of formality and syntax are so low as to present very little challenge, other CSRs easily usurp predominance because there is not enough challenge in the formality or syntax of the actions to maintain momentum. In typical flow activities, habit is an ally because it allows you to execute part of a complex action or set of actions while paying attention to other, more subtle, features of the activity. In open-ended activities, habit is the enemy because there are no subtleties of form or syntax of the activity to move on to.

We discussed above that introducing artificial challenges to an activity is one way to overcome low challenge. Another way is through the practice of mindfulness. Mindfulness is a form of meditation in which one keeps various elements of an otherwise habituated activity in attention. Meditation, in all its stripes, does one thing well—it destroys habits of mind. One of the most intransigent and difficult to identify habits is the very process in which attention transitions rapidly, successively, repeatedly, and unnoticeably from one CSR to the next (let's call it *attention substitution*). Traditionally, the first step in Buddhist meditation is to recognize the process of attention substitution (phrased in different terms) and prevent the attention from following the ascending CSR. Attention substitution is easy enough to experience. Simply sit still and do nothing, paying attention only to your natural breathing and noticing how often your attention shifts to something else. Each "something else" is a competing CSR.

In this *breath meditation*, one has formed a *meditation* CSR, which is so devoid of both formality and syntax that it is nearly empty of any content, whatsoever. Of course, this is difficult to maintain against other more established, richer, or more urgent CSRs. The method of this kind of meditation more generally (terminology varies, so I'll call it *open meditation* for simplicity) is to allow a competing CSR to arise but then to abandon it and come back to the *meditation* CSR. In effect, this type of meditation CSR is a meta-activity that takes attention, itself, as its subject. There are two important ways in which the activation of CSRs is habituated. One lies in how various CSRs are interlinked, and so repeatedly moving from one to the next by virtue of these connections will be habituated. The second way is through the very process of allowing different CSRs to arise one after another, which is a deep habit that goes back to infancy. The practice of abandoning a newly ascendant CSR serves to dishabituate the meta-activity (attentional substitution) in which CSRs spontaneously compete with each other, to diminish the chance of the ascendant CSR's attempting to gain ascendance again—like an action that fails to receive positive feedback. Over time—weeks, months, and even years—the meditation CSR, during the activity of meditation, expands to monopolize all of attention, and competing CSRs fail to arise. The anomaly of this kind of meditation is that it can be maintained despite so little apparent complexity of content and so little information flow; however, this is, of course, explained by the understanding that the activity of attentional substitution has itself been modified such that competing CSRs no longer compete as vigorously.

From open meditation, let us return to mindfulness meditation, a form of meditation adopted during active life. Mindfulness is said to be most effective when it is coupled with sitting meditation as just described. If competing CSRs have been muted through the successful cultivation of a meditation CSR, then when performing normal habituated tasks, competing CSRs are less likely to arise. As mentioned above, actions naturally concatenate in syntactic series, and in the process of habituation these cognitive processes are tucked away for automatic processing. Mindfulness practices bring these processes back to the foreground. While walking, one notices one's balance, one's gait, one's breathing, and as many elements of these that one can bring to mind. The challenge lies in identifying these elements, attending to them in turn, noticing subtle characteristics, and even fine-tuning them. In this way, one reconstructs the CSR, enriching both its syntax and formality, moving it from an open-ended activity further toward the center of the action diagram, where enjoyment and sustained attention will more likely ensue. This is how mindfulness mediation can assist in achieving flow in low-challenge/high-skill situations.

In this section, we have circled back to the topic of the first section ("Interest and Effortless Attention")—the neglected role of interest in accounting for effortless attention in flow. The original intention was to begin to see how the ADS model of attention can yield new insights into the diverse phenomena associated with attention. This was done by further explicating interest with respect to CSRs and then considering how interest, enjoyment, and flow may reinforce each other in activities that have a moderate amount of formality and syntax of actions. Also, not only did the model make sense of how mindfulness exercises can be useful in raising the level of challenge in order to facilitate flow but it also made sense of meditation, itself. Finally, this model helped account for the phenomenon of effortless attention itself, conceived as the highly automated negotiation of a tightly constructed, complex syntax with a very high flow of information. Combined, these provide a momentum in a CSR that inhibits competing CSRs.

Conclusion

The purpose of presenting the formality–syntax diagram (figure 11.9) is to demonstrate how understanding attention via the aperture, draw, syntax model can lead to a more fruitful theoretical engagement of features of cognition that are associated with attention. As discussed, effortless attention becomes quite a bit less mysterious when it is understood as the inhibition of competing CSRs in the normal process of attention substitution, either by momentum of the ascendant CSR, as in flow, or by the diminution of the substitution process, itself, through meditation. The hope is that this model will open up new avenues of profitable exploration for future research on attention.

Limitations of This Model

One obvious potential limitation of this model is that it claims no direct correspondence to neurophysiology, and for this reason, it may be open to objections from readers attempting to apply it to human neurophysiology. For instance, one might object that neurophysiologists have demonstrated that attention is not a unitary phenomenon, and yet the ADS model of attention presumes that it is. It must be kept in mind, however, that this model is a functional model, the aim of which is to account for human cognitive functions that are underpinned by neurophysiological processes. Thus, any neurophysiological processes that underpin functions that contradict it would invalidate it. In the case of the nonunitary nature of attention, the ADS model posits not that there must necessarily be one physical location in the brain that is a channel of all attentional processes but that the neurophysiological processes that underpin attention act as one functional channel, *as if* there were only one physiological channel. Just as physicists include a notion of a center of gravity in models of physical motion even though one cannot locate a center of gravity in the physical universe, so this model posits a central channel of information flow even though no such physical channel exists in the brain.

Another potential limitation is that this model is purported to apply to conscious attention, and consciousness is a notion only tenuously supported by the cognitive scientific literature. By "conscious," I am simply referring to the explicit–implicit, controlled–automatic distinction common in the literature (but see Blais, chapter 6, this volume). I am suggesting that in this model of attention, there is neither explicit nor implicit activity alone but necessarily both together. If it were all implicit, there would be no attention, as such. (This is not to say that there would be no processing.

It is a matter of stipulation—attention to one's actions is understood here as involving awareness of some of the relevant events, by definition.) If it were all explicit, the perception–action cycle would slow to a snail's pace.

Finally, the model is limited by the lack of empirical data supporting it, particularly with respect to the formal–syntactic distinction in the last section. As suggested at the beginning of the chapter, this limitation is due partly to the constraints placed upon attention research by the laboratory emphasis. The suggestion here is that such an approach has limited our understanding of attention due to a lack of empirical studies of attention in naturalistic, ecologically valid activities. Therefore, it is not that the model lacks empirical support but that the model predicts empirical findings from studies that have not yet been conceived due to the inferential poverty of current, implicit and explicit, models of attention.

Notes

1. I ignore the possibility of divided attention but only for the sake of brevity. One may note that in the diagram, a second aperture is larger than the other minor apertures, and one may take this to be attentive to a second domain more or less simultaneously.

2. Researchers often stress neurophysiological evidence that attention is not a unitary process. This is true at the preconscious level, which this model takes into account via the subapertures. There is no accounting here for the actual systems of attention because this is a higher level functional model rather than a lower level physiological or computational model.

3. Edelman (1987) was the first to suggest Darwinian-type competition among neuronal processes. Calvin (1993, 238) later posited the brain as a "Darwin machine" in which "the brain selects the sequences of schema."

4. Anthropological inaccuracies notwithstanding.

5. Again, specifying a position on divided attention is not important. It could be that two CSRs are simultaneously open halfway or are more fully open but only in succession. What matters is the proportion of their averages compared over a short period of time and that an increase of intensity in one CSR leads to a decrease in sensitivity in others.

6. Of course, the monikers postulated to indentify CSRs may be taken as more or less appropriate. While a sustenance CSR, for example, may have an emphasis on genuine nutrition at one point in time, it may have an emphasis on pleasure at another point, or any combination of the two.

7. Botvinick and Plaut state that "there are many types of routine behavior for which it is not straightforward to identify discrete, explicit goals, for example, taking a walk or playing the violin" (Botvinick and Plaut 2004, 423) and that such activities may be driven, instead, by external cues. How correct this claim is depends on what one means by "discrete, explicit goals." In the model offered here, by *goals*, I mean any directedness in an activity such that action in the activity can be judged in at least a tenuous way successful or not. Routine activities may be acti-

vated by external cues, but they will still have a directedness to them, even though such directedness may be as general as preserving homeostasis, satisfying curiosity, alleviating stiffness, or killing time. Further, it should be stressed that I make no claim as to whether the goals guiding activities are conscious nor to their number. It may be that a goal is unconscious while the behavior, itself, is conscious, and it may be that multiple goals within a CSR are driving an activity.

This deserves a bit more discussion. Consider John Conway's Game of Life (Gardner 1970). In this game, a simple set of instructions leads to temporally unfolding, complex, patterned movement. We can accurately say that these are parameter-constrained "movements" but not goal-driven ones. This would be equivalent to a decontextualized human action, such as raising a hand. I suggest that such actions in humans are always embedded in goal-directed activities and do not arise solely due to external cues. A domain of activity (CSR), which contains the encoding for potential actions, may arise from attentional ascendency prompted by external cues but only in conjunction with internal sensitivity, which is itself tied to some general or specific goal or goals.

8. It is true that neural network researchers often exploit nonlinear dynamics in their models of cognition (as in gradient descent learning) and that some cognitive scientists have had great success with stochastic equations that result in simulated behavior that appears to mimic features of human cognition. Nevertheless, such cognitive processes in a normal human being are still fundamentally goal driven (i.e., directed), are parameter bounded, and are related in nonrandom ways to other goal-driven, parameter-bounded cognitive processes. Thus, my claim of the syntactic nature of cognition is not damaged by the prospect of stochastic processes in cognition. If such processes occur, they likely occur at one or two stages in the cognition of attention: (1) in the online approximations of an unfolding action—as such they still occur at a level that is subservient to nonrandom, syntactic processes; (2) in the ongoing spontaneous neural activity that subtends endogenous CSR fluctuations. If both of these are the case, there would be a beautiful hierarchy of levels, with randomness embedded in syntax and syntax embedded in randomness, and so on.

9. In attention research, a cue is often understood as a preliminary stimulus that precedes a target stimulus and directs attention to it. Here, however, I am replacing the term *stimulus* with the term *cue*, to emphasize that there is no stimulus without context. Cues are primary.

10. The correctness of a formal action can be judged on either normative grounds (e.g., movements in classical ballet) or instrumental grounds (a correct golf swing, for instance, is an effective one).

11. There is only one way to swallow that I can think of, but there are an infinite number of ways to move the grape to the mouth and to chew, even if we habitually choose only one. For easy verification, observe children at the table.

References

Bindra, D. 1974. A motivational view of learning, performance, and behavior modification. *Psychol. Rev.* 81:199–213.

Borghi, A. 2005. Object concepts and action. In *Grounding cognition: The role of perception and action in memory, language, and thinking*, ed. D. Pecher and R. A. Zwaan. Cambridge: Cambridge University Press, 8–34.

Botvinick, M., and D. C. Plaut. 2004. Doing without schema hierarchies: A recurrent connectionist approach to normal and impaired routine sequential action. *Psychol. Rev.* 111:395–429.

Broadbent, D. E. 1957. A mechanical model for human attention and immediate memory. *Psychol. Rev.* 64:205–215.

Broadbent, D. E. 1958. *Perception and communication*. New York: Pergamon Press.

Calvin, W. H. 1993. The unitary hypothesis: A common neural circuitry for novel manipulations, language, plan ahead, and throwing? In *Tools, language, and cognition in human evolution*, ed. K. R. Gibson and T. Ringold. New York: Cambridge University Press, 230–250.

Csikszentmihalyi, M. 1975. *Beyond boredom and anxiety*. 1st ed. San Francisco: Jossey-Bass.

Csikszentmihalyi, M. 1990. *Flow: The psychology of optimal experience*. 1st ed. New York: Harper & Row.

Csikszentmihalyi, M. 1997. *Finding flow: The psychology of engagement with everyday life*. New York: Basic Books.

Csikszentmihalyi, M., and I. S. Csikszentmihalyi. 1988. *Optimal experience: Psychological studies of flow in consciousness*. Cambridge: Cambridge University Press.

Edelman, G. M. 1987. *Neural Darwinism: The theory of neuronal group selection*. New York: Basic Books.

Faglioni, P. 1990. The frontal lobe. In *Handbook of clinical and experimental neuropsychology*, ed. G. Denes and L. Pizzamiglio. Hove, UK: Psychology Press, 525–569.

Gardner, M. 1970. The fantastic combinations of John Conway's new solitaire game "Life." *Sci. Am.* 223:120–123.

Gopnik, A., and L. Schulz. 2004. Mechanisms of theory formation in young children. *Trends Cogn. Sci.* 8:371–377.

Houghton, G., and T. Hartley. 1995. Parallel models of serial behaviour: Lashley revisited. *Psyche* 2 (25).

Kahneman, D. 1973. *Attention and effort*. Englewood Cliffs, NJ: Prentice-Hall.

Mack, A., Z. Pappas, M. Silverman, and R. Gay. 2002. What we see: Inattention and the capture of attention by meaning. *Conscious. Cogn.* 11:488–506.

Mack, A., and I. Rock. 1998. *Inattentional blindness*. Cambridge: MIT Press.

Millikan, R. G. 1989. Biosemantics. *J. Philos.* 86:281–297.

Parasuraman, R. 1998a. The attentive brain: Issues and prospects. In *The attentive brain*, ed. R. Parasuraman. Cambridge: MIT Press, 3–15.

Parasuraman, R. 1998b. *The attentive brain.* Cambridge: MIT Press.

Pashler, H., ed. 1998. *Attention.* Hove, UK: Psychology Press.

Posner, M. I. 2004. *Cognitive neuroscience of attention.* New York: Guilford.

Pylyshyn, Z. 1989. The role of location indexes in spatial perception: A sketch of the FINST spatial-index model. *Cognition* 32:65–97.

Silvia, P. J. 2006. *Exploring the psychology of interest.* New York: Oxford University Press.

Treisman, A. M., and G. Gelade. 1980. A feature-integration theory of attention. *Cognit. Psychol.* 12:97–136.

Underwood, G. 1993. *The psychology of attention.* New York: New York University Press.

12 Toward an Empirically Responsible Ethics: Cognitive Science, Virtue Ethics, and Effortless Attention in Early Chinese Thought

Edward Slingerland

The two models of ethics that have been dominant in the West since the Enlightenment—and continue to serve as the default in both academic philosophy and public ethical debate—are deontology and utilitarianism. The former is best captured in Kant's classic rule-based approach, where ethical behavior is to be guided by a hierarchy of maxims, which can be applied to properly classified situations in a fairly straightforward manner. For instance, consider the maxim, "It is wrong to lie." When presented with a situation, we can consult our definition of a *lie* to determine whether act X in this given situation was or was not an instance of lying, and having made this determination, we can then decide whether it was right or wrong depending on where this particular maxim is located in a hierarchy of maxims—for example, perhaps it is trumped by the maxim that we should strive to preserve life. If we are utilitarians, in any situation we should be able to unproblematically tally up the costs and benefits of proposed courses of action, do the math, and thereby figure out which course of action maximizes whatever good our brand of utilitarianism deems important (happiness, justice, gross national product, etc.).

Despite their differences, both models of ethics might be characterized as *cognitive control* or *high reason* (Damasio 1994) models: In order to be effectively implemented, they require the agent to be consciously aware of all of the relevant factors, to suppress emotional reactions and social biases, and to arrive at and carry out an objective, dispassionately rational decision. The reasoning process drawn upon is amodal, involving the manipulation of abstract maxims or mathematical values. In both cases, the entire process of moral reasoning is transparent and under our conscious control and has nothing to do with the details of our embodiment, or with emotions, implicit skills, or unconscious habits. In other words, effortless attention and action—automatic, nonconscious, embodied engagement with the world—play no role in either model of ethics.

Problems with Cognitive-Control Ethical Models

The extent to which disembodied, purely rational convictions could realistically be expected to guide ethical behavior has been questioned at least since the early Chinese philosopher Mencius (4th c. B.C.E.) and his criticism of the Mohists, who defended a form of rational utilitarianism.[1] More to the point of this volume, recent developments in the cognitive sciences have begun to call into question the model of the self upon which both deontology and utilitarianism are based. This model, which we might term *objectivist*,[2] involves conceiving of the self as a disembodied, unitary consciousness, housed within a body but distinct from it and all of the phenomena—emotions, habits, somatic skills—that come along with a body. This disembodied intelligence finds itself confronting a world with a fixed, pregiven structure. This world contains discrete objects, which make themselves known to the disembodied self through (somehow) translated sensory impressions; on the basis of these sensory impressions, the objects can be classified into clearly demarcated categories, with sufficient and necessary conditions for category membership. Categories are then labeled with arbitrary symbols (words), and by our combining these words into sentences, the logical relationships between categories of things in the world can be directly represented and communicated. Reasoning, on this model, consists of "a rule-governed manipulation of connections among symbols ... [whereby] connections among symbols and rule-governed combinations of symbols are established and traced out according to various logical canons or principles" (Johnson 1987, xxiv).

Of course, there exist in the Western tradition older, more pragmatic models of rationality that can be traced back to Aristotle (trans. 1999) and that involve a mind always already in direct, constant contact with a messy world of tangible things. The strongly dualistic model of a disembodied mind really takes rigid hold on Western thought in the Enlightenment. Since at least the 18th century, however, it has become entrenched as the sole proper model of ontology and epistemology in most areas of academic philosophy, including ethics. The purpose of this chapter is, first of all, to review how the picture of human reasoning and decision making that is emerging from the cognitive sciences calls into question some of the basic assumptions of objectivism–rationalism and, therefore, models of ethics based upon "high reason." I will then argue that the importance in everyday human cognition of effortless attention and action suggests that virtue ethics, a model of ethics characteristic of many world traditions (including pre-Enlightenment Europe), might be preferable to deontology and utilitarianism both descriptively and normatively. Finally, I will illustrate how effortless attention and action might be cultivated and manifested in ethical behavior by looking at a text from early China, the *Analects* of Confucius, which provides one of the earliest accounts of a virtue ethic in world literature.

Problems with the Objectivist Self and Effortful Attention

The consensus coming out of recent work in cognitive science suggests that pure, bloodless, fully conscious rationality plays a limited role in everyday decision making, and indeed an absence of emotion—a hallmark of the ideal moral agent for Plato or Kant—apparently transforms us into ethical incompetents. We are rarely fully conscious or in control of what "we" are doing, and indeed the very idea of a unitary, conscious "I" in control of the dumb, animal-like nonself (the body, the emotions) appears to be an illusion. Even such quotidian achievements as ordinary language comprehension and basic perception of our surroundings rely heavily upon tacit know-how and fast and frugal heuristics, guided by embodied and mostly unconscious emotional reactions to our environment. Perception is not concerned primarily with representation but rather with action, and the concepts we acquire from interacting with the world seem to be based primarily upon imagery and sensorimotor schemas. Concepts are therefore not amodal, abstract, and propositional, but perception and body based. Even when dealing with "abstract" concepts or complicated, novel situations, somatic knowledge appears to plays a fundamental role.[3] Below I will touch upon each of these themes, noting their relevance for ethics.

The Importance of Tacit Know-How

Tacit *know-how* has been an increasingly important theme in philosophy, especially among philosophers with some knowledge of cognitive science. John Searle, for instance, asks his readers to consider the sentences "Sally cut the cake," "Bill cut the grass," or "The tailor cut the cloth." None of these sentences are characterized by lexical ambiguity or obvious metaphorical usage,

> but in each case the same verb will determine different truth conditions or conditions of satisfaction generally, because what counts as cutting ... will vary with the context.... If somebody tells me to cut the cake and I run it over with a lawn mower or they tell me to cut the grass and I rush and stab it with the knife, there is a very ordinary sense in which I did not do as I was told to do. Yet nothing in the literal meaning of those sentences blocks those wrong interpretations. (Searle 1995, 130–131)

What *does* block the wrong interpretation of these sentences is our recourse to what Searle calls *the Background*: a reservoir of tacit social and ontological assumptions and skills for coping with the world (Searle 1995, 129–137). Involving a type of inarticulable know-how, this Background cannot, according to Searle, be translated into a finite set of explicit sentences, which means that the comprehension of human sentences cannot be reduced to simply the algorithmic transformation of strings of symbols.

A similar point is made by Hilary Putnam, who notes that the ease with which we access our background knowledge disguises the potential ambiguity of most of the sentences that we nonetheless effortlessly and correctly process; it is clear, upon reflection, that we need recourse to "good judgment" in order to figure out what almost any given string of words means in any given context. Putnam points out that this need for contextual judgment undermines the algorithmic model of sentence processing, for "as Kant long ago said (if not in those terms), there isn't a recursive rule for 'good judgment'" (Putnam 1999, 89). He summarizes a point made by Stanley Cavell (1979), in *The Claim of Reason*, that "our 'attunement' to another, our shared sense of what is and what is not a natural projection of our previous uses of a word into a new context, is pervasive and fundamental to the very possibility of language—without being something that can be captured by a system of 'rules'" (89). It is thus apparent that the understanding of even quite pedestrian human utterances involves reliance on a huge reservoir of tacit, nonalgorithmic knowledge and a pragmatic "feel" for the conversational environment. The objectivist paradigm does not seem to capture either how knowledge of the world is stored nor how it is processed online, and this fact is not surprising considering what knowledge is supposed to *do* for creatures such as ourselves—that is, help us to survive long enough to pass on our genes most effectively.

Philosophers such as Gilbert Ryle and Michael Polanyi have developed theoretical accounts of the function of know-how and the distinction between explicit and tacit knowledge, and the importance of implicit, bodily skills for human flourishing can be traced in the West as far back as Aristotle (trans. 1999).[4] Here I would like to focus on a growing body of empirical work coming out of social psychology and behavioral neuroscience that bolster these theoretical accounts by highlighting the crucial role that tacit, nonpropositional forms of knowledge play in everyday human cognition. In their review of the social psychology literature on "automaticity," for instance, John Bargh and Tanya Chartrand discuss studies revealing the power of priming to affect modes of behavior, the effect of stereotype priming on social judgments, the unconscious acquisition of goals from external stimulation, and the unconscious mimicry of behavior and its effect on social judgments. For instance, subjects whose movements—crossing their legs, playing with their hair—were subtly mimicked by an interviewer subsequently rated the interviewer as more likeable, and the interview process itself as having gone more smoothly, than if the interviewer maintained a relaxed, neutral physical posture. Bargh and Chartrand conclude that, in many areas, people "classify their experience as either good or bad and do so immediately, unintentionally, and without awareness that they are doing it" (Bargh and Chartrand 1999, 474). They describe this process as follows:

Automatic evaluation of the environment is a pervasive and continuous activity that individuals do not intend to engage in and of which they are largely unaware. It appears to have real and functional consequences, creating behavioral readiness within fractions of a second to approach positive and avoid negative objects, and, through its effect on mood, serving a signaling system for the overall safety versus danger of one's current environment. All of these effects tend to keep us in touch with the realities of our world in a way that bypasses the limitations of conscious self-regulation capabilities. (475–476)

In other words, the social psychology literature documents the pervasive importance of automatic, tacit, and unformulizable heuristics ("good judgment") on human behavior and attitude formation.

It is also apparent that there are separate human cognitive systems that work on the implicit and explicit levels, with know-how functioning primarily at the former level. Robert Zajonc and colleagues have demonstrated that people can have affective responses to stimuli without being able to consciously recognize them,[5] and Antonio Damasio has shown that skin conductance reactions to emotionally charged stimuli *precede* conscious awareness of emotion: Emotional states happen first, and conscious feelings follow (Damasio 2003, 101). Joseph LeDoux has postulated the existence of two systems of memory, an unconscious, implicit "emotional memory" and an explicit "declarative" memory, and reviews studies indicating that priming, manual skills, and cognitive skills (such as the ability to solve a particular type of puzzle) are preserved in amnesiac patients, suggesting that implicit "know-how" is developed and stored in brain systems separate from those that subserve conscious memory (LeDoux 1996, 195–198).

Of course, it is obvious that the brain systems associated with abstract reasoning and cognitive control can, at least sometimes, bring implicit biases and other sorts of emotions into consciousness in order to modify or override them. Indeed, there is evidence that cortical control is necessary for the normal conscious experience and expression of emotion. Animals that have had their cortex removed, for instance, are still capable of having emotional reactions, but they are not entirely normal—such creatures are easily provoked and seem entirely incapable of regulating their emotional reactions, which suggests that cortical areas normally rein in and control emotional reactions (LeDoux 1996, 80). However, it is equally clear that conscious self-control is something of a limited resource. The work of Roy Baumeister and his colleagues (Baumeister, Bratslavsky, Muraven, and Tice 1998; Muraven, Tice, and Baumeister 1998) has shown that when conscious control is exerted in one domain, this depletes the individual's ability to exert it in another unrelated domain. This suggests that conscious self-control must be a relatively rare occurrence, since it seems to require a lion's share of cognitive resources. There is also considerable evidence that conscious intervention in automatic processes can be counterproductive. Baumeister's work has shown that automatic behaviors are disrupted when people analyze and decompose them (Baumeister 1984). Similarly, Timothy Wilson and Jonathan Schooler have shown in a series of studies that, in many domains, people form automatic and apparently quite adaptive evaluations that can then be disrupted when these people are asked to reflect on their reasons for their evaluative feelings. Untrained subjects who were asked to spontaneously rate the taste of a variety of jams, for instance, assigned ratings that best matched their demonstrated future satisfaction, as well as the ratings of food industry expert tasters; when asked to rationalize their rankings by analyzing their reasons as they went along, however, the optimality of their ratings decreased significantly.[6] In summary, evolution seems to have off-loaded the vast bulk of our everyday decision making and judgment formation onto automatic, unconscious systems, because such systems are fast, computationally frugal, and reliable.

No Unitary Subject: The Objectivist Knower Is Not Master of His Own House
The objectivist model of reasoning and conscious decision making assumes the presence of a unitary, conscious self—the locus of rationality and will—whose job is to evaluate incoming sense data, classify it, and enforce appropriate conclusions and behavioral decisions on the dumb, recalcitrant emotions or body. While it is acknowledged that this rational self is not always successful in exerting control over other portions of the self, it is assumed that the self is at least *aware* of what "it" is doing and why.

The phenomenon of automaticity discussed above calls this assumption into question, and the outline of the human neural architecture emerging from neuroscientific research indeed calls into question the very idea of a unitary ego as the locus of consciousness. One of the main Cartesian "errors" at which Antonio Damasio takes aim in his famous 1994 book, *Descartes' Error*, is the concept of a Cartesian theater: a central area of consciousness that experiences the world and the self in a unified fashion and serves as a kind of headquarters of knowledge and decision making. As Damasio notes, there is no single region in the human brain equipped to act as such a central theater; although there are various intermediate-level "convergence zones" that coordinate information coming in from more specialized sensorimotor regions, there is no "master" convergence zone that has an overall view of the entire process (Damasio 1994, 94–96; cf. Damasio 1989). Of course, in our everyday experience we certainly *feel* a strong sense of mental integration—the intuition of a unified self in charge of and informed about everything is very powerful and universal. This is, however, "a trick of timing," Damasio argues, an illusion "created from the concerted action of large-scale systems by synchronizing sets of neural activity in separate brain regions" (1994, 95; cf. Damasio and Damasio 1994). How this sort of "binding" occurs is still not precisely understood, but what is clear is that there is no little homunculus collecting data and running a central command post in the brain. It is also likely that each of the various interconnected subsystems that together make up the mind encode and process information in their own task-specific manner, merely transmitting the results of their processing to other appropriate subsystems, which means that there is probably not even the kind of central, universal representational format that such a homunculus would need to function (Clark 1997, 136–141).

One of the more dramatic illustrations of the decentered nature of the self emerges from a series of experiments with split-brain patients performed by Michael Gazzaniga and his colleagues. In these patients the corpus callosum, which normally connects the left and right hemispheres, has been severed (this has been found to be an effective, if last resort, treatment for certain severe forms of epilepsy). The left brain is the seat of verbal ability and interpretative synthesis—in other words, the locus of our sense of unified self—and Gazzaniga and his colleagues found that the illusion of an in-control, unified self that the left hemisphere weaves persists even when it is most certainly *not* in control. For instance, in one experiment, images were selectively presented to each hemisphere: The left hemisphere was shown a chicken claw, the right a snow scene. Subjects were then presented with an array of objects and asked to choose an object "associated" with the image they were shown. A representative response was that of a patient who chose a snow shovel with his left hand (controlled by the right hemisphere and prompted by the snow scene) and a chicken with the right (controlled by the left hemisphere and prompted by the chicken claw). Asked why he chose these items, "he" (that is, his left hemisphere "spin doctor") replied, "Oh, that's simple. The chicken claw goes with the chicken, and you need a shovel to clean out the chicken shed" (Gazzaniga 1998, 25). Gazzaniga and LeDoux found a similar effect with normative judgments: In one particular patient referred to as P.S., the left hemisphere could correctly identify the emotional valence of a stimulus presented to right hemisphere ("good" or "bad") without any conscious awareness of the nature of the stimulus (reported in LeDoux 1996, 14–15). In other words, the left hemisphere "was making emotional judgments without knowing what was being judged" (LeDoux 1996, 15).

As Gazzaniga concludes, "The left brain weaves its story in order to convince itself and you that it is in full control" (1998, 25). He argues that, in place of the all-powerful legislator or canny calculator, a more appropriate metaphor for the conscious, verbal self might be a "harried playground monitor, a hapless entity charged with the responsibility of keeping track of multitudinous brain impulses running in all directions at once" (1998, 23), and also responsible for concocting an ex post facto story of unified control for the consumption of both itself and others. One is reminded of Nietzsche's claim that the idea of free will is "the expression for the complex state of delight of the person exercising volition, who commands and at the same time identifies himself with the executor of the order," taking pleasure in the illusion that *"L'effet c'est moi"* (Nietzsche, 1886/1966, 26).

Lest one think this sort of illusion of self-control is confined to people with extreme trauma, such as a severed corpus callosum, a large body of psychological experimental evidence has demonstrated the existence of a rather deluded "spin doctor" in neurologically normal individuals. The pioneering experiments in this field were performed by Richard Nisbett and Timothy Wilson (Nisbett and Wilson 1977; T. Wilson and Nisbett 1978), who demonstrated in a series of experiments that people often report having thoughts and desires that they could not, in fact, possibly have, and that the verbal reports given by subjects concerning the effects of stimuli on their judgments and behavior in experiments are often highly inaccurate. In a now classic experiment, Nisbett and Wilson presented shoppers at a mall with a display of identical nylon stockings, laid out from left to right. They observed the well-attested phenomenon that, given such a horizontally oriented presentation of otherwise identical items, people display a preference for the items on their right-hand side: in this experiment, the rightmost stocking was preferred almost four to one over the leftmost. What they found most interesting, however, was the confabulated rationales the subjects concocted to justify their choices—swearing, for instance, that their preferred stocking was clearly of better quality than the identical stocking to its left. None of the subjects mentioned the position of the article, and virtually all of the subjects absolutely denied the possible effect of the article's position on their judgment when directly questioned about it by the researchers, "usually with a worried glance at the interviewer suggesting that they had misunderstood the question or were dealing with a madman" (1977, 244).

Studies of subjects given posthypnotic suggestions show a similar effect. For instance, Philip Zimbardo (Zimbardo, Laberge, and Butler 1993) found that subjects in which both hypnotic arousal and amnesia were induced generated a range of plausible explanations for their mental state that had nothing to do with the actual context of the experiment, and Paul Rozin and Carol Nemeroff (Rozin and Nemeroff 1990) found that subjects justified disgust-based attitudes with rationalizations that proved upon examination to be poor predictors of their actual behavior. Jonathan Haidt and his colleagues have found a similar effect with regard to moral judgments: Judgments resulting from emotional reactions or posthypnotic suggestions are invariably given ex post facto—and utterly specious—rational justifications by experimental subjects.[7] Together with the vast literature on the unconscious effects of stereotype, mood, and emotional priming,[8] these results suggest that the deontological or utilitarian self is not, in fact, master of its own house, or even of "itself."

Thought Is Image-Based
One of the most fundamental challenges to the disembodied, amodal model of human reason is the increasing consensus in the fields of neuroscience and cognitive science that human thought is primarily image-based and modal in character—that is, deriving its structure from sensorimotor patterns. As opposed to a picture of thought as the manipulation of arbitrary, abstract symbols, cognitive scientists such as Lawrence Barsalou have been arguing for a "perceptual symbol" account of human cognition.[9] According to this model, the symbols manipulated in human thought are understood not as pictures but as "records of neural activation that arises during perception" (Barsalou 1999, 583). These records can be abstracted from and combined in various ways in areas of the brain "upstream" from the sensorimotor cortices (what Damasio

1989 refers to as "convergence zones"), but they always remain to some extent grounded in sensorimotor systems.

There is a huge and constantly growing body of evidence in favor of at least some version of the perceptual symbol account.[10] To begin with, it is clear that offline reasoning and language comprehension is imagery based. In a series of classic experiments on the mental rotation of three-dimensional objects, Roger Shepard, Lynn Cooper, and Jacqueline Metzler showed that reaction times for subjects asked to match objects varied consistently as a function of the angular difference of the objects, suggesting that subjects were mentally simulating physical rotation of the objects in real time.[11] Observation of eye saccades during sentence comprehension reveals that subjects' eyes react to a described situation in an attenuated but similar manner, as they would if the situation were actually in front of them, suggesting that descriptive sentences are serving as cues for imagistic reconstruction of scenarios (Spivey and Geng 2001). It is also apparent that imagination involves the activation of the appropriate sensorimotor regions. Damasio and his colleagues, for instance, have found that achromatopsia (the loss of color perception) also precludes imaging color in recall (Damasio 1985), and Wexler, Kosslyn, and Berthoz (1998) found that the premotor cortices utilized in actual physical rotation of objects are also activated in mental rotation.[12] Further, this sort of sensorimotor simulation is necessary in processing even less obviously perceptual concepts. Damage to sensorimotor systems, for instance, results in category-specific deficits in cognition: Damage to visual areas selectively disrupts the conceptual processing of categories specified by visual features (e.g., birds), while damage to the motor regions selectively disrupts use of categories specified by motor programs (e.g., tools; Warrington and Shallice 1984). Work on imitation has similarly found that both the perception and conceptualization of action and action-related words requires the activation of the appropriate sensorimotor regions of the brain (e.g., Rizzolatti, Fogassi, and Gallese 2001), and Ronald Langacker's and Leonard Talmy's work on cognitive grammar and semantics has demonstrated the superior explanatory power of image-schematic over formal analyses of natural language use (Langacker 1987, 1991; Talmy 2000).

Perhaps the strongest argument in favor of something like the perceptual symbol account is that it avoids two fundamental problems that plague amodal symbolic accounts, the transduction problem (how perceptual signals could get "translated" into amodal symbols) and the grounding problem (how arbitrary, abstract symbols could ever come to refer to something in the world.) As Spivey and his colleagues note:

True digital symbol manipulation would require a kind of neural architecture that is very different from the analog two-dimensional maps that might implement image-schematic representations (cf. Regier, 1996) and that we know populate much of the cortex (e.g., Churchland & Sejnowski, 1992; Swindale, 2001). (Spivey, Richardson, and Gozalez-Marquez 2005, 272)

They argue that Occam's razor therefore favors a view whereby much of perception and cognition "is implemented in two-dimensional spatial formats of representation that we know exist in the brain, without the use of discrete symbolic representations that we have yet to witness." Barsalou sums up this argument against classical amodal theories of meaning by concluding that such theories "are unfalsifiable, they are not parsimonious, they lack direct support, they suffer conceptual problems such as transduction and symbol grounding, and it is not clear how to integrate them with theory in neighboring fields, such as perception and neuroscience" (1999, 580).

Prototype Categories
Objectivist philosophy relies upon classic Aristotelian categories, which have sharp boundaries and clearly defined sufficient and necessary conditions for category membership. If something like the perceptual symbol account of concepts is correct, this would entail the need for a different model of categorization, and evidence from cognitive psychology and linguistics has long suggested that the mode of categorization generally relied upon by human beings differs significantly from the classical account. Much of the early work in this field was done by Eleanor Rosch and her colleagues,[13] who developed a theory of "radial" categorization based upon a "prototype effect." Categories as they are usually active in human minds are based upon certain exemplars or prototypes; membership in the category is then based upon family resemblance and can be a matter of degree (there can be "better" or "worse" members of a given category). For example, most North Americans have an understanding of the category "bird" that is based upon an image of a sparrow, robin, or jay. Most people can switch into a "logical category" mode and acknowledge that chickens, penguins, and ostriches are "birds," but will continue to insist that these are not particularly "good" examples of birds. The same effect can be seen with social categories such as "bachelor": the Pope, for instance, is not a particularly good instance of a "bachelor" (Lakoff 1987).

The dominance in everyday thought of prototype-based categorization is to be expected from the perspective of the perceptual symbol account of cognition. If concepts are a form of sensorimotor simulation, categorization will be based upon imagined exemplars and family resemblances. As Barsalou (1999, 587) notes, categorization understood from this perspective will also not be designed as a rigid net for exhaustively cataloguing and organizing sets of clearly defined objects in the world but rather as a dynamic, contextual, and embodied means of gaining access to categorical inferences—that is, suggestions as to how to interact successfully with encountered objects and situations and to reason about absent (future) entities. Experimental work by W. Kyle Simmons and colleagues[14] found that functional magnetic resonance imaging (fMRI) images of brain activity in sensory regions of subjects asked to confirm the property of categories corresponded significantly with the predicted sensory profile of the category, and studies by Pecher, Zeelenberg, and Barsalou (2003) on property verification tasks found significant temporal costs in shifting from one sensory modality to another—suggesting that subjects are activating sensorimotor prototype images in processing categories. As Raymond Gibbs (2006, 83) concludes, "prototypes are not summary abstractions based on a few defining attributes, but are rich, imagistic, sensory, full-bodied mental events."

Metaphor and the Importance of Imaginative Extension

If categories as they generally function in human minds are *not* classic Aristotelian categories, this means that reasoning—the classification of events or objects into categories, and the relating of these categories to one another—must involve something other than propositional transformation. The most likely suspect for this "something other" is sensorimotor-based imagination.

That imagination is crucial for moral reasoning has been the central argument of Mark Johnson for two decades,[15] and it has also been argued by philosophers such as Martha Nussbaum. In a discussion of the importance of imagination and literature for morality, Nussbaum notes that moral knowledge

is not simply intellectual grasp of propositions; it is not even simply intellectual grasp of particular facts; it is perception. It is seeing a complex, concrete reality in a highly lucid and richly responsive way; it is taking in what is there, with imagination and feeling. (Nussbaum 1990, 152)

Part of what this sort of moral perception involves is the categorization of novel situations in terms of learned prototypes, which in turn involves a kind of intuitive pattern matching rather than conscious rule following. Johnson discusses the work of Linda Coleman and Paul Kay (Coleman and Kay 1981; refined by Sweetser 1987) on the prototype semantics of the English word *lie*, which seems to demonstrate radial category structure: There are better and worse instances of what constitutes a lie, and subjects' judgment of whether or not a given act constitutes a lie depends upon a set of implicit criterion that are contextually weighted, as well as upon what Sweetser refers to as "idealized cognitive models" of knowledge and communication.[16] Applying these models to novel situations involves the reactivation of previous sensorimotor experiences, the identification of relevant features in the novel situation, and the recruitment of both implicit and explicit social knowledge. This process cannot be captured in a propositional maxim-following or cost–benefit analysis.

What this means is that moral education will involve training individuals—explicitly or implicitly—to develop more and more sophisticated imagistic models, as well as the ability to extend them in a consistent manner. As Johnson explains, in any kind of reasonably complex situation, "moral reasoning cannot consist merely in the rational unpacking of a determinate concept. Instead, it requires imaginative extensions to nonprototypical cases" (Johnson 1993, 100). Such extension often involves the use of metaphors or analogies, and thus both internal moral reasoning and public moral debate will often take the form of battling metaphors—which metaphor or analogy best captures the current situation? Is the current U.S. position in Iraq a "quagmire" like Vietnam, or is it like the difficulties encountered in the early period of implementing the Marshall Plan? When a senator vetoes an aid bill to help Sudanese famine victims, is he snatching food out of the mouths of hungry children, or is he helping the Sudanese to learn to stand on their own two feet? How we choose to metaphorically frame a situation is probably the single most crucial element in how we will morally reason and morally *feel* about it, which leads us to our next point.

Embodied Emotions in Human Cognition
As Gerd Gigerenzer and Reinhard Selten (2001) explain in an introductory essay on the concept of "bounded rationality," economists and psychologists have, since the 1950s, been moving away from models of behavior that assumed humans are optimal calculators toward models that assume that, in most situations, human beings rely upon domain-specific, "fast and frugal" heuristics.[17] These heuristics generally do not result in rationally optimal results but often outperform general-purpose, time-consuming, and "information-greedy" optimizing strategies, especially in the specific situations of partial knowledge and computational limitations for which they have evolved. A representative example is the "recognition heuristic" (Goldstein and Gigerenzer 2002), whereby an organism presented with a choice between two options—say, two potential food items—simply chooses the one that has been previously encountered over the one that is unknown. It is not hard to imagine how this strategy might be adaptive: Items that have been consumed before by you or by a conspecific are more likely to be edible than an item chosen randomly from the environment, and this might very well outweigh any potential advantage derived from discovering a superior new foodstuff. What is perhaps less intuitively obvious is how such crude heuristics can outperform more "rational" strategies even in quite complex and evolutionarily novel situations, such as stock market investment (Borges, Goldstein, Ortmann, and Gigerenzer 1999).

These heuristics and biases often take the form of tacit skills, unformulizable hunches, or—the focus of this section—emotional reactions. In the last decade there has been an explosion of literature on the role of emotions in human reasoning in such fields as behavioral neuroscience, cognitive science, economics, social psychology, and philosophy.[18] Because of space restrictions, I will focus here on the work of perhaps the best known pioneer in this field, Antonio Damasio, and in particular his theory of "somatic marking." In his discussion of the "body-minded brain," Damasio points out that the mind evolved in order to ensure the survival of the entire mind–body unit, and he argues that the best way to do this is by *"representing the outside world in terms of the modifications it causes in the body proper,* that is, representing the environment by modifying the primordial representations of the body proper whenever an interaction between organism and environment takes place" (Damasio 1994, 230). The result is a set of "somato-motor maps" that provide a "dynamic map of the overall organism anchored in body schema and body boundary" (Damasio 1994, 231). Thus, when we are presented with a situation—or called upon to imagine a situation (neurophysiologically not that different a process)—we rely upon the "dispositional representations" (Damasio 1994, 104) that constitute our full repository of knowledge in order to comprehend it, and these representations inevitably include emotional information. As Damasio (1999, 161) observes, "When we recall an object ... we retrieve not just sensory data but also accompanying motor and emotional data.... We recall not just sensory characteristics of an actual object but the past reactions of the organism to the object." In other words, the images that form the basis of our concepts are somatically "marked" with visceral and often unconscious feelings of "goodness" or "badness," urgency or lack of urgency, and so on, and these feelings play a crucial role in everyday, "rational" decision making.[19]

In *Descartes' Error* (1994), Damasio describes his work with patients suffering from damage to the ventromedial prefrontal cortex, a center of decision making in the brain. The accidents or strokes that had caused this damage had spared these patients' "higher" cognitive faculties—their short- and long-term memories, abstract reasoning skills, mathematical aptitude, and performance on standard IQ tests were completely unimpaired. They were also perfectly physically healthy, with no apparent motor or sensory disabilities. Nonetheless, these patients had been brought to Damasio's attention as a physician because, despite their apparent lack of physical or cognitive impairment, they were no longer functional members of society. In real-life decision-making contexts they were appallingly inept, apparently incapable of efficiently choosing between alternate courses of action, taking into account the future consequences of their actions, or accurately prioritizing the relative importance of potential courses of action.

One representative example is the patient Damasio refers to as "Elliot." Formerly a successful businessman and respected husband and father, Elliot's life began to unravel after he was operated on for a brain tumor, a procedure that involved removing parts of his ventromedial prefrontal cortex. As Damasio (1994, 36) describes it, "Elliot's smarts and his ability to move about and use language were unscathed. In many ways, however, Elliot was no longer Elliot." Elliot needed to be prompted to get up and prepare to go to work in the morning and, once there, seemed incapable of managing his time properly, focusing his attention effectively, or completing even the most routine of tasks:

Imagine a task involving reading and classifying documents of a given client. Elliot would read and fully understand the significance of the material, and he certainly knew how to sort out the documents according to the similarity or disparity of their content. The problem was that he was likely, all of a sudden, to turn from the sorting task he had initiated to reading one of those papers, carefully and intelligently, and to spend an entire day doing so. Or he might spend a whole afternoon deliberating on which principle of categorization should be applied: Should it be date, size of document, pertinence to the case, or another? The flow of work was stopped. (Damasio 1994, 36)

Understandably, Elliot was soon fired. He proved no more successful in negotiating his way through unemployed life. He developed bizarre collecting habits, took up a bewilderingly diverse array of projects (often dropping them almost as quickly as he had picked them up), entered into questionable financial ventures with disreputable individuals, lost his life's savings, divorced several times, and finally was reduced to living off of social security disability payments.

In the view of Damasio and his colleagues, the problem with ventromedial prefrontal cortex patients such as Elliot is that they lack "somatic markers"—the unconscious, visceral normative weights that ordinarily accompany our representations of the world. This prevents them from unconsciously assigning different values to different options, thereby rendering their "decision-making landscape hopelessly flat" (1994, 51). In any given situation, the number of theoretically possible courses of action is effectively infinite, and the human mind is obviously not capable of running simultaneous analyses of all of them at once. Therefore, the body contributes by biasing the reasoning process with somatic markers—often unconsciously—before it even begins. Patients such as Elliot perform well on abstract moral reasoning and utilitarian calculation tasks because such abstract analyses are artificially simplified. Thrown into a real-life situation, but deprived of the biasing function of somatic markers, they seem to attempt to dispassionately consider *all* of the options theoretically open to them, with the result that they become paralyzed by indecision or simply commit themselves to what appear to outside observers as poorly considered and capriciously selected courses of action.[20] Some researchers have compared their situation to that of alcoholics or compulsive gamblers, in that mere conceptual knowledge that something is harmful is not necessarily adequate—in the absence of the appropriate somatic markers—to motivate a person to actually avoid those harmful things. The problem with impulsive behavior may thus not be too much emotion but rather not *enough* emotion.

Of course, it is important to note that, despite the crucial importance of somatic markers for normal decision making, navigating through the world by means of hunches and know-how does not necessarily lead to advantageous results. Damasio remarks upon the ability of one of his prefrontal patients to calmly steer his way through a skid on icy roads: one sort of scenario where a person's immediate emotional response to a perceived danger (slamming on the brakes) typically leads to unhelpful behavior. More generally, it is clear that human beings are sometimes quite *bad*—that is, not rationally ideal—decision makers, especially when operating in modern industrial societies, far outside of their ancestral environment. In the field of economics, Daniel Kahneman and the late Amos Tversky have been the best known proponents of a move away from rational choice theory toward more psychologically realistic models that take into account the role of the nonrational heuristics and biases that guide everyday decision making.[21] Dispassionate calculation makes it clear that we are likely to achieve a much better payoff investing $20 weekly in some conservative mutual fund rather than using that money to buy lottery tickets, but the reasoning processes of many are (incorrectly, in this case) biased by the powerfully positive somatic marker attached to the image of the multimillion-dollar payoff. Similarly, the powerfully negative image of a jetliner falling in flames from the sky prevents many from making the "rational" decision to fly rather than drive, even though commercial airline travel is statistically much safer than automobile travel. George Loewenstein and his colleagues have formulated a "risks as feelings" hypothesis very similar to Damasio's somatic marker theory, finding that human risk assessment of an imagined scenario is driven largely by vividness, not probability of that scenario actually occurring. In one study (Loewenstein, Weber, Hsee, and Welch 2001), they found that people are willing to pay more for airline travel insurance covering death from "terrorist acts" than for insurance covering death from "all possible causes"! At the other extreme, people tend to be underinsured against emotionally "pallid" risks like floods. Other studies have found that people are also much more responsive to warnings that are linked to individuals and anecdotes than those put in statistical terms.

Thus, while navigating by means of powerful, reasoning-biasing somatic markers must have been adaptive in our dispersed, hunter–gatherer environment of evolutionary adaptation, it sometimes leads us into errors of judgment in the more complex world of settled agricultural societies, especially when modern technology is thrown into the mix. More generally, recognizing the importance of somatic markers in no way requires us to neglect the crucial importance of good old-fashioned "offline," bloodless rational calculation and algorithmic reasoning—indeed, the fact that humans are even *capable* of such forms of reasoning indicates that they have proven their worth over evolutionary time. The best way to view the work of Damasio and his colleagues is as a corrective to the fetishization of reason in the post-Enlightenment period and as an indication that the objectivist–rationalist model as it has been traditionally formulated has some serious and fundamental limitations.

Relating this work to ethics, a growing number of cognitive scientists and philosophers have come to agree with David Hume and the Stoics that normative judgments are ultimately derived from human emotional reactions. Damasio has argued that our sense of "goodness" corresponds to our sense of bodily wellness, which is not surprising considering that "achieving survival coincides with the ultimate reduction of unpleasant bodily states and the attaining of homeostatic ones, i.e., functionally balanced biological states" (1994, 179). Martha Nussbaum has similarly argued for a "neo-Stoic" "cognitive-evaluative" view of emotions, which views them as "intelligent responses to the perception of value" (Nussbaum 2001, 1).[22] Although he explicitly wishes to distance himself from "naturalists" who would apply scientific reasoning to the realm of the human, the work of Charles Taylor (1989) is nonetheless very helpful when it comes to the relationship of emotions to ethical values. One of Taylor's most important points is that human beings, by their very nature, can only operate within the context of a normative space defined by a framework of empirically unverifiable beliefs. The Enlightenment conceit that one can dispense with belief or faith entirely, and make one's way through life guided solely by the dictates of objective reason, is nothing more than that—a conceit, itself a type of faith in the power of a mysterious faculty, "reason," to reveal incorrigible truth. In addition to the panoply of "weak evaluations"—such as a preference for chocolate over vanilla ice cream—that we are familiar with, humans are also inevitably moved to assert "strong," or normative, evaluations. This latter type of evaluation is based on a set of explicit or implicit ontological claims and therefore is perceived as having objective force rather than being a merely subjective whim. For instance, I don't particularly like chocolate ice cream and believe that the flavor of vanilla ice cream is superior. I don't, however, expect everyone to share my preference, and am certainly not moved to condemn my wife for preferring chocolate. I am also not inclined to sexually abuse small children, but this feels like a different sort of preference to me: Abusing small children seems *wrong*, and I would condemn and be moved to punish anyone who acted in a manner that violated this feeling. If I were pressed on the matter, this condemnation would be framed, moreover, in terms of beliefs about the value of undamaged human personhood and the need to prevent suffering and safeguard innocence.

In the fields of cognitive science and social psychology, there is a growing set of empirical literature supporting Taylor's position, showing that people distinguish between "response-dependent" evaluations (Taylor's weak evaluations), merely conventional evaluations, and moral evaluations (Taylor's strong evaluations), the last of which are seen even by young children as having an objective quality and being universally applicable.[23] According to Taylor, the distinguishing feature of a strong evaluation is that it is based upon an ontological claim—a claim about how the world really *is*, which gives the evaluation objective force. Evidence from cognitive science and psychology has, however, called into question the directionality of the causal link between ontological belief and moral emotion, suggesting that in many cases the causality may derive from the emotion, with the ontological belief tacked on as an ex post facto justification. Jonathan Haidt et al. (1993) found that, when people are presented with verbal scenarios, their affective reactions to them were better predictors of their moral judgments than their claims about harmful consequences, and that people who have a strong negative affective reaction to a scenario often have to struggle to provide a rational justification, with sometimes rather silly results. Similarly, Shaun Nichols (2002) has shown that affectively charged but conventionally neutral scenarios are judged along the same dimensions as moral violations, while Kari Edwards and William von Hippel (1995) found that social attitudes are best changed by altering people's affectively charged intuitions rather than by rational argument and that affectively based opinions were held with much more confidence than rationally based ones. In a recent study, Thalia Wheatley and Jonathan Haidt (2005) demonstrated that judgments of both how disgusting and how morally wrong a given behavior is were made more severe by a flash of hypnotically induced queasiness—directly implicating the importance of "gut reactions" for moral judgments.

In defense of his "social intuitionist" approach to moral judgment, Haidt sums up a vast body of literature suggesting that conscious moral reasoning "is usually a post hoc construction, generated after a judgment has been reached" (2001, 814).[24] These results strongly support the idea that Taylorian strong evaluations arise from affectively laden sensorimotor intuitions, such as disgust, which are then justified through the invocation of ontological claims or rational justification. As Haidt (2001, 814) remarks, "Faced with a social demand for a verbal justification, one becomes a lawyer trying to build a case rather than a judge searching for the truth." This has led the neuroscientist Joshua Greene, who has studied the various brain regions involved in moral decision making, to conclude that deontological moral principles are ultimately "a kind of moral confabulation" (Greene 2007, 63).

Gut Reactions and Cognitive Control
As important as work on moral "gut reactions" has been as a corrective to objectivist models, one should not be tempted into dismissing the importance of cognitive control for ethical reasoning and behavior. First of all, although emotional reactions can inspire the creation of ex post facto conscious beliefs, it is also clear that causality often flows in the opposite direction: Explicit beliefs, for instance, frequently engender affective responses in otherwise affectively neutral situations. To take a case of religious belief, being touched by a low-caste Indian on the street is not likely to inspire much of an emotional–moral response in me, while it is likely to inspire physical revulsion and moral outrage in a conservative high-caste Hindu, for whom the caste system is part of the normative structure of the cosmos. Even here, though, we should note that this type of culturally specific ontological belief can elicit strong evaluations from an individual only because it is metaphorically tied into basic physiological responses to uncleanliness, contamination, and disgust: Physical "mixing" of castes is revolting to a conservative Hindu because of a worldview in which lower castes are understood as metaphorically "unclean," which then inspires innate affective responses to pollution and contamination.

Another problem with taking too strongly the affective determination of conscious moral reasoning is that the process can be blocked: It is clear that top–down control, based on rational beliefs, can override affective reactions. In a cross-cultural study of disgust and moral reactions to various scenarios performed by Haidt et al. (1993), interesting differences were found in the reactions of individuals from cultures varying in their degree of "Westernization" and from various socioeconomic classes. The results suggest that conscious reference to an "ethics of autonomy"—the framework of beliefs concerning the importance of diversity, individual freedom, rights, and so forth that forms the basis of the Western liberal conception of the self—allowed individuals from high socioeconomic classes and living in Westernized cultures to resist converting their affectively negative responses to moralized ones. When presented with certain scenarios—such as a person cutting up the national flag to use as a toilet-cleaning rag or eating a family dog that had been killed in an accident—these individuals felt at least mild disgust or disapproval but often overrode this feeling to declare that these actions were not morally wrong, no matter how much they might personally feel uncomfortable with them.[25]

Joshua Greene et al. (Greene, Sommerville, Nystrom, Darley, and Cohen 2001) document a similar phenomenon in an fMRI study of moral reasoning, where subjects have quite divergent reactions to two versions of a classic thought experiment. In the trolley version, the subject is asked to imagine a runaway trolley rolling down a track toward a Y-shaped rail junction, with one person tied to one set of tracks and five people tied to another set. The subject controls a switch that determines which set of tracks the trolley will be diverted to, and most subjects fairly quickly conclude that they would switch the trolley away from the five people and toward the lone person. In the footbridge version, the subject is asked to imagine being on a footbridge over a single track to which five people have been tied, standing next to a single but rather large individual. The only way to stop the trolley is to push this large person off the bridge to certain death (the subject being too small to stop the trolley), but this will have the effect of saving the other five. The utilitarian calculus is the same, but in this scenario most subjects say they would not be willing to push the person off the bridge. Greene et al. found that emotional regions of the brain were strongly implicated in subjects' reactions to the footbridge scenario but not to the trolley version, which suggests that the differing responses are the result of a visceral, negative response to the idea of actively pushing a person off a bridge. Interestingly, a subset of subjects in this experiment did endorse the "proper" utilitarian response to the footbridge scenario, and the timing of the activation of various brain regions as documented in the fMRI results suggests that this response involved activating brain regions associated with abstract reasoning and cognitive control in order to override the affective responses triggered by the scenario.[26] These sorts of results provide empirical support for the "high-reason" conviction, endorsed by philosophers since the time of Plato and Xunzi, that the rational faculties *can* and *should* supervise and—when appropriate—override the reactions of our more emotional faculties.

An important question for someone interested in an empirically grounded and practically plausible model of morality is, however, the proper degree of *salience* to be given to this type of conscious, rational control. It is clearly possible. What is less clear is how much of an effect it has, and can be expected to have, on the quotidian functioning of a real moral agent making his or her way through the world. It is important to note that the sort of conscious overriding of automatic emotional responses documented in the Greene et al. 2001 study significantly interfered with the reaction time of participants, which suggests that cognitive control is a fairly costly and time-consuming process. In a recent follow-up study, Greene and his colleagues (Greene, Morelli, Lowenberg, Nystrom, and Cohen 2008) found increased reaction times for utilitarian judgments under cognitive load. This accords with the work of Baumeister et al. (1998), cited above, documenting the so-called "ego-depletion" phenomenon: Conscious supervision is a limited cognitive resource.

It is even more important to note that the sort of moral dilemmas that are the staple of deontological and utilitarian theorizing are radically simplified decision-making frames—ethical decision making in the real world takes place in an environment characterized by time pressure, limited and often inaccurate information, indistinct physical and temporal boundaries, and often only limited or entirely nonexistent conscious involvement.[27] Part of the problem with the scenarios such as the footbridge case examined by Greene et al. is that they are artificially simplified (in real life, would a person *really* know for sure that the large man's body will stop the train or that he or she would be able to get him over the railing in time?), are unmotivated (some subjects *say* they would push the man off, but that does not mean they would actually do it in real life, faced by the real human being), and focus attention on dramatic moments of conscious choice, when in fact most of what counts as moral judgment in real life is probably automatic, or at best semiconscious. Am I performing a conscious utilitarian calculation (or deontic reasoning) every time I pass a homeless person on my way to the bus? I am a professor and catch a student plagiarizing. The rules say he should get an "F" for the class, but he is the first generation in his family to go to college; my "impression" of him is that he is a basically honest, extremely hard-working kid driven to cheat as an act of desperation under extreme pressure; he seems to be experiencing genuine, excruciating remorse; throwing the book at him will result in his scholarship's being taken away and expulsion from school, and so forth. When I decide what to do about his case, can I really be said to be performing a utilitarian calculation? What are the numerical parameters I am supposed to be working with? (How many points for remorse? Is it a sliding scale, depending on intensity?) It seems that these sorts of situations, rather than the trolley or footbridge situations, are what people face most often as the noticeable tip of the iceberg of moral decision making. Then, of course, there is a huge hidden iceberg of moral "choice" that is operating unconsciously all the time when we simply move through the world:

Are we nice to the check-out girl at the supermarket? Do we notice the old person getting on the bus and give him or her our seat? Do we pay attention when our spouse is talking to us about something important to her, although we have not yet had our coffee and are thinking intensely about utilitarianism and really just want to get back to our writing?

As William Casebeer has noted, the problem with "experimental regimens that isolate 'dry' thinking-about-moral-things from 'wet' here-I-am-doing-moral-things" is that they "can unnecessarily restrict the scope of the neural mechanisms that are activated" (Casebeer 2003) and produce a distorted picture of what real-life moral reasoning is like.[28] It is clear that the kind of dispassionate reflection and cognitive control required to override somatic–emotional reactions is a very limited resource, which suggests that active attention—though an important human ability—is a rather fragile foundation on which to build an ethical theory. We now turn to a model of ethics that does *not* rely primarily on active cognitive control and algorithmic reasoning but instead aims to cultivate self-activating, automatic, effortless dispositions to act in virtuous manner.

Virtue Ethics and Effortless Attention

In light of the work on human cognition reviewed above, a model of ethics generally referred to as *virtue ethics*—the dominant model of ethics in many world cultures for thousands of years and one that relies much less on cognitive control than modern Western ethical theories—might begin to look rather appealing. There is some disagreement about what constitutes a virtue ethic, and there are stronger and weaker ways of understanding how virtue ethics differs from deontology or consequentialism.[29] Here I would like to focus on a set of features most relevant to the phenomenon of effortless attention and which might be seen as central, and distinguishing, features of a virtue ethic: the idea that ethical behavior results not from rational, conscious rule following or calculation but rather through the activation of stable, spontaneous, and at least partially emotional dispositions, which cause one to respond ethically to specific situations and to reliably perceive the world in certain normatively desirable ways. For instance, someone possessing the virtue of courage can be counted on to correctly recognize situations that call for courageous action, effortlessly grasp what the appropriate "courageous" response would be, and put that response into action in a spontaneous and unselfconscious manner.

Many, if not most, virtue ethics hold that such virtues do not develop naturally but require various forms of cultural training—a process that begins with some conception of raw human nature and aims to transform it in accordance with some conception of what a "flourishing" or proper human life looks like. This training will inevitably involve some general rules and principles, but because the goal is to produce a self-activating disposition and a particular mode of perception, the primary tools tend to be role modeling, mentor-guided imaginative extension, and cultural practices that engage the body and the emotions, such as ritual and music. Properly developed virtuous dispositions have been compared to a kind of "know-how," or skill, and display a degree of flexibility, context sensitivity, and effortlessness that is absent in behavior strictly guided by rules or abstract calculations. As such, virtues would seem to rely on the sort of implicit knowledge and automaticity that, as the research reviewed above suggests, play such a large role in everyday human activity. One might say that the very essence of virtue ethics is a suspicion of the power of cognitive control and a consequent desire to get at and reshape the vast iceberg of human cognition that lies beneath the surface of active consciousness.

As one would expect, the virtue ethical model is not without its problems. In particular, the circularity of the so-called "good person criterion"—the definition of *courage* in any given situation is what the courageous person would do—gives deontologists and utilitarians fits. The reliance upon tradition and social norms to provide models of virtue can easily lead—and historically has lead—to authoritarianism and hidebound conservatism, precisely the ills that deontology and utilitarianism were formulated to counteract. Nevertheless, given the features of human cognition outlined above, it may very well be the case that we do not have much of a choice when it comes to ethical models. As attractive as deontology and utilitarianism may be in certain respects, if human beings are simply incapable of consistently employing deontological or utilitarian principles in everyday life, we may be stuck with virtue ethics whether we like it or not.

One of many services that a knowledge of cognitive science can offer scholars in the humanities is a chance to finally settle certain perennial, and previously interminable, theoretical debates (Slingerland 2008). Since the Mencius–Mohist debates in 4th c. B.C.E. China, virtue ethicists have been arguing for the theoretical and practical limitations of rationalist ethics—the latest and most local iteration of this argument kicking off with G. E. M. Anscombe's "Modern Moral Philosophy" (Anscombe 1958)— and there seems no a priori way to settle the debate. If even some of the discoveries about human cognition outlined above hold up to further scrutiny, this might decisively tilt the balance toward virtue ethics, at least with regard to particular subissues. If emotions play a crucial role in everyday human decision making, a model of ethical training aimed at shaping and properly directing the emotions begins to look quite attractive.[30] If much of our everyday decision making and judgment formation is automatic, nonconscious, and not easily amenable to cognitive control, we might be justifiably concerned about the efficacy of ethical models that rely exclusively on conscious reasoning. If bodily based metaphors and metaphoric blends are central and ineliminable features of human thought, ethical models based on amodal, propositional cognitive processes begin to appear radically inadequate—not necessarily a knockout blow to deontology and utilitarianism (whatever their cognitive plausibility, one might continue to argue for them as unattainable but crucially regulative ideals) but certainly progress of sorts. Virtue ethics may be characterized by its own theoretical problems and prone to various types of social abuses, but it may be, realistically speaking, the only ethic we've got.

The modern revival of virtue ethics has traditionally looked back to Aristotle for inspiration, and many of the features of human psychology discussed above can be easily accommodated by the Aristotelian conception of the self. As some scholars of Chinese thought have argued, however,[31] there are other virtue ethicists besides Aristotle, and looking beyond Aristotle to traditions such as early Confucianism can give us a broader, richer picture of what a cognitively plausible ethic in action might look like. I will conclude with a very brief sketch of an early Chinese virtue ethic, paying particular attention to the central role given to effortless attention.

Effortless Attention in Confucian Virtue Ethics

In a previous work on Warring States Chinese thought (Slingerland 2003b), I argued that the "mainstream"[32] thinkers of this period share as a spiritual goal the ideal of *wu wei,* or *effortless action*. Literally meaning no doing or no effort, *wu wei* refers to an ideal state whereby the individual acts, effortlessly and unselfconsciously, in a manner that harmonizes with the normative order of the cosmos. In the case of the Confucians, *wu wei* also involves effortlessly and spontaneously according with the dictates of traditional ethical and ritual standards. In this work I argued that the question of how to achieve *wu wei* is the central religious problematic in early Chinese thought and that the tension involved in consciously striving to achieve effortlessness—trying not to try—drives much of the secondary theorizing about issues such as the character of human nature, the best metaphoric models for self-cultivation, and the relationship of the individual to inherited cultural traditions.

Here I will focus on the case of Confucius, as portrayed in the *Analects*,[33] arguably the earliest detailed account of a virtue ethic in action. The *Analects* clearly portrays effortless action and effortless attention as a goal to be reached only after a long period of intense training and personal reformation, although it is somewhat inconsistent concerning the issue of how the ethically ideal state relates to one's innate nature. Certain passages suggest that cultural training merely refines and "adorns" an already-present innate potential, while others seem to endorse a model whereby cultural forms fundamentally reshape an inherently crude natural endowment.[34] For the purposes of this discussion, I will leave these differences to the side in order to focus on the *Analects*'s portrayal of the state of effortless action and effortless attention as personified in the figure of Confucius near the end of his life.

The Confucian project of self-cultivation, aimed at producing an individual (the "gentleman" or "sage") endowed with the virtue of Goodness (*ren* 仁),³⁵ involves a strict regimen of training in which the individual subordinates himself to traditional standards of practice and judgment. This training advances along several fronts, including practice in religious and social rituals, intensive learning of transmitted classics, and training in music and other traditional cultural forms. The aim is to achieve a state where outer form and inner state are perfectly harmonized. As Confucius observes in *Analects* 6.18, commenting on the relationship between inborn nature ("native substance") and the refinement created by cultural training:

> When native substance overwhelms cultural refinement, the result is a crude rustic. When cultural refinement overwhelms native substance, the result is a foppish pedant. Only when culture and native substance are perfectly mixed and balanced do you have a gentleman.³⁶

This passage is perhaps the earliest expression of an ideal that later became very important in Confucian writings: the doctrine of holding fast to the "mean" (*zhong* 中). A perfect balance between native substance and cultural refinement is thus the ideal state, although if one is to err it should be on the side of substance.

Flexibility and Autonomy

One clear virtue ethical characteristic of Confucius's thought is that his program of self-cultivation is designed to transform the student into a particular type of person, not to merely win assent to a set of principles or teach a method of calculation. For instance, in 9.24 the Master remarks:

> When a man is rebuked with exemplary words after having made a mistake, he cannot help but agree with them. However, what is important is that he change himself in order to *accord* with them. When a man is praised with words of respect, he cannot help but be pleased with them. However, what is important is that he actually *live up* to them. A person who finds respectful words pleasing but does not live up to them, or agrees with others' reproaches and yet does not change—there is nothing I can do with one such as this.

Nominal assent to the Confucian Way is insufficient—one must love the Way and strive to embody it in one's person. This is why Confucian moral training involves long periods of time engaged in concrete, embodied practices such as ritual and music—the latter of which included singing, the playing of musical instruments, and dancing.³⁷

The "offline," theoretical aspect of Confucian training emphasizes the absorption of proper language and cognitive models acquired through study of the classics, memorized and rehearsed until they become fully internalized and unconscious patterns of thought. It also includes the consideration and group discussion of case examples from the past. Here is a typical exchange:

5.19 Zizhang said, "Prime Minister Ziwen[38] was given three times the post of prime minister, and yet he never showed a sign of pleasure; he was removed from this office three times, and yet never showed a sign of resentment. When the incoming prime minister took over, he invariably provided him with a complete account of the official state of affairs. What do you make of Prime Minister Ziwen?"

The Master said, "He certainly was dutiful."

"Was he not Good?"

"I do not know about that—what makes you think he deserves to be called Good?"

We have to imagine that this conversation, though initiated by the disciple Zizhang, is taking place in the company of assembled disciples, and Confucius's judgment of this historical figure is thus intended as a general lesson for them all. One of the most interesting—and to some analysts, most infuriating—aspects of the *Analects* is Confucius's failure to precisely define his supreme virtue of Goodness, as well as his reluctance to pronounce any particular person to be Good. When asked if a particular individual might be considered Good, Confucius typically goes no farther than conceding to the person one of the lesser virtues as in the exchange above. The reason for this is not only that true Goodness is extremely difficult to obtain, but also that—as the master virtue of being a perfected person—it involves a kind of flexibility and grace that is hard to perceive in second-hand accounts of contemporaries or historical figures.

The difficulty of conveying genuine Goodness in words is also the reason that much of Confucius's pedagogy is focused on context-specific injunctions or bits of advice tailored to the needs of individual disciples. Indeed, some commentators believe that the reservations Confucius expresses about Prime Minister Ziwen in 5.19 may have less to do with his actual opinions of this figure than with his concerns about the moral qualities of the disciple Zizhang himself. His flexibility in tailoring his pedagogical message to the needs of the student is famously illustrated in 11.22:

Zilu asked, "Upon learning of something that needs to be done, should one immediately take care of it?"

The Master replied, "As long as one's father and older brothers are still alive, how could one possibly take care of it immediately?"[39]

[On a later occasion] Ran Qiu asked, "Upon learning of something that needs to be done, should one immediately take care of it?"

The Master replied, "Upon learning of it, you should immediately take care of it."

Zihua [having observed both exchanges], inquired, "When Zilu asked you whether or not one should immediately take care of something upon learning of it, you told him one should not, as long as one's father and elder brothers were still alive. When Ran Qiu asked the same question, however, you told him that one should immediately take care of it. I am confused, and humbly ask to have this explained to me."

The Master said, "Ran Qiu is overly cautious, and so I wished to urge him on. Zilu, on the other hand, is too impetuous, and so I sought to hold him back."

This is a paradigmatic example of how the Master's teachings were variously formulated depending upon the individual needs of his students—a Confucian version of the Buddhist practice of *upaya*, or "skillful means."⁴⁰

This is not to deny that Confucius taught his disciples certain general principles, such as the famous "negative Golden Rule"—"Do not do to others what you would not want done to you"—described in 15.24 as "a single teaching that can be a guide to conduct throughout one's life." Modern Western students of the text, especially those with backgrounds in analytic philosophy, often make such general principles the central focus of their interpretations of the *Analects*,⁴¹ but I believe this leads to a distortion of how the text was traditionally intended and used in premodern China. Rather than focusing primarily on such principles, Confucius's pedagogical technique is designed to create in his students an ability to apply Confucian ideals in a context-sensitive and flexible manner. This *feel*—a type of rational emotion or embodied know-how—allows the perfected Confucian sage to act in accordance with the ethical ideals and rules while at the same time displaying a level of autonomy and flexibility impossible for one who is merely going by the book. Indeed, one cannot be said to have properly mastered a set of principles until one knows how to apply them skillfully and in a context-sensitive manner. As Confucius notes in 13.5:

Imagine a person who can recite the several hundred Odes by heart but, when delegated a governmental task, is unable to carry it out, or when sent abroad as an envoy, is unable to engage in repartee. No matter how many Odes he might have memorized, what good are they to him?

The goal is to develop a *sense* for the practice and not to be overly constrained by its formal structure. This sort of situation-centered reasoning resembles Aristotelian *phronesis* (practical wisdom), and ultimately what is right in the ethical realm corresponds to what the gentleman (i.e., the good person) would do.

Indeed, the entirety of Book Ten of the *Analects*—an extended account of Confucius's ritual behavior—can be seen as a model of how the true sage flexibly adapts the principles of ritual to concrete situations. While this chapter is often skipped over in embarrassment by Western scholars sympathetic to Confucianism but nonetheless appalled by the seemingly pointless detail and apparent rigidity of behavior ("With a black upper garment he would wear a lambskin robe; with a white upper garment he would wear a fawnskin robe; and with a yellow upper garment he would wear a fox-fur robe."—10.6), this discomfort is based upon a fundamental misunderstanding.

While the scope and detail of Confucian ritual certainly (and quite rightly) seem alien to a modern Westerner, it is important to understand that what is being emphasized in this chapter is the ease and grace with which the Master embodies the spirit of the rites in every aspect of his life—no matter how trivial—and accords with this spirit in adapting the rites to new and necessarily unforeseeable circumstances.

Consider some snapshots of Confucius in action from Book Ten, with occasional comments interposed for the sake of clarification:

10.2 At court, when speaking with officers of lower rank, he was pleasant and affable; when speaking with officers of upper rank, he was formal and proper. When his lord was present, he combined an attitude of cautious respect with graceful ease.

Confucius effortlessly adapted his countenance and behavior to the demands of the social situation; he was not overly familiar with his colleagues nor obsequious to his superiors.

10.3 When called upon by his lord to receive a guest, his countenance would become alert and serious, and he would hasten his steps. When he saluted those in attendance beside him—extending his clasped hands to the left or right, as their position required—his robes remained perfectly arrayed, both front and back. Hastening forward, he moved smoothly, as though gliding upon wings. Once the guest had left, he would always return to report, "The guest is no longer looking back."

According to most commentators, Confucius is here serving as the "Master of Reception"; to his left would be the "Master of Introductions" and to his right the "Supreme Master of Ceremonies." Each had a set speech to deliver, and after each speech they would bow both to their guests and to one another. As for his final report, it was the custom in ancient China for the guest to turn around and bow repeatedly as he left; the host (or the host's proxy, in this case Confucius) could return to his place only after this process was over. Here we see Confucius fulfilling his ritual duties with both precision and grace.

10.23 When receiving a gift from a friend—even something as valuable as a cart or a horse—he did not bow unless it was a gift of sacrificial meat.

There was apparently no specific clause in the rites that dictates this specific response to this particular situation; rather, Confucius, by virtue of his sensitivity to the ritual value of sacrificial meat relative to a sumptuous—but nonceremonial—gift, simply knows how to respond properly.

That Confucius's flexibility in applying ritual is the theme of Book Ten is made clear in the last passage, 10.27:

Startled by their arrival, a bird arose and circled several times before alighting upon a branch. [The Master] said, "This pheasant upon the mountain bridge—how timely it is! How timely it is!" Zilu saluted the bird, and it cried out three times before flying away.

This poetic, somewhat cryptic passage seems like a non sequitur at the end of a chapter devoted to short, prosaic descriptions of ritual behavior—unless, that is, it is seen as a thematic summary of the chapter as a whole. Timeliness (*shi*) is Confucius's particular forte, and indeed he is known to posterity (through the efforts of Mencius) as the "timely sage": the one whose ritual responses were always appropriate to circumstances. As Mencius explains in 5:B:1:

> When Confucius decided to leave Qi, he emptied the rice from the pot before it was even done and set out immediately. When he decided to leave Lu he said, "I will take my time, for this is the way to leave the state of one's parents." Moving quickly when it was appropriate to hurry, moving slowly when it was appropriate to linger, remaining in a state or taking office when the situation allowed—this is how Confucius was…. Confucius was the sage whose actions were timely.

We have thus seen that, by internalizing the rules and conventions that define a practice such as the rites, one is able at the same time to achieve a certain degree of autonomy in applying them. This autonomy, in turn, can allow one a certain degree of critical distance: Once the meaning embodied in the norms is grasped, the norms themselves can potentially be evaluated, criticized, or even altered. Hence we have the famous passage, *Analects* 9.3, where Confucius accedes to a modification in the rites:

> The Master said, "A ceremonial cap made of linen is prescribed by the rites, but these days people use silk. This is frugal, and I follow the majority. To bow before ascending the stairs is what is prescribed by the rites, but these days people bow after ascending. This is arrogant, and—though it goes against the majority—I continue to bow before ascending."

According to commentators, the linen cap specified by ritual was an elaborate affair—consisting of many layers and involving intricate stitching—and Confucius's contemporaries had begun replacing it with a simpler silk version. Confucius apparently feels that this does not interfere with its basic function. When approaching a ruler or other superior sitting on a raised dais, ritual dictates bowing before ascending the stairs, but Confucius's contemporaries had taken to ascending the stairs and only bowing when directly before their ruler. This is a more substantial change, and Confucius rejects it as not ritually proper. This passage thus describes the sort of judgment and flexibility that can be exercised by an accomplished ritual practitioner. Rites are expressive of a certain sense or feeling, and thus an alteration in the actual rite is permissible if it will not—in the opinion of one who has fully mastered the rites and thus internalized it—alter its essential meaning.

Spontaneity, Harmony, and Ease

After extended training in traditional cultural practices, the emotions are ultimately harnessed by Confucians to produce moral behavior that springs spontaneously from personal inclination. This means that, for the ethically perfected person, proper action requires no conscious thought or effort and is governed spontaneously by what we might term effortless attention. Music was considered by the early Confucians to be one the most powerful tools for affecting this sort of emotional transformation, and the metaphor of musical perfection also served for Confucius as a metaphor for the perfected spiritual state:[42]

3.23 The Master was discussing music with the Grand Music Master of Lu. He said, "What can be known about music is this: when it first begins, it resounds with a confusing variety of notes, but as it unfolds, these notes are reconciled by means of harmony, brought into tension by means of counterpoint, and finally woven together into a seamless whole. It is in this way that music reaches its perfection."

Music here serves as a model or metaphor for the process of self-cultivation: starting in confusion, passing through many phases and culminating in a state of *wu wei* perfection. Music as a model of harmony is also the theme of 8.8, which succinctly summarizes the process of Confucian self-cultivation in three phrases: "The Master said, 'Find inspiration in the *Odes*,[43] take your place through ritual, and achieve perfection with music.'" Steps 1 and 2 represent, respectively, cognitive shaping through learning and behavioral shaping through ritual training. In the third stage, the joy inspired by the powerfully moving music of the ancients brings the cognitive and behavioral together into the unselfconscious, effortless perfection that is *wu wei*. *Mencius* 4:A:27, which invokes the metaphor of dance, represents perhaps the best commentary on this passage:

The substance of benevolence (*ren*) is the serving of one's parents; the substance of rightness is obeying one's elders; the substance of wisdom is to understand benevolence and rightness and to not let them go; the substance of ritual propriety is the regulation and adornment of benevolence and rightness; and the substance of music is the joy one takes in benevolence and rightness. Once such joy is born, it cannot be stopped. Once it cannot be stopped, then one begins unconsciously to dance it with one's feet and wave one's arms in time with it.

That the inner state of the actor be harmonized with outer behavior, to the point that it becomes effortless and unselfconscious, is crucial for Confucius. This is a clear point of departure from most classic formulations of deontology. In a famous passage from the *Groundwork of the Metaphysics of Morals* (Kant, 1785/1964, 65–66), for instance, Kant argues that a shopkeeper who refrains from cheating his customers simply because he is honest—that is, he is unselfconsciously honest "out of inclination" (*aus Neigung*)—cannot be considered genuinely moral. True morality requires consciously acting "out of duty" (*aus Pflicht*), not merely "in conformity with duty" (*Pflichtmäßig*): consciously rehearsing the moral law, and then deliberately putting that law into practice through an act of cognitive control. In the *Analects*, there is not only no place for duty-bound action in the Kantian sense, but such behavior would be looked down upon as forced and inauthentic. The praise for the sage-king Shun by Mencius—that "his actions flowed from benevolence and rightness, he did not merely put them into practice" (4:B:19)—is in this sense quite anti-Kantian: Shun is considered virtuous precisely *because* he acted *aus Neigung* rather than *aus Pflicht*. As the famous Song commentator Zhu Xi explains in his commentary on *Mencius* 4:B:19, "Benevolence and rightness were already rooted in Shun's heart, and all of his actions sprang from there; it is not the case that he merely valued benevolence and rightness and therefore forced himself to put them into practice."

Conscious deliberation and cognitive control, though necessary in the early stages of self-cultivation, are thus hallmarks of inauthenticity and ethical clumsiness. Despite the importance of hard work, struggle, and endurance in the early stages of Confucian self-cultivation, it is fully expected that any Confucian gentleman worth the title will have come to fully internalize—behaviorally automatize—such practices as ritual and music. The result will be an individual with an entirely transformed set of dispositions. This theme is captured in Confucius's spiritual autobiography in *Analects* 2.4:

The Master said, "At fifteen I set my mind upon learning; at thirty I took my place in society; at forty I became free of doubts; at fifty I understood Heaven's Mandate; at sixty my ear was attuned; and at seventy I could follow my heart's desires without overstepping the bounds of propriety."

We can see the reshaping of Confucius's initial dispositions as taking place in three pairs of stages. In the first pair (stages 1 and 2), the aspiring gentleman commits himself to the Confucian Way, submitting to the rigors of study and ritual practice until these traditional forms have been internalized to the point that he is able to "take his place" among others. In the second pair, the practitioner begins to feel truly at ease with this new manner of being and is able to understand how the Confucian Way fits into the order of things and complies with the will of Heaven. The clarity and sense of ease this brings with it leads to the final two stages, where one's dispositions have been so thoroughly harmonized with the dictates of normative culture that one accords with them spontaneously. In such a state of *wu wei*, one can "follow one's heart's desires"—that is, surrender to automaticity and effortless attention—while still according perfectly with the dictates of traditional etiquette and morality. Some of the work on automaticity and spontaneous judgment formation reviewed above concludes that, in certain situations, automatic judgments may be more accurate than those arrived at through tortuous reasoning, and automatic behaviors may be both more efficacious than those under active cognitive control and easily disrupted by conscious interference. All of the early Confucians believed, realistically or not, that the state of supreme effortlessness enjoyed by the gentlemen would endow him with perfect efficacy in the world, including the ability to influence and transform others. Confucian *wu wei* is thus not merely a personal ideal but also has crucial political and soteriological effects,[44] all of them flowing from a state of unselfconscious and effortless attention.

Conclusion

Allow me to quote an apropos call to arms issued by David Hume over 200 years ago:

> Men are now cured of their passion for hypotheses and systems in natural philosophy, and will hearken to no arguments but those which are derived from experience. It is full time that they should attempt a like reformation in all moral disquisitions; and reject every system of ethics, however subtle or ingenious, which is not founded on fact and observation. (Hume, 1777/1976, 174–175)

What I would like to suggest is that the body of empirical evidence emerging from cognitive science, cognitive linguistics, neuroscience, social psychology, and primatology that I have reviewed above indicates that the so-called "virtue ethical" model best describes how real human beings actually *engage* in moral reasoning (a descriptive claim) and therefore provides us with the best framework for formulating a psychologically realistic model of moral reasoning and moral education (a normative claim).[45] Since we are invoking Hume, we must, of course, guard against the error of slipping from *is* into *ought*. I think, however, that psychological feasibility is an important desideratum for any ethical theory. If deontology and utilitarianism require us to think or behave in manners that are simply not possible or sustainable in quotidian life, this should temper our enthusiasm for adopting them as moral ideals.

Traditional world cultures, such as early Confucianism, provide us with a variety of virtue ethical models replete with profound psychological insights, as well as clever and effective methods for transforming and redirecting our nonconscious selves. As we learn more about how the human mind works, such ethical traditions take on a more than merely antiquarian interest, helping us to fill in an enormous blind spot that has hindered modern Western ethical thinking for the past several hundred years. The transformation required in ethics is similar to that currently taking place in certain pubic health campaigns, which have traditionally tended to focus on conveying specific bits of conscious knowledge ("wearing condoms prevents transmission of the AIDS virus"). As a recent *New York Times* piece (Duhigg 2008) observes, some of these campaigns are now borrowing techniques from corporate marketing departments[46] and focusing more on changing unconscious habits rather than transmitting conscious knowledge. If much of our everyday behavior is driven by effortless attention and spontaneous habits, modern ethical theorists need, in a similar way, to pay more attention to how such tacit modes of perceiving and acting function, how they are formed, and how—when our cognitive control systems deem it necessary—they can be reformed or redirected.

Notes

1. Van Norden (2007) provides a helpful summary of the Mencius–Mohist debate.

2. See Johnson (1987, ix–xiii) for a characterization of "objectivism" as I am using the term.

3. For a helpful, recent discussion of the objectivist model of concepts and the embodied alternative, with a wealth of experimental evidence, see Gibbs (2006, chapter 4).

4. See especially Ryle's famous distinction between "knowing how" and "knowing that" (Ryle 1949; Polanyi 1967).

5. See Kunst-Wilson and Zajonc (1980) and the literature review in Zajonc (1980). For a very helpful review article on the topic of emotional processing and automaticity, see Pessoa (2005), which concludes that emotional processing appears to enjoy a degree of autonomy from conscious "top–down" processes, but not complete automaticity.

6. T. Wilson and Schooler (1991); cf. T. Wilson, Kraft, and Dunn (1989) and T. Wilson (2002).

7. See especially Haidt, Koller, and Dias (1993), Haidt (2001), and Wheatley and Haidt (2005).

8. For a recent literature survey and account of the role and power of the "adaptive unconscious," see T. Wilson (2002).

9. Also see Johnson (1987), Lakoff (1987), and Langacker (1987) for similar arguments that linguistic representations have an analog, spatial component, as well as Damasio's claim that "images are the main content of our thought" (1994, 107).

10. For recent reviews, see the essays collected in Pecher and Zwaan (2005).

11. See the essays collected in Shepard and Cooper (1982).

12. Cf. the recent study by Winawer, Witthoft, Huk, and Boroditsky (2005) demonstrating that imagined and implied motion appear to recruit the same neural circuits as are involved in viewing actual motion.

13. Rosch (1973) and Rosch, Mervis, Gray, Johnson, and Boyes-Braem (1976); also see Lakoff (1987).

14. W. K. Simmons, Pecher, Hamann, Zeelenberg, and Barsalou (2003), reviewed and discussed in K. W. Simmons and Barsalou (2003).

15. See especially Johnson (1987, 1993), as well as Lakoff and Johnson (1999).

16. See Johnson (1993, 91–98) for a discussion of this work.

17. The term "bounded rationality" was coined by Herbert Simon in 1956. For more on the topic, see the essays gathered in Gigerenzer, Todd, and Group (1999) and Gigerenzer and Selten (2001).

18. For just a sampling, see Damasio (1994), LeDoux (1996), Nussbaum (2001), Prinz (2007), Sinnott-Armstrong (2008a, 2008b), and Solomon (2003, 2004).

19. Cf. Gerald Edelman's (1992, 121) concept of "value memory," where "current value-free perceptual categorization interacts with value-dominant memory" through the online construction of scenes.

20. Cf. Gigerenzer and Selten's (2001, 9) characterization of emotions as "effective stopping rules for search and a means for limiting search spaces."

21. See especially the essays gathered in Kahneman, Slovic, and Tversky (1982) and Kahneman and Tversky (2000). Kahneman and Tversky tend to emphasize the suboptimal nature of ordinary decision making. In contrast, the "bounded rationality" movement discussed above contends that, in ecologically realistic situations, the rationally optimal decision (the economist's usual standard for the "right" decision) is not necessarily the best or most adaptive because of the costs of information gathering and processing or lost opportunities.

22. Cf. Lakoff and Johnson's argument that normative judgments arise from background feelings and that bodily ease or "well-being" is the basic source domain for our understanding of "goodness" (Lakoff and Johnson 1999, 290–292). For representative recent works on morality and emotion, see the essays collected in Solomon (2004), Nichols (2004), and Prinz (2007).

23. See the literature reviewed in Nichols (2002, 221–222) and Nichols and Folds-Bennett (2003) for results with 4- to 6-year-old children.

24. See Haidt (2007) for a more recent literature review.

25. See Jones (2007) for a recent review article on disgust and moral judgments.

26. Greene, Nystrom, Engell, Darley, and Cohen (2004) also found increased activity in brain regions associated with cognitive control prior to utilitarian judgments.

27. Daniel Dennett's (1995, 495–502) example of a philosophy fellowship competition is a helpful illustration of some of the features of realistic, "myopic and time-pressured" decision making.

28. He and Patricia Churchland (Casebeer and Churchland 2003, 187–188) have argued for a more "ecologically valid experimental regime" that takes into account that real moral reasoning is "hot" (affective states are a crucial part), social (decisions are not made in a social vacuum but are subject to social cues), distributed (embedded in a large web of stimulation), organic (context sensitive), genuine (personally involved rather than abstract), and directed (about actual things in the world).

29. The essays in Crisp and Slote (1997) provide a helpful introduction to virtue ethics. Also see Van Norden (2007, 33–37) for a discussion of "radical" versus "moderate" versions of virtue ethics.

30. In a piece composed some years ago that included a discussion of the relative advantages of virtue ethics and deontology (Slingerland 2001), an anonymous referee pointed out to me that Kant, to take one example, recognized the need for pragmatic, situation-specific judgment in applying universal principles to specific situations and that, therefore, the gulf between a sophisticated Kantianism and virtue ethics is not as large as it might at first seem. Indeed, defenders

of the Kantian tradition have long argued that what is attacked by virtue ethicists is often a caricature of the true Kantian position, which in fact gives a prominent role to practical reason (e.g., Schneewind 1990). However we understand Kantian practical reason, one point on which Kant was absolutely unequivocal is that emotions and habits—as accidental, empirical, *heteronomous* qualities of human beings—can have absolutely nothing to do with morality. To the extent that more recent takes on Kant attempt to give a positive role to emotions or to analogical imagination (e.g., Johnson 1987), they seem to simply confirm the point that traditional deontology is plagued by deep problems.

31. For example, S. Wilson (1995), Chong (1998), Ivanhoe (2000), Slingerland (2001), and Van Norden (2007).

32. A somewhat anachronistic term for the so-called Daoists and Confucians whose worldview later came to dominate East Asian thought.

33. The *Analects* (*lunyu* 论语; lit. "Classified Sayings") was probably put together sometime after the death of the historical Confucius (551–479 B.C.E.). Our present version is a somewhat heterogeneous collection of material from different time periods, probably representing different lineages of disciplines, although scholars differ in their identification of the different strata, as well as in the significance they attribute to these differences.

34. Confucius's two immediate followers in the Warring States, Mencius and Xunzi, each focus on and develop one of these two themes, with Mencius advocating a more thoroughgoing "internalism" and Xunzi formulating a fairly extreme "externalist" model of self-cultivation.

35. In the *Analects*, *ren* refers to the highest of virtues, the overarching virtue of being truly good or truly human (being cognate with the term for person, *ren* 人). In post-*Analects* texts, it has the more specific sense of empathy or kindness between human beings—especially for a ruler toward his subjects—and in such contexts is usually translated as *benevolence*. Although we see hints of this later usage in the *Analects* (12.22, 17.21), it is much more commonly used there in the more general sense of goodness.

36. All citations from the *Analects* are taken from Slingerland (2003a).

37. On the role of the arts in Confucian self-cultivation, see Eno (1990) and Gier (2001).

38. A prime minister who was renowned for his integrity and devotion to the state.

39. That is, one should continue to defer to the judgment of one's elders and not take the initiative.

40. For more on the contextual nature of Confucius's teachings, refer to Setton (2000).

41. For a classic example of Confucius interpreted as a deontologist, with a particular focus on the Negative Golden Rule, see Roetz (1993, especially 133–148).

42. See Cook (1995) and Brindley (2006) for excellent discussions of this themes. In this context, it is very telling that the utilitarian Mozi rejected Confucian music, failing to see the moral value

of music because the cultivation of emotions and dispositions played no role in his extremely rationalistic ethical scheme.

43. One of the classic Confucian texts.

44. See Slingerland (2003b) for more on *wu wei* as a spiritual and political ideal.

45. Observations along these lines have been made by neuroscientifically literate philosophers such as Flanagan (1991), Churchland (1998), and Casebeer (2003). John Doris (1998, 2002) and Gilbert Harman (1999) have famously argued that findings in social psychology suggest that stable human character traits do not exist, which, of course, would call into question the very raison d'être of virtue ethics (This was first brought to my attention by Eric Hutton, personal communication, September 2005). In fact, large-scale meta-analyses—for example, Roberts, Kuncel, Shiner, Caspi, and Goldberg (2007)—show that, while situational effects can be quite strong, stable personality traits have at least as strong an effect. Also see Kupperman (2001), Kamtekar (2004), and Hutton (2006) for philosophical responses to Doris's and Harman's positions.

46. The marketing departments, of course, were, in turn, inspired by precisely the sort of social psychology research reviewed above. The fact that people flogging toothpaste and air fresheners are more empirically up-to-date when it comes to human cognition than most philosophers says much about the ivory tower quality of contemporary academic ethics.

References

Anscombe, G. E. M. 1958. Modern moral philosophy. *Philosophy* 33 (124):1–19.

Aristotle. 1999. *Nicomachean ethics*. 2nd ed. Indianapolis: Hackett.

Bargh, J., and T. Chartrand. 1999. The unbearable automaticity of being. *Am. Psychol.* 54:462–479.

Barsalou, L. 1999. Perceptual symbol systems. *Behav. Brain Sci.* 22:577–609.

Baumeister, R. 1984. Choking under pressure: Self-consciousness and paradoxical effects of incentives on skillful performance. *J. Pers. Soc. Psychol.* 46:610–620.

Baumeister, R., E. Bratslavsky, M. Muraven, and D. Tice. 1998. Ego depletion: Is the active self a limited resource? *J. Pers. Soc. Psychol.* 74:1252–1265.

Borges, B., D. Goldstein, A. Ortmann, and G. Gigerenzer. 1999. Can ignorance beat the stock market? In *Simple heuristics that make us smart*, ed. G. Gigerenzer, Peter Todd, and the ABC Research Group. New York: Oxford University Press.

Brindley, E. 2006. Music, cosmos, and the development of psychology in early China. *Toung Pao* 92:1–49.

Casebeer, W., and P. Churchland. 2003. The neural mechanisms of moral cognition: A multi-aspect approach to moral judgment and decision-making. *Biol. Philos.* 18:169–194.

Casebeer, W. D. 2003. Moral cognition and its neural constituents. *Nat. Rev. Neurosci.* 4:840–845.

Cavell, S. 1979. *The claim of reason.* New York: Oxford University Press.

Chong, K.-C. 1998. Confucius' virtue ethics: Li, Yi, Wen and Chih in the Analects. *J. Chin. Philos.* 25:101–130.

Churchland, P. 1998. Toward a cognitive neurobiology of the moral virtues. *Topoi* 17:83–96.

Churchland, P., and T. Sejnowski. 1992. *The computational brain.* Cambridge: MIT Press.

Clark, A. 1997. *Being there: Putting brain, body and world together again.* Cambridge: MIT Press.

Coleman, L., and P. Kay. 1981. Prototype semantics: The English word lie. *Language* 57:26–44.

Cook, S. 1995. *Unity and diversity in the musical thought of warring states China.* Unpublished Ph.D. dissertation, University of Michigan.

Crisp, R., and M. Slote, eds. 1997. *Virtue ethics.* New York: Oxford University Press.

Damasio, A. 1985. Disorders of complex visual processing: Agnosias, achromatopsia, Balint's syndrome, and related difficulties of orientation and construction. In *Principles of behavioral neurology*, ed. M. M. Mesulam. Philadelphia: Davis, 259–288.

Damasio, A. 1989. The brain binds entities and events by multiregional activation from convergence zones. *Neural Comput.* 1:123–132.

Damasio, A. 1994. *Descartes' error: Emotion, reason, and the human brain.* New York: Putnam.

Damasio, A. 2003. *In search of Spinoza: Joy, sorrow, and the feeling brain.* New York: Harvest House.

Damasio, A., and H. Damasio. 1994. Cortical systems for retrieval of concrete knowledge: The convergence zone framework. In *Large-scale neuronal theories of the brain*, ed. C. K. J. Davis. Cambridge: MIT Press, 61–74.

Dennett, D. 1995. *Darwin's dangerous idea: Evolution and the meaning of life.* New York: Simon & Schuster.

Doris, J. 1998. Persons, situations, and virtue ethics. *Nous* 32:504–530.

Doris, J. 2002. *Lack of character: Personality and moral behavior.* New York: Cambridge University Press.

Duhigg, C. 2008. Warning: Habits may be good for you. *New York Times.* (Business, July 13).

Edelman, G. 1992. *Bright air, brilliant fire: On the matter of the mind.* New York: Basic Books.

Edwards, K., and W. von Hippel. 1995. Hearts and minds: The priority of affective versus cognitive factors in person perception. *Pers. Soc. Psychol. Bull.* 21:996–1011.

Eno, R. 1990. *The Confucian creation of heaven.* Albany: State University of New York Press.

Flanagan, O. 1991. *Varieties of moral personality: Ethics and psychological realism.* Cambridge: Harvard University Press.

Gazzaniga, M. 1998. *The mind's past.* Berkeley: University of California Press.

Gibbs, R. 2006. *Embodiment and cognitive science.* Cambridge: Cambridge University Press.

Gier, N. 2001. The dancing Ru: A Confucian aesthetics of virtue. *Philos. East West* 51:280–305.

Gigerenzer, G., and R. Selten, eds. 2001. *Bounded rationality: The adaptive toolbox.* Cambridge: MIT Press.

Gigerenzer, G., P. M. Todd, and A. R. Group. 1999. *Simple heuristics that make us smart.* New York: Oxford University Press.

Goldstein, D., and G. Gigerenzer. 2002. Models of ecological rationality: The recognition heuristic. *Psychol. Rev.* 109:75–90.

Greene, J. 2007. The secret joke of Kant's soul. In *Moral psychology: The neuroscience of morality: Emotion, disease, and development.* vol. 3. ed. W. Sinnott-Armstrong. Cambridge: MIT Press, 35–79.

Greene, J. D., S. A. Morelli, K. Lowenberg, L. E. Nystrom, and J. D. Cohen. 2008. Cognitive load selectively interferes with utilitarian moral judgment. *Cognition* 107:1144–1154.

Greene, J. D., L. E. Nystrom, A. D. Engell, J. M. Darley, and J. D. Cohen. 2004. The neural bases of cognitive conflict and control in moral judgment. *Neuron* 44:389–400.

Greene, J. D., R. B. Sommerville, L. E. Nystrom, J. M. Darley, and J. D. Cohen. 2001. An fMRI investigation of emotional engagement in moral judgment. *Science* 293:2105–2108.

Haidt, J. 2001. The emotional dog and its rational tail: A social intuitionist approach to moral judgment. *Psychol. Rev.* 108:814–834.

Haidt, J. 2007. The new synthesis in moral psychology. *Science* 316:998–1002.

Haidt, J., S. Koller, and M. Dias. 1993. Affect, culture, and morality, or is it wrong to eat your dog? *J. Pers. Soc. Psychol.* 65:613–628.

Harman, G. 1999. Moral philosophy meets social psychology: Virtue ethics and the fundamental attribution error. *Proceedings of the Aristotelian Society* 99:315–331.

Hume, D. (1777/1976). *Enquiries concerning human understanding and concerning the principles of morals.* 3rd ed. Oxford: Clarendon.

Hutton, E. 2006. Character, situationalism, and early Confucian thought. *Philos. Stud.* 127:37–58.

Ivanhoe, P. J. 2000. *Confucian moral self cultivation.* 2nd ed. Indianapolis: Hackett.

Johnson, M. 1987. *The body in the mind: The bodily basis of meaning, imagination, and reason.* Chicago: University of Chicago Press.

Johnson, M. 1993. *Moral imagination: Implications of cognitive science for ethics.* Chicago: University of Chicago Press.

Jones, D. 2007. The depths of disgust. *Nature* 447:768–771.

Kahneman, D., P. Slovic, and A. Tversky, eds. 1982. *Judgement under uncertainty: Heuristics and biases.* Cambridge: Cambridge University Press.

Kahneman, D., and A. Tversky. 2000. *Choices, values, and frames.* Cambridge: Cambridge University Press.

Kamtekar, R. 2004. Situationalism and virtue ethics on the content of our character. *Ethics* 114:458–491.

Kant, I. (1964). *Groundwork of the metaphysic of morals.* Translated by H. J. Paton. New York: Harper Torchbooks. (Original work published 1785)

Kunst-Wilson, W., and R. Zajonc. 1980. Affective discrimination of stimuli that cannot be recognized. *Science* 207:557–558.

Kupperman, J. 2001. The indispensability of character. *Philosophy* 76:239–250.

Lakoff, G. 1987. *Women, fire and dangerous things: What categories reveal about the mind.* Chicago: University of Chicago Press.

Lakoff, G., and M. Johnson. 1999. *Philosophy in the flesh: The embodied mind and its challenge to Western thought.* New York: Basic Books.

Langacker, R. 1987. *Theoretical prerequisites.* vol. 1. *Foundations of cognitive grammar.* Stanford: Stanford University Press.

Langacker, R. 1991. *Descriptive applications.* vol. 2. *Foundations of cognitive grammar.* Stanford: Stanford University Press.

LeDoux, J. 1996. *The emotional brain: The mysterious underpinnings of emotional life.* New York: Simon & Schuster.

Loewenstein, G., E. Weber, C. Hsee, and N. Welch. 2001. Risk as feelings. *Psychol. Bull.* 127:267–286.

Muraven, M., D. Tice, and R. Baumeister. 1998. Self-control as a limited resource: Regulatory depletion patterns. *J. Pers. Soc. Psychol.* 74:774–789.

Nichols, S. 2002. Norms with feeling: Towards a psychological account of moral judgment. *Cognition* 84:221–236.

Nichols, S. 2004. *Sentimental rules: On the natural foundations of moral judgment.* New York: Oxford University Press.

Nichols, S., and T. Folds-Bennett. 2003. Are children moral objectivists? Children's judgments about moral and response-dependent properties. *Cognition* 90 (23–N):32.

Nietzsche, F. (1966). *Beyond good and evil*. Translated by W. Kaufmann. New York: Vintage. (Original work published 1886)

Nisbett, R. E., and T. D. Wilson. 1977. Telling more than we can know: Verbal reports on mental processes. *Psychol. Rev.* 84:231–259.

Nussbaum, M. 1990. *Love's knowledge: Essays on philosophy and literature*. Oxford: Oxford University Press.

Nussbaum, M. C. 2001. *Upheavals of thought: The intelligence of the emotions*. Cambridge: Cambridge University Press.

Pecher, D., R. Zeelenberg, and L. Barsalou. 2003. Verifying different-modality properties for concepts produced switching costs. *Psychol. Sci.* 14:119–124.

Pecher, D., and R. Zwaan, eds. 2005. *Grounding cognition: The role of perception and action in memory, language and thinking*. Cambridge: Cambridge University Press.

Pessoa, L. 2005. To what extent are emotional visual stimuli processed without attention and awareness? *Curr. Opin. Neurobiol.* 15:188–196.

Polanyi, M. 1967. *The tacit dimension*. Garden City, NY: Doubleday.

Prinz, J. 2007. *The emotional construction of morals*. New York: Oxford University Press.

Putnam, H. 1999. *The threefold cord: Mind, body, and world*. New York: Columbia University Press.

Regier, T. 1996. *The human semantic potential: Spatial language and constrained connectionism*. Cambridge: MIT Press.

Rizzolatti, G., L. Fogassi, and V. Gallese. 2001. Neurophysiological mechanisms underlying the understanding and imitation of action. *Nat. Rev. Neurosci.* 2:661–670.

Roberts, B., N. Kuncel, R. Shiner, A. Caspi, and L. Goldberg. 2007. The power of personality: The comparative validity of personality traits, socioeconomic status, and cognitive ability for predicting important life outcomes. *Perspect. Psychol. Sci.* 2:313–345.

Roetz, H. 1993. *Confucian ethics of the Axial Age*. Albany: State University of New York Press.

Rosch, E. 1973. Natural categories. *Cognit. Psychol.* 4:328–350.

Rosch, E., C. Mervis, W. Gray, D. Johnson, and P. Boyes-Braem. 1976. Basic objects in natural categories. *Cognit. Psychol.* 8:382–439.

Rozin, P., and C. Nemeroff. 1990. The laws of sympathetic magic. In *Cultural psychology: The Chicago Symposia on Human Development*, ed. R. S. G. H. James Stigler. Cambridge: Cambridge University Press, 205–232.

Ryle, G. 1949. *The concept of mind*. London: Hutchinson.

Schneewind, J. 1990. The misfortunes of virtue. *Ethics* 101:42–63.

Searle, J. 1995. *The construction of social reality*. New York: Free Press.

Setton, M. 2000. Ambiguity in the Analects. *J. Chin. Philos.* 27:545–569.

Shepard, R., and L. Cooper. 1982. *Mental images and their transformations*. Cambridge: MIT Press.

Simmons, K. W., and L. Barsalou. 2003. The similarity-in-topography principle: Reconciling theories of conceptual deficits. *Cogn. Neuropsychol.* 20:451–486.

Simmons, W. K., D. Pecher, S. Hamann, R. Zeelenberg, and L. Barsalou. 2003. *fMRI evidence for modality-specific processing of conceptual knowledge on six modalities*. Paper presented at the Meeting for the Society of Cognitive Neuroscience, New York.

Sinnott-Armstrong, W., ed. 2008a. *Moral psychology: The cognitive science of morality: Intuition and diversity*. vol. 2. Cambridge: MIT Press.

Sinnott-Armstrong, W., ed. 2008b. *Moral psychology: The neuroscience of morality: Emotion, brain disorders, and development*. vol. 3. Cambridge: MIT Press.

Slingerland, E. 2001. Virtue ethics, the Analects, and the problem of commensurability. *J. Relig. Ethics* 29:97–125.

Slingerland, E. 2003a. *Confucius: Analects: With Selections from traditional commentaries*. Indianapolis: Hackett.

Slingerland, E. 2003b. *Effortless action: Wu-wei as conceptual metaphor and spiritual ideal in early China*. New York: Oxford University Press.

Slingerland, E. 2008. *What science offers the humanities: Integrating body and culture*. New York: Cambridge University Press.

Solomon, R., ed. 2003. *What is an emotion? Classic and contemporary readings*. New York: Oxford University Press.

Solomon, R., ed. 2004. *Thinking about feeling: Contemporary philosophers on emotion*. New York: Oxford University Press.

Spivey, M., and J. Geng. 2001. Oculomotor mechanisms activated by imagery and memory: Eye movements to absent images. *Psychol. Res.* 65:235–241.

Spivey, M., D. Richardson, and M. Gozalez-Marquez. 2005. On the perceptual-motor and image-schematic infrastructure of language. In *Grounding cognition: The role of perception and action in memory, language and thinking*, ed. D. Pecher and R. Zwaan. Cambridge: Cambridge University Press, 235–241.

Sweetser, E. 1987. The definition of lie. In *Cultural models in language and thought*, ed. D. N. Q. Holland. Cambridge: Cambridge University Press, 43–66.

Swindale, N. 2001. Cortical cartography: What's in a map? *Curr. Biol.* 11:R764–R767.

Talmy, L. 2000. *Towards a cognitive semantics*. Cambridge: MIT Press.

Taylor, C. 1989. *Sources of the self: The makings of modern identity*. Cambridge: Harvard University Press.

Van Norden, B. 2007. *Virtue ethics and consequentialism in early Chinese philosophy*. New York: Cambridge University Press.

Warrington, E., and T. Shallice. 1984. Category-specific impairments. *Brain* 107:829–854.

Wexler, M., S. Kosslyn, and A. Berthoz. 1998. Motor processes in mental rotation. *Cognition* 68:77–94.

Wheatley, T., and J. Haidt. 2005. Hypnotic disgust makes moral judgments more severe. *Psychol. Sci.* 16:780–784.

Wilson, S. 1995. Conformity, individuality, and the nature of virtue: A classical Confucian contribution to contemporary ethical reflection. *J. Relig. Ethics* 23:263–289.

Wilson, T. 2002. *Strangers to ourselves: Discovering the adaptive unconscious*. Cambridge: Harvard University Press.

Wilson, T., D. Kraft, and D. Dunn. 1989. The disruptive effects of explaining attitudes: The moderating effect of knowledge about the attitude object. *J. Exp. Soc. Psychol.* 25:379–400.

Wilson, T., and R. Nisbett. 1978. The accuracy of verbal reports about the effects of stimuli on evaluations and behavior. *Soc. Psychol.* 41:118–131.

Wilson, T., and J. Schooler. 1991. Thinking too much: Introspection can reduce the quality of preferences and decisions. *J. Pers. Soc. Psychol.* 60:181–192.

Winawer, J., N. Witthoft, A. Huk, and L. Boroditsky. 2005. Common mechanisms for processing of perceived, inferred, and imagined visual motion. *J. Vis.* 5:491.

Zajonc, R. 1980. Feeling and thinking: Preferences need no inferences. *Am. Psychol.* 35:151–175.

Zimbardo, P., S. Laberge, and L. Butler. 1993. Psychophysiological consequences of unexplained arousal: A posthypnotic suggestion paradigm. *J. Abnorm. Psychol.* 102:466–473.

13 Flow Experience Explained on the Grounds of an Activity Approach to Attention

Yuri Dormashev
Translated by Evgeny N. Osin

In a number of works, Mihaly Csikszentmihalyi and his colleagues described their research that investigated the content of flow experience and its necessary conditions (e.g., Csikszentmihalyi and Csikszentmihalyi 1988; Csikszentmihalyi 1975, 1990, 1993, 1997). They discovered that concentration of attention without any mental effort is a primary and a universal characteristic of this experience. However, *the existing theoretical models of flow are mostly descriptive, rather than explanatory* (Csikszentmihalyi 1975; Massimini and Carli 1988; Nakamura and Csikszentmihalyi 2002). In a discussion of future perspectives and methodological issues of flow research, Csikszentmihalyi wrote:

> Until a consistent and coherent theory of attention is developed, research results will continue to be trivial, no matter how brilliant are the techniques we devise. Only a new conceptual paradigm will be able to inspire new research, direct it along the most promising paths and then relate findings to each other and explain them in a meaningful context. (1978, 356)

In my opinion, the lack of such a theory of attention still, after 30 years, remains the main obstacle on the way toward a psychological explanation of flow experience.[1]

A certain gap between description and explanation of observed phenomena can be found in any area of psychology, not only in flow research. This gap keeps shrinking thanks to an ongoing integration of different theoretical approaches and the development of new research methods. However, in the psychology of attention this gap is especially wide and seemingly insurmountable. In other areas of psychology, as knowledge progresses, issues are successively resolved, and the understanding of the principal problems advances. But if we follow the philosophical and psychological studies of attention from remote ages to the most recent works, we find that an unvarying question remains: *Does attention even exist*? (e.g., Hamilton 1880; Bradley 1886; James 1890; Rubin 1926; Galperin 1958; Johnston and Dark 1986; Bäumler 1991; Fernandez-Duque and Johnson 2002). In different works attention is understood either as a separate human ability *or* as a manifestation of other abilities, as a separate process *or* as a characteristic of other processes of consciousness, as a specific *or* a total attuning of an organism, as a set of certain mechanisms and resources *or* as a characteristic of information processing, as a separate activity *or* as an aspect of any activity. Different authors have been giving two opposite answers to this question: a positive one, affirming that attention does exist, and a negative one, explaining attentional phenomena as manifestations or properties of other mental and physiological processes.

One of the reasons why the problem of attention is so difficult is that the researchers are unable to point out the phenomena that would reflect a primary effect, or product, of attention within the diverse phenomenology traditionally related to this process. It is generally reckoned that, at present, attentional phenomena are all described completely, which makes it impossible to find anything new or of importance in understanding the process of attention. Another reason is a lack of a psychological theory that could provide a sound basis for the solution of this problem. The question of existence of attention can be answered affirmatively on the grounds of Leontiev's[2] (1975, 1978, 1981a, 1981b) psychological theory of activity, which can also be used to explain the flow phenomenon. However, in order to assimilate the results of the flow research, the theory of activity has to accommodate by expanding its conceptual apparatus. The aim of this chapter is to provide a theoretical basis needed to explain attentional phenomena, rather than to review the actual state of affairs within the psychological theory of activity, psychology of attention, or flow research. *This chapter aims to provide an explanation of the flow experience using a hypothesis that views the process of attention as an act of activity.*

The first section of this chapter, "The Psychological Theory of Activity," outlines the main concepts of Leontiev's psychological theory of activity and includes a discussion and elaboration of its principal points. In the second section, "Activity and Attention," an account of Dobrynin's theory of attention is given, and the hypothesis about the nature of attention as an act of activity is proposed. In the third section, "The Role of Attention within Autotelic Activity," the flow phenomenon is explained on the grounds of the statements set forth in the first two sections, thus providing indirect evidence of their consistency.

The Psychological Theory of Activity

An Overview of the Psychological Theory of Activity
Aleksei Nikolaevich Leontiev (1903–1979) proposes *activity*,[3] rather than behavior or conscious and unconscious processes, to be the subject matter of psychology, which "includes activity in its function, rather than in some of its 'parts' or 'elements.' This is the function of situating the subject within objective reality and of transforming this reality into a subjective form" (Leontiev 1975, 92).[4] The word *situating* denotes not only the processes of localization and orientation of an organism within its natural, material environment. When it is applied to human beings, it implies also

the definition of their place within the social and cultural settings of their life, activity, and development.

An *object of activity*[5] is defined by Leontiev in a philosophical sense "as something opposing..., resisting..., that which an action is directed at, that is, something a living being relates to, *an object of its activity*, whether that activity be external or internal" (1981b, 49). Anything that exists independently of a subject can determine its activity and, therefore, its mind and behavior by becoming an object of its activity. These objects can be "substantial, or material," as well as "those characterized by ... their intellectual content" (Leontiev 2000, 428). The basic vital relationships of an organism with its environment are manifested through activity, which determines the process of development of mind and of its physiological mechanisms.

Vital activity is defined as a whole, a system, or a hierarchy of activities. *Specific activities* are differentiated according to the difference in their objects and constitute principal units of the vital process (Leontiev 1975, 105). The object of an activity in a psychological sense is its motive, defined as an *objectified need*.[6] A *motive* is something for which an activity is carried out, a mental representation of a certain object. A motive corresponds to a need by motivating and directing the activity toward the object that can be used to satisfy this need or by simply matching it, as in the case of *insatiable needs*, such as the need for cognition. Leontiev states that all needs are object related, with the exception of *functional needs* (such as the need for movement), which "constitute a specific class of [mental] states that are either related to conditions arising, so to say, in the course of the 'inner housekeeping' of organisms (the need for rest after intensive activity, etc.), or derived—arising as object-related needs are pursued (for instance, the need for completion of an act)" (Leontiev 1971, 1).

Organic needs—that is, needs for something an organism requires—are *primary needs*. However, primary needs are only initial prerequisites and intrinsic conditions of activity. Human needs keep developing as their objects change. According to Leontiev, in the course of material and intellectual (mental) production, society keeps creating new needs, as well as new ways of need satisfaction. In a human mind, needs become *ideational*, which means they can motivate an activity directed toward relevant objects even when these needs are not actually present. For instance, a man who is not actually hungry can nevertheless go shopping in order to buy food for dinner. In practice, almost any human activity is *polymotivated*—it corresponds to several needs at the same time and becomes a realization of several different relationships of a human being to the world.

As he approached the classical problem of origins and development of mind in phylogenesis, Leontiev introduced the concepts of action and operation—structural units into which a specific activity can be analyzed (Leontiev 1981b, 219–349). He stated that the structure of human activity changes in the course of the biological evolution of the species. At the primary stages, activity was comprised of *operations* carried out by unconscious mental processes. This type of activity is called *simple* (Leontiev 1994, 188).

A qualitative change in the structure of activity (and, as a result, in the development of the psyche) took place at the human level as a consequence of a gradual "inversion" of relationships between organisms and the environment. Whereas other living organisms can only adapt to the environment using their specific and accumulated individual experience, humans can change the environment in the course of their collective labor activity, which is carried out using social tools, signs, and symbols. A human activity becomes *complex* when actions emerge distinctly within its structure. *Actions* are directed toward consciously represented goals.[7] A *goal* does not possess any motivating force; it arises as a mental representation of a distinct role an individual plays within a collective activity. According to Leontiev, consciousness emerged as a phylogenetic stage of psychic development as a result of collective labor activity. In other words, goals represent the person's relationships to other people (Leontiev 1981b, 477). From this point on, ontogenetic development of the psyche becomes determined by the process of appropriation of the sociohistoric experience that is contained in the domains of production, art, and science.

A goal defines what a person is doing or is intending to do; "it is the anticipated result that my action is aiming to attain" (Leontiev 2000, 45). A goal situated within a specific set of internal and external conditions is a *task*. A task determines the way an action will be carried out, that is, the set of operations that will implement the action.

Operations on the ontogenetic level are distinguished by Leontiev into *primary operations* (either innate or formed early in ontogenesis by unconscious attuning of activity to the conditions in which it takes place) and *secondary operations* (formed later in ontogenesis from actions that shift to the operational level, becoming automatic and unconscious). Generally, action-level processes directed at a goal are consciously represented, but secondary operations (and their related conditions) may become conscious in the case of an impediment to activity—for instance, if the conditions in which it is carried out change abruptly. Primary operations, as a rule, cannot become conscious.

The three main *constituents* of consciousness, according to Leontiev (1975, 2005), are sensory fabric, meaning, and personal sense. *Sensory fabric*, determined by the anatomy and physiology of an individual's sensory systems, is a conscious representation of the real existence of objects that surround the individual, as well as of his or her own bodily processes. *Meanings* are social by nature and are appropriated by individuals in the course of instrumental and collective activity mediated by interpersonal communication. A person appropriates the system of meanings that is conserved by means of special objects—that is, social instruments, such as language and cultural artifacts. In the course of this appropriation one has to "carry out such an activity in relation to these [objects], which, in a manner of speaking, reproduces in itself the essential features of the activity embodied and accumulated in the given object" (Leontiev 1981b, 418). The *personal sense*, or the *meaning to me* (Leontiev 1994, 209), of an action reflects the relation between the action's goal and the motive of the overlying activity that this action implements. In a polymotivated activity, such a motive (called a *sense-forming motive*) plays a leading role.

According to Leontiev, one action can be associated with different activities. The actual personal sense of an action depends on the activity in which this action is currently being executed. Personal sense becomes apparent in emotional experiences that arise in the course of an action or reflect the evaluation of its results. A personal sense can be expressed in a set of meanings.[8] It becomes conscious as soon as a person is able to find relevant meanings and, more importantly, to recognize the real motives that lie behind his or her actions—in Leontiev's terms, "to solve a problem of personal sense" (Leontiev 1975, 206). In case this inner work is not undertaken, or when its results are substituted by some ready-made meanings borrowed from an ideology, one is only able to recognize the *quasi-motives* of their actions, which leads to a superficial understanding of oneself, the world, and one's place within it.

In addition to the above outlined psychological analysis of the structure of human activity, Leontiev (1975, 113–123) proposed *two more levels of analysis* necessary for an adequate understanding of the human mind and behavior. An overlying level of analysis of a specific activity can be called *social*, as it involves consideration of the systems of an individual's social and interpersonal relationships in order to understand an individual's personality and the role a given activity plays in a person's vital activity more generally. The other, underlying level of analysis can be called *physiological*, as it involves a study of elementary psychophysiological functions and their groupings into *functional organs*, also called *functional physiological systems* (Leontiev 1975, 116; 1981b, 400–401, 549–550).

Functional physiological systems are socially determined physiological mechanisms of secondary operations. They develop in ontogenesis in the course of activity, at first external and practical, mediated by objects and by the dialog that takes place between a child and its caregivers. The development of functional physiological systems is determined by the type of activity an individual carries out and is supported, as well as limited, from above (by society) and from below (by the physiological mechanisms). The process that is most important for the formation of functional physiological systems is *internalization*[9]—the transition of an originally external activity into an internal form. The structure of internal activity is the same as that of its external counterpart, and the dynamics, or the way the activity processes shift from the level of specific activity to the action and operational levels and back, also remain the same. During these transitions, the peripheral motor components of the functional physiological systems are retained so that they can later be unfolded or reduced again

(Leontiev 1981b, 550–551). Various psychophysiological indicators of these transitions can be studied in order to analyze the functional physiological systems, yielding objective data about the structure and dynamics of a specific activity.[10] Leontiev referred to the level approach to movement regulation and formation of motor skills developed by Nikolai Aleksandrovich Bernstein (1896–1966) as a model for this type of study of the structure of functional physiological systems (Bernstein 1967, 1990).

An individual's set of specific activities defines one's *personality*, which is defined as a hierarchy of socially significant motives of a person's activity. It is formed in the course of one's life as one's motivational sphere develops. According to Leontiev, personality is born twice. Its *first birth* takes place in early childhood, when some motives become subordinated by other ones for the first time. A prerequisite for the *second birth of personality* is an individual's insight into the existing hierarchy of one's own motives, which enables the person to carry out acts that change the world around one and change one's own personality. As a result of these acts, the motivational structure begins to change, and in this way a personality is born for the second time (Leontiev 1983, 382).

According to Leontiev, the structure of a personality can be described by three parameters: its span, the complexity of its hierarchy, and the type of its overall structure. The *span* of personality is defined by the number of active motives it embraces. It can expand, thanks to the psychological mechanism of "shifting the motive to the goal," whereby the goal of an action that takes place within one activity may become a motive of another specific activity (Leontiev 1981b, 310–313, 520–523). The *complexity* of the personality hierarchy is determined by the way some motives are subordinated to other ones. A top-level motive, or *leading motive*, not only defines the general direction of one's activity by defining a range of possible goals but also provides personal sense to the actions that implement this activity. The sense-forming motives "'evaluate' the significance that objective circumstances and the subject's actions in these circumstances have for the individual's own life, providing one with personal sense that does not directly correspond to one's understood objective meaning" (Leontiev 1975, 150). The remaining motives, called *stimulating motives*, "might only perform a stimulating function, determining, in a way, the dynamics of action: its activation, its maintenance, its level of intensity and so on, that is, its dynamic characteristics" (Leontiev 2000, 446). The *overall structure* parameter of a personality implies that motives can be grouped into one or several relatively independent hierarchies, which allows us to distinguish single-apex and multi-apex types of personality structure.

The psychological theory of activity was based upon a wide range of empirical research studies and theoretical work undertaken by Leontiev's colleagues, students, and followers (see, e.g., Leontiev 1976). However, as is probably evident from the outline above, the epistemological status of Leontiev's theory is beyond that of a specific theory or a model. It reaches the level of a general theory, or a system, that includes a number of metatheoretical recommendations (Valentine 1982, 90–104; Madsen 1988, 453–475) and provides a general approach to the study of psychological phenomena which may be termed a *level-activity approach*.[11] This is the reason why direct application of its ideas may not be extremely productive. The potential of the psychological activity theory is unveiled when its ideas are applied to general psychological problems, such as the problem of attention. Such theoretical work may require some additional elaboration of activity theory's conceptual apparatus in order to suit the specific character of the phenomena studied—in our case, the phenomenon of flow.[12]

Elaboration of the Psychological Theory of Activity

Two negative tendencies can be observed in the ways Leontiev's psychological theory of activity is understood. While some of its principal concepts are groundlessly narrowed, others are expanded without proper justification.[13] Among those narrowed is the very concept of activity; among those expanded is the concept of personality. A balanced position avoiding both of these tendencies could begin with understanding activity as a gestalt and make use of the concepts of the subject of activity and object of activity at the second stage, in order to approach, finally, the concept of personality.

The scope of the notion of activity, as it was introduced by Leontiev in psychology, is wider than that of traditional notions of activity found in philosophy and biology, but, more importantly, the content of his notion is also richer. Leontiev provides a definition of activity that is structural, functional, and genetic:

Activity is a molar, non-additive unit of life of a corporeal, material subject. In a narrower sense—that is, on a psychological level—it is a unit of life that is mediated by mental representation, which serves to orient the subject within the world of objects. In other words, activity is neither a reaction, nor a set of reactions, but a system with its own structure, its own internal transitions and transformations, its own development. (Leontiev 1975, 81–82)

This definition allows us to understand activity as a gestalt. The term *gestalt* itself is well-established in psychology by the works of Max Wertheimer, Kurt Koffka, Wolfgang Köhler, and Kurt Lewin. The word *gestalt* denotes a whole, the essence and properties of which cannot be discovered by way of analyzing the whole into components and studying these components and their relationships separately (e.g., English and English 1968, 225). The components constituting a gestalt gain properties and functions that they do not possess in an isolated state, or, as the saying goes, the whole lives in each of its parts. I propose to consider the subject and the object of an activity as two components of an *activity gestalt*.

The range of specific activities to be chosen follows from the activity gestalt. Depending on the gestalt, within the subject's actions[14], operations and psychophysiological functions are selected, activated, or developed, and from the subject's environment, relevant objects are selected or created. An activity gestalt is a general form of human activity that is specified by external and internal conditions in which the activity of an individual takes place. Some properties of the subject and the object of activity cannot be described completely in an isolated way, outside the overarching activity gestalt; they are not completely definite before the activity takes place (because an activity, according to Leontiev, is always richer than its mental representation). The process leading to an appropriate, complete definition of the subject and the object within the gestalt of activity can be called *up-definition* (in the sense of amplification, addition to the original definition of some of its necessary characteristics).

The concept of up-definition was introduced by Valery Viktorovich Petukhov (1950–2003) in order to describe a creative product, such as a work of art (Petukhov 2008). A creative product is created twice—for the first time within the activity of its creator and for the second time within an act of its understanding, through appropriation by another person. Appropriation of a creative product can be called cocreation, because the activity relevant to this product may activate or develop certain personal qualities within its subject, as well as reveal within the creative product some new object–content, unknown to its creator. Thus, within an act of creation both the subject and the object of activity are redefined, or up-defined, by each other. The notion of activity gestalt allows us to apply this principle of up-definition to any activity in general. In this up-definition the subject and the object of activity obtain certain qualities relevant to the whole gestalt—that is, to the activity.

Petukhov approaches the notion of personality by relating the subject of activity to the environment of objects, where the subject may search for and find his or her own unique position. Petukhov distinguishes natural, social, and cultural environments as "effective conditions (settings) of human existence and development, sources of different kinds of human experience, and different life problems and means of their solution" (Petukhov 1996, 8). The natural environment includes not only the surrounding natural settings, living and lifeless, but also one's own body. The social environment comprises other people, social instruments and knowledge, social institutions, customs and traditions, and historically specific (as opposed to universal) norms of law and morals—that is, all means by which the sociohistoric experience of humanity is conserved. Culture is comprised of universal values unconfined to any predefined and concrete form of expression. Culture contains principles, models, and means for the solution to the most important life problems. It is "an absolute form that defines different ways and means of social organization, transformation, and protection of the natural characteristics (needs) of each individual" (Petukhov 1996, 62). On a philosophical level, this distinction between environments allows us to see three distinct sides or roots of human nature: biological, social, and cultural. On the psychological level, the subject of activity can be divided into three levels: that of *organism, social individual,* and *personality* (Petukhov and Stolin 1989; Petukhov 1996, 2001). The activity processes determined at the level of the organism are involuntary, those at the level of the social individual are voluntary, and those at the personality level are postvoluntary (to be explained in the following section).

Personality in an exact sense is "a subject capable of autonomous and responsible solutions to one's own problems by means of universal cultural principles, that is, those common to all mankind" (Petukhov 1996, 74). This definition may seem overly individualistic, but it is implied that life problems of an individual are determined by the society he or she lives in. When one is a personality in an exact sense, the problems of the society and those of other people become one's own problems. The development of an individual can be called positive when the motives relevant to the organism and social individual levels are subordinated to those of the personality level.

As discussed above, personality, according to Leontiev, can be represented as a system including one or several hierarchies of motives. An activity gestalt can be understood as a form that determines which of the three motivational subdomains (corresponding to personality, social individual, or organism) plays the leading role, that is, operates as a set of sense-forming motives, while the motives relevant to the other subdomains shift to the background and become subordinated. Thus, one can distinguish between three distinct and persistent types of activity gestalt—with personality, social individual, or organism on the side of the subject. This gestalt notion of activity allows us to understand personality as a limited-capacity pool of possible motivational dispositions. The motives that are not active within the current activity and remain in the background might still influence the dynamics of this activity, depending on their relation to the active activity gestalt (as any activity is polymotivated).

Each of the three possibly dominating levels within the subject of activity corresponds to a certain *principal function* of an activity gestalt. This principal function determines which properties of the subject (as an organism, social individual, or personality) are expressed, transformed, or developed within a given activity. The function of the organism-level activity gestalt is to provide adaptation to the natural environment, the criterion of a successful adaptation being satisfaction of physiological and material needs. The function of the activity gestalt of the social individual–level is to provide adaptation to the social environment. The condition for such adaptation is appropriation of certain sociohistoric experience; the criterion of success is satisfaction of the needs for safety, belonging, and respect. The function of the personality-level activity gestalt is commitment and creation that are directed, in the end, toward expression and maintenance of the universal values. The condition for this activity is appropriation of the cultural experience, and the criterion of success is satisfaction of the need for self-actualization and making one's unique contribution to the culture.

The principal function is the defining characteristic of an activity gestalt; the latter can even be called the *functional gestalt*. According to the famous example of gestalt provided by Christian von Ehrenfels and Max Wertheimer, the same melody can be played on different instruments and in different keys; similarly, the same activity gestalt can be manifested through different specific activities, in different actions and ways, and by different people. The particular objects related to the motives, goals, and conditions of these specific activities may be completely different, their functional gestalt still being the same.

The principal function may be discovered either on the side of the subject or the object of activity. On the subject's side, the analysis aimed at discovering it involves finding out the leading, sense-forming motive of the activity in question and finding out the motivational subdomain of which this motive is a part. On the object side, it involves finding out the product of the activity in question and its immediate and long-term consequences. Following the gestalt theorists' metaphor, one could say that the principal function defines an activity's melody, instruments, and musicians (the latter representing personality broadly understood). But what conducts the orchestra? Following Petukhov (1996), I suppose that this role is played by the rules, norms, limitations, and prohibitions at the level of organism, the social individual, and the personality.[15] In this light, the meaning of the up-definition concept includes also the idea of imposing limitations on the specific activity. An example of such limitations at the level of organism can be provided by the limitations of central information processing. The problem of existence of such limitations has been raised in the cognitive psychology of attention: "If the brain had infinite capacity for information processing, there would be little need for attentional mechanisms" (Mesulam 1985, 125). At the same time, it is often said that attention in itself is limited. Thus, Michael Posner states, "The key to understanding the nature of conscious attention is its limited capacity" (1986, 153). In my view, the role of attention is, on the contrary, to cope with these limitations.

Several alternate hypotheses about the nature of attention have been proposed based on the notion of activity.[16] However, in view of the aim of this chapter proposed above, only two of these hypotheses are covered here: Dobrynin's personality approach to attention and the author's hypothesis viewing attention as an act within the structure of activity.

Activity and Attention

Activity as the Object of Attention

The problem of attention was the central interest of Nikolaj Fyodorovich Dobrynin (1890–1981). He formulated his principal ideas on attention in the 1930s. Back then, as he considered different definitions of attention, he already used the notions of personality and activity (although in a more general sense of *aktivnost'* than *deyatel'nost'* used by Leontiev).

He defines attention as "*directedness* and *concentration* of our *mental* activity," elaborating, "Directedness is understood here as *selection* of an activity and *maintenance* of that selection once made. Concentration is understood as *immersion* into the chosen activity and *removal,* or distraction, from any other activity" (Dobrynin 1938, 118).

The first part of this definition describes attention as a phenomenon expressed in two characteristics of mental activity, directedness and concentration.[17] The second part of the definition explains these characteristics as selection and maintenance of an activity, immersion into it, and distraction from all other activities. In fact, this statement postulates a set of attentional processes that have activity as their object and that function to direct it and to keep it within its course.

Therefore, attention, according to Dobrynin, does not exist as an independent, separate process. It always functions in relation to a specific activity, which makes it "unproductive to propose a study of pure attention as such, outside of an activity of a personality" (Dobrynin 1958a, 39). Attention is a specific process which is included in all kinds of mental activity, apart from those that are completely automatic. Dobrynin explained this definition in order to defend against incorrect interpretations, which either disposed of the specific nature of attention or separated it from activity (Dobrynin 1975, 1977).

In order to find a causal explanation for the processes of attention, Dobrynin referred to affective and volitional spheres, utilizing the concepts of needs, drives, interests, and strivings. He distinguished between *primary needs* and *secondary needs*, noting that the latter can be and must be cultivated. Primary needs are organic, or material needs; a vague emotional experience of a primary need is a *drive*. The most permanent of secondary, or *spiritual*, needs are needs for communication, cognition, and activity (Dobrynin 1971). Primary needs are expressed in emotions, and secondary needs are expressed in feelings, which are more prolonged and more expressive of one's personality. Needs serve as a basis for the development of *interests*. Dobrynin proposed to distinguish at least two kinds of interests: Some interests are directed toward doing a certain activity, while others are directed toward reaching certain goals. "It is possible, though, and quite typical for a human being, that an interest for the result becomes an interest for the process itself, in a sense, transferred onto the process" (Dobrynin 1958a, 11). Human *strivings* involve having a well-considered conscious goal and undertaking volitional efforts toward it.

Beliefs influence the subjective significance of one's needs and interests and are formed with the development of an individual worldview. Dobrynin introduced the *significance principle,* which states that environmental stimuli and their related sets of associations, as well as different kinds of activity, differ in their social and personal significance. In his view, the significance principle "allows us to establish the causes of human behavior and therefore to control it" (Dobrynin 1971, 138). He notes that "personal significance is objective;[18] it is a vital necessity for the personality. Sometimes it might not be consciously represented, when a person does not know why ... [he or she] acts in one way rather than another. But for the most part one is conscious of this objective significance, which amplifies it rather than weakens it" (Dobrynin 1957, 46). The aim of education, in his view, is to make personally significant that which is socially significant and to ensure that the socially significant dominates in cases in which it is discrepant with or contradicts the personally significant. A person's worldview determines the ideological direction of one's personality and, therefore, of one's attention.[19]

One's needs, drives, interests, and strivings form a personality.[20] Personality as a system is characterized by its activity and its degree of organization (regularity), determined, according to Dobrynin, by the ensemble of social relationships it implements. He states:

The organization of a personality is expressed in an active and ideologically firm attitude a person has towards everything he/she perceives and does; in a capacity to maintain consistency and coherence of one's actions, to perform what is necessary, not to hesitate when hesitation is inadmissible, to consider one's decisions and persistently strive for their fulfillment, and also to be able to admit and correct one's own mistakes. (Dobrynin 1958a, 16)

Attention is one of the forms in which organization and activity of personality are expressed. The organization of personality determines the *organization of attention*, which, in its turn, determines the former. The development of personality which happens within a certain social setting guides the development of attention. Therefore, the development of attention, in general, "comes to *formation of interests* and *formation of volitional effort*" (Dobrynin 1938, 122). Two decades later Dobrynin wrote that "development of attention, first of all, is related to the development of personality as a whole, of its strivings, interests and worldview" (Dobrynin 1958b, 5). According to Dobrynin, attention does not require any special training; it develops naturally within properly organized settings of play and study activities of a child.

Based on the ideas outlined above, Dobrynin's approach can justly be called a *personality approach to attention*. Consistent application of this approach to attention research led Dobrynin to a phenomenological classification of different varieties of attention based on two criteria: the extent of personality activity (quantitative criterion) and the nature of this activity (qualitative criterion). The first three "stages" of his "scale" are occupied by the varieties of attention that are usually grouped under the label of *involuntary attention*. Dobrynin distinguished three varieties of involuntary attention; he notes that these varieties can be transformed into one another successively or arise simultaneously, in combination. The process of (1) *forced attention* is determined by the features of the stimuli (intensity, extensiveness, duration, movement, discontinuity, etc.); the extent of personality activity is minimal; (2) *emotional attention* is determined by one's actual needs and drives and also by the extent to which actual stimuli correspond to one's current state; (3) *habitual attention* is determined by past experience and the extent to which actual stimuli are matching it. Dobrynin (1938, 120) stressed that involuntary attention may be developed, although in an indirect way. Forced attention can be developed by developing one's powers of observation by means of cultivating one's senses, which leads one to become more aware and deeply sensitive to different stimuli. Emotional attention can be developed by means of cultivation of one's feelings. Habitual attention develops with the widening and deepening of one's knowledge and, as a result, of one's interests.

In the case of voluntary attention, personality is confronted by consciously represented needs, wishes, desires, and strivings. The setting of a conscious goal is a feature that makes voluntary attention different from its involuntary counterpart. Personality is active: Its activity expresses itself in *volitional efforts* undertaken in order to reach the goal that has been set. Thus, hiding behind voluntary attention are conscious goals and conscious will. This kind of attention develops with the development of one's conscientiousness and will and can also develop as a result of one's conscious efforts of self-education. The extent of personality activity within voluntary attention is determined by the development of one's motivational sphere, which takes place within a specific social setting, thanks to organized education and training. Voluntary attention appears first during preschool years, when a child "makes him/herself do the things that are necessary, instead of those he/she desires" (Dobrynin 1958a, 45).

During the school-age years, this activity of personality increases in quantity and changes in quality. The social significance of studies and new demands and responsibilities become conscious and personally significant. A teacher promotes the cognitive processes in the students and supports and encourages the joy they experience when gaining new skills and knowledge. At the same time, the teacher sets tasks that can be completed with a certain *effort*, yet are not too difficult, and encourages the students' successes:

It is important that the task set before the students be significant, objectively significant to them, then there is no need for the teacher to worry about attention. The attention will be caused and supported by the significance of the task itself. (Dobrynin 1958a, 52)

However, objective significance of the material being taught

should become significant to the person who receives it.... The teacher's task is to create this significance—to evoke a flow of interrelated systems of associations, their development, and the creation of new systems on a foundation of actual experience. (Dobrynin, 52)

New systems of reactions necessary in order to reach a goal are formed with a certain degree of difficulty, which is accompanied by an experience of volitional effort. On a physiological level, the formation of new associative connections and systems involves a straining of nervous activity, an increase in (and competition between) the processes of arousal and inhibition within the central nervous system:

> Complicated systems of associations that exist within a person and are expressed in one's actions, develop throughout the course of a person's life. They are secured by the significance that these connections have for one's life. The association systems can compete, because at a given time and within given conditions some of them are more significant for the personality than other ones. Their significance can change along with the change of the given life conditions or with the change and development of the personality's needs, interests, and strivings. (Dobrynin 1963, 116)

Later he noted:

> Personality is a unity of a multitude of intercompeting tendencies. Each of these tendencies might have a certain significance for the personality.... As a result of this competition within the personality and also of a competition with external influences, a certain tendency or a system of tendencies gains the highest significance and determines the actions of a person. (Dobrynin 1971, 139)

As early as 1938, Dobrynin wrote:

> At the same time, we should not forget about the third variety of attention, which arises as a transition of voluntary attention supported by successive efforts into an attention that is also related to the present goal but does not require such constant efforts. One should strive to develop, along with one's immediate interests, also mediated interests, that is, those related to the very process of work or to its result. The more "labor captivates the worker by its content and its way of execution," the more the worker "enjoys labour as a play of his physical and intellectual powers," and the less effort is required to maintain attention during the work.[21] (Dobrynin, 122)

New associations can be formed within the existing systems of associations; "they follow, as if involuntarily, from the existing systems, developing and strengthening them, ...[and this] strengthening and development of temporary association systems that have become sufficiently steady can be accompanied by the feelings of joy, satisfaction, and triumph" (Dobrynin 1958a, 54). The attention remains intentional, but volitional efforts once necessary to direct and maintain it are no more required. A person becomes interested not only in the result, but in the very process of activity:

> an interest for the goal can pass onto the activity related to this goal rather easily. Reading a difficult book or solving a complicated math problem might seem to be completely uninteresting from the beginning. But it is necessary, and therefore attention is directed at reading or at the process of solving. However, once the student comes to know the text of the difficult book and starts gaining a better and better understanding of it, or as the student grasps the problem and steadily begins to approach the correct way of its solution, the very process of doing this work

becomes more and more captivating. This enthusiasm is joined with an understanding of the importance of the task and with a creative approach to it.... [and] an interest for the goal becomes an interest for the activity itself.... Is this kind of attention possible in primary schoolers? Quite possible. (Dobrynin 1958b, 13–14)

This form of activity of the personality is named *postvoluntary attention*[22] by Dobrynin. When attention becomes postvoluntary, the intention that has led to it remains actively pursued, but the experience of *effort significantly decreases or disappears completely*. Dobrynin (1958b) distinguished between two kinds of postvoluntary attention, one supported by elementary feelings, another one by the creative process itself. He believed that this highest form of postvoluntary attention, creative attention, results from the development of a conscious worldview: "Post-voluntary attention ... is the superior type of attention; it expresses the personal strivings that have reached a high level of development, are not imposed upon the person, but have become a necessary part of his/her life" (14). The task of the teacher is to make children "more and more inspired by the joy of studying, the joy of learning more and more new things, the joy of being capable of doing what they could not do before" (14).

Empirical studies were conducted under Dobrynin's direction in order to investigate the conditions and the dynamics of this transition of voluntary attention into postvoluntary attention (e.g., Dobrynin 1966). These studies confirmed the hypothesis that postvoluntary attention in students can be promoted by the teacher with the help of certain teaching techniques. However, the psychological mechanisms of the transition were not clarified. In 1958 Dobrynin urged his colleagues, students, and followers to "avoid limiting our studies to descriptions, even though well done ones, but to go beyond, towards the explanations of the data, which necessarily should be related to the study of personality as a whole, rather than of its specific mental processes" (1958a, 65). This is the reason why he directed his subsequent efforts to the development of the significance principle, which "allows us to make psychological studies more explanatory, rather than limiting oneself to description" (Dobrynin 1957, 50).

Even this short exposition of psychological theories by Leontiev and Dobrynin allows us to see their resemblance due to the fact that both authors adhere to the same ideas of Marxist philosophy.[23] However, on a psychological level, they explicate its philosophical categories, as well as corresponding psychological concepts, in different ways and using different empirical data. Dobrynin's views on personality and its development are to a large extent declarative, while Leontiev proposes a personality theory that allows for empirical validation and development of its principal ideas. At the same time, Leontiev's works do not contain any hypotheses concerning the nature of attention,[24] while Dobrynin tried to develop his own theory of it. In my view, Dobrynin's hypothesis of attention as a form of personality activity that is directed at the activity currently carried out can well be interpreted on the grounds of Leontiev's psychological theory of activity. In order to do this, a hypothesis of attention as an act of activity (within activity theory) is needed.

Attention as an Act of Activity
Within the psychological theory of activity, the problem of attention can be put as a question of existence (actual or potential) of attention as a specific activity, that is, an activity having its own object.

At the end of 1970s, the author of the present chapter proposed a hypothesis that *attention is an act directed at the functional physiological system underlying an activity*—that is, the functional physiological system is the object of attention (Dormashev 1979). According to this hypothesis, activity and its functional physiological system are interrelated: On the one hand, activity determines the composition, the dynamics, and the properties of the functional physiological system; on the other hand, intrinsic mechanisms and properties of the latter determine the formal and dynamic aspects of the activity and impose limits upon it. The subject of attention has to reckon with the reality of a functional physiological system and, more importantly, to influence it in order to carry out the activity successfully.

At present, there are sound grounds to suppose that the concept of a functional physiological system corresponds in many respects to the concept of *cognitive schema* widely used and discussed within cognitive psychology (e.g., Mandler 1985, 36–38; Rumelhart and Norman 1988; Kampinnen 1993). Donald Norman and David Rumelhart consider a cognitive schema to be an active data-processing structure which organizes the content of memory and guides the processes of perception, action execution, and thinking (Norman and Rumelhart 1981). In addition to generalized knowledge, a cognitive schema also includes knowledge of the way and of the conditions in which this knowledge can be appropriately and effectively applied (Norman 1982). In short, a cognitive schema is knowledge utilized in action and for action (Neisser 1976, 54). I propose that a cognitive schema is the object, concrete and material, of attention.

We arrive at the following definition: *Attention is an act directed at the cognitive schema of activity*. It should be noted that from the point of common sense this definition seems rather unusual at first glance.[25] Indeed, we usually specify objects of attention situated in our environment or in our consciousness: For instance, I can direct my attention to a rose and then to the memories that it evokes in my consciousness. However, according to the hypothesis proposed here, at first my attention was directed at the physiological mechanisms (schemas) of perception and then at the physiological mechanisms (schemas) of remembering. That is, attention is an act of activity that is directed at the schema itself rather than at the stimuli or the products of the schema's functioning. Phenomenologically, this direction is experienced in the conscious characteristics of these products (in our example, images resulting from perception and from memory): They are now experienced clearly and distinctly, which signifies that the act of attention was successful.

The functions of attention include activation of the cognitive schemas, their maintenance, modification, construction, inhibition, and perhaps destruction. A special analysis is needed in order to find out the functions of attention within any given situation. For example, in vigilance tasks, which require continuous and uninterrupted observation, attention functions to activate and maintain the cognitive schema that implements the detection activity. In a skill-learning situation, attention enables the creation of new cognitive schemas or transformation of existing ones.[26] When a skill is applied, attention serves to activate the appropriate schemas. Within meditation and certain psychotherapy practices, the schema inhibition and destruction functions of attention become important.

Attention can be viewed as an executive action, just like a motor action directed at an external object. However, unlike a motor action, attention transforms an internal object rather than an external one. It can be hypothesized that attention acts upon the schemas in a motoric-like way. The well-known motor theories of attention tried to understand its nature by postulating a direct correspondence between consciousness and physiological mechanisms (Lange 1893; Ribot 1890; Smith 1969). According to these theories, within any cognitive content of consciousness there is a component of motoric origin, such that by means of motor activity the subject can amplify or inhibit that content and thus regulate the flow of associations (Théodule Ribot) or improve the conditions for cognition (Nikolai Nikolayevitch Lange).

The psychological theory of activity allows a different view on the role of motor activity in the attentional processes. Its statements about the development of internal (mental) activity on the basis of external (practical) activity and about motor components of functional organs imply that functional physiological systems underlying any type of activity have motor driving input points. In order to develop a theoretical explanation of the mechanism by which attention influences the functional physiological systems (that is, cognitive schemas), the principal ideas of the hierarchical theory of movement coordination and regulation by Bernstein (1967, 1990) have to be assimilated. This influence can be carried out in accordance with his circular and hierarchical principles of movement regulation, following the internal circuit of the sensory corrections ring, that is, the circuit which does not include the external object or the working point of the organ in motion (Bernstein 1990, figure 55, 384). Some schema theorists also propose or imply that cognitive schemas have motor inputs and outputs: Thus, within Neisser's theory of the perceptual cycle, when a schema performs its anticipatory function, it tunes its sensory inputs by means of motor activity, and it also drives the motor outputs in order for the environment to be explored (Neisser 1976).[27]

An act of attention can take place at the level of operations, actions, or activity, developing in accordance with the rules of activity transformations in the course of human development described by Leontiev. *The place of an attentional act within the structure of activity is the real basis for the classification of the kinds of attention.*

Forced attention can be understood in terms of primary operations, which respond selectively to a certain, rather narrow set of stimulus conditions. When such conditions arise, attention inhibits the schema of the activity that was carried out at the moment and activates the schema of perception corresponding to the unexpected stimulation. Emotional attention arises when a stimulus matches a desire, a drive, or an unsatisfied need of the subject. In this case, the attentional act also takes place at the level of operations and is also determined by conditions, which are internal, rather than external, as in the case of forced attention. The operations of emotional attention can develop within an individual either by means of unconscious attuning or with the help of a conscious effort; that is, they can be primary or secondary operations. The function of emotional attention in relation to cognitive schemas is the same as that of forced attention. Habitual attention belongs to secondary operations that are determined by the past experience of an individual. In this case, attention serves to activate the existing schemas that specialize in reception and processing of a certain type of stimuli. To summarize, the phenomena of involuntary attention are implemented by the acts of attention that work at the operational level. The attentional processes of this level serve mainly to activate preexisting schemas matched to a certain type of stimuli and to inhibit the schemas relevant to the current activity.

Acts of voluntary attention occupy the level of actions within the structure of an activity. The conscious goal of attentional actions is to *be attentive*. To accommodate this idea, the psychological theory of activity should be supplemented with a notion of the *goal state* of the subject. A goal state is not related to any particular set of objects and cannot provide a direction to one's actions. But it can become a motive of activity when it is related to the objects relevant to activities which led (as a result or simply as a by-product) to emergence of the desired state within the subject previously. It is worth noting that a number of different activities, rather than one, can be conducive to the same state; in this sense, a goal state is rather indifferent to its objects, unlike the goal.

The goal state *to be attentive* can be set in the course of activity as its necessary condition or can be imposed from the outside by order or request of other participants of a collective activity. The attentional action is implemented in a set of operations and therefore takes into account both external and internal conditions. At the level of actions, however, the scope of possible objects of attention, that is, of possible schemas, is much wider. Acting at this level, one has more control of oneself. Attention at this level has a wider range of functions: It mainly serves to enable modification of the existing schemas and construction of new ones. An act of attention undertaken at the level of actions is represented in consciousness as a feeling of effort, which has a motor origin.

In short, the effective objects of attention are functional–physiological systems, which I presently believe correspond to cognitive schemas, as long as there is no theoretical or empirical evidence against this. But who is the subject, or the agent, of attention? The subject of involuntary attention is an organism; in the case of voluntary attention, a social individual; and the subject of postvoluntary attention is a personality. Only when attention takes place at the level of activity can it be deemed to exist as a specific, self-dependent process, and only then can the problem of existence of attention be given an unambiguous affirmative answer.

The transition from voluntary to involuntary attention can be explained by *shifting the motive to the goal*. This is the way the state of absorption arises, for instance, as we read a fascinating book. A transition of another kind takes place when an attentional action gains its own motive as a result of *shifting the goal to the motive*. In this case, attention becomes postvoluntary, and we experience flow. In both cases, experienced *effort sharply decreases or disappears*. I shall now discuss the conditions and possible psychological mechanisms of both transitions.

The Role of Attention within Autotelic Activity

The concentration of attention is a common characteristic or a necessary condition of many subjectively valued states of consciousness. A general trait of such states is that people want to repeat such an experience once they have had it. These experiences become *goal states*, so that one is ready to invest quite an effort, overcoming numerous obstacles and sacrificing benefits, in order to enter these states again. In other words, these states become strong motivational factors impelling people to perform or to abandon other activities, occasionally at the expense of their health. There is a wide range of states of consciousness, from satiety and drug intoxication to aesthetic delight to love and poetic inspiration, that can potentially become goal states. Actions that lead to the emergence of goal states may have different personal senses (meaning to oneself), but they always have either positive or negative social meaning. The lack of coincidence (or even the presence of a contradiction) between social meaning and personal sense of the actions carried out by a subject entails a wide range of intrapersonal and interpersonal conflicts. The way these conflicts are resolved influences the quality of life of an individual, as well as well-being at the social level. The psychological mechanisms behind goal states still remain rather obscure, as the relevant research is impeded by the lack of theoretical explanation of a number of general psychological problems, including the problem of attention.

Attention as a Key Characteristic of the Flow Experience

Among potential goal states, or experiences that can be of subjective and social value, is the phenomenon of immersion into activity. The experience of enjoyment is an important feature of this state of consciousness. The word *enjoyment*, apart from the pleasure itself, denotes also the process of its attainment. The fact that certain kinds of activity are essentially conducive of pleasure was already noted by Aristotle in his *Nicomachean Ethics*. These activities were later labeled *autotelic*, as they are undertaken for the sake of the positive experience related to the process itself rather than any result thereof. The subjective experience that accompanies an autotelic activity was already known in the 19th century and named *excitation of activity* (excitement related to activity; e.g., Snegiryov 1893, 447–448).

In the twentieth century, autotelic activities were observed and described in detail by many prominent developmental psychologists, including Maria Montessori (see, e.g., Sobe 2004), Karl Bühler (1928), and Jean Piaget (1951/2001). Since then, intrinsic motivation research has become the field where the phenomenon of autotelic experience was especially well recognized (e.g., Heckhausen 1991).

The group led by Mihaly Csikszentmihalyi is one of the most prominent in the intrinsic motivation field, in view of the large span of research data they have accumulated, as well as fruitfulness and high level of generalization of their ideas (Csikszentmihalyi and Csikszentmihalyi 1988; Csikszentmihalyi 1990, 1993, 1997; Nakamura and Csikszentmihalyi 2002). Csikszentmihalyi coined the term *flow* to designate his characterization of autotelic experience (Csikszentmihalyi 1975). At present, based on the analysis of thousands of subjective self-reports in the above-mentioned works and a number of others, the complex phenomenon of flow is described as having the following features: (1) *clear goals* (clear and step-by-step awareness of the most immediate goals of actions being performed); (2) *immediate feedback* (awareness of the results of actions undertaken is instantaneous, not postponed); (3) perceived *balance between* actual *challenges and* available *skills* necessary to meet them; (4) *merging of action and awareness* (actions are consciously represented in an immediate manner); (5) *concentration on the task at hand* (effortless concentration of attention on the actions performed); (6) *a sense of potential control* and confidence of success of current and future actions; (7) *loss of self-consciousness*, or self-forgetfulness; (8) *altered sense of time* (a feeling that time passes at a different pace than usual); and (9) *acute and continuous enjoyment* related to the process of activity that makes the experience autotelic (Csikszentmihalyi 1975, 1990, 1993, 1997; Csikszentmihalyi and Csikszentmihalyi 1988).

Prolonged effortless concentration of attention is the principal characteristic of the flow experience, as it is most closely related to all the other aspects of autotelic experience (Csikszentmihalyi 1975; Nakamura and Csikszentmihalyi 2002). However, the explanatory models of flow were based on another *descriptive* characteristic of this experience, namely, balance between challenges of the task at hand and the subject's relevant skills (Csikszentmihalyi 1975; Massimini and Carli 1988; Nakamura and Csikszentmihalyi 2002). This characteristic, once considered to be a necessary condition of flow, within these models has become (and still remains) an explanatory principle. Csikszentmihalyi emphasized that this characteristic concerns *perceived* challenges and skills: A flow situation is experienced by the subject as problematic, challenging, and, at the same time, solvable, as long as the subject knows that he or she possesses the necessary skills and abilities. Thus, the source of autotelic experience lies neither within the subject nor within the situation or task but within the interaction between the subject and the environment. The most entertaining games might seem very boring at times, while some extremely routine activity might eventually bring enjoyment. Any activity can become autotelic, and the decisive role in this transformation is played by attention. The balance between challenges and skills is formed as a result of attentional activity that provides for a cognitive restructuring of the problematic situation.

This idea was developed by Jean Hamilton (1981), who supported it with vast empirical evidence. Instead of developing further in this direction and studying the influence that attention has on the human emotional sphere, however, flow research followed an extensive route of cross-cultural comparisons and of the study of flow within different kinds of activities, including everyday life, learning, and professional and creative activity. The resulting data indicate that the phenomenon of flow is not unique to any particular activity or culture and that its characteristics are universal: Flow was discovered within members of different cultural, social, and age groups. Csikszentmihalyi considered flow experience to be a principal, primary motivating force behind individual development and social progress (Csikszentmihalyi 1988, 367).

New data required some refinement and elaboration of the explanatory model of flow (Massimini and Carli 1988; Nakamura and Csikszentmihalyi 2002). In addition to an evolutionary explanation of the motivation behind flow experience, a notion of situational motivation emerging in the course of an activity was proposed. An activity might initially be quite boring, but later on, "when the opportunities for action become clearer or the individual's skills improve, the activity begins to be interesting and, finally enjoyable" (Csikszentmihalyi, Abuhamdeh, and Nakamura 2005, 603). In this case, "motivation is emergent in the sense that *proximal goals* arise out of the interaction" (Nakamura and Csikszentmihalyi 2002, 91).

However, the ideas concerning the nature of attention and its role in the processes leading to a flow experience remained unchanged. When Csikszentmihalyi set forth his view of attention, he still referred only to its selective function in relation to a limited psychic energy resource metaphor (Csikszentmihalyi 1990, 33; Nakamura and Csikszentmihalyi 2002, 92).

This metaphoric and, as a result, overly wide and vague interpretation of attention as a limited source of psychic energy has led Csikszentmihalyi to a number of extremely broad generalizations he used to explain different social and cultural phenomena (Csikszentmihalyi 1978). In my opinion, the notion of attention in this case serves, in the words of German psychologists, as *eine Mädchen für Alles* [one maid for everything], creating an overall illusion of explanation and understanding of heterogeneous subjective and objective phenomena. However, more importantly, the explanation of flow still remains *descriptive and biological in that it does not go beyond the limits of psychological hedonism*, "which postulates that men do, in fact, act so as to attain pleasure and to avoid pain" (Young 1936, 319; see also Leontiev 1975, 196–197).[28]

An Activity-Level Approach to Attention as a Psychological Explanation of Flow

It was shown in the previous section that the explanation of the flow experience revolves around one of its central characteristics—the concentration of attention; however, the definition of attention that the authors of this explanation adhere to appears to be rather inconsistent. Attention is described as a limited reservoir of psychic energy.[29] Even if such a reservoir exists, it seems logical to suppose that psychic energy is necessary for the process of selection (cf. Schmeichel and Baumaister, chapter 1, this volume); it turns out that attention understood as a selective function requires psychic energy, which is another way attention is understood, and thus the notion becomes ambiguous.[30]

The concentration of attention has two aspects, attention selectivity and intensity. It can be explained from a commonsense point of view using an archer as a metaphor: The direction of the arrow symbolizes the direction or selectivity of attention, and attentional intensity is represented by the bend of the bow and the tension of the bowstring. Thus, two rather distinct phenomena are united within this metaphor, and a theory of attention is indispensable in order to justify their relationship. An additional question arising from this metaphor is that of the archer's identity. Attempts to answer this question within cognitive psychology have led to the homunculus dead end (e.g., Dennett 1978; Newell 1980), and this problem appears to be especially evident and acute within attention studies (e.g., Navon 1989). At the same time, the development and critique of selection and limited-resource models have led to a new gradual disappearance of attention as a specific process and a psychological mechanism from psychological theory.[31]

If an *affirmative* (positive) answer to the question of the existence of attention is given, the flow phenomenon seems to be especially interesting and relevant to such an answer because it is the most well-studied state of consciousness in which attention becomes a specific activity.[32] As was discussed above, only a specific activity can be considered to be an autonomous unit of the vital activity of human beings. When an attentional process unfolds at the level of actions or operations, its object and its effects are completely masked by other processes, which leads to different variants of a negative answer to the problem of attention.

"We do not call every process an activity. We apply this term only to processes that, by implementing a certain relationship of a human to the world, answer a corresponding specific need" (Leontiev 1981b, 518). The hypothesis of attention as an act of activity extends the definition of specific activity given by Leontiev. Attention as an activity implements a relationship of a human to oneself, rather than to one's environment. This relationship of self-modification and self-determination may only be implemented at a certain stage of cognitive and personal development. In this sense, attention can be given its own place among other specific activities within the general system of human vital activity. The consequences of attention's becoming a specific activity should be investigated by moving to the social level of analysis proposed by Leontiev.

On the other hand, the definition of attention proposed here also fits the definition of activity in regard to answering a specific need. Attention, as a specific activity, answers a functional need that is organic and vital. Just as all other needs, this functional need develops within activity as its object changes, but in its core it remains organic, like the needs for food and water. Like other human needs, in the course of its development it becomes ideational, in other words, able to motivate different kinds of activity when the need is not actually present. Moreover, there are good reasons to suppose that in most cases this need only becomes actualized when the activity is already taking place, quite in line with the emergent flow motivation proposed by flow theorists. The research into the motivating power, or intensity, of this need can be undertaken at the level of psychophysiological mechanisms of activity, although, in accordance with Leontiev's theory, this need will be determined "top–down," that is, from the psychological level of activity processes. Such a study could utilize psychophysiological indicators, for example, blood circulation in brain areas relevant to the activity served by a given cognitive schema. The functional need differs from other physiological needs in that it is practically insatiable.

Thus, according to the hypothesis proposed here, *attention as a specific human activity answers to a functional need and is directed at the cognitive schemas within the subject of this activity*. Attention may turn into a specific activity whenever acts of attention (that are usually directed at some cognitive schemas relevant to other activities) shift from the level of actions to the activity level. This happens as a result of the process of shifting the goal to the motive mentioned above. The cognitive schema that previously was the object of the attentional act gets included into the polymotivation of the activity within which the attentional act used to occupy the action level. In this case, voluntary attention becomes postvoluntary, and flow emerges within conscious experience. The state of voluntary attention, when one has to undertake significant efforts in order to remain attentive, is familiar to each of us from the beginning of school age. Nevertheless, the flow experience that was so well described by Csikszentmihalyi is comparatively rare in the everyday life of an average person. Why? In my opinion, it is because attentional actions are much more likely to shift to the level of operations rather than to that of activity. This will be examined in more detail in the following paragraphs.

In one kind of voluntary attention, a person performs attentional actions in order to retain a schema or a system of schemas that are necessary within a given activity that has a certain motive. The goal of these actions is to reach the state of *being attentive*. The work undertaken to meet this goal is represented in the consciousness as a feeling of effort. The executive chain of these actions is motoric, involving movements of the sense organs as well as changes in breathing patterns and vasomotor reactions. When these actions are executed repeatedly, attention becomes automatic (just like any other motor skill), which leads to a sharp decrease of experienced effort.

In another kind of voluntary attention, the subject's goal or intention is determined by the activity which includes this attentional action. In this case, *to be attentive* might mean, for example, to grasp a complicated matter or to perform a complicated movement correctly. In fact, a person undertakes the effort in order to *change*, unknowingly, one's existing schemas. The actions of attention directed at these cognitive schemas are performed until the necessary change in schemas is accomplished and, thus, the goal is reached. After this, the feeling of effort decreases, because the attentional actions are not needed anymore; they shift to the level of operations and perform other functions. In both cases described above the experience of effort is comprised of a feeling of activity, a feeling of displeasure, and cutaneous (kinaesthetic) sensations (Ribot 1890, Lange 1893; Wundt 1897/1999; Titchener 1910).[33]

The described shifting of attentional acts from the action to the operational level can induce states of consciousness that are *similar to flow* and usually called *states of absorption*. An example of such a state can be found in the case of a continuous, almost obsessive observation of the constantly changing bonfire flame. At first, a person voluntarily directs and keeps one's attention on the flame but then might start looking at it quite involuntarily, with an "enchanted" gaze, for a prolonged period of time. Another example of absorption can be found in the reading activity of a professional proofreader. In this case, the voluntary attentional act serves to activate the existing schemas and might take a very short time. A proofreader works on a book continuously and without any felt effort. A third example can be provided by a student who reads the same book rather unwillingly in order to give a presentation in a seminar. The student starts reading with difficulty and has to maintain a continuous effort in order to keep reading. These efforts, indicative of attentional action taking place, are motivated by another motive, which has no direct relation to the book or to the process of reading itself. But, later on, the content of the book may carry the student along, so that after a certain point in time no more effort is required on the student's side in order to keep reading. On the contrary, an effort might be needed to turn away from the book. These are cases of absorption but not of flow.

In my opinion, the psychological mechanisms of attention are the same in all three examples above in the sense that the acts of attention take place at the operational level, such that attention at some point or other becomes an involuntary and "passive" process—no longer monitored by the subject and requiring no effort. The difference between these examples lies in the types of the objects of attention, that is, the cognitive schemas. In the case of fire, the schemas are either primitive and innate or formed early by unconscious attuning. These schemas implement primary operations. In the two examples of reading, the schemas are those formed comparatively late in ontogenesis in the course of education within conscious activity. These schemas implement secondary operations. The attentional operations will also be primary or secondary.

Because the acts of attention that take place at the operational level are either not consciously represented at all (as in the case of fire) or only controlled consciously (as in the two cases of reading), I can only infer that they are taking place by looking at the products of the cognitive schemas at which the attentional operations are directed. The only experience they are related to is an experience of continuity of the activity implemented by means of these operations. In view of the hypothesis proposed here, the phenomena of attentional direction, intensity, and span result from the cognitive schemas rather than from attention itself. A real psychological difference between the attentional operations may follow from their relation to the motives of the activity. I shall come back to this later, as this difference is relevant to the kinds of operations, or ways, an action can be executed. Phenomenologically, these states of absorption can only be characterized negatively, as lacking both an experience of effort and enjoyment.

One can argue that enjoyment might be present in our third example. Surely, experiences similar to enjoyment may arise in the course of reading a fascinating novel, but they only appear episodically and in relation to changes in the content and motivation of the activity of reading, not of the attentional process. Indeed, absorption that takes place during the reading of a detective novel happens thanks to the craft of the author, who is able to keep supplying the reader's existing cognitive schemas with new information. The range of emotions arising in the reader depends on twists in the storyline, on the extent to which the reader identifies with the characters, and also on the spontaneous reproduction of the reader's own memories: The reader may experience pleasure, sorrow, regret, and many other feelings. I should emphasize that these processes and experiences happen automatically in a way, so that the reader's own thought remains mostly idle. The reader in this state remains rather passive and will not experience any enjoyment. When the environment is favorable, the dynamics and extent of such absorption are completely determined by the text being read. However, in the course of reading, one's unconscious motives may become actualized, entering the polymotivation of the activity of reading. These motives may later become consciously represented if the subject makes an effort to solve the "problem of personal sense," and this is the reason why reading fiction is an indispensable part of education that may induce personality development. This might happen as a result of shifting the motive to the goal, which results in a new motive's being formed—a motive related to the object at which the former goal was directed.

In the different states of absorption, a continuous positive emotional tone may be present that can easily be confused with enjoyment. Indeed, a person can be completely absorbed in a horror film, experiencing fear and pleasure at the same time. This pleasure can partly be explained by continuous satisfaction of the functional need in relation to the schemas: Within our examples, these are schemas of perception (flame or film) and reading (student and proofreader). However, this weak feeling of pleasure will not be transformed into enjoyment as long as attentional acts remain at the operational level.[34]

The difference between absorption and flow is the difference between passive and active (although not necessarily effortful) attention. In order to differentiate these states more clearly, one could compare any description of hypnotic trance, a passive "enchantment," with that of the state of immersion in activity (Gaylin 1979, 206–207).

To summarize, the type of attention that comes *after* voluntary attention is not always *post*voluntary attention, as the name suggests, but might be involuntary attention as well. This transition was theoretically suggested by a number of authors within the classical psychology of consciousness (e.g., James 2005, 101), but its psychological mechanisms remain obscure to the present day.[35] I explain this transition through the shifting of attentional acts from the action level to the operational level. Following Leontiev's distinction between primary and secondary operations, we obtain three different forms of involuntary attention described by Dobrynin: Primary operations correspond to forced attention, and secondary ones correspond to emotional and habitual varieties of attention. The proposed downward "shift" of the attentional actions to the operational level explains the existing formal and dynamical similarities between these states, which allows us to classify them all into one group of absorption states.

A more detailed differentiation between different varieties of absorption, for example, those arising in the course of watching a fire, reading a detective story, and proofreading a book, involves analysis of the object-related content of the conditions, goals, and motives of the corresponding activity. From the point of view of psychological activity theory, an analysis of the activity's relation to objects is fundamental. Indeed, such an analysis would allow us to explain *why* an attentional action shifts to the operational level. However, the limited scope of this chapter only allows us to suggest that the primary reason for this shift does not lie within the formal and dynamic characteristics of an activity and is not caused by automatization of attentional actions but rather is caused by modification of the object-related content of activity.

More complicated causal links can be supposed in the case of an upward transition, when an attentional action shifts to the activity level. This transition can as well be metaphorically described as *shifting of the goal to the motive* (an inverse variant of Leontiev's shifting of the motive to the goal). In this case the arising state is flow, which is different from absorption and involves a higher level of activity for the subject, as well as intense enjoyment. Absorption can be described as a passive *imbibing* of the objective (external or internal) environment, whereas flow is an active *immersion* in it.

Thus, during the state of flow, an attentional process occupies the level of activity, which has a cognitive schema or a system of such schemas as its object (or motive). Behind the motive, there is a functional and vital need for activity, which is, in a way, "built into" the cognitive schema. The cognitive schema (which is an object related to the goal) shifts to the motive position, and the way it is experienced also changes.[36] Initially, during the voluntary attention phase, the state of "being attentive" was a goal within an activity directed at some other motive, but after the shift the goal state itself becomes the motive. From the subject's point of view, enjoyment becomes the motive, and *the experience becomes autotelic*. In fact, the motive of attentional activity (the cognitive schema) enters the polymotivation of the activity accompanied by flow experience. As a result, the structure of activity is determined by the schema and becomes quasi-simple: This happens because operations also shift upward, to the actions level, but nevertheless they remain operations, as they are still determined by the conditions in which they are executed rather than by some external goal. Thus, one can say that in the state of flow the goal of each action is the following action:[37] *Action and awareness merge.*

The processes of goal setting are also altered in the way determined by the schema which, being a motive, performs the structuring function in relation to activity.[38] As a result, goals become more fragmented, and operations, along with their object content (the conditions), occupy the focus of consciousness. Thus, flow obtains another one of its characteristics, *clear goals*. Because the goal setting and selection of conditions are determined by the cognitive schema itself, these goals, as a rule, are reached within the activity. As a result, the subject experiences a nearly continuous feeling of success, *a sense of potential control*, perhaps to the degree of omnipotence. The continuous, full-fledged satisfaction of the functional need objectivated in the given schema results in an *experience of intense enjoyment*. Only those inputs are selected from the environment and from memory that match the schema perfectly or that can be assimilated by its immediate development. This process automatically provides for *balance between challenges and existing skills*. Because the schema only feeds from the memory inputs that are necessary for its functioning, a person forgets about his or her problems and social position. Activity becomes, in fact, automatic, so that it *does not require any mental effort* or conscious control. This is how the principal constituting characteristics of flow can be explained.

Flow as Postvoluntary Attention: Some Implications

According to Leontiev, an analysis of the relation of any specific activity to other activities existing within an individual's overall vital activity system is necessary. In our case, such analysis involves a consideration of the possible consequences of schemas entering the motivational sphere. Attention can be seen as a sharp knife that could be used for one's benefit or harm. The consequences of postvoluntary attention and flow experience might be especially important for the development of one's personality.

When personality is defined, according to Leontiev, as a hierarchy of motives of socially significant activities, it can be said that in the case of flow, attention enters the motivational system of activity primarily as a stimulating motive. As discussed above, within the psychological theory of activity, three basic constituents of consciousness were proposed, sensory fabric, meaning, and personal sense. Leontiev considered them to be primary but not the only ones (Leontiev 1981b, 302). In light of the hypothesis of attention as an act of activity directed at cognitive schemas, I propose to supplement the psychological theory of activity with a notion of *personal taste*, which *reflects the relationship between the stimulating motives of activity and its internal and external conditions*. Personal taste characterizes the way an action is executed, that is, *how* a subject does it. Personal taste is reflected in positive or negative emotional experiences, and within conduct and communication it is expressed as *personal tact*.

A *taste-forming motive* can occupy different positions within the personality structure. Within a personality in the exact sense (of a subject of universal norms), it is always subordinated; cases in which it is leading personality development can be considered anomalous. In the latter situation, personal senses and personal tastes may well contradict each other, and resolution of these intrapersonal conflicts leads to certain ways of personality development. In such cases, the development of attentional skills and habits that implement personal tastes can lead to positive experiences that are no less important than such human values as honor, dignity, freedom, or meaning. The values related to personal tastes are manifold: They include zest, vitality, attachment to life, purposeless joy of existence, self-irony, and respect toward the life of other beings and one's own. A particularly wide diversity of personal taste phenomena can be found within the domain of aesthetic experience. By underestimating this constituent of individual consciousness, psychological research leaves behind the vital experience of millions of people. Just as one speaks of an individual *life meaning*, understood as the personal sense derived from the whole system of one's vital activity, similarly one can speak of an individual *life taste*. A criterion of positive life taste is experiencing frequent positive emotions that result from paying attention to things, people, and circumstances unrelated to the current activity.

A cognitive schema is a necessary internal condition and means of activity. When it becomes a motive, personal taste results from the relation of attention to the activity it was originally serving. *In the flow phenomenon, personal taste is expressed especially brightly*. When a schema enters the system of motives of human personality, the existing hierarchy is temporarily transformed. The vital functional need that is being satisfied within flow fits into the gestalt of activity that has the organism as its subject, and the personal sense of actions is replaced with their personal taste. The situation is different when the schema assumes a subordinated position within activity polymotivation: In this case, the personal sense of actions is retained, although personal taste imparts to them a bright positive tint. However, in both cases, because personal taste is related to the conditions of the activity, the subject remains peripherally conscious of these conditions, even if they are irrelevant to the execution of current operations.

The activity gestalt that has the social individual as its subject can also include attention (a cognitive schema) as one of its motives. When the schema assumes a leading position, it leads to conflicts or friction with members of one's immediate social environment. If the schema is subordinated, the person enters communication and cooperation with other people even within an autotelic activity, thanks to a variety of personal taste called personal tact. As a result of personal tact, the person remains peripherally aware of social circumstances and individual features of the other participants of social interaction. This awareness influences the way the person cooperates and communicates with other people, no matter what the object of their collective activity may be.

The consequences of a cognitive schema's being included in the activity gestalt that has personality as its subject are always positive because, as a result of limitations and universal cultural norms that determine this level, a cognitive schema can never assume a leading position here.[39] Instead, it promotes creative activities, because the widening of the periphery of consciousness that happens thanks to personal taste and personal tact helps a person notice the details necessary for problem solving.

In short, flow arises when a cognitive schema (or functional physiological system), which is the object of attention, enters the motivational sphere. Depending on which of the three activity gestalts (or motive hierarchies) it falls into, and also on the place (leading or subordinated) the schema assumes within the gestalt, different subjective and behavioral phenomena ensue. The consequences of these phenomena can be evaluated as positive or negative; therefore, a distinction between *positive and negative flow experience* can be made.

A cognitive schema may firmly assume a leading position within the hierarchy of motives and entail different results for society and for the individual's personal development, depending on which of the three gestalts of activity it is in. Autotelic personalities, who are able, according to Csikszentmihalyi, "to enjoy the least autotelic of activities" (Csikzentmihalyi 2000, 22), are determined by the gestalt of activity that has the organism as its subject. The life of such people might be filled with meaningless sensual pleasures (e.g., Macbeth 1988; Minto 2004, 24–25).

At the social individual level, the taste-forming and sense-forming motives can support or contradict each other. When autotelic activity assumes a firm place within the vital activity of an individual, it results in the possibility of motivational conflict, from which anomalous personality development may ensue if its resolution goes awry. In such a case, personal life meaning is substituted by personal life taste, and the flow experience may be regarded as negative. When the flow is positive, life meaning does not contradict life taste.

The conflict of taste-forming and sense-forming motives becomes especially acute at the level of personality. In a situation of inner conflict (called *the struggle of motives* in the classical psychology of consciousness), the role of an attentional act undertaken as a specific activity is to resolve this conflict. This is where the schema motive, which is always strong due to its relationship to a vital functional need, confronts the motives corresponding to cultural norms that form the core of human morality. In relation to this, William James proposed that attention is a process of volitional retention of a weaker, "ideal" motive (James 2005, chapter 15). The human will is free, according to James, and one can always make a decision in favor of a weaker motive, but the fulfillment of this decision is a function of attention. James equated attentional effort and volitional effort, emphasizing the motoric origins of both. A human being makes a multitude of efforts, each effort retaining the weaker motive for a short period of time. Because the flow of consciousness is continuous and constantly changing, the stronger motive will at some point or other decrease in intensity or temporarily escape consciousness, while the weaker one will still remain, developing its associative links; at this point a person will commit an act in accordance with the weaker motive. James called a person capable of such multitudinal efforts "a heroic mind" (James 1890, vol. 2, 578–579).

Within the conceptual framework of this chapter, this heroic mind corresponds to personality in an exact sense. I propose that in such a situation of a motive struggle, postvoluntary attention can be transformed into *volitional attention*. Quite like voluntary attention, and yet distinct, volitional attention is accompanied by an experience of effort that reflects the functioning of the motor mechanisms of attention. One can say that *voluntary* attention is needed when a person *wants to but is unable to* do something, for lack of adequate schemas (which are, effectively, means for activity), so that existing schemas have to be changed or new ones created. The acts of attention necessary for this change or creation will take place at the level of actions. *Volitional* attention is needed when there is something *one has chosen to do and is able to do but for which the person lacks a sufficient motive.* In this case, the necessary schemas are all available, but a person has to modify his or her own motivational sphere in order to act, and this requires a specific activity of attention. Because volitional attention is caused by this particular type of relationship between the motives, it seems more productive to distinguish it from voluntary attention, thus supplementing Dobrynin's classification with one more, top level of personality activity, which is volitional attention.

This explanation of flow is based on a theoretical analysis and is, therefore, preliminary. It does, however, provide a sufficient basis for empirical research that could help to clarify, develop, or perhaps disprove the hypotheses proposed above. A rare example of flow research conducted with regard to the hypothesis of the activity nature of attention is being conducted by my colleague, Aleksandra Guramovna Makalatiya (2003). She has supposed that people who experience difficulties in controlling their attention within conventional everyday activities are inclined to compensate for the unsatisfied functional need (objectivated in their cognitive schemas) by engaging in computer games. It was shown that computer-game fans who spend more than 10 hours a week at play demonstrate in their everyday behavior the symptoms of attention-deficit/hyperactivity disorder more often and in a more pronounced way than those who do not play computer games at all. This is one example of negative flow that may inhibit the development of attention and personality in everyday life. People inclined to value computer games and game addicts experience a shortage of flow in their everyday lives; that is, their relevant functional needs remain unsatisfied. Computer games serve as an outlet, a unique, or one of the few, activities where they can reach a state of optimal functioning.

To summarize, voluntary attention may be followed by a state of absorption, which does not have the principal characteristic of flow, namely, the activity of the subject and resulting enjoyment. This happens when attentional actions shift to the operational level, resulting in three possible varieties of involuntary attention: forced, emotional, and habitual attention. If an attentional action shifts to the level of a specific activity, a state of flow ensues. In view of my hypothesis, the postvoluntary attention taking place at this level is spontaneous and automatic, or self-acting. In addition, two kinds of postvoluntary attention may be distinguished: *dependent postvoluntary* attention (positive flow) and *independent postvoluntary* attention (negative flow). This distinction is based on an analysis of the subject's motivation: In the case of dependent attention, its motive (the cognitive schema) assumes a subordinated position within the structure of autotelic motivation, whereas in the case of independent attention, it becomes autonomous or assumes a leading motive position. Both of these varieties of attention are effortless. At the highest level of personality activity, dependent postvoluntary attention turns into volitional attention, which is executed with significant effort.

Conclusion

Ingmar Bergman, the Swedish film director, used to say that happiness lies in knowing one's capabilities and trying to expand them. Flow involves the knowledge of one's capabilities. An attempt to expand or increase them implies that a person is willing to invest efforts in order to perfect one's skills and abilities. However, according to flow theory, what motivates these efforts and flow activities is intense and continuous enjoyment that can be experienced in the course of the activity. This idea has become central within different explanations of the complex phenomenon of flow. A close link that exists between flow states and corresponding activities enables us to approach flow from the position of psychological activity theory using the hypothesis presented here that allows us to understand attention in terms of activity rather than psychic energy.

Attention is understood here to be an act of activity directed at cognitive schemas. Flow arises when the object of attentional action, that is, a cognitive schema, shifts into the motivational domain. As a result, a person experiences a continuous satisfaction of a functional need and his or her attention becomes postvoluntary: When attention is a specific activity and its own motive at the same time, no more effort is experienced. The consequences of this shift for the development of personality and for society depend on the position of the motive relevant to flow within the personality structure. Flow has positive consequences when its relevant motive is subordinated within the hierarchy, and it is negative when the attentional motive dominates within the hierarchy or becomes autonomous.

Voluntary attention, which is effortful, can shift from the level of actions to the operational level. In such a case, a person enters the state of absorption, and one's attention becomes involuntary. An experience of effort disappears because attentional acts directed at the cognitive schema become automated. Experiences similar, but not identical, to flow may arise in a state of absorption; they are caused by the objects situated in the focus of consciousness and their relation to satisfaction of other needs of the individual.

On the whole, it is shown that Csikszentmihalyi's phenomenological approach to flow and Dobrynin's personality approach to attention can be integrated into the level-activity approach to human mind and behavior proposed by Leontiev. In order to assimilate these theories, the psychological theory of activity has to accommodate them by expanding its conceptual framework. The theory presented here introduces the notion of personal taste into activity theory in order to explain the flow experience. A study of personal taste phenomena, their relationship to personal sense of actions, and their development can enrich the psychological theory of activity by providing it with a hedonistic tint that it was lacking.

Flow research holds an important place within the field of positive psychology (e.g., Seligman and Csikszentmihalyi 2000). In my opinion, the advancement of positive psychology in general, as well as that of attention research, is impeded by the ever-growing "contradiction between the vastness of factual evidence accumulated by psychology ... and the pitiful state of its theoretical and methodological foundations" that Leontiev (1975, 4) spoke about and tried to overcome. Rather recently, Stuart Sutherland has compared attention research by psychologists to the study of black holes by cosmologists over the past 50 years. In his opinion, both have achieved very modest results, as "after many a thousand of experiments we know only marginally more about attention than about the interior of a black hole" (Sutherland 1998, 350).

The gap between the theory and the multitude of empirical data that exists within the psychology of attention and flow research keeps increasing. It can be overcome, at least to some extent, by means of empirical studies based upon the psychological theory of activity and the hypothesis of the activity nature of attention.

The proposed explanation of the flow experience may provide a new direction for empirical research into the conditions and psychological mechanisms of flow: The level transitions of attentional acts within the structure of activity can be studied using the extensive methodological arsenal of cognitive psychology. Based on the hypothesis postulating the existence of attention on the grounds of psychological activity theory, this research direction seems quite promising. The conceptual apparatus of positive psychology may benefit from the new concepts of personal taste and volitional attention.

Acknowledgments

I am grateful to Dmitry A. Leontiev, who helped me to get in touch with the editor of this book; to Anna A. Leontieva, who kindly provided some materials for this chapter; to Olga N. Subbotina, who helped me in obtaining some sources difficult to access. I am especially grateful to Evgeny N. Osin for his valuable remarks and excellent translation of this chapter from Russian and to Brian Bruya for his thoughtful and careful editorial work on this text. The translation of this paper was supported by a Visiting Research Fellowship from the Leverhulme Trust to the translator (EO).

Notes

1. It is similarly an obstacle with respect to the study of such phenomena as attention-deficit/hyperactivity disorder (Barkley 1998), joint attention (Eilan et al. 2005), mindfulness (Langer 1989), human errors (Reason 1990), and self-focused attention (Ingram 1990), to name only a few other research directions which depend on the way the problem of attention is treated.

2. The transliteration of all Russian names and terms is given in accordance with the BGN/PCGN standard, except for some names that have an established tradition of English transliteration (e.g., Leontiev instead of Leont'yev). All citations of Leontiev's works refer to A. N. Leontiev unless noted otherwise.—Trans.

3. The Russian term *deyatel'nost'*, central to the psychological theory of activity, corresponds to German *Tätigkeit* and denotes a process of interaction between an active living being and the world. Although it is translated here as *activity*, it should be distinguished from a more general term *aktivnost'* (corresponding to German *Aktivität*), which may denote any activity in general, including that of inorganic materials (e.g., radioactivity).—Trans.

4. Because the English translations of A. N. Leontiev's works are difficult to find and vary in quality and in choice of English terms, the quotations from his works are translated here anew, with references to Russian sources.—Trans.

5. The Russian term *predmet*, translated here as *object of activity* (or simply *object*) corresponds to German *Gegenstand*, rather than *Objekt* (*Ob"ekt* in Russian), and denotes an integral and defined object singled out from the world in the course of activity of a living being and mentally represented by it. *Predmet* can be immaterial (intellectual), in which case it corresponds to the English *subject matter* or *subject* (of thoughts). When human activity is concerned, *predmet* within activity theory often implies a *mentally represented* object (see Vasilyuk 1991). The word *objective* will be used in this translation in a traditional sense, meaning independent of the subject, while the terms *object content* or *object-related* refer here to the object in a *predmet* sense.—Trans.

6. Leontiev explains the term *objectivated* in the following passage: "A need only becomes definite in an object of activity: it must, in a way, discover itself within it. Since the need finds its definiteness (gets objectivated) in an object, the latter becomes the motive of activity, by the very fact of motivating it" (Leontiev 1981, 312). Elsewhere he writes: "It is exactly in its directing function that need becomes an object of a psychological inquiry.... Only as a result of its 'meeting' with a corresponding object the need initially becomes capable of directing and regulating activity. The meeting between a need and an object is an extraordinary act" (A. N. Leontiev 1975, 312).

7. Often also translated as *aims*.—Trans.

8. It should be emphasized that personal sense is only expressed in meanings but is not defined by them: "The [personal] sense is by no means contained in the meaning potentially, and it cannot arise within consciousness from a meaning. The source of the personal sense is not meaning, but life itself.... The personal sense cannot be taught— it is nurtured" (A. N. Leontiev 1975, 279, 286).

9. Also translated as *interiorization*.—Trans.

10. For instance, minute eye movements during fixation were shown to be such an indicator (Gippenreiter, Romanov, and Samsonov 1976; Dormashev, Romanov, and Skorikov 1985, 1986).

11. Vladimir Petrovich Zinchenko maintains that the activity principle allowed Soviet psychology to achieve a high degree of liberation from the shackles of ideology:

> The activity *approach*, in fact, turned out to be an activity *way out*—fortunate for psychology. At the same time, we have to remember that activity as a philosophical category was borrowed (and substantially impoverished in the process) by Marxism from German classical philosophy, where it played a very productive role. The notion of *activity* and that which is called the activity approach also have deep roots within the history of Russian natural science, Russian philosophy, and psychology.... Activity plays two roles within the activity approach that should be distinguished: it is a general explanatory principle for the psyche, consciousness, and personality, as well as a subject matter of psychological research. The claims and pretensions to explain everything using the activity category turned out to be excessive. At the same time, the research into what Leontiev called specific activities, while, in fact, they were mental actions (in the terms of P. I. Zinchenko), turned out to be extremely productive. (Zinchenko 2003, 106–107)

12. In 1969 Leontiev said that the conceptual framework of the psychological theory of activity "has become frozen, without any movement" (A. N. Leontiev 1994, 247). During Leontiev's lifetime, the most significant input into his theory was made, in my opinion, by Vladimir Petrovich Zinchenko's studies of perception and by Oleg Konstantinovich Tikhomirov's (1933–2001) research on problem solving. Zinchenko (1976) proposed one more (microstructural) level for the psychological analysis of activity, and Tikhomirov (1984) introduced the concepts of *nonverbalized operational tacit meaning* and the *structuring function* of motives. Later on, researchers' efforts were directed mostly at the development of the conception of personal sense and toward an assimilation of the ideas of humanistic psychology (see D. A. Leontiev 1999, 2005). An article by the philosopher Vladislav Aleksandrovich Lektorsky might be useful to readers interested in the present state of affairs within the activity approach in general, and particularly within the psychological theory of activity. The ideas and conclusions of that article remain valid to the present day, and some of them are worthy of being quoted, as they are directly related to the aims of our research. Lektorsky writes:

> Within the present situation, the activity approach not only makes sense but also offers interesting perspectives. However, this requires, in my opinion, that its ideas be reconsidered and its narrow interpretation rejected. It requires also that the activity approach (or, rather, activity research programme) be distinguished from specific theories of activity (philosophical, methodological, psychological, etc.) developed within its framework. These specific theories can and should be developed, transformed, re-interpreted, could as well be rejected, but all of this does not necessarily involve a rejection of the activity approach as a general framework for new activity theories.... The activity approach can only show itself to be viable in the present situation if within its framework attempts are undertaken to understand the phenomena discovered within non-activity and anti-activity approaches, such as phenomenology, a range of varieties of analytical philosophy of consciousness and analytical philosophical psychology, and cognitive psychology based on a computer metaphor of mental processes. (Lektorsky 2001, 86–87; see also: Lektorsky 1999)

13. This section cannot include the multitude of opinions and discussions concerning approaches to the development of the psychological theory of activity or critical evaluations of its present state and future prospects. There are a number of publications treating these issues (e.g., Zaporozhets et al. 1983; Kasavin 1990; Voiskunsky et al. 1999; Hakkarainen 2004).

14. The notion of *action* should be distinguished from a broader notion of *act*, which simply means "a unit of activity" and can denote an operation, an action, and even a separate activity.—Trans.

15. Thus, at the level of organism, an activity directed at satisfaction of physiological needs can be limited by surfeit. A striking example of this is shown in an observation made by the poet V. Ya. Bryusov and used by Leontiev (A. N. Leontiev 1971, 10–11): "A little girl, who was very fond of candies, was permitted by her mother to eat as many candies as she wanted during her birthday party. After a while, the girl started to cry. 'Why are you crying?' she was asked. 'I want one more candy,' the girl replied. 'So have it, mommy is allowing you to.' 'But I cannot eat any more,' answered the girl, crying." An uplifting of a social prohibition and the resulting "dehumanization" of the need for food lead to a biological limitation being enacted. Leontiev quotes this episode to illustrate the ideational character of human needs and the positive function of human emotions, which make one independent of objective states caused by needs by providing their anticipatory representation. Within the conflict "I want but I cannot," Leontiev emphasizes the *want* part, whereas for us the *cannot* is more important here. A little girl at the level of *first birth of personality* is helped by innate biological limiting mechanisms. In adults, the mechanisms limiting the satisfaction of biological and social needs do not always function. If biological limitations, social norms, and cultural prohibitions are rejected or absent, the activity becomes perverted and the personality development retrogressive or anomalous.

16. The most important among these are the theory of attention proposed by Pyotr Yakovlevich Galperin (1902–1988) and the hypothesis proposed by Yuliya Borisovna Gippenreiter and Valeriy Yakovlevich Romanov. These hypotheses are worthy of a detailed account and a comparative analysis, as they propose opposite answers to the problem of attention. According to Galperin (1958), attention is a reduced and automatized mental action that functions to control activity. It is worth noting that Galperin did not consider mental effort to be significant, as, in his opinion, it was not a distinguishing feature of voluntary attention. On the grounds of Leontiev's psychological theory of activity and Bernstein's physiology of activity, Gippenreiter and Romanov proposed a hypothesis in which attention is understood as a phenomenal and productive expression of the leading level within the structure in which the current activity is organized (Gippenreiter 1983; Romanov and Dormashev 1993); the existence of attention as a specific process is denied. According to the authors, the quantitative ratio between the leading and the background levels of activity organization is experienced as tension, or attentional effort. On the same grounds and at approximately the same time, Dormashev (1979, unpublished manuscript) proposed an alternative hypothesis later called the "essential" definition of attention, as it proposes the existence of attention as a specific process (Romanov and Dormashev 1993). The authors supposed that in the course of subsequent empirical research these two hypotheses would turn out to be complementary, each of them better explaining a certain range of attention phenomena. Unfortunately, owing to a number of subjective and objective reasons, that research was never carried out. In the present chapter only one of these hypotheses is being expounded, which postulates attention as a specific process of activity.

17. This concentration characteristic of attention has two sides, according to Dobrynin. On one hand, it expresses itself as attentional intensity, which is relative to the extent of involvement

or immersion of a person in the current activity. On the other hand, it expresses itself as removal of distraction from everything irrelevant to the activity. In other words, attention (or, in Dobrynin's terms, personality) performs the double work of (1) immersion in activity and (2) inhibition of everything foreign to it. Dobrynin defines another characteristic of attention, its *coalescence*, in terms of its directedness: Attention is coalescent when it is directed at one object, and it is distributed when it is directed at two or more objects (Dobrynin 1958b).

18. In the sense of "independent of the subject," rather than "related to object(s)" as used previously in the context of activity theory.—Trans.

19. Still, Dobrynin mentions that not all human actions have a relation to ideological direction (Dobrynin 1977, 96).

20. Dobrynin did not consider contemporaneous theories of personality that existed in the West, behind the "Iron Curtain." This may be the reason why, unlike Leontiev, his own theory of personality, which was based on Marxist philosophy, was not very successful.

21. Quotations in this passage are from Karl Marx's *Kapital* (Marx and Engels 1937, 198).

22. Within classical psychology of consciousness, a form of attention similar to postvoluntary was labeled *unvolitional*, or *spontaneous*:

The two sorts of attention commonly distinguished are: "reflexive" (or "passive"—sometimes inappropriately called "spontaneous") and "voluntary" (or "active")—attention being reflexive when drawn without the subject's foreknowledge by an unexpected stimulation and voluntary when (1) it follows a purpose to attend or (2) pursues an object intrinsically interesting. If we call the first of these cases [of voluntary attention] "volitional," the second may be named "unvolitional" or "spontaneous," both being voluntary. (Baldwin 1925, 86; emphasis added)

In Ribot's (1890) theory, the most highly developed form of artificial, that is, voluntary, or active, attention is habitual attention, characterized by absence of effort. Although Titchener (1910, 1922) denied the existence of attention as a specific process of consciousness, he discussed the transition of attention as a state of consciousness from "secondary" attention into "derived primary" attention. In the case of the latter, there is no more effort, so that attention can be kept up for hours, and one's activity becomes productive to the highest degree.

23. The psychological science in the Soviet Union developed under the close ideological control of the ruling Communist Party. Notwithstanding this fact, most Soviet psychologists treated Marxism as a valid philosophical basis for their scientific research rather than a set of ideological clichés.

24. In my opinion, Leontiev avoided raising and solving the problem of attention. Perhaps the reason for this was his otherwise productive idea of the relationship of any mental process (activity) to objects, which had a gnoseological inflection: The subject was seen as cognizing, the object as being cognized. Although this understanding is productive when applied to cognition, it begins to stumble when it faces attention. As a result of this inflection, the problem of attention, which traditionally was classified as a cognitive process, becomes complicated for Leontiev. However, as soon as we suppose that the object of attentional activity is the attending individual (which, of course, requires making some additional definitions and solving some questions), the

problem of attention becomes no more complicated than it really is and takes its proper place within the psychological theory of activity as a necessary and still lacking part.

25. The idea of attention's influencing brain structures has been proposed more than once within philosophy and psychology (e.g., Bonnet, 1760/1966, 336).

26. Donald Norman and David Rumelhart discuss three principal ways of learning: accretion, tuning, and restructuring of cognitive schemas (Rumelhart and Norman 1978). They do not discuss, however, the potentially decisive role of attention in learning.

27. When they discuss consciousness and especially attention, cognitive psychologists keep confronting the homunculus problem. In our case, the real agent of attention is the physical subject, which can control its movements. In this light, we can say that the executive homunculus of attention is the Penfield homunculus! Extending this analogy, we can say that attention is behavior carried out in the internal environment, more precisely, in the brain (cf. Tolman 1928).

28. When a positive emotional state is seen as a principal motivating factor behind human activity, this view overlooks personal values. The activity related to values may be accompanied by or lead to emotional states that are clearly perceived as negative by the subject, but the latter might still proceed with this activity or resume it even if it is unsuccessful. A reference to positive subjective experience is clearly insufficient in order to explain why a value-related activity is chosen or why a flow activity unrelated to values can be refused despite all the enjoyment. Recently Jeanne Nakamura and Mihalyi Csikszentmihalyi (2003) have addressed this issue by introducing the concept of lifetime engagement.

29. Within psychology this psychic energy metaphor is implemented in a large number of constructs jointly classified as energetics. The notion of energetics in a traditional sense applies to the motivation of behavior (Hockey, Gaillard, and Coles 1986), as well as to that of attention (Beckmann, Strang, and Hahn 1993). The notion of psychic energy has a long history, and attempts at applying it in order to explain attentional phenomena have often, ever since early works by Freud (1916/1961) and Rapaport (1951), been made with different reservations and have been strongly criticized. A detailed theoretical discussion of this issue is not within the scope of this chapter, but the efforts to define the ontological status of psychic energy have led researchers to an investigation of physiological mechanisms of attention (Hirst 1995). I do not deny the importance of this kind of study, as long as the results help us understand the nature of attention as a *psychological* process, a process of activity that is carried out by the subject rather than simply taking place only physiologically. Otherwise, we are led back to a variety of physiological reductionism, which, in my opinion, is what interdisciplinary cognitive neuroscience is trending toward (Dehaene 2001; Gazzaniga 2000; Parks et al. 1998; Posner 2004; Schulkin 2007).

30. Instead of resolving this controversy, William Johnston and Steven Heinz dispose of it by narrowing down the notion of attention. In their view, other authors, such as Kahneman (1973), rightly use the term attention "in the sense of effort to pay attention in the sense of selective perception" (Johnston and Heinz 1978, 422).

31. A review and analysis of contemporary attention studies is beyond the scope of this chapter. I shall merely mention the two principal tendencies that can be observed within these studies. The first is a tendency toward physiological reductionism, which expresses itself in the movement within the cognitive psychology of attention toward cognitive neuroscience (see, e.g., Posner 2004) and leads to a complicated psychophysiological problem. As Ivan Petrovich Pavlov used to say, "first of all it is important to understand psychologically, and then to translate to the physiological language" (as quoted in Leontiev 1975, 114–115). A second tendency, more essential for the problem of attention, consists in a quantitative increase in selection mechanisms and mental effort resource types. This tendency expresses itself in flexible and multiple selection models (e.g., Erdelyi 1974; Johnston and Heinz 1978), as well as multiple resource models (e.g., Navon and Gopher 1979; Wickens 1987). This potentially limitless increase inevitably leads to a denial of the existence of attention as a specific process or resource of information processing. This tendency is supported by an empirically based critique provided by a skills and habits approach, which denies the existence of limitations in central information processing (e.g., Neisser 1976; Allport 1989). As a result, cognitive psychology finds itself in the problematic situation described by William James (1890, vol. 1, 447– 454) and is drawn to interpreting the empirical data as evidence of attentional phenomena resulting from processes and mechanisms of different kinds that do not have any common essence (see also Johnston and Dark 1986).

32. According to Leontiev, perception can be a specific human activity:

First of all, such a naïve question arises before me: can perception operate as a proper activity, that is, as a process motivated and directed by some object or other, we will call it a motive, which specifies some need.... Is there perception for perception itself? This means just the following: does perception exist as a specific human activity, as a process having its specific motive? Yes, it exists. And we can see it if we think for a moment of aesthetic activity. (Leontiev 2000, 152–153)

In my opinion, acts of attention are carried out at an activity level within the practices of spiritual self-perfection, meditation, and psychotherapy. Extensive research into the phenomena of altered states of consciousness arising within these practices is needed in order to provide support for this hypothesis.

33. The question of the genesis, composition, and function of attentional effort has been a point of heated discussions for many years; however, these discussions have not led to any conclusion (see, e.g., Titchener 1910).

34. Enjoyment is a form of pleasure, which is a more generic term. The experience of enjoyment does not motivate activity but reflects its dynamics, tempo, and successfulness. According to my hypothesis, when an attentional act takes place at the activity level, enjoyment emerges as an indicator of the fact that a cognitive schema has become a motive of the present activity. If that motive also assumes a leading position within the hierarchy of motives (i.e., within the personality), this type of motivational structure becomes essentially hedonistic. It satisfies a physiological need of the organism: the functional need corresponding to an artificially formed organ—that is, the functional physiological system. Thus, Csikszentmihalyi's theory can be understood as an instance of an activity approach to attention.

35. The mechanism of shifting the motive to the goal proposed by Leontiev might be the cause of certain states of absorption. According to Leontiev, this mechanism also enables expansion

and conscious recognition of human motives. Research into this mechanism could have been very important, but, as far as I know, it was never undertaken within Leontiev's school in a rigorous empirical way.

36. According to schema theorists, schemas, as such, never enter consciousness. This could be agreed with, as long as focal, rather than peripheral, awareness is implied. In my opinion, working schemas can be represented within consciousness as vague emotional experiences. Among these is the experience of enjoyment, which can be particularly intensive and prolonged. In some cases, for example, as a result of psychotherapy, certain kinds of schemas can become consciously represented in a more clear way.

37. This idea was stated by John Dewey quite early, as he compared work and play: "When the intended act is another activity, it is not necessary to look far ahead and it is possible to alter it easily and frequently" (Dewey 1916/2007, 165).

38. This structuring function of motives was empirically demonstrated within cognitive activity by the Tikhomirov school researchers (Tikhomirov 1984).

39. Such limitations also exist within the social individual activity gestalt (e.g., traditions or legal regulations), but they are not willingly obeyed and thus not always effective.

References

Allport, D. A. 1989. Visual attention. In *Foundations of cognitive science*, ed. M. I. Posner. Cambridge: MIT Press, 631–682.

Baldwin, J. M., ed. 1925. *Dictionary of philosophy and psychology.* vol. 1. New York: Macmillan.

Barkley, R. A. 1998. *Attention-deficit hyperactivity disorder.* New York: Guilford.

Bäumler, G. 1991. Auf dem Weg zur operationalen Definition von Aufmerksamkeit [On the way towards operational definition of attention]. In *Konzentration und Leistung*, ed. J. Janssen, E. Hahn, and H. Strang. Göttingen: Hogrefe, 11–26.

Beckmann, J., H. Strang, and E. Hahn, eds. 1993. *Aufmerksamkeit und Energetisierung: Facetten von Konzentration und Leistung* [Attention and activation: Aspects of concentration and performance]. Göttingen: Hogrefe.

Bernstein, N. 1967. *The coordination and regulation of movement.* Oxford: Pergamon.

Bernstein, N. A. 1990. *Fiziologiya dvizheniy i aktivnosti* [The physiology of movements and activity]. Moscow: Nauka.

Bonnet, Ch. 1966. Abstract of the analytical essay upon the faculties of the soul. In *The classical psychologists*, ed. B. Rand. Gloucester, MA: Peter Smith, 331–340. (Original work published 1760)

Bradley, F. H. 1886. Is there any special activity of attention? *Mind* 43:305–323. doi:10.1093/mind/os-XI.43.305

Bühler, K. 1928. Displeasure and pleasure in relation to activity. In *Feelings and emotions: The Wittenberg Symposium*, ed. C. Murchison. Worcester, MA: Clark University Press, 195–199.

Csikszentmihalyi, M. 1975. *Beyond boredom and anxiety*. San Francisco: Jossey-Bass.

Csikszentmihalyi, M. 1978. Attention and the holistic approach to behavior. In *The stream of consciousness*, ed. K. S. Pope and J. L. Singer. New York: Plenum, 335–358.

Csikszentmihalyi, M. 1988. The future of flow. In *Optimal experience: Psychological studies of flow in consciousness*, ed. M. Csikszentmihalyi and I. S. Csikszentmihalyi. Cambridge: Cambridge University Press, 364–383.

Csikszentmihalyi, M. 1990. *Flow: The psychology of optimal experience*. New York: Harper & Row.

Csikszentmihalyi, M. 1993. *The evolving self: A psychology for the third millennium*. New York: HarperCollins.

Csikszentmihalyi, M. 1997. *Finding flow: The psychology of engagement with everyday life*. New York: Basic Books.

Csikszentmihalyi, M. 2000. *Beyond boredom and anxiety: Experiencing flow in work and play*. San Francisco: Jossey-Bass.

Csikszentmihalyi, M., and I. S. Csikszentmihalyi, eds. 1988. *Optimal experience: Psychological studies of flow in consciousness*. Cambridge: Cambridge University Press.

Csikszentmihalyi, M., S. Abuhamdeh, and J. Nakamura. 2005. Flow. In *Handbook of competence and motivation*, ed. A. J. Elliot and C. S. Dweck. New York: Guilford, 598–608.

Dehaene, S., ed. 2001. *The cognitive neuroscience of consciousness*. Cambridge: MIT Press.

Dennett, D. C. 1978 *Brainstorms: Philosophical essays on mind and psychology*. Hassocks, UK: Harvester Press.

Dewey, J. 2007. *Democracy and education: An introduction to the philosophy of education*. Sioux Falls, SD: NU Vision. (Original work published 1916)

Dobrynin, N. F. 1938. O teorii i vospitanii vnimaniya [On the theory and training of attention]. *Sovetskaya pedagogika* 8:108–122.

Dobrynin, N. F. 1957. Problema znachimosti v psikhologii [The problem of significance in psychology]. In *Materialy soveshchaniya po psikhologii*. Moscow: Izdatel'stvo APN RSFSR, 45–50.

Dobrynin, N. F. 1958a. Proizvol'noe i posleproizvol'noe vnimanie [Voluntary and post-voluntary attention]. *Uchenyye zapiski Moskovskogo gorodskogo pedagogicheskogo instituta imeni V.P. Potyomkina* 81:5–65.

Dobrynin, N. F. 1958b. *Vnimanie i pamyat'* [Attention and memory]. Moscow: Znanie.

Dobrynin, N. F. 1963. Problema aktivizatsii vnimaniya [The problem of activization of attention]. In *Tezisy dokladov na s"yezde Obshchestva psikhologov. Vypusk 1. Obshchaya psikhologiya. Istoriya psikhologii*. Moscow: Izdatel'stvo APN RSFSR, 115–116.

Dobrynin, N. 1966. Basic problems of the psychology of attention. In *Psychological science in the USSR*. Washington, DC: U.S. Dept. of Commerce, Clearinghouse for Federal Scientific and Technical Information, 274–291.

Dobrynin, N. F. 1971. Aktivnost' lichnosti i printsip zhachimosti [The activity of personality and the significance principle]. In *Sovetskaya psikhologiya v svete leninskikh idei. Vsesoyuznyi simpozium, posvyashchyonnyi stoletiyu so dnya rozhdeniya V. I. Lenina*. Perm': Permskii pedagogicheskii institut, 124–140.

Dobrynin, N. F. 1975. O selektivnosti i dinamike vnimaniya [On the selectivity and dynamics of attention]. *Vopr. Psikhol.* 2:68–80.

Dobrynin, N. F. 1977. Deyatel'nost' i vnimaniye [Activity and attention]. In *Problema deyatel'nosti v sovetskoi psikhologii. Tezisy dokladov k V Vsesoyuznomu s"ezdu Obshchestva psikhologov: Chast' 1 (27 iyunya – 2 iyulya)*, ed. F. I. Yurchenko. Moscow, 93–100.

Dormashev, Y. B. 1979. *Rassuzhdeniye o metode vyzvannogo nistagma* [Discourse on the method of induced nystagmus]. Unpublished manuscript.

Dormashev, Y. B., V. Ya. Romanov, and V. B. Skorikov. 1985. Ob"ektivnaya identifikatsiya funktsional'nykh edinits kratkovremennoi pamyati [Objective identification of functional units of short-term memory]. *Vestnik Mosckovskogo gosudarstvennogo universiteta. Ser. 14. Psikhologiya* 2:17-30.

Dormashev, Y. B., V. Ya. Romanov, and V. B. Skorikov. 1986. Objective identification of functional units of short-term memory. *Soviet Psychol.* 25:28–49.

Eilan, N., P. Hoerl, T. McCormack, and J. Roessler, eds. 2005. *Joint attention: Communication and other minds: Issues in philosophy and psychology*. Oxford: Clarendon Press.

English, H., and A. English. 1968. *A comprehensive dictionary of psychological and psychoanalytical terms*. New York: David McKay.

Erdelyi, M. H. 1974. A new look at the new look: Perceptual defense and vigilance. *Psychol. Rev.* 81:1–25. Medline:4812878 doi:10.1037/h0035852

Fernandez-Duque, D., and M. L. Johnson. 2002. Cause and effect theories of attention: The role of conceptual metaphors. *Rev. Gen. Psychol.* 6:153–165. doi:10.1037/1089-2680.6.2.153

Freud, S. 1961. *The interpretation of dreams*. New York: Wiley. (Original work published 1916)

Galperin, P. Ya. 1958. K probleme vnimaniya [On the problem of attention]. *Doklady APN RSFSR* 3:33–38.

Gaylin, W. 1979. *Feelings*. New York: Ballantine Books.

Gazzaniga, M. S., ed. 2000. *The new cognitive neurosciences*. Cambridge: MIT Press.

Gippenreiter, Yu. B. 1983. Deyatel'nost' i vnimaniye [Activity and attention]. In *A. N. Leont'yev i sovremennaya psikhologiya: sbornik statey pamyati A. N. Leont'yeva*, ed. A. V. Zaporozhets. Moscow: Izdatel'stvo Moskovskogo Universiteta, 165–177.

Gippenreiter, Yu. B., V. Ya. Romanov, and I. V. Samsonov. 1976. Metod vydeleniya edinits deyatel'nosti [A method to distinguish units of activity]. In *Vospriyatie i deyatel'nost'*, ed. A. N. Leontiev. Moscow: Izdatel'stvo Moskovskogo Universiteta, 55–67.

Hakkarainen, P. 2004. Editor's introduction: Challenges of activity theory. *J. Russ. East Eur. Psychol.* 42 (2):3–11.

Hamilton, J. A. 1981. Attention, personality and the self-regulation of mood: Absorbing interest and boredom. In *Progress in experimental personality research*. vol. 10. ed. B. A. Maher. New York: Academic Press, 281–315.

Hamilton, W. (1880). On the history of the terms consciousness, attention and reflection. In *The works of Thomas Reid*. vol. 2. Edinburg: MacLachlan and Stewart, 940–948.

Heckhausen, H. 1991. *Motivation and action*. Berlin: Springer-Verlag.

Hirst, W. 1995. Cognitive aspects of consciousness. In *The cognitive neurosciences*, ed. M. S. Gazzaniga. Cambridge: MIT Press, 1307–1319.

Hockey, G. R. J., A. W. K. Gaillard, and M. G. H. Coles, eds. 1986. *Energetics and human information processing*. Dordrecht: Nijhoff.

Ingram, R. E. 1990. Self-focused attention in clinical disorders: Review and a conceptual model. *Psychol. Bull.* 107:156–176. Medline:2181521 doi:10.1037/0033-2909.107.2.156

James, W. (1890). *Principles of psychology*. vol. 1 and 2. New York: Holt.

James, W. 2005. *Talks to teachers on psychology and to students on some of life's ideals*. Whitefish, MT: Kessinger. (Original work published 1899)

Johnston, W. A., and S. P. Heinz. 1978. Flexibility and capacity demands of attention. *J. Exp. Psychol. Gen.* 107:420–435. doi:10.1037/0096-3445.107.4.420

Johnston, W. A., and V. J. Dark. 1986. Selective attention. *Annu. Rev. Psychol.* 37:43–75. doi:10.1146/annurev.ps.37.020186.000355

Kahneman, D. 1973. *Attention and effort*. Englewood Cliffs, NJ: Guilford.

Kampinnen, M. 1993. Cognitive schemata. In *Consciousness, cognitive schemata and relativism: Multidisciplinary explorations in cognitive science*, ed. M. Kampinnen. Dordrecht: Kluwer, 131–168.

Kasavin, I. T., ed. 1990. *Deyatel'nost': Teorii, metodologiya, problemy* [Activity: Theories, methodology, problems]. Moscow: Politizdat.

Lange, N. N. (1893). *Psikhologicheskiye issledovaniya. Zakon pertseptsiy. Teoriya volevogo vnimaniya* [Psychological studies. The law of perceptions. The theory of volitional attention]. Odessa: Tipografiya Shtaba Odesskogo voennogo okruga.

Langer, E. J. 1989. *Mindfulness*. Reading, MA: Addison-Wesley/Addison Wesley Longman.

Lektorsky, V. A. 1999. Activity theory in a new era. In *Perspective on activity theory*, ed. Y. Engeström, R. Miettinen, and R. L. Punamaki. Cambridge: Cambridge University Press, 65–69.

Lektorsky, V. A. 2001. Deyatel'nostnyi podkhod: Smert' ili vozrozhdenie? [Activity approach: Death or renaissance?]. In *Epistemologiya klassicheskaya i neklassicheskaya*, ed. V. A. Lektorsky. Moscow: Editorial URSS, 75–87.

Leontiev, A. N. 1971. *Potrebnosti, motivy, emotsii* [Needs, motives, emotions]. Moscow: Izdatel'stvo Moskovskogo Universiteta.

Leontiev, A. N. 1975. *Deyatel'nost', soznanie, lichnost'* [Activity, consciousness, personality]. Moscow: Politizdat.

Leontiev, A. N., ed. 1976. *Vospriyatie i deyatel'nost'* [Perception and activity]. Moscow: Izdatel'stvo Moskovskogo Universiteta.

Leontiev, A. N. 1978. *Activity, consciousness, and personality*. Englewood Cliffs, NJ: Prentice-Hall.

Leontiev, A. N. 1981a. *Problems of the development of mind*. Moscow: Progress.

Leontiev, A. N. 1981b. *Problemy razvitiya psikhiki* [Problems of the development of the psyche]. Moscow: Izdatel'stvo Moskovskogo Universiteta.

Leontiev, A. N. 1983. Nachalo lichnosti–postupok [Conscious act is a beginning of personality]. In *Izbrannye psikhologicheskie proizvedeniya* [Selected psychological works], ed. V. V. Davydov, V. P. Zinchenko, A. A. Leontiev, A. V. Petrovsky. vol. 1. Moscow: Pedagogika, 381–385.

Leontiev, A. N. 1994. *Filosofiya psikhologii* [The philosophy of psychology], ed. A. A. Leontiev and D. A. Leontiev. Moscow: Izdatel'stvo Moskovskogo Universiteta.

Leontiev, A. N. 2000. *Lektsii po obshchey psikhologii* [Lectures on general psychology], ed. D. A. Leontiev and E. E. Sokolova. Moscow: Smysl.

Leontiev, A. N. 2005. Lecture 14: The structure of consciousness. *J. Russ. East Eur. Psychol.* 43 (5):14–24.

Leontiev, D. A. 1999. *Psikhologiya smysla: Priroda, stroeniye i dinamika smyslovoy real'nosti* [The psychology of meaning: Nature, structure and dynamics of meaning reality]. Moscow: Smysl.

Leontiev, D. A., ed. 2005. *Problema smysla v naukakh o cheloveke (k 100-letiyu Viktora Frankla)* [The problem of meaning in human sciences (the 100th anniversary of Viktor Frankl)]. Moscow: Smysl.

Macbeth, J. 1988. Ocean cruising. In *Optimal experience: Psychological studies of flow in consciousness*, ed. M. Csikszentmihalyi and I. S. Csikszentmihalyi. Cambridge: Cambridge University Press, 214–231.

Madsen, K. B. 1988. *A history of psychology in metascientific perspective*. Amsterdam: Elsevier Science.

Makalatiya, A. G. 2003. Vnimanie kak motivoobrazuyushchiy faktor [Attention as a motive-forming factor]. In *Teoriya deyatel'nosti: fundamental'naya nauka i sotsial'naya praktika (k 100-letiyu A. N. Leont'yeva). Materialy mezhdunarodnoi konferentsii 28–30 maya 2003 g*, ed. A. A. Leontiev. Moscow, 89–91.

Mandler, G. 1985. *Cognitive psychology: An essay in cognitive science*. Hillsdale, NJ: Erlbaum.

Marx, K., and F. Engels. 1937. Kapital. In *Sochineniya* [Collected works]. vol. XVII. ed. K. Marx and F. Engels. Moscow: Politizdat.

Massimini, F., and M. Carli. 1988. The systematic assessment of flow in daily experience. In *Flow: The psychology of optimal experience*, ed. M. Csikszentmihalyi and I. S. Csikszentmihalyi. Cambridge: Cambridge University Press, 266–287.

Mesulam, M. M. 1985. Attention, confusional states, and neglect. In *Principles of behavioral neurology*, ed. M. M. Mesulam. Philadelphia: F. A. Davis, 125–133.

Minto, W. 2004. *Logic: Inductive and deductive*. Whitefish, MT: Kessinger. (Original work published 1893)

Nakamura, J., and M. Csikszentmihalyi. 2002. The concept of flow. In *Handbook of positive psychology*, ed. P. R. Snyder and S. J. Lopez. Oxford: Oxford University Press, 89–105.

Nakamura, J., and M. Csikszentmihalyi. 2003. The construction of meaning through vital engagement. In *Flourishing: Positive psychology and the life well-lived*, ed. C. L. M. Keyes and J. Haidt. Washington, DC: American Psychological Association, 83–104.

Navon, D. 1989. The importance of being visible: On the role of attention in a mind viewed as an anarchic intelligence system: II. Application to the field of attention. *Eur. J. Cogn. Psychol.* 1 (3):215–238. doi:10.1080/09541448908403082

Navon, D., and D. Gopher. 1979. On the economy of the human processing system. *Psychol. Rev.* 86:214–255. doi:10.1037/0033-295X.86.3.214

Neisser, U. 1976. *Cognition and reality*. San Francisco: Freeman.

Newell, A. 1980. Reasoning, problem solving, and decision processes. In *Attention and performance VIII*, ed. W. A. Nickerson. Hillsdale, NJ: Erlbaum, 693–718.

Norman, D. A. 1982. *Learning and memory*. San Francisco: Freeman.

Norman, D. A., and D. E. Rumelhart. 1981. The LNR approach to human information processing. *Cognition* 10:235–240. Medline:7198542 doi:10.1016/0010-0277(81)90051-2

Parks, R. W., D. S. Levine, and D. L. Long, eds. 1998. *Fundamentals of neural network modeling: Neuropsychology and cognitive neuroscience*. Cambridge: MIT Press.

Petukhov, V. V. 1996. *Priroda i kul'tura* [Nature and culture]. Moscow: Trivola.

Petukhov, V. V. 2001. Ponyatiye lichnosti: Funktsional'nye razlichiya prirody i kul'tury [The notion of personality: Functional differences between nature and culture]. In *Obshchaya psikhologiya. Teksty. T. 1. Vvedeniye*, ed. V. V. Petukhov. Moscow: UMK Psikhologiya, Genezis, 274–284.

Petukhov, V. V. 2008. Opredeleniye tvorcheskogo voobrazheniya i osnovnyye kharakteristiki ego produkta [The definition of creative imagination and principal characteristics of its product]. In *Obshchaya psikhologiya. Teksty. T. 3. Sub"yekt poznaniya. Kniga 3*. ed. V. V. Petukhov. Moscow: UMK Psikhologiya; Genezis, 606–627.

Petukhov, V. V., and V. V. Stolin. 1989. *Psikhologiya. Metodicheskiye ukazaniya* [Psychology. Methodical guidelines]. Moscow: Izdatel'stvo Moskovskogo Universiteta.

Piaget, J. 2001. *The psychology of intelligence*. New York: Routledge. (Original work published 1951)

Posner, M. 1986. *Chronometric explorations of mind*. New York: Oxford University Press.

Posner, M. I., ed. 2004. *Cognitive neuroscience of attention*. New York: Guilford.

Rapaport, D. 1951. Toward a theory of thinking. In *Organization and pathology of thought*, ed. D. Rapaport. New York: Columbia University Press, 689–770.

Reason, J. 1990. *Human error*. Cambridge: Cambridge University Press.

Ribot, Th. 1890. *The psychology of attention*. Chicago: Open Court.

Romanov, V. Ya., and Yu. B. Dormashev. 1993. Postanovka i razrabotka problemy vnimaniya s pozitsii teorii deyatel'nosti [The formulation and development of the attention problem on the grounds of psychological activity theory]. *Vestnik Moskovskogo universiteta. Ser.14. Psikhologiya* 2:51–62.

Rubin, E. 1926. Die Nichtexistenz der Aufmerksamkeit [The non-existence of attention]. In *Bericht über den IX. Kongreß für Experimentelle Psychologie in München, 1925*, ed. K. Bühler. Jena: G. Fischer, 211–212.

Rumelhart, D. E., and D. A. Norman. 1978. Accretion, tuning, and restructuring: Three modes of learning. In *Semantic factors in cognition*, ed. J. W. Cotton and R. L. Klatzky. Hillsdale, NJ: Erlbaum, 37–53.

Rumelhart, D. E., and D. A. Norman. 1988. Representation in memory. In *Steven's handbook of experimental psychology*. vol. 2. ed. R. C. Atkinson, R. J. Herrnstein, and G. Lindzey. New York: Wiley, 511–587.

Seligman, M., and M. Csikszentmihalyi. 2000. Positive psychology: An introduction. *Am. Psychol.* 55:5–14. Medline:11392865 doi:10.1037/0003-066X.55.1.5

Schulkin, J. 2007. *Effort: A behavioral neuroscience perspective on the will*. Mahwah, NJ: Erlbaum.

Smith, M. O. 1969. History of the motor theories of attention. *J. Gen. Psychol.* 80:243–257. Medline:4891927

Snegiryov, V. A. 1893. *Psikhologiya* [Psychology]. Kharkov: Tip. A. Darre.

Sobe, N. W. 2004. Challenging the gaze: The subject of attention and a 1915 Montessori demonstration classroom. *Educ. Theory* 54:281–297. doi:10.1111/j.0013-2004.2004.00020.x

Sutherland, S. 1998. Feature selection. *Nature* 392:350. doi:10.1038/32817

Tikhomirov, O. K. 1984. *Psikhologiya myshleniya* [The psychology of thinking]. Moscow: Izdatel'stvo Moskovskogo Universiteta.

Titchener, E. B. 1910. *A textbook of psychology*. New York: Macmillan.

Titchener, E. B. 1922. *A beginner's psychology*. New York: Macmillan.

Tolman, E. C. 1928. A behaviorist's definition of consciousness. *Psychol. Rev.* 34:433–439.

Valentine, E. R. 1982. *Conceptual issues in psychology*. London: George Allen and Unwin.

Vasilyuk, F. E. 1991. *The psychology of experiencing: The resolution of life's critical situations*. Hemel Hempstead: Harvester Wheatsheaf.

Voiskunsky, A. E., A. N. Zhdan, and O. K. Tikhomirov, eds. 1999. *Traditsii i perspektivy deyatel'nostnogo podkhoda v psikhologii: Shkola A. N. Leont'yeva* [The traditions and perspectives of activity approach within psychology: A. N. Leontiev's school]. Moscow: Smysl.

Wickens, C. D. 1987. Attention. In *Human factors in psychology*, ed. P. A. Hancock. Amsterdam: Elsevier, 29–80.

Wundt, W. 1999. *Outlines of psychology*. Bristol: Thoemmes. (Original work published 1897)

Young, P. T. 1936. *Motivation and behavior*. New York: Wiley.

Zaporozhets, A. V., V. P. Zinchenko, O. V. Ovchinnikova, and O. K. Tikhomirov, eds. 1983. *A. N. Leont'yev i sovremennaya psikhologiya: Sbornik statei pamyati A. N. Leont'yeva* [A. N. Leontiev and the contemporary psychology: A collection of articles in memoriam A. N. Leontiev]. Moscow: Izdatel'stvo Moskowskogo Universiteta.

Zinchenko, V. P. 1976. Mikrostrukturnyy analiz pertseptivnykh protsessov. [Micro-structural analysis of perceptive processes]. In *Psikhologicheskiye issledovaniya, Vypusk 6* [Psychological research, Issue 6], ed. A. N. Leontiev. Moscow: Izdatel'stvo Moskovskogo Universiteta, 19–31.

Zinchenko, V. P. 2003. Prekhodyashchiye i vechnyye problemy psikhologii [Passing and perpetual problems of psychology]. In *Trudy Yaroslavskogo metodologicheskogo seminara (metodologiya psikhologii), Tom 1*, ed. V. V. Novikov. Yaroslavl': MAPN, 98–134.

14 Two to Tango: Automatic Social Coordination and the Role of Felt Effort

Joshua M. Ackerman and John A. Bargh

What do jazz bands, sports teams, construction crews, and SeaWorld dolphins have in common? To succeed at their jobs, these groups of people (and other gainfully employed animals) require a high degree of social coordination. For many complex tasks, such as those above, the ability to effectively coordinate with others requires intensive training. However, social coordination also occurs automatically, nonconsciously, and effortlessly throughout our daily encounters with other people. Just as walking down the street involves the coordinated action of muscles, nerves, and control centers in the brain, having a conversation with someone involves coordinated actions like speaking at the right time, understanding the intentions of the speaker, and, often, mimicking facial expressions and posture (Clark 1996). Coordination can even be anticipatory, as when people alter their mood state prior to interacting with unfamiliar others (Erber, Wegner, and Therriault 1996). The ubiquity and automatic nature of such processes suggests that social coordination may be a fundamental property of social interaction.

In this chapter, we consider why social coordination is, and has evolved to be, so fundamental. Indeed, coordination may be the default response in any situation, and across any modality, in which information is socially transmitted. This possibility may help to explain why social coordination processes typically occur outside of conscious awareness and are associated with the absence of feelings of subjective effort.

To begin, we will consider the wide range of coordination experiences that occur in social interactions and the functions these experiences might serve. We will also outline several routes to automatic social coordination, including their neural and social cognitive substrates. We will then review some of our own research highlighting coordination processes in some novel content areas. Finally, we will address how the experience of effortlessness, characterized by processing fluency (Reber, Schwarz, and Winkielman 2004) and flow (Csikszentmihalyi 1975), serves as a functional indicator of successful coordination.

In What Ways Do We Coordinate?

The hallmarks of social coordination emerge in virtually all situations involving more than one person. In our view, social coordination represents a matching process exemplified either by imitation of action or by complementation of action (see also Bandura 1977; Bernieri and Rosenthal 1991; Carson 1969; Clark 1996). Thus, coordination represents a suite of potential actions which are tied together by interpersonal influence. For instance, babies exhibit behavioral coordination when they mimic the facial expressions of their mothers. Adults exhibit coordination when they take turns speaking during a conversation. In essence, we can say that "two (or more) people are coordinated to the extent that the actions, thoughts, and feelings of one person are related over time to the actions, thoughts, and feelings of the other person or persons" (Vallacher, Nowak, and Zochowski 2005, 36).

Perhaps the most easily recognized form of coordination, and thus the most studied, involves the synchronization of *behavior*. According to Bernieri and Rosenthal (1991), there are two subtypes of behavioral coordination—behavior matching–mimicry and interactional synchrony. Mimicry refers to the direct imitation of actors by perceivers (e.g., Chartrand and Bargh 1999; Dimberg 1982; LaFrance 1982), while interactional synchrony refers to the coordination of rhythmic and timing elements (e.g., Bernieri 1988; Condon and Sander 1974). We would also add complementation to the mix, referring to behaviors that represent the natural or rule-based counterparts to other behaviors (e.g., one person holding open a door is complemented by another person walking through the open doorway; e.g., Fiske 2000; Markey, Funder, and Ozer 2003; Tiedens, Chow, and Unzueta 2007; Tiedens, Unzueta, and Young 2007; Tracey, Ryan, and Jaschik-Herman 2001). Social psychological research on automatic behavioral coordination has tended to focus on the role of mimicry in interpersonal interactions. For example, people are more likely to rub their faces and shake their feet when interacting with someone who exhibits those same behaviors (e.g., Chartrand and Bargh 1999). People may also adopt others' facial expressions (e.g., Bush, Barr, McHugo, and Lanzetta 1989; Dimberg 1982; Vaughan and Lanzetta 1981), word usage (e.g., Garrod and Anderson 1987), and speech patterns (e.g., Neumann and Strack 2000; Pickering and Garrod 2004). Interactional synchrony can also be expressed in a variety of ways (Bernieri and Rosenthal 1991), from the simultaneous movement of performing musicians to the cyclic rise and fall of conversational speaking (Hayes and Cobb 1982). Examples of complementary behaviors abound as well, such as those that occur during financial transactions or when people are deferent to authority figures (Fiske 1992), and even when we respond with a "you're welcome" to a "thank you."

Evidence suggests that humans are naturally predisposed to behavioral coordination. Simple forms of this coordination emerge quite early in life. Infants as little as 3–6 weeks old show evidence of mimicked facial displays and gestures, even when the original displays are no longer visible (Meltzoff and Moore 1977, 1994; Meltzoff 2004). Over the next two to four years, children develop the capacities for more complex forms of motor imitation and complementary action (e.g., Ashley and Tomasello 1998; Jones 2007; Warneken and Tomasello 2006). One of the most recognizable and important consequences of this developmental process is the ability to engage in coordinated language use (Clark 1996).

Despite the prevalence of such research, behavior is not the only medium by which people coordinate. Evidence also exists for the synchronization of thoughts, feelings, and even basic physiological processes. With respect to the coordination of *affect*, research on emotional contagion indicates that people can "catch" the feelings of others (Hatfield, Cacioppo, and Rapson 1994). Instantiations of this process may occur at a very early age, as when infants cry in the presence of other crying infants (e.g., Simner 1971). Similar forms of automatic, empathetic responses continue to occur throughout life (see Hodges and Wegner 1997; Preston and de Waal 2002). It has been proposed that emotional contagion might sometimes emerge as a consequence of behavioral mimicry. People often nonconsciously imitate the facial expressions and postures of interaction partners; these behavioral cues can generate feedback that influences the affective experiences of the imitators (Darwin 1872; Hatfield, Cacioppo, and Rapson 1992; Levenson and Ruef 1997; Niedenthal 2007; Vaughan and Lanzetta 1980, 1981). However, people do not always mimic the emotional expressions of others. When these expressions signal certain interpersonal affordances (Fridlund 1997; Frijda 1986), perceivers may instead coordinate their internal states with actors' expressions in a complementary (or correspondent) fashion. For instance, anger in another's face can produce fear in observers, and conversely, feeling fear can lead observers to mistakenly "see" anger in relevant targets (Maner et al. 2005; Murray 1933).

With respect to the coordination of *cognition*, there is relatively less evidence for direct mimicry of thoughts and beliefs. However, activating interpersonal or relational concepts can produce forms of cognitive synchronization. For instance, reminding people about their family or friend relationships can lead them to evaluate situations in a manner consistent with the norms of those relationships (Baldwin and Holmes 1987). Similarly, nonconsciously activating an "elderly" mental representation can lead individuals to think and act as though they were elderly themselves. Kawakami, Young, and Dovidio (2002) primed the concept of elderly by having participants categorize photographed targets and showed that people took longer to make decisions, in line with the idea that the thought processes of older people are slower than those of younger people. This study built on an earlier one by Bargh, Chen, and Burrows (1996) in which participants were primed with words related to the stereotype of elderly (e.g., "Florida," "wrinkle"). Although none of the words involved the concept of slowness, after leaving the experiment, these participants walked more slowly down the hall than did participants not primed with this stereotype. Such studies suggest that the activation of mental representations (either of a target category or a category stereotype) may automatically involve coordination with those representations. This process may also have the benefit of preparing individuals to interact with others in a coordinated fashion (Cesario, Plaks, and Higgins 2006).

People can also automatically adopt the goals of others. When observing others' actions, people encode these actions in terms of the goals they represent (Hassin, Aarts, and Ferguson 2005). This process can lead to the activation of those same goals in observers. For instance, in one study, male participants who read a story about a man and a woman interacting (designed to prime the goal of seeking casual sex) spent more effort helping a female researcher than did participants who read a control story (Aarts, Gollwitzer, and Hassin 2004). Cognitive coordination can also proceed through assortative techniques (e.g., Buss 1984), as when romantic partners select each other on the basis of shared personality traits. Of course, we can also consider social learning more generally to be a case of cognitive coordination.

Finally, one of the most plainly nonconscious types of social coordination involves the coordination of basic *physiological* processes. Perhaps the most well-known example is the synchronization of ovulatory cycles that occurs between women who are cohabitating or living in close proximity (McClintock 1981; Weller and Weller 1993). Additionally, other processes over which people have little executive control show the tendency to coordinate as well. Levenson and Ruef (1997) review the extensive work done on the synchrony of autonomic nervous system activity. For instance, studies of therapists and their patients have shown that these individuals' heart rates often vary in matched or inversely matched patterns (e.g., DiMascio, Boyd, Greenblatt, and Solomon 1955; Kaplan and Bloom 1960). Similar findings have been uncovered for heart rate synchronization between mothers and infants (Field, Healy, and LeBlanc 1989), skin conductance within small groups (Kaplan, Burch, and Bloom 1964), and a variety of physiological measurements within married couples (Gottman and Levenson 1985).

In aggregate, these findings indicate that coordination is a wide-ranging, multimodal phenomenon. People coordinate their behaviors, thoughts, feelings, and even basic physiological activities. They begin to show inclinations to coordinate shortly after birth and continue to do so over the life span. It seems likely, therefore, that researchers will continue to uncover forms of coordination emerging (under the right conditions) within any and every social domain. But just how do these processes work?

Three Routes to Social Coordination

Research into the elicitors of social coordination has suggested the plausibility of at least three causal routes. These routes vary in the degree of cognition they entail, yet it is likely that they jointly influence (and mutually constrain) the emergence of coordinated activity.

Route 1: Dynamical Systems

In many ways, human interactions, as well as those of other organisms, follow the same principles that underlie interactions between elements of nonliving systems. For instance, elements of a system share some degree of similarity and connection whether those elements are players on a basketball team, planets in a solar system, or (literally) peas in a pod. These elements achieve a degree of synchrony through shared changes in external or internal state. Often, however, this synchrony is achieved nonlinearly such that changes in one element do not proportionately match the changes in other elements.

From the perspective of dynamical systems, social coordination occurs as a product of self-organizing, natural forces that require no cognitive-representational substrate (cf., Richardson, Marsh, and Schmidt 2005). Coordination in this case involves entrainment of dynamic processes—the directional or mutual influence between elements that creates alterations in individual (intrinsic) dynamics (Bernieri and Rosenthal 1991; Schmidt and Turvey 1994). For instance, two pendulums that are hung from the same bar but swinging out of sync will gradually match each other's rhythm without input from outside sources (Bennett, Schatz, Rockwood, and Wiesenfeld 2002). Similarly, a motionless tuning fork held near a vibrating one of comparable frequency will begin vibrating, itself (McGrath and Kelly 1986). People show similar patterns of entrainment when asked to swing their legs (e.g., Schmidt, Carello, and Turvey 1990) or rock in rocking chairs near one another (e.g., Richardson, Marsh, Isenhower, Goodman, and Schmidt 2007). The behaviors in these examples usually result in either in-phase (behavior matching) or antiphase (behavior complementation) synchronization and may occur spontaneously (e.g., Oullier, de Guzman, Jantzen, Lagarde, and Kelso 2008). In addition to motor movements, other phenomena exhibit entrainment as well. For example, the common vernacular that people use to describe their everyday experiences is a product of mutual influence (e.g., Garrod and Anderson 1987).

From this perspective, any two people with some connection (e.g., proximity, prior relationship, visual line of sight, etc.) have mutual influence over one another. As this influence increases, such as when proximity or relationships become closer, coordination will increase (Vallacher et al. 2005). The same is true when two people share a high degree of preexisting similarity (e.g., in body shape, educational background, mood). As influence increases, synchronization of states will become more fixed, and often mutual entrainment will give way to unidirectional entrainment (e.g., the less dominant person will model the more dominant person in an interaction; Markey et al. 2003). Of course, the manner in which this process will play out, including the particular dynamics and end states involved, is also constrained by aspects of the social context (Kenrick, Li, and Butner 2003).

Interestingly, fixation of synchronized states may be more likely to occur for behavioral coordination than for other, more internal forms of coordination (e.g., beliefs). Vallacher and colleagues (2005) report a series of computer simulations in which they varied the degree of influence and preexisting state similarity between "participants." In their studies, a high degree of influence produced extremely tight behavioral synchronization but, at the same time, prevented interpersonal convergence of a parameter representing internal state. The researchers conclude that, with respect to people, "very strong influence… is likely to prevent the development of a relationship based on mutual understanding and empathy" (46). Thus, institutions that mandate strict behavioral coordination, including many companies and families, may in fact be instilling the seeds of disobedience, providing some support for the aphorism that "the more you tighten your grasp, the more will slip through your fingers."

A dynamical systems perspective therefore provides one important route to social coordination. This route involves naturally self-organizing synchronization that, although requiring some degree of perceptual connection between individuals, is not necessarily mediated by the activation of cognitive representations (Richardson et al. 2005). We now turn to a route that is so mediated.

Route 2: Direct Perception–Action Link

A second route to social coordination also involves a perception–action link, but one that is mediated by shared mental representations. That is, the same representations are involved in both perceiving some activity and performing that activity (which includes behavior, cognition, and emotion). This route has its origins in Carpenter's (1874) and James' (1890/1981) notions of ideomotor action, which posit that simply thinking about performing an action makes it more likely that you will perform that action. In fact, one need not "think" in the conscious, effortful sense, at all. The link between perception and action is a passive and automatic one. Perceiving an action activates representations associated with that action, making that action more accessible and thus likely to be exhibited (Bargh et al. 1996; Dijksterhuis and Bargh 2001). Following from this link, people coordinate not intentionally but as a natural by-product of perceiving the actions of others.

Prinz (1990, 2003) described this linkage as the result of common coding—the mental representations that code for *perception* of action are the very same ones that code for *production* of action. A wide variety of studies support the notion that perception and action often rely on the same mental procedures. For instance, watching another person grasp an object activates the same neural regions (e.g., Buccino et al. 2001) and muscular responses (e.g., Fadiga, Fogassi, Pavesi, and Rizzolatti 1995) that are active when people perform these grasping motions; seeing emotional expressions on others' faces triggers matching neural and facial reactions (e.g., Hatfield et al. 1994; Niedenthal 2007; Wicker et al. 2003); and listening to speech activates brain regions associated with speech production (e.g., Wilson, Saygin, Sereno, and Iacoboni 2004). In fact, this perception-to-action process occurs even when perception is in the mind's eye—when it is imagined. Imagining the actions of others involves mentally simulating both the perception of those actions and their actual execution (Goldman 2006) and can lead to a multimodal reenactment of that experience in the imaginer (Niedenthal 2007). Thus, people automatically coordinate with others, even when those others are simply figments of the mind. This mental simulation process may help people to prepare for social interaction by "precoordinating," as when people adjust their moods to match those of future interaction partners (e.g., Erber et al. 1996).

In a reversal of the perception-to-action chain, performing actions can also facilitate perception. Participants induced to help another person in one part of an experiment subsequently perceived greater helpfulness in a target person in an ostensibly unrelated impression formation task; in another study, participants induced to feel they'd been "nosy" by looking at an apparently private note subsequently rated a target person as being more "nosy" compared to participants in a control condition (Kawada, Oettingen, Gollwitzer, and Bargh 2004). Cognitive processing is also influenced by physical action. In one classic study (Strack, Martin, and Stepper 1988), for example, participants who held a pen between their teeth (facilitating smiling) rated cartoons as funnier than participants who held a pen between their lips (inhibiting smiling). Moreover, moving one's arm improves memory for the arm movements of others (Reed and Farah 1995). So-called embodied effects on emotion have been demonstrated in a number of other studies (see Niedenthal 2007). Interfering with automatic mimicry can also inhibit the cognitive processing of other people. For instance, having people chew gum while looking at (encoding) faces can reduce memory for those faces (Zajonc, Pietromonaco, and Bargh 1982; but see Graziano, Smith, Tassinary, Sun, and Pilkington 1996).

The idea of a shared representational system also suggests that people should not (easily) be able to both perceive and perform the same action at the same time. Confirming this prediction, in one study (Müsseler and Hommel 1997), participants viewed a series of four arrows on a computer screen (e.g., "< > > <") and rapidly identified each arrow in succession by pressing the corresponding key on the keyboard. During each series that was presented, a fifth arrow appeared at the exact moment that the second arrow was being identified. Participants were required to identify this new arrow as quickly as possible after responding to the first four. For this final judgment, participants made more errors identifying the fifth arrow when it was identical to the second arrow than when the two were different, indicating that initial perception of the fifth arrow had been interfered with by the simultaneous action of identifying the second arrow.

The perception–action link suggests that social coordination often involves a passive, automatic process. People adjust their behaviors, thoughts, and feelings as a function of perceiving (or imagining) those same constructs in others. In fact, this process is at the root of priming phenomena more generally—mental constructs are made more accessible by relevant features of the environment (Bargh et al. 1996). Therefore, we can infer that the simple perception of others primes social coordination. It appears from this framework of the perception–action link that coordination would be a necessary and inevitable consequence of social perception. Obviously, though, we do not coordinate our internal and external states with everyone we run across. Why not?

Dijksterhuis and Bargh (2001) identified two classes of explanations for humans' relative flexibility in circumventing the direct perception–action link. The first involves a facilitation process—perception is likely to lead to action only in the presence of additional input (e.g., an active motivation). The second involves an inhibition process—perception is sufficient to create action but is typically prevented from doing so by the presence of a roadblock (e.g., an active motivation). While debate continues as to which class is more applicable, new evidence suggests that the answer may be "both." Researchers have identified a brain rhythm labeled the *phi complex* that is involved in social coordination and consists of two oscillatory components, one that facilitates the perception–action link and one that inhibits it (Tognoli, Lagarde, DeGuzman, and Kelso 2007). This suggests the possibility that some input may act on one component and other input on the other component, and thus social coordination may be both inhibited and facilitated by additional forces. One of the most significant and well-researched of these forces is the presence of active motivations, to which we now turn.

Route 3: Active Motivations

A third route to social coordination involves the influence of active goal states. Two types of goal states are relevant here—those whose completion is arrived at by deliberate coordination and those whose completion is arrived at by incidental coordination. These goals can both be temporarily or chronically active and can both be triggered consciously (e.g., by reflecting about a problem) or nonconsciously (e.g., by the presence of an eliciting environmental stimulus) (Chartrand, Maddux, and Lakin 2005). The extensive similarities in functioning between conscious and nonconscious goals suggest that the level at which they are active will make little difference in outcome (e.g., Bargh and Huang 2009; Bargh and Morsella 2008; Chartrand and Bargh 2002), though we suspect that conscious goals may have a stronger influence on deliberate coordination and nonconscious goals on incidental coordination.

People often generate goals whose ends involve psychological matching or synchronization (such as conformity; Epley and Gilovich 1999). This deliberate form of coordination can be relatively difficult when it concerns complex, high-skill tasks. Formal dancing is one example, as anyone who has had their toes crushed by a clumsy partner knows all too well. Team sports are another example: Learning the fundamentals of a sport like basketball or soccer takes a considerable amount of time and effort, and individual mastery is no guarantee that one will be able to effectively function within the team environment. However, other forms of goal-directed coordination have higher success rates. Consider the goal to communicate with others. Having a conversation with someone is a process of turn taking (or role-playing) that emerges quite naturally (Clark 1996), even when people speak different dialects or languages. Rarely do we hear conversations fail because one conversant directly imitates what's being said at the same instant it's being said (mockery among children notwithstanding). Interestingly, behavior matching is itself sometimes considered to be a communicative act. Mimicking another's behavior may signal a sense of similarity or connection with the person being mimicked (Bavelas, Black, Lemery, and Mullett 1986, 1987), and thus mimicry *is* the desired behavioral end.

In addition to these deliberate forms of social coordination, coordination often emerges incidentally as a function of goal-driven behavior. Language use again plays a prominent role here. Most forms of social activity require communication to proceed effectively, and language thus provides the medium by which actions become synchronized (Clark 1996). For instance, a couple who goes out to a nice restaurant is not necessarily interested in coordinating their own actions with those of the restaurant employees. They simply want to eat a good meal. Yet, this meal is acquired through back-and-forth conversation, and often a meshing of judgments, with the waiter or waitress.

A number of studies demonstrate that coordination can emerge as a result of priming a goal that is not explicitly coordinative in nature. For example, the goal to be liked does not require coordination for its completion, yet people who have this goal are more likely to mimic the behavior of others (e.g., Lakin and Chartrand 2003). This typically occurs automatically and nonconsciously, suggesting that mimicry functions as social glue, binding people more closely together (Chartrand et al. 2005; van Knippenberg and van Baaren 2006). In another setting, Griskevicius and colleagues (2006) conducted a series of experiments in which participants were primed with either a physical self-protection goal, a romantic goal, or a control goal and then were given the opportunity to evaluate an object (e.g., a piece of abstract art). Before this evaluation, participants were shown the (bogus) responses of other people in the study, giving participants the opportunity to either conform to those responses or not. Those participants with an active self-protection goal conformed more than those participants with a control goal. This likely occurred because, in dangerous situations, matching the behavior of others reduces how conspicuous one is (Dijksterhuis, Bargh, and Miedema 2000; Hamilton 1971). However, this mimicry was incidental to the active goal and even to the evaluative task, especially considering that mimicking others' evaluations of abstract art is unlikely to effectively lessen one's vulnerability to threat. Interestingly, an active romantic goal led male participants to conform less in these studies, but only when participants' image would not be damaged by failing to conform. This presumably occurred because, just as coordination can act as a signal of similarity, not coordinating helps one to stand out from the crowd and thus attract (romantic) attention (Griskevicius et al. 2006).

Thus, a goal, whether temporarily or chronically active, can modulate the extent to which people coordinate their actions (see also Ackerman and Kenrick 2008). This may occur when coordination is the desired outcome of that goal or when it is only the means to successful goal pursuit. As the two prior routes suggest, though, an active goal may not be a necessary feature for social coordination. Instead, the degree to which goals play a facilitatory or inhibitory role in the expression of coordination (Dijksterhuis and Bargh 2001) may depend on the particular goal and the context in which it is being pursued. Consistent with this, recent research suggests that the basic neural architecture involved in social coordination may be innate, but the expression of particular forms of coordination may often be moderated by goal-relevant features of the social interaction (see Chartrand and van Baaren 2009).

Benefits of Social Coordination

Many of the forms of coordination we have just reviewed require the concurrent use of multiple online processes. People need to monitor others' actions, regulate their own actions away from their current state and into line with what is being observed, and continually monitor the discrepancy between actions of the self and the other (though these all may occur at a nonconscious level; Chartrand and Bargh 2002). Use of these processes can divert cognitive resources away from other primary goals. Thus, one might wonder, why bother?

A wide array of benefits has been proposed to stem from automatic coordination, reflecting both evolutionary selection pressures and more proximate challenges. Perhaps the most commonly discussed benefit involves the fostering of social bonds (e.g., Chartrand et al. 2005; Galinsky, Ku, and Wang 2005). People are inherently social and possess a fundamental motivation to establish coalitions with others (Ackerman and Kenrick 2008; Baumeister and Leary 1995; Caporael and Baron 1997). Coordination can help to both cement existing relationships and lubricate new social interactions. For example, mirroring the posture and behaviors of others is associated with, and can even produce, liking and a sense of rapport between individuals (e.g., Chartrand and Bargh 1999; LaFrance and Broadbent 1976; LaFrance 1982). Appropriately synchronizing behaviors can help individuals get along, while failures to do so may produce detrimental outcomes (e.g., Bernieri and Rosenthal 1991; Finkel et al. 2006). Further, the emotional convergence associated with this synchronization (Hatfield et al. 1994) may underlie the development of empathic bonds.

When in Rome...

The creation of close, affiliative relationships is certainly a fundamental enterprise; however, it may be that social bonding is simply one instantiation of coordination's primary adaptive function(s). We suggest a broader possibility. The cognitive substrate that underlies interpersonal coordination may have evolved to aid individual goal achievement within a social world. Social living allows creatures to capitalize on the information provided by other creatures in situations where the correct course of action is uncertain (importantly, we are not implying conscious indecision or uncertainty). By following in the footsteps of others who share the same goals, imitators may find more efficient solutions to immediate and future problems than they would on their own. These problems need not be social (e.g., a person may need to decide which color berries to eat and which not to eat). More derived forms of coordination (e.g., complementarity) again function to aid individual goal achievement, though the problems involved may be more social in nature. The notion that social coordination evolved to facilitate the rather broad concepts of goal achievement or problem solving may appear to be an appeal to the contentious idea of domain-general evolution (for reviews of this literature, see Ackerman and Kenrick 2008; Barrett and Kurzban 2006; Pinker 2002). However, uncertainty *is* a domain-general feature inherent to problem solving and goal pursuit (e.g., Dawes 1993). The specific ways in which coordination actually emerges would, in turn, be susceptible to domain-specific features of the problem or goal. Thus, we suggest that social coordination aids in the successful pursuit of chronic and temporarily active goals, of which the formation of coalitions is but one, and consequently in preparation for future action as well.

With respect to immediate goal achievement, coordination can serve as an end in and of itself, as when effectively coordinating with others communicates one's membership and value in a group (Bavelas et al. 1986; Kurzban and Neuberg 2005; Scheflen 1964). Additionally, people face a number of critical individual and social problems (Ackerman and Kenrick 2008; Barkow, Cosmides, and Tooby 1992; Kenrick, Li, et al. 2003) whose solutions may be facilitated through interpersonal coordination. People may learn faster by utilizing shared intelligence, gather resources more efficiently through division of labor, defend themselves by mimicking group behaviors, evaluate the desirability of romantic partners based on others' preferences, read the intentions of others by mentally simulating their actions, and so on. For example, mimicking the behavior and posture of others in business negotiations can increase both the odds of making a deal and the monetary gain garnered from that deal (e.g., Maddux, Mullen, and Galinsky 2008). Additionally, recognizing and instigating coordinated activities may vault one into leadership roles (e.g., Van Vugt, Hogan, and Kaiser 2008). Coordination can therefore provide for better outcomes than individuals would be able to achieve on their own. These outcomes may often benefit the group (e.g., division of labor results in more efficiency for everyone), but this is not a prerequisite for useful coordination.

Humans are also creatures of habit. We repeatedly encounter situations that involve similar problems and solutions. By synchronizing our reactions to these situations with the reactions of others, people may condition the emergence of such reactions within similar future situations, thus helping to prepare for future action. One of the earliest examples of this process concerns emotional synchronization between parent and child. Proper mother–infant coordination of emotional expression helps the infant with effective emotion regulation (Field 1994). Lack of this coordination during early development can lead to future problems with emotion management (Tronick 1989).

Co-opting Coordination

To the degree that social coordination provides a powerful tool for goal pursuit, people have likely evolved sensitivities to capitalize on its use. That is, the foundations of social coordination probably did not evolve for many of the specific purposes coordination currently serves—it is unlikely that such diverse functions would have simultaneously created selection pressures for coordination. Instead, many of these current functions may represent what Buss and colleagues (1998, 539) label co-opted adaptations ("features that evolved by selection for one function are co-opted for another function"). Co-option is a common process whereby new structures or functions are "built on top of" preexisting ones (see Bargh and Morsella 2008 for an example involving conscious and nonconscious goal pursuit, and Williams, Huang, and Bargh, forthcoming for an example involving basic and derived goals). We have suggested (above) that coordination may have evolved to facilitate individual goal pursuit. Much of coordination's social utility may have been co-opted from this original function. We now discuss three possibly derivative functions—rapport building, reverence–leadership, and ostracism.

Interpersonal synchronization may not only facilitate individual outcomes but, as a consequence, may also build rapport by signaling similarity between parties (Bavelas et al. 1986, 1987; Chartrand and Bargh 1999). The functional utility of signaling similarity (including knowing whose goals are like yours, creating relational closeness, etc.) would likely have created pressure to capitalize on the communicative aspects of coordination. Consistent with this idea, acts of coordination can produce a number of positive interpersonal outcomes. People who are behaviorally mimicked report liking the mimicker more, even when they are not aware of having been mimicked (e.g., Chartrand and Bargh 1999; Maurer and Tindall 1983). Complementation of behavior may produce even stronger feelings of liking and comfort than mimicry does (e.g., Tiedens and Fragale 2003). Emotional synchronization can also lead to closer peer relationships and increased romantic relationship satisfaction (e.g., Anderson, Keltner, and John 2003; Dryer and Horowitz 1997). Social coordination can bind individuals together through the shared positive experiences people undergo. Many forms of cultural and religious ritual involve groups of people performing synchronized, rhythmic, and repetitive actions (Fiske 2000; Wiltermuth and Heath 2009) that in turn produce states of ecstasy and awe (Haidt 2007).

People also tend to react quite powerfully to individuals who communicate expertise in some of the more difficult forms of coordination (e.g., Haidt 2003; Morgan 1941; Meindl, Ehrlich, and Dukerich 1985). For example, we treat with reverence those sports teams whose play resembles a single, cohesive unit. We consider the epitome of musical collaboration to be the time when a group's members create and perform in harmony. We also idolize leaders whose ideas resonate with our ideals. These experts often acquire legions of followers who are quite fanatical in their devotion. The reverence and popularity accorded to natural coordinators may vault them into leadership positions (Van Vugt et al. 2008). As observers, it may be that we derive pleasure from mentally synchronizing our actions with those who can do the things we only wish we could do.

The communicative aspect of social coordination also provides a useful tool for identifying those people with whom we do *not* wish to affiliate. The communication of similarity and closeness through coordination is largely an unintended, nonconscious act (Scheflen 1964), and in fact, deliberate, conscious imitation attempts can produce a negative backlash against imitators (e.g., Thelen, Miller, Fehrenbach, and Frautschi 1983). Additionally, a demonstrated inability to effectively coordinate with others is a clear predictor of problematic group functioning and thus may lead to individuals' being devalued as group members (Chartrand and Bargh 1999; Cottrell, Neuberg, and Li 2007). People lacking indicators of coordination ability, as with unpredictability (Kurzban and Leary 2001), antisocial tendencies (Dunn and Hughes 2001), stuttering (Whaley and Golden 2000), and autism (Rogers and Pennington 1991), may face ostracism and expulsion from social groups (Kurzban and Neuberg 2005; Williams, Forgas, and von Hippel 2005). Consistent with this, people are less likely to mimic members of outgroups compared to members of the ingroup (Yabar, Johnston, Miles, and Peace 2006). The presence of outgroup competitors, itself, may even motivate forms of ingroup coordination (e.g., Bornstein and Erev 1994; Van Vugt et al. 2008).

Emerging Research

Despite a large literature on imitation and synchronization effects, and their concordant benefits, social coordination remains relatively unexamined within a number of domains. Here, we present two independent lines of investigation that reveal new forms of coordination involving romantic relationship formation and self-regulatory processes.

Cooperative Courtship

Researchers concerned with romantic relationship formation have tended to ignore the role of the broader social environment or concentrate solely on its more competitive aspects (e.g., Buss 1988; Kenrick and Trost 1997; Schmitt 2005). However, it is certainly feasible that coordinated action between people (e.g., cooperation) has played a role in shaping the courtship process. Research examining cooperative courtship is virtually nonexistent in humans, but the phenomenon has been documented in a variety of other social species. For example, wild male turkeys form coalitions to display their fitness to females (Krakauer 2005), male common chimpanzees occasionally cooperate in guarding mates (Watts 1998), and female alliances among bonobo chimpanzees help to reduce male sexual coercion (Smuts and Smuts 1993).

Following from the examples set by other species, we investigated the possibility that humans socially coordinate to improve their own romantic outcomes (Ackerman and Kenrick 2009). We conducted several studies in which people reported both their past experiences and projective future actions in (social) romantic situations. These initial studies suggested that, despite the inherent motivation to compete for romantic partners (Buss 1988), people were still willing to help each other achieve successful mating outcomes. This help was exemplified by a suite of cooperative strategies that included assistance with self-esteem support, information management, and social networking. Thus, coordination took a variety of complex forms, all of which promoted individual romantic goal achievement.

We also uncovered evidence for sex-specific forms of cooperation indicative of coordination *between* the sexes. This evidence fit with the basic premise of parental investment theory (Trivers 1972), which suggests that within a species, the sex that invests more in (potential) offspring will be more romantically choosy than the sex that invests less. In humans, women tend to invest more in children than do men, and consistent with this investment, they tend to be more selective in choosing mates (e.g., Buss and Schmitt 1993; Gangestad and Simpson 2000; Kenrick, Sadalla, Groth, and Trost 1990; Schmitt 2003). Indeed, in our studies, women were more likely to cooperate in creating romantic barriers and in giving barrier-building help to their same-sex friends. Men, on the other hand, were more likely to cooperate in attempting to achieve romantic access and in giving barrier-breaking help to their same-sex friends. However, the type of help given to opposite-sex friends was reversed for men and women, suggesting that people are sensitive to the intended outcomes of their friends' romantic goals. These patterns indicate a behavioral complementarity between the sexes such that men and women synchronize their cooperative strategies to counter the role of the other sex (e.g., women build thresholds, men try to overcome these, etc.).

Cooperative courtship tendencies were also found in a study in which people expected to *actually* meet potential romantic partners (Ackerman and Kenrick 2009). In this study, participants took part in an experiment modeled after the TV game show *The Dating Game*. Participants (two same-sex friends or two strangers) became "contestants" in a game to win a date with a (fictitious) opposite-sex Dater in each round of the game. However, in one condition this Dater was described as very desirable, and in another condition as less desirable. Before participants met the Dater, they were allowed to choose a behavioral strategy that was either competitive (e.g., meeting with the Dater to try and win the date) or cooperative (e.g., giving their meeting time with the Dater to the other contestant), though not described in these terms. As above, women primarily attempted to help the other contestant avoid undesirable Daters, and men primarily attempted to help the other contestant attract desirable Daters. However, these patterns of cooperation emerged only when the contestants were friends and not when they were randomly paired strangers. We might therefore say that "the mating game" (Nettle 2005) is, in fact, a team sport. Thus, social coordination as exemplified by romantic cooperation is a function of a preexisting close relationship, just as coordination (in other forms) is more often found between people who share rapport (e.g., Chartrand et al. 2005; LaFrance and Broadbent 1976; Scheflen 1964).

This research, as well as newly emerging work, highlights many of the specialized forms of coordination that occur in the romantic realm. For instance, we found that people are also willing to have friends act as counterfeit relationship partners in order to stimulate social coordination with potential mates and thus promote barrier-building and access goals (Ackerman and Kenrick 2009). Other researchers (e.g., Hill and Buss 2008; Jones, DeBruine, Little, Burriss, and Feinberg 2007) have found that people synchronize their romantic preferences with same-sex individuals in the social environment, effectively copying these others' mating choices (a similar process also occurs in animals like birds and fish). Further examples of romantic coordination surely await discovery.

Vicarious Self-Control
One method of prompting rapport between two individuals is by having one person take the perspective of the other (Galinsky, Ku, and Wang 2005). Perspective taking also makes it more likely that one person will mentally simulate the actions of the other (Goldman and Sebanz 2005). That is, imagining what another person is experiencing (the mental simulation) elicits a form of internal replication involving much the same neural and pre-motor activity that would occur if perspective takers performed the actions, themselves (e.g., Decety and Sommerville 2008; Goldman 2006; Niedenthal, Barsalou, Winkielman, Krauth-Gruber, and Ric 2005).

This cognitive synchronization not only can lead to greater empathic understanding between individuals but can also result in a variety of downstream effects. For instance, simulating another's experience can produce feelings of pain (e.g., Jackson, Brunet, Meltzoff, and Decety 2006) and cognitive dissonance (e.g., Norton, Monin, Cooper, and Hogg 2003) and even lead people to attribute qualities associated with an actor's behavior to themselves (e.g., people who read about a self-sacrificing person may rate themselves as more self-sacrificing; Goldstein and Cialdini 2007). These downstream effects may occur because, when people engage in actions, they encode associations between these actions and the sensory and affective effects that result from the actions (Hommel 2004; Niedenthal 2007). Simulation of these actions generates a multimodal response (e.g., muscle movements, facial expressions, physiological changes) through retrieval of these experiences. We applied these findings to the question of whether simulating the experience of another's *self-control* might result in such downstream responses.

Self-control is not a limitless resource. Exercising it to avoid temptation, make decisions, and act appropriately temporarily depletes executive control abilities, leading people to perform worse on subsequent tasks requiring self-control (e.g., Baumeister, Bratslavsky, Muraven, and Tice 1998; Muraven and Baumeister 2000; Vohs et al. 2008). What would this mean for other people in the social environment? If cognitive coordination tends to make goals "contagious" (Aarts et al. 2004; Hassin et al. 2005), then perceiving another person's self-control should prime a self-control goal in observers. However, if simulating that self-control activity produces downstream effects, imagining what that person experiences may result in the consequence of that self-control activity—depletion—even in observers.

We investigated these alternate possibilities in two studies (Ackerman, Goldstein, Shapiro, and Bargh 2009). In the first, participants read a story about a waiter who worked at a restaurant selling high-quality food and who arrived to work hungry but unable to eat on the job (thus necessitating self-control). Half of the participants simply read this story with no further instructions, and the other half were instructed to take the perspective of the waiter while reading. Later, the participants were asked to judge the amount of money they would be willing to spend on a series of luxury goods as a measure of self-control over impulse buying. Those participants who took the perspective of the waiter reported being willing to spend an average of $6,000 more on the products, indicating that their ability to control their impulses was depleted.

In the second study, both the original waiter story and another in which the waiter was not hungry and worked at an undesirable restaurant (thus necessitating no self-control) were used. Participants were either instructed to take the perspective of a waiter or not and then completed a word-construction task in which they had to create new words using the letters from a source word. Again, there was vicarious depletion, as participants' taking the perspective of the hungry waiter led to a decline in word-construction performance compared to those participants who did not take the perspective of the hungry waiter, and compared to those participants who took the perspective of the full waiter. However, among non-perspective-taking participants, reading the hungry waiter story improved word-construction performance relative to reading the full waiter story (indicative of a goal-contagion effect).

We have found similar effects across a range of other measures. For instance, vicarious depletion can undo people's resistance to persuasive messages, leading them to view unwelcome requests more favorably and even agree to changes espoused in those requests. In one study, vicariously depleted students were twice as likely to agree to a change in their school's grading system (instituting the dreaded "curve") as were typical students. Vicarious depletion can also affect people's perception of time, leading them to overestimate how long a task involving mental self-control takes relative to a task not involving mental control. Such patterns suggest that simple perception can inspire others to exert a greater amount of self-control, but mentally simulating self-control use can instead deplete people vicariously.

Future Directions

As demonstrated above, social coordination can result in quite different outcomes depending on the type of activity being coordinated and the extent to which coordination takes place. Researchers have tended to operationalize coordination in terms of a single modality (e.g., behavioral mimicry, emotional contagion, etc.), yet synchronized responses can take place all they way down the psychological stream, from behavior to affect to cognition, and back up again. Studies revealing that facial mimicry is associated with affective changes resulting from facial feedback are one useful step in understanding this process (e.g., Bush et al. 1989; McIntosh 1996; Vaughan and Lanzetta 1980, 1981). However, we suspect that further investigation of social coordination's multimodal nature will continue to reveal important insights. For instance, are people equally likely to synchronize thoughts, feelings, and actions with others; is it easier to synchronize certain modalities than others? What does the synchronization of one modality imply for the subsequent synchronization of other modalities? What forms of perception best facilitate interpersonal coordination, and within which modalities? While the objective answers to such questions remain to be uncovered, some insights might be gained by considering the subjective sense of ease with which coordination proceeds.

The Role of Felt Effort

Many commonly recognized forms of social coordination require intensive training. Consider the willpower required for basketball players to master the triangle offense or for operating room personnel to effectively collaborate during eight-hour surgeries. Yet, in virtually any domain, as people gain expertise in their roles, coordination becomes easier and more automatic. In fact, these features characterize the vast majority of instances of social coordination. As we have seen, people both mimic and complement the thoughts, feelings, and behaviors of others, often without even realizing it. The nonconscious nature of these examples guarantees, by definition, that they require both little attention and little effort. Why would this be? Why is social coordination often so effortless?

The answer may lie with automaticity (Bargh and Chartrand 1999; Moors and De Houwer 2006). Goals, plans for completing these goals, and even the consequences of goal pursuit can, through repeated pairings, become associated with the situations in which these goals typically arise, such that the presence of relevant situational features can automatically (unintentionally, autonomously) activate the associated goal representations (Bargh 1990, 1994, 1997). This automaticity allows for the diversion of cognitive resources away from repetitive (mental and physical) actions (Jastrow 1906; Shiffrin and Schneider 1977), resulting in greater efficiency and a reduction in subjective effort (Bargh 1989). Without this diversion, we would have trouble managing more complex tasks. Consider the wide array of cognitive and behavioral actions necessary to simply walk across a room (Clark and Phillips 1993; Sutherland 1997). Walking requires the simultaneous coordination of depth, obstacle, and rate perception, as well as the use of over 200 muscles. If walking, and all such activities, were not largely automatized, we would have a tough time simply getting out of bed in the morning (Miller, Galanter, and Pribram 1960).

The same is true with respect to social coordination. There is a virtually infinite number of ways that people can coordinate their thoughts, feelings, and behaviors. Indeed, "most human activity involves coordinating one's actions with the actions of others" (Reis and Collins 2004, 233). Thankfully, social coordination is also highly automatized. In fact, we can draw a rather direct parallel between the coordination required for individual movement and for social life. People must learn how to walk effectively (and build the muscles necessary to do so), and they must also learn how to engage others socially (and build the self-awareness and language skills necessary to do so). These developmental processes are aided by adaptive predispositions that make learning specific procedures (like walking) more rapid and resistant to extinction (e.g., Cosmides and Tooby 1994; Kenrick, Ackerman, and Ledlow 2003; Seligman 1970). An evolved need to belong—to form and maintain social relationships (Baumeister and Leary 1995; Brewer 1991; Fiske, 2008)—also creates pressure to automate the majority of ways people synchronize their interactions. Although proficiency in walking and social coordination can be and are intentionally developed, many aspects of such activities are automatically (unintentionally) automatized (Bargh and Chartrand 1999). In fact, the basic features of individual motion and social coordination, such as leg swinging and behavior matching, may be automatic from the get-go, without needing to be learned (Chartrand and Bargh 1999). To draw a simple analogy, coordination *with* others is akin to coordination *within* oneself. The result is interactions that are typically as effortless as walking across the room.

This fact is perhaps most readily demonstrated by the phenomenal state experienced during times of faulty coordination. Within the individual, conflicts of intention and action (e.g., wanting to carry a hot plate but feeling one's hand burning) or of cognitive integration (e.g., attempting to accept two opposing ideas) are often a source of mental strife (Festinger 1957; Morsella 2005). Similarly, attempting to interact with unfamiliar others, especially those with whom we have trouble synchronizing, requires dynamic entrainment and is likely to bring the lack of coordination into consciousness (Jeannerod 2006). In the short term, uncoordinated interaction may frustrate the pursuit of chronic affiliation goals and is often an aversive experience. Self-regulatory resources are drained, tension sets in, and suspicion of others may increase (e.g., Finkel et al. 2006; Kurzban and Neuberg 2005; Richeson and Trawalter 2005). These reactions are also evident in people who face problems with social coordination as a function of certain individual differences. For instance, high self-focus can both reduce coordination and call attention to this reduction (e.g., Van Baaren, Maddux, Chartrand, de Bouter, and van Knippenberg 2003)), resulting in a variety of negative feelings (e.g., Kowalski 1996). These effects may be exaggerated in people with social anxiety who have difficulty synchronizing their behaviors with interaction partners and may react to social interactions by fidgeting and excessively seeking reassurance (e.g., Heerey and Kring 2007).

In contrast, effective coordination is characterized by a feeling of smoothness and positive social reactions (Chartrand and Bargh 1999). People often derive pleasure from engaging in coordinated activities like team sports, musical performance, and dance (e.g., Ehrenreich 2006; Haidt, Seder, and Kesebir, 2008; Levenson and Ruef 1997; McNeill 1995). Importantly, to effectively and skillfully engage in such activities requires a relatively high degree of automaticity from all of the interaction partners (Ehrenreich 2006; Fitts and Posner 1967). The positive responses associated with coordinated interactions may occur because the negative aspects of the self (Leary 2004) are transcended in favor of a connection with others (Ehrenreich 2006; Haidt et al., 2008). Additionally, it may be that coordination acts as a signal of interpersonal fluency, the social equivalent of processing fluency (e.g., Reber et al. 2004). Fluent processing involves a subjective sense of ease (Clore 1992; Whittlesea, Jacoby, and Girard 1990), resulting in elevated feelings of familiarity and trust with the fluently processed stimuli (e.g., Reber and Schwarz 1999; Whittlesea 1993). Indeed, the experience of fluency is associated with highly automatized behaviors (Dougherty and Johnston 1996).

Flow

These facts may help to link the process of social coordination to the experience of effortlessness as described by the state of *flow*. Flow is considered to be a feeling of reduced subjective effort in the face of maintained objective effort, often coupled with feelings of happiness and intrinsic motivation to continue engaging in an activity (Csikszentmihalyi 1975; Hektner, Schmidt, and Csikszentmihalyi 2007). For instance, a trained musician described this state as "you lose your sense of time, you're completely enraptured, you are completely caught up in what you're doing" (Csikszentmihalyi 1996, 121). The flow state tends to emerge during activities that are highly automatized and involve either individual coordination (e.g., driving) or social coordination (e.g., language use; Csikszentmihalyi and LeFevre 1989). In fact, some evidence indicates that with coordinated activities such as conversations, people are more likely to experience flow when talking to high coordinators (e.g., kin, friends) than less-high coordinators (e.g., strangers; Csikszentmihalyi and LeFevre 1989).

The state of flow is intimately tied to a reduction in felt effort. Often, reduced effort is accompanied by a reduction in conscious attention to the immediate task (Dehaene, Kerszberg, and Changeux 2001); however, the effortless nature of flow is exclusively subjective, with attention preserved or even enhanced (Csikszentmihalyi 1975). From this perspective, many of the automatic forms of social coordination discussed here do not meet the criteria of "effortless attention" because they do not involve conscious awareness. Yet coordinated activities such as talking or walking in lockstep certainly feel effortless. This raises a dilemma as to the nature of effortless attention and action. Is there something fundamentally unique about activities in which attention can be focused on those activities without a corresponding increase in felt effort?

Not necessarily, perhaps. There are at least two important points to consider with respect to this question. First, it is worth recognizing that increases in attention are not inevitably tied to increases in subjective effort. Kahneman (1973, 33) noted that states featuring high levels of arousal (and thus focused attention) may be characterized by "a pattern of relaxed acceptance of external stimulation," with a focus on motor inhibition, in addition to the more promotion-oriented arousal typically thought to characterize flow states. Focused attention on a task may only entail the subjective experience of increased effort when one's performance is insufficient or when one's expectations are violated. Effort is thus determined by the demands of the processing task and not necessarily by either intuitive notions of task difficulty or the degree of voluntary intention or attention devoted to that task (Kahneman 1973). For instance, when a person is in a state of perceptual and response readiness (e.g., prior to engaging in a well-practiced task), or when attention is driven by external stimuli (e.g., when visual attention is captured by angry faces), subjective effort is minimized.

Second, conscious control of attention does not equate with the awareness of particular stimuli or actions but instead with the awareness of the influence and effects of those stimuli or actions (Bargh and Morsella 2008). The "unconscious" acts as a behavioral guidance system that drives attention and action; people are often aware of what they are doing, but they also are often not consciously aware of the reasons for those actions. For example, people may be aware that they are completing a sentence-unscrambling task (to use a classic priming manipulation) yet still not be conscious of how the linguistic content of those sentences is influencing downstream thoughts, feelings, and behaviors. Similarly, people may perceive the actions of others without understanding that this perception produces entrainment and coordination between self and other.

These two pieces of information suggest that the conscious awareness accorded to flow states may not be the driving force for the actions performed within those states. Consider that many of the elements associated with flow are not reliant on conscious awareness. For example, emotions (Ruys and Stapel 2008), motivation (Bargh and Huang 2009; Burton, Lydon, D'Alessandro, and Koestner 2006), and even creativity–flexibility (Hassin, Bargh, and Zimerman, 2009; Sassenberg and Moskowitz 2005) can all be experienced and utilized without conscious executive control. The intrinsic motivation that drives attention and the feeling of decreased subjective effort associated with flow are both hallmarks of (nonconscious) automaticity (Bargh 1989, 1990). Thus, virtually every element of flow can, and may typically, occur without conscious processing (the only element requiring consciousness is the awareness of one's current experience).

In fact, given the enormous complexities of mental processing involved in flow activities, it is highly unlikely that consciousness is in control. Consider the processing requirements for two people to engage in a coordinated conversation (see Clark 1996). A conversation typically entails multiple levels of co-occurring mental representations with respect to the words uttered, the syntax used, the overall goal of the discussion, the perceptual and verbal feedback provided by the other conversant, and so on. The activities commonly considered representative of flow experiences also include such processing requirements. All of this processing must be done simultaneously, or in parallel, despite the fact that the actions produced proceed in serial fashion. The manner in which this parallel distributed processing occurs is described by *cascade models* of cognition (which are typically applied to language production; e.g., Bargh 2006; Morsella and Miozzo 2002; Navarette and Costa 2004). Activities involving effortless action and attention are likely the result of this parallel processing, resulting in behavioral outcomes that are nonconsciously "selected for" the individual (e.g., Dell, Burger, and Svec 1997). This notion appears consistent with subjective descriptions of flow states, as when a former poet laureate described working in such a state as "you have the feeling that there's no other way of saying what you're saying" (Csikszentmihalyi 1996, 121). Consciousness is simply too slow a mechanism to effectively manage the processing requirements for such tasks.

From this perspective, conscious awareness may instead play the role of outside observer (Johnson and Reeder 1997. The state of flow would thus entail awareness of one's automatized responses without that awareness's being involved at a more causal level. Automatized behavior, by definition, does not require conscious elicitation, but it also does not preclude awareness of action. Thus, a person in a state of effortless attention and action may be experiencing something like a minor out-of-body experience, or, consistent with the poet laureate's quote above, an understanding that one's actions are not entirely under one's control. [This conceptualization is similar to James's description of consciousness as "express fiat" (1890/1981, 1131), not the originator of behavioral impulses, but their gatekeeper. Drawing on this account, consciousness may still play a role in flow experiences but at the level of behavioral inhibition]. Feelings of subjective effort would follow from task performance, not from attention–awareness for that task, allowing for focused attention without the depleting effects typically ascribed to elevated executive control. The positive feelings that result from flow experiences (Csikszentmihalyi, Abuhamdeh, and Nakamura 2005; Massimini, Csikszentmihalyi, and Carli 1987) could be explained as a combination of those typically accorded to observers of high-quality performances (e.g., awe, delight) as well as those that accompany rapid progress toward the current goal (Carver and Scheier 1981) and goal attainment itself (Förster, Liberman, and Friedman 2007). For example, during a basketball game, a player might become completely absorbed in the experience of the game, including the movements of the other players, a feeling that the basket is larger and time is moving slower, a loss of fatigue, and an intuitive sense of what actions to perform in order to score—in other words, the state of flow. If the player's actions are successful moment to moment, he or she might be enraptured by the experience, just as observers in the crowd would be (Haidt 2007; Haidt et al., 2008). A sense of effortlessness would result because the actions being performed, including those involving physical and social coordination, are highly automatized and thus require very little subjective effort. This perspective may also suggest that the awareness accorded to one's behaviors within flow states is in essence an enhancement or impairment of proprioception—the sense of bodily movements and positioning (e.g., Bermúdez, Marcel, and Eilan 1995; Farrer, Franck, Paillard, and Jeannerod 2003; Maxwell, Masters, and van der Karnp 2007). A more general implication is that effortless actions lie within the purview of the unconscious as demarcated by Bargh and Morsella (2008). Although one may be intensely aware of one's actions, and attentionally caught up in them, this does not imply that those actions are being controlled by that awareness.

The automaticity and the feelings of both effortlessness and positive affect that accompany flow states appear quite encouraging. Indeed, a high degree of interpersonal automaticity probably *is* beneficial in many circumstances (e.g., Fitts and Posner 1967; Singer 2002). For instance, the ability to coordinate under conditions of high objective effort without the correspondent increase in subjective effort is characteristic of high-performing sports teams (e.g., Jackson and Csikszentmihalyi 1999). Additionally, redirecting the cognitive resources typically involved with self-monitoring to other-monitoring (where the self becomes an observer) may help prevent "choking" under pressure (e.g., Baumeister 1984). Feeling effortlessly in sync with others may also aid both in predicting their future behavior and subsequently adjusting one's own behavior in an appropriate fashion. Such outcomes are surely beneficial for cooperative coalitions such as military units, hospital staff, and so on. However, there is also a potential downside to the allure of effortlessness. The self-reinforcing properties of this form of social coordination may make us susceptible to exploitation, and the lack of conscious awareness associated with many instantiations of coordination (e.g., behavioral mimicry) makes this prospect especially pernicious. Consider that individuals who are able to coordinate with us in a relatively effortless manner are likely to automatically build rapport and trust. These feelings of closeness may, in turn, increase our vulnerability to the wiles of salespeople (e.g., Wood 2006), social cheaters (e.g., Cummins 1999), and bad leaders (e.g., Bennis 2007; Lipman-Blumen 2006).

In sum, much of social coordination is highly automated, associated with subjective ease, and reinforced by the positive individual and interpersonal experiences resulting from it. With respect to effortless attention (which requires some degree of conscious attention), we suspect that a state of effortlessness is likely to emerge between individuals who have automatized their roles in the particular social interaction and who are able to easily coordinate with others, thereby freeing up conscious resources for the appreciation of this interpersonal activity. Whether or not this effortlessness will truly lead to positive or negative outcomes may depend on who is doing the interacting and on the goals and agendas of those individuals.

Conclusions

Interpersonal coordination is a fundamental property of social interaction. Automatic forms of coordination help to lubricate new social interactions and cement existing relationships. Though social coordination often emerges nonconsciously, it produces powerful effects on interpersonal cognitions and actions while at the same time making the sensory experience of complex social dynamics seem easier. Here, we have tried to answer several basic questions about social coordination, including what it is, how it emerges, and why people continue to so readily match, complement, and synchronize with others. In doing so, we have proposed that social coordination exists primarily to promote individual goal achievement. The mechanisms that drive this process may also underlie the experience of effortlessness in social interaction, for good or for ill. Social coordination is a topic that has received empirical attention in a wide range of psychological subdisciplines, and yet the implications of this topic remain absent from a number of potentially fruitful areas of inquiry. As such, we expect that (coordinated teams of) researchers will continue to uncover novel forms of interpersonal coordination within virtually any domain they examine.

Acknowledgments

Preparation of this chapter was supported in part by grant R01-MH60767 from the U.S. Public Health Service. We thank Julie Huang, Randy Stein, and the rest of the Automaticity in Cognition, Motivation, and Evaluation lab for their feedback.

References

Aarts, H., P. M. Gollwitzer, and R. R. Hassin. 2004. Goal contagion: Perceiving is for pursuing. *J. Pers. Soc. Psychol.* 87:23–37.

Ackerman, J. M., N. J. Goldstein, J. R. Shapiro, and J. A. Bargh. 2009. You wear me out: The vicarious depletion of self-control. *Psychol. Sci.* 20:326–332.

Ackerman, J. M., and D. T. Kenrick. 2008. The costs of benefits: Help-refusals highlight key trade-offs of social life. *Pers. Soc. Psychol. Rev.* 12:118–140.

Ackerman, J. M., and D. T. Kenrick. Forthcoming. Cooperative courtship: Helping friends raise and raze relationship barriers. *Pers. Soc. Psychol. Bull.* 35:1285–1300.

Anderson, C., D. Keltner, and O. P. John. 2003. Emotional convergence between people over time. *Journal of Personality and Social Psychology* 84:1054–1068.

Ashley, J., and M. Tomasello. 1998. Cooperative problem solving and teaching in preschoolers. *Soc. Dev.* 7:143–163.

Baldwin, M. W., and J. G. Holmes. 1987. Salient private audiences and awareness of the self. *J. Pers. Soc. Psychol.* 52:1087–1098.

Bandura, A. 1977. *Social learning theory*. Englewood Cliffs, NJ: Prentice Hall.

Bargh, J. A. 1989. Conditional automaticity: Varieties of automatic influence on social perception and cognition. In *Unintended thought*, ed. J. Uleman and J. Bargh. New York: Guilford, 3–51.

Bargh, J. A. 1990. Auto-motives: Preconscious determinants of social interaction. In *Handbook of motivation and cognition*. vol. 2. ed. E. T. Higgins and R. M. Sorrentino. New York: Guilford, 93–130.

Bargh, J. A. 1994. The four horsemen of automaticity: Awareness, intention, efficiency, and control in social cognition. In *Handbook of social cognition*. 2d ed. Ed. R. S. Wyer, Jr., and T. K. Srull. Hillsdale, NJ: Lawrence Erlbaum Associates, 1–40.

Bargh, J. A. 1997. The automaticity of everyday life. In *Advances in social cognition*. vol. 10. ed. R. S. Wyer, Jr. Mahwah, NJ: Erlbaum, 1–61.

Bargh, J. A. 2006. What have we been priming all these years? On the development, mechanisms, and ecology of nonconscious social behavior. *Eur. J. Soc. Psychol.* 36:147–168.

Bargh, J. A., and T. L. Chartrand. 1999. The unbearable automaticity of being. *Am. Psychol.* 54:462–479.

Bargh, J. A., M. Chen, and L. Burrows. 1996. Automaticity of social behavior: Direct effects of trait construct and stereotype activation on action. *J. Pers. Soc. Psychol.* 71:230–244.

Bargh, J. A., and J. Y. Huang. 2009. The selfish goal. In *The psychology of goals*, ed. G. Moskowitz and H. Grant. New York: Guilford, 127–152.

Bargh, J. A., and E. Morsella. 2008. The unconscious mind. *Perspect. Psychol. Sci.* 3:73–79.

Barkow, J., L. Cosmides, and J. Tooby, eds. 1992. *The Adapted Mind: Evolutionary psychology and the generation of culture*. New York: Oxford University Press.

Barrett, H. C., and R. Kurzban. 2006. Modularity in cognition: Framing the debate. *Psychological Review* 113:628–637.

Baumeister, R. F. 1984. Choking under pressure: Self-consciousness and paradoxical effects of incentives on skillful performance. *J. Pers. Soc. Psychol.* 46:610–620.

Baumeister, R. F., E. Bratslavsky, M. Muraven, and D. M. Tice. 1998. Ego depletion: Is the active self a limited resource? *J. Pers. Soc. Psychol.* 74:1252–1265.

Baumeister, R. F., and M. R. Leary. 1995. The need to belong: Desire for interpersonal attachments as a fundamental human motivation. *Psychol. Bull.* 117:497–529.

Bavelas, J. B., A. Black, C. R. Lemery, and J. Mullett. 1986. "I show how you feel": Motor mimicry as a communicative act. *J. Pers. Soc. Psychol.* 50:322–329.

Bavelas, J. B., A. Black, C. R. Lemery, and J. Mullett. 1987. Motor mimicry as primitive empathy. In *Empathy and its development*, ed. N. Eisenberg and J. Strayer. Cambridge: Cambridge University Press, 317–338.

Bennett, M., M. F. Schatz, H. Rockwood, and K. Wiesenfeld. 2002. Huygens' clocks. *Proc. R. Soc. Lond. A* 458:563–579.

Bennis, W. 2007. The challenges of leadership in the modern world. *Am. Psychol.* 62:2–5.

Bermúdez, J. L., A. J. Marcel, and N. Eilan, eds. 1995. *The body and the self*. Cambridge: MIT Press.

Bernieri, F. J. 1988. Coordinated movement and rapport in teacher–student interactions. *J. Nonverbal Behav.* 12:120–138.

Bernieri, F. J., and R. Rosenthal. 1991. Interpersonal coordination: Behavior matching and interactional synchrony. In *Fundamentals of nonverbal behavior*, ed. R. S. Feldman and B. Rime. Cambridge: Cambridge University Press, 401–432.

Bornstein, G., and I. Erev. 1994. The enhancing effect of intergroup competition on group performance. *Int. J. Conflict Manage.* 5:271–283.

Brewer, M. B. 1991. The social self: On being the same and different at the same time. *Pers. Soc. Psychol. Bull.* 17:475–482.

Buccino, G., F. Binkofski, G. R. Fink, L. Fadiga, L. Fogassi, V. Gallese, R. J. Seitz, G. Rizzolatti, and H. J. Freund. 2001. Action observation activates premotor and parietal areas in somatotopic manner: an fMRI study. *European Journal of Neuroscience* 13:400–404.

Burton, K. D., J. E. Lydon, D. U. D'Alessandro, and R. Koestner. 2006. The differential effects of intrinsic and identified motivation on well-being and performance: Prospective, experimental and implicit approaches to self-determination theory. *J. Pers. Soc. Psychol.* 91:750–762.

Bush, L. K., C. L. Barr, G. J. McHugo, and J. T. Lanzetta. 1989. The effects of facial control and facial mimicry on subjective reactions to comedy routines. *Motiv. Emot.* 13:31–52.

Buss, D. M. 1984. Toward a psychology of person–environment correspondence: The role of spouse selection. *J. Pers. Soc. Psychol.* 47:361–377.

Buss, D. M. 1988. The evolution of human intrasexual competition: Tactics of mate attraction. *J. Pers. Soc. Psychol.* 54:616–628.

Buss, D. M., M. G. Haselton, T. K. Shackelford, A. L. Bleske, and J. C. Wakefield. 1998. Adaptations, exaptations, and spandrels. *American Psychologist* 53:533–548.

Buss, D. M., and D. P. Schmitt. 1993. Sexual strategies theory: An evolutionary perspective on human mating. *Psychol. Rev.* 100:204–232.

Caporael, L. R., and R. M. Baron. 1997. Groups as the mind's natural environment. In *Evolutionary social psycholog*, ed. J. A. Simpson and D. T. Kenrick. Mahwah, NJ: Erlbaum Associates, 317–343.

Carpenter, W. B. 1874. *Principles of mental physiology*. London: John Churchill.

Carson, R. 1969. *Interaction concepts of personality*. Chicago: Aldine.

Carver, C. S., and M. F. Scheier. 1981. *Attention and self-regulation: A control-theory approach to human behavior*. New York: Springer.

Cesario, J., J. E. Plaks, and E. T. Higgins. 2006. Automatic social behavior as motivated preparation to interact. *J. Pers. Soc. Psychol.* 90:893–910.

Chartrand, T. L., and J. A. Bargh. 1999. The chameleon effect: The perception–behavior link and social interaction. *J. Pers. Soc. Psychol.* 76:893–910.

Chartrand, T., and J. A. Bargh. 2002. Nonconscious motivations: Their activation, operation, and consequences. In *Self and motivation: Emerging psychological perspectives*, ed. A. Tesser, D. A. Stapel, and J. W. Wood. Washington, DC: APA, 13–41.

Chartrand, T. L., W. M. Maddux, and J. L. Lakin. 2005. Beyond the perception–behavior link: The ubiquitous utility and motivational moderators of nonconscious mimicry. In *The new unconscious: Oxford series in social cognition and social neuroscience, ed. R. R. Hassin, J. S. Uleman, and J. A. Bargh. New York: Oxford University Press, 334–361.

Chartrand, T. L., and R. van Baaren. Human mimicry. 2009. In *Advances in experimental social psychology*, ed. M. Zanna. New York: Academic Press, 219–274.

Clark, H. H. 1996. *Using language*. Cambridge: Cambridge University Press.

Clark, J. E., and S. J. Phillips. 1993. A longitudinal study of intralimb coordination in the first year of independent walking: A dynamical systems analysis. *Child Dev.* 64:1143–1157.

Clore, G. L. 1992. Cognitive phenomenology: Feelings and the construction of judgment. In *The construction of social judgment*, ed. L. L. Martin and A. Tesser. Hillsdale, NJ: Erlbaum, 133–163.

Condon, W. S., and L. W. Sander. 1974. Synchrony demonstrated between movements of the neonate and adult speech. *Child Dev.* 45:456–462.

Cosmides, L., and J. Tooby. 1994. Origins of domain specificity: The evolution of functional organization. In *Mapping the mind: Domain specificity in cognition and culture*, ed. L. A. Hirschfeld and S. A. Gelman. Cambridge: MIT Press, 85–116.

Cottrell, C. A., S. L. Neuberg, and N. P. Li. 2007. What do people desire in others? A sociofunctional perspective on the importance of different valued characteristics. *Journal of Personality and Social Psychology* 92:208–231.

Csikszentmihalyi, M. 1975. *Beyond boredom and anxiety*. San Francisco: Jossey-Bass.

Csikszentmihalyi, M. 1996. *Creativity: Flow and the psychology of discovery and invention*. New York: HarperCollins.

Csikszentmihalyi, M., S. Abuhamdeh, and J. Nakamura. 2005. Flow. In *Handbook of competence and motivation*, ed. A. J. Elliot and C. S. Dweck. New York: Guilford, 598–608.

Csikszentmihalyi, M., and J. LeFevre. 1989. Optimal experience in work and leisure. *J. Pers. Soc. Psychol.* 56:815–822.

Cummins, D. D. 1999. Cheater detection is modified by social rank: The impact of dominance on the evolution of cognitive functions. *Evol. Hum. Behav.* 20:229–248.

Darwin, C. 1872. *The expression of the emotions in man and animals*. London: John Murray.

Dawes, R. M. 1993. Prediction of the future versus an understanding of the past: A basic asymmetry. *Am. J. Psychol.* 106:1–24.

Decety, J., and J. A. Sommerville. 2008. Action representation as the bedrock of social cognition: A developmental neuroscience perspective. In *The Oxford handbook of human action*, ed. E. Morsella, J. A. Bargh, and P. M. Gollwitzer. New York: Oxford University Press.

Dehaene, S., M. Kerszberg, and J. Changeux. 2001. A neuronal model of a global workspace in effortful cognitive tasks. In *Cajal and consciousness: Scientific approaches to consciousness on the centennial of Ramón y Cajal's textura*, ed. P. C. Marijuán. New York: New York Academy of Sciences, 152–165.

Dell, G. S., L. K. Burger, and W. R. Svec. 1997. Language production and serial order: A functional analysis and a model. *Psychol. Rev.* 104:123–147.

Di Mascio, A., R. W. Boyd, M. Greenblatt, and H. C. Solomon. 1955. The psychiatric interview (a sociophysiologic study). *Dis. Nerv. Syst.* 16:4–9.

Dijksterhuis, A., and J. A. Bargh. 2001. The perception–behavior expressway: Automatic effects of social perception on social behavior. In *Advances in experimental social psychology*, ed. M. P. Zanna. San Diego, CA: Academic Press, 1–40.

Dijksterhuis, A., J. A. Bargh, and J. Miedema. 2000. Of men and mackerels: Attention and automatic behavior. In *Subjective experience in social cognition and behavior*, ed. H. Bless and J. P. Forgas. Philadelphia: Psychology Press, 36–51.

Dimberg, U. 1982. Facial reactions to facial expressions. *Psychophysiology* 19:643–647.

Dougherty, K. M., and J. M. Johnston. 1996. Overlearning, fluency, and automaticity. *Behav. Anal.* 19:289–292.

Dryer, D. C., and L. M. Horowitz. 1997. When do opposites attract? Interpersonal complementarity versus similarity. *J. Pers. Soc. Psychol.* 72:592–603.

Dunn, J., and C. Hughes. 2001. "I got some swords and you're dead!": Antisocial behavior, friendship, and moral sensibility in young children. *Child Development* 72:491–505.

Ehrenreich, B. 2006. *Dancing in the streets*. New York: Metropolitan.

Epley, N., and T. Gilovich. 1999. Just going along: Nonconscious priming and conformity to social pressure. *J. Exp. Soc. Psychol.* 35:578–589.

Erber, R., D. M. Wegner, and N. Therriault. 1996. On being cool and collected: Mood regulation in anticipation of social interaction. *J. Pers. Soc. Psychol.* 70:757–766.

Fadiga, L., L. Fogassi, G. Pavesi, and G. Rizzolatti. 1995. Motor facilitation during action observation: A magnetic simulation study. *J. Neurophysiol.* 73:2608–2611.

Farrer, C., N. Franck, J. Paillard, and M. Jeannerod. 2003. The role of proprioception in action recognition. *Consciousness and Cognition: An International Journal* 12:609–619.

Festinger, L. 1957. *A theory of cognitive dissonance*. Oxford: Row, Peterson.

Field, T. 1994. The effects of mother's physical and emotional unavailability on emotion regulation. *Monographs of the Society for Research in Child Development* 59:208–227.

Field, T., B. T. Healy, and W. G. LeBlanc. 1989. Sharing and synchrony of behavior states and heart rate in nondepressed versus depressed mother–infant interactions. *Infant Behav. Dev.* 12:357–376.

Finkel, E. J., W. K. Campbell, A. B. Brunell, A. N. Dalton, S. J. Scarbeck, and T. L. Chartrand. 2006. High-maintenance interaction: Inefficient social coordination impairs self-regulation. *J. Pers. Soc. Psychol.* 91:456–475.

Fiske, A. P. 1992. The four elementary forms of sociality: Framework for a unified theory of social relations. *Psychol. Rev.* 99:689–723.

Fiske, A. P. 2000. Complementarity theory: Why human social capacities evolved to require cultural complements. *Pers. Soc. Psychol. Rev.* 4:76–94.

Fiske, S. T. 2008. Core social motivations: Views from the couch, consciousness, classroom, computers, and collectives. In *Handbook of motivation science*, ed. J. Y. Shah and W. L. Gardner. New York: Guilford, 3–22.

Fitts, P. M., and M. I. Posner. 1967. *Learning and skilled performance in human performance.* Belmont, CA: Brooks/Cole.

Förster, J., N. Liberman, and R. S. Friedman. 2007. Seven principles of goal activation: A systematic approach to distinguishing goal priming from priming of non-goal constructs. *Pers. Soc. Psychol. Rev.* 11:211–233.

Fridlund, A. J. 1997. The new ethology of human facial expressions. In *The psychology of facial expression: Studies in emotion and social interaction, 2nd series,* ed. J. A. Russell and J. M. Fernández-Dols. New York: Cambridge University Press, 103–129.

Frijda, N. H. 1986. *The emotions.* Cambridge: Cambridge University Press.

Galinsky, A. D., G. Ku, and C. S. Wang. 2005. Perspective-taking and self–other overlap: Fostering social bonds and facilitating social coordination. *Group Process. Intergroup Relat.* 8:109–124.

Gangestad, S. W., and J. A. Simpson. 2000. The evolution of human mating: Trade-offs and strategic pluralism. *Behav. Brain Sci.* 23:573–587.

Garrod, S. C., and A. Anderson. 1987. Saying what you mean in dialogue: A study in conceptual and semantic co-ordination. *Cognition* 27:181–218.

Goldman, A. I. 2006. *Simulating minds: The philosophy, psychology and neuroscience of mindreading.* New York: Oxford University Press.

Goldman, A., and N. Sebanz. 2005. Simulation, mirroring, and a different argument from error. *Trends Cogn. Sci.* 9:320.

Goldstein, N. J., and R. B. Cialdini. 2007. The spyglass self: A model of vicarious self-perception. *J. Pers. Soc. Psychol.* 92:402–417.

Gottman, J. M., and R. W. Levenson. 1985. A valid procedure for obtaining self-report of affect in marital interaction. *J. Consult. Clin. Psychol.* 53:151–160.

Graziano, W. G., S. M. Smith, L. G. Tassinary, C. R. Sun, and C. Pilkington. 1996. Does imitation enhance memory for faces? Four converging studies. *J. Pers. Soc. Psychol.* 71:874–887.

Griskevicius, V., N. J. Goldstein, C. M. Mortensen, R. B. Cialdini, and D. T. Kenrick. 2006. Going along versus going alone: When fundamental motives facilitate strategic (non)conformity. *J. Pers. Soc. Psychol.* 91:281–294.

Haidt, J. 2003. Elevation and the positive psychology of morality. In *Flourishing: Positive psychology and the life well-lived*, ed. C. L. Keyes and J. Haidt. Washington, DC: American Psychological Association, 275–289.

Haidt, J. 2007. The new synthesis in moral psychology. *Science* 316:998–1002.

Haidt, J., P. Seder, and S. Kesebir. 2008. Hive psychology, happiness, and public policy. *J. Legal Stud. 37:133–156.*

Hamilton, W. D. 1971. Geometry for the selfish herd. *J. Theor. Biol.* 31:295–311.

Hassin, R. R., H. Aarts, and M. J. Ferguson. 2005. Automatic goal inferences. *J. Exp. Soc. Psychol.* 41:129–140.

Hassin, R. R., J. A. Bargh, and S. Zimerman. 2009. Automatic and flexible: The case of nonconscious goal pursuit. *Soc. Cogn.* 27:20–36..

Hatfield, E., J. Cacioppo, and R. L. Rapson. 1992. Emotional contagion. In *Review of personality and social psychology.* vol. 14. ed. M. S. Clark. Newbury Park, CA: Sage, 151–177.

Hatfield, E., J. T. Cacioppo, and R. L. Rapson. 1994. *Emotional contagion.* Cambridge: Cambridge University Press.

Hayes, D. P., and C. Cobb. 1982. Cycles of spontaneous conversation and long term isolation. In *Interaction rhythms: Periodicity in communicative behavior*, ed. M. Davis. New York: Human Sciences Press, 319–339.

Hektner, J. M., J. A. Schmidt, and M. Csikszentmihalyi. 2007. *Experience Sampling Method: Measuring the quality of everyday life.* Thousand Oaks, CA: Sage.

Heerey, E. A., and A. M. Kring. 2007. Interpersonal consequences of social anxiety. *J. Abnorm. Psychol.* 116:125–134.

Hill, S. E., and D. M. Buss. 2008. The mere presence of opposite-sex others on judgments of sexual and romantic desirability: Opposite effects for men and women. *Personality and Social Psychology Bulletin* 34:635–647.

Hodges, S., and D. M. Wegner. 1997. Automatic and controlled empathy. In *Empathic accuracy*, ed. W. J. Ickes. New York: Guilford, 311–339.

Hommel, B. 2004. Event files: Feature binding in and across perception and action. *Trends Cogn. Sci.* 8:494–500.

Jackson, P. L., E. Brunet, A. N. Meltzoff, and J. Decety. 2006. Empathy examined through the neural mechanisms involved in imagining how I feel versus how you feel pain. *Neuropsychologia* 44:752–761.

Jackson, S., and M. Csikszentmihalyi. 1999. *Flow in sports: The keys to optimal experiences and performances*. Champaign, IL: Human Kinetics.

James, W. 1890/1981. *The principles of psychology*. Cambridge: Harvard University Press.

Jastrow, J. 1906. *The subconscious*. New York: Houghton Mifflin.

Jeannerod, M. 2006. *Motor cognition: What actions tell the self*. Oxford: Oxford University Press.

Johnson, M. K., and J. A. Reeder. 1997. Consciousness as meta-processing. In *Scientific approaches to consciousness*, ed. J. D. Cohen and J. W. Schooler. Mahwah, NJ: Erlbaum, 261–293.

Jones, B. C., L. M. DeBruine, A. C. Little, R. P. Burriss, and D. R. Feinberg. 2007. Social transmission of face preferences among humans. *Proceedings. Biological Sciences* 274:899–903.

Jones, S. S. 2007. Imitation in infancy: The development of mimicry. *Psychol. Sci.* 18:593–599.

Kahneman, D. 1973. *Attention and effort*. Englewood Cliffs, NJ: Prentice-Hall.

Kaplan, H. B., N. R. Burch, and S. W. Bloom. 1964. Physiological covariation and sociometric relationships in small peer groups. In *Psychobiological approaches to social behavior*, ed. P. H. Leiderman and D. Shapiro. Stanford, CA: Stanford University Press, 92–109.

Kaplan, H. B., and S. W. Bloom. 1960. The use of sociological and social-psychological concepts in physiological research: A review of selected experimental studies. *J. Nerv. Ment. Dis.* 131:128–134.

Kawada, C. L. K., G. Oettingen, P. M. Gollwitzer, and J. A. Bargh. 2004. The projection of implicit and explicit goals. *J. Pers. Soc. Psychol.* 86:545–559.

Kawakami, K., H. Young, and J. F. Dovidio. 2002. Automatic stereotyping: Category, trait, and behavioral activations. *Personality and Social Psychology Bulletin* 28:3–15.

Kenrick, D. T., J. M. Ackerman, and S. Ledlow. 2003. Evolutionary social psychology: Adaptive predispositions and human culture. In *Handbook of social psychology*, ed. J. DeLamater. New York: Kluwer Academic/Plenum, 103–122.

Kenrick, D. T., N. L. Li, and J. Butner. 2003. Dynamical evolutionary psychology: Individual decision rules and emergent social norms. *Psychol. Rev.* 110:3–28.

Kenrick, D. T., E. K. Sadalla, G. Groth, and M. R. Trost. 1990. Evolution, traits, and the stages of human courtship: Qualifying the parental investment model. *J. Pers.* 58:97–116.

Kenrick, D. T., and M. R. Trost. 1997. Evolutionary approaches to relationships. In *Handbook of personal relationships: Theory, research, and interventions*, ed. S. Duck. Chichester, UK: Wiley, 151–177.

Kowalski, R. M. 1996. Complaints and complaining: Functions, antecedents, and consequences. *Psychol. Bull.* 119:179–196.

Krakauer, A. H. 2005. Kin selection and cooperative courtship in wild turkeys. *Nature* 434:69–72.

Kurzban, R., and M. R. Leary. 2001. Evolutionary origins of stigmatization: The functions of social exclusion. *Psychological Bulletin* 127:187–208.

Kurzban, R., and S. L. Neuberg. 2005. Managing ingroup and outgroup relationships. In *Handbook of evolutionary psychology*, ed. D. Buss. New York: Wiley, 653–675.

LaFrance, M. 1982. Posture mirroring and rapport. In *Interaction rhythms: Periodicity in communicative behavior*, ed. M. Davis. New York: Human Sciences Press, 279–298.

LaFrance, M., and M. Broadbent. 1976. Group rapport: Posture sharing as a nonverbal indicator. *Group and Organization Studies* 1:328–333.

Lakin, J. L., and T. L. Chartrand. 2003. Using nonconscious behavioral mimicry to create affiliation and rapport. *Psychol. Sci.* 14:334–339.

Leary, M. R. 2004. *The curse of the self: Self-awareness, egotism, and the quality of human life*. New York: Oxford University Press.

Levenson, R. W., and A. M. Ruef. 1997. Physiological aspects of emotional knowledge and rapport. In *Empathic accuracy*, ed. W. Ickes. New York: Guilford, 44–73.

Lipman-Blumen, J. 2006. *The allure of toxic leaders: Why we follow destructive bosses and corrupt politicians—And how we can survive them*. New York: Oxford University Press.

McClintock, M. K. 1981. Social control of the ovarian cycle and the function of estrous synchrony. *Am. Zool.* 21:243–256.

McGrath, J. E., and J. R. Kelly. 1986. *Time and human interaction: Toward a social psychology of time*. New York: Guilford.

McIntosh, D. N. 1996. Facial feedback hypotheses: Evidence, implications, and directions. *Motivation and Emotion* 20:121–147.

Maddux, W. W., E. Mullen, and A. D. Galinsky. 2008. Chameleons bake bigger pies and take bigger pieces: Strategic behavioral mimicry facilitates negotiation outcomes. *J. Exp. Soc. Psychol.* 44:461–468.

Maner, J. K., D. T. Kenrick, D. V. Becker, T. E. Robertson, B. Hofer, S. L. Neuberg, A. W. Delton, J. Butner, and M. Schaller. 2005. Functional projection: How fundamental social motives can bias interpersonal perception. *J. Pers. Soc. Psychol.* 88:63–78.

Markey, P. M., D. C. Funder, and D. J. Ozer. 2003. Complementarity of interpersonal behaviors in dyadic interactions. *Pers. Soc. Psychol. Bull.* 29:1082–1090.

Massimini, F., M. Csikszentmihalyi, and M. Carli. 1987. The monitoring of optimal experience: A tool for psychiatric rehabilitation. *J. Nerv. Ment. Dis.* 175:545–549.

Maurer, R. E., and J. H. Tindall. 1983. Effects of postural congruence on client's perceptions of counselor empathy. *J. Couns. Psychol.* 30:158–163.

Maxwell, J. P., R. S. W. Masters, and J. van der Karnp. 2007. Taking a conscious look at the body schema. *Behav. Brain Sci.* 30:216–217.

McNeill, W. H. 1995. *Keeping together in time: Dance and drill in human history.* Cambridge: Harvard University Press.

Meindl, J. R., S. B. Ehrlich, and J. M. Dukerich. 1985. The romance of leadership. *Adm. Sci. Q.* 30:78–102.

Meltzoff, A. N. 2004. The case for a developmental cognitive science: Theories of people and things. In *Theories of infant development*, ed. G. Bremner and A. Slater. Oxford: Blackwell, 145–173.

Meltzoff, A. N., and M. K. Moore. 1977. Imitation of facial and manual gestures by human neonates. *Science* 198:75–78.

Meltzoff, A. N., and M. K. Moore. 1994. Imitation, memory, and the representation of persons. *Infant Behav. Dev.* 17:83–99.

Miller, G., E. Galanter, and K. Pribram. 1960. *Plans and the structure of behavior.* New York: Holt, Rinehart and Winston.

Moors, A., and J. De Houwer. 2006. Automaticity: A theoretical and conceptual analysis. *Psychol. Bull.* 132:297–326.

Morgan, J. J. B. 1941. The acquisition of motor skills. In *Psychology*, ed. J. J. B. Morgan. New York: Farrar & Rinehart, 202–245.

Morsella, E. 2005. The function of phenomenal states: Supramodular interaction theory. *Psychological Review* 112:1000–1021.

Morsella, E., and M. Miozzo. 2002. Evidence for a cascade model of lexical access in speech production. *J. Exp. Psychol. Learn. Mem. Cogn.* 28:555–563.

Muraven, M., and R. F. Baumeister. 2000. Self-regulation and depletion of limited resources: Does self-control resemble a muscle? *Psychol. Bull.* 126:247–259.

Murray, H. A. 1933. The effect of fear upon estimates of the maliciousness of other personalities. *Journal of Social Psychology* 4:310–329.

Müsseler, J., and B. Hommel. 1997. Blindness to response-compatible stimuli. *J. Exp. Psychol. Hum. Percept. Perform.* 23:861–872.

Navarette, E., and A. Costa. 2004. How much linguistic information is extracted from ignored pictures? Further evidence for a cascade model of speech production. *J. Mem. Lang.* 53:359–377.

Nettle, D. 2005. The wheel of fire and the mating game: Explaining the origins of tragedy and comedy. *J. Cult. Evol. Psychol.* 3:39–56.

Neumann, R., and F. Strack. 2000. "Mood contagion": The automatic transfer of mood between persons. *J. Pers. Soc. Psychol.* 79:211–223.

Niedenthal, P. M. 2007. Embodying emotion. *Science* 316:1002–1005.

Niedenthal, P. M., L. W. Barsalou, P. Winkielman, S. Krauth-Gruber, and F. Ric. 2005. Embodiment in attitudes, social perception, and emotion. *Pers. Soc. Psychol. Rev.* 9:184–211.

Norton, M. I., B. Monin, J. Cooper, and M. A. Hogg. 2003. Vicarious dissonance: Attitude change from the inconsistency of others. *J. Pers. Soc. Psychol.* 85:47–62.

Oullier, O., G. C. de Guzman, K. J. Jantzen, J. Lagarde, and J. A. S. Kelso. 2008. Social coordination dynamics: Measuring human bonding. *Soc. Neurosci.* 3:178–192. Medline:18552971

Pickering, M. J., and S. Garrod. 2004. Towards a mechanistic psychology of dialogue. *Behav. Brain Sci.* 27:169–190.

Pinker, S. 2002. *The blank slate: The modern denial of human nature*. New York: Viking-Penguin.

Preston, S. D., and F. B. M. de Waal. 2002. Empathy: Its ultimate and proximate bases. *Behav. Brain Sci.* 25:1–71.

Prinz, W. 1990. A common coding approach to perception and action. In *Relationships between perception and action*, ed. O. Neumann and W. Prinz. Berlin: Springer-Verlag, 167–201.

Prinz, W. 2003. Experimental approaches to action. In *Agency and self-awareness*, ed. J. Roessler and N. Eilan. Oxford: Oxford University Press, 175–187.

Reber, R., and N. Schwarz. 1999. Effects of perceptual fluency on judgments of truth. *Conscious. Cogn.* 8:338–342.

Reber, R., N. Schwarz, and P. Winkielman. 2004. Processing fluency and aesthetic pleasure: Is beauty in the perceiver's processing experience? *Pers. Soc. Psychol. Rev.* 8:364–382.

Reed, C. L., and M. J. Farah. 1995. The psychological reality of the body schema: A test with normal participants. *J. Exp. Psychol. Hum. Percept. Perform.* 21:334–343.

Reis, H. T., and W. A. Collins. 2004. Relationships, human behavior, and psychological science. *Curr. Dir. Psychol. Sci.* 13:233–237.

Richardson, M. J., K. L. Marsh, R. Isenhower, J. Goodman, and R. C. Schmidt. 2007. Rocking together: Dynamics of intentional and unintentional interpersonal coordination. *Hum. Mov. Sci.* 26:867–891.

Richardson, M. J., K. L. Marsh, and R. C. Schmidt. 2005. Effects of visual and verbal couplings on unintentional interpersonal coordination. *J. Exp. Psychol. Hum. Percept. Perform.* 31:62–79.

Richeson, J. A., and S. Trawalter. 2005. Why do interracial interactions impair executive function? A resource depletion account. *J. Pers. Soc. Psychol.* 88:934–947.

Rogers, S. J., and B. F. Pennington. 1991. A theoretical approach to the deficits in infantile autism. *Development and Psychopathology* 3:137–162.

Ruys, K. I., and D. A. Stapel. 2008. The secret life of emotions. *Psychol. Sci.* 19:385–391.

Sassenberg, K., and G. B. Moskowitz. 2005. Don't stereotype, think different! Overcoming automatic stereotype activation by mindset priming. *J. Exp. Soc. Psychol.* 41:506–514.

Scheflen, A. E. 1964. The significance of posture in communication systems. *Psychiatry* 27:316–331.

Schmidt, R. C., C. Carello, and M. T. Turvey. 1990. Phase transitions and critical fluctuations in the visual coordination of rhythmic movements between people. *J. Exp. Psychol. Hum. Percept. Perform.* 16:227–247.

Schmidt, R. C., and M. T. Turvey. 1994. Phase-entrainment dynamics of visually coupled rhythmic movements. *Biol. Cybern.* 70:369–376.

Schmitt, D. P., L. Alcalay, J. Allik, L. Ault, I. Austers, K. L. Bennett, et al. 2003. Universal sex differences in the desire for sexual variety: Tests from 52 nations, 6 continents, and 13 islands. *Journal of Personality and Social Psychology* 85:85–104.

Schmitt, D. P. 2005. Fundamentals of human mating strategies. In *The handbook of evolutionary psychology*, ed. D. M. Buss. Hoboken, NJ: Wiley, 258–291.

Seligman, M. E. P. 1970. On the generality of the laws of learning. *Psychological Review* 77:406–418.

Shiffrin, R. M., and W. Schneider. 1977. Controlled and automatic human information processing: II. Perceptual learning, automatic attending, and a general theory. *Psychol. Rev.* 84:127–190.

Simner, M. L. 1971. Newborns' response to the cry of another infant. *Dev. Psychol.* 5:136–150.

Singer, R. N. 2002. Preperformance state, routines, and automaticity: What does it take to realize expertise in self-paced events? *J. Sport Exerc. Psychol.* 24:359–375.

Smuts, B. B., and R. W. Smuts. 1993. Male aggression and sexual coercion of females in nonhuman primates and other mammals: Evidence and theoretical implications. *Adv. Stud. Behav.* 22:1–63.

Strack, F., L. Martin, and S. Stepper. 1988. Inhibiting and facilitating conditions of the human smile: A nonobtrusive test of the facial feedback hypothesis. *Journal of Personality and Social Psychology* 54:768–777.

Sutherland, D. 1997. The development of mature gait. *Gait Posture* 6:163–170.

Thelen, M. H., D. J. Miller, P. A. Fehrenbach, and N. M. Frautschi. 1983. Reactions to being imitated: Effects of perceived motivation. *Merrill-Palmer Quarterly* 29:159–167.

Tiedens, L. Z., R. M. Chow, and M. M. Unzueta. 2007. Complementary contrast and assimilation: Interpersonal theory and the social functions of contrast and assimilation effects. In *The Social Psychology of Contrast and Assimilation*, ed. D. Stapel and J. Suls. New York: Psychology Press.

Tiedens, L. Z., and A. R. Fragale. 2003. Power moves: Complementarity in submissive and dominant nonverbal behavior. *Journal of Personality and Social Psychology* 84:558–568.

Tiedens, L. Z., M. M. Unzueta, and M. J. Young. 2007. An unconscious desire for hierarchy? The motivated perception of dominance complementary in task partners. *J. Pers. Soc. Psychol.* 93:402–414.

Tognoli, E., J. Lagarde, G. C. De Guzman, and J. A. S. Kelso. 2007. The phi complex as a neuromarker of human social coordination. *Proc. Natl. Acad. Sci. USA* 104:8190–8195.

Tracey, T. J., J. M. Ryan, and B. Jaschik-Herman. 2001. Complementarity of interpersonal circumplex traits. *Pers. Soc. Psychol. Bull.* 27:786–797.

Trivers, R. L. 1972. Parental investment and sexual selection. In *Sexual selection and the descent of man, 1871–1971*, ed. B. H. Campbell. Chicago: Aldine, 136–179.

Tronick, E. 1989. Emotions and emotional communication in infants. *American Psychologist* 44:112–119.

Vallacher, R. R., A. Nowak, and M. Zochowski. 2005. Dynamics of social coordination: The synchronization of internal states in close relationships. *Interact. Stud.* 6:35–52.

Van Baaren, R. B., W. W. Maddux, T. L. Chartrand, C. de Bouter, and A. van Knippenberg. 2003. It takes two to mimic: Behavioural consequences of self-construals. *Journal of Personality and Social Psychology* 84:1093–1102.

Van Knippenberg, A., and R. B. van Baaren. 2006. Baboons, brains, babies and bonding: A multidisciplinary approach to mimicry. In *Bridging social psychology: Benefits of transdisciplinary approaches*, ed. P. van Lange. Mahwah, NJ: Erlbaum, 173–178.

Van Vugt, M., R. Hogan, and R. Kaiser. 2008. Leadership, followership, and evolution: Some lessons from the past. *Am. Psychol.* 63:182–196.

Vaughan, K. B., and J. T. Lanzetta. 1980. Vicarious instigation and conditioning of facial expressive and autonomic responses to a model's expressive display of pain. *J. Pers. Soc. Psychol.* 38:909–923.

Vaughan, K. B., and J. T. Lanzetta. 1981. The effect of modification of expressive displays on vicarious emotional arousal. *Journal of Experimental Social Psychology* 17:16–30.

Vohs, K. D., R. F. Baumeister, B. J. Schmeichel, J. M. Twenge, N. M. Nelson, and D. M. Tice. 2008. Making choices impairs subsequent self-control: A limited-resource account of decision making, self-regulation, and active initiative. *J. Pers. Soc. Psychol.* 94:883–898.

Warneken, F., and M. Tomasello. 2006. Altruistic helping in human infants and young chimpanzees. *Science* 311:1301–1303.

Watts, D. P. 1998. Coalitionary mate guarding by male chimpanzees at Ngogo, Kibale National Park, Uganda. *Behav. Ecol. Sociobiol.* 44:43–55.

Weller, L., and A. Weller. 1993. Human menstrual synchrony: A critical assessment. *Neurosci. Biobehav. Rev.* 17:427–439.

Whaley, B. B., and M. A. Golden. 2000. Communicating with persons who stutter: Perceptions and strategies. In *Handbook of communication and people with disabilities: Research and application*, ed. D. O. Braithwaite and T. L. Thompson. Mahwah, NJ: Erlbaum.

Whittlesea, B. W. A. 1993. Illusions of familiarity. *J. Exp. Psychol. Learn. Mem. Cogn.* 19:1235–1253.

Whittlesea, B. W. A., L. L. Jacoby, and K. Girard. 1990. Illusions of immediate memory: Evidence of an attributional basis for feelings of familiarity and perceptual quality. *J. Mem. Lang.* 29:716–732.

Wicker, B., C. Keysers, J. Plailly, J. P. Royet, V. Gallese, and G. Rizzolatti. 2003. Both of us disgusted in My insula: the common neural basis of seeing and feeling disgust. *Neuron* 40:655–664.

Williams, K. D., J. P. Forgas, and W. von Hippel, eds. 2005. *The social outcast: Ostracism, social exclusion, rejection, and bullying*. New York: Psychology Press.

Williams, L. E., J. Y. Huang, and J. A. Bargh. (Forthcoming). The scaffolded mind: Higher mental processes are grounded in early experience of the physical world. *European Journal of Social Psychology*.

Wilson, S. M., A. P. Saygin, M. I. Sereno, and M. Iacoboni. 2004. Listening to speech activates motor areas involved in speech production. *Nat. Neurosci.* 7:701–702.

Wiltermuth, S. S., and C. Heath. 2009. Synchrony and cooperation. *Psychological Science* 20:1–5.

Wood, J. A. 2006. NLP revisited: Nonverbal communications and signals of trustworthiness. *J. Pers. Sell. Sales Manage.* 26:197–204.

Yabar, Y., L. Johnston, L. Miles, and V. Peace. 2006. Implicit behavioural mimicry of an in-group and an out-group member. *Journal of Nonverbal Behavior* 30:97–113.

Zajonc, R. B., P. Pietromonaco, and J. Bargh. 1982. Independence and interaction of affect and cognition. In *Affect and cognition*, ed. M. S. Clark and S. Fiske. Hillsdale, NJ: Erlbaum, 211–227.

15 The Thalamic Gateway: How the Meditative Training of Attention Evolves toward Selfless Transformations of Consciousness

James H. Austin

The faculty of voluntarily bringing back a wandering attention, over and over again, is the very root of judgment, character, and will.
William James (1918, 424)

William James did more than emphasize attention's salient attributes. He foresaw the current trend to apply rigorous research methods to investigate the contemplative path. Back in 1901, James even chose "Religion and Neurology" as his title for the first lecture in the series that would later expand into his classic, *The Varieties of Religious Experience*.

In this new millennium, a cadre of neuroscientists has taken up the challenging task of studying how the brain responds during a formal meditative practice of training attention. These pages explore a central question: How could such a training program not only enable meditators to experience sudden, brief, extraordinary states of selfless insight but also help them gradually to transform their traits of judgment, character, and will?

Selfless insight is not a new topic, though its intimate relationship with attention becomes the central theme of this essay. Early exemplars of a meditative approach to this general topic area were Siddhartha, the Buddha—who became enlightened while meditating two-and-a-half millennia ago—and then Jesus of Nazareth, whose spiritual path included 40 days and nights in solitude in the desert wilderness.

In the 20th century, writings by the psychiatrist Richard Bucke, about "cosmic consciousness," and by D. T. Suzuki, about the selfless Zen Buddhist states of *kensho* and *satori*, emphasized that these "awakened states" were not culture bound. They were states characterized by extraordinary degrees of wordless insight–wisdom (Sanskrit: *prajna*), and their liberations from overconditioning were often followed by salutary changes in traits of character.

Are we to disregard enlightened "peak experiences" as esoteric glimpses of unreality that mystics have overinterpreted for centuries? Or can we view the basic phenomena of the advanced states from a more neurobiological perspective? If the latter, then these states can also be seen to illuminate the ways that long-term meditative training helps sponsor substantial psychophysiological transformations of consciousness (Austin 1998, 2006, 2009a,b).

A Working Hypothesis

The hypothesis developed here proposes, first, that the meditative training of attentiveness sets the stage for deep tectonic events to occur in the thalamus and, second, that these thalamic changes then create a physiological shift so pivotal that the whole sense of self drops out of consciousness. Topics will begin to unfold in pairs, starting with our two cortical systems of attention, followed next by the two basic styles of meditation, and then by our two versions of processing ordinary reality. Initially, these sets of paired concepts might seem to be in mutual opposition. Later, however, they will converge on a fourth crucial fact: The human thalamus has two tiers of nuclei. This observation makes possible the proposal that all four overlapping topic areas coalesce in interactions that are mutually complementary. Indeed, such pairings can be reconciled, almost like yin and yang, in the context of their larger creative partnership.

The main hypothesis and its corollaries represent the perspectives of an academic neurologist. After starting Zen meditative practice late in life, the author happened to experience two representative extraordinary states of consciousness, *kensho* and internal absorption. Interested readers can access lines of evidence elsewhere that amplify each sequence of the explanations being proposed (Austin 1998, 2006, 2008, 2009a,b).

Why begin with attention? Because attention is our vanguard mental function. Indeed, whether we conceptualize attentiveness as effortful or effortless, as directed internally or externally, consciously or unconsciously, attention's sharp point serves as the foremost tip that impales stimuli, anchors them, and permits them to be processed as perceptions.

Dorsal–Ventral: Our Two Lateral Cortical Systems of Attention

When you read this sentence, you are probably looking *down* at a printed page or computer screen close to your body. Our brain's *dorsal* attention system directs these more *voluntary* forms of attention (Fox, Corbetta, Vincent, and Raichle 2006). The "top–down" executive functions of this dorsal system usually focus on things that are nearby, helping us reach out and respond to tasks that we might anticipate will be reasonably well-defined. The dorsal system's first assignment is to pay attention selectively to any *earlier* cues that might prove helpful. Next we deploy this system to monitor each increment of the data as it comes in. The results help us adjust our ongoing responses, for the first target could have moved slightly, and new packets of incoming data can be conflicting.

Figure 15.1 illustrates that this dorsal attention network arches upward toward the parietal lobe and follows a trajectory rising high up over the cerebral convexity. Two major modules reside on this upper, occipital → *parietal* → frontal path: (1) the intraparietal sulcus (IPS) and (2) the region around the frontal eye field (FEF). The right dorsal system attends chiefly to the *left* side of its spatial environment. The left dorsal system attends chiefly to the *right* side.

The *ventral* attention system serves other needs. It specializes in reflexive, *involuntary* types of diffuse attention (Fox, Corbetta, Vincent, and Raichle 2006). Its "bottom–up" functions respond automatically to each fresh need to *disengage* attention. Remaining on standby alert, this lower system is poised effortlessly to detect and to shift attention. Where? Toward *any kind of novel stimulus that might enter unexpectedly*. Enter from where? *From either the right or left side* of the environment. Figure 15.1 illustrates how the cortical networks of this ventral system pursue a *downward* and forward course as they stream from the occipital lobe on through the temporal and frontal lobes.

Please note a crucial asymmetry. It will be two major modules over on the right side (*not* those that figure 15.1 shows here on the left) that mediate this ventral system's dominant *global* physiological commitment to *both* sides of the environment. These modules are (1) the *right* temporoparietal junction (TPJ) and (2) the *right* inferior frontal cortex (IFC). Why is the right-sided cerebral dominance of this bilateral, wide-open attentiveness so important? Because it implies that the right ventral system is free from that heavy commitment to language with which evolution burdened our left frontotemporal cortex. It also suggests one reason why profound insights can strike wordlessly.

The Two Basic Categories of Meditation Cultivate Attention in Different Ways

Meditation does not follow a single monolithic tradition. Still, most systems of Buddhist meditative training serve essentially to cultivate, exercise, and refine one's attentive capacities. Worth emphasizing in this respect is the fact that the two generic categories of meditation—concentrative and receptive—are mutually reinforcing.

• *Concentrative* meditation can be viewed as a *voluntary*, top–down practice. Meditators often begin by lowering their gaze, focusing on one spot, and attending to the simpler sensations associated with the way air passes in and out as they breathe. Further mental effort is required to focus narrowly and exclusively. When applying such a keen mental edge to still greater degrees of intention, it also feels like one is "paying" attention. When meditators choose to intensify their practice, the momentum of this

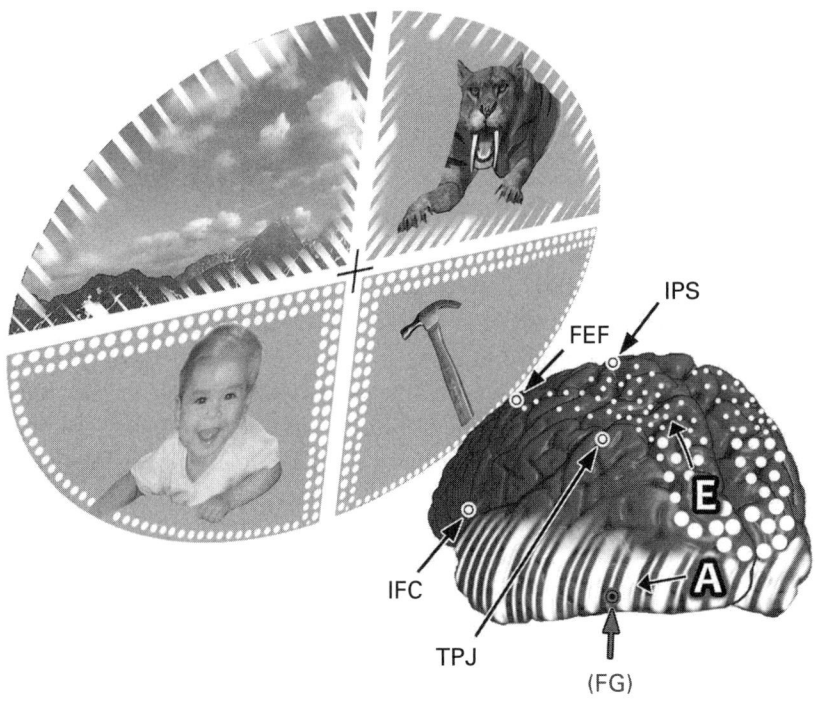

Figure 15.1
Inherent visual efficiencies of the dorsal and ventral attention systems. This view imagines the different kinds of scenery a brain might attend to with optimum visual efficiency as observed from a vantage point behind its left hemisphere. The smaller black letters at the top of the brain identify two major *dorsal* regions: the intraparietal sulcus (IPS) and the frontal eye field (FEF). We activate both modules during our executive, "top–down" visual attention. Running through each of them, in turn, is the overlapping trajectory of the upper parietal → frontal processing system (shown as white circles). Why do rows of similar white circles also surround the *lower* visual quadrants containing the baby (at left) and the hammer (at right)? This is to suggest that this dorsal attention system can attend to the handling of items somewhat more efficiently when they are located down in the corresponding *lower* parts of the visual field *closer* to our body. In contrast, the two other modules identified reside at a lower level. They are the temporoparietal junction (TPJ) and the inferior frontal cortex (IFC). We activate them (chiefly on the *right* side) during involuntary "bottom–up" attention. The diagonal white lines suggest the temporal and frontal networks that can interact with each lower module of this ventral attention system. Why do similar arrays of diagonal white lines also surround the upper visual quadrants? The purpose is to suggest that this *ventral* temporal → frontal system stays on the alert, ready to detect items at a distance in the *upper* parts of the visual (and auditory) field. There's an obvious survival advantage in quickly seeing a sabertooth tiger and in detecting its noises while this tiger is still *a long distance away* from one's body. The *FG* in parentheses points toward the left fusiform gyrus, hidden on the undersurface of the temporal lobe. (The next figure, figure 15.2, goes on to illustrate certain aspects of the related egocentric (E) and allocentric (A) processing streams when their pathways partially overlap and their processing functions are governed by these modules of the adjacent dorsal and ventral attention systems, respectively.)

more highly focused concentration sometimes carries them into one-pointed modes of attention. These can evolve into preliminary states termed absorptions (Austin 1998, 470–518, 589–590; Austin 2006, 313–325, 451).

• *Receptive* meditation is more *effortless, involuntary,* and *inclusive.* With practice, one learns to relax, *let go,* and tap "bottom–up" *pr*eattentive, intuitive mechanisms. These remain so openly available, so diffusely attuned, that they notice any stimulus arising from *anywhere* in the environment. Having begun as the open expression of a bare interest, receptive modes of automatic processing later evolve into more universal forms of choiceless awareness. Some of their increasing clarity reflects the fact that they then also become empty of thoughts. It is this clear wordless, thought-free, spacious orientation that characterizes the much later spontaneous shifts into the advanced states of insight–wisdom (Austin 1998, 519–624; 2006, 327–387; 2009b, 123–219).

In actual practice, meditators tend not only to drift back and forth from one style to the other but discover how often discursive word–thoughts and emotions enter their mental field. The way such intrusive events leap from one branching topic to the next has led to this familiar phenomenon's being known as "monkey mind."

Self–Other; Dorsal–Ventral: Our Two Versions of Processing Ordinary "Reality"

The skin surface divides what's inside our body from what's obviously outside. Brain circuits are programmed to perceive this personal "Self" inside as separate from that "other" world outside. Our pathways along the dorsal trajectory evolved in practical ways. They specialized in grasping things close at hand (like a hammer) and in performing skilled tasks *down near our own bodies* (like holding a baby; see figure 15.1). Using two accurate senses—touch and proprioception—we become highly efficient in solving these nearby sensorimotor tasks.

In contrast, the ventral pathways evolved in other ways. Some of their circuits were specialized to detect and discern faint stimuli arriving from events *off at a distance.* Surviving generations became increasingly skilled at using their two distant early warning channels: vision and hearing. We call these our "special senses." Vision and hearing each have a processing advantage for detecting a faint potential threat from the outside world while it is still far away and often located *above* the visual or auditory horizon. Figure 15.1 includes clouds high in the sky, far above distant mountains, to reinforce this point.

Note that when you return to scan figure 15.1, you'll need to adjust your mental set. As you examine the anatomical origins of each dorsal or ventral processing stream carefully, you can begin to appreciate why each one might be associated with its own particular reduced "wiring cost." For example, the *upper* part of the occipital cortex is the part that helps us "see" things down in the *lower* quadrants of the visual environment. Note that it lies closest to the parietal stream. In contrast, the *lower* part of the occipital cortex (the part that helps us "see" things out there in the *upper* visual quadrants) lies closest to the temporal stream. Could each of these shorter circuits translate into greater processing efficiencies? The shorter transit time inherent in the (upper) occipital → parietal path could confer a physiological advantage designed instantly to service one's task-solving behaviors in the lower visual fields. Less so the distant early warning capacities of its lower counterpart. Its reaction times may take a few more milliseconds to process events seen in the upper visual fields (Sdoia, Couyoumdjian, and Ferlazzo 2004).[1]

These slight differences in reaction times are only the preamble. They serve to introduce us to the next topic: Crucial psychophysiological differences exist between the two frames of reference. Many parietal functions are *Self*-referential, meaning Self-centered. In contrast, many temporal functions are *other*-referential, meaning anything external that lies outside a person's skin.

Egocentric–Allocentric Distinctions

The same two versions—Self–other—also go by two different names. Only the first of these names is likely to sound familiar.

• This *egocentric* version establishes an implicit Self-referential point of view. The witnessing viewer is always in the center. Why is our egocentric perspective so viewer-centered? Because when sensory signals come in from external items, the brain refers them immediately back into hardwired circuits that represent our body image, our *soma*. These pages capitalize the *S* in our personal construct of Self solely as an expedient to emphasize the inevitable biological result: Consciousness keeps assigning its highest priority to these Self-centered processes that directly reinforce our personal frame of reference. Suppose, for example, we are holding a hammer in one hand and a nail in the other. Our normal Self-centered point of view helps us ask, and then answer, a practical spatial question: "*Where* is each item in relation to me and my body?"

Let us follow the successive somatic steps in this normal egocentric processing (E) along their parietal path. We see them ascend through the angular gyrus on an upward trajectory. Soon they will be further incorporated into the somatosensory association functions of the superior partial lobule (to be shown later in figure 15.2).[2]

• In contrast, the other-referential version proceeds from an *allocentric* perspective (*allo* meaning other; A in figure 15.1). Its first role is simply to identify. Having asked, "*What* is it?" its pattern recognition functions now identify unfamiliar objects. Adjacent circuits interpret the nuances of what such objects *mean*. From this first allo-vantage point, each target exists both as a *separate* object "out there" and in relation to *other* things out there in *that* environment. Moreover, as just discussed, evolution sculptured a different role for the nearby temporal lobe networks. Temporal networks are programmed by experience to detect and discern the particular stimuli that enter from our two other special sensory avenues: seeing and hearing. The relay for auditory information is the shorter of the two. After auditory impulses speed from the medial geniculate nucleus up to the primary auditory cortex, we decode the meaning of what we hear in other regions of the temporal lobe. Our three-dimensional listening skills are even more globally attuned than our visual skills. For example, they are keenly sensitive to the faint rustling sounds that can arise far *behind* the listener (say, from a sabertooth tiger lurking in the remote underbrush to the rear).

The object-centered perspective inherent in allocentric processing begins anonymously during its early milliseconds, and its pathway pursues a lower course. Figures 15.1 and 15.2 suggest that its initial downward trajectory leads toward the fusiform gyrus hidden on the undersurface of the temporal–occipital junction. Its branches then stream forward on through the rest of the temporal lobe toward the inferior frontal region.

Two versions of reality? Do these two different cortical systems of attention that we identified earlier really initiate two different frames of reference that process perceptions in such a curious manner? Is any other evidence more convincing?

Data from Stroke Patients Confirm the Separate Ego- and Allo-Pathways

Obviously, to meet the needs of our ordinary perceptions, consciousness must quickly integrate these two dissimilar versions. Normally, this merger happens seamlessly as our brain quickly blends its other-centered version into our Self-centered processing. The result: A single image (the Self-referential version) dominates consciousness in "our mind's eye." (A precedent exists: The brain asserts one preeminent image—that of our "master eye"—over the visuospatial percepts of the other, subordinate eye.) However, the basic fact that two versions exist and that the Self-centered path pursues a different course emerges clearly in the evidence reported by Hillis and colleagues (Hillis, Newhart, Heidler, Barker, Herskovits, and Degaonkar 2005). They collected two groups of neurological patients who had small strokes. Parietal blood vessels were blocked acutely in one group, and temporal blood vessels in the other.

Suppose the stroke damaged the parietal functions of the *right* angular gyrus. Neurological examination then disclosed a characteristic Self-centered visual defect. The patients could no longer attend to one entire area of visual space—namely, their whole left visual field. This visual defect was a hemineglect referable to their own *left* side. Imagine that you were one such patient and that you were instructed to look at the

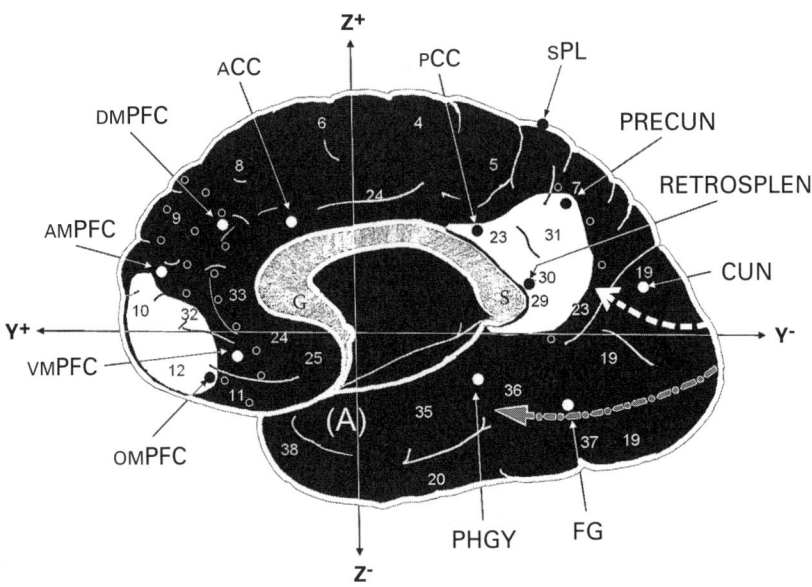

Figure 15.2
Directions of the two processing streams in a medial view of the right hemisphere. This view represents the inside surface of the *right* side of the brain. The large white area at the viewer's left (and its halo of small open circles) occupies much of the medial prefrontal cortex. Here, normal subjects show high levels of metabolic activity in positron-emission tomography scans even when they are resting passively. At right, the other large white area represents our second major metabolic "hot spot." It lies deep in the medial parietal region near the splenium of the corpus callosum. This extensive region includes the *precuneus, retrosplenial cortex*, and the *posterior cingulate cortex*). When presented with an external stimulus in daily life, we often need to know the following: *Where* is *it* in relation to *Me*? To answer this question, cortical sequences along this whole Self-centered path contribute multiple circumstantial details. Off to the right, a short, curved white dashed line hints at the course taken by a medial branch that could add to the flow of answers supplied by this dorsal *egocentric* processing stream (E in figure 15.1). In daily life, we also need to identify objects and other stimuli. Therefore, we ask different questions— those of the "*What* is it?" type. Beginning lower down is the longer, gray, arrowheaded, dashed *and* dotted line. This represents the major initial, ventral direction of the *allocentric* stream (A in figure 15.1). The early course of this pathway runs along the undersurface of the temporal lobe. The pattern-recognition sequences along this ventral path provide the other frame of reference that answers our question about identity. More often than not, illustrations in the literature use the left hemisphere to show standard anatomical details, the side that seems more familiar to the general reader. The medial view of the *right* hemisphere is shown here instead. The point is to emphasize that this right side is involved in crucial representations of bottom–up attention and allocentric processing, both normally and as the diverse mechanisms of *kensho* unfold— through activations and deactivations—into selfless insight. Starting at the left, in the frontal

Figure 15.2

(continued)

lobe, mPFC refers to four subdivisions of the medial prefrontal cortex: orbital, ventral, anterior, and dorsal. Elsewhere, aCC, anterior cingulate cortex; pCC, posterior cingulate cortex; sPL, superior parietal lobule; PRECUN, precuneus; RETROSPLEN, retrosplenial cortex; CUN, cuneus; FG, fusiform gyrus; PHGY, parahippocampal gyrus; (A), amygdala, in parentheses to indicate that it is a *sub*cortical structure. The long, gray curved area in the center represents the corpus callosum. Its fibers cross over, constantly linking this right hemisphere in a dialogue with its partner. In front, G refers to its genu; S refers to its splenium. The lines of the vertical Z and horizontal Y axes suggest how it becomes possible to specify the locations of different sites on the cortical surface by using numbers that describe their spatial coordinates.

cross-hair (+) centering four quadrants of scenes similar to those illustrated in figure 15.1. You would neglect seeing everything on the left half of external space—the entire baby, the mountains, and the clouds. It is important to note that this defect of visual *attention* involves the right dorsal attentional system and stops all egocentric processing. It is *not* the absolute blindness caused by a different lesion that would block visual processing because it had destroyed the left optic nerve or the right visual cortex.

However, the other neurological patients had a distinctively different visual defect. It did not involve a Self-centered frame of reference, because these patients had occluded a ventral blood vessel. As a result, their dominant allocentric pathway had been interrupted lower down in their *right inferior* temporal lobe (the lower arrow in figure 15.2). These patients could no longer use their bottom–up system of attention and allocentric processing to decode the visual stimuli from external objects into patterns that could be recognized and identified (Austin 2009b, 49–83).

Why was this other-referential defect so different? Remember that the right side of the ventral attention system is dominant for *both* sides of the environment. This helps us understand why the patients were inattentive in a particular way. Why couldn't they detect the left half of any discrete object, anywhere? This defect wasn't restricted to only one half of the outside space in which that object happened to be located (right or left, as viewed from the patients' standpoint). To appreciate this seemingly counterintuitive finding, suppose, again, you were a patient with such an allocentric defect and were also instructed to look at the same central cross-hair. Now, you would neglect seeing (1) the tiger's right eye, ear, and right paw; (2) the head of the hammer beneath; (3) the baby's right eye, ear, and right arm; and (4) the darker mountains and clouds in the scenery off to the left.

To summarize, recent evidence suggests that normally—in the early milliseconds— important physiological events unfold in our cortex along separate dorsal and ventral pathways. Two separate sets of conceptual links start to emerge from the partial overlappings within each of these two diverging upper and lower processing pathways:

- One cluster of shared concepts links our *dorsal* cortical system of top–down attention with the concentrative category of meditation, and with the two upper pathways (on the right and left sides equally) through which we process incoming messages that we refer to our Self.
- Another cluster of shared concepts links the *ventral* cortical system of bottom–up attention with the receptive category of meditation, and with the lower pathway—especially on the right side—through which flow the messages that serve global versions of other-referential processing.

Perception becomes infinitely more complicated during later milliseconds, as soon as sensory messages spread from the more hardwired image of our soma to ramify farther into the softer domains of the psyche.

How the Psychic Self Relates to Its Exteroceptive and Interoceptive Environment

The early constructs of our somatic Self are easy to appreciate. When reaching out to grasp an apple, we can actually feel our arm move, see our soma in action. In contrast, the attributes of our psychic Self are intangible and more elusive, because their blend of softer functions has interactive origins that are cognitive, emotional, and instinctual (Austin 1998, 37–47).

The imperatives of this psychic Self might be described further using psychological categories loosely equivalent to those of an "*I–Me–Mine*." While this triad's assets have survival value, their liabilities generate serious problems. For example, our sovereign *I* often expresses its arrogance and aggressive instincts. Its partner, the fearful *Me*, can be battered physically and feels besieged emotionally. The *Mine* is our possessive Self, readily captured by its greedy cravings and cherishing each of its rigid opinions.

Recent neuroimaging research correlates relevant higher level functions of our psychic Self with the networking activities of several major regions in the brain. In figure 15.2, the large white areas emphasize two of the larger sites. First, note their internal location—deep along the midline of the brain. This medial location is a sharp contrast with the way the two attention systems are represented over the lateral surface of the brain.

Here, along this inner surface on both sides, one large active area of the Self occupies the *medial prefrontal* region, whereas the other resides back in the *medial posterior parietal* region. A smaller coactive site is located over the brain's outer surface. It lies in the angular gyrus and adjacent parts of the inferior parietal lobule.

Next, remember that these three Self-referential regions are unusually active, even when normal subjects seem to be resting passively. Indeed, resting positron-emission tomography (PET) scans confirm that these are the three most significant "hot spots" in the brain, showing exceptionally high metabolic activities. Moreover, the medial prefrontal region becomes even more active when normal subjects respond to brief phrases that describe introspective and other psychic aspects centering on their own personal *I–Me–Mine* (Fox and Raichle 2007). In contrast, the deep medial posterior parietal region increases its functional magnetic resonance imaging (fMRI) signals when the subjects perform navigational tasks. These tasks require a frame of Self-reference that also includes details of the external environment. Therefore, such a frame of "self–othering" addresses itself to much more than what subjects know about the specific nature of their own psychological identity per se (Austin 2009b, 70–76).

What basic function of selfhood could these three cortical regions perform that leads them to remain so highly active—even at rest? One descriptive phrase, commonly applied, calls it "autobiographical memory." Examine, however, what happens when you retrieve a personal event. Your memory doesn't service the needs of an isolated person, some entity who exists inside a vacuum of otherwise empty space. Instead, autobiographical implies your capacity to register and retrieve—into one composite narrative—highly detailed blendings of *Self-plus-other*. Why do both coexist simultaneously?

They coexist because you always recorded a host of other circumstantial details in relation to your own personal history whenever each new event unfolded. These details document the time sequences and narrative flavor of the whole setting in which other people and other things occupied the scenery outside your body.

Thus, there is a reasonable explanation for some of the high levels of activity within this joint frontal–parietal networking system. It is plausible to consider that this system's high activities represent the normal, ongoing coactive integrative transactions of a kind of "self-othering personal memory bank." In this role, it is a system that incorporates and consolidates relevant details about time, place, and person. After the medial temporal lobe has first helped us file away and index a lifetime of such daily deposits, we can return to them later whenever we need to access some (semifictional) remembrances of our own life story.

A recent review suggests that when we integrate our *I–Me–Mine* ego representations with their allocentric versions, some Self-centered personalized frames of reference (e.g., left, right, ahead, behind) become translatable into coordinates that also refer to more other-centered, global terms, such as West, East, North, and South (Burgess 2008). These normal self-otherings can occur when the head direction nerve cells in the limbic system (Austin 2006, 172–174) interact with their counterparts in the retrosplenial cortex and adjacent regions.

Meditators soon discover that their habitual access to lifetime accumulations of such trivia has the downside cited earlier: All too often, their repeated mind wanderings swirl into a turmoil of spontaneous intrusive thoughts that retrieve the past, imagine the future, and neglect the present moment.

Deactivations When Attention Shifts toward Externalized Goals

Thus far, this discussion of functional imaging has focused on two aspects of our normal brain activity: (1) Certain regions maintain unusually high activities at rest, and (2) these mostly medial regions become further activated when attention turns *inward*, toward Self-referential forms of introspection. From here on, the emphasis shifts. In order to grasp the implications of the main hypothesis and its corollaries, it becomes essential to understand why certain physiological functions drop off when the brain is *deactivated*. Furthermore, it remains essential to remember that there exist crucial distinctions between the attention we direct *externally* toward other things, and the attention we direct *internally* that directly involves aspects of the Self.

Let us proceed by posing, and answering, seven exploratory questions:

• *Where* do such deactivations occur? They chiefly involve the same deep *medial* regions just discussed, those of the anterior prefrontal cortex, the posterior parietal cortex (figure 15.2), and the angular gyrus as well (figure 15.4).

• *When* do these deactivations occur? At two very different times. One kind of deactivation occurs at the same instant that our sharp tip of attention shifts just as we start to impale and process new *externalized* goals. This quick shift of heightened externalized attention appears to be evoking a brief *reactive* deactivation of the Self-referential network just described.

• *What purpose* could such a reactive deactivation serve? Perhaps this evoked deactivation implies that when attention turns externally, it initiates a useful brief reorganization, one that governs the access to one's Self-referential networks. It could be that a brain's first job is to shed certain kinds of old baggage before it takes on the next round of new responses. Accordingly, we might view reactive deactivations as a first practical step, a "clearing of the decks" for action, as it were. In any case, the sudden *decrease* of signals in egocentric regions becomes noteworthy, because these mostly medial deactivations occur at the same instant that the lateral attention system develops the sharp *increase* in fMRI signals as it becomes activated.

• Normally, is some other kind of deactivation also going on continually? Yes. This second type of deactivation occurs *spontaneously*. No obvious sensory stimulus drives it. In fact, it is a normal part of similar up-and-down intrinsic fluctuations that recur three to four times a minute on their own very slow independent cycle.

• When did researchers discover that fMRI signals were normally undergoing these slow spontaneous reciprocal activations and deactivations? They discovered this only after they stopped assigning "goal-oriented" tasks and simply monitored their subjects with fMRI at rest for several minutes continually (Buckner, Andrews-Hanna, and

Schacter 2008). Meditating subjects, resting passively, show similar slow spontaneous ongoing, reciprocal fluctuations—when one network activates, the other deactivates. Under such passive conditions, fMRI signals keep rising and falling, consistently shifting—in opposite directions—the "functional connectivity" of their separate lateral attention systems and their Self-referential networks. To be specific, the patterns of these normal, slow, spontaneous intrinsic fluctuations are also reciprocal. They closely resemble the way the first kind of seesaw patterns react in a reciprocal manner to an external stimulus. In that first instance, during goal directed tasks, when modules *increase* their spontaneous activity in the lateral regions known to mediate attention, we've seen that modules included in the standard Self-referential networks simultaneously *decrease* (deactivate) their activity (and vice versa).

• Why devote so much discussion to either the first kind of stimulus-prompted (reactive, exogenous) shift or to this second kind of ongoing (slow, endogenous) fluctuation, let alone to both of them? There are two reasons. First, even though such shifts clearly differ, we need to understand why their reciprocal effects are so similar and why both kinds are manifested on both sides of the brain. (A deep *central* mechanism will soon offer plausible explanations.) Second, the acute reactive shift takes on immediate implications for any person seriously interested in reducing the unfruitful side effects of the overactive Self. Why? Because, as we've now observed, the instant a novel situation activates attention, it triggers a reflex deactivation that reduces the functions of the person's Self-relational regions.

• Then, what kinds of deep, central, seismic changes could enable a brain suddenly to shift into a state of *total* selflessness, as it does in *kensho*? The requisite twofold mechanisms would (1) be stimulus sensitive and (2) have the capacity to enhance both the normal amplitude and duration of the reciprocal deactivations. This raises a practical corollary issue: Because meditation trains attention, it might be possible for such reciprocal shifts to occur more frequently and to become most effective after long-term meditative training practices had served to cultivate attentiveness.

A Triggering Stimulus: How Could It Upset the Equilibrium between Self-Referential and Other-Referential Functions?

Triggers help us understand why both insight–wisdom and selflessness occur at the same time. For centuries, the annals of Zen have recorded remarkably similar stories. In each instance, when an unexpected sensory stimulus arrives, it catalyzes a monk's abrupt awakening into an extraordinary state of consciousness (Austin 1998, 452–460; 2006, 303–306). Yet, years of meditative training usually precede such a trigger. The central question remains: What ingredients in this prior training had enabled a relatively minor sensory stimulus to strike so deeply that it finally triggered a sensitized person into the advanced states called *kensho* or *satori*? And how could such a punctuated disequilibrium then evolve in ways that would subsequently transform that person's preexisting traits of character?

A plausible theory is that regular training programs that include receptive forms of meditation could set the stage for globally sensitized, reciprocal brain responses of increased amplitude to develop as a reaction to random external sights and sounds. Finally, let some novel triggering stimulus arrive—one that captures and fully activates the person's sensitized ventral attentional and allocentric processing resources. Simultaneously, Self-referential networks could then topple over into the kind of sudden major, extended deactivation that figure 15.3 suggests.

Moreover, suppose it happens that the person's two sets of enhanced activations and deactivations are brought simultaneously into their reciprocal phases—the first one reacting briskly to this sudden exogenous triggering stimulus, the second one already fluctuating on its own slow, independent, covert, endogenous cycle. Now, each of the two polar extremes of activation might reinforce each of the other two reciprocal extremes of deactivation. In this moment of syzygy, when high amplitude peaks are rising abruptly out of deep deactivated valleys, all prior Self-centered functions could briefly drop out of that person's mental field (Austin 1998, 346–347). Yet, even allowing for such rare overlapping coincidences to occur, could this dual reciprocal shift empty one's psyche, cut off every old overconditioned construct that had supported egocentric consciousness? No. It couldn't accomplish such a conversion—not without several pivotal contributions from the thalamus (Austin 1998, 610–611).

A Crucial Role for the Thalamus in Effortless Attention and Selfless Insight–Wisdom

The preceding discussion outlines a plausible sequence of mechanisms that could yield selfless states of insight–wisdom and transform consciousness. It is a proposal based on two further observations: (1) The thalamus serves as a normal gateway for our separate ego- and allo-processing streams, and (2) triggering events that capture attention can cause this pivotal thalamic gate to open selectively—to close off the E pathway while opening up the A pathway (see figure 15.1).

Under normal everyday circumstances, how can any such gateway deep in the brain shape the ways we attend, perceive, feel, think, and behave? To begin with, our thalamus gates the entry of all stimuli coming from our perceptual pathways (except for smell). After the thalamus selects which sensory impulses will first pass through its antechambers, it then relays them elsewhere while reshaping them in the process (see figure 15.4).

These selective closings and openings of the thalamic gate exert a major, dynamic influence on the way we live. Let's begin in the back of the thalamus with a key nucleus.

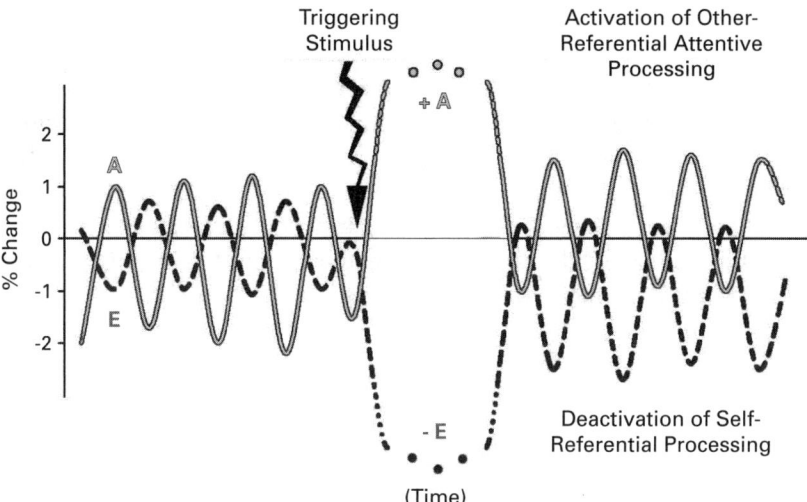

Figure 15.3
The postulated response to a random stimulus that triggers *kensho*. In this schematic diagram, the up-and-down course of the two wavy lines represents the usual spontaneous, ongoing *reciprocal* fluctuations of intrinsic functional magnetic resonance imaging signals. At rest, the peaks of these endogenous rhythms recur slowly, only three to four times a minute or so. Starting at the left, the wavy *gray* line represents the signal fluctuations referable to the anatomical locations of the other-referential (allocentric) networks and lateral attentive systems (A). Note the timing of each such peak of activation. It rises directly above a corresponding low valley of *de*activation—as shown by dashed *black* lines—representing the spontaneous, reciprocal signals from the separate Self-referential (egocentric) networks (E). Suppose a triggering stimulus (↓) now happens to capture the attention of a meditator, one whose sensitivities had been honed and attuned during a long-term program of meditative training. Two physiological reactions are shown unfolding simultaneously: (1) A major activating surge enhances the amplitude of attentive processing within the ventral allocentric pathway (+A). The resulting experience—reaching the level of insight–wisdom—conveys the impression of "suchness." All things are experienced "as THEY really are." (2) A major *de*activation stops all Self-referential processing (-E). This selective inhibition dissolves all prior egocentric constructs of the *I–Me–Mine*. It is experienced as selfless emptiness, timelessness, and fearlessness. Lingering in the immediate afterglow is a heightened allocentric appreciation that encompasses the whole external environment (higher peaks of the gray A line). Simultaneously, the reduction of Self-centeredness leaves the impression of a much lower profile i–me–mine (as represented here by the lower peaks of the black dashed E line).

The Pulvinar; Its Dorsal and Ventral Levels

The pulvinar is the biggest thalamic nucleus. Its large size is in keeping with its immense responsibilities. Preconsciously, it must decode both routine and "hotline" messages. Effortlessly, the pulvinar's antennae of association functions sense the essence of a particular stimulus event. How? In a synthesis informed both by nature and nurture, its networkings instantly highlight each salient ingredient in the foreground while relegating all incidental items to the background. Survival messages enter the pulvinar from the superior colliculus at top speed (SC in figure 15.4). This circuit serves as our primal visual hotline. When the pulvinar detects a situation of urgent visual interest, it forwards this message instantly to the amygdala (A in figure 15.2). The amygdala starts decoding the gist of such an urgent impression in the first 25 milliseconds. Its signals resonate in the form of anxious conditioned responses. They relay coarse, preconscious anticipations of fear throughout our cerebrum and brain stem.

Importantly, the pulvinar's subnuclei are arranged into two levels: upper (dorsal) and lower (ventral). This anatomical division has functional consequences that are crucial to the main themes of this chapter. Their implications are relevant to our dorsal and ventral cortical systems for attention, to their respective roles in the two categories of meditation, and to the two different versions of Self-referential and other-referential processing just discussed.

To cite an example, let us follow two major projections that the dorsal pulvinar sends up to activate the parietal cortex. Begin with those two long arrows rising on the right side of figure 15.4. They illustrate that each projection contributes vital messages to the dialog that unfolds along the Self-centered path. Thus, one projection informs our angular gyrus on the outside of the inferior parietal lobule. The other leads to the precuneus (PRECUN) deep inside the posterior parietal region. The pulvinar serves as the bridge that integrates such shared bidirectional associations. Its deep central position enables it both to draw on the old entries in our personal journal and to link these past experiences with fresh stimulus events that unfold in the present moment.

For contrast, note the next two projections. As they ascend from the *ventral* pulvinar, they relay up through the *lower* occipital → temporal pathway. As this ventral stream flows along through the fusiform gyrus, it can inject its portent of salience into the way the temporal lobe processes its incoming visual and auditory data into a fresh other-referential version. When this allocentric version first identifies objects, why aren't they distorted by old Self-centered memories? Because the impulses flowing forward along this lower pathway are not connected during the earlier milliseconds with any observer's somatic axis farther up in the parietal lobe. Therefore, at this early stage, objects register anonymously, leaving the lower temporal lobe compartments relatively free to register their independent version of objects "out there."

The lateral posterior nucleus (LP) is another thalamic nucleus. From its position in the dorsal tier, just in front of the dorsal pulvinar, its messages rise to interact with the whole superior parietal lobule. This superior lobule serves as a major cortical hub for an elaborate framework of somatic associations. One might envision the joint efforts of the dorsal pulvinar and its neighboring LP nucleus as helping to incorporate the higher order images of our own head, body, and extremities. These constructs then become a basis for projecting their somatic capacities out into the matrix of our environment, enabling us to "embody" such Self-oriented associations as our agency in outside space.

Farther Forward in the Dorsal Thalamus: The Limbic Nuclei and Their Cortical Targets

Three vitally important nuclei occupy the whole front part of the dorsal thalamus (see figure 15.4). They are called *limbic nuclei* because they maintain strong interconnections with the limbic system. Most of their contributions to our psyche's ongoing higher order emotional, instinctual, and memory functions tend to be subtle and to emerge subconsciously.

What parts of the cortex receive affect-laden projections from these limbic nuclei of the thalamus?

- The large *medial dorsal thalamic nucleus* (MD) infuses its limbic resonances into the whole prefrontal cortex. (Like the others, these projections are bidirectional.)
- The *anterior thalamic nucleus* interacts with the posterior cingulate cortex and also with the rest of the cingulate gyrus, including its anterior cingulate extension.
- The *lateral dorsal nucleus* enhances the activities of the retrosplenial region and adjacent areas deep in the medial cortex (Buckwalter, Parvizi, Morecraft, and van Hoesen 2008).

What happens normally when these limbic nuclei stimulate our cortex? If the words elicit a sense of déjà vu, it is because the earlier discussion of figure 15.2 anticipated the answer. It pointed to the two large white areas that serve as our major Self-referential "hot spots." These two medial regions—deep in the frontal and parietal cortex—maintain the highest ongoing metabolic activities of our whole cortex, even at rest. On the other hand, figure 15.4 just illustrated a potential remedy. What is the normal role of the three *inhibitory* nuclei at the bottom of this figure? Their function is to "cool" any overheating that could occur when this dorsal thalamocortical circuitry becomes excessively activated. Could these inhibitory nuclei serve some additional role? They have the capacity to block our whole dorsal stream of Self-centered processing.

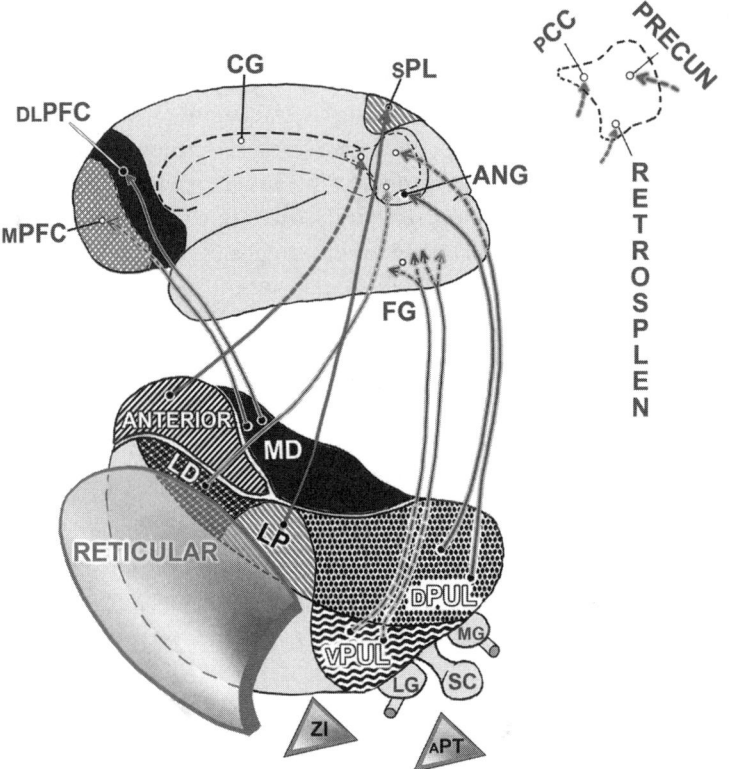

Figure 15.4
The normal thalamus: separate contributions to the dorsal egocentric and ventral allocentric streams. The arrows in this composite view emphasize our normal ascending pathways. These connections are shown linking specific nuclei of the left thalamus with their cortical targets on the outside and inside of the left hemisphere. Pathways (usually bidirectional) predominate from the dorsal tier of thalamic nuclei. Thus, at bottom right, one path leads up from the *dorsal* pulvinar (dPUL) to the angular gyrus (ANG) on the *outer* cortical surface. A second path from this dorsal pulvinar leads up to the *precuneus* (PRECUN). This and each of the other dashed arrow lines indicates a medial path, one that is projecting to the *inner* cortical surface. A separate projection from the adjacent *lateral posterior* (LP) nucleus supplies the *superior parietal lobule* (sPL). This is our somatosensory association cortex. It contributes to the subliminal sensate impression that we exist and are poised to act as a physically articulated image, as a *physical* Self. In front, the *medial dorsal* (MD) thalamic nucleus projects to the prefrontal cortex (PFC) through two pathways. One path is shown supplying its entire outer, dorsal lateral (dL) surface. The other supplies its medial (m) surface. In back is the second deep *medial* region (both are also illustrated in figure 15.2). This region is now shown enlarged at the top right. Here it is easier to see that this large "hot spot" region in the back of the brain also receives dashed projections from the two other adjacent dorsal nuclei that are also part of the limbic thalamus. Thus, one dashed line

Figure 15.4

(continued)

rises up from the *anterior nucleus* to supply the *posterior cingulate cortex* (pCC). The other dashed line projects from the *lateral dorsal nucleus* (LD) to the *retrosplenial cortex* (RETROSPLEN). This figure shows fewer pathways rising up from the ventral tier of the thalamic nuclei to serve the allocentric processing stream. Observe, however, that messages from the *ventral pulvinar* (vPUL) pass first through the region of the *fusiform gyrus* (FG) on the undersurface of the temporal lobe. These messages contribute to our other-referential processing as they stream forward through the rest of the temporal lobe, proceed on up toward the superior temporal gyrus, and also continue on into the inferior frontal region. Three important inhibitory nuclei are illustrated at the bottom, contracted and artificially detached. They are the large *reticular nucleus*, the small *zona incerta* (ZI), and the small *anterior pretectal nucleus* (aPT). Why was the back of the reticular nucleus removed? In order to reveal two important sensory relay nuclei concealed under the back of the thalamus (bottom right). One is the *lateral geniculate nucleus* (LG). This is the major thalamic avenue through which we relay visual information up to the primary visual cortex for finer degrees of discriminative processing. The other is the *medial geniculate nucleus* (MG). It relays auditory information up to the temporal lobe for processing by the primary auditory cortex. After further decoding, the messages in both of these visual and auditory streams can filter into consciousness. In contrast, the *superior colliculus* (SC) in the midbrain relays its coarse, reflexive visual and related polymodal messages quickly through both the dorsal and ventral pulvinar to the amygdala and beyond. CG, cingulate gyrus.

Our Normal Subcortical Sources of Inhibition

Under normal everyday circumstances, we mobilize a standard array of ongoing oscillations that enhance and unify our normal thalamo ↔ cortical functions. When all their reverberating frequencies arrive at times that are *in phase,* their synchronies unite our thalamocortical functions. To maintain the necessary balance, we depend on the crucial opposing roles played by the reticular nucleus, the zona incerta, and the anterior pretectal nucleus. Sensitive to any excessive excitation, their inhibitory functions act normally as a "shield." This prevents the other thalamic nuclei from overfiring and stops them from becoming "overheated."

Precisely how does such a thalamic "cooling effect" also quench hot spots up in the cortex? As a first step, the inhibitory nuclei release gamma aminobutyric acid (GABA), an inhibitory transmitter. This GABA inhibition disorganizes the synchronized firing rhythms of these usual oscillations. This renders the thalamocortical oscillations grossly out of phase and physiologically ineffectual. It is by blocking the interactive links that connect the dorsal thalamic nuclei with their counterparts up in the association cortex that these three GABA nuclei *can delete the higher order cortical functions of the Self.*

Why wouldn't consciousness be lost if the person's psychic functions and affiliated somatic associations were both deleted? Because other standard excitatory pathways remain that can still go on generating bottom–up arousal and attention. These circuits pursue the several other routes that bypass a blockade limited to the dorsal thalamus per se.

Kensho: Deactivations of the Dorsal Nuclei of the Thalamus Can Block the Higher Association Functions of the Psychic Self

Figure 15.5 envisions a selfless state that develops suddenly.

For simplicity, let's describe the sequence that leads to deactivation in three steps. First, activity increases in the dorsal aspect of the reticular shield. Second, in keeping with the way in which this acts to "tighten" the *dorsal* segment of the so-called GABA "cap," all five nuclei in the dorsal thalamus beneath are inhibited and shown here in a darker shade. Third, similar darker areas of deactivation are also shown higher up among their copartner regions in the cortex. These suggest that the resulting loss of synchronized thalamocortical oscillating activities reduces the functions of particular portions of the frontoparietal cortex.

Figure 15.5 illustrates that only certain interactions stop when the whole dorsal tier of thalamic nuclei is inhibited:

- The egocentric stream that would rise normally up through the angular gyrus is shown as deactivated (-E). Egocentric messages no longer flow toward the somatic associations of the superior parietal lobule.
- The Self-centered psychic functions of both the medial prefrontal and medial posterior parietal cortex are also suspended, as is indicated by the deactivation (-E) of these darker regions.

In contrast, the ventral thalamic tier remains unshaded. (Figure 15.5 makes no attempt to show the degree to which some of its functions are also *dis*inhibited—that is, further *excited* because they are released from prior inhibition.)

At this critical moment, all the brain's habitual Self-referential pathways are deactivated. Therefore, consciousness lacks any witnessing compartment that is exclusively Self-centered. Distorted *I–Me–Mine* priorities no longer dominate dorsal thalamocortical circuits. Freed from a lifetime of hidden limbic overconditioning, a novel dimension of *other*-consciousness can now open up. The white arrows suggest that this version of enhanced allocentric processing takes over (+A). For a timeless moment, *other*-consciousness is the single unifying operating mode. Consciousness registers clearly, directly, no longer divided into Self versus other.

This total dissolution of the prior sense of Self is not a new idea. *Anatta* is the ancient Pali term for such an unconditioned state of non-I. Zen Buddhist traditions have long regarded the nondual version of *kensho's* awakened consciousness as a state of "no self." Only during moments of total selflessness do such states of existential insight–wisdom arrive (Austin 2008, 2009a). Moreover, the total blockade of limbic angst during this state adds a profound sense of release and emptiness to the resulting impression of that deepest peace "which passeth all understanding."

The following phenomena are prominent among the several qualities blended into this deconditioned state: (1) It is fearless—troubled no longer by primal anxieties relayed from the amygdala (Fox, Shelton, Oakes, Davidson, and Kalin 2008); (2) it is conflict free and effort free—liberated from the constraints imposed by prior conflicts and from the sense of mental effort that arises when the dorsal anterior cingulate gyrus monitors performance (Mulert et al. 2007); and (3) it is deeply satisfied—driven no longer by the disturbing sense of disappointments that can arise from the nucleus accumbens (Austin 2006, 79–82).

The Dutch Door—A Metaphor for the Thalamus

Until the early 17th century, a door meant a solid barrier. It blocked your entry from top to bottom. Then a Dutchman invented a different kind of door. It was divided horizontally into upper and lower halves (see figure 15.6). Top and bottom could now be opened or closed independently.

When such an upper door opens (at left), a busy parent might look down to monitor children playing on the doorstep nearby. Or perhaps the occupant might feel a need, in solitude, to receive fresh breezes from afar. Then the lower door swings open, inviting this cool draft to enter and freely displace the stale air within. At night, both halves join in closure when the household retires in privacy. The Dutch door is a convenient visual metaphor. It illustrates the several options our thalamic gateway has to open and close its dorsal and ventral divisions selectively.

Potential Thalamic Contributions to Rarer Qualities of Awakening: To "Oneness," "Unity," and "Moonlight"

The mechanisms causing Selflessness are only one part of our puzzle. There exist other ways to interpret the role of the thalamus in relation to certain phenomena associated with advanced, extraordinary states of consciousness. After Edward Carpenter defined "cosmic consciousness" back in 1892, he went on to characterize its special perspective of "oneness" (Austin 2006, 393). It meant that the person could finally see things from a "more universal standpoint." From this vantage point, "sight and touch and hearing are all fused in identity." This could lead to an impression that one actually *is* those objects, things, and persons that one is perceiving.

Among the other subtle phenomena that can interpenetrate states of insight–wisdom, some are relatively rare. For example, certain qualities of so-called "unitive" experiences usually tend to emerge during later stages of the meditative path, and

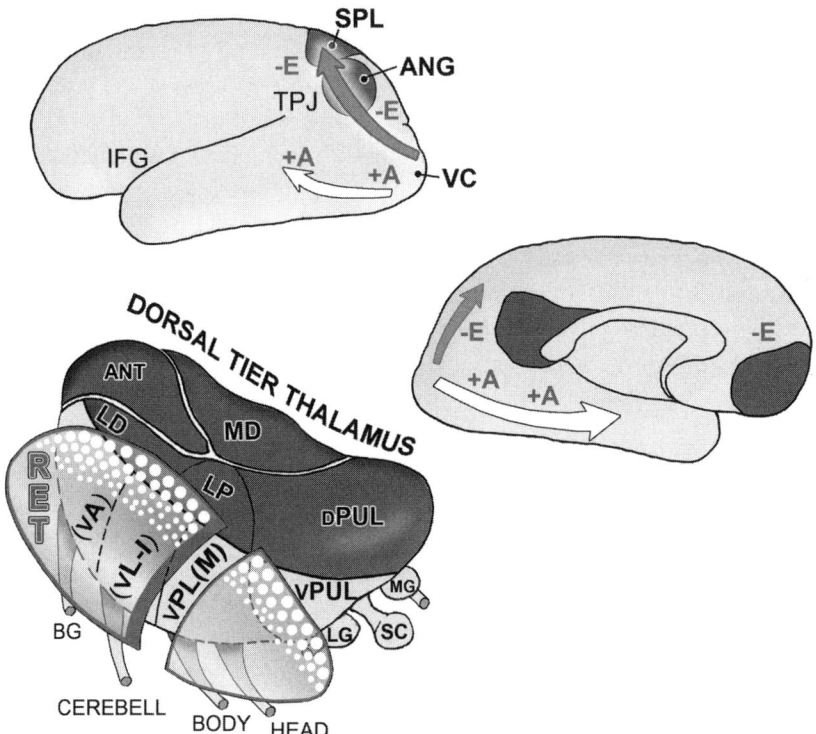

Figure 15.5
Kensho: a deactivated psychic Self. In this composite view, the dark areas up in the cortex suggest what can happen in a left hemisphere when all five of its specific dorsal thalamic nuclei are deactivated. The top of the figure indicates, by its large gray arrow, that the egocentric stream is deactivated (-E). Its Self-centered messages can no longer rise from the visual cortex (VC), pass through the angular gyrus (ANG), and stream up toward the superior parietal lobule (SPL). This stream of egocentric processing stops when the back portion of the reticular nucleus (RET) is excited in its dorsal portion (white circles) and releases gamma aminobutyric acid (GABA). The resulting GABA inhibition blocks the major input that the dorsal pulvinar (dPUL) and lateral posterior nuclei (LP) had been projecting up to this Self-centered, *lateral* association cortex. A similar sequence of events also unfolds in the *medial* cortex (at far right). Dark areas are shown in both the prefrontal and deep posterior parietal cortex. They represent deactivations of the *medial* Self-centered regions (-E). In this instance, GABA is released from the more anterior parts of the reticular nucleus (and its inhibitory allies). The resulting inhibition blocks all three limbic nuclei farther forward in the dorsal thalamus. Why does selflessness occur? Primarily because all the usual Self-relational interactions between the thalamus and these specified cortical regions have stopped at the *dorsal* thalamic level. In contrast, the white arrows suggest that other pathways of the allocentric processing system are spared (+A). This other-referential processing stream flows unchecked through the *lower* occipital → temporal cortex. Why isn't this pathway inter-

The Thalamic Gateway

Figure 15.5
(continued)
rupted? Because the corresponding portions of the reticular nucleus have not released their inhibitory transmitter, GABA. (The reticular nucleus is portrayed here only schematically, taking the form of a shield that has been artificially sectioned.) Also depicted as spared are messages rising from the cerebellum (CEREBELL) into the ventral lateral and ventral intermediate nucleus (vL-I), and messages en route from the basal ganglia (BG) that rise into the ventral anterior nucleus (vA). These sparings in the ventral tier hint that options remain open for avenues through which deep covert resonances of the psyche might infuse subtle, ineffable, quasi-perceptual qualities into awakening that reflect mature behavioral programming. ANT, anterior thalamic nucleus; IFG, inferior frontal gyrus; LG, lateral geniculate nucleus; MD, medial dorsal thalamic nucleus; MG, medial geniculate nucleus; SC, superior colliculus; TPJ, temporoparietal junction; VPL(M), ventral posterior and medial; vPUL, ventral pulvinar.

Figure 15.6
The Dutch door. At left, the upper half-door opens in a manner suggesting the way the *dorsal* tier of our thalamic nuclei open to enhance the normal thalamocortical flow toward top–down attention and Self-referential processing. At right, the lower half-door opens in a manner comparable with the way nuclei of the *ventral* tier open to enhance the normal thalamocortical flow toward bottom–up attention and other-referential (allocentric) processing.

they are not all the same. Why not? A corollary of the present hypothesis might venture a general principle. It could help us understand how a few uncommon "varieties" could arise of these more advanced experiences to which William James and Carpenter had referred. It suggests that some of their phenomena could (1) reflect particular combinations of activation–deactivation, (2) arise from the different hierarchical levels of thalamic nuclei that share distinctive functions with their respective cortical partners, and (3) be referable more to the right and/or left sides of the brains of individual subjects.

To offer specific examples of such a general approach, let us first consider two varieties that represent different subcategories of the quality of "oneness" (Austin 2006, 333–401):

1. Some phenomena added to the state of awakening appear to project quasi-physical representations of the person. When these impressions are infused into the larger open field of consciousness, they seem consistent with "mirror-like" projections of that individual's residual somatic Self. Perhaps some of this subtle additional sense of self-recognition could arrive via the resonances from two of the spared ventral posterior nuclei. These ventral lateral and medial nuclei are located just in front of the ventral pulvinar nucleus. Figure 15.5 raises the possibility that the sparing of these more elementary somatic sensory functions might go on (in some of their further ramifications) to nourish residual impressions of recognizable identity related to residual sensibilities representing that person's body and head.

2. However, other phenomena added to an awakened state appear much more abstract and much less explicitly physical. Some might seem referable to subtle distant resonances involving the psychic Self. As our brains mature normally over the decades, we slowly refine into behavior many attributes resonating from our psyche. Moreover, only after decades of superimposed meditative training do meditators develop the mental attitudes of compassion accompanied by procedural memory routines that go on to transform their actual sensorimotor behavior. These attitudinal and postural transformations emerge involuntarily. The person remains unaware how thoroughly the deep behavioral nuances of their traits of compassion have been thus transformed.

In such instances one wonders how such subtle ongoing subconscious expressions of the person's psyche could become manifested during a brief, advanced alternate state of consciousness. Could they emerge as indirect, almost holographic reflections of prior deep, covert, sensorimotor reprogramming? Figure 15.5 hints that such corresponding kinesthetic resonances—lingering among distant coordinating networks in the cerebellum (arriving via the ventral lateral and ventral intermediate nucleus) and also buried among the postural engrams in the basal ganglia (via the ventral anterior nucleus)—might still contribute to these remote impressions. If so, perhaps traces of such distant procedural links could be conveyed via these most rostral of the thalamic nuclei that are spared in the ventral tier. (A subsequent section expands on these speculations.)

Very different perceptual phenomena can occur as *kensho* closes. On rare occasions, the scenery shifts into a late colorless phase—a black-and-white illusion—as if illuminated by moonlight (Austin 2006, 403–463). Nothing esoteric is implied by this brief "moonlight phase." It is interpretable as a delayed inhibitory rebound. This kind of inhibitory response could be expected to follow a major prior excitatory interval of enhanced allocentric processing. The brief phase when color vision drops out is consistent with such a selective inhibition of other-referential processing. It suggests that the V4 color complex regions have been deactivated, perhaps more on the right than on the left side. These regions lie on the lower occipital → temporal allocentric pathway where it passes through the fusiform gyrus (shown as FG in figure 15.1).

Beyond *kensho-satori* lies the advanced state of "Being" (Austin 1998, 627–632; 2006, 392–393). It is an ineffable awareness, lacking every ordinary frame of reference to Self–other, subject–object: no person inside, no world outside. Can such a "nirvana-like" extinction be conceptualized? No. However, if pressed to speculate, perhaps it might resemble the third option of the Dutch door: a further expanded degree of GABA inhibitory "shielding" that could deactivate both the dorsal *and* ventral tier of the thalamic nuclei—thus disconnecting them from the cortex—yet also sparing the residual activations arising from their ancient innermost medial core of interoceptive and nonspecific nuclei (Austin 1998, 266–267).

Nitric Oxide: Its Implications for Functional Imaging and for the Thalamus

The discussion now returns to the slower, endogenous fMRI signals, because their spontaneous fluctuations relate in an intriguing way to the thalamic hypothesis. Why do these normal blood-oxygen-level-dependent signals keep reversing themselves so slowly back and forth between activation and deactivation? Nitric oxide (NO·) is one candidate molecule that can enter into part of an explanation (Austin 2006, 170, 279–288, 449–450, 452). NO· is a highly reactive free radical gas. Not only do its multiple effects clearly influence cerebral blood flow but some effects also change the brain's bioelectric potentials (Austin 2009b, 260–261).

NO· is a key intermediate molecule in a large, complex metabolic cycle. Inside the brain, several major excitatory neurotransmitters—including glutamate and acetylcholine—engage in their individual dynamic turnovers within this large, endogenous cycle. The whole metabolic cycle also includes small calcium ions as well as larger molecules, such as NO·-synthase, cyclic GMP, and phosphodiesterase.

Inside such a large cycle, several seconds can elapse before each single moiety is regenerated to reach its own peak level. Suppose we begin by taking the total number of seconds required before all such sequences develop their optimum individual metabolic regenerations to such a peak level and then superimpose this number on the timing cycles representing the way the whole brain expresses its separate bioelectric rhythms of excitation and inhibition. The later harmonic intervals emerging from such a summation of results might contribute to what is observed: fMRI signals that change periodically from activation to deactivation: a slow endogenous cycle that keeps recurring every 15 to 20 seconds or so.

NO· has other actions that directly affect the thalamus. Pertinent to this topic of bioelectric mechanisms is the way that NO· preferentially excites certain GABA nerve cells of the reticular nucleus. These reticular neurons fire in strong burst discharges (Yang and Cox 2008). When they release bursts of GABA, its inhibitory effects create major changes in thalamo ↔ cortical oscillating rhythms. Moreover, when NO· is released into the basal ganglia nearby, it offers an additional way for the brain to transform old dysfunctional motor patterns. Here in the striatum, the glutamate–nitric oxide–cyclic GMP system can reshape outworn conditioned physiological responses, enabling the person to shed dysfunctional habits and develop newly adaptive behavioral options (Austin 1998, 676).

Several aspects of this dual metabolic–bioelectric NO· proposal are testable. For example, preclinical studies might begin by adding selective NO· precursors, NO· donors, and other pertinent molecules that are known to modify each step in these larger interacting cycles. Subsequent investigations could test whether the changing amplitudes and rhythms of the brain's endogenous fMRI signals, plus those resonating as overtones from its changing electrophysiological potentials, occur at the predictable times and in the appropriate directions.

A PET Scan during Receptive Meditation

Suppose that a person were to settle into a sustained interval of receptive meditation. Could the results first influence the reticular nucleus, then adjust the way it inhibits the thalamus, and finally be reflected among the functional layers of the thalamocortical interactions just discussed? In 1988, the author was the subject of a radioactive deoxyglucose PET scan (Austin 1998, 282–284). During an unusually long interval (two to three hours), he relaxed into a passive, nonconcentrative mode of awareness. This meant attending gently to the kinesthetic risings and fallings of the lower abdomen during slow, quiet respiration. Eyes were masked, and ears were plugged with cotton. Discursive thoughts fell to a minimum.

Under these settled waking conditions, the medial frontal activities were reduced on both sides symmetrically. However, in general, it was the other cortical regions on the right side that displayed the greater metabolic activity. Importantly, this trend toward relatively greater right-sided activity predominated in the regions lower down: the right middle temporal and fusiform gyri, the right inferior fronto-opercular region, and the deep medial regions of the right posterior parietal cortex.

In contrast, the thalamic nuclei on this right side tended to show lesser degrees of metabolic activity. The asymmetrical decreases in this right thalamus became increasingly apparent within the lowest thalamic levels. These corresponded with the nuclei of the right ventral tier. Wouldn't we expect thalamic nuclei ("simply") to share their coactivations with the cortex? If so, then why didn't this subject's right lower thalamus also coactivate to the same asymmetrical degree as did its cortical partners that had shown greater activation in the right inferior frontotemporal (other-referential) region?

The previous discussion suggests ways to reconcile this paradox. The explanations remain speculative for three reasons: first, because no thalamocortical interactions are "simple"; second, because dynamic interpretations are limited when only a single set of static PET scans is available; and third, because current neuroimaging methods cannot yet visualize the thin cap of the reticular nucleus, even though physiological studies clearly show how much it (and its allies) inhibits the underlying thalamus.

Accepting these reservations, the following interpretations are consistent with this summary of the set of reciprocal lateralized findings just described:

- In the cortex, the *right* lower temporal and inferior frontal regions developed the greater degrees of cortical activation during this long interval of openly receptive meditation. Such an asymmetry of cortical activity is compatible with a spontaneous trend toward right-sided, bottom–up other-referential processing. Furthermore, there slowly evolved a major spontaneous reduction in the subject's discursive thoughts. This passive letting go of Self-centered thoughts would be accompanied by a corresponding reduction of activity in the language areas of the opposite *left* temporal and inferior frontal regions (not only in the medial frontal regions, where it appeared to be reduced equally on both sides).
- In the right lower levels of the thalamus, lesser degrees of activation were observed. This could be consistent with some normal, inhibitory attempts by the *right* reticular nucleus to shield the corresponding thalamic nuclei of the ventral tier when their right cortical counterparts were tending to become overactive.

In brief, the asymmetrical thalamic activity (left > right) is interpretable as the kind of covert compensatory effect that one might expect from the right reticular nucleus. Two decades have elapsed since this scan. A well-designed, high-resolution large-scale fMRI investigation of prolonged receptive meditation is essential to resolve these complex issues.

Along a Spectrum of Selflessness

What does it mean to be "liberated" from overconditioning? It implies that one's behaviors become spontaneous, effortless, fluid, flexible, and efficient. Meditators who totally surrender—who let go of all their top–down supervisory efforts and attendant mental friction—finally drop effortlessly into extraordinary alternate states of consciousness. Zen uses the terms *kensho* or *satori* when referring to these deep so-called "peak experiences" that realize existential insights. Do these major Selfless states also illustrate phenomena along a broad spectrum that might include our shallower creative moments of intuition, as well as those peak athletic performances called "playing in the zone," the times when athletes let go "into the flow?" (Austin 1998, 670–677)? Probably, because the evidence increasingly suggests that a variety of globally distributed networks employ bottom–up parallel processing once we let go and open up effortlessly into coherent moments of enhanced attention, clarity, and skillful behavior (Volz and von Cramon 2006).

Internal Absorption: Thalamic Origins of a Deafferented Somatic Self

Meditators who intensify concentrative meditation techniques can undergo the several varieties of absorptions (Austin 1998, 467–518). States of absorption tend to occur earlier on the meditative path, but they do not penetrate consciousness to depths sufficient to permanently transform traits of behavior. However, during the state termed *internal absorption*, two phenomena occur that are relevant to this discussion: (1) Thalamic inhibitory mechanisms appear to delete the *somatic* sense of Self in a way that clearly distinguishes this internalized absorption from the major egocentric loss of the psyche so characteristic of *kensho*, and (2) late residues of liberated motor behavior also occur (Austin 1998, 508–509). This effortless lightness of the body is of interest to other chapters in this volume in the general context of "flow."

Figure 15.7 illustrates the initial somatic deactivations of the brain that could occur during a state of internal absorption (Austin 2008, 2009a).

It envisions them as deletions of the person's elementary sensory percepts. Note, however, that the figure represents relatively few of the GABA nerve cells in the whole shield as being overactive. Back in the lowermost part of the caudal reticular nucleus, it is these cells' normal inhibitory role to deactivate only our *first-order* sensory relay nuclei. These smaller thalamic nuclei relay elementary visual, auditory, and somatic sensory messages. Their simpler functions differ from those of our association nuclei higher up in the dorsal thalamus. Relay nuclei are also located much lower down: under the ventral pulvinar, or just in front of it down in the ventral tier of thalamic nuclei.

Moreover, when the reticular nucleus deactivates these simpler sensory nuclei of the thalamus, it deprives corresponding regions of their afferent supply up in the sensory cortex. Accordingly, figure 15.7 shows that the three dark areas representing this deafferentation all reside in the primary sensory cortex. These dark deprived areas are shown occupying only its primary visual (1° VC), auditory (1° AC), and somatosensory regions (1° SSC). This pattern is very different from that shown for *kensho* in figure 15.5.

Though the meditator does undergo a heightened plenitude of awareness during internal absorption, the experience also includes a vast encompassing vacuum of space that is blacker than black, absolutely silent, and devoid of every former sense of a central *physical* axis of Self. These deafferentiations reflect major initial inhibitory deactivations that begin in lower regions of the thalamus.

Assets of a Thalamic Hypothesis

How did this vast domain of current spiritual inquiry seem to observers far back in 9th century China? At that time, to Zen Master Huang-Po, it was "an inexpressible mystery." Twelve centuries later, researchers now have the advantage of correlating computerized techniques of functional imaging with their meditators' first-person experiential reports. This chapter has presented the bare outlines of a preliminary thalamic hypothesis. Of what practical use is an approach that ventures to correlate several core aspects of attention and meditation with Selfless states of consciousness?

- First, the message of these pages strongly reemphasizes the training of attention. Because one's initial motivations tend to fade, it can be useful to have a unifying rationale that keeps encouraging meditators to cultivate and refine their several powers of attention. Those meditators who have already adopted a consistent long-term approach to formal practice have discovered how concentrative techniques can contribute to the clarity, vividness, and stability of their attentive focusing. However, receptive meditative techniques are more nuanced. They evolve less conspicuously, on a slower timetable. It takes a very long time to learn the subtle ways to genuinely "let go" and to become more effortless. To accomplish this, regular extended meditative retreats are recommended. In this regard, a detailed follow-up EEG report has just analyzed how 17 mature practitioners improved on the so-called "attentional blink" test after they had completed a three-month meditative retreat (Slagter, Lutz, Greischar, Nieuwenhuis, and Davidson 2009). This intensive retreat had combined a mixture of concentrative, receptive, and "metta" (kindness and compassion) approaches. The test improvements appear (1) to reflect the kinds of problem-solving techniques that are Self-directed and focused on the sensorimotor task and (2) to have enlisted other

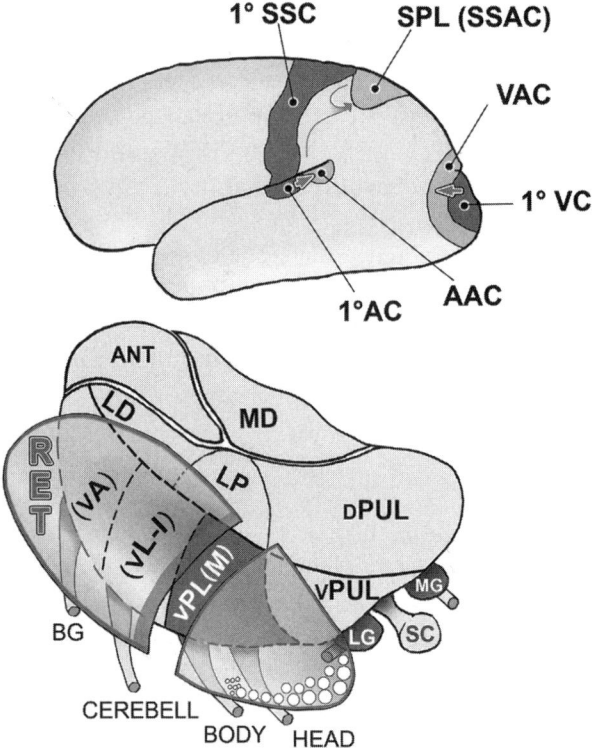

Figure 15.7
Internal absorption: a deafferented somatic Self. In this instance, the dark areas suggest deactivations that are chiefly confined to the early sensory *relay* nuclei of the thalamus and to their target regions up in the primary sensory cortex. The net result is to dissolve the person's *physical* sense of Self. These dissolutions of one's soma offer a sharp contrast with those affecting the psyche that are illustrated in figure 15.5. (Figure 15.5 proposed that deactivations of the dorsal tier of thalamic *association* nuclei and their cortical *association* areas were responsible for deletions of the *psychic* Self.) Here, in the left thalamus, note that only a small area of excitation (white circles) is shown to occupy the detached portion at the back of the reticular nucleus (RET). As is shown, this inhibits (deactivates) only three relatively small thalamic nuclei in the lower and most posterior part of the thalamus. Which sensory messages would normally enter through these three deep relay nuclei, later to be refined into conscious perceptions? (1) The lateral geniculate nucleus (LG) relays visual information; (2) the medial geniculate (MG) relays auditory messages; (3) the ventral posterior nuclei (vP) relay somatosensory information about the person's body (vPL) and head (vPM). At the bottom of the figure, however, the gamma aminobutyric acid inhibitory gate has closed, blocking these elementary sensory messages at the level of the thalamus. Corresponding regions up in the cortex are secondarily deafferented. Accordingly, three darker areas of cortical deactivations are shown: in the primary visual cortex (1° VC), the primary auditory cortex (1° AC), and the primary somatosensory cortex (1° SSC). Small arrows hint that these initial corti-

Figure 15.7
(continued)
cal deactivations might subsequently reduce discriminative functions in their respective areas of the *association* cortex (VAC, AAC, SSAC). ANT, anterior thalamic nucleus; BG, basal ganglia; CEREBELL, cerebellum; dPUL, dorsal pulvinar; LD, lateral dorsal nucleus; LP, lateral posterior nucleus; MD, medial dorsal thalamic nucleus; SC, superior colliculus; SPL, superior parietal lobule; VA, ventral anterior nucleus; vL-I, ventral lateral and ventral intermediate nucleus; vPUL, ventral pulvinar.

ventral attention resources, the kinds that are of bottom–up origin and are directed reflexively toward the stimulus. For example, the subjects' EEG responses showed prominent theta activities that were phase-locked not only over the frontal areas along the midline of the scalp (Austin 2006, 42–43) but also over areas on the *right* side in the ventral frontal and central parietal regions.
• Second, it is crucial to understand that receptive meditative practices do not simply mean sitting on a cushion indoors. Receptive techniques are broadly inclusive. They incorporate a wide variety of mindful practices that openly engage mindful attentive behavior in each and every aspect of daily life (Austin 2006, 57–57; 2009b, 8–13). In Zen, this is called *daily life practice (shugyo)*.
• Third, to cite a specific practical example, it can be helpful to learn to celebrate the world of nature outdoors (Austin 1998, 664–667). Meditators can literally "raise their sights" above the horizon by adopting the more spacious, actual "sky watching" practices that they engage in naturally when they are outdoors. That such explicit allocentric approaches could play a beneficial role in meditative training seems insufficiently emphasized at present. However, practices that cultivate incremental degrees of spaciousness could have a salutary effect. Openly receptive practices could gradually enhance one's range of auditory and visual receptivities in ways that encourage more diffuse, bottom–up kinds of intuitive processing. When such routine practices of elevating attention above the horizontal plane gradually become more expansive in scope, they might enable practitioners to tap into hidden other-referential resources that become genuinely insightful. That said, the nondual qualities of advanced states of awakening expand into unbounded, language-free comprehensions that are inherently horizonless.
• Fourth, several observations are relevant to the wider application of such a broad-based, receptive allocentric approach:
1 It was when this Zen meditator happened to look up—into a bit of distant, open sky—that the state of *kensho* began (Austin 1998, 536–539).
2 A different Zen meditator recently reported an impressive state of consciousness. The episode began with the following quasi-physical projection: "I looked up at the sky and that experience was exactly like looking at a mirror.... It was a physical

sensation, as if the sky had my eyes and could see me staring up at it" (Austin 2006, 345).

3 A third Zen meditator recently reported dropping into an extraordinary emotionless state. What triggered its interpenetrating "emptiness" and "Oneness"? An auditory stimulus: the natural sound of a birdcall outside his window (Austin 2006, 354–355).

• Fifth, human brains are already working overtime. Examples from our language demonstrate how often the excesses inherent in this word, "over," carry dysfunctional implications. To illustrate: Nowadays, many persons become both overstressed and sleep deprived. Long-term regular meditative practices confer ongoing calming effects, and they reshape one's priorities (Austin 1998, 141–145). These measures help cut back on the urgencies that dopamine and norepinephine nerve cells in the brain stem are prone to release in ways that excite our limbic system. The thalamic hypothesis enables one to understand how meditation's general calming effects could then cut back on the impulses projected from this overemotional limbic system that would otherwise rise up to overactivate its three specific thalamic nuclei in ways that constantly drive certain higher regions of the cortex. By reducing the habitual overactivity of this overstimulated Self-referential cortical stream, consciousness could become clarified, free from the many distractions that the overconditioned *I–Me–Mine* had imposed on the psyche.

Limitations of the Present Thalamic Hypothesis

The proposals outlined here are gross simplifications. As caveats, it is important to include a sample of omissions and complexities. These figures do not show the nonspecific nuclei of the thalamus (Austin 1998, 264). Among them are the anterior intralaminar nuclei and the thalamic nuclei next to the midline of the brain. The ventral medial nucleus is one of these midline nuclei, and it relays interoceptive information up to the cortex of our insula (Austin 2006, 95–99). Exciting, inhibiting, or disinhibiting these several nonspecific nuclei would also infuse diverse experiential influences into our complex spectrum of arousal–awareness–attention (Austin 1998, 265–277; Buckwalter, Parvizi, Morecraft, and van Hoesen 2008).

Dopamine and norepinephrine receptors obviously contribute to the energies that drive the emotions of the limbic system and enhance their motor expressions by the striatum. Only recently were dopamine fibers detected in pertinent sectors of the reticular nucleus. To the degree that these dopamine nerve terminals could then stimulate adjacent reticular nerve cells to release GABA, this GABA might in turn neutralize some of the untoward effects caused by excessive dopamine functions elsewhere (Garcia-Cabezas, Rico, Sanchez-Gonzales, and Cavada 2007).

Clearly, these pages raise more questions than they resolve. In particular, can long-term meditative training selectively enhance the plasticity that governs the brain's attentive responses, thereby increasing the likelihood, the duration, and the amplitude of the reactive and endogenous responses illustrated in figure 15.3? These critical issues remain to be tested.

Worldwide, relatively few centers are currently organized and fully equipped to address—let alone answer—such challenging interdisciplinary questions (Lutz, Slagter, Dunne, and Davidson 2008; Buckner, Andrews-Hanna, and Schacter 2008). Still, the experimental designs of months-long meditation research programs have recently become increasingly rigorous. Moreover, the temporal and spatial resolving powers of magnetoencephalography are now greatly enhanced. When human subjects respond to affective stimuli, researchers can now measure the pertinent gamma synchrony peaks as each sequence unfolds along their colliculo → pulvinar → amygdala → cortical pathways (Luo, Holroyd, Jones, Hendler, and Blair 2007).

Using simultaneous EEG and fMRI of high magnetic field strength (4 Tesla), it is now possible (during seemingly "relaxed states") to detect "widespread activation of the dorsal thalamus" at times when other deactivations are described chiefly involving the fusiform gyrus and adjacent lower regions of the visual association cortex (Difrancesco, Holland, and Szaflarski 2008).

Given the remarkable rates at which other novel imaging methods, such as diffusion tensor imaging, are being invented and refined, it seems increasingly likely that future researchers will be able to measure accurately the results of several key interactions between the thalamus, other subcortical nuclei, and the cortex. Therefore, the premises underlying a thalamic hypothesis and its corollaries can be subjected to rigorous testing in the future. Those proposals that survive such testing, when further modified, can help clarify the inexpressible mystery of how the age-old meditative path actually does transform various aspects of our attentiveness, consciousness, and behavior.

Conclusion

The Selfless insight–wisdom of *kensho* is interpretable as a lack of egocentric, top–down attentive processing. It occurs during a simultaneous, reciprocal enhancement of allocentric, bottom–up attentive processing. Both events reflect pivotal underlying changes that shift the gating functions of the thalamus.

Acknowledgments

It is a pleasure to thank Lauren Elliott for her invaluable contributions in preparing this chapter and Scott Greathouse for his skillful efforts in creating its illustrations, as well as James W. Austin, Scott Austin, and Brian Bruya for their helpful comments.

Notes

1. Visual fibers relay back from the lateral geniculate nucleus into the occipital cortex. Those fibers destined to serve our upper fields of vision pursue a slightly longer course through Meyer's loop in the temporal lobe.

2. Figure 15.1 identifies the IPS and FEF as key modules in the system that generates top–down *attentive* functions. The superior parietal lobule (figures 15.2, 15.4, 15.5, and 15.7) and angular gyrus are modules that contribute to the *processing* of our egocentric functions. Attention first initiates. Subsequently, it helps sustain processing. For present purposes, it's useful to separate these two concepts.

References

Austin, J. 1998. *Zen and the brain: Toward an understanding of meditation and consciousness.* Cambridge: MIT Press. (The frontispiece of this hardcover edition contains a full-color version of the subject's PET scan. Pages 263–277 discuss the functions of different thalamic nuclei. Pages 519–624 discuss the outward turning of attention into *kensho*. Pages 467–518 discuss the states of absorption.)

Austin, J. 2006. *Zen-brain reflections: Reviewing recent developments in meditation and states of consciousness.* Cambridge: MIT Press.

Austin, J. 2008. Selfless insight–wisdom; a thalamic gateway. In *Measuring the immeasurable: The scientific case for spirituality.* Louisville, CO: Sounds True, 211–230.

Austin, J. 2009a. Our ordinary sense of self: Different aspects of "no self" during states of absorption and kensho. In *Self and no-self: Continuing the dialogue between Buddhism and psychotherapy*, ed. D. Mather, M. Miller, and O. Ando. London: Routledge, 59–65.

Austin, J. 2009b. *Selfless insight: Zen and the meditative transformations of consciousness.* Cambridge: MIT Press.

Buckner, R., J. R. Andrews-Hanna, and D. Schacter. 2008. The brain's default network: Anatomy, function, and relevance to disease. *Ann. N. Y. Acad. Sci.* 1124:1–38.

Buckwalter, J., J. Parvizi, R. Morecraft, and G. van Hoesen. 2008. Thalamic projections to the posteromedial cortex in the macaque. *J. Comp. Neurol.* 507:1709–1733.

Burgess, N. 2008. Spatial cognition and the brain. *Ann. N. Y. Acad. Sci.* 1124:77–97.

Difrancesco, M., S. Holland, and J. Szaflarski. 2008. Simultaneous EEG/functional magnetic resonance imaging at 4 Tesla: Correlates of brain activity to spontaneous alpha rhythm during relaxation. *J. Clin. Neurophysiol.* 25:255–264.

Fox, A., S. Shelton, T. Oakes, R. Davidson, and N. Kalin. 2008. Trait-like brain activity during adolescence predicts anxious temperament in primates. *Proceedings of the Library of Science ONE* 3:e2570.

Fox, M., M. Corbetta, J. Vincent, and M. Raichle. 2006. Spontaneous neuronal activity distinguishes human dorsal and ventral attention systems. *Proc. Natl. Acad. Sci. USA* 103:10046–10051.

Fox, M., and M. Raichle. 2007. Spontaneous fluctuations in brain activity observed with functional magnetic resonance imaging. *Nat. Rev. Neurosci.* 8:700–711.

Garcia-Cabezas, M., B. Rico, M. Sanchez-Gonzalez, and C. Cavada. 2007. Distribution of the dopamine innervations in the macaque and human thalamus. *Neuroimage* 34:965–984.

Hillis, A., M. Newhart, J. Heidler, P. Barker, E. Herskovits, and M. Degaonkar. 2005. Anatomy of spatial attention: insights from perfusion imaging and hemispatial neglect in acute stroke. *J. Neurosci.* 25:3161–3167.

James, W. [1902] 1982. *The Varieties of Religious Experience: A Study in Human Nature*. New York: Penguin.

James, W. 1918. *The principles of psychology*. vol. 1. New York: Holt, 424.

Luo, Q., T. Holroyd, M. Jones, T. Hendler, and J. Blair. 2007. Neural dynamics for facial threat processing as revealed by gamma band synchronization using MEG. *Neuroimage* 34:839–847.

Lutz, A., H. Slagter, J. Dunne, and R. Davidson. 2008. Attention regulation and monitoring in meditation. *Trends Cogn. Sci.* 12:163–169.

Mulert, C., G. Leicht, O. Pogarell, R. Mergl, S. Karch, G. Juckel, et al. 2007. Auditory cortex and anterior cingulate cortex sources of the early evoked gamma-band response: Relationship to task difficulty and mental effort. *Neuropsychologia* 45:2294–2306.

Sdoia, S., A. Couyoumdjian, and F. Ferlazzo. 2004. Opposite visual field asymmetries for egocentric and allocentric spatial judgments. *Neuroreport* 15:1303–1305.

Slagter, H., A. Lutz, L. Greischar, S. Nieuwenhuis, and R. Davidson. 2009. Forthcoming. Theta phase synchrony and conscious target perception: Impact of intensive mental training. *J. Cogn. Neurosci.*

Volz, K., and D. von Cramon. 2006. What neuroscience can tell about intuitive processes in the context of perceptual discovery. *J. Cogn. Neurosci.* 18:2077–2087.

Yang, S., and C. Cox. 2008. Excitatory and anti-oscillatory actions of nitric oxide in thalamus. *J. Physiol.* 586:3617–3628.

16 Training Effortless Attention

Michael I. Posner, Mary K. Rothbart, M. R. Rueda, and Yiyuan Tang

Concept of Effort

The concept of effort is familiar in daily life. It involves the subjective experience of strain in connection with striving for a goal. Effort has also been given a technical definition within psychology that overlaps with the lay idea but is also somewhat different. In experimental psychology, effort has been defined as the amount of energy needed to accomplish a task. As such, effort is one of a cluster of motivational concepts that carry the idea of underlying energizing systems involved in task performance (Hockey, Gaillare, and Coles 1986). These include drive, arousal, activation, stress, alertness, vigilance and capacity. Effort can be measured by bodily changes and by interference between a primary and secondary task, and it can be reported subjectively by the person involved.

In this chapter we first summarize the concept of effort as it arose in experimental and cognitive psychology and as it has been translated into studies of brain activity. We argue that effortful control can be measured in daily life from psychometrically sound self- and parent reports and by cognitive tasks. These tasks can be related to specific nodes of neural networks that include frontal midline and lateral frontal areas as well as autonomic and central nervous system activity. We next examine where individual differences arise in the efficiency of brain networks related to effortful control, and we review educational training methods used with children that can alter these networks. We then describe state changes achieved in adults through meditation training. Meditation produces improved attentional performance while also changing the subjective state related to effort. Finally, we speculate on how these training methods are related to the concept of flow (Csikszentmihalyi 1990).

Physical and Psychological Measures of Effort
In the book *Attention and Effort*, Kahneman (1973) proposed converging psychological and physiological measures of effort. Effort is varied by manipulating the information-processing load in the task. In a classic study, people were given four digits to hold in

mind. They then were required to transform the digits by adding 0, 1, or 3 to them and then recall the transformed digits after being given a signal. Adding 3 was more difficult than adding 1; adding 0 was the easiest. Kahneman measured various autonomic indices such as pupil size, heart rate, and galvanic skin response over the 20-second interval of the task, finding that all three indices are related to subjective effort. Both objective and subjective effort were particularly high during the time when the digits were being transformed and during recall.

Posner (1978) sought to distinguish between automatic and effortful performance. Automatic effects can be obtained by priming a representation of a word (physical, phonological, or semantic) even if the person is unaware of the prime. Automatic priming has the effect of activating all representations related to the prime. If the person attends to the prime, the attended representation has priority while other representations fade. Attended representations require capacity and thus interfere with other tasks. For example, the probability of detecting a masked letter occurring during the interval when the participant is transforming the digits in Kahneman's experiment varied systematically with the difficulty of the transformation on the digits. In general, task difficulty on one task can be measured by reduced levels of performance on a secondary task. While controlled attention is similar to effort, it is less clear that automatic performance is the only way to achieve reduced effort.

Measures of central nervous system activity during mental effort have often been taken from scalp electrical recording. Several components of the EEG have been shown to be related to mental effort. For example, increased P300 amplitude has been used to index the degree of mental effort shown in a task (Posner 1978), while the frontal recorded N2 has been used as an index of the degree of conflict present (van Veen and Carter 2002). There is evidence that the N2 can be localized to the anterior cingulate gyrus, which is a part of the executive attention network (Posner et al. 2007). Partly for this reason the anterior cingulate has been associated with an executive attention network for the resolution of conflict and the control of effort (Posner et al. 2007).

Glucose metabolism has also been used as a measure of mental effort (Fairclough and Houston 2004). One study used the well-known Stroop effect as a measure of mental effort. The Stroop task asks the person to name the color of ink of words that designate either the same or a conflicting color (e.g., the word red in blue ink color). This conflict task has been used in many neuroimaging studies and has been shown to activate the dorsal anterior cingulate gyrus (Bush, Luu, and Posner 2000). The anterior cingulate has most often been activated when conflict is produced, as in the Stroop effect; however, it is likely activated whenever mental effort is involved, even if there is little or no conflict (Posner et al. 2007).

In summary, effort has been assessed through interference between primary and secondary tasks, through autonomic or central nervous system activity, or through subjective report. Reduced effort would be reflected in lowered or absent responses with these various methods.

Dissociating Objective and Subjective Effort

Koriat, Ma'ayan, and Nussinson (2006) discuss the distinction between reactive and regulatory aspects of effort in a recent paper on metacognition. In this paper they try to separate the monitoring of effort (phenomenal experience) from the control of effort (regulation) and to determine their causal sequence. Participants learned a series of associations between words and, in the same session, judged their probability of having learned each pair. If control efforts are the basis for phenomenal experience, people should judge items on which they spent more time as less likely to have been learned than those on which they spent little time. This is because effort is expended on more difficult items, which are harder to remember. If, however, phenomenal experience influences control, people should report items on which they spent more time as more likely to have been learned. In general, people conformed to the first model in which experience was at least partly influenced by control. However, subsequent experiments by the same authors indicated that, depending on task demands, phenomenal experience can either arise from the effort to exert control or can directly exercise influence on control.

Koriat and colleagues argue that the feeling of effort is driven to a larger than expected degree by the feedback from efforts to control. In other words, our perception of an effortful task depends upon analyzing the degree of our control of the task. They do not deny that perception can in some cases drive control, but empirical studies lead them to stress the position that perception is influenced from control operations. A separation between monitoring and control has also been observed in neuroimaging studies. The monitoring of effort, particularly in the cases of conflict and error detection, has usually been associated with the medial frontal areas like the anterior cingulate (Botvinick, Braver, Barch, Carter, and Cohen 2001), while more lateral frontal areas are thought to be involved in the actual control operations, including operations involved in working memory (Bush, Luu, and Posner 2000).

Another clue to dissociations between objective and subjective measures of effort comes from a recent patient study (Naccache et al. 2005). The patient, with a large left-hemisphere frontal lesion that included the anterior cingulate, was able to peform tasks requiring effort like the Stroop task but had no subjective feeling of difficulty and was unable to rate incongruent trials as more difficult than congruent ones. The authors suggest that the dissociation of performance from subjective impression was due to a disconnection involving the cingulate. Since the cingulate is an important structure in tasks that, like the Stroop effect, involve conflict and has also been important in regulating other brain networks (Posner, Rothbart, Sheese, and Tang

2007), this finding might indicate that the cingulate is involved in the subjective state related to mental effort.

In the next sections, we examine individual differences in the efficiency of attentional networks. We then consider two different ways of altering the efficiency of executive attention. One way is to train the network through exercises in conflict resolution. The other is a meditation-based state training.

Individual Differences

While the general brain network related to our feelings of effort is common to all people, there are differences in the efficiency of this network between people. Such differences could rest in part upon genetic variation among individuals and in part upon differences in cultural or individual experience. The study of temperament examines individual differences in reactivity and self-regulation that are biologically based (Rothbart and Bates 2006; Rothbart and Sheese 2007).

Effortful Control
Effortful control is a broad dimension of individual difference in temperament that can be measured in a person's self-report and in the report of caregivers of infants or children (Rothbart and Rueda 2005). Effortful control is defined as the ability of a person to select a nondominant response in preference to a dominant one, and questionnaires have been developed from year 2 to adulthood to measure it (Putnam, Ellis, and Rothbart 2001). Effortful control has been linked to the brain areas involved in self-regulation by imaging studies (Whittle 2007; Whittle et al. 2008). Whittle had 155 adolescents fill out a temperament scale (Ellis and Rothbart 2001) and also measured the size of different brain structures and their activity. She found that dorsal anterior cingulate size was positively correlated with effortful control. As mentioned above, the dorsal anterior cingulate is also the area found to be active during the Stroop task. During childhood, measures of effortful control have been shown to be related to the difficulty a child has in resolving conflict during Stroop like tasks (Rothbart and Rueda 2005). Effortful control and executive attention are, in turn, related to important aspects of children's social and emotional behavior, including empathy, prosocial behavior, and theory of mind (Posner and Rothbart 2007).

Attention Network Test
In our research we have used the Attention Network Test (ANT) to examine the efficiency of three brain networks underlying attention: alerting, orienting, and the executive attention network related to effort (Fan, McCandliss, Sommer, Raz,& Posner 2003). The ANT requires the participant to press one key if a central arrow appearing on the monitor points to the left and another if it points to the right. Conflict is

introduced by having surrounding flankers either point in the same (congruent) or opposite (incongruent) direction. Cues presented prior to the target provide information on either where or when the target will occur. Reaction times for the separate conditions are subtracted to provide three scores representing the efficiency of each individual in the alerting, orienting, and executive networks. In a sample of 40 adults (Fan, Flombaum, McCandliss, Thomas, et al. 2003), we found each of these measures to be reliable over repeated presentations. In addition, we found no correlation among the scores.

A subsequent study using functional magnetic resonance imaging (fMRI; Fan, McCandliss, Fossella, Flombaum, et al. 2005) showed that the anatomy of these three networks was, for the most part, independent. Different networks of neural areas represent the sources of the alerting, orienting, and executive (conflict) attention network. In the case of the executive network, the areas involve the anterior cingulate, lateral prefrontal cortex, and the underlying basal ganglia. Each of the networks has a dominant neuromodulator arising from subcortical brain areas. In the case of the executive network, this is dopamine. Although the networks clearly work together in many tasks, they do seem to have a large degree of independence.

Scores on the executive network of the ANT are correlated with the measures of temperamental effortful control (EC) at several ages during childhood. Gerardi-Caulton (2000) carried out some of the first research linking EC to underlying brain networks of executive attention, using a spatial conflict task. Similar findings linking parent-reported temperamental EC to performance on laboratory attention tasks have been shown for 24-, 30-, and 36-month-olds (Rothbart, Ellis, Rueda, and Posner 2003), 3- and 5-year-olds (Chang and Burns 2005), 7- to 10-year-olds (Simonds, Kieras, Rueda, and Rothbart 2007), and adults (Kanske 2008).

Genes and Experience

Since the success of the human genome project, it has become increasingly possible to suggest which genes are related to specific neural networks. To determine genes that might be related to building an attentional network, we used the ANT to examine individual differences in the efficiency of executive attention (Fan, McCandliss, Sommer, Raz, and Posner 2002).

We then used the association of the executive network with the neuromodulator dopamine as a way of searching for candidate genes that might relate to the efficiency of the network (Fossella et al. 2002). To do this, 200 persons performed the ANT and were genotyped to examine frequent gene polymorphisms related to dopamine. We found significant association of two genes, the dopamine receptor D4 (DRD4) gene and the monoamine oxidase A (MAOA) gene, with executive attention. We then conducted a neuroimaging experiment in which persons with different alleles of these two genes were compared while they performed the ANT (Fan, Fossella, Sommer, and

Posner 2003). Groups with different alleles of these genes showed differences in the ability to resolve conflict as measured by the ANT and produced significantly different activations in the anterior cingulate, a major node of the executive attention network.

Recent studies have extended these observations. In two different studies employing conflict-related tasks other than the ANT, alleles of the catechol-O-methyltransferase (COMT) gene were related to the ability to resolve conflict (Blasi et al., 2005; Diamond, Briand, Fossella, and Gehlbach 2004). A study using the child ANT also showed a significant relation between the dopamine transporter (SLC6A3/DAT1) gene and executive attention (Rueda, Rothbart, McCandliss, Saccamanno, and Posner 2005). In addition, research has suggested that genes related to serotonin transmission also influence executive attention (Canli, Omura, Haas, Fallgatter, Todd, Constable, and Lesch 2005; Reuter, Ott, Vaidl, and Henning 2007). Future studies should determine other genetic influences and examine their interaction and modes of operation.

The relation of genetic factors to the functioning of the executive attention system does not mean that the system cannot be influenced by experience. Rather, it appears that some genetic variation allows for additional influence from parenting and other experience (Sheese, Voelker, Rothbart, and Posner 2007). In a longitudinal study conducted in our lab, we found that the 7-repeat allele of the dopamine 4 Receptor D4 gene interacted with the quality of parenting to influence such temperamental variables in the child as activity level, sensation seeking, and impulsivity. With high-quality parenting, 2-year-old children with the 7-repeat allele showed average levels of these temperamental traits, whereas with lower quality parenting, children with the 7-repeat allele showed high levels of the same traits Children without the 7-repeat had average levels of these traits irrespective of parenting quality. Other research has shown similar findings for parenting effects of the DRD4 7-repeat allele on externalizing behaviors of the child, as rated by the parents in the Child Behavior Checklist (Bakermans-Kranenburg and van Ijzendoorn 2006).

There is evidence that the 7-repeat allele of the DRD4 gene is under positive selective pressure (Ding et al. 2002). Our results suggest a possible reason for this. Genetic variation may make it more likely that children will be influenced by their culture through parenting style. This idea could be important for understanding why the frequency of genetic alleles has changed during human evolution. In accord with this idea, a recent study showed that only those children with the 7-repeat allele of the DRD4 showed the influence of a parent training intervention (Bakermans-Kranenburg, van Ijzendoorn, Pijlman, Mesman, and Juffer 2008).

In our experiments, the DRD4 7-repeat allele did not influence the executive attention network but seemed to act more directly on temperamental characteristics. However, our results with 18- to 20-month-old children show that toddlers with high-quality parenting and different alleles of the COMT and cholinergic receptor, nicotinic, alpha 4 (CHRNA4) genes showed significant differences in our assessments of the efficiency of executive attention (Voelker et al. 2009). These results highlight the idea that the development of attention networks reflects both genetic instructions and early environmental inputs.

Genes do not directly produce attention. What they do is code for proteins that influence the efficiency with which modulators such as dopamine are produced and/or bind to their receptors. These modulators are, in turn, related to individual differences in the efficiency of the attention networks. There is a great deal in common among humans in the anatomy of high-level networks, and this must have a basis within the human genome. The same genes that are related to individual differences in attention are also likely to be important in the development of the attentional networks common to all humans. Some of these networks are also common to nonhuman animals. By examining these networks in animals, it should be possible to better understand the role of genes in shaping networks.

The parenting-by-gene interactions suggest that experience is important for developing regulation of attention and behavior. In the next section we describe our efforts to influence executive attention in two different studies. One involves young children and the other undergraduate students.

Training Attention

Training Attention in Young Children

To examine the effect of experience on the executive attention network, we developed and tested a five-day training intervention that uses computerized exercises (Rueda, Rothbart, et al. 2005). We tested the effect of training during the period of major development of executive attention between 4 and 7 years of age (Rueda, Posner, and Rothbart 2005). We hoped to develop methods that could be used to improve the efficiency of children's executive attention network.

The training began with the children's learning to use a joystick. First, they used the joystick to move a cat shown on the monitor to the grass so as to avoid mud. Over trials, the grass area shrank and the mud area increased, requiring more careful control of the cat. These joystick skills were then used to teach prediction, to exercise working memory, and finally to give children practice in resolving conflict. Children who went through the training were compared with a randomly selected control group who were engaged with interactive videos.

Recording of brain activation before and after training showed clear evidence of improvement in the executive attention network following training. The N2 component of the scalp-recorded averaged electrical potential has been shown to arise in the anterior cingulate and is related to monitoring or resolution of conflict (van Veen and Carter 2002; Jonkman, Sniedt, and Kemner 2007). We found N2 differences between congruent and incongruent trials of the ANT in trained 6-year-olds that resembled differences found in adults. In 4-year-olds, training seemed to influence more anterior electrodes that might relate to emotional control areas of the cingulate (Bush et al. 2000). These data suggest that training altered the network for the resolution of conflict in the direction of being more like what is found in adults.

We also found a significantly greater improvement in a measure of intelligence in the trained group compared to the control children. This finding suggested that training effects had generalized to a measure of cognitive processing that is far removed from the training exercises. It also suggests that the network related to IQ, which includes both medial and lateral frontal brain areas (Duncan et al. 2000), would be improved, probably due to the training involving working memory as well as conflict resolution.

Recently, a replication of this study was carried out for 5-year-olds in a Spanish preschool (Rueda, Checa, and Santonja 2008). Several additional exercises were added, and 10 days of training were provided for the experimental group. As in the previous study, the randomly assigned control group viewed child-appropriate videos for the same amount of time as the training group. A follow-up session for all children was also given two months after the training. The experimental group showed a significant improvement in the matrices scale of the intelligence test following training that was maintained over the two months without further training, while the control group did not show any significant improvement. Since the training included working memory, we suspect that both medial and lateral frontal areas were affected. Training of attention also produced beneficial effects on performance of tasks involving affective regulation, such as delay of reward tasks and regulation of wins and loses in a gambling task for children.

The training in children seemed to work primarily on the executive attention network, which is closely associated with our feelings of effort. Improvement in this network could have widespread influence on behavior. For example, attentional difficulties are a very frequent symptom related to failure in school and to different forms of psychopathology (Rothbart and Posner 2007). However, without a real understanding of the neural substrates of attention, there have not been systematic efforts to remedy attentional problems. This situation has been changed with the application of our understanding of attentional networks to the development of the interventions discussed in this section. We hope our training method will be evaluated along with other such methods as a means of improving attention prior to school and for children diagnosed with attention-deficit/hyperactivity disorder and other attention-related disorders. We do not have any expectation that our exercises are optimal or even better than other methods but conclude that the study of attention training as a whole suggests that networks can be improved by training. With an understanding of which training method improves what aspect of network function, it might be possible to design more appropriate methods for children of various ages and with various forms of disabilities.

Improving Attention through Meditation

There is considerable evidence that training exercises provided by meditation might improve aspects of attention in adults (Jha, Klein, Krompinger, and Baime 2007; Slagter, Lutz, Greischar, Francis, Nieuwenhuis, Davis, and Davidson 2007). While some of this evidence is impressive, it has not used brief training or random assignment to examine changes, as we have done for attention training in children.

To accomplish this goal, a training method called Integrative Body–Mind Training (IBMT) was adopted from traditional Chinese medicine (Tang et al. 2007). In this method the trainee concentrates on achieving a balanced state of mind through training by a trainer and a CD containing instructions and background music. Trainees are taught to relax, adjust their breathing, use mental imagery, and achieve a state of calm balance. Because this approach is suitable for novices, it was hypothesized that a short period of training and practice might influence the efficiency of the executive attention network related to self-regulation (Tang et al. 2007). The study used a random assignment of 40 Chinese undergraduates to an experimental group and 40 to a control group for five days of training, requiring 20 minutes per day. The experimental group was given a short-term version of IBMT. The control group was given relaxation training (Benson 1975; Bernstein and Borkoved 1973). Training was presented in a standardized way via a CD and guided by a skillful IBMT trainer. Because of the importance of the trainer, each of the trainers in this study had considerable experience with IBMT.

The two groups were given a battery of tests a week before training and immediately after the final training session. Tests included the ANT, the Raven's Standard Progressive Matrices (a standard culture-neutral intelligence test), a measure of mood state (the Profile of Mood States, POMS), and a stress challenge (mental arithmetic task) followed by assays of cortisol release as a measure of stress. All of these are standard measures scored objectively by experimenters who were blind to the experimental condition.

The experimental group showed significantly greater improvement in executive attention than the control group. Similar results were obtained for self-reports of lower negative affect and fatigue on the POMS. The experimental group also showed less cortisol response to a cognitive challenge following training than did the control group, suggesting that training improved the handling of the stressor. Results of our studies (Tang et al. 2007) indicated that meditation changes important aspects of mood as well as the efficiency of executive attention. Studies underway using fMRI during meditation training may help our understanding of the brain changes involved. In an additional study, either five days or five weeks of training was given. Five weeks of IBMT improved both alerting and executive attention significantly more than did five days. In addition, the regulation of cortisol secretion was much stronger after the longer period of training.

Since participants were randomly assigned to experimental and control groups and objective tests were used by researchers blind to the condition, we conclude that IBMT improved executive attention more than the relaxation control. The reaction to a mental stressor was also significantly improved in the experimental group, which showed less cortisol excretion than the control group after the additional training. These outcomes after only five days of training open a new door for simple and effective investigations of meditation effects. The IBMT provides a convenient method for studying the influence of meditation training using appropriate experimental and control methods similar to those used to test drugs or other interventions. The findings also indicate the potential of IBMT for stress management, body–mind health, and improvement in cognitive performance and self-regulation (Tang 2005; Tang et al. 2007).

Why does the IBMT work after only a few days of practice while studies with other methods often require months? The following are possible reasons. First, the IBMT integrates several key components of body–mind techniques, including body relaxation (Benson 1975), breathing adjustment, mental imagery (Watanabe, Fukuda, and Shirakawa 2005), and mindfulness training, which have shown broad positive effects on attention, emotion, and social behavior in previous studies. This combination may amplify the training effect over the use of only one of these components. Second, since everyone experiences mindfulness sometimes a qualified coach can help each participant increase the amount of this experience and thus guarantee that each practice session achieves a good result (Tang 2005; Tang et al. 2007). For participants with months to years of meditation, there has been the opportunity to make mistakes, correct them, and gradually find the right way. Recent findings indicate, however, that the amount of time participants spend meditating each day, rather than the total number of hours of meditative practice over their lifetime, is related to their performance on attentional tasks (Chan and Woollacott 2007).

In order for meditation practice to improve attention and self-regulation in only five days, a very high quality of training is needed. To ensure this quality, a trainer is needed to help trainees with problems in obtaining a balanced state of mind and body. Although trainers are not present during the training sessions, they observe the trainees over TV and help them after the session with problems. The trainers could well be a part of the effective ingredient of IBMT, and their role requires additional research.

Why should IBMT improve executive attention? One possibility is that IBMT works by allowing the trainee to maintain the alert state longer and thus improve performance. However, evidence suggests that alertness improves with IBMT more slowly than does executive attention. Another possibility is that it occurs via the tendency of IBMT to improve mood. Positive moods produce greater fluency, but that may not be true for more general cognitive processes. Another possibility is that IBMT reduces the feelings of stress involved with difficult tasks. It is known that IBMT reduces cortisol secretion, so this mechanism would be a reasonable possibility. More research will be needed to establish the exact mechanism leading from IBMT training to executive attention improvements.

Meditation and Flow

Flow appears to be defined primarily as the absence of subjective effort while still accomplishing a task or goal that might at another time or by another person seem effortful. As Csikszentmihalyi puts it in his volume *Finding Flow,* "The metaphor of 'flow' is one that many people have used to describe the sense of effortless action they feel in moments that stand out as the best in their lives" (Csikszentmihalyi 1990).

Csikszentmihalyi recognizes that the flow experience requires effort as defined by objective measures, but subjectively the effort is not noticed because the mind is occupied with the task at hand. Does the evidence for training attention provide a basis for deciding whether flow can be improved?

Because flow involves being totally occupied with the present task so as to suspend evaluations, it has many similarities to the state of mindfulness which involves being completely in the current moment. In his book on mindfulness, Siegel (2007, 119) suggests that when midline cortical regions (e.g., the anterior cingulate) are engaged without activation of lateral prefrontal areas involved in working memory, a mindful state might be obtained without effort.

Siegel's effortless mindfulness is very much like flow. It seems to involve activity in the anterior cingulate not accompanied by lateral frontal activation. We do not yet know whether either training of executive attention can actually produce this state. However, practice in tasks involving conflict resolution is likely to produce increased activity in both medial and lateral brain areas involved in general cognitive processes. This form of training may be similar to reducing the difficulty of a task. Making the task easier would reduce effort but also reduce the feelings of accomplishment in carrying out a difficult task.

Flow shares similar components with deep meditation, which has been described as including occupied, effortless, joyful, and satisfied feelings (Tang 2005, 2007). Meditation training has been described as proceeding from effortful practice to effortless practice. In initial stages, a practitioner devotes mental effort to achieve a quiet and relaxed state which is quite different from daily life with a restless, wandering mind and diverse emotions. This requires strong executive function and capacity. This can be termed the "actor stage." With practice, the person experiences a deeply relaxed state, meaning that one enters the midstage of meditation. This process still requires effortful control, but at this stage the autonomic system starts to work in parallel with the central nervous system. We speculate that the anterior cingulate cortex plays an important role in this stage to maintain the balance of cognitive control and autonomic activity. We term it the "actor and director stage." In later meditation stages, the practitioner doesn't need strong effort to maintain the meditative state. The mind is deeply in this state, and one totally forgets the body, oneself, and the environment. We term this the "director stage."

While the late stage of meditation training is appropriate to the appearance of the "flow" feeling, we don't have direct evidence that meditation will increase the likelihood of reported mindful flow experiences on the part of the trained person. However, the increase of flow reports in trained meditators would be a prediction from the association between flow and the late stage of meditation. Based on Siegel's speculation, one might predict that meditation, as in our adult studies, would have its influence primarily on the anterior cingulate, which is associated with medial frontal activity. On the other hand, practice in specific computer exercises, as in our studies with children, might have its effect on the coordination of medial and lateral frontal activity and not result in increased flow experience. In the future, imaging data and subjective report data might provide an opportunity to examine the relation between attention training, mindfulness, and flow in more detail.

Acknowledgment

This research was supported by National Institute of Child Health and Human Development grant HD35801 to Georgia State Universities, by the James S. Bower and John Templeton Foundation Grants, and by a grant from the Spanish Government.

References

Bakermans-Kranenburg, M. J., and M. H. van Ijzendoorn. 2006. Gene–environment interaction of the dopamine D4 receptor (DRD4) and observed maternal insensitivity predicting externalizing behavior in preschoolers. *Dev. Psychobiol.* 48:406–409.

Bakermans-Kranenburg, M. J., M. H. V. van Ijzendoorn, F. T. Pijlman, J. Mesman, and F. Juffer. 2008. Experimental evidence for differential suscetibiliy: Dopamine DRD4 (VNTR) Moderates intervention effects of toddlers' externalizing behavior in a randomized control trial. *Dev. Psychol.* 44:293–300.

Benson, H. 1975. *The relaxation response.* New York: Avon.

Bernstein, D. A., and T. D. Borkoved. 1973. *Progressive relaxation training.* Champaign, IL: Research Press.

Blasi, G., G. S. Mattay, A. Bertolino, B. Elvevåg, J. H. Callicott, S. Das, et al. 2005. Effect of cCatechol-O-Methyltransferase val ^{158} met genotype on attentional control. *J. Neurosci.* 25:5038–5045.

Botvinick, M. M., T. S. Braver, D. M. Barch, C. S. Carter, and J. D. Cohen. 2001. Conflict monitoring and cognitive control. *Psychol. Rev.* 108:624–652.

Bush, G., P. Luu, and M. I. Posner. 2000. Cognitive and emotional influences in the anterior cingulate cortex. *Trends Cogn. Sci.* 4:215–222.

Canli, T., K. Omura, B. W. Haas, A. Fallgatter, R. Todd, R. T. Constable, and K. P. Lesch. 2005. Beyond affect: A role for genetic variation of the serotonin transporter in neural activation during a cognitive attention task. *Proc. Natl. Acad. Sci. USA* 102:12224–12229.

Chan, D., and M. Woollacott. 2007. Effects of level of meditation experience on attentional focus: Is the efficiency of executive or orientation networks improved? *J. Altern. Complement. Med.* 13:651–658.

Chang, F., and B. M. Burns. 2005. Attention in preschoolers: Associations with effortful control and motivation. *Child Dev.* 76:247–263.

Csikszentmihalyi, M. 1990. *Flow*. New York: Harper & Row.

Diamond, A., L. Briand, J. Fossella, and L. Gehlbach. 2004. Genetic and neurochemical modulation of prefrontal cognitive functions in children. *Am. J. Psychiatry* 161:125–132.

Ding, Y. C., H. C. Chi, D. L. Grady, A. Morishima, J. R. Kidd, K. K. Kidd, P. Flodman, et al. 2002. Evidence of positive selection acting at the human dopamine receptor D4 gene locus. *Proc. Natl. Acad. Sci. USA* 99:309–314.

Duncan, J., R. J. Seitz, J. Kolodny, D. Bor, H. Herzog, A. Ahmed, et al. 2000. A neural basis for general intelligence. *Science* 289:457–460.

Ellis, L., and M. K. Rothbart. 2001. Revision of the early adolescent termperament questionnaire. Paper presented 2001 meeting SRCD, Minneapolis, MN.

Fan, J., J. I. Flombaum, B. D. McCandliss, K. M. Thomas, and M. I. Posner 2003. Cognitive and brain consequences of conflict. *Neuroimage* 18:42–57.

Fan, J., J. A. Fossella, T. Sommer, and M. I. Posner. 2003. Mapping the genetic variation of executive attention onto brain activity. *Proc. Natl. Acad. Sci. USA* 100:7406–7411.

Fan, J., B. D. McCandliss, J. Fossella, J. I. Flombaum, and M. I. Posner. 2005. The activation of attentional networks. *Neuroimage* 26:471–479.

Fan, J., B. D. McCandliss, T. Sommer, M. Raz, and M. I. Posner. 2002. Testing the efficiency and independence of attentional networks. *J. Cogn. Neurosci.* 3 (14):340–347.

Fairclough, S. H., and K. Houston. 2004. A metabolic measure of mental effort. *Biol. Psychiatry* 66:177–190.

Fossella, J., T. Sommer, J. Fan, Y. Wu, J. M. Swanson, D. W. Pfaff, and M. I. Posner. 2002. Assessing the molecular genetics of attention networks. *BMC Neurosci.* 3:14.

Gerardi-Caulton, G. 2000. Sensitivity to spatial conflict and the development of self-regulation in children 24–36 months of age. *Dev. Sci.* 3:397–404.

Hockey, G. R. J., Gaillard, A. W. K., and Coles, M. G. H. 1986. *Energetics and human information processing.* Dodrecht: Matinus/Nijhoff.

Jha, A., R. Klein, J. Krompinger, and M. Baime. 2007. Mindfulness training modifies subsystems of attention. *Cogn. Affect. Behav. Neurosci.* 7:109–119.

Jonkman, L. M., F. L. F. Sniedt, and C. Kemner. 2007. Source localization of the Nogo-N2: A developmental study. *Clin. Neurophysiol.* 118:1069–1077.

Kahneman, D. 1973. *Attention and effort.* Englewood Cliffs, NJ: Prentice Hall.

Kanske, P. 2008. Exploring executive attention in emotion: ERP and fMRI evidence. Unpublished dissertation, University of Dresden.

Koriat, A., H. Ma'ayan, and R. Nussinson. 2006. The intricate relationships between monitoring and control in metacognition: Lessons for the cause-and-effect relation between subjective experience and behavior. *J. Exp. Psychol. Gen.* 135:36–69.

Naccache, L., S. Dehaene, L. Cohen, M. O. Habert, E. Guichart-Gomez, D. Galanaud, and J. C. Willer. 2005. Effortless control: Executive attention and conscious feelings of mental effort are dissociable. *Neuropsychologia* 43:1318–1328.

Posner, M. I. 1978. *Chronometric explorations of mind.* Hillsdale, NJ: Erlbaum.

Posner, M. I., and M. K. Rothbart. 2007. Attention as a model system for the integration of cognitive science. *Annu. Rev. Psychol.* 58:1–23.

Posner, M. I., M. K. Rothbart, B. E. Sheese, and Y. Tang. 2007. The anterior cingulate gyrus and the mechanisms of self regulation. *Cogn. Affective Behav. Neurosci.* 7:391–395.

Putnam, S. P., L. K. Ellis, and M. K. Rothbart. 2001. The structure of temperament from infancy through adolescence. In *Advances/proceedings in research on temperament*, ed. A. Eliasz and A. Angleitner. Berlin: Pabst Scientist, 165–182.

Reuter, M., U. Ott, D. Vaidl, and J. Henning. 2007. Impaired executive attention is associated with a variation in the promotor region of the tryptophan hydroxylase-2 gene. *J. Cogn. Neurosci.* 19:401–408.

Rothbart, M. K., and J. E. Bates. 2006. Temperament in children's development. In *Handbook of child psychology.* vol. 3. *Social, emotional, and personality development.* 6th ed. W. Damon and R. Lerner (book eds.) and N. Eisenberg (vol. ed.). New York: Wiley, 99–166.

Rothbart, M. K., L. K. Ellis, M. R. Rueda, and M. I. Posner. 2003. Developing mechanisms of temperamental effortful control. *J. Pers.* 71:1113–1143.

Rothbart, M. K., and M. R. Rueda. 2005. The development of effortful control. In *Developing individuality in the human brain: A tribute to Michael I. Posner*, ed. U. Mayr, E. Awh, and S. W. Keele. Washington, DC: American Psychological Association, 167–188.

Rothbart, M. K., and B. Sheese. 2007. Temperament and emotion regulation. In *Handbook of emotion regulation*, ed. J. J. Gross. New York: Guilford, 331–350.

Rueda, M. R., P. Checa, and M. Santonja. 2008. *Training executive attention: Lasting effects and transfer to affective self-regulation*. Paper presented at the Annual Meeting of the Cognitive Neuroscience Society.

Rueda, M., M. I. Posner, and M. K. Rothbart. 2005. The development of executive attention: Contributions to the emergence of self-regulation. *Dev. Neuropsychol.* 28:573–594.

Rueda, M. R., M. K. Rothbart, B. D. McCandliss, L. Saccamanno, and M. I. Posner. 2005. Training, maturation and genetic influences on the development of executive attention. *Proc. Natl. Acad. Sci. USA* 102:14931–14936.

Sheese, B. E., P. Voelker, M. K. Rothbart, and M. I. Posner. 2007. Caregiver quality interacts with genetic variation to influence aspects of toddler temperament. *Dev. Psychopathol.* 19:1039–1046.

Siegel, D. J. 2007. *The mindful brain: Reflection and attunement in the cultivation of well-being*. New York: Norton.

Simonds, J., J. E. Kieras, M. Rueda, and M. K. Rothbart. 2007. Effortful control, executive attention, and emotional regulation in 7–10-year-old children. *Cogn. Dev.* 22:474–488.

Slagter, H. A., A. Lutz, L. L. Greischar, A. D. Francis, S. Nieuwenhuis, J. M. Davis, and R. J. Davidson. 2007. Mental training affects use of limited brain resources. *Public Library of Science* 5:e138.

Tang, Y. 2005. *Health from brain, wisdom from brain*. Dailan, China: Dailan University Press.

Tang, Y. 2007. *Multi-intelligence and unfolding the full potentials of brain*. Dalian, China: Dalian University of Technology Press.

Tang, Y. Y., Y. Ma, J. Wang, Y. Fan, S. Feng, Q. Lu, et al. 2007. Short-term meditation training improves attention and self regulation. *Proc. Natl. Acad. Sci. USA* 104:17152–17156.

van Veen, V., and C. S. Carter. 2002. The timing of action-monitoring processes in the anterior cingulate cortex. *J. Cogn. Neurosci.* 14:593–602.

Voelker, P., B. E. Sheese, M. K. Rothbart, and M. I. Posner. 2009. Variations in catechol-O-methyltransferase gene interact with parenting to influence attention in early development. *Neuroscience.* 164:121–130.

Watanabe, E., S. Fukuda, and T. Shirakawa. 2005. Effects among healthy subjects of the duration of regularly practicing a guided imagery program. *BMC Complement. Altern. Med.* 5:21.

Whittle, S. L. 2007. *The neurobiological correlates of temperament in early adolescents*. Unpublished doctoral dissertation, University of Melbourne, Australia.

Whittle, S., M. Yücel, A. Fornito, A. Barrett, S. J. Wood, D. I. Lubman, et al. 2008. Neuroanatomical correlates of temperament in early adolescents. *J. Am. Acad. Child Adolesc. Psychiatry* 47:682–693.

Contributors

Joshua M. Ackerman Sloan School of Management, Massachusetts Institute of Technology, Cambridge, Massachusetts

James H. Austin Department of Neurology, University of Florida College of Medicine, Gainesville, Florida

John A. Bargh Department of Psychology, Yale University, New Haven, Connecticut

Roy F. Baumeister Department of Psychology, Florida State University, Tallahassee, Florida

Sian L. Beilock Department of Psychology, The University of Chicago, Chicago, Illinois

Chris Blais Helen Wills Neuroscience Institute, University of California, Berkeley, California

Matthew M. Botvinick Department of Psychology, Princeton University, Princeton, New Jersey

Brian Bruya Department of History and Philosophy, Eastern Michigan University, Ypsilanti, Michigan

Mihaly Csikszentmihalyi School of Behavioral and Organizational Sciences, Claremont Graduate University, Claremont, California

Marci S. DeCaro Department of Psychology and Human Development, Vanderbilt University, Nashville, Tennessee

Örjan de Manzano Division of Neuropediatrics, Department of Women's and Children's Health, Karolinska Institutet, Stockholm, Sweden

Arne Dietrich Department of Social and Behavioral Sciences, American University of Beirut, Lebanon

Yuri Dormashev Department of Psychology, Lomonosov Moscow State University, Moscow, Russia

László Harmat Institute of Behavioural Sciences, Semmelweis University, Budapest, Hungary

Bernhard Hommel Leiden University Institute for Psychological Research and Leiden Institute for Brain and Cognition, Leiden, The Netherlands

Rebecca Lewthwaite Physical Therapy Department, Rancho Los Amigos National Rehabilitation Center, Downey, California; Division of Biokinesiology and Physical Therapy, University of Southern California, Los Angeles, California

Joseph T. McGuire Department of Psychology, Princeton University, Princeton, New Jersey

Brian P. Meier Department of Psychology, Gettysburg College, Gettysburg, Pennsylvania

Arlen C. Moller Department of Preventive Medicine, Northwestern University, Chicago, Illinois; Department of Psychology, Gettysburg College, Gettysburg, Pennsylvania

Jeanne Nakamura School of Behavioral and Organizational Sciences, Claremont Graduate University, Claremont, California

Evgeny N. Osin Department of Psychology, Higher School of Economics, Moscow, Russia

Michael I. Posner Institute of Cognitive and Decision Sciences, Department of Psychology, University of Oregon, Eugene, Oregon

Mary K. Rothbart Department of Psychology, University of Oregon, Eugene, Oregon

M. R. Rueda Department of Experimental Psychology, University of Granada, Granada, Spain

Brandon J. Schmeichel Department of Psychology, Texas A&M University, College Station, Texas

Edward Slingerland Department of Asian Studies, University of British Columbia, Vancouver, British Columbia

Oliver Stoll Department of Sport Sciences, University of Halle-Wittenberg, Halle, Germany

Yiyuan Tang Institute of Neuroinformatics and Laboratory for Body and Mind, Dalian University Technology, Dalian, China

Töres Theorell Stress Research Institute, Stockholm University, Stockholm, Sweden

Fredrik Ullén Division for Neuropediatrics, Department of Women's and Children's Health, Karolinska Institutet, Stockholm, Sweden

Robert D. Wall Care Code, Inc., Leesburg, Virginia

Gabriele Wulf Department of Kinesiology and Nutrition Sciences, University of Nevada, Las Vegas, Nevada

Index

absorption, state of, 310–311, 312–313, 325–326n35
  versus flow, 312
  following voluntary attention, 317
  internal, 400–401, 402–403
achievement motivation, 200–201
Ackerman, Joshua, 17
action
  versus activities, 237–238
  adjustment of, 126–127
    action planning and, 128–130
  attention and performance of, 159–160
  in cognitive control, 142
  deliberative, 8–9
  drivers of, 242–243n7
  effort and, 1
  facilitating perception, 340–341, 342
  formality in, 237, 238–239, 240–241
  intentional control of, 121–136
  nonagentive, 14
  operation and, 289–290
  orientation of, volatility-persistence component of, 200
  perception and, 340–342
  syntax of, 9–12, 240–241
action-at-a-distance effect, 231
action-awareness merging, 205, 306, 312
action motivations, 342–344
action planning
  action adjustment and, 128–130
  neural pathways for, 126–127
  perception and, 133–134
  perceptual events and, 124–125
  visual processing and, 128–130
action-related processing, 125–127
action representation, driving attention, 10–11
activity, 293. *See also* expertise, skills and syntax
  versus action, 237–238
  attention as act of, 302–305
  complex, 290
  degree of syntax of, 237–238
  domain of, 10–12, 16–18, 20, 28n2, 51, 58, 65, 66, 68, 108, 209, 210, 212, 224, 227, 228, 232, 243n7, 251, 258, 345, 352 (*see also* contextual structure of reference)
  excitation of, 306
  in flow experience, 287–319
  gestalt, 293–294, 295, 315
  motive in, 289
  object of, 289
  as object of attention, 296–302
  organism level of, 295
  person level of, 15
  polymotivated, 289
  psychological theory of, 288–296, 321n11, 323–324n24
  simple, 289–290
  structure of, 289–290
  unit of, 322n14
  value-related, 324n28

Activity Experience Scale, 206
activity-level attention, 308–314
adaptation, attention in, 179–180
adaptive unconscious, 277n7
ADS. *See* Aperture, Draw, Syntax model of attention
affect coordination, 212, 337
agency,
  ethics and, 15
  intentional, 16
  research on, 12–15
  sense of, 13
agent
  of attention, 305, 324
  individual, 14
  moral, 249, 265
  multimodal, 16
  rational, 15
  social, 14
allocentric perspective, 378–379
  receptive, 403–404
  in stroke patients, 379–382
Analects (Confucius), 248, 275, 279n33, 279n35–n36
  virtue ethics in, 268–276
anatta, 392–393
Anscombe, G. E. M., 267–268
anterior cingulate cortex (ACC)
  activity of in demand-based decision making, 107
  in conflict monitoring, 115–116
  demand level and activity of, 109
  demand monitoring by, 107–108
  demand-related bodily arousal and, 111–113
  lesions of in subjective feelings, 411–412
apertures, 224–227
  draw
    implications of, 234–241
    limitations of, 241–242
  diffuse attention, 225–229
Aperture, Draw, Syntax model of attention, 220, 226–229, 234–236, 240–241

Aristotle, 248, 250, 268, 306
  categories of, 256–257
arousal, 220, 409
  attention and, 392, 404
  demand-related, 111–113
  in flow experience, 206–207, 211
  high level of, 354
  hypnotic, 254
  inhibition and, 300
  joyous, 18
  physiological/bodily, 111–112
  valence and, 206
associations, systems of, 299–301
associative maps, 226–227
associative processing, 65–66, 67
atherosclerotic process, flow and, 213
athlete burnout syndrome, 171
attachment style
  anxious-ambivalent, 38–39
  avoidant, 38–39
attention. *See also* dorsal attention system, effortlessness; emotional attention; executive attention; flow; visual attention
  as act of activity, 302–305
  action control and, 127–128
  action representation driving, 10–11
  activity approach to, 287–319
  activity as object of, 296–302
  anticipated cognitive demand and, 103–116
  apertures of, 224–229
  in autotelic activity, 305–318
  awareness and, 355–357
  beam-of-light metaphor for, 225–226
  bottom-up versus top-down influences on, 30
  cognitive draw and, 229–232
  cognitive schemas in, 318
  concentration characteristic of, 322–323n17
  contextual structures of reference and, 227–229
  coordinative and administrative functions of, 122
  current theories of, 6

Index   431

in daily life, 181–186
decreasing objective effort during, 7
definition of, 297
diffuse, 222
  as aperture, 225–229
  versus selective attention, 223–224
distributed representations and common coding of, 123–125
divided, 242n1, 242n5
draw of, 11–12, 229–232
drivers of, 227–232
early onset, 15
effortful, 1, 135–136, 354
  control of, 29–47
  objectivist self and, 248–249
effortless, 19. *See also* effortlessness; flow
  automaticity and, 186
  conditions for, 186–188
  in Confucian virtue ethics, 268–276
  control of, 33–34
  in decision making, 8
  definition of, 5
  direct path to, 188
  in early Chinese thought, 247
  enhancement of, 188
  in everyday life, 179–188
  indirect path to, 188
  individual differences in, 412–415
  interest and, 220–221
  laboratory research on, 11
  mechanisms of, 159–160
  neurocognitive underpinnings of, 161–165
  perfectionism and, 170–174
  physiology of, 205–213, 210–211
  quality of life and, 181–186
  thalamus in, 386–387, 386–405
  training, 409–420
  transient hypofrontality and, 165–170
  virtue ethics and, 266–268
exogenous versus endogenous control of, 30
expertise and, 17–18
external focus in movement effectiveness and efficiency, 75–96

eye movement programming and, 128
in flow experience, 222–223
flow proneness and, 207–208
focused, 182–186
forced, 298–299, 304
function of, 121–123
gap between description and explanation of, 287–288
grounding in action control, 121–136
intensity of, 308
intentional control framework for, 128–134
involuntary, 298–299
as key characteristic of flow experience, 306–308
limited capacity of, 122–123
meditation improving, 375–377, 417–419
mental training and, 21
models of, 221–224
multiple processing pathways of, 125–127
organization of, 298
personality approach to, 298–299
phenomena of, 322n16
physiological mechanisms of, 324n29
postvoluntary, 4, 5, 300–301, 316–318, 323n22
  flow as, 314–318
  persona level in, 15
psychological approach to, 219, 288–296
as psychological resource, 180
in quality of life, 181
remodeling of, 219–242
selective, 31, 221–222, 308
  versus diffuse attention, 223–224
  versus diffuse under flow conditions, 223–224
  metaphors for, 224–226
  tasks of, 144–145
self-regulation and, 6–7
sensitivity in, 230–232
shifting to activity level, 312
shifting toward externalized goals, 384–385
spatial limitations of, 122
studies of, 325n31

attention (cont.)
  sustained, 31, 236
  syntax and, 232–234
  top-down control of, 5
  training of, 401–403
  triangular circuit theory of, 12
  volitional/voluntary, 299, 309–310
    acts of, 304–305
    in flow, 318
    postvoluntary attention transformed to, 316–317
    transition to involuntary, 301, 305
    transition to involuntary attention, 305
attention control
  benefits and perils of, 51–69
  in category learning, 59–62
  cognitive aftereffects of, 34–38
  in correlation perception, 63–64
  depleting resources, 32–34
  executive attention in, 51
  forms of, 31
  glucose levels and, 47
  interpersonal consequences of, 38–40
  in language learning, 62–63
  physiological consequences of, 42–44
  in problem solving, 52–59
  resources need for, 46–47
  rule-based and associative processing in, 65–68
  self-control undermining, 44–46
  task persistence and, 40–42
  undermining problem solving, 64–65
  undermining subsequent self-control, 34–44
  working memory and, 51–52
attention-control video task, 32–36
attention deficit/hyperactivity disorder, attention training and, 416–417
Attention Network Test (ANT), 412–413
  genetics and experience effects on, 413–414
  meditation and performance on, 417
attention substitution, 239, 240
attention training, 21
  in children, 415–417

attentional bias, action-induced, 131–133
attentional focus
  in automaticity, 88–91
  EMG activity as function of, 81–87
  explanations of, 92–93
  external, 76–80
  external and internal determinants of, 29–30
  internal, 76–80
  motor system effects of, 85
  movement effectiveness and, 77–78
  movement efficiency and, 78–81
  self-control in, 30–32
  in skilled performance speed, 91–92
  visual information in, 92–93
attentional processing pathways, 125–127
attentional systems, 121
  dorsal and ventral, 376
    in processing reality, 377–378
attentiveness
  dorsal-ventral cortical systems of, 374–375
  goal of, 304–305
  meditative training and, 374
  state of, 310
attunement, 250
Austin, James, 14, 19
automaticity
  in conscious control, 251–252
  in daily life, 186
  versus effortful action, 410
  in expertise, 209
  external attentional focus in, 88–91
  felt effort and, 354–357
  know-how and, 250–251
  in movement control, 87–88
  versus objectivist reasoning model, 252–254
  processes of, 144
  research on, 15–17
  response inhibition level in, 7–8
  social, 17
  in social coordination, 352–353
autonomy
  in Confucian virtue ethics, 269–273
  context-level support of, 198–199
  ethics of, 264

Index

autopoiesis, 19
autotelic experience, 1–4
  attention within, 305–318
  in decision making, 8
  definition of, 5
  enjoyment and, 312
  in flow, 205
  mechanisms of, 159–160
autotelic personality, 206
aversion learning, colocalization of, 113
awakened states, 373
awareness
  attention and, 355–357
  cognitive schemas and, 326n36
  function of, 150–153
  implicit versus deliberate cognitive control and, 141–153

Background, 249
balance, learning
  attentional focus in, 87–88
  external focus in, 88–91
balance tasks, 78
ballistic thought, 233
Bargh et al. elderly stereotype study, 337–338
Bargh, John, 16, 17, 144, 250–251
Barsalou, Lawrence, 254–255, 256
baseball problem-solving task, 58–59
Baumeister, Roy, 6–7, 40, 42, 47, 251–252
Bechara, Antoine, 7–8
behavior
  cascade model of, 16
  temporal integration of, 9
behavior synchronization (coordination), 336–337
behavioral demand avoidance, 110–113
Beilock, Sian, 9, 17
Beilock and Carr working memory research, 53–54
Beilock and DeCaro problem solving study, 57
Being, state of, 397
beliefs, 297–298
benevolence, harmony in, 274–275

Bergman, Ingmar, on flow experience, 318
Bernieri and Rosenthal behavioral coordination research, 336
Bernstein, Nikolai Aleksandrovich, 292
Blais, Chris, 9
Blais et al. item-specific control model, 148–150
blood pressure, in flow experience, 208
bodily motion, effortless attention in, 165–170
boredom coping, 206
Borg, Gunnar, 6
Botvinick, Matthew, 8–10, 106, 108, 111–113, 115, 143, 242–243n7
Botvinick et al. number-judgment task, 108–109
brain
  body-minded, 258–259
  coding of representation in, 123–124
  as Darwin machine, 242n3
  individual differences in, 412–415
  as intentional system, 12
  measuring activity of, 168–169
  Self-referential regions of, 382–383
  structure and processing characteristics of, 122
brain hemispheres
  processing streams in, 380–381
  severed, 252–253
Broadbent, D. E., 122, 231, 344, 349
Bruya, Brian, 11–12, 19
Bryusov, V. Ya., 322n15
Bucke, Richard, 373
Buddha, 373
Buddhism, 19–20. *See also* meditation; Zen Buddhism

Cabo et al. flow experiments, 194
Cahn, B. Rael, 19–20
Calvin, William, 233
Camerer and Hogarth demand cost metaphor, 108
capital-labor-production framework, 104
Carpenter, Edward, 393, 396

Cartesian errors, 252, 259
Casebeer, William, 266, 278n28
category learning
　associative-based, 65
　attention control in, 59–62
　dual-process theories of, 65, 68
　rule-based, 59–62
Cavell, Stanley, 250
central nervous system, in mental effort, 410
challenge (see also demand, cognitive), 115
　artificial, 239
　high level of, 173, 182, 191, 228n2, 236, 239
　low level of, 235, 236, 239, 240
　increasing/raising, 235, 240
　perceived, 183, 307
　resources for self-control and, 44, 47
challenge-skill balance, 183, 184, 187, 191, 192, 193–196, 197, 198, 306, 307, 312–313
　in flow, 205, 208–209, 211, 235–236
　psychological states related to, 220–221
Changeux, J., 17, 18
character traits, 280n45
Chartrand, Tanya, 250–251
children, training attention in, 415–417
Chinese philosophy, 247–248
　virtue ethics in, 267–268
choice, versus decision making and action, 8
Churchland, Patricia, 278n28
coalescence, 323n17
coding, in attention, 123–125
cognition
　embodied emotions in, 258–263
　in flow state, 212
　need for, 114–115
　preventing overload of, 122–123, 134
　self-control in, 34–35
　symbolic representations in, 123–124
　syntactic nature of, 243n8
cognitive aftereffects, 34–38
cognitive control
　brain activity in, 278n26
　cycle of, 142–143

　in decision making, 9
　definition of, 141
　formula for, 144–145
　gut reactions and, 263–266
　implicit versus deliberate, 141–153
　top-down, 142–143
cognitive-control ethics model, 247–248
cognitive demand
　anticipated cognitive demand
　　in attention and behavioral choice, 103–116
　　mechanisms for, 110–112
　costliness of, 104, 108–109
　levels of in information processing, 103
cognitive draw, 229–232
cognitive resources
　in language learning, 62
　in probability matching, 63–64
cognitive schemas, 325n31
　in activity gestalt, 315–316
　awareness and, 326n36
　in flow, 318
cognitive science ethics, 247–276
cognitive synchronization, 337–338
　vicarious self-control in, 349–351
Coleman, Linda, 257
communication
　psychological synchronization in, 343
　social coordination in, 346
competition, Darwinian, 242n3
competitive anxiety, 171–172, 173
complementary behavior, 336–337
complexity, in activity syntax, 236–237
COMT gene, 414
concentration, 297
　in attention, 322–323n17
　effortless, 187, 306
　in expertise, 209
　in flow, 205
　prolonged effortless, 306–307
　quality of life and, 182–186
conflict
　in absence of awareness, 153
　monitoring

computations of, 107
  in demand-based decision making, 115–116
  hypothesis of, 146, 148
conformity, 342–343
Confucianism
  spontaneity, harmony, and ease in, 273–276
  virtue ethics and, 268–276
Confucius, 248, 279n33–n41
consciousness
  constituents of, 290–291
  function of, 150–153
  limits of, 122–123
  transient hypofrontality in altered states of, 165–170
constrained action hypothesis, 76–77
  mechanisms underlying, 92–95
constraints, and syntax, 232
contextual judgment, 249–250, 251
contextual structure of reference (CSRs), 227–229. *See also* activity, domain of
  analyzing the game CSR, 228
  attention and, 227–228, 229
  ascendancy CSR, 227–228
  cheering CSR, 228
  competition of, 227
  complexity of, 236–237
  curiosity CSR, 227
  defense fight or flight CSRs, 227, 228
  dilation and contraction of, 227
  kinds of, 227
  meditation, 239–240
  meditation CSRs, 239–241
  romance CSR, 227, 228
  salience and, 229–230
  socializing with elders CSR, 228–229
  sustenance CSRs, 228, 242n6
  syntax and, 233–234
continuous positive emotional tone, 311–312
control
  deliberate, 144
  effortful, individual differences in, 412
  modulation of, 105–107

sense of
  in flow, 205
  potential, 306, 312–313
  sequential adjustment effects on, 106
convergence zones, 252, 254–255
Conway, A. R., dichotic listening study of, 52, 57
Conway, John, 243n7
Cooper, Lynn, 255
cooperative courtship, 348–349
co-option, 345–346
correlation perception, 63–64
cortical systems. *See also* prefrontal cortex
  dorsal-ventral, 374–376
  limbic nuclei targets in, 389–391
Cosmides, L., 180
Craighero et al. manual action planning study, 129–130
creative expression, flow in, 191–192, 198
Csikszentmihalyi, Mihalyi, 1–4, 6, 11, 13–14, 17, 114–115, 173, 191, 192–193, 287, 306–308, 310, 316, 318–319, 324n28, 325n34
  flow theory of, 220, 234–235, 419
cues, 232–233
  driving activities, 242–243n7
  as preliminary stimulus, 243n9
  recognition of, 233–234
culture
  in health and flow proneness, 212–213
  personality and, 294–295
  in virtue ethics, 266–267, 269

Damasio, Antonio, 7–8, 8, 251, 252, 255, 258–261, 277n9
dancing, psychological synchronization in, 342–343
Darwinian competition, 242n3
The Dating Game, 349
de Manzano, Örjan, 18
deactivations, 384–385
  of psychic Self, 392–393, 394–395
deafferented somatic Self, 400–401, 402–403

death thoughts
  suppressing, 35, 36
  undermining attention control, 45–46
DeCaro, Marci, 9, 53, 57, 61–62
decision making, 7–8
  attentional processing pathways in, 125–127
  demand-based, 103–104
    modulating control in, 105–107
  nonrational heuristics and biases in, 258–262
  objectivist model of, 252–254
  prefrontal cortex damage affecting, 259–260
  reasoning in, 247–249
  recurrent connectionist network model of, 9–10
  research on, 8–9
  response conflict and effort in, 8–9
  suboptimal, 278n21
  theories of, 8
Dehaene, Stanislaus, 7, 8, 17, 18
delayed retention tests, 77–78
demand, cognitive. *See also* challenge
  avoidance of, 107–108
  behavioral, 110–113
  costliness of high demand in, 108–109
  conflict monitoring and, 115
  competition of, 226
  versus effort, 1–2
  high levels of
    costliness of, 108–109
    pursuit of, 114–115
    subjective effort and performance in, 115–116
  demand, economic, 231
Dennett, Daniel, 278n27
deontology
  advantages of, 278–279n30
  virtue ethics and, 265–268
determinism, free will and, 152
Dewey, John, 12, 16, 326n37
dichotic listening, 52, 57
Dietrich, Arne, 8, 18

Dijksterhuis and Bargh perception-action link research, 342
directedness, 297
disgust-based attitudes, 254
dispositional representations, 259
distractions
  minimizing, 199–200
  as obstacle to flow, 235–236
divided attention, 31
Dobrynin, Nikolai Fyodorovich, 1, 4, 6, 13, 322–323n17, 323n19, 323n20
  activity model of, 296–305
  attention theory of, 288
domain. *See* activity, domain of
dopamine
  in executive network, 413–414
  receptors for in emotions and limbic system, 404
Doris, John, 280n45
Dormashev, Yuri, 15, 322n16
dorsal attention system, 374–375, 376
  kensho and, 392–393
  in processing reality, 377–378
  in stroke patient, 380–382
draw of attention. *See* attention
DRD4 gene, 414
drives, 297
  in personality, 298
dual-process theories, 65, 68
  epiphenomenalism and, 150–152
dual-task methodology, 64
Dukas, Reuven, 17
Dutch door metaphor, 393, 395
duty, acting out of, 274–275
dynamic systems theory, 13
  in social coordination, 339–340

ease, 273–276
Edelman, Gerald, 242n3, 278n19
Edwards, Kari, 263
effort. *See also* attention, effortful; control, effortful; effortfulness
  versus attention, 222–223

attentional, neuronal model of, 5
versus automatic action, 410
concept of, 409–412
in decision making, 8–9
in deliberative problem solving, 9
versus demand, 1–2
discounting, 109
felt, 8
  reduction of in flow experience, 354–357
  in social coordination, 351–358
in intensity of focus, 222–223
justification of, 114
kinds distinguished in literature, 5
monitoring versus controlling, 411
objective, 1, 5, 411–412
  correlated with subjective, 6
  decreasing during attention, 7
  versus subjective, 411–412
physical, 5, 81–87
physical and psychological measures of, 409–411
positive reinforcers of, 114–115
reactive versus regulatory aspects of, 411
subjective, 1, 5, 6
  versus objective, 411–412
volitional, 299–300
effort-related aversion, 115–116
effortfulness, 3. *See also* attention, effortful
  definition of, 5
effortlessness, 3, 16. *See also* attention, effortless; automaticity; flow
  action syntax and, 10
  agency and, 13–14
  of attentional processes, 135–136
  as autotelic experience, 1–4
  domain specific, 11
  experimental induction of, 191–202
  in expertise, 19–20
  focused attention and, 18
  movement efficiency and, 81
  paradox of, 28n2, 159, 164, 186
  phenomenon of, 6
  in social coordination, 354–357

egocentric perspective, 378–379
  in stroke patients, 379–382
"elderly" mental representation, 337–338
electromyographic (EMG) activity
  as function of attentional focus, 81–87
  internal versus external focus in, 81–82
emotion inhibition task, 37
emotional attention, 299
  operations of, 304
emotional contagion, 337
emotional memory, 251
emotional stability, 212
emotional synchronization, 344–346
emotions
  attention control and regulation of, 46
  cognitive-evaluative view of, 261–262
  convergence of in social coordination, 344
  embodied, 258–263, 341
  in flow proneness, 206–207
  in focus of attention, 29–30
  in moral reasoning, 263–266
emptiness, sense of, 404
energetics, 324n29
energy expenditure
  in mental effort, 87–91
  in physical effort, 81–87
  time and, 91–92
Engeser and Rheinberg studies
  of flow, 200–201
  of task instrumentality, 197
enjoyment, 306, 325n34
  acute and continuous, 306
  in flow, 206–207, 311–312
  intense, 312–313
  intrinsic, 206
  versus pleasure, 235
enlightenment, 373–374
environment
  in focus of attention, 29–30
  imbibing of, 312
epiphenomenalism, 150–152
ethics
  agency and, 15

ethics (cont.)
  cognitive-control models of, 247–248
  in decision making, 261–262
  emotions and, 261–262
  empirically responsible, 247–276
  spontaneity, harmony, and ease in, 273–276
  strong evaluations and, 261–263
  virtue, 266–268
    Confucian, 268–276
  etiquette. *See* syntax
evaluations
  response-dependent, conventional, and moral, 262–263
  weak versus strong, 261–263
executive attention
  in category learning, 59–60
  in children, 416–417
  and effortful control, 412
  function of, 51
  meditation improving, 417–419
  neuromodulators in, 413–414
executive control network, 9
  in decision making, 8
  testing of, 413
experience, in effortless attention, 413–414
Experience Sampling Method (ESM) study, 181–185
Expertise. *See also* activity, skills, and syntax
  in attentional control, 67–68
  effortless attention/flow and, 164–165, 208–209
  intelligence and, 212
  mental training and, 19–21
  research on, 17–18
explicit system, 18
external stimuli, 29–30
eye movements, programming of, 128

Fagioli et al. reaching movement study, 131–132
feedback, immediate, 306
  in flow, 187, 197–198, 205

feelings synchronization, 337
figure-tracing puzzle, 41
flanker task, 105, 145
flexibility, in Confucian virtue ethics, 269–273
flow. *See also* attention, effortless; automaticity; effortlessness
  versus absorption, 312
  activity-level approach to, 287–319, 308–314
  actor stage of, 419–420
  attention as key characteristic of, 306–308
  attention versus effort in, 222–223
  autonomy support in, 198–199
  balancing challenge and skill in, 193–196
  complexities of, 355–356
  correlates of, 209–210
  effortless attention training and, 409
  experimental induction of, 191–202
  expertise and, 208–209
  flow proneness and, 205–206
  gap between description and explanation of, 287–288
  implicit information-processing system in, 160–165
  meditation and, 419–420
  minimizing distractions in, 199–200
  motivation and, 234–235
  neurocognitive mechanisms of, 159–165
  obstacles to, 235–237
  in open-ended activity, 239
  perfectionism and, 170–172, 173–174
  person-level moderators of, 200–201
  person-level variables in, 192
  personal taste in, 314–315
  phenomenology of, 186–187
  physiology of, 18, 210–211
  positive and negative, 315–316
  as postvoluntary attention, 314–318
  psychophysiology of, 212–213
  quality of life and, 181
  research literature on, 191–192
  research on, 319

selective versus diffuse attention under, 223–224
in social coordination, 354–357
task instrumentality in, 197
task structure in, 197–198
flow channel, 220
flow proneness
 attention and, 207–208
 correlates of, 210
 emotion and, 206–207
 flow state and, 205–206
Flow Short Scale questionnaire, 194
Flow State Scale, 196
focus, 17–18
 in expertise, 209
 intensity of, 222–223
force production, external focus in, 86–87
formality, 237, 240–241, 243n10
 versus syntax, 237–239
free will, versus determinism, 152
Freeman, Walter, 12, 13, 14
Freudenheim et al. swimming speed study, 92
functional connectivity, 385
functional gestalt, 296
functional imaging, nitric oxide in, 397–398
functional needs, 289
functional physiological systems, 291–292, 302–303
Fuster, Joaquín, 9

GABA
 excitation of, 398
 inhibition of, 391–392, 394–395, 397
Gailliot attention control study, 42–45, 47
Gaissmaier et al. correlation perception study, 63–64
Galperin, Pyotr Yakovlevich, 322n16
Game of Life, 243n7
Garrity, Pat, 191
Gatkevich, D.I., 4
Gazzaniga, M., 253

genetic factors, in effortless attention, 413–414
gestalt, 293–294, 295
 cognitive schema in, 315–316
 functional, 296
Gibbs, Raymond, 257
Gigerenzer, Gerd, 258, 278n20
Gippenreiter, Yuliya Borisovna, 322n16
glucose
 in attention control, 7, 42–44, 47
 in mental effort, 410
 in self-control, 47
 in self-regulation, 7
goal-directed activity, 12
goal orientation, 171–172
goal setting processes, 312–313
goal states
 active, 342–344
 shifting to motive, 304–305
goals
 action optimization and, 234
 clear, 306, 312–313
 in flow, 197–198, 205
 contagious, 350
 coordination of, 338
 defining action, 290
 driving activities, 242–243n7
 in effortless attention, 187
 effortless selection of, 135–136
 externalized, attention shifting toward, 384–385
 motives shifting to, 325–326n35
 shifting to motive, 312
 social coordination in achieving, 345–346
 syntax and, 233
Golden Rule, negative, 271
golf swing, learning, 78
good person criterion, 267
Goodness, virtue of, 269, 270, 278n22
Govorun and Payne attention control study, 35–36, 45
Graduate Record Exam (GRE) Reading Comprehension subtest, 34

grasping action
  planning, 129–130
  size information in, 135
Gratton effect, 145–146, 147–150
Green, C., 152
Greene, Joshua, 263, 264–265, 278n26
gut reactions, 263–266
Guthrie, E.R., 75, 78

habitual attention, 299
habituation, 233–234
Haidt, Jonathan, 254, 262–263, 264, 277n7
Hamilton, Jean, 307
Harman, Gilbert, 280n45
Harmat, László, 18
harmony, 273–276
health, psychophysiology of flow and, 212–213
heart rate
  synchronization of, 338
  variability of in flow, 208, 211
hedonism, limits of, 308
Heinz, Steven, 324n30
heroic mind, 316
high reason model, 247, 248, 264
Hillis et al. stroke patient studies, 379
Hommel, Bernhard, 4, 11, 16, 124, 128, 130, 131, 133, 135
human nature, roots of, 294–295
Hume, David, 261–262, 276
Hurley, Susan, 12
hypofrontality, transient, 165–170
hypothesis testing
  cognitive resources in, 63–64
  working memory in, 61–62

I-Me-Mine, 382–383
  distorted priorities of, 392–393
  egocentric constructs of, 387
ideal moral agents, 248–249
idealized cognitive models, 257–258
ideational needs, 289
ideomotor action, 340

imaginative extension, 257–258
immersion, 297, 312
implicit control, 143–147
incongruent trial, 146
inefficient behavior, 144
information flow
  economic demand and, 231
  projectile view of, 230
  sensitivity and, 232
information-integration category learning, 61
  dual-process theories in, 68
information potential, 231
information-processing system
  biologically predetermined, 179–180
  cognitive demand levels in, 103
  explicit, 161, 162–163
    inhibition of, 164–165
  flexibility-efficiency trade-off in, 162–163
  implicit, 161–165
insight-wisdom
  balanced with selflessness, 385–386
  thalamus in, 386–387
  total selflessness and, 392–393
instruction wording, performance and learning effects of, 92–95
Integrative Body-Mind Training (IBMT), 417–419
intelligence
  attention training and, 416
  in flow state, 210, 212
intentional action model, 12
intentional control framework, 128–134
  theoretical implications of, 134–136
intentional selection control, 121–136
interactional synchrony, 336
interest
  effortless attention and, 220–221
  lack of, 236–237
  as motivation, 234–235
Interests, 297
  beliefs and, 297–298
  in personality, 298
interference effect, 145–146

internalization, 291–292
interpersonal style
unlikable/maladaptive, 38–39
item-specific control, 147–150

James, William, 5, 166, 180, 232, 236, 316, 373, 396
Jeannerod, Marc, 13, 15, 16, 20
Jesus, meditative approach of, 373
Johnson, Mark, 257–258, 277n2, 277n9, 278n22
Johnson, Samuel, 182
Johnston, William, 324n30
judgment
  brain hemispheres in, 253
  dual-process theories of, 65
  emotional, 261–262
  moral, 262–263
  normative, 278n22
jump performance, attentional focus in, 86
justification, rational and emotional, 262–263

Kabat-Zinn, John, 20
Kahneman, Daniel, 4, 5, 15, 160, 180, 261, 278n21, 324n30, 409–410
Kant, Immanuel, 250, 274–275, 278–279n30
Kareeve et al. correlation perception study, 63
Kawakami et al. elderly stereotype study, 337–338
Kay, Paul, 257
Keller and Bless flow induction study, 194–195
kensho, 380–381
  closing, 397
  deactivations in, 394–395
  dorsal deactivations and, 392–393
  triggers for, 385–386, 387
Kersten and Earles language learning study, 62
know-how, importance of, 249–252
knowledge
  explicit versus tacit, 250–252
  moral, 257–258

Koriat et al. effort studies, 411
Kubey, R., 191
Kunst-Wilson, W., 277n5

LaBerge, David, 12, 13
Lakoff, G., 277n9, 278n22
Langacker, Ronald, 255, 277n9
Langer, Ellen, 19
language
  attunement and, 250
  learning
    attention control in, 62–63
    dual-process theories in, 68
    holistic, 65
    limited cognitive resources in, 62
    psychological synchronization in, 343–344
Lavrova, N.V., 4
learned industriousness theory, 114–115
learning, attention in, 16
least mental effort, law of, 108
LeDoux, Joseph, 251, 253
Lektorsky, Vladislav Aleksandrovich, 321n12
Leontiev, Aleksei Nikolaevich, 301–318, 320–326nn
  activity theory of, 288–296
Lewthwaite, Rebecca, 7, 164
limbic nuclei, cortical targets of, 389–391
Loewenstein, George, 261
Logan and Gordon executive control study, 131–132

Maddox category learning study, 62
Makalatiya, Aleksandra Guramovna, 317
Mannell and Bradley task structure study, 197, 198–199
Marchant et al. force production study, 82, 86–87
Markman et al. category learning study, 61–62
Massimini and Carli flow channel model, 220
math problem solving, 55–56
Mauss, Iris, 144
maximizing strategy, 64

McGuire, Joseph, 8–9, 108, 112
meanings, in consciousness, 290–291
meditation, 19, 159, 165, 166, 170, 181, 188, 211, 239, 240, 241, 303, 325, 374, 401, 404, 405, 411, 412. *See also* Zen Buddhism
breath, 239–240
categories of, 375–377
concentrative, 375–377, 400
Eastern, 19–20
flow and, 419–420
in improving attention, 417–419
mindful, 188
neurological studies of, 19–20
PET scan during, 398–399
receptive, 377
  PET scan during, 398–399
  techniques of, 403
meditative training
in attentiveness, 374
Meier, Brian, 11
Mencius, 247–248, 274–275, 279n34
Mencius-Mohist debates, 267–268
mental effort, 5
  energy expenditure in, 87–91
  glucose metabolism in, 410
mental training, 19–21
meridian effect, 127–128
metacognitive processes, 164–165
metamental training, 20
metaphors, 257–258
  in moral reasoning, 258
Metzinger, Thomas, 12
Metzler, Jacqueline, 255
Milner and Goodale action-planning study, 127
mimicry, 336
  in action motivation, 343–344
mind-body dualism, 152
mindfulness, 188, 240
  effortless, 419–420
Moller, Arlen, 11, 195–196
momentum, in flow, 236
monkey mind, 181

"moonlight" phase, 397
moral behavior
  music and, 279–280n42
  spontaneity, harmony, and ease in, 273–276
moral education, 257–258
moral evaluations, 262–263
moral reasoning
  affective states in, 278n28
  gut reactions in, 263–266
motivational forces, 30
motivations
  action, 289, 342–344
  in action optimization, 234–235
  in attentional effort, 5
  in flow, 200–201, 309
  hierarchy of, 292, 295
  leading, 292
  sense-forming, 291
  shifting to goals, 325–326n35
  stimulating, 292
  structuring function of, 321n12, 326n38
  struggle of, 316
  taste-forming, 314–315
  taste-forming versus sense-forming, 316
motor skills, learning, 75–96
movement
  control of
    automaticity in, 87–88
    smoothness and fluidity of, 91
    social-cognitive variables in, 94–95
  economy of, 81
  effectiveness of, 77–78
  efficiency of
    attentional focus and, 78–81
    external focus in, 85–86
    internal versus external focus in, 81–82
  external attention focus in effectiveness and efficiency of, 75–96
  reaching, saccades and, 130–131
Mozi, 279–280n42
music
  in emotional transformation, 274
  moral value of, 279–280n42

performance of
  health and flow in, 213
  physiological factors in, 211
Müsseler et al. manual action planning studies, 128–130

Nakamura, Jeanne, 11, 191, 324n28
Narcissistic Personality Inventory, 39–40
native substance, 269
nature, meditation on, 403
needs
  beliefs and, 297–298
  insatiable, 289
  objectified, 289, 320n6
  in personality, 298
  physiological, satisfaction of, 322n15
  primary, 289
  primary and secondary, 297
  satisfaction of, 322n15
  social, satisfaction of, 322n15
  spiritual, 297
Neitzsche, F., 253
Nemeroff, Carol, 254
NEO Personality Inventory-Revised, 210
neural cost-benefit analysis, 108–109
neural pathways, action-related versus perception-related, 125–127
neuromodulators, 413–414
neurons, electrochemical activity of, 12
Newport language learning study, 62
Nichols, Shaun, 263
Nisbett, Richard, 253–254
nitric oxide, in functional imaging, 397–398
non-I state, 392–393
norepinephrine receptors, 404
Norman, Donald, 324n26
novice skills, in attentional control, 67–68
number-judgment task, 108–109
Nussbaum, Martha, 257–258, 261–262

object-centered perspective, 378–379
object matching, reaction times in, 255

objectivist model, 248–249
  moral gut reactions and, 263–266
  prototype categories in, 256–257
oneness
  subcategories of, 396
  thalamus in, 393–397
  triggering sense of, 404
"onion-peeling" principle, 165
open-ended activity, 239
operations
  action and, 289–290
  of emotional attention, 304
  primary and secondary, 290, 311
optimal experience studies, 181
organic needs, 289
organism, 294–295
OSPAN task, 36–38
  emotion regulation and, 46
  working memory in, 53
other-referential perspective, 377–379
  defect in, 381–382
other-referential/self-referential function equilibrium, 385–386
outcome measures, 77–78
oxygen consumption, in physical effort, 81

Pac-Man game
  challenge-skill balance in playing, 193–194
  task instrumentality in, 197
parasympathetic activation
  in flow, 208, 211
  flow and, 213
parietal function
  dorsal and ventral processing in, 376–378
  ego- and allocentric pathways in, 378–382
pattern-recognition pathways, 380
Pavlov, Ivan Petrovich, 325n31
peak experiences, 373–374
pedalo riding performance, 91–92
Penfield homunculus, 324n27
perception
  action planning and, 124–125, 133–134
  actions facilitating, 341, 342

perception (cont.)
  genesis and function of, 325n33
  as human activity, 325n32
perception-action cycle, 340–342
  momentum in, 236
  syntax and, 234
perception-related processing, 125–127
perceptual dimensions
  priming of, 130–132
  selective use of, 134–135
perceptual symbols, 254–256
perfection, effortless, 274–276
perfectionism, 18, 170–174
  negative, 171–172, 174
  positive, 170–172, 173–174
performance monitoring, 5
  in cognitive control, 142–143
person-level factors, in flow, 200–201
personal sense, 320n8
  in consciousness, 290–291
personal significance, 297–298
personal taste, 314–315
personality
  activity and, 15, 294–295
  attention organization and, 298–299
  in exact sense, 295
  expanded concept of, 293
  in flow proneness, 210
  intercompeting tendencies in, 300
  levels of, 294–295
  motive hierarchy in, 295
  organization of, 298
  second birth of, 292
  span of, 292
  taste-forming motive in, 314–315
PET scan, during receptive meditation, 398–399
Petukhov, Valery Viktorovich, 294–295, 296
phenomenological subtraction, 165–166
phenomenology, 321
  of attention, 288
  of flow, 161, 186

in effortful versus effortless attention, 182
in normal versus altered consciousness, 165–169
systematic, 179
phi complex, 342
physical activity
  energy expenditure during, 81–87
  neural activation during, 168–169
physical sensations, 29–30
physiological measures, in flow state, 209–210
physiological processes
  attention control and, 42–44
  coordination of, 338
  in flow state, 210–212
Plaut, D. C., 242–243n7
pleasure, versus enjoyment, 235, 325n34
Polanyi, Michael, 250
Polich, John, 19–20
Posner, Michael, 21, 296, 410
prajna (insight-wisdom), 373
precoordination, 341
prefrontal cortex
  in cognitive control, 141–142
  decision making center of, 259–260
  hypoactivity of, 165–170
  susceptibility to change, 165
principal function, 295–296
Prinz perception-action research, 340–341
probability matching, 63–64
problem solving
  attention control in, 52–59
  cognitive resources undermining, 64–65
  deliberative, 9
  dual-process theories in, 65–68
processing-filtering, selective, 15
Profile of Mood States (POMS), 417–418
projectile view of information flow. *See* information flow
proportion effects, 145, 146
  deliberate control hypothesis and, 147, 148–150
prototype categories, 256–257

psychic capacity, 180
psychic energy, 180, 324n29
psychic Self
  blocking association functions of, 392–393
  deactivations of, 394–395
  exteroceptive and interoceptive environments in, 382–383
psychological matching, 342–343
psychological states
  in attention, 219–220
  challenge-skill balance and, 220–221
psychology
  of attention, 180, 288–296
  in flow proneness, 206–207
psychophysiological factors, in flow, 212–213
pulvinar, 388–389, 390
Putnam, Hilary, 249–250

quality of life, attention and, 181
quasi-motives, 291

racially biased response, attention control and, 35–36, 45
rapport building, 345–346
  vicarious self-control in, 349–351
rational justifications, 254
rationality, bounded, 258, 277n17, 278n21
Raven's Standard Progressive Matrices, 417
Raven's Standard Progressive Matrices Plus, 210
readiness potential, 151–152
Reading Span (RSPAN) task, working memory in, 53
reasoning, 247–248
  in decision making, 261–262
  deontological, 265–266
    in virtue ethics, 267–268
  emotions and, 251–252
  judgment, 65
  Kantian, 278–279n30
  objectivist model of, 252–254
recognition heuristic, 258

reference, contextual structures of, 11–12
reflective self-consciousness, loss of, 199
Relationship Closeness Induction Task (RCIT), 39
relationships, social coordination enhancing, 345–346
religious beliefs, gut reactions in, 263
Remote Associates Task (RAT), 58–59
representational systems
  distributed, 123–125
  shared, 341
research, challenges and gaps in, 6, 8
response
  conflict
    in decision making, 8–9
    sensitivity to in monitoring demand, 106–107
  execution of, 233
  inhibition of, 7–8
    attention control and, 45–46
  selection of in cognitive control, 142
  steps of, 233–234
response representations, 124
responsiveness, 16, 230, 232
Rheinberg and Vollmeyer flow experiments, 193–194
Ribot, Henri, 180, 323n22
Richeson and Shelton attention control study, 45
Ricks et al. problem solving task, 58–59
ritual behavior, flexibility in, 272–273
Roboguard game, flow in playing, 193–194
Romanov, Valerly Yakovlevich, 322n16
romantic relationship, social coordination in, 346, 348–349
Rosche, Eleanor, 256
Rothbart, Mary, 5, 21
Rozin, Paul, 254
Rueda, M. R., 21
rule-based processes, 59–62, 65–66
  conceptualizing, 67
Rumelhart, David, 324n26
Ryle, Gilbert, 250

saccades, reaching movements and, 130–131
salience, 229, 230
Sanders attention theory, 160
Sarter, M. W., 5
satori (awakened state), 373
  triggers for, 385–386
Schall, J. D., 8
Schmeichel, Brandon, 6–7
  attention control studies of, 34–37
  emotion regulation study of, 46
Schooler, Jonathan, 251–252
schoolwork experience, attention and quality of, 184–186
Schubotz and von Cramon oddball task study, 131–132
Schücker et al. movement efficiency study, 87
Searle, John, 249
selection, intentional control of, 121–136
self. *See also* psychic Self
  deafferented somatic, 400–403
  decentered, 252–254
    versus unitary, 252–254
  objectivist, 248–249
  thalamus and, 14–15
self-actualization, need for, 295
self-awareness, dropping away of, 13, 14–15, 19
self-centered perspective, 381, 383, 388
self-consciousness, loss of, 306
  in flow, 205
self-control, 5–6
  in attention focus, 30–32
  benefits of, 31
  definition of, 30–31
  resources need for, 46–47
  testing of, 32
  undermining subsequent attention control, 44–46
  vicarious, 349–351
self-cultivation
  Confucian, 269
  music as metaphor for, 274
self-determination theory, 198–199
self-directing capacity, 179–180

self-focus
  in movement efficiency, 78–81
  in self-regulatory processes, 94–95
self-forgetfulness, 306
selfhood, transient, 12
self-invoking trigger, 93–94
selfless insight-wisdom, 373–374
  parietal pathways of, 380–381
  thalamus in, 386–387, 386–405
selflessness
  balanced with insight-wisdom, 385–386
  in insight-wisdom, 392–393
  spectrum of, 400
  total state of, 385
self-modification, 309
self-other dichotomy, 377–378
self-othering personal memory bank, 383
Self-plus-other, 383
self-referential networks, 377–379, 382–383
  deactivation of, 392–393
  equilibrium with other-referential functions, 385–386
  reciprocal activations and deactivations in, 384–385
self-regulation, 5–6
  and effortful control, 412
  limited resources for, 350–351, 353
  meditation improving, 417–418
  in movement efficiency, 78–81
  resources of, 6–7
  self-focus in, 94–95
self-representation, 13
Selten, Reinhard, 258, 278n20
sensitivity, 230–232
sensitivity-responsiveness, 16
sensitization mechanism, 11–12
sensorimotor system
  damaged, 255
  imaginative extension of, 257–258
  perceptual symbols and, 254–256
sensory fabric, 290–291
sequential actions
  in decision making, 9–10
  neural timing mechanisms in, 10

Index

sequential adjustment effects, 106
Shepard, Robert, 255
Shun (sage-king), 275
Siddhartha, 373
Siegel effortless mindfulness, 419
Sigman, Mariano, 7, 8
significance principle, 297–298
Silvia, Paul, 220–221
Simmons, W. Kyle, 256–257
Simon, Herbert, 277n17
Simon task, 144–145
  proportion effects in, 145
ski-simulator task, 77–78
skiing. *See* syntax
skilled performance
  attentional focus in, 78–81
  instruction wording differences in, 92–95
  speed of, 91–92
skills. *See also* activity, expertise, and syntax
  challenge balanced with, 193–196, 205, 208–209, 211, 235–236, 306, 307, 312–313
  psychological states related to, 220–221
  task instrumentality and, 197
Slingerland, Edward, 15, 19
Sloan Study of Youth and Social Development, 182
smoothness, in social coordination, 353
social agent, 14
social behavior
  agency and, 13
  automaticity of, 16
  complexity of, 14
social cognition
  dual-process theories in, 65
  in movement control, 94–95
social coordination, 335
  automatic, 336–358
  benefits of, 344–347
  co-opting, 345–346
  emerging research on, 347–351
  felt effort in, 351–358
  flow in, 354–357
  hallmarks of, 336–338
  routes to, 338–339

  active motivation, 342–344
  direct perception-action link, 340–342
  dynamical, 339–340
  sex-specific, 348–349
social individual, 294–295
social intuition, 263
social motivations, 15
social norms
  disinhibition of, 165
  utilitarianism and, 267
social psychology
  in marketing, 280n45
  virtue ethics and, 280n45
somatic markers, 258–259, 260–261
  of demand anticipation, 111–112
  reasoning-biasing, 261–262
somato-motor mapping, 259
specific activities, 289
Spivey, M., 255–256
spontaneity, 273–276
sports performance
  explicit and implicit information processing in, 163–165
  flow in, 159
  focus in learning skills for, 77–78, 79–80
  perfectionism in, 170–172
  stabilometer task, 77–78, 87–88
stimulus representations, 124
Stoicism, 261–262
Stoll, Oliver, 18, 172
strivings, in personality, 298
stroke patients, ego- and allocentric pathways in, 379–382
Stroop color-naming task, 33–34, 35–36, 39, 41–42
  awareness in, 153
  cingulate lesions effect in, 411–412
  to manipulate cognitive demand, 105–106
  proportion effects in, 145
  racial bias and performance of, 45
  selective attention in, 144–145
Stroop effect, 146
  item-specific control and, 148–150
  size of, 151, 152

structures of reference, 226–229
  contextual, 227–229
stylized activity, 239
subapertures, 242n2
subcortex, inhibitory functions of, 391–392
subjective effort
  demand and, 115–116
  versus objective effort, 411–412
suchness, impression of, 387
Suzuki, D. T., 373
Sweetser, E., 257–258
swimming speed, attentional focus in, 92
symbols
  as basic units of cognition, 123–124
  rule-governed combinations of, 248
sympathetic activation, in flow state, 211
syntactic activity, 237–239
syntax. *See also* activity, expertise, and skills
  action optimization and, 234–241
  attention and, 232–234
  in cognition, 243n8
  complexity in, 236–237
  degree of, 237–238
  draw of attention and, 11–12
  etiquette and, 232
  hierarchy of goals in, 10
  linguistic, 9
  as set of constraints, 232
  skiing and, 232
systematic phenomenology, 179–188

Talmy, Leonard, 255
Tang, Yiyuan, 21
Tart, Charles, 166
task instruction, external versus internal foci in, 77–78, 79–80
task instrumentality, in flow induction, 197
task performance
  attention and performance of, 159–160
  attention control and persistence in, 40–42
  flow in, 173
  goals and, 290
  perfectionism in, 170–172, 173–174

task structure
  autonomy and, 198–199
  in flow, 197–198
Taylor, Charles, 262
team sports, psychological synchronization in, 342–343
temperament, individual differences in, 412
terror management theory, 35
Tetris computer game, flow in playing, 194–196
thalamus
  deafferented somatic self and, 400–401
  in effortless attention and selfless insight-wisdom, 386–405
  inhibitory functions of, 391–392
  nitric oxide effects on, 397–398
  normal, 390–391
  sense of self and, 14–15
Theorell, Töres, 18
thought
  image-based, 254–256
  synchronization of, 337
time
  altered sense of, 306
  energy expenditure and, 91–92
  transformation of in flow, 205
Timliness *(shi)*, 273
Titchener, E. B., 323n22
Tooby, J., 180
top-down control, 142–143
  in flow, 208–209
  in Stroop performance, 149
transient hypofrontality theory (THT), 164–170
Treisman, Anne, 4, 15
triggering stimulus, 385–386
Tversky, Amos, 261, 278n21

Ullén, Fredrik, 18, 19
unitary subject, in objectivist reasoning model, 252–254
unity experience, thalamus in, 393–397
unselfconscious behavior, 274–275

up-definition, 294
utilitarianism
  judgment in, 278n26
  reasoning in, 265–266
  versus traditional virtue models, 267–268

valence-arousal dimension, 206–207
Vallacher et al. social coordination study, 340
value memory, 278n19
Van Norden, B., 277n1
Vance et al. energy expenditure study, 82
ventral attention system, 374–375, 376
  in processing reality, 377–378
  in stroke patient, 380–382
vicarious depletion, 350–351
video games
  challenge-skill balance in playing, 11
  flow in playing, 193–196
vigilance, 221–222
  intensity of, 222
virtue ethics, 278n29
  advantages of, 278–279n30
  Confucian, 268–276
  effortless attention and, 266–268
  human character traits and, 280n45
  multiple cultural models of, 276
visual attention
  action planning and, 127–128
  eye movement programming in, 128
  manual action planning and, 128–130
  selective, 123
visual search tasks, 133–134
vital activity, 289
Vohs and Faber attention control study, 38–40
volatility-persistence factor, 200
von Ehrenfels, Christian, 296
von Hippel, William, 263

Waldron and Ashby category learning study, 60
Wall, Robert, 11

Wallace, B. Alan, 19–20
Wallace and Baumeister attention-control study, 40–42
Webb and Sheeran attention-control study, 41–42
Wertheimer, Max, 296
Westernization, affective reactions and, 264
will, 5–6
Wilson, Timothy, 251–252, 253–254, 277n6, 277n8
Winawer, J. N., 277n12
Wolford et al. dual-task study, 64
working memory
  in attention control, 68–69
  in category learning tasks, 60–61
  as central processing unit, 122
  in cognitive control, 142
  in complex hypothesis testing, 61–62
  function of, 51–52
  individual differences in, 52–53
  in language learning, 62–63
  in problem solving, 52–59
wu wei (effortless action/perfection), 268–276, 274–276
Wulf, Gabriele, 7, 76, 82, 164
Wulf and Dufek jump performance study, 86
Wulf et al. automaticity studies, 87–91
Wykowska et al. visual search study, 133–134

Xunzi, 279n34

Zachry et al. energy expenditure study, 82–85
Zajonc, Robert, 251, 277n5
Zen Buddhism
  awakening *kensho* in, 392–393
  enlightenment experience in, 14–15
  meditation in, 188
    allocentric approach in, 403–404
  selflessness in, 373–374
Zhu Xi, 275
Zimbardo, Philip, 254
Zinchenko, Vladimir Petrovich, 321n11, 321n12